# BACK
## TO THE
# LAKE

# BACK
## TO THE
# LAKE

A READER
AND GUIDE

## Thomas
## Cooley

THIRD EDITION

W · W · NORTON & COMPANY · NEW YORK · LONDON

**W. W. Norton & Company** has been independent since its founding in 1923, when William Warder Norton and Mary D. Herter Norton first published lectures delivered at the People's Institute, the adult education division of New York City's Cooper Union. The firm soon expanded its program beyond the Institute, publishing books by celebrated academics from America and abroad. By midcentury, the two major pillars of Norton's publishing program—trade books and college texts—were firmly established. In the 1950s, the Norton family transferred control of the company to its employees, and today—with a staff of four hundred and a comparable number of trade, college, and professional titles published each year—W. W. Norton & Company stands as the largest and oldest publishing house owned wholly by its employees.

*Editor:* Marilyn Moller
*Managing editor:* Rebecca Homiski
*Associate editor:* Tenyia Lee
*Editorial assistant:* Claire Wallace
*Marketing manager:* Lib Triplett
*Emedia editor:* Cliff Landesman
*Emedia editorial assistant:* Cara Folkman
*Production manager:* Andrew Ensor
*Design director:* Rubina Yeh
*Text design:* Jillian Burr
*Composition:* Graphic World
*Manufacturing:* R. R. Donnelley—Crawfordsville

Permission to use copyrighted material is included in the credits section of this book, which begins on p. 836.

Library of Congress Cataloging-in-Publication Data

Cooley, Thomas, 1942–
  Back to the lake : a reader and guide / Thomas Cooley. — Third edition.
    pages cm
  Includes bibliographical references and index.
  **ISBN 978-0-393-93736-7 (pbk.)**
    1. College readers. 2. English language—Rhetoric—Problems, exercises etc. 3. Report writing—Problems, exercises, etc. I. Title.
  PE1417.C6549 2015
  808'.0427—dc23

                                2014030852

W. W. Norton & Company, Inc., 500 Fifth Avenue, New York, NY 10110
www.wwnorton.com
W. W. Norton & Company Ltd., Castle House, 75/76 Wells Street, London W1T 3QT
1 2 3 4 5 6 7 8 9 0

# Preface

I first read E. B. White's classic essay "Once More to the Lake" with awe and wonder as a freshman in a college writing course. Only years later did I realize that White worked his magic with common rhetorical techniques—narration, description, comparison, and the other modes of writing discussed in this book— that good writers use every day in all kinds of texts and contexts. Far from magic, these standard techniques could be applied to my own writing, whether to structure a paragraph or an entire essay, or, even more essentially, to generate ideas and organize my thoughts throughout the writing process.

We now take it for granted that the process of writing is one we can learn—and teach. This was not the case in White's day, however, as I discovered when, as a young associate professor of English, I rashly fired off a letter asking him to explain how he composed "Once More to the Lake." To my astonishment, White not only responded to my letter, he said he didn't really know how he wrote anything. "The 'process,'" White confided, "is probably every bit as mysterious to me as it is to some of your students—if that will make them feel any better."

Fortunately for today's students and teachers, the scene has changed; we now know a lot more than we once did about how the writing process works and how to teach it. *Back to the Lake*—which takes its title from White's essay—applies this understanding of the process to show students how to make the basic moves that seasoned writers make, whether consciously or otherwise, in their writing.

## An Overview of the Book

*Back to the Lake* is a reader and guide for writers. It contains more than 75 readings— from the classic ("Grant and Lee") to the most current ("A Zombie Is a Slave Forever")—all demonstrating that the rhetorical methods taught in this book are ones that all good writers use. Each mode is represented by 6 or 7 readings, including at least one annotated student example and one story or poem. In this new edition, we also show how the modes are used in reports, analyses, position papers, and all the kinds of writing students are expected to do.

**Chapter 1** introduces students to the principles of analytical reading, taking them through the basic steps of reading with a critical eye.

**Chapter 2** covers the basic moves of academic writing, helping students research a topic, synthesize ideas, respond with ideas of their own, consider counterarguments, and explain why their ideas matter.

**Chapter 3** shows how the methods discussed in this book can be used in all kinds of academic writing, including reports, position papers, rhetorical analyses, evaluations, and proposals.

**Chapter 4** gives an overview of the writing process, preparing students to analyze assignments; come up with topics and generate ideas; draft and revise an essay with a particular audience and purpose in mind; and edit and proofread.

**Chapter 5** provides guidance on writing paragraphs, with an in-depth discussion of topic sentences, transitions, and parallel structures—and how to use the modes to develop coherent paragraphs, including introductory and concluding paragraphs.

**Chapters 6 through 14** each focus on one of the rhetorical modes as a basic method of discovery and development. Practical guidelines lead students through the process of composing a text using that mode: generating ideas, organizing and drafting, getting feedback, and revising and editing a final draft.

**Chapter 15** demonstrates how much real-world writing combines those methods.

An **appendix on using sources** offers guidance in finding, incorporating, and documenting sources MLA-style—and includes an annotated student research paper.

A **glossary / index** completes the book, providing definitions of all the key terms along with a list of the pages where they are covered in detail.

## Highlights

**An engaging, teachable collection of readings,** from classic ("Ain't I a Woman?") to current ("Superhero Smackdown") to humorous ("My Education: Repossessed")— all demonstrating the patterns taught in this book. Each chapter includes an annotated student essay, and a story or poem.

**Readings and writing instruction are explicitly linked** with notes in the margins that make this book work well in courses taking an *integrated reading-writing approach*. See pp. 94 and 129 for two examples.

**Everyday examples,** showing that the methods taught in this book are familiar ones—and that they are not used just in first-year writing: that crossing a street, for example, relies on process analysis; and that a coffee mug can make a comparison.

**Templates for drafting,** providing language to help students get started with the fundamental moves of describing, comparing, defining, and so on.

**Practical editing tips,** to help students check for the kinds of errors that frequently occur with each of the rhetorical methods taught in this book—for instance, to check that verb tenses accurately reflect when actions occur in a narrative.

**Help for students whose primary language is not English,** with glosses for unfamiliar terms and cultural allusions, templates for getting started, and tips for dealing with predictable stumbling points, such as adjective order or the use of the present perfect.

## What's New

**38 new readings,** including Paul Krugman's "E Pluribus Unum," Mindy Kaling's "Types of Women in Romantic Comedies Who Are Not Real," and a chapter from Marjane Satrapi's *Persepolis*. Of the new readings, 29 are appearing in a composition reader for the first time.

**A new chapter on writing paragraphs.** Paragraphs are the building blocks of essays, yet few other modes readers devote sufficient attention to them. *Back to the Lake* provides a whole chapter focusing in particular on how the modes can be used to organize and develop coherent paragraphs.

**Expanded coverage of academic writing,** with a new chapter showing how the modes are used in the kinds of writing college students are most often assigned, along with academic examples and writing prompts—all serving as a bridge between the patterns taught in this book and the academic writing students need to do. An index of readings arranged by common academic genres makes it easy to locate examples.

**New design elements make the book especially easy to use.** Color-coding highlights key information: green for writing instruction; red for online resources; tan for the Glossary / Index, Contents, and other reference materials. Templates and other materials students may refer to often are in boxes and checklists. Color-coded citation templates make even MLA documentation easy to do. A menu of readings on the inside back cover helps students find readings quickly.

**A free and open student website (wwnorton.com/write)** includes links to resources related to the readings, exercises on editing common errors, download-able templates for drafting and worksheets for reading with a critical eye, bio-graphical notes on each author in the book, sample student papers, and tutorials on research writing and avoiding plagiarism.

**Now available as an ebook.** An affordable and convenient alternative, the ebook lets students search, highlight, and take notes with ease; and collaborate and share notes with teachers and classmates. It can be used on any device—laptop, tablet, phone, even a public computer—and will stay synced between devices.

## Acknowledgments

For help in the preparation of a new edition of this book, I wish to thank a number of people. As always, I am most grateful to Barbara Cooley, who deals equally well with issues of water quality and murky prose. Marilyn Moller, without your inspi-ration and experience at the editorial helm there would be no *Back to the Lake*; I thank you for keeping us all on course during a longer voyage than anyone expected. Thanks as well to Rebecca Homiski, my wonderful hands-on editor at Norton, who took care of development, photo research, and copyediting, as well as overseeing the book's typesetting and layout. I am also grateful to Darren DeFrain for his work on the instructor's notes. In addition, I wish to thank Jillian Burr for the beautiful design; Bethany Salminen for clearing the many permissions; Andrew Ensor for getting the book produced in good form despite the many deadlines some of us missed; and Marian Johnson and Julia Reidhead for their support of this ambitious project all along the way.

Thanks go as well to the following teachers who reviewed the second edition: Heidi Ajrami, Victoria College; Don Boes, Bluegrass Community and Technical College; Jennifer Browne, Frostburg State University; Larry O. Dean, Northeastern Illinois University; Beth Heim de Bera, Rochester Community and Technical College; Justin Eatmon, Coastal Carolina Community College; George Edwards, Tarrant County College—Northwest Campus; Jennifer Eimers, Missouri Valley College; Kelley D. McKay Fuemmeler, Missouri Valley College; Curtis Fukuchi, Tarrant County College—Northwest Campus; Loren C. Gruber, Missouri Valley College; Sylvia Holladay, Hillsborough Community College; Tina Hultgren, Kishwaukee College; Malvina King, Hillsborough Community College; Anne M. Kuhta, Northern Virginia Community College; Mary E. Lounsbury, Tarrant County College—Northwest Campus; Matthew Masucci, State College of Florida; Jeanne-Marie Morrissey, Castleton State College; Betty J. Perkinson, Tidewater

Community College; Gregg Pratt, North Country Community College; Rodney Rather, Tarrant County College—Northwest Campus; James Rawlins, Sussex County Community College; Louis Riggs, Hannibal-LaGrange University; Kelly Terzaken, Coastal Carolina Community College; Margaret Vallone Gardineer, Felician College; April Van Camp, Indian River State College; Julie Vega, Sul Ross State University; Maryann Vivolo-Sclafani, Felician College.

I am grateful as well to the instructors who took time to share their thoughts on the new readings: Heidi Ajrami, Victoria College; Dawn Marie Bergeron, St. Johns River State College; Darci Cather, South Texas College; Larry O. Dean, Northeastern Illinois University; Beth Heim de Bera, Rochester Community and Technical College; Margaret V. Gardineer, Felician College; Tina Hultgren, Kishwaukee College; Matthew Masucci, State College of Florida; Kelly Terzaken, Coastal Carolina Community College.

Thanks also to the many teachers across the country who have reviewed various previous versions and offered valuable input and encouragement: Kellee Barbour, Virginia Western Community College; Andrea Bates, Coastal Carolina Community College; Judy Bello, Lander University; Mark Bernier, Blinn College at Brenham; Kathleen Collins Beyer, Farmingham State College; Patricia Bostian, Central Piedmont Community College; Jonathan Bradley, Concord University; Mary Jane Brown, Miami University Middletown; Sarah Burns, Virginia Western Community College; Marian Carcache, Auburn University; Amy Cooper, St. Cloud State University; Lily Corwin, Kutztown University; Darren DeFrain, Wichita State University; Kathleen Dixon, University of North Dakota; MaryBeth Drake, Virginia Western Community College; Jean M. Evans, Norwalk, Connecticut, Public Schools; Lynn Ezzell, Cape Fear Community College; Richard Farias, San Antonio College; Adam Fischer, Bowie State University; Gabriel Ford, Penn State–University Park; Hannah Furrow, University of Michigan at Flint; Bill Gahan, Rockford College; Judy Gardner, University of Texas at San Antonio; Mary Ellen Ginnetti, Hillsborough Community College; Peggy Hach, SUNY New Paltz; Monica Hatchett, Virginia Western Community College; Catherine F. Heath, Victoria College; James M. Hilgartner, Huntingdon College; Gina L Hochhalter, Clovis Community College; Jo Ann Horneker, Arkansas State University; Laura Jensen, University of Nebraska; Sandra Kelly, Virginia Western Community College; Aaron Kimmel, Penn State; Jim LaBate, Hudson Valley Community College; Henry Marchand, Monterey Peninsula College; Howard Mayer, University of Hartford; Mary Murray McDonald, Cleveland State University; Scott Moncrieff, Andrews University; Stephen Monroe, University of Mississippi; Bryan Moore, Arkansas State University; Angela Mustapha, Penn State; Daniel Olson, North Harris College; Joyce O'Shea, Wharton County Junior College; Jeffrey Powers-Beck, East Tennessee State University; Gregg Pratt, North Country Community College/SUNY Adirondack; Lisa Riggs,

Oklahoma Wesleyan University; Jacquelyn Robinson, Victoria College; Craig-Ellis Sasser, Northeast Mississippi Community College; Anne Taylor, North Dakota State College of Science; Julian Thornton, Gadsden State Community College; Nann Tucker, Hillsborough Community College; Anita Tully, Nicholls State University; April Van Camp, Indian River State College; Karina Westra, Point Loma Nazarene University; Lea Williams, Norwich University; Mark Williams, California State University at Long Beach; Daniel Zimmerman, Middlesex County College; and Jamie L. Zorigian, Lehman College.

It is a great pleasure to name the teachers of writing and experts in the field of composition and rhetoric who have given advice, or otherwise assisted me, at various stages in the evolution of this book. They include my colleagues at Ohio State, particularly Beverly Moss, Sara Garnes, and the late Edward P. J. Corbett; the late Dean McWilliams of Ohio University; Roy Rosenstein of the American University of Paris; and, for his great generosity in allowing me to use the fruit of his research and experience in the appendix, Richard Bullock of Wright State University. For a clean, well-lighted place to write away from home, thanks to Ron and Elisabeth Beckman of Syracuse University and Paris.

Finally, I say a big thank you to Gerald Graff and Cathy Birkenstein for showing me—particularly in *"They Say / I Say": The Moves That Matter in Academic Writing*—how to represent sophisticated intellectual and rhetorical strategies in a shorthand, generative way that teachers can actually use to help students make those moves in their own writing. I believe, with them, that writing and reading are "deeply reciprocal activities" and that "imitating established models" is one of the best ways to learn how to write.

# Contents

• Student writing

◆ Student writing

# 7 Description 165

JUDITH ORTIZ COFER, *More Room*  197
"As each of their eight children were born, new rooms were added. After a few years, the paint didn't exactly match, nor the materials, so there was a chronology to it, like the rings of a tree."

PAUL CRENSHAW, *Storm Country*  203
"Sometimes it will stop raining when the funnel falls. Sometimes the wind stops and the trees go still and the air settles on you as everything goes quiet."

MICHAEL J. MOONEY, *The Most Amazing Bowling Story Ever*  209
"All you have to do is say the words 'That Night' and everyone at the Plano Super Bowl knows what you're talking about."

E. B. WHITE, *Once More to the Lake*  219
"I felt the same damp moss covering the worms in the bait can, and saw the dragonfly alight on the tip of my rod as it hovered a few inches from the surface of the water. It was the arrival of this fly that convinced me beyond any doubt that everything was as it always had been, that the years were a mirage and that there had been no years."

RITA DOVE, *American Smooth*  227
"We were dancing—it must have / been a foxtrot or a waltz, / something romantic but / requiring restraint"

# 8 Example 231

• Student writing

## 9 Process Analysis 281

**JOSHUA PIVEN, DAVID BORGENICHT, AND JENNIFER WORICK,**
*How to Pull an All-Nighter*  307
"Do not stay up with someone you know will distract you with either idle chatter or sexual tension."

**ALEX HORTON, *On Getting By: Advice for College-Bound Vets*  311**
"I guarantee you've done something harder than a five-page essay."

**DAVE BARRY, *How to Jump-start Your Car When the Battery Is Dead*  317**
"When you drive, be alert for further signs of trouble, such as a flickering of your head-lights, which is an indication of a problem in your electrical system; or a collision with a building, which is an indication that you forgot to put the hood back down."

**CHARLES DUHIGG, *How to Create New Habits*  321**
"The company had spent millions of dollars developing a spray that could remove bad smells from almost any fabric. And the researchers in that tiny, windowless room had no idea how to get people to buy it."

**BILLY COLLINS, *Fishing on the Susquehanna in July*  331**
"I have never been fishing on the Susquehanna / or on any river for that matter / to be perfectly honest."

## 10 Comparison and Contrast 335

◆ JAMIE GULLEN, *The Danish Way of Life* 349

EVERYDAY COMPARISON / A Souvenir Coffee Mug 354

PATRICIA PARK, *Where Are You From?* 357
"Despite the fact that I recited the pledge of allegiance at school each morning, despite my blue U.S. passport, I never self-identified as American while growing up; it had never occurred to me that I was."

DOUGLAS WOLK, *Superhero Smackdown* 361
"At a tender age, most fans of superhero comics start honing their arguments in an ancient debate: 'Which is better—Marvel or DC?'"

DAVID SEDARIS, *Remembering My Childhood on the Continent of Africa* 369
"Certain events are parallel, but compared with Hugh's, my childhood was unspeakably dull. When I was seven years old, my family moved to North Carolina. When he was seven years old, Hugh's family moved to the Congo."

BRUCE CATTON, *Grant and Lee* 377
"They were two strong men, these oddly different generals, and they represented the strengths of two conflicting currents that . . . had come into final collision."

WILLIAM SHAKESPEARE, *Sonnet 130* 383
"My mistress' eyes are nothing like the sun"

◆ Student writing

## 12 Definition 449

"H is unique in that she is both a dead person *and* a patient on the way to surgery. She is what's known as a 'beating-heart cadaver, alive and well everywhere but her brain.'"

"There seem to be more and more zombies every Halloween, more zombies than princesses, fairies, ninjas or knights. In all probability, none of them knows what a zombie really is."

"What most non-dyslexics don't know about us, besides the fact that we simply process information differently, is that our early failures often give us an important edge as we grow older."

"I couldn't have put it in words when I was growing up, but what I observed in my mother's restaurant defined the world of adults, a place where competence was synonymous with physical work."

"I believed progress meant freedom from the field and the range. That meant moving to town, I thought."

"The grandmother shrieked. She scrambled to her feet and stood staring. 'You're The Misfit!' she said. 'I recognized you at once!' "

◆ Student writing

◆ Student writing

◆ Student writing

# Guide to the Readings by Theme

## Cultures and Ethnicities

## Ethics and Religion

## Fiction and Poetry

## Gender

## History

## Humor and Satire

## Language and Identity

## Life, Death, and Illness

## Love and Marriage, Home and Family

## Memories of Youth

## Nature, Science, and Technology

## Public Policy

## Reading and Writers

## Sociology and Anthropology

## Sports and Leisure

## Student Writing

You'll find additional examples of student writing at: wwnorton.com/write/back-to-the-lake.

# Guide to the Readings by Academic Genre

## Personal Narratives

## Position Papers

## Profiles

## Reflections

## Writing That Reports Information

## Rhetorical Analyses

## Textual Analyses

# CHAPTER 1

# Good Writers Are Good Readers

The more that you read, the more things you will know.
The more that you learn, the more places you'll go.

—Dr. Seuss

Learning to write is similar to learning to play the piano.
You have to practice daily to improve your skills. Studying good examples also helps.

—Juha Haataia

L et's start with the alphabet. By the time you learned the alphabet song, you were already proficient at what linguists call *first order* language skills— listening and speaking. We pick up these skills naturally as young children simply by hearing other people talk and by imitating the sounds we hear. The *second order* language skills, reading and writing, take much longer to learn, and they require more formal instruction—just as it took you more time and study to learn the written (as opposed to spoken or sung) alphabet. This is especially true if we are to achieve real competence with the written word. To a degree, however, we learn to write as we first learned to speak—by imitating the words of others.

Consequently, good writers are usually good readers. They may not read every book in the library; but they read critically, paying close attention to the strategies and techniques that accomplished writers use all the time for presenting their ideas. This chapter focuses on how to engage in such close reading and provides some guidelines to help you read the essays in this book with an eye for what they can teach you about your own writing.

## Reading Closely—and Critically

Like writing, reading is an active process. Even when you take a thriller to the beach and read for fun, your brain is at work translating words into mental images and ideas. When you read more purposefully, as with the essays in this book, your brain will get even more of a workout. In both instances, however, the words on the page form a text that can be analyzed and interpreted. The word *text*, like the word *textile*, derives from the Latin word for weaving. A text is a written fabric of words. When you read a text with a critical eye, you unravel that fabric, looking at how the words fit together to make meaning. You also question what you're reading and think more deeply about your own ideas on the subject.

Reading a text critically does not mean that you have to be judgmental. Instead, it means that you analyze the text as carefully and objectively as you can. This is why critical reading will be defined in this book as *close* reading: it sticks to the text as closely as possible and avoids reading too much (or too little) into the text.

## The Reading Process

When you read any text, you engage in a number of activities. Among these are previewing, reading, and responding. *Previewing* a text means looking it over generally to get a rough sense of its subject, scope, and context. When you actually *read* the text, you comb through it systematically from beginning to end, trying to discern the author's main point, how it's supported, and whether any pertinent information is missing. As you *respond* to the text, you think about whether you agree or disagree (or both) with the author's ideas; you may reread parts of the text that you have questions about. Let's take a closer look at each of these activities.

## Previewing a Text

Before you plunge into a text, it's a good idea to take a few moments to survey the territory. Get your pencil ready, but resist the urge to underline until you have a better sense of where the text is going and what you want to focus on.

### TIPS FOR PREVIEWING A TEXT

**Look at the introduction or headnote** to find out about the author and the original context—the time, place, and circumstances in which the text was written and published. For example, a soldier's firsthand account of a battle has a far different context than a historian's account of the same battle written ten years later.

**Think about the title.** What does it reveal about the topic and tone of the text? Are you expecting a serious argument or an essay that pokes fun at its subject?

**Skim the text for an overview,** noting any headings, boldfaced words, illustrations, charts, or footnotes.

**Skim the introduction and conclusion.** What insight do they give into the purpose and message of the text?

**Think about your own expectations and purpose for reading.** Are you reading to obtain information? for entertainment? to fulfill an assignment? How will your purpose and prior knowledge affect what you take from the text?

## Reading a Text

Reading a text closely is a little like investigating a crime scene. You look for certain clues; you ask certain questions. Your objective is to determine, as precisely and accurately as you can, both what the text has to say and how it says it. Your primary clues, therefore, are in the text itself—the actual words on the page.

If you've previewed the text carefully, you already have some idea of what it's about. Now is the time to examine it closely. So pull out your pencil, and perhaps a highlighter (whether physical or electronic), and be ready to annotate the text as you go along—to jot down questions or comments in the margins, underline important points, circle key words, and otherwise mark places in the text that you may want to come back to.

The following example shows how a student writer, Judy Vassey, has annotated a paragraph from an essay reprinted later in this chapter. Notice that she has identified and underlined the author's main point, circled a few words and phrases that she wants to investigate further, and raised a key question about the many questions in the passage.

| | |
|---|---|
| begets = Bible? | For some of us, reading begets rereading, and rereading begets |
| main point | writing. (Although there is no doubt which is first, and supreme; as |
| who's Manguel? | Alberto Manguel writes in his wonderful A History of Reading, "I |
| | could perhaps live without writing. I don't think I could live without |
| what story? | reading.") After a while the story is familiar, the settings known, the |
| | characters understood, and there is nothing left to discover but tech- |
| | nique. Why that sentence structure and not something simpler, or |
| why all the questions? | more complex? Why that way of ordering events instead of something |
| | more straightforward, or more experimental? What grabs the reader |
| | by the throat? What sags and bags and fails? There are only two ways, |
| | really, to become a writer. One is to write. The other is to read. |

—Anna Quindlen, *How Reading Changed My Life*

Vassey is a good close reader, but even she can't decipher all the important clues on her first run through a relatively complex passage. How does a good detective ensure that she hasn't missed any important evidence? She returns to the scene of the crime—she rereads the text.

When Vassey reread the Quindlen text, she answered her own query about the number of questions the author asks, noting that they show how a writer habitually reads with an eye for methods and technique. To discover not only *what* a text is saying but *how* and *why*—this is your goal as a writer reading the work of others.

## QUESTIONS FOR CLOSE READING

**What is the writer's main point?** Is it clearly stated in a thesis? If so, where? If the main point is not stated directly, is it clearly implied?

**What is the primary purpose of the text?** To provide information? Sell a product or service? Argue a point of view? Make us laugh? Tell a story?

**Who is the intended audience?** Readers familiar with the topic? Those who know little about it? People who might be inclined to agree—or disagree?

**What is the tone and style of the text?** Serious? Informal? Inspirational? Strident?

**How and where does the writer support the main point?** Can you point out specific details, facts, examples, visuals, expert testimony, personal experience, or other kinds of evidence?

**Is the evidence sufficient?** Or does the supporting evidence fail to convince you? Are sources clearly identified so you can tell where quotations, paraphrases, or summaries are coming from?

**Has the writer fairly represented—and responded to—other points of view?** Has any crucial perspective been left out?

**How is the text organized?** Do ideas flow logically from one to another? Where, if anywhere, is the text difficult to follow? Why?

**What is the larger historical and cultural context of the text?** Who is the author? When was the text written and published? By whom? What other ideas or events does it reflect?

## Responding to What You've Read

Once you've read a text closely—questioning point by point what it says and how— you're in a good position to judge what the text adds up to and how you feel about it, both emotionally and intellectually. That is, you're ready to respond—preferably in writing—to the text as a whole. Go back over the text once more and try the following tips.

## TIPS FOR RESPONDING

**Summarize what you've read in your own words.** If you can write a SUMMARY of the main points, you probably have a good grasp of what you've read.

**Think about and record your own reactions.** To what extent do you agree or disagree—or both—with what the author is saying? It is usual, of course, to accept some statements in a text—including the THESIS, or main point—and still question others. And it is possible to like (or dislike) the tone and style of a text even if you reject (or accept) the argument.

**Consider what you learned about writing.** Make note of any techniques used in the text that you might want to incorporate into your own writing. For example, does the piece have a catchy introduction, interesting and pertinent examples, or striking visuals? If the text has elements you don't want to emulate—such as a weak conclusion—you might write those down as well.

## Reading Visual Texts

Almost everywhere we look these days, we are surrounded by visuals—on blogs and websites, in magazines and textbooks, on billboards and subways. It is essential, then, to be able to read visuals closely, to look at them with a critical eye.

In many ways, reading a visual is similar to reading a written text: you have to think critically about its purpose, its main point, and so on. Some visuals consist only of images—photographs, drawings, paintings—whereas other visuals—like graphs and diagrams—include words. Many advertisements, for example, combine images and words to create an explicit message, urging us perhaps to buy a Honda, support the NRA, or quit smoking.

## QUESTIONS FOR READING VISUALS

**What is the specific message of the visual?** Does the message come across clearly, and does it do so with words as well as images?

**How does the visual support its message?** For example, does it use a poignant photograph, a quotation from an expert, or relevant statistics?

**What is the source and purpose?** Was it developed by an individual? A corporation? A government agency? Is the source reputable? What does the nature of the source tell you about the purpose of the visual? Is the purpose to sell you something? to provide information? to persuade you to support a cause?

**Who is the intended audience?** Is it aimed at a general audience or at a more specialized one: college students, parents, sports enthusiasts, experts in a particular field? How do you think the intended audience affects the argument the text makes?

**What is the tone of the overall design—and what does that say about the message?** What word would you use to describe the design—bold? lively? tranquil? gloomy? cluttered? something else?

This book cover has been annotated by a student writer; a passage from the book begins on the next page. After you've read the passage, look back at this cover and think about how (and how well) the illustration supports the written text.

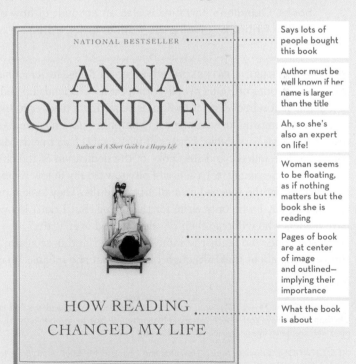

NATIONAL BESTSELLER ········· Says lots of people bought this book

ANNA QUINDLEN ········· Author must be well known if her name is larger than the title

Author of *A Short Guide to a Happy Life* ········· Ah, so she's also an expert on life!

········· Woman seems to be floating, as if nothing matters but the book she is reading

········· Pages of book are at center of image and outlined—implying their importance

HOW READING ········· What the book is about
CHANGED MY LIFE

ANNA QUINDLEN

# How Reading Changed My Life

Anna Quindlen (b. 1952) grew up in the suburbs of Philadelphia in a neighborhood that was "the sort of place in which people dream of raising children—pretty, privileged but not rich, a small but satisfying spread of center-hall colonials, old roses, rhododendrons, and quiet roads." After graduating from Barnard College, Quindlen worked as a reporter, first for the *New York Post* and then for the *New York Times*, where her regular column, "Public and Private," won a Pulitzer Prize in 1992. Between 2000 and 2009, she contributed a biweekly column, *The Last Word,* to *Newsweek.* Quindlen gave up full-time journalism in 1995 to concentrate on writing fiction. Her novels include *Black and Blue* (1998), *Blessings* (2002), *Every Last One* (2010), *and Still Life with Breadcrumbs* (2014).

In addition to a memoir, *Lots of Candles, Plenty of Cake* (2012), Quindlen is the author of *How Reading Changed My Life* (1998), from which this reading is taken. The personal story of her private life with books, Quindlen's narrative is also an account of how a writer learns the craft of writing by reading the work of other writers.

I N 1997 KATHERINE PATERSON, whose novel *Bridge to Terabithia* has engaged several generations of young people with its story of friendship and loss—and also led to a policy in a school district in Kansas requiring a teacher to list each profanity in required reading and forward the list to parents—gave the Anne Carroll Moore[1] Lecture at the New York Public Library. It was a speech as fine as Ms. Paterson's books, which are fine indeed, and she spoke of the dedication of the children who are her readers: "I increasingly feel a sense of pity toward my fellow writers who spend their lives writing for the speeded-up audience of adults. They look at me, I realize, with a patronizing air, I who only write for the young. But I don't know any of them who have readers who will read their novels over and over again."

As someone who reads the same books over and over again, I think Ms. Paterson is wrong about that, although I know what she means. I have sat on the edge

---

1. *Anne Carroll Moore* (1871–1961): An author of children's books and the first supervisor of Work with Children at the New York Public Library in Manhattan. *Bridge to Terabithia* (1977): A novel about two children who create an imaginary kingdom in a forest.

MLA CITATION: Quindlen, Anna. "How Reading Changed My Life." 1998. *Back to the Lake.* Ed. Thomas Cooley. 3rd ed. New York: Norton, 2015. 8–9. Print.

of several beds while *Green Eggs and Ham* was read, or recited more or less from memory; I read *A Wrinkle in Time* three times in a row once, when I was twelve, because I couldn't bear for it to end, wanted them all, Meg and Charles Murry and even the horribly pulsing brain called It,[2] to be alive again as they could only live within my mind, so that I felt as if I killed them when I closed the cover and gave them the kiss of life when my eyes met the words that created their lives. I still reread that way, always have, always will. I suspect there are more of us than Ms. Paterson knows. And I think I know who we are, and how we got that way. We are writers. We danced with the words, as children, in what became familiar patterns. The words became our friends and our companions, and without even saying it aloud, a thought danced with them: I can do this. This is who I am.

For some of us, reading begets rereading, and rereading begets writing. 3 (Although there is no doubt which is first, and supreme; as Alberto Manguel writes in his wonderful *A History of Reading*,[3] "I could perhaps live without writing. I don't think I could live without reading.") After a while the story is familiar, the settings known, the characters understood, and there is nothing left to discover but technique. Why that sentence structure and not something simpler, or more complex? Why that way of ordering events instead of something more straightforward, or more experimental? What grabs the reader by the throat? What sags and bags and fails? There are only two ways, really, to become a writer. One is to write. The other is to read. ◆

2. *A Wrinkle in Time* (1962): A novel by Madeleine L'Engle (1918–2007) about three children who are transported through the galaxy by transcendental beings to fight an evil force known as It. The manuscript took a while to find a publisher because, according to L'Engle, many considered it "too different." *Green Eggs and Ham* (1960): A popular children's book written and illustrated by Dr. Seuss (Theodor Seuss Geisel, 1902–1991), who believed that children learn to read through repetition and familiarity.

3. *Alberto Manguel* (b. 1948): A writer and editor living in Buenos Aires. *A History of Reading* (1996) is his enthusiastic, thematic tour through the library imagined in a story by the Argentinean writer Jorge Luis Borges (1899–1986).

## Reading the Essays in This Book

Even if reading doesn't change your life, it will change your writing. Good writers are good readers because many of the basic skills of writing can only be learned by reading the work of other writers. Before we come back to the example of Anna Quindlen and the specific methods and techniques she uses in her brief essay, let's look ahead to the rest of the essays in this book.

In *Back to the Lake*, you will be reading and analyzing numerous essays by many different writers on a variety of topics. The essays are grouped into chapters according to the principal methods of development they use: NARRATION, DESCRIPTION, EXAMPLE, PROCESS ANALYSIS, COMPARISON AND CONTRAST, CLASSIFICATION AND DIVISION, DEFINITION, CAUSE AND EFFECT, and ARGUMENT. Experienced writers often employ more than one method in the same essay, so there is also a final chapter called "Combining the Methods."

Your main goal in reading the essays in this book is to master the methods of development they demonstrate so you can use those methods in your own writing. As you study these model essays in detail, however, you will encounter many other useful strategies and techniques—ways of beginning, of using transitions to move a text along, of presenting certain kinds of information in lists or charts, and so on.

Each selection in *Back to the Lake* is introduced with a headnote—like the one before the Quindlen piece—that provides information about the author of the text and its historical, social, or cultural context; and each selection is followed by study questions and writing prompts. The following questions and suggestions for writing pertain to "How Reading Changed My Life," but they are typical of the ones you will find after every other selection in this book (except they include sample answers after the questions).

### FOR CLOSE READING

1.  Anna Quindlen thinks that "Ms. Paterson is wrong about that" (2). About what? What's at issue between these two writers—one who writes exclusively for children, the other who writes both for children and adults?

    *At issue is the nature of today's reading audience. Katherine Paterson claims that adult readers are too busy to reread anything. Thus, she feels "a sense of pity toward my fellow writers" who do not write for children, because children read their favorite authors again and again (1).*

2.   In her debate with Katherine Paterson, what **POSITION** does Quindlen take?

*Quindlen thinks there is at least one class of adult readers—those who are also writers—who read a favorite book over and over again. "I still reread that way," says Quindlen, "always have, always will" (2).*

3.   In paragraph 3, Quindlen tells how her childhood reading inspired her to become a writer. What, according to Quindlen, do writers learn from reading and rereading a familiar text?

*They learn "familiar patterns" of writing (2).*

## Strategies and Structures

1.   Quindlen begins by disagreeing with a fellow writer. How, and how fairly, does she represent the opposing point of view?

*Before saying that Ms. Paterson is wrong, Quindlen praises her as a "fine" writer and speaker (1). She also says that she understands the opposing point of view and gives herself as an example of a repeat reader of children's books.*

2.   What evidence does Quindlen give to support her contention that at least some adult readers are rereaders? How convincing do you find this evidence? Why?

*Most of Quindlen's evidence comes from her childhood reading. She might have given more examples of her reading as an adult, or cited the experiences of others, to support her statement, "I suspect there are more of us than Ms. Paterson knows" (2).*

3.   The chair on the cover of Quindlen's book (p. 6) looks at first like it's upside down. Why do you think the designer chose this particular angle?

*It looks like the reader is floating—and could go anywhere as she reads. The viewing angle shows the woman from above, focusing our gaze on the book in the woman's lap. From a different angle, the book would be less central to the picture.*

4.   *Other Methods.* Quindlen's personal **NARRATIVE** not only tells the story of how reading changed her life, it analyzes the **EFFECTS** of a life-changing experience. What are they?

*The main effect was to make her want to be a writer as well as a reader: "I can do this" (2). But Quindlen cites other effects as well: an exciting mental life filled with imaginary companions—and rich memories to savor as an adult.*

## Thinking about Language

1.   Ms. Paterson pities writers who must write for an audience that is "speeded-up" (1). Why do you think she chose this word instead of *sped up* or *hurried*?

*By emphasizing the word speed, she draws the reader's attention to how fast-paced contemporary life has become, how we are accustomed to completing daily activities—including reading—as quickly as possible.*

2. Look up *"begets"* in a dictionary (3). What are the CONNOTATIONS of the term? Why do you think Quindlen chose it to describe how writing comes from reading?

   *Beget means "to father" or "to cause to exist." It connotes a close and natural relationship. Perhaps she is suggesting that writing is a natural progression from reading.*

3. What does Quindlen mean by "technique" (3)?

   *From the examples she gives, it means practically every choice—sentence structure, overall organization, audience appeal—that a writer makes to achieve the desired effect on the reader.*

4. Quindlen is recalling her childhood from memory. Which particular phrases and sentences in her narrative do you find most memory-like in their flow and structure? Explain.

   *Most of Quindlen's sentences are long, but when she recalls how reading enchanted her as a child—and still does—the words become almost dreamlike in the way they mimic her thought processes. The best example is the sentence beginning, "I have sat on the edge of several beds" (2).*

## FOR WRITING

1. Write a paragraph or two explaining how you typically read a text.

2. Write a LITERACY NARRATIVE about an early reading (or other) experience from your childhood and how it has shaped your present-day attitudes toward reading and writing.

3. Write a detailed DESCRIPTION of the cover of Quindlen's book (or of some other book, video, or album you're familiar with). EVALUATE and explain how, and how well, the illustration fits the text it's intended to illustrate. In addition to focusing on key words and images, be sure to include such elements of the design as color and shading, size and style of the print, and the use of space.

4. As a child reading and rereading one of her favorite books, Quindlen felt that she killed the characters when she closed the book "as they could only live within my mind." What view of the reader's role in constructing a text does this statement imply? COLLABORATE with one or more of your classmates on a POSITION PAPER that supports or questions this view of reading and writing.

5. As you read the essays and commentary in *Back to the Lake*, keep a JOURNAL focusing on what you're learning about the processes of reading and writing. Each time you dip into the book, make an entry, however brief, in your journal.

# CHAPTER 2

# Putting in Your Oar:
# Learning the Basic Moves
# of Academic Writing

You listen for a while, until you decide that you have
caught the tenor of the argument; then you put in your
oar. —KENNETH BURKE, *The Philosophy of Literary Form*

You come late to a party. A lively conversation is going on around you. You aren't sure what it's about at first—a class, a movie, the merits of two teams? Academic writing is like this, except the discussion began long ago, and—as suggested by philosopher Kenneth Burke's famous parlor analogy—it never ends. Here's the scene as Burke describes it:

> Imagine that you enter a parlor. You come late. When you arrive, others have long preceded you, and they are engaged in a heated discussion, a discussion too heated for them to pause and tell you exactly what it is about. You listen for a while, until you decide that you have caught the tenor of the argument; then you put in your oar. Someone answers; you answer him; another comes to your defense; another aligns himself against you. . . . The hour grows late, you must depart. And you do depart, with the discussion still vigorously in progress.

Like Burke's parlor, academic writing is the site of an ongoing conversation—about ideas. The ultimate purpose of that conversation is the advancement of human knowledge. More immediately, you can learn a lot about any field of study that interests you, from physics to dance, just by listening to what knowledgeable people in that field have to say.

Specific kinds of academic writing are discussed in Chapter 3 (p. 27).

Academic writing, like other social activities and forms of conversation, has its own rules and conventions. Don't leave a party without properly thanking the hostess; don't turn in a paper without properly citing your sources. This chapter covers some of the basic conventions and strategies (or "moves") of academic writing:

- researching what's been said about your topic
- synthesizing the ideas you find with your own ideas
- presenting your ideas as a response to the ideas of others
- considering other views
- saying why your ideas matter
- using description, comparison, and the other methods taught in this book

## Finding Out What's Been Said about Your Topic

Before you put in your oar, you need to get your bearings. So before you leap into a discussion on a topic that's new to you, test the waters by attending lectures, talking with your teachers and fellow students, and reading and thinking about what others have written on the topic under discussion. In short, you need to do some preliminary research.

With many kinds of academic writing—a brief answer on an essay exam, for example—your research will consist mostly of thinking about your topic and figuring out what you want to emphasize. For a research paper, however, you will need to find out what experts in the field are saying. So you'll need to look for authoritative written sources of information, such as academic books and peer-reviewed articles. Remember that all the sources you consult when you write a research paper should be identified in a reference list at the end of your paper—and you'll also name many of your most important sources as you go along.

Refer to the Appendix (p. 799) for information on finding, evaluating, and citing sources.

Academic writing is about much more than amassing sources, however. With even the most informal research paper, you'll be expected to show what you've learned and even to contribute ideas of your own to the discussion. Coming up with ideas, in fact, is the main reason you join in the give and take of an academic conversation in the first place.

In some cultures, it is impolite to disagree directly and openly with others, especially if they are older than you are, or are your hosts at a social event. But imagine a conversation in which every assertion ("the earth is flat," "printing new money will ease the financial crisis") is always met with polite assent ("I agree"; "yes, that's right"). Academic discourse should always be courteous, but in most U.S. academic contexts, the conversation goes more like this: "I see what you're saying, but what about . . . ?" "No, that's not my point. My point is. . . ." In other words, this tradition of academic discourse is based on a synthesis of different—even conflicting—ideas and viewpoints.

## Synthesizing Ideas

Suppose you're writing a paper on how the internet has changed our lives. You've begun to do your research, and you're finding lots of good ideas, some of which you plan to weave into your paper—with full attribution, of course. You don't want to simply repeat what others have said on your topic, however. You want to synthesize their ideas and come up with some new ones of your own.

Here's how that process might work. As you read through your many sources, you keep running into various arguments to the following effect: "The internet is making us stupid." You don't agree with this view; but you find it thought-provoking. You may even mention it in your paper as an idea that helped nudge you into taking a different (more positive) position on your topic.

As you mull over such negative statements about the effect of the internet on the human brain, you come upon others that are virtually the antithesis of the first.

They run, more or less, as follows: "The internet is making us all smarter because it places more information at our fingertips more quickly than ever before."

You do not agree entirely with these ideas, either; but by bringing them together—which is what *synthesis* means—with other, opposing ideas on your topic, a spark is struck in your mind. You now have a clearer conception of what you want to say.

You jot down some notes before you forget: "Both of these positions are flawed. The internet's not really making us smarter or dumber. Just speeding up our access to information. Conclusion: the internet is not fundamentally changing how we think; it's simply making us more efficient."

This last statement is a synthesis of the opposing views you have encountered in your research. It will make a dandy THESIS, or main point, for the paper you want to write about the internet. And it came to you out of the intellectual give and take that is the heart, or rather, the brain, of academic writing. As you present this proposition to your readers, you may also want to explain some of the other, contrasting ideas that inspired it.

## Presenting Your Ideas as a Response to Those of Others

Starting with the ideas of others is so basic to academic writing that some teachers and theorists of writing consider it to be *the* underlying pattern of much academic prose, cutting across all disciplines and majors. The following is an elegant statement of this view:

> For us, the underlying structure of effective academic writing . . . resides not just in stating our own ideas, but in listening closely to others around us, summarizing their views in a way that they will recognize, and responding with our own ideas in kind. Broadly speaking, academic writing is argumentative writing, and . . . to argue well you need to do more than assert your own ideas. You need to enter a conversation, using what others say (or might say) as a launching pad . . . for your own ideas.
>
> —GERALD GRAFF AND CATHY BIRKENSTEIN,
> *"They Say / I Say": The Moves That Matter in Academic Writing*\*

In the following passage from an Op-Ed piece in the *New York Times*, for example, a psychology professor starts by summarizing the views of other writers—and then disagrees, advancing his own view.

---

\*In fact, the work of Graff and Birkenstein in demystifying the argumentative aspect of academic writing has served not only as a launching pad for this chapter but for the templates throughout the book. As these scholars demonstrate, such templates "do more than organize students' ideas; they help bring those ideas into existence."

Media critics write as if the brain takes on the qualities of whatever it consumes, the informational equivalent of "you are what you eat." As with primitive peoples who believe that eating fierce animals will make them fierce, they assume that watching quick cuts in rock videos turns your mental life into quick cuts or that reading bullet points and Twitter postings turns your thoughts into bullet points and Twitter postings. . . . Far from making us stupid, these technologies are the only things that will keep us smart.

—STEVEN PINKER, "Mind Over Mass Media"

Although Pinker disagrees completely with those who say that electronic media are making us stupid, he nonetheless puts forth his own views as a response to their views. In particular, he does so by COMPARING—a common pattern in academic writing—their respective ideas with those of "primitive peoples."

For a lively debate on this issue, read the group of essays beginning on p. 715.

In any academic writing you do, there are many ways of introducing the ideas of others. Three of the most common ones are:

• *Quoting another writer's exact words.* "Media critics," says Steven Pinker, "write as if the brain takes on the qualities of whatever it consumes, the informational equivalent of 'you are what you eat.' "

• *Paraphrasing another writer's ideas.* According to Steven Pinker, critics of the new media have a faulty view of the human brain as an organ that must be fed a constant diet of intellectual red meat.

• *Summarizing another writer's ideas.* Steven Pinker attacks the views of media critics as a primitive form of superstition.

Now let's look at a more complicated example. In the following passage, a student writer both summarizes and quotes from the work of writers with whom she agrees:

Pioneering evolutionary psychologist Robert L. Trivers has observed that having and rearing children requires women to invest far more resources than men do because of the length of pregnancy, the dangers of childbirth, and the duration of infants' dependence on their mothers (145). According to Helen Fisher, one of the leading advocates of this theory, finding a capable mate was a huge preoccupation of all prehistoric reproductive women, and for good reason: "A female couldn't carry a baby in one arm and sticks and stones in the other arm and still feed and protect herself on the very dangerous open grasslands, so she began to need a mate to help her rear her young" (Frank 85). . . . [T]hese are the bases upon which modern mate selection is founded, and there are many examples of this phenomenon to be found in our own society.

—CAROLYN STONEHILL, "Modern Dating, Prehistoric Style"

For tips on determining when to quote, paraphrase, or summarize, see p. 807 in the Appendix.

In this passage, Stonehill is not simply reporting what she learned about human mating behavior by reading the work of experts in the field of evolutionary biology, such as Trivers and Fisher. Having synthesized their views in her own mind, she uses them as a framework to support *her* thesis, stated in the previous paragraph, about the origins of "modern mate selection": "Driven by the need to reproduce and propagate the species, these ancestors of ours formed patterns of mate selection so effective in providing for their needs and those of their offspring that they are mimicked even in today's society."

As you introduce the ideas of others into your writing, you can present your own ideas by responding to theirs in many different ways. These three are the most common: agree with what they say (as Stonehill did), disagree (like Pinker), or both. The templates on p. 19 suggest some ways to structure your response.

## Considering Other Views

You can read the complete version of this paper on p. 21.

Carolyn Stonehill's paper on mate selection is a good example of academic writing that both agrees and disagrees with the views of other writers. Stonehill is aware that evolutionary psychology is a controversial field. So after building on the work of such evolutionary psychologists as Trivers and Fisher, she anticipates other possible arguments: "There is, however," she writes, "a good deal of opposition to evolutionary theory. Some critics say that the messages fed to us by the media are a larger influence on the criteria of present-day mate selection than any sort of ancestral behavior."

As Steven Pinker does when he disputes critics of mass media, Stonehill introduces the views of potential opponents ("some critics") for the purpose of acknowledging other views, a rhetorical move known as *planting a naysayer*. Stonehill does not simply disagree with the naysayers' position, however; she carefully refutes it by summarizing and then directly quoting arguments on *her* side of the debate about which has the greater influence—modern media or ancestral behavior—on how we date and mate today.

First her summary: "Evolutionary psychologists argue that research has not determined what is cause and what is effect." Then the quotation (from the work of Leda Cosmides and John Tooby): "In the absence of research on the particular topic, there is no way of knowing." These arguments do not conclusively prove Stonehill's point, of course. But they may cast a reasonable doubt on the position she is challenging.

## TIPS AND TEMPLATES FOR DRAFTING

**Agree.** When you agree with others, do more than just echo their arguments—point out unnoticed implications, or explain a concept that you think needs to be better understood.

▸ One of the most respected experts in the field is X, who says essentially that _____.

▸ Advocates of this view are Y and Z, who also argue that _____.

▸ Persuaded by these arguments, I agree with those who say _____.

**Disagree.** Don't just contradict the views of others: offer persuasive reasons why you disagree. Justify your reason for writing, and move the conversation forward.

▸ In my view, these objections do not hold up because _____.

▸ Like some critics of these ideas, particularly X and Y, I would argue instead that _____.

▸ Z's focus on _____ obscures the underlying issue of _____.

**Both agree and disagree.** This approach works well when your topic is complex. It avoids a yes/no standoff and displays your thorough understanding of the issues. You don't have to give equal weight to all aspects of the topic — just the main points under debate. This approach invites COMPARISON, for example, when you want to list pros and cons.

▸ Although I concede that _____, I still maintain that _____.

▸ Whereas X and Y make good points about _____, I have to agree with Z that _____.

▸ X may be wrong about _____, but the rest of her argument is persuasive.

## Saying Why Your Ideas Matter

Who cares? Why does it matter? Whatever you're writing about, you also need to explain the *significance* of your ideas. Stonehill does so by explicitly stating that her thesis "would explain why women of our time are preoccupied with plastic surgery, makeup, and . . . a quick hair check as a potential date approaches." Most aspects of "our mating behavior," in fact, can be better understood, she argues, if we recognize that they derive from "the complex mating strategies developed by our ancestors." These last three templates suggest some ways to explain why your ideas matter:

> ▸ The prevailing view has long been _____; but now we can see that _____.
>
> ▸ This conclusion is significant because _____.
>
> ▸ In particular, X and Y should be interested in this view because _____.

## Using the Rhetorical Methods in Academic Writing

The basic purpose of most academic writing is to prove a point. The writer makes a claim in the form of a thesis and then supports that claim throughout the rest of his or her paper. The basic strategies and methods of ARGUMENT are, therefore, particularly useful in academic writing.

In addition to argument, however, the other basic methods of development taught in this book—NARRATION, DESCRIPTION, EXAMPLE, PROCESS ANALYSIS, COMPARISON AND CONTRAST, CLASSIFICATION, DEFINITION, and CAUSE AND EFFECT—can also help you figure out and present what you have to say in any piece of academic writing. Useful as these methods of development can be for presenting your ideas in an academic paper, they can also serve as ways of discovering what you have to say in the first place—as you do research and begin to write. Much of the rest of this book, in fact, is about that process of discovery and the use of these methods  as ways of thinking as well as strategies for writing.

See Chapter 3 (p. 27) for more on using these methods in academic writing.

## A Sample Academic Essay

In "Modern Dating, Prehistoric Style," Carolyn Stonehill draws on her research in the field of evolutionary psychology to argue that many of the dating habits of modern humans derive from behaviors developed by our ancient ancestors as they struggled to survive and reproduce in dangerous environments. Since Stonehill's paper was written for a first-year college writing class, she uses MLA style to cite her sources. Styles of documentation vary from discipline to discipline, however, so consult your instructor if you're not sure which style you should use.

## Modern Dating, Prehistoric Style

Consider the following scenario: It's a sunny afternoon on campus, and Jenny is walking to her next class. Out of the corner of her eye, she catches sight of her lab partner, Joey, parking his car. She stops to admire how tall, muscular, and stylishly dressed he is, and she does not take her eyes off him as he walks away from his shiny new BMW. As he flashes her a pearly white smile, Jenny melts, then quickly adjusts her skirt and smooths her hair.

> Introduction uses NARRATION and DESCRIPTION to give an EXAMPLE of "modern dating"

This scenario, while generalized, is familiar: Our attraction to people—or lack of it—often depends on their physical traits. But why this attraction? Why does Jenny respond the way she does to her handsome lab partner? Why does she deem him handsome at all? Certainly Joey embodies the stereotypes of physical attractiveness prevalent in contemporary American society. Advertisements, television shows, and magazine articles all provide Jenny with signals telling her what constitutes the ideal American man. Yet she is also attracted to Joey's new sports car even though she has a new car herself. Does Jenny find this man striking because of the influence of her culture, or does her attraction lie in a more fundamental part of her constitution? Evolutionary psychologists, who apply principles of evolutionary biology to research on the human mind, would say that Jenny's responses in this situation are due largely to mating strategies developed by her prehistoric ancestors. Driven by the need to reproduce and propagate the species, these ancestors of ours formed patterns of mate selection so effective in providing for their needs and those of their offspring that they are mimicked even in today's society. While cultural values and messages clearly play a part in the process of mate selection, the genetic and psychological predispositions developed by our ancestors play the biggest role in determining to whom we are attracted.

> Raises a key question about CAUSE AND EFFECT

> DEFINES the field of evolutionary psychology, which may be unfamiliar to Stonehill's AUDIENCE

> States the main point, or THESIS, of Stonehill's paper

> Anticipates views of potential opponents

## Women's Need to Find a Capable Mate

Pioneering evolutionary psychologist Robert L. Trivers has observed that having and rearing children requires women to invest far more resources than men do because of the length of pregnancy,

SUMMARIZES
and QUOTES
the views of
other writers
whose ideas
Stonehill plans
to build on

the dangers of childbirth, and the duration of infants' dependence on their mothers (145). According to Helen Fisher, one of the leading advocates of this theory, finding a capable mate was a huge preoccupation of all prehistoric reproductive women, and for good reason: "A female couldn't carry a baby in one arm and sticks and stones in the other arm and still feed and protect herself on the very dangerous open grasslands, so she began to need a mate to help her rear her young" (Frank 85). So because of this it became advantageous for the woman to find a strong, capable man with

SYNTHESIZES the
views of other
writers as a basis
for Stonehill's
own claim

access to resources, and it became suitable for the man to find a healthy, reproductively sound woman to bear and care for his offspring. According to evolutionary psychologists, these are the bases upon which modern mate selection is founded, and there are many examples of this phenomenon to be found in our own society.

Returns to
Stonehill's
opening
NARRATIVE and
reads it in the
light of ideas in
evolutionary
psychology that
support her
position

One can see now why Jenny might be attracted by Joey's display of resources—his BMW. In our society, men with good job prospects, respected social positions, friends in high places, or any combination thereof have generally been viewed as more desirable mates than those without these things because they signal to women that the men have resources (Buss and Schmitt 226). Compared with males, females invest more energy in bearing and raising children,

SUMMARY
statement
about origins of
female behavior
leads to
COMPARISON
with male
behavior in
next section

so it is most advantageous for females to choose mates with easy access to resources, the better to provide for their children.

### Men's Need to Find a Healthy Mate

For men, reproductive success depends mainly on the reproductive fitness of their female counterparts: No amount of available resources can save a baby miscarried in the first month of gestation. Because of this need for a healthy mate, men have evolved a particular attraction "radar" that focuses on signs of a woman's health and youth, markers that are primarily visual (Weiten 399). Present-day attractiveness ratings are based significantly on this primitive standard: "Some researchers have suggested that cross-cultural standards of beauty reflect an evolved preference for physical traits that are generally associated with youth, such as smooth skin, good muscle tone, and shiny hair" (Boyd and Silk 625). This observation would explain why women of our time are preoccupied with plastic surgery, makeup, and—in Jenny's case—a quick hair check as a potential date approaches. As Michael R. Cunningham et al. noted, "A focus on outer beauty may have stemmed from a need for desirable inner qualities," such as health, strength, and fertility, and "culture may build on evolutionary dynamics by specifying grooming attributes that signal successful adaptation" (262–63).

> Introduces more expert opinion in support of Stonehill's thesis—and explains the broader significance of that thesis

### The Influence of the Media on Mate Selection

There is, however, a good deal of opposition to evolutionary theory. Some critics say that the messages fed to us by the media are a larger influence on the criteria of present-day mate selection than any sort of ancestral behavior. Advertisements and popular media have long shown Americans what constitutes a physically ideal mate: In general, youthful, well-toned, symmetrical features are considered more attractive than aging, flabby, or lopsided ones. Evolutionary psychologists argue that research has not determined what is cause and what is effect. Leda Cosmides and John Tooby offered the following analogy to show the danger of assigning culture too powerful a causal role:

> Introduces naysayers in order to anticipate and refute views of potential opponents

> Explains Stonehill's point in directly quoting two more writers with whom she agrees

> For example, people think that if they can show that there is information in the culture that mirrors how people behave, then *that* is the cause of their behavior. So if they see that men on TV have trouble crying, they assume that their example is *causing* boys to be afraid to cry. But which is cause and which effect? Does the fact that men don't cry much on TV *teach* boys to not cry, or does it merely *reflect* the way boys normally develop? In the absence of research on the particular topic, there is no way of knowing. ("Nature and Nurture: An Adaptationist Perspective," par. 16)

We can hypothesize, then, that rather than media messages determining our mating habits, our mating habits determine the media messages. Advertisers rely on classical conditioning to interest consumers in their products. For instance, by showing an image of a beautiful woman while advertising a beauty product, advertisers hope that consumers will associate attractiveness with the use of that particular product (Weiten 684). In order for this method to be effective, however, the images depicted in conjunction with the beauty product must be ones the general public already finds attractive, and an image of a youthful, clear-skinned woman would, according to evolutionary psychologists, be attractive for reasons of reproductive fitness. In short, what some call media influence is not

an influence at all but merely a mirror in which we see evidence of our ancestral predispositions.

### If Not Media, Then What?

Ian Tattersall, a paleoanthropologist at the American Museum of Natural History, offered another counterargument to the evolutionary theory of mate selection. First, he argued that the behavior of organisms is influenced not only by genetics, but also by economics and ecology working together (663). Second, he argued that no comparisons can be made between modern human behavior and that of our evolutionary predecessors because the appearance of *Homo sapiens* presented a sudden, qualitative change from the Neanderthals—not a gradual evolution of behavioral traits:

> As a cognitive and behavioral entity, our species is truly unprecedented. Our consciousness is an emergent quality, not the result of eons of fine-tuning of a single instrument. And, if so, it is to this recently acquired quality of uniqueness, not to the hypothetical "ancestral environments," that we must look in the effort to understand our often unfathomable behaviors. (665)

The key to Tattersall's argument is this "emergent quality" of symbolic thought; according to his theories, the ability to think symbolically is what separates modern humans from their ancestors and shows the impossibility of sexual selection behaviors having been passed down over millions of years. Our sexual preferences, Tattersall said, are a result of our own recent and species-specific development and have nothing whatsoever to do with our ancestors.

Opponents of the evolutionary theory, though, fail to explain how "unfathomable" mating behaviors can exist in our present society for no apparent or logical reason. Though medicine has advanced to the point where fertility can be medically enhanced, Devendra Singh observed that curvy women are still viewed as especially attractive because they are perceived to possess greater fertility—a perception that is borne out by several studies of female fertility, hormone levels, and waist-to-hip ratio (304). Though more and more women are attending college and achieving high-paying positions, women are still "more likely than men to consider economic prospects a high priority in a mate" (Sapolsky 18). While cultural norms and economic conditions influence our taste in mates, as Singh showed in observing that "the degree of affluence of a society or of an ethnic group within a society may, to a large extent, determine the prevalence and admiration of fatness [of women]" (304-05), we still react to potential mates in ways determined in Paleolithic times. The key to understanding our mating behavior does not lie only in an emergent modern quality, nor does it lie solely in the messages relayed to us by society; rather, it involves as well the complex mating strategies developed by our ancestors.

Attacks that assumption as unfounded and draws support from additional sources

Conclusion acknowledges the validity of opposing views but stipulates that Stonehill's argument is also valid

Works Cited

Boyd, Robert, and Joan B. Silk. *How Humans Evolved*. 6th ed. New York: Norton, 2012. Print.

Buss, David M., and David P. Schmitt. "Sexual Strategies Theory: An Evolutionary Perspective on Human Mating." *Psychological Review* 100.2 (1993): 204-32. Print.

Cosmides, Leda, and John Tooby. "Evolutionary Psychology: A Primer." *Center for Evolutionary Psychology*. University of California, Santa Barbara, 1997. Web. 14 Oct. 2014.

Cunningham, Michael R., Alan R. Roberts, Anita P. Barbee, Perri B. Druen, and Cheng-Huan Wu. " 'Their Ideas of Beauty Are, on the Whole, the Same as Ours': Consistency and Variability in the Crosscultural Perception of Female Physical Attractiveness." *Journal of Personality and Social Psychology* 68.2 (1995): 261-79. Print.

Frank, C. "Why Do We Fall in—and Out of—Love? Dr. Helen Fisher Unravels the Mystery." *Biography* Feb. 2001: 85+. Print.

Sapolsky, Robert M. "What Do Females Want? Does a Male's Long Tail or Flashy Coloration Advertise His Good Genes? New Research Challenges the Old Answers" *Natural History* 110.10 (2001): 18-21. Print.

Singh, Devendra. "Adaptive Significance of Female Physical Attractiveness: Role of Waist-to-Hip Ratio." *Journal of Personality and Social Behavior* 65.2 (1993): 293-307. *PubMed*. Web. 14 Oct. 2014.

Tattersall, Ian. "Evolution, Genes, and Behavior." *Zygon: Journal of Religion & Science* 36.4 (2001): 657-66. Web. 29 Sept. 2014.

Trivers, Robert L. "Parental Investment and Sexual Selection." *Sexual Selection and the Descent of Man: The Darwinian Pivot*. Ed. Bruce G. Campbell. New Brunswick, NJ: AldineTransaction, 2006. 136-79. Print.

Weiten, Wayne. *Psychology: Themes & Variations* 9th ed. Belmont, CA: Wadsworth/Cengage, 2013. Print.

CHAPTER 3

# Using the Methods Taught in This Book in Academic Writing

Writing and learning and thinking are the same process.

—WILLIAM ZINSSER

The basic purpose of most academic writing, as we noted in the last chapter, is to make a point and support it throughout the rest of your text. Thus the strategies and methods of argument are particularly important. Just as indispensable, however, are the other basic methods taught in this book—narration, description, example, process analysis, comparison and contrast, classification, definition, and cause and effect.

In a research **REPORT** on modern dating, for example, the writer had a point to make in the field of evolutionary biology. Here is her thesis:

> Driven by the need to reproduce and propagate the species, these ancestors of ours formed patterns of mate selection so effective in providing for their needs and those of their offspring that they are mimicked even in today's society.    —CAROLYN STONEHILL, "Modern Dating, Prehistoric Style"

Read Stonehill's **REPORT** on p. 21 to see how she draws on most of the methods.

To support this claim, Stonehill uses mostly strategies of **ARGUMENT**, but she also uses other methods of development as well. For example, she begins her essay on "mate selection" by **NARRATING** the story of a young woman who is attracted to her lab partner because he drives a BMW; she **DESCRIBES** the young woman as having "a pearly white smile" and the young man as "tall, muscular, and stylishly dressed"; she analyzes **CAUSE AND EFFECT** to explain the origins and consequences of their attraction; and she gives specific **EXAMPLES** of the woman's instinctive interest in the man's "resources."

**DEFINING** key concepts with precision is fundamental to most academic writing. Stonehill does this when she explains what she means by such terms as "evolutionary psychologists" and "mating behavior." And she **COMPARES AND CONTRASTS** different theories of mating behavior when reporting the research she did.

Each of the methods discussed in this book can be used in all kinds of academic writing. This chapter focuses on how you can learn to use them in some of the most fundamental types of academic writing, including **REPORTS**, **POSITION PAPERS**, **RHETORICAL ANALYSES**, **PROPOSALS**, and others.

## Using Narration

Narration is storytelling; it tells what happened, usually in chronological order. In academic writing, narration is seldom an end in itself—but it can be a great strategy for supporting a point in many kinds of academic writing. For example, you can use narration for presenting information in a **REPORT** or for making a point in a **POSITION PAPER**.

## In a Report on Texting and Writing

In the following example, Michaela Cullington uses narration to explain some of the research she did on the question of whether texting has a negative effect on student writing:

> I decided to conduct my own research into this controversy. I wanted to get different, more personal, perspectives on the issue. First, I surveyed seven students on their opinions about the impact of texting on writing. Second, I questioned two high school teachers, as noted above. Finally, in an effort to compare what students are actually doing to people's perceptions of what they are doing, I analyzed student writing samples for instances of textspeak.
>
> —MICHAELA CULLINGTON, "Does Texting Affect Writing?"

Ultimately, Cullington concluded that texting does not carry over into the more formal writing that students are asked to do. "They recognize the difference," she writes, "between texting friends and writing formally and know what is appropriate in each situation." To support this conclusion, Cullington tells about—narrates—what she did that led her to it.

Read Cullington's REPORT about the effects of textspeak on formal writing at wwnorton.com/write/back-to-the-lake.

## In a Position Paper on Walmart

Narration can also be useful for supporting a particular claim in a POSITION PAPER. In the following example, Matthew Douglas gives an account of a typical visit to Walmart as a way of supporting his argument that Walmart is not so "evil" as it has sometimes been made out to be:

> "Hi, welcome to Walmart," says the greeter. You smile back politely in acknowledgement before you quickly enter the store. . . . It was just a quick visit today. You make your way to the register and the cashier rings up your items and tells you the total damage to your wallet. You smile to yourself knowing you saved a bundle of time and money. Walmart is your one stop shop. You leave the store with bags in hand, only to find a chanting mob outside the store: volunteers for the union. They yell out many of Walmart's faults: its discrimination toward women, its dismal health care benefits, and its barely livable wages. . . . Has the company been singled out unfairly?
>
> —MATTHEW DOUGLAS, "The Evil Empire?"

You can see where this narrative is headed—it's arguing for a more sympathetic view of the company's retailing practices than some readers may have been willing

Read the rest
of Douglas's
POSITION PAPER
on p. 624.

to entertain before they heard Douglas's story about visiting Walmart and finding all the things he needed at good prices. Douglas's personal narrative doesn't completely prove his point, of course, but it skillfully sets the stage for his audience to lend an ear to his argument.

## Using Description

Description appeals to a reader's senses; it tells what something looks, sounds, smells, feels, or tastes like. Catalogs, advertisements, and menus use descriptions extensively to sell their wares. In more formal writing, such as a **PROFILE** or a **MEMOIR**, description can be especially helpful for capturing the physical and other distinctive characteristics of a person or a place.

### In a Profile of "Well-Behaved Women"

The historian Laurel Thatcher Ulrich uses description to introduce us to a remarkable but obscure woman who kept a diary of her routine activities more than two hundred years ago:

> Martha Moore Ballard was the stuff from which funeral sermons were made. . . . She cherished social order, respected authority, and abhorred violence. As a midwife and healer, she relied on home-grown medicines little different from those found in English herbals a century before her birth. Her religious sentiments were conventional; her reading was limited to the Bible, edifying pamphlets, and newspapers. Although she lived through the American Revolution, she had little interest in politics. She was a care-giver and a sustainer rather than a mover and shaker.
> —LAUREL THATCHER ULRICH,
> "Well-Behaved Women Seldom Make History"

Ulrich
DESCRIBES
Ballard and
others on
p. 267.

Ulrich's purpose in describing Ballard and some of the other women in her paper, such as the Civil Rights demonstrator Rosa Parks, is to analyze how they "made history" despite the appearance of being utterly conventional. To do this, Ulrich must first describe what made these extraordinary women seem so ordinary.

## In a Memoir about Making Butter

In the following passage from an essay written for a college writing course, Melissa Hicks describes the farmhouse in Maine where she grew up; she and her sisters have just finished the noisy and exhausting task of making butter:

> Now the kitchen is quiet, without the rolling and thudding. I suddenly fantasize about flaky biscuits melting on my tongue. My sisters and I are yawning, but our stomachs growl at the smell. On the cutting board are the scraps from the last block of butter. They are not grocery-store squares, but long strips, thick and round on one side. The image of a delightfully buttery slug comes to mind slithering onto a hot roll before leaving a slick buttery trail down my throat. The best part of the butter is that there was plenty.
>
> —MELISSA HICKS, "The High Price of Butter"

In her MEMOIR, Hicks is not just recalling the place where she grew up, she is *recreating* it—through vivid descriptive passages like this one. Physical description appeals directly to the reader's senses, and here the dominant sense is taste. By recreating the taste of the "buttery slug" on her tongue, Hicks brings back not only an earlier time and place but herself in it—for the ultimate purpose of showing us something about life in rural Maine.

Read the full text of Hicks's MEMOIR on p. 182.

# Using Examples

Giving examples is fundamental to academic writing. Examples make abstract ideas more concrete and general statements more specific. In a RHETORICAL ANALYSIS, for instance, concrete details in a story or poem can serve to illustrate the larger meaning of the text as a whole. And in a research PROPOSAL, specific examples of how the research will be conducted can give an overall sense of the project that is being proposed.

## In a Rhetorical Analysis of Persepolis

In the following passage, part of a longer project she wrote while a student at Stockton College, Stephanie Cawley gives examples of how the younger girls refuse to wear their veils in the well-known graphic narrative *Persepolis*:

At the bottom of the page, in perhaps one of the most iconic images from *Persepolis*, the group of girls is shown refusing to wear their veils—some complaining it is too hot, others using their veils to play-act political or fantastical games, and others jumping rope with them.

—STEPHANIE CAWLEY, "The Veil in *Persepolis*"

Read the rest of Cawley's RHETORICAL ANALYSIS on p. 243.

In Cawley's analysis, the portrayal of the veiled woman in *Persepolis* "runs counter to the images presented in the Western media of passive, victimized women who are oppressed and flattened into a monolithic group by wearing the veil." To support this thesis, she points out numerous examples like these that show girls and women wearing the veil as a "trope of resistance" throughout the narrative.

## In a Proposal for a Physics Experiment

One way of explaining what you plan to do in an experiment or other project is to give examples of the intended work, as in this PROPOSAL for an experiment on the physics of a falling Slinky:

The proposed project will examine the basic physics of wave propagation in a tension spring, especially the timing. A good, working example of a tension spring might be the child's toy commonly known as a Slinky. Using high speed video, we will film falling slinkies and measure how long it takes for the bottom loop to begin falling once the top loop is released. Existing models, for example, Calkin, Am. J. Phys. 61, 261–264 (1993), do a good job of explaining why there is a delay in the total collapse: the bottom loop of the spring doesn't know the tension has been released until the resulting wave propagates through the spring. What is missing in the literature is an exact calculation of the time typically required for the top loops to collide with the

bottom. Based on preliminary observations in the lab, we anticipate that the total collapse time (tc) will be approximately a third of a second (~o:3s). If this proves to be correct, it will represent a significant modification of the existing model.                    —AFTER R. C. CROSS AND M. S. WHEATLAND,
"Modeling a Falling Slinky"

To demonstrate how a wave propagates through a tension spring, the two physics professors who originally dreamed up this experiment propose to use the example of a toy Slinky. The Slinky possesses all the main characteristics of the subject it exemplifies (tension springs)—and it uses something familiar (a child's toy) to introduce a less familiar concept (the basic physics of wave propagation).

> The abstract of the Slinky experiment proposed here appears on p. 168.

## Using Process Analysis

Process analysis is how-to writing; when you analyze a process, you break it into steps so that the reader can replicate (or simply understand) the process. Process analysis can be used in many kinds of academic writing. In an **EVALUATION**, for example, it can help to show how and how well a particular study was conducted or a new product was marketed. Or it can serve as part of a larger analysis, such as a **CULTURAL ANALYSIS** of a particular group or profession.

### In an Evaluation of a Marketing Campaign

When you analyze something—whether it's a written text, a physical object such as a consumer product, or a set of ideas—you break it down into its constituent parts. Consider Febreze, the fabric deodorizer developed by Procter & Gamble. The following passage comes from an analysis of the marketing process by which the company hoped to sell this (then) new product:

> They designed two television commercials. The first showed a woman talking about the smoking section of a restaurant. Whenever she eats there, her jacket smells like smoke. A friend tells her if she uses Febreze, it will eliminate the odor. The cue: the smell of cigarettes. The reward: odor eliminated from clothes. The second ad featured a woman worrying about her dog, Sophie, who always sits on the couch. "Sophie will always smell like Sophie," she says, but with Febreze, "now my furniture doesn't have to." The cue: pet smells, which are familiar to the seventy million households with animals. The reward: a house that doesn't smell like a kennel.
> —CHARLES DUHIGG, "How to Create New Habits"

Read the rest of Duhigg's EVALUATION on p. 321.

The marketing executives who designed the Febreze campaign, as Duhigg analyzes it, were relying on a simple two-step process. Follow that process, they believed, and the customer would inevitably take the next step: cue → reward → purchase. They were wrong, as Duhigg points out. Febreze was a flop at first because the ads promised the wrong reward.

## In a Cultural Analysis of Blue-Collar Work

A CULTURAL ANALYSIS is an analysis of the behavior of a particular society, group, or profession. Here a professor of education analyzes the work patterns of a waitress who happens to be his mother:

> A waitress acquires knowledge and intuition about the ways and rhythms of the restaurant business. Waiting on seven to nine tables, each with two to six customers, Rosie devised memory strategies so that she could remember who ordered what. And because she knew the average time it took to prepare different dishes, she could monitor an order that was taking too long at the service station. . . . She'd sequence and group tasks: What could she do first, then second, then third as she circled through her station? What tasks could be clustered? She did everything on the fly, and when problems arose—technical or human—she solved them within the flow of work, while taking into account the emotional state of her co-workers.
>
> —MIKE ROSE, "Blue-Collar Brilliance"

Read the rest of "Blue-Collar Brilliance" on p. 497.

Rose is not simply analyzing the process of waiting on tables here. Taking apart that process—first, second, third—is part of a larger analysis of blue-collar work in general. Rose's conclusion is that it demands just as much "brilliance" as other, more apparently "intellectual," kinds of work.

## Using Comparison and Contrast

When you compare two or more things, you examine their similarities and differences. Comparison is such a useful method of writing and thinking, in fact, that many kinds of academic writing are basically comparative studies. For example, in a history REPORT you might compare (and contrast) two presidential campaign styles; or in a CRITICAL ANALYSIS of two giant entertainment companies, you might focus on the styles and powers of their biggest superheroes.

## In a Report on a Presidential Campaign

In the 1948 campaign for president of the United States, many pollsters were so sure that the Republican candidate, Thomas E. Dewey, would defeat his Democratic opponent, Harry S. Truman, that they stopped taking polls before the election. Here's why Dewey lost—and why Truman won:

> With all indications pointing to an easy victory, Dewey and his staff believed that all he had to do was bide his time and make no foolish mistakes. Dewey himself said, "When you're leading, don't talk.". . . Eventually, Dewey began to be perceived as aloof and stuffy. One observer compared him to the plastic groom on top of a wedding cake.
>                       . . .
> As a former farmer and relatively late bloomer, Truman was able to connect with the public. He developed an energetic style, usually speaking from notes rather than from a prepared speech, and often mingled with the crowds that met his train. These crowds grew larger as the campaign progressed.                                   —DYLAN BORCHERS,
>          "Against the Odds: Harry S. Truman and the Election of 1948"

History recorded Truman's victory, of course. Explaining why he won, however, has fallen to the historians, and they usually cite the contrasting campaign styles of the two men as the deciding factor in the election.

Read this REPORT about the 1948 election on p. 827.

## In a Critical Analysis of Two Entertainment Companies

When a business writer compares the bottom lines of giant corporate entities, he or she runs the risk of losing the reader in a cloud of abstraction. To avoid that problem in an ANALYSIS of two entertainment giants, Douglas Wolk compared the companies themselves to two of their most famous products:

> At a tender age, most fans of superhero comics start honing their arguments in an ancient debate: "Which is better—Marvel or DC?" They may not yet realize that the fight has long been waged not just on the page, but also in boardrooms and on the NYSE. To understand the battle between the two major American mainstream comic book companies, we can go straight to the source material, because each is very much like one of its biggest franchise players. Marvel, it's fair to say, is Iron Man; DC is Batman.
>                   —DOUGLAS WOLK, "Superhero Smackdown"

Follow the epic conflict between DC and Marvel on p. 361.

Batman may be darker and more complex than Iron Man. However, says Wolk, if you compare how the parent companies have positioned their heroes in the universe of finance, Iron Man and his friends come out on top in any market analysis. By "fitting their stories together into the 'Marvel Cinematic Universe,'" says Wolk, Marvel rules. Or, as he puts the results of his comparative analysis more concretely, "Right now, DC's Batarangs don't stand a chance against Marvel's repulsor rays."

## Using Classification

When you classify plants and animals—or other things—you put them into categories based on their shared characteristics. Classification is common in scientific writing, but it's useful in other kinds as well, for example in a socioloy REPORT on the ways in which men and women fail to communicate, or a POSITION PAPER on what it means to be an American.

### In a Report on How Men and Women Miscommunicate at Work

Are women from Venus and men from Mars? Not necessarily, says the sociolinguist Deborah Tannen—but they do talk differently. They also inhabit different universes when it comes to joking around, especially at work:

> The types of humor women and men tend to prefer differ. Research has shown that the most common form of humor among men is razzing, teasing, and mock-hostile attacks, while among women it's self-mocking. Women often mistake men's teasing as genuinely hostile. Men often mistake women's mock self-deprecation as truly putting themselves down.
> —DEBORAH TANNEN, "But What Do You Mean?"

Read Tannen's REPORT on p. 437.

Classification is all about categories, but those categories should help you think outside the box. Tannen's purpose in classifying humor according to gender is not just to distinguish different types but to encourage the respective sides to communicate better with each other.

### In a Position Paper on What Makes an American

Classification deals with categories. Sometimes the main purpose of a POSITION PAPER is to question whether a familiar category still means what it used to. In this passage from an Op-Ed column, the author asks whether America is, "in any meaningful sense, the same country that declared independence in 1776":

And ethnically we are, of course, very different from the founders. Only a minority of today's Americans are descended from the WASPs and slaves of 1776. The rest are the descendants of successive waves of immigration: first from Ireland and Germany, then from Southern and Eastern Europe, now from Latin America and Asia. We're no longer an Anglo-Saxon nation; we're only around half-Protestant; and we're increasingly nonwhite.

Yet I would maintain that we are still the same country that declared independence all those years ago.     PAUL KRUGMAN, "E Pluribus Unum"

Why is Krugman so confident that all these different categories—Irish, German, European, Latin American, Asian—can still be meaningfully classified within the single overarching category called American? His position is that we still believe in "the democratic ideal that 'all men are created equal'—all men, not just men from certain ethnic groups or from aristocratic families." In this context, of course, "men" also means "women."

Read Krugman's POSITION PAPER on p. 433.

# Using Definition

When you define something, you tell what is by identifying the traits and characteristics that set it apart from others like it. In a Shakespearean play, for example, both soliloquies and monologues can be defined as speeches by a single character. A *soliloquy*, however, is spoken in private, whereas a *monologue* is addressed to other characters. Defining key terms like this is fundamental to virtually all forms of academic writing, from a commencement address to a CULTURAL ANALYSIS of a renowned school of dance.

## In a College Commencement Address

In his celebrated address to the class of 2013 at Syracuse University, George Saunders's main purpose was to give advice to the new graduates. First, however, he felt the need to define the type of speech he was giving:

Down through the ages, a traditional form has evolved for this type of speech, which is: Some old fart, his best years behind him, who over the course of his life has made a series of dreadful mistakes (that would be me) gives heartfelt advice to a group of shining, energetic young people with all of their best years ahead of them (that would be you).

And I intend to respect this tradition.          —GEORGE SAUNDERS,
"Congratulations, by the Way"

Link to Saunder's speech via wwnorton. com/write/ back-to- the-lake.

This is a common way of commencing in many different academic genres: before you tell the audience what you're going to tell them, orally or in writing, you define the form you're going use—in this case the traditional commencement address. That way they'll know what to expect in the minutes (or hours) ahead.

## In a Cultural Analysis of Body Image in Ballet

What lies beneath the sequins, tulle, and satin shoes of the fantasy world of ballet? Intense cultural pressures upon dancers to conform to an unhealthy body image based on a dubious aesthetic, according to Paula T. Kelso. Kelso defines a specific ideal of body image in this CULTURAL ANALYSIS, which she wrote, using APA style, as an undergraduate:

> Almost everyone credits George Balanchine, the renowned dancer, teacher, and choreographer, with the current aesthetic of ballet in the West, referred to by most as the "Balanchine body," or the "anorexic look" (Gordon, 1983). He has promoted the skeletal look by his costume requirements and his hiring practices, as well as the treatment of his dancers (Gordon, 1983). The ballet aesthetic current consists of long limbs and a skeletal frame, which accentuates the collarbones and length of the neck, as well as absence of breasts and hips (Benn & Walters, 2001; Gordon, 1983; Kirkland, 1986).
> —PAULA T. KELSO, "Behind the Curtain: The Body, Control, and Ballet"

Read Kelso's CULTURAL ANALYSIS on p. 550.

The purpose of Kelso's paper is to analyze how the pressure to be physically thin exposes many dancers to the dangers of verbal harassment, injury, and malnourishment. She goes on to examine this problem through subculture and paradox theory. First, however, Kelso must define the body image idealized by modern dance culture.

## Using Cause-and-Effect

Understanding the relationship between cause and effect—fire burns; step off a wall, and you'll fall down—is fundamental not only to dealing with the physical world but with the universe of ideas. In academic writing, we analyze causes and effects whenever we need to explain—for example in a LITERACY NARRATIVE or a RHETORICAL ANALYSIS of a visual—why one action or condition produced another action or condition.

## In a Literacy Narrative

A **LITERACY NARRATIVE** usually tells about a formative personal experience with reading or writing. In the following passage, from a literacy narrative she wrote in college, Shannon Nichols analyzes the lasting effects of her struggles with a standardized proficiency test that she took back in high school:

> After I failed the test the first time, I began to hate writing, and I started to doubt myself. I doubted my ability and the ideas I wrote about. Failing the second time made things worse, so perhaps to protect myself from my doubts, I stopped taking English seriously. Perhaps because of that lack of seriousness, I earned a 2 on the Advanced Placement English Exam, barely passed the twelfth-grade proficiency test, and was placed in developmental writing in college. I wish I knew why I failed that test, because then I might have written what was expected on the second try, maintained my enthusiasm for writing, and continued to do well.     —SHANNON NICHOLS, "Proficiency"

Nichols is not just telling about a troubling experience she had with testing in high school—she is trying to understand and explain that experience. So she analyzes its negative effects in some detail ("began to hate writing," "stopped taking English seriously"). The ultimate cause ("why I failed that test"), however, is still not clear to her, though she can imagine more positive effects had she done better on the test.

Read Nichols's LITERACY NARRATIVE at wwnorton.com/write/back-to-the-lake.

## In a Rhetorical Analysis of a Photograph

When you analyze a written text, you look at how that text communicates a message to its audience. The same is true when you're analyzing a visual text, such as a painting or a photograph. Often you need to determine why one event in the tet causes another. In the following **RHETORICAL ANALYSIS** of a black and white photo of a fashion show, Alex Ryan Bauer not only assigns motives to the onlookers, he speculates about the causes and effect of a mysterious presence on the runway:

> I come across a photograph from a spring runway show. In it, a model stands before rows of on-lookers, editors and high-society types: women wearing chic minimalist outfits, holding notepads and Fiji water bottles. A fashion show is beautiful people in expensive clothing watching beautiful people in expensive clothing move across a stage. . . . The photograph—perhaps because of some optical illusion, the reflection of dozens of camera flashes all going off at once, the model's sequined or metallic dress—shows the model engulfed in brilliance: a piece of clothing composed entirely of light, a haute couture dress that walks all on its own.

—Alex Ryan Bauer, "A History of Men's Fashions"

Read the rest of Bauer's RHETORICAL ANALYSIS at wwnorton.com/ write/back-to-the-lake.

The point of Bauer's study of men's and women's clothing is to show that fashion can have a life of its own. The "haute couture dress" in this photo is a perfect case in point, but someone looking at this photograph for the first time might think they're seeing a ghost at a séance instead of a model on a runway. So Bauer has to analyze what CAUSES this strange luminescence—the photo itself does not tell us—before he can use the image to make his point about fashion.

## Using Argument

There are many strategies for arguing a point in academic writing. One of them is to narrow the scope of your claim to a one you can reasonably support. Another is to cite facts and figures that support your point. In a POSITION PAPER, the first strategy is essential when you're addressing a controversial issue.

### In a Position Paper on the Sale of Human Organs

In the following paragraph, Joanna MacKay argues what seems at first to be a freewheeling POSITION on a difficult issue:

There are thousands of people dying to buy a kidney, and thousands of people dying to sell a kidney. It seems a match made in heaven. So why are we standing in the way? Governments should not ban the sale of human organs; they should regulate it. Lives should not be wasted; they should be saved.
—JOANNA MACKAY, "Organ Sales Will Save Lives"

MacKay is not actually calling for unbridled traffic in human organs; she knows that such a wild proposition would never get out the gate with most readers. Instead, she is making the more limited claim that organ sales should be legalized so they can be properly regulated:

> If the sale of organs were made legal, it could be regulated and closely monitored by the government and other responsible organizations. In a regulated system, education would be incorporated into the application process.

Limiting a claim to a more defensible scope like this is one of the most effective steps you can take when arguing a controversial position. It's a rhetorical marriage made in heaven: a reasonable show of restraint in a cause the writer passionately believes in.

Read MacKay's ARGUMENT at wwnorton. com/write/ back-to-the- lake.

## In a Magazine Article about the Value of a College Education

Is a college education worth the cost? This is an issue you might expect to be settled with facts and figures. We all know, however, that facts and figures can be cited on both sides of an argument. The editors of the *Economist* magazine tend toward statistical gloom, although they agree that college pays a premium in the job market:

> While this is still broadly true . . . it is easily possible to overspend on one's education: just ask the hundreds of thousands of law graduates who have not found work as lawyers. And this premium is of little comfort to the 9.1% of borrowers who in 2011 had defaulted on their federal student loans within two years of graduating. There are 200 colleges and universities where the three-year default rate is 30% or more.          —THE ECONOMIST,
> "Higher Education: Not What It Used to Be"

In contrast to the *Economist's* negative view, the author of a piece from the business pages of the *New York Times* takes the position that going to college makes financial sense:

So, despite the painful upfront cost, the return on investment on a college degree remains high. An analysis from the Hamilton Project at the Brookings Institution in Washington estimated that the benefits of a four-year college degree were equivalent to an investment that returns 15.2 percent a year, even after factoring in the earnings students forgo while in school.

—CATHERINE RAMPELL,
"College Graduates Fare Well, Even through Recession"

For a group of POSITION PAPERS on the issue of college costs, see p. 675.

Assuming all the facts and figures to be correct in these two arguments, who's right about the cost benefits of college? Chances are, the answer depends on which way the reader is already leaning. The point, however, is that citing facts and figures in a position paper is a good way to make a point.

# CHAPTER 4

# The Writing Process

I think I did pretty well, considering I started out
with nothing but a bunch of blank paper.
—STEVE MARTIN

To learn to do anything well, from baking bread to programming a computer, we usually break it down into a series of operations. Writing is no exception. This chapter introduces all the steps of the writing process that will take you from a blank page to a final draft: planning; generating ideas; organizing and drafting; revising your draft as it progresses, both on your own and with the help of others; and editing and proofreading your work into its final form.

Keep in mind, however, that writing is a recursive process—that is, it involves a certain amount of repetition. We plan, we draft, we revise; we plan, we draft, we revise again. Also, we tend to skip around as we write. For example, if we suddenly think of a great new idea, we may go back and redraft what we have already written, perhaps revising it completely. Often, in fact, we engage in the various activities of writing more or less at the same time—and many times we perform these various activities in collaboration with others.

## Planning

Most of the writing we do—and not just in school—starts with an assignment. An English teacher asks you to analyze a poem by Billy Collins. A college application includes an essay question, asking you to explain why you want to go to that school. A prospective employer wants to know, on a job application form, why he or she should hire you. Before you plunge headlong into any writing assignment, however, you need to think about where you're going. You need to plan.

To plan any piece of writing effectively, think about your purpose in writing, the audience you're writing for, and the nature and scope of your topic. If a topic hasn't already been suggested or assigned to you, of course, you'll have to find one. You'll also need to budget your time.

### Managing Your Time

When is the assignment due? As soon as you get a writing assignment, make a note of the deadline. Some teachers deduct points for late papers; some don't accept them at all. Even if your instructor is lenient, learning to meet deadlines is part of surviving in college—and beyond. And remember that it's hard to plan well if you begin an assignment the night before it's due. Especially with research papers and other long-range projects, you should begin early so you have plenty of time to do everything the assignment requires.

What kind of research will you need to do? If you are writing a personal narrative or analyzing a process you know well (such as teaching an Irish setter to catch a Frisbee), you may not need to do much research at all before you begin to write.

On the other hand, if you are preparing a full-scale research paper on climate change or the fiction of Henry James, the research may take longer than the actual writing. Most college assignments require at least some research. So as you plan any piece of writing, think about how much and what kind of research you will need to do, and allow plenty of time for that research.

## Finding a Topic

Though we often use the words interchangeably, a *subject*, strictly speaking, is a broad field of study or inquiry, whereas a *topic* is a specific area within that field. If you are writing a paper for an ecology class, the subject of your paper is likely to be ecology. However, if your teacher asks what you're planning to write on and you reply simply, "ecology," be prepared for a few more questions.

Even if you said "climate change" or "global warming," your teacher would still want to know just what approach you planned to take. A good topic not only narrows down a general subject to a specific area within that field, it addresses a particular aspect of that more limited area, such as what climate change is or what causes climate change or what effects climate change has on the environment or how to stop climate change.

With many writing assignments, you may be given a specific topic or choice of specific topics. For example, an essay exam in Ecology 101 might ask, "Can climate change be stopped? How? Or why not?" Or it might say, more specifically, "Describe the key principles of the Kyoto Protocol." In a literature course, you might get a topic like this: "The narrator of Henry James's *The Turn of the Screw:* heroine or hysteric?" Or in a political science course, you might be asked to compare Marx's theory of revolution with Lenin's.

When you're given such a specific topic, make sure you read the assignment carefully and know just what you are being asked to do. Pay close attention to how the assignment is worded. Look for key terms like *describe, define, analyze, compare and contrast, evaluate, argue.* Be aware that even short assignments may include more than one of these directives. For example, the same assignment may ask you not only to define climate change but to analyze its causes and effects or to compare and contrast present-day climate conditions with those of an earlier time or to construct an argument about what should be done to stop climate change.

Many teachers provide lists of possible topics. With longer assignments, however, you may have to work out a topic yourself, perhaps after meeting with your teacher. Start the conversation as soon as you get the assignment. Let your instructor know if there are any areas within your field of study you find particularly interesting or would like to learn more about. Ask for guidance and suggestions— and start looking on your own. If your school has a writing center, it might be useful to discuss possible topics with someone there.

## Thinking about Purpose and Audience

We write for many reasons: to organize and clarify our thoughts, express our feelings, remember people and events, solve problems, persuade others to act or believe as we think they should.

For example, let's look at a passage from a recent government report on climate change:

> Climate change, once considered an issue for a distant future, has moved firmly into the present. Corn producers in Iowa, oyster growers in Washington State, and maple syrup producers in Vermont are all observing climate-related changes that are outside of recent experience. So, too, are coastal planners in Florida, water managers in the arid Southwest, city dwellers from Phoenix to New York, and Native Peoples on tribal lands from Louisiana to Alaska. This National Climate Assessment concludes that the evidence of human-induced climate change continues to strengthen and that impacts are increasing across the country.
>
> —U.S. GLOBAL CHANGE RESEARCH PROGRAM,
> *Climate Change Impacts in the United States: Highlights*

The main purpose of this passage, and the report it introduces, is to persuade the reader that serious climate change, far from an issue to be addressed in the distant future, has already occurred.

As you think about *why* you're writing, however, you also need to consider *who* your readers are. In this report on climate change, for example, the authors speak directly to their intended audience:

> Climate change presents a major challenge for society. This report advances our understanding of that challenge and the need for the American people to prepare for and respond to its far-reaching implications.

The intended audience here is ordinary citizens in communities across the country. Your intended audience can be yourself; someone you know, such as your roommate or your teacher; or someone you can't know immediately and directly, such as "the American people." These different audiences have different needs, which you'll want to take into account as you write. If *you* are the intended audience—as when you write in a diary or journal, or jot down a reminder for yourself—you can be as cryptic as you like:

> CC lecture tonight @ 8 in Denney.
> Joy @ Blue Dube, get notes, ask her to feed cat.

## QUESTIONS ABOUT PURPOSE AND AUDIENCE

**What is the occasion for writing?** Are you writing a research paper? Applying for a job? Responding to an email? Commenting on a blog? Planning a wedding toast?

**What is your purpose?** Do you want to tell your readers something they may not know? Entertain them? Convince them to do something? Change their minds?

**Who is going to read (or hear) what you write?** Your classmates? Your teacher? Readers of a blog? Guests at a wedding?

**What do you know about your audience's background?** For example, if you are writing an argument on how to stop climate change, you can expect readers who come from coal-mining regions to be more sympathetic if you suggest reducing carbon emissions than if you propose shutting down all coal-burning power plants.

**How much does your audience already know about your subject?** If you are writing for a general audience, you may need to provide some background information and explain terminology that may be unfamiliar. For example, if you are writing about climate change for a newsmagazine, you might note that sequestration is one way to reduce carbon emissions—and then define *sequestration* for those who don't already know. If you're writing for an audience of environmental scientists, though, you may be able to assume that they are familiar with carbon sequestration and you don't have to define it.

**What should you keep in mind about the demographics of your audience?** Does the gender of your audience matter? How about their age, level of education, economic status, or religion? Once you have sized up your audience, you're in a better position to generate ideas and evidence that will support what you have to say *and* appeal to that audience.

**Who do you want your audience to be?** The language you use can let your readers know that you are writing to them—or not. In particular, be careful how you use the personal pronouns *we, us,* and *our.* For instance, if you write, "As Christians, we need to have compassion for others," be sure you want to limit your audience to Christians, for this language excludes anyone who is not.

Once you plan to address someone else in writing, no matter what your purpose, you will need to fill in more blanks for the reader, even if you know that person well and are simply, as in the following example, leaving an informal message:

> Joy,
>
> I have to go to a lecture on climate change tonight in Denney. Meet you at the Blue Danube at 6. May I borrow your ecology notes? Please feed Gen. Burnsides for me. Friskies in cabinet above fridge. Half a can. Thanks!
>
> Fred

Obviously, the writer of this message is familiar with his audience. He can assume, for example, that she knows Denney is the name of a building on campus and that General Burnsides is the name of a cat—but even Joy has to be told where the cat food is stashed and how much to serve. When you don't know your audience, or when you can't be sure they know what you're talking about, you need to supply them with even more information.

In each chapter that follows, you'll find a section that will help you think about purpose and audience as you write. For now, refer to the checklist of general guidelines on p. 47 to help you think about your intended audience and your purpose.

## Collaborating with Others

Listen to Wiley's "Last Kind Words Blues" at wwnorton. com/write/ back-to-the-lake.

From a brief check-in on Facebook or Twitter ("Listening to an *amaazzing* tune by Geeshie Wiley. Who was she?") to a full-scale research project on, for example, early black female blues singers—most of the writing you do in the digital age invites collaboration with others. Whether you're working online or face to face, follow these general guidelines:

*Set clear goals and deadlines.* One way to do this is to draw up a "contract" that spells out the purpose, scope, and schedule of the project—and have everyone sign it. Update this document periodically.

*Be flexible and open minded.* The whole point of collaboration is to encourage everyone to contribute. Listen carefully and be respectful of other people's ideas. You're working for consensus, not total agreement.

*Appoint a group manager.* Although everyone needs to take responsibility for the efforts of the group, one well-organized person should be chosen to coordinate those efforts and be in charge of communication within the group. Otherwise, deadlines will be missed and potholes will go unfilled.

*Appoint a chief editor.* This may or may not be the same person as the group manager, but it should be someone who writes well. Without a general editor, collaborative writing becomes writing by committee.

*Assign specific tasks to each member.* These should include all aspects of research, writing, editing, and distribution. Tasks should be assigned according to the skills and preferences of each member of the group, and everyone should willingly agree to accept his or her assignment. No (heavy) arm-twisting.

*Confer regularly and do periodic progress checks.* In addition to talking things over throughout the writing process, this is best done by scheduling regular meetings, whether online or in person, and by requiring (and sharing) written samples of everyone's work.

## ADDITIONAL TIPS FOR COLLABORATING FACE TO FACE

*Sit in a circle or around a table.* Collaboration is a form of conversation, and most people converse best when speaking face to face—or ear to ear.

*Appoint a discussion leader.* Someone needs to be in charge of moving the discussion along, while keeping it on point and making sure that everyone participates. Unlike that of group manager or chief editor, however, this job can be assigned to different members of the group at different meetings, or as the topic of discussion changes.

*Appoint a scribe.* Someone else should take notes and write a SUMMARY of the proceedings.

## ADDITIONAL TIPS FOR COLLABORATING ONLINE

*Decide on a method of exchange.* For example, you can agree to cut and paste contributions directly into email; or send them as attachments; or post them to an online discussion board inside or outside of your course's learning management system.

*Name files clearly and consistently.* You need to be able to find each other's work and know what you're looking at.

*Be polite; proof before you send.* Collaboration should always be synonymous with courtesy. But remember: anything you post to the internet could end up being read by your grandmother.

Aside from the internet itself, one of the most comprehensive sites for the collaborative exchange of ideas in human history is *Wikipedia*, the online universal encyclopedia. As an example of how collaboration, particularly online collaboration, can shed light on the most elusive of topics, consider the brief *Wikipedia* entry for the early blues singer Geeshie Wiley—and its sequel.

In 2007 a researcher identified as "John" made the following appeal in the Talk thread accompanying the Wiley article: "Help me Geeshie Wiley Fans! I have undertaken an impossible research project: Find out more about Geeshie Wiley." When accessed in April 2014, Wiley's sketchy biography still included these words: "Further details of Wiley's early and later life, her career, and her legal name are unknown." In the Talk thread, however, an unnamed contributor noted (on April 12) that the entire article needed "to be ripped out and rewritten . . . which I am considering."

Thanks to the collaborative efforts of a host of writers and researchers over more than fifty years, we now know not only Wiley's legal name (Lillie Mae Scott Wiley) but why she disappeared. The key to the mystery came in another on-line exchange, between the musicologist John Jeremiah Sullivan—the initiator, perhaps, of the *Wikipedia* thread on Wiley—and his research assistant Caitlin Love, an undergraduate at a university in Arkansas.

Love's urgent text messages to Sullivan ("!!!!!!!" and "Check your email") pertained to Geeshie Wiley's husband (or lover). In the following words from the latest chapter in the ongoing Wiley saga, Sullivan describes what his youthful collaborator had found in a Houston archive:

> I opened the message and the attachment. It was an official form, like a birth certificate. No, a death certificate. State of Texas. Thornton Wiley. Not that exciting. Not "!!!!!!!" Of course he died. Wait, though — it was from 1931, just a year after she was living with him on Saulnier Street in the Fourth Ward. Not long after they made the records. He died young. That was sad. . . . Maybe she is thinking of him in "Last Kind Words" when she sings, "What you do to me, baby, it never gets out of me / I believe I'll see you after I cross the deep blue sea."
>
> I'm reading down through the crowded handwriting. "Inquest." "Homicide." He had been murdered.
>
> Manner of injury: "Stab wound in between collarbone and neck. . . ."
>
> Then the form got to the cause of death. "Knife wound inflicted by Lillie Mae Scott." —JOHN JEREMIAH SULLIVAN AND OTHERS, "The Ballad of Geeshie and Elvie"

# Generating Ideas

Once you have a topic, purpose, and audience clearly in mind, it's time to start generating ideas. Where do you look for ideas? How do you go from nothing to something in a systematic way?

Over the years, writing teachers have developed a number of techniques to help writers find ideas. Freewriting, looping, listing, and brainstorming are ways to probe what you already know; clustering can help you connect ideas and begin organizing a text around them; questioning can be particularly useful when you're trying to make a topic more specific; and keeping a journal can be helpful at any stage. All of these techniques, in fact, may come in handy at various points in the writing process, not just at the outset.

## Freewriting

When you freewrite, you simply put pen to paper (or fingers to keyboard), and force yourself to jot down whatever pops into your head.

1. Write nonstop for a short period of time, say five or ten minutes. If nothing comes to mind at first, just write: "Nothing. I'm getting nothing. The words aren't coming." Eventually, the words *will* come—if you keep writing and don't stop until time runs out.

2. This is freewriting—so skip around freely and don't get bogged down.

3. Circle or underline words and ideas that you might want to revisit, but don't stop freewriting until your time is up. Then go back over what you have written and mark any passages that stand out as promising.

4. Freewrite again, using something you have marked in the previous session as your starting point. Do this over and over until you find an idea you want to explore further.

Here's an example of a five-minute freewriting session by Zoe Shewer, a first-year writing student at Vanderbilt University who was given the assignment "Write about an experience that has taught you something new about yourself."

> Write write write. Five minutes. Okay, something I learned about myself. Yikes, what a question. I'm me. Blond, not too tall—okay, looks really aren't the point here. I'm a pretty good athlete, love riding horses. I have a brother named Max and 2 dogs named Oz and Jazz. I tutor kids in Harlem—I like volunteering. I had a great time at Camp Robin Hood last summer. Working with all those different nonprofits was great. But did I learn anything about myself? I learned how to clean gutters, some American Sign Language, how to make spaghetti sauce. I learned that I'm not a good cook. Time.

Freewriting like this is more than a stretching exercise. It can lead to many new ideas if you take something you have just said as the point of departure for more probing. Shewer's freewriting session led her to a possible source for an essay topic: her volunteer work.

## Looping

To narrow down the subject you are exploring, try the more directed form of freewriting called *looping*. Looping not only helps you turn up a specific topic, it nudges you into writing sentences about it. Later on, you may want to use some of these sentences in your essay.

1. Freewrite for five or ten minutes, focusing on a single subject or idea and putting down everything about that subject that you can think of.

2. When you've finished that first loop, look over what you've written and summarize the most important part in a sentence: "I learned a lot volunteering last summer."

3. Use this summary sentence as the point of departure for your next loop. Write for another five or ten minutes without stopping. Then reflect on what you've just written, and compose another sentence summing it up: "Volunteering last summer taught me that I have a lot to learn."

4. Do as many loops as necessary until you have a direction in mind. If you already know the final destination of your essay, so much the better; but for now you're mainly looking for ways of refining your topic along the way.

Looping can be especially useful when you are trying to make an ABSTRACT subject more CONCRETE. Shewer summed up her freewriting exercise with the sentence "I learned a lot volunteering last summer" and used that sentence as the starting point for a new loop that helped her explore what she learned about herself.

*Summary sentence from freewriting*: I learned a lot volunteering last summer.

Loop 1: I learned a lot volunteering last summer through Camp Robin Hood. At Ready, Willing & Able, Seymour taught me to clean gutters. At ABC, I learned some American Sign Language, and I learned how strong those kids were. Every day, they came in determined to do everything. At the homeless shelter, I learned so much from Elsie about the city and how to survive in it. But did I learn anything about *myself*? At the end of the summer I had more admiration for Seymour, Elsie, and the kids at ABC. They all had so much more experience with life—even the kids. They had a lot of hard knocks and kept getting back up. Maybe I learned just how lucky I've been. But I think I already knew that. Maybe it was mostly that I learned that I really haven't experienced all that much.

*Summary sentence:* Volunteering taught me that I have a lot to learn.

Loop 2: Volunteering taught me that I have a lot to learn. Seymour told me a lot of stuff that I didn't know before, not just how to drain gutters but what his life was like. Elsie didn't talk much about her personal life, but she did tell me a lot about being homeless. And just being with the kids at ABC gave me insight into what it's like to be disadvantaged. They had to have so much determination. So did Seymour and Elsie. I don't have that kind of determination.

*Summary sentence:* Volunteering taught me to admire the determination of Seymour, the children at ABC, and Elsie.

As these excerpts show, looping brings ideas into sharper focus. By writing out her thoughts and looping back over them several times, Shewer was able to come up with concrete ideas about what she learned through volunteering.

## Listing

Most writing is better and clearer if it is detailed and specific instead of general and abstract. Keeping lists is a good way to generate ideas—and to illustrate those ideas with interesting examples and specific details.

1. A list can be written anywhere: on paper, on a computer, in a notebook, on a napkin. Keep your lists handy so you can add to them at any time.

2. Don't worry about the form of your lists. But if the lists start to get long, group related items into piles, as you would if you were sorting your laundry.

3. Look for relationships not only *within* those piles but *between* them. Later, if you decide to construct a formal outline for your essay, you can build on the loosely arranged lists you already have.

## Brainstorming

Brainstorming is a form of listing, but you write down words and ideas in one sitting rather than over time.

1. If you are brainstorming by yourself, first jot down a topic at the top of your page or screen. Then make a list of every idea or word that comes to mind.

2. Brainstorming is often more effective when you do it collaboratively, as part of a team, with everyone throwing out ideas and one person acting as scribe.

3. If you brainstorm with others, make sure everyone contributes. If one person monopolizes the session, the purpose of brainstorming is lost.

## Clustering

Clustering helps you to make connections among ideas.

1. Write down your topic in the center of the page, and circle it.

2. Outside this nucleus, jot down related topics and ideas, and circle each one. Draw a line from each of these satellite ideas to the central topic.

3. As you think of additional ideas, phrases, facts, or examples, group them in clusters and connect them to one another.

Zoe Shewer created the following cluster to group her ideas.

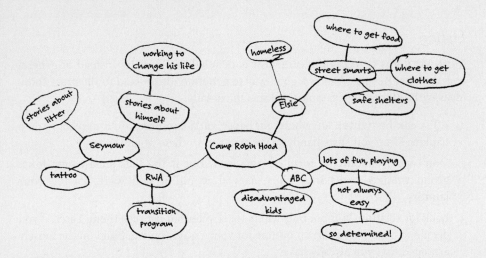

## Questioning Who, What, Where, When, Why, and How

Journalists ask *who, what, where, when, why,* and *how* to uncover the basic information that readers look for in a news story. These standard journalistic questions can be useful for all kinds of writing. Here is how you might use them in an essay about a car accident involving a member of your family:

1. *Who* was involved in the accident? What should I say about my sister (the driver)? About the passengers in the car (including the dog)? The police officer who investigated? The witnesses on the sidewalk?

2. *What* happened? What were the main events leading up to the crash? What did my sister do to avoid hitting the other car head-on? Should I mention that the dog got out of the car first?

3. *Where* did the accident occur? How much of the scene should I describe? The intersection itself? The hill leading up to it?

4. *When* did the accident take place? What time did my sister leave the party? Was it still raining?

5. *Why* did the accident happen? Did the other car swerve into her lane?

6. *How* could it have been avoided? Would my sister have reacted sooner if she hadn't been on her cell phone? Should I write about cellphone usage as a contributing cause in traffic accidents?

Asking key questions like these early in the writing process will help you turn up ideas and figure out which aspects of your subject you want to write about. Later on, the questions you choose to answer will determine, in part, the methods you use to organize your essay. For example, if you decided to explain in detail what happened on the day of your sister's accident, you would draw extensively on the techniques of NARRATION. Or if you decided to focus on the scene of the accident, you would write a largely DESCRIPTIVE essay.

## Keeping a Journal

A personal journal can be a great source of raw material for your writing. Here, for example, is part of a journal entry that Annie Dillard kept when she went on a camping trip in Virginia:

> Last night moths kept flying into the candle. They would hiss & spatter & recoil, lost upside down & flopping in the shadows among the pans on the table. Or—and this happened often, & again tonight—they'd burn their wings, & then their wings would stick to the next thing they'd touch—the edge of a pan, a lid. . . . These I could free with a quick flip with a spoon or something.

Two years after she made this journal entry, Dillard used some of those same details in an essay entitled "The Death of a Moth." In the published essay, the moth-drawn-to-the-flame becomes a vivid image of the dedicated writer who devotes all her energy to her work. Obviously, however, Dillard did not begin the writing process with a big idea like this in mind, and neither should you. She started with the homely details of pots and pans and ordinary moths as recorded in her journal. If you keep a journal regularly, as many writers do, you will have at your fingertips a world of concrete details to think and write about.

You can learn a lot about keeping a journal from an entry like Dillard's:

1. Write down your observations as close to the time of the event as possible; don't wait until you get home from a camping trip to note what happened while you were camping.

2. The observations in a journal don't have to deal with momentous events; record your everyday experiences.

3. Make each journal entry as detailed and specific as possible; don't just write "the bugs were bad" or "another beautiful day."

4. The entries don't have to be long or formally composed; they are for your eyes alone, so be as informal as you like.

5. You may not know the significance of a particular entry until months, even years, after you've written it.

## Organizing and Drafting

Once you accumulate enough facts, details, and other raw material, your next job is to organize that material and develop it into a draft. The method (or methods) of development that you use will be determined by the main point you want your draft to make.

### Stating Your Point

As you begin gathering materials for an essay, you probably won't know exactly what your THESIS—your main point—is going to be (unless, of course, you've been given a specific one as part of your assignment). Before you begin writing, however, try to state your thesis in one sentence. You may find as you go along that you need to revise it, but you should start with a thesis in mind.

What makes a good thesis statement? First, let's consider what a thesis statement is not. A general announcement of your topic—"in this paper I plan to write about how you can fight climate change"—is *not* a thesis statement. A thesis statement tells the reader what your topic is, and it makes an interesting CLAIM *about* your topic, one that is open to further discussion. This is why statements of fact aren't thesis statements either: "The effects of climate change were first predicted in the 1890s by a little-known Swedish chemist." Historical and scientific facts may help support your thesis, but the thesis itself should say something about your subject that requires further discussion. For example:

The best way you can fight climate change is by reducing your personal carbon footprint.

The fight against climate change will be won or lost in developing nations such as India and China.

The United States is still the biggest energy hog on the planet.

When you draft an essay, make sure you state your thesis clearly, usually near the beginning. Like these examples, your thesis statement should be direct and specific, and it should let readers know what you'll be discussing in your essay.

## Making an Outline

An informal outline is simply a list of your main points in the order they might appear in your draft. For example, after grouping her ideas into clusters, Zoe Shewer created this informal outline for her essay on an unexpected lesson:

Volunteering
    three nonprofits
    learned about myself
Ready, Willing & Able
    Seymour
    draining gutters
    telling stories
    his plans
Association to Benefit Children
    disadvantaged kids
    loved to play
    persevered
Homeless shelter
    Elsie
    street smarts
Learned that I have a lot to learn

For longer projects, such as a research paper, you may need a more detailed outline, indicating the order of both the main ideas and the less important ones. When you make a formal outline, you also show—by indenting and using letters and numbers—how all of your ideas fit together to support your thesis.

*Thesis statement*: Volunteering taught me to admire the determination of Seymour, the children at ABC, and Elsie.

  I. Camp Robin Hood
    A. Crash course in volunteering
    B. Ready, Willing & Able
    C. Association to Benefit Children
    D. Homeless shelter
 II. Ready, Willing & Able
    A. Seymour
    B. Taught me to drain gutters
    C. Told me about his own life
III. Association to Benefit Children (ABC)
    A. Played with disadvantaged kids
    B. Read to them
    C. Admired their determination
 IV. Homeless shelter
    A. Elsie
    B. Depended on handouts and shelters
    C. Had figured out the system
  V. Conclusion
    A. Wanted to give something back
    B. Hope I helped others
    C. Sure I learned a lot myself

When you construct a formal outline like this, try to keep items that are at the same level in more or less the same grammatical form. Also, include at least two items for each level, otherwise you don't need to subdivide. Whatever kind of outline you make, however, change it as necessary as you write and revise.

## Using the Basic Methods of Development

Once you've accumulated enough material to write about, have narrowed your subject down to a manageable topic, and have a workable thesis, you should choose one or more methods of development.

Zoe Shewer, for example, ultimately chose to develop her topic by writing a narrative that shows what she learned from doing volunteer work over the summer. Within a narrative framework, however, she also incorporated some description and analyzed cause and effect. Whatever you're writing about, you can draw on the following methods, as Shewer did, to help you develop your topic:

- *Tell a story.* NARRATION (Chapter 5) is one of the oldest ways of making a point.

- *Help the reader see, hear, feel, smell, or taste* what you're writing about. Good DESCRIPTIONS (Chapter 7) include specific details that appeal to the senses and help to create some dominant impression in the reader's mind.

- *Give a "for instance."* Giving EXAMPLES (Chapter 8) is one of the best ways to make general statements more specific and abstract statements more concrete.

- *Break an activity into steps* in order to figure out and systematically explain how something works or is made. The purpose of a PROCESS ANALYSIS (Chapter 9) like this is often to enable the reader to replicate the process, as with a recipe for baking cookies or instructions for using a new app on your phone.

- *Trace similarities and differences.* As a method of development, COMPARISON AND CONTRAST (Chapter 10) tells readers how two subjects are alike or different or both.

- *Divide a subject into types or kinds.* CLASSIFICATION (Chapter 11) helps to explain a complex subject by breaking it down into basic categories.

- *Identify the main characteristics of your subject.* DEFINITION (Chapter 12) tells the reader what something is (or is not) by identifying the particular qualities and attributes that set it apart from others like it.

- *Trace causes and effects.* This method of development is a fundamental way of understanding and explaining relationships among actions and events. How to analyze CAUSE AND EFFECT is examined in Chapter 13.

- *Make a claim and give evidence to support it.* How to state a claim, choose the best evidence you can find to support it, and present that evidence in a logical way are all discussed in ARGUMENT (Chapter 14).

The methods you choose for developing your essay will depend on the nature of your topic and your purpose in writing. If your purpose is simple—to give someone written directions for finding the nearest grocery store, for example—a single method may suffice. Often, however, you will want to use several methods together, as best-selling author Michael Lewis does in *Liar's Poker*, which we will examine part by part, method by method in Chapter 15 ("Combining the Methods").

# The Parts of an Essay

No matter what methods of development you use, any essay you write should have a beginning, a middle, and an end. These three basic parts are usually referred to as the introduction, the body, and the conclusion.

In the introduction, you introduce the topic and state your thesis. That is, you tell the reader exactly what you're writing about and what your main point is. In the body—which may run anywhere from a few sentences or paragraphs to many pages—you offer evidence in support of your thesis. In the conclusion, you wrap up what you have to say, often by restating the thesis—but with some variation based on the evidence you have just cited.

For example, here is a brief essay about alligators with its parts indicated in the margins. The author states her thesis in the first two paragraphs. In the middle paragraph—the body of her essay—she cites facts and figures to support her thesis. And in the final paragraph, she concludes by restating that thesis—with a twist.

*Introduction* States the thesis.

At the Congregational Church, Pastor John puts on puppet shows for the children. One of the star characters is Chompers, a crocodile who talks, attends church, and could go to City Hall if he wanted to.

In the real world, however, the alligators on this sanctuary island can't speak for themselves. So maybe it's time for the rest of us to do it for them and ask if we should reevaluate our alligator policy.

*Body* Supports the thesis with facts, figures, and other evidence.

In 2004, responding to two fatal attacks, the city changed how it deals with alligator complaints. Under that policy, not only nuisance alligators can be destroyed but *any* alligator in the area that exceeds four feet in length. More than 200 alligators have been killed since the 2004 policy was initiated.

Since alligators don't breed until they're about six feet long, we could be on our way to eliminating these reptiles from the island and dramatically altering the natural balance among its wildlife. Fewer alligators mean more raccoons, snakes, and other natural prey left to feed on birds' eggs and hatchlings. Is that what we want?

*Conclusion* Restates the thesis with a twist.

Now that the alligator population on the island is clearly under control, perhaps even threatened, let's ask City Hall to reconsider its "targeted harvest" policy. Attend Tuesday's Council meeting and speak up for the alligators. Tell 'em Chompers sent you.

—BARBARA JOY WHITE, "Speaking Up for Alligators"

As in this reptilian example, any essay you write should have an introduction and a conclusion that state and restate your main point. In addition, you'll want to include, in the main body of your essay, at least one paragraph for each supporting point you make. If you are writing about how individuals can combat climate change, for example, you might include a body paragraph for each way of reducing carbon consumption that you propose, such as recycling old clothes, eating less red meat, planning a green wedding, and making fewer left turns when driving.

More tips for writing effective introductory, body, and concluding paragraphs can be found on pp. 86–92.

## Using Visuals

In addition to giving your essay a clear beginning, middle, and ending, you may want to consider using visuals. Illustrations such as graphs and charts can be especially effective for presenting or comparing data, and photographs can help readers see things you describe in your written text.

Visuals should never be mere decoration or clip art, however. Any visuals should be directly relevant to your topic and must support your thesis in some way. For example, if you are writing about conserving energy by carrying a reusable shopping bag, you might include an illustration showing the kind of bag you have in mind.

As with a written text, any visual material you include should be appropriate for your audience and purpose. A picture of a raven, for example, would not add much to an essay for a literature class on Edgar Allan Poe's famous poem—but it might be appropriate, if properly labeled, for a biology paper or a field guide to birds.

This reusable bag lets you avoid using plastic shopping bags, thereby conserving energy and reducing landfill waste. © Doug Steley B / Alamy.

If you do decide that a visual will genuinely enhance your argument, be sure to refer to it in your text and number it, if necessary, so that readers can find it ("see Fig. 1"). Position the visual as close as you can to the part of your text that it illustrates, and provide a caption that identifies and explains its point. If you found the visual in another source, identify the source and provide documentation in a Works Cited or References list.

To cite visual sources MLA-style, see p. 824.

## Revising

Revising is a process of re-vision, of looking again at your draft and making necessary changes in content, organization, or emphasis. Occasionally when you revise, you discover only a few minor scrapes and bruises that need your attention. More often, however, revising requires some major surgery: adding new evidence, narrowing a thesis, cutting out paragraphs or entire sections, rewriting the beginning to appeal better to your audience, and so on.

Revising is not generally the time to focus on words or sentences, though you may change some words and smooth out awkward or unclear sentences as you go. Nor is revising a matter of correcting errors, but rather of more general shaping and reshaping. Many writers try to revise far too soon. To avoid this pitfall, put aside your draft for a few hours—or better still, for a few days—before revising.

### Reading a Draft with a Critical Eye

Start by reading the draft yourself, and then try to get someone else to look it over—a classmate, a writing tutor, your roommate, your grandmother. Whoever it is, be sure he or she is aware of your intended audience and purpose. Here's what you and the person with fresh eyes should look for as you read:

**AN EFFECTIVE TITLE.** Is the title more than a label? How does it pique the reader's interest? Does it indicate the point of the essay—and if not, should it?

**A CLEAR FOCUS.** What is the main point? Is it clearly stated in a **THESIS** statement— and if not, should it be? Is the thesis too broad? too narrow?

**SUFFICIENT INFORMATION FOR YOUR AUDIENCE.** How familiar is the topic likely to be to your readers? Is there sufficient background information? Are there clear definitions for any terms and concepts readers might not know? Will readers find it interesting?

**ADEQUATE SUPPORT FOR THE THESIS.** What evidence supports the thesis? Is the evidence convincing and the reasoning logical? Could the draft be strengthened by adding more facts or specific details?

**ORGANIZATION.** Is the draft well organized? Does it have a clear beginning, middle, and ending? Are paragraphs related to each other by clear TRANSITIONS? Does each paragraph contribute to the main point, or are some paragraphs off the topic? Does the ending give a sense of closure?

**METHODS OF DEVELOPMENT.** What is the main method of development—is the draft primarily a NARRATIVE? a DESCRIPTION? an ARGUMENT? Is this method effective? If not, which other methods might be introduced? For instance, would more EXAMPLES, or DEFINITIONS, or a discussion of CAUSES be beneficial?

**SOURCES.** Is there material from other sources? If so, how are those sources incorporated—are they quoted? paraphrased? summarized? How are they acknowledged? In other words, is it clear to the reader whose words or ideas are being used? How does the source material support the main point? Have all source materials been properly cited and documented?

**PARAGRAPHS.** Does each paragraph focus on one main idea and have a clear topic sentence? Does the structure of paragraphs vary, or are they too much alike? If they all begin with a topic sentence, should you consider rewriting some paragraphs to lead up to the topic sentence instead of down from it? Does every sentence in a paragraph support the point that the rest of the paragraph is making? Are there any long or complex paragraphs that should be subdivided?

> For more on writing paragraphs, see Chapter 5 (p. 75).

The more common problem, however, is that paragraphs are too short. Are there paragraphs that should be combined with other paragraphs or developed more fully? How well does the draft flow from one paragraph to the next? If any paragraphs seem to break the flow, look to see if you need to add transitions or to use repetition to help the reader follow the text.

**SENTENCE LENGTH AND VARIETY.** Check the length of your sentences. If they are all approximately the same length, try varying them. A short sentence among long sentences can provide emphasis. On the other hand, too many short sentences, one after another, can sound choppy. Try combining some of them.

**VISUALS.** Does the draft include any visuals? If not, is there any material in the text that would be easier to understand as a chart or table? Any descriptive passages where a photo might help readers see what you're talking about? If there are visuals, are they relevant to the topic? How do they support your thesis?

## A Sample Student Essay

Here is Zoe Shewer's first draft of an essay on what she learned about herself from a summer program. It is based on her formal outline on p. 58.

### FIRST DRAFT

How should I spend my summer vacation? Many college students have internships or summer jobs. Some travel. I spent last summer volunteering with three nonprofits through Camp Robin Hood.

Camp Robin Hood is a hands-on summer crash course in New York City nonprofit organizations. Every week, I worked at a different nonprofit: a day care center, a homeless shelter, and a transitional lifestyle program for ex-convicts and former addicts. At every organization, I learned something about working with the underprivileged, but at the end of the summer, I realized that I had also learned something about myself.

I began by working at Ready, Willing & Able, where ex-convicts and former addicts clean streets as part of a transitional lifestyle program. I'll never forget the street cleaning attendant I worked with there. Seymour was tall, tattooed, and a former addict. He was also calm and completely at ease in his RWA jumpsuit, sweeping the sidewalks and wheeling a huge blue trash can through the streets. Seymour taught me how to drain gutters by diverting the flow of water with a rolled-up towel. He also taught me to "read" the back stories in the litter. It was like he saw a story in every piece of trash: a schoolgirl who discarded a bracelet in a temper tantrum, a closet eater who ate Twinkies in the street. He talked about his family, too, and his dreams and plans. I grew to respect him and admire his perseverance and determination, despite all the setbacks in his life.

That respect and admiration was something I would come to feel at each of the nonprofits. At the Association to Benefit Children, an organization that provides services to underprivileged children, I played with and taught children who had many challenges. Like any kids, they loved singing, finger painting, and playing with toys. But there was no escaping the fact that these activities didn't always come easily to them. They worked hard for what they wanted. It was impossible not to admire their determination.

At a homeless shelter, where I handed out clean clothes and tickets for showers, I met people from every walk of life. Some had addiction problems or other illnesses, but many had simply fallen on hard times. The loss of a job or an unexpected medical problem ended up costing them their homes, and they had nowhere else to go. I spent many evenings talking to one woman in particular, Elsie. She had been homeless for several years and knew the streets of New York better than anyone I've ever met. She knew which restaurants would give out their leftover food and when you should appear at their back door for dinner. She knew which churches had the best soup kitchens, and which shelters were safest, and where to find the best cast-off clothing. I never found out how she'd become homeless, but she'd figured out the system and made it work for her. Although I grew up in New York City, her street smarts made me feel like I'd never really known the city.

I volunteered for Camp Robin Hood because I wanted to give something back. I know that my upbringing has been privileged, and I've been lucky to have never gone without. I wanted to do something for those who weren't so lucky. But I discovered that while I may have more tangible goods than those I was volunteering to help, they had a lot to teach me about the intangible: qualities like perseverance, determination, optimism and cheerfulness no matter what the circumstances. They taught me that I have a lot to learn.

## Getting Response before Revising

After finishing her first draft, Shewer set it aside for a few hours and then reread it, using the guidelines for reading a draft with a critical eye (pp. 62–63). She also asked a classmate to read it, and he offered her the following comments:

I really like the topic of your essay, and I think it meets the assignment well. But maybe it would be more effective if you picked one of the three places you worked to focus on, so that you could talk about it more in depth. I'd like to know more about them.

You kind of state a thesis—"At every organization, I learned something about working with the underprivileged, but at the end of the summer, I realized that I had also learned something about myself"—but then you state it more directly at the end of the paper—"They taught me that I have a lot to learn." That works pretty well, and the body paragraphs do support this idea.

You describe the people you meet, but it might be more interesting if there was more of a story.

Shewer agreed with her classmate's suggestions to focus on just one of the places she worked, and to incorporate more narration. She chose to write about her experience at Ready, Willing & Able, and to focus on her day working with Seymour. After some **BRAINSTORMING** about that day, she decided to add a **NARRATIVE** about one incident in particular. She then revised her **THESIS** to reflect her narrower focus on that specific day. She also added a title, which she hadn't included in her first draft.

## SECOND DRAFT

Ready, Willing, and Able

July is stifling in New York City, and I was not looking forward to wearing an oversized jumpsuit in ninety-degree heat. I was suited up to clean streets as part of the Camp Robin Hood program. I was at the headquarters of Ready, Willing & Able. Most RWA employees are ex-convicts or former addicts for whom street cleaning is both a job and part of a transitional lifestyle program.

The program coordinator waved me toward a tall man who had apparently been waiting for me. His name was Seymour, and he was the street cleaning attendant I would be working with all day. As he reached out to shake my hand, I noticed that he had a tattoo on his forearm.

We headed out to the street, and while I fidgeted with the broom I carried, Seymour calmly wheeled a bright blue trash can behind him. As we began sweeping the sidewalks, Seymour not only showed me how to drain the gutters, he talked about who might have dropped certain kinds of trash and why and told me about his family and his desire to get his life back on track. Though I had lived in the city my entire life, I began to see things in a new light. I became so absorbed in Seymour's stories that I heard some girls laughing and almost didn't realize they were laughing at me. "I wonder what *she* did to deserve *that*!"

I looked up and saw a group of girls about my age laughing at me as they walked past. They obviously thought I was serving a juvenile court sentence. Ordinarily I may have laughed at the idea that I could be mistaken for a juvenile delinquent, but on this day I felt butterflies in my stomach.

What if Seymour thought I was just like those other girls? What if he thought I didn't want to be there and was counting down the minutes until the day would be over? I wanted to tell him that I had a lot of respect for his work and that I knew I couldn't possibly understand what he does just by shadowing him for a day. I wanted to tell him that I was not simply doing a day of community service so I could include it on a résumé.

But Seymour broke the silence, saying, "Put some muscle in it, Goldilocks."

## Revising a Second Draft

After setting her revision aside for a day, Shewer came back to her essay and reread it, again following the questions for revision on pp. 62–63. She liked the story of her day working with Seymour, but she thought that now there was too much narration, and she needed to have more DESCRIPTIVE details. She also decided that she needed to explain more about the incident with the girls—how she felt and how that moment taught her something. Finally, she revised some of her sentences to keep them from being the same length and tried to make some of her language more precise.

FINAL DRAFT

Ready, Willing, and Able

Introduction

Wearing a canvas jumpsuit zipped up to my neck, I must have looked as though I was stepping onto the set of *ET: The Extra-Terrestrial*, but my actual destination was Madison Avenue, home to some of the fanciest boutiques in New York City. The bright blue jumpsuit I wore was far from high fashion: it was sized for a full-grown man, and it ballooned about my slender frame. My blond hair was pulled back in a ponytail, and the only label I displayed was the bold-lettered logo on my back: Ready, Willing & Able. I was suited up to collect trash from the sidewalks of New York.

Beginning of narrative: the first day

July is stifling in New York City, and I was not looking forward to wearing the oversized jumpsuit in ninety-degree heat. As I made my way through the Ready, Willing & Able (RWA) headquarters, I passed colorfully decorated bulletin boards bearing smiley-faced reminders: "Drug testing is on Monday!" "Curfew is midnight!" Most fulltime employees of RWA are ex-convicts or former addicts for whom street cleaning is the work-for-housing component of a transitional lifestyle program. For me, street cleaning was day one of Camp Robin Hood, a hands-on summer crash course in New York nonprofit organizations. As I selected a broom from the supply closet, I reminded myself that I had volunteered to do this. Feeling like a new kid on the first day of school, I stood nervously next to the program supervisor who would introduce me to the street cleaning attendant I would be helping.

Description of key character, with concrete details

If I was the awkward new kid, the street cleaning attendant to whom I was assigned, a tall man named Seymour, was undoubtedly the Big Man on Campus. Seymour wore his RWA cap slightly askew, and, as he reached out to shake my hand, I caught a glimpse of a tattoo under his sleeve. We headed out to the street together, and, while I nervously fidgeted with the broom I carried, he calmly wheeled a bright blue trash can behind him. Seymour began sweeping the sidewalks, and I followed his lead. He not only showed me how to drain the gutters by diverting the flow of water with a

Fig. 1. Homeless men get back to work and self-respect with help from the Ready, Willing & Able program sponsored by the DOE Fund.

rolled-up towel, he also taught me how to "read" the back stories in the litter. To Seymour, a torn hemp bracelet on the curb was a schoolgirl's temper tantrum; a Twinkie wrapper in the street was a closet eater's discarded evidence. Though I have lived in New York my entire life, I began to see my surroundings in a new light. The streets that had always felt so familiar seemed full of surprises. As our afternoon continued, Seymour also told me stories about his sister, his desire to get his life back on track after some time on the wrong side of the law, his love of Central Park, and his aspiration to travel across the country.

    After several hours, I had more or less forgotten about my tent-sized RWA jumpsuit when suddenly I heard someone laughing at me: "I wonder what *she* did to deserve *that*?!"

    I looked up and saw a group of girls my age looking in my direction and laughing as they walked past. My stomach tightened.

Dialogue and climax of narrative

Effect of incident They obviously thought I was being punished, perhaps serving a juvenile court sentence. Ordinarily I might have laughed at the idea that I could be mistaken for a juvenile delinquent, but on this day I felt a jumble of feelings—panic, shame, sadness, and admiration for a man whose history is suggested by his jumpsuit and the logo on his back. I will admit that a few hours earlier I was embarrassed about my ill-fitting uniform. Halfway through the workday, however, the Thesis indicated indirectly girls' rude comments caused an entirely different kind of shame: What if Seymour thought *I* was anything like those girls? What if he thought that I was faking a smile and counting down the minutes until the day was over?

Significance of narrative I suddenly wanted to thank Seymour for this experience. I wanted to tell him that he was probably the best guide through these streets I had ever had, and that I knew I could not possibly understand what he does by shadowing him for a day in a borrowed uniform. I wanted to explain to him that I volunteer regularly in New York: I am committed to working with at-risk children, and have done so for years at an after-school program in Harlem. I wanted to share how much I relate to his closeness with his family, his desire to travel, and his love of Strawberry Fields in Central Park. But the girls' mocking comments and laughter had left us in an uncomfortable silence, and I felt that anything I might say would make us feel even more awkward.

It was Seymour who broke this silence. As I stood next to the trash can and tried to avoid staring off in the direction of the latte-carrying girls, Seymour caught my eye, smiled, and nodded Conclusion with dialogue toward my broom with one excellent piece of advice: "Put some muscle in it, Goldilocks."

This final draft, Shewer felt, better blended the modes of narration and description, and it fulfilled the assignment to write about an experience that taught her something new about herself. She especially liked the concrete details she included and the dialogue that ended the essay.

# Editing and Proofreading

When you finish revising your essay, you're still not quite done. You've put the icing on the cake, but you need to make sure all the candles are straight and wipe the edge of the plate. That is, you need to edit and proofread your final draft before presenting it to the reader.

When you edit, you add finishing touches and correct errors in grammar, sentence structure, punctuation, and word choice that affect the sense and meaning of your text. When you proofread, you take care of misspellings, typos, problems with your margins and format, and other minor blemishes in the appearance of your document.

Certain types of problems are common to certain types of writing. Chapters 6–14 include sections on "Editing for Common Errors"—the kinds that are likely with the method being discussed. Here are some tips that can help you check your drafts for some common mistakes.

## TIPS FOR EDITING SENTENCES

**Check to be sure that each sentence expresses a complete thought**—that it has a subject (someone or something) and a verb performing an action or indicating a state of being.

**Check capitalization and end punctuation.** Be sure that each sentence begins with a capital letter and ends with a period, a question mark, or an exclamation point.

**Look for sentences that begin with *it* or *there*.** Often such sentences are vague or boring, and they are usually easy to edit. For example, if you've written *There is a doctor on call at every hospital*, you could edit it to read *A doctor is on call at every hospital*.

**Check for parallelism.** All items in a list or series should have parallel forms—all nouns (*Lincoln, Grant, Lee*), all verbs (*dedicate, consecrate, hallow*), all phrases (*of the people, by the people, for the people*).

**Check adjective order.** Adjectives usually go in the following order: number, size, shape, age, color, nationality (*a pair of small round hand-me-down navy earrings*).

## TIPS FOR EDITING WORDS

**There, their.** Use *there* to refer to place or direction or to introduce a sentence: *Who was there? There was no answer.* Use *their* as a possessive: *Their intentions were good.*

**It's, its.** Use *it's* to mean "it is": *It's difficult to say what causes dyslexia.* Use *its* to mean "belonging to it": *Each car has its unique features.*

**Lie, lay.** Use *lie* when you mean "recline": *She's lying down because she's tired.* Use *lay* when you mean "put" or "place": *Lay the book on the table.*

## TIPS FOR EDITING PUNCTUATION

**Check for commas after introductory elements in a sentence**

The day he disclosed his matrimonial ambitions for me, my uncle sat me at his right during lunch.     —SAIRA SHAH, "Longing to Belong"

**Check for commas before *and, but, or, nor, so,* or *yet* in compound sentences**

They divorced when I was in junior high school, and they agreed on little except that I was an impossible child.   —RICHARD RUSSO, "Dog"

**Check for commas in a series**

A circuit of the courthouse square took you past the grand furniture stores, the two dime stores, the shoe stores, the men's stores, the ladies' stores, the banks, the drugstores.     —BOBBIE ANN MASON, "Being Country"

**When you quote other people's words, be sure to put quotation marks at the beginning and end of the quotation**

Instead of offering an abject apology, Ms. Hegemann insisted, "There's no such thing as originality anyway, just authenticity."
   —TRIP GABRIEL, "Plagiarism Lines Blur for Students in Digital Age"

**Check to be sure that you've put commas and periods inside quotation marks**

"Put some muscle in it, Goldilocks."                    —ZOE SHEWER,
                                                "Ready, Willing, and Able"

"You know," Dave told his grandmother, "I'm responsible for the lives
of 40 men."                              —ANNE BERNAYS, "Warrior Day"

**Check your use of apostrophes with possessives.** Singular nouns should
end in 's, whereas plural nouns should end in s'. The possessive pronouns
*hers, his, its, ours, yours,* and *theirs* should not have apostrophes.

Robert Bergman's radiant portraits of strangers provoked this meditation.
                                    —TONI MORRISON, "Strangers"

Morrison's meditation was provoked by the strangers' faces.

Theirs was the life I dreamt about during my vacations in eastern
North Carolina.                                    —DAVID SEDARIS,
                "Remembering My Childhood on the Continent of Africa"

## Proofreading and Final Formatting

Proofreading is the only stage in the writing process where you are *not* primarily concerned with meaning. Of course you should correct any substantive errors you discover, but your main concerns when you proofread are small technicalities and the appearance of your text. Misspellings, margins that are too narrow or too wide, unindented paragraphs, missing page numbers—these are the kinds of imperfections you're looking for as you put the final touch on your document.

Such minor blemishes are especially hard to see when you're looking at your own work. So slow down as you proofread, and view your document more as a picture than as a written text. Use a ruler or piece of paper to guide your eye line by line as you scan the page; or read your entire text backward a sentence at a time; or read it out loud word by word. Use a spellchecker, too, but don't rely on it: a spellchecker doesn't know the difference, for example, between *spackling* and *spacing* or *Greek philosophy* and *Geek philosophy*.

After you've proofread your document word for word, check the overall format to make sure it follows any specific instructions that you may have been given. If your instructor does not have formatting requirements, follow these tips based on the Modern Language Association (MLA) guidelines.

## TIPS FOR FORMATTING AN ESSAY MLA-STYLE

**Heading and title.** Put your name, your instructor's name, the name and number of the course, and the date on separate lines in the upper-left-hand corner of your first page. Center your title on the next line, but do not underline it or put it in quotation marks. Begin your first paragraph on the line that follows.

**Typeface and size.** Use ten-, eleven-, or twelve-point type in an easy-to-read font, such as Times New Roman, Palatino, or Cambria.

**Spacing.** Double-space your document.

**Margins.** Set one-inch margins at the top, bottom, and sides of your text.

**Paragraph indentation.** Indent the first line of each paragraph one-half inch.

**Page numbers.** Number your pages consecutively in the upper right-hand corner of the page, and include your last name with each page number.

**Long quotations.** When quoting more than three lines of poetry, more than four lines of prose, or dialogue between characters in a drama, set off the quotation from the rest of your text, indenting it one inch from the left margin. Do not use quotation marks, and put any parenthetical documentation *after* the final punctuation.

Turn to pp. 827–35 in the Appendix for further information about formatting a paper using MLA style.

# CHAPTER 5

# Writing Paragraphs

I didn't have the vocabulary to say "paragraph," but I
realized that a paragraph was a fence that held words.
—SHERMAN ALEXIE

Just as an essay is made up of a number of related paragraphs, a paragraph is made up of a number of related sentences on the same topic. In any piece of writing longer than a few sentences, paragraphs are necessary to indicate when the discussion shifts from one topic to another. Just because a group of sentences is on the same topic, however, doesn't mean they're all closely related. All of the following sentences, for example, are about snakes:

> There are no snakes in Ireland. Ounce for ounce, the most deadly snake in North America is the coral snake. Snakes are our friends; never kill a snake. North America is teeming with snakes, including four poisonous species. Snakes also eat insects.

Although they make statements about the same topic, these sentences do not form a coherent paragraph because they're not closely related to each other: each one snakes off in a different direction. In a coherent paragraph, all the sentences work together to support the main point.

## Supporting the Main Point

Suppose the main point we wanted to make in a paragraph about snakes was that, despite their reputation for evil, snakes should be protected. We could still mention snakes in North America, even the deadly coral snake. We could say that snakes eat insects. But the sentence about snakes in Ireland would have to go. Of course, we could introduce additional facts and figures about snakes and snakebites—so long as we made sure that every statement in our paragraph worked together to support the idea of conservation. For example, we might write:

> Snakes do far more good than harm, so the best thing to do if you encounter a snake is to leave it alone. North America is teeming with snakes, including four poisonous species. (Ounce for ounce, the most deadly snake in North America is the coral snake.) The chances of dying from any variety of snakebite, however, are slim—less than 1:25,000,000 per year in the United States. Snakes, moreover, contribute to a healthy ecosystem. They help to control the rodent population, and they eat insects. (Far more people die each year from the complications of insect bites than from snakebites.) Snakes are our friends and should be protected; never kill a snake.

This is a coherent paragraph because every sentence contributes to the main point, which is that snakes should be protected.

## Don't Go Off on a Tangent

Anytime the subject of snakes comes up, it is tempting to recall the legend of Saint Patrick, the patron saint of Ireland who, in the second half of the fifth century, is said to have driven the snakes from the land with his walking stick. Beware, however, of straying too far from the main point of your paragraph, no matter how interesting the digression may be. That is, be careful not to go off on a tangent. The term *tangent*, by the way, comes from geometry and refers to a line that touches a circle at only one point—on the periphery, not the center.

> Every sentence in Molly Hennessy-Fiske's essay (p. 261) makes the point that "Texas Talk Is Losing Its Twang."

And, incidentally, did you know that St. Patrick used a three-leaf clover to explain the Christian doctrine of the Trinity to the Irish people? Which is why shamrocks are associated with St. Patrick's Day. Also, there's another really interesting legend about St. Patrick's walking stick. . . . But we digress.

## Writing Topic Sentences

To help you stay on track in a paragraph, state your main point in a **TOPIC SENTENCE** that identifies your subject (snakes) and makes a clear statement about it ("should be protected"). Most of the time your topic sentence will come at the beginning, as in this paragraph from an essay about the benefits of working at McDonald's:

> Working at McDonald's has taught me a lot. The most important thing I've learned is that you have to start at the bottom and work your way up. I've learned to take this seriously—if you're going to run a business, you need to know how to do all the other jobs. I also have more patience than ever and have learned how to control my emotions. I've learned how to get along with all different kinds of people. I'd like to have my own business someday, and working at McDonald's is what showed me I could do that.
>
> —MARISSA NUÑEZ, "Climbing the Golden Arches"

When you put the topic sentence at the beginning of a paragraph like this, every other sentence in your paragraph should follow from it.

Sometimes you may put your topic sentence at the end of the paragraph. Then, every other sentence in the paragraph should lead up to the topic sentence. Consider this example from an essay on hummingbirds that ultimately makes a statement about all living things:

Mammals and birds have hearts with four chambers. Reptiles and turtles have hearts with three chambers. Fish have hearts with two chambers. Insects and mollusks have hearts with one chamber. Worms have hearts with one chamber, although they may have as many as eleven single-chambered hearts. Unicellular bacteria have no hearts at all, but even they have fluid eternally in motion, washing from one side of the cell to the other, swirling and whirling. No living being is without interior liquid motion. We all churn inside.

—BRIAN DOYLE, "Joyas Voladoras"

All of the statements in this paragraph are about hearts, or otherwise pertain to the circulation of fluid ("liquid motion") within the body of living creatures. Thus, they all contribute to the topic sentence at the end: "We all churn inside."

Sometimes the main point of a paragraph will be implied from the context, and you won't need to state it explicitly in a topic sentence. This is especially true when you're making a point by telling a story. In both of the following paragraphs from her essay about working at McDonald's, Marissa Nuñez explains how she got the job in the first place:

Two years ago, while my cousin Susie and I were doing our Christmas shopping on Fourteenth Street, we decided to have lunch at McDonald's.

"Yo, check it out," Susie said. "They're hiring. Let's give it a try." I looked at her and said, "Are you serious?" She gave me this look that made it clear that she was.

Nuñez doesn't have to tell the reader that she is explaining how she came to work for McDonald's because that point is clear. (Also, she later writes that "finally one day the manager came out and said we had the job.")

Topic sentences not only tell your reader what the rest of a paragraph is about; they help, collectively, to tie all your ideas together in support of the main point of your essay. In Nuñez's case, the main point is what she learned about people, business, and herself from working at a fast-food restaurant, as she states clearly at the beginning: "Working at McDonald's has taught me a lot."

## Using Parallel Structures

See how parallel structure is used in "Grant and Lee" (p. 377).

Another way of tying ideas together in a paragraph is by using parallel structures. Brian Doyle does this in his paragraph about hearts and liquid motion: "Reptiles and turtles have hearts with three chambers. Fish have hearts with two chambers. Insects and mollusks have hearts with one chamber." The similarities in form among these sentences (subject + verb + phrase) tie them together in support of the topic sentence about churning inside with liquid motion.

Parallel structures indicate key elements in a paragraph, or even in an entire essay. They do not, however, tell the reader exactly how those pieces of the puzzle fit together. For this we need transitions.

## Using Transitions

Paragraphs are all about connections. The following words and phrases can help you to make TRANSITIONS that clearly connect one statement to another—within a paragraph and also between paragraphs.

- *When describing place or direction:* across, across from, at, along, away, behind, close, down, distant, far, here, in between, in front of, inside, left, near, next to, north, outside, right, south, there, toward, up

- *When narrating events in time:* at the same time, during, frequently, from time to time, in 2015, in the future, now, never, often, meanwhile, occasionally, soon, then, until, when

- *When giving examples:* for example, for instance, in fact, in particular, namely, specifically, that is

- *When comparing:* also, as, in a similar way, in comparison, like, likewise

- *When contrasting:* although, but, by contrast, however, on the contrary, on the other hand

- *When analyzing cause and effect:* as a result, because, because of, consequently, so, then

- *When using logical reasoning:* accordingly, hence, it follows, therefore, thus, since, so

- *When tracing sequence or continuation:* also, and, after, before, earlier, finally, first, furthermore, in addition, last, later, next

- *When summarizing:* in conclusion, in summary, in the end, consequently, so, therefore, thus, to conclude

Consider how transitional words and phrases like these work together in the following paragraph about perpetuating a family tradition; the transitions are indicated in **bold**:

> One summer, **along about** 1904, my father rented a camp on a lake in Maine and took us all there for the month of August. We all got ringworm from some kittens and had to rub Pond's Extract on our arms and legs night

and morning, and my father rolled over in a canoe with all his clothes on; **but outside of** that the vacation was a success and **from then on** none of us ever thought there as any place in the world like that lake in Maine. We returned summer after summer—**always on** August 1 for one month. I have **since** become a salt-water man, but **sometimes** in summer there are days **when** the restlessness of the tides and the fearful cold of the sea water and the incessant wind that blows across the afternoon and into the evening make me wish for the placidity of a lake in the woods. **A few weeks ago** this feeling got so strong I bought myself a couple of bass hooks and a spinner and returned to the lake **where** we used to go, for a week's fishing and to revisit old haunts.                          —E. B. WHITE, "Once More to the Lake"

Without transitions, the statements in this paragraph would fall apart like beads on a broken string. Transitions indicate relationships: they help to tie the writer's ideas together—in this case by showing how they are related in time, the passage of which is the grand theme of White's essay.

## Developing Paragraphs

There are many ways—in addition to supporting a topic sentence and using parallel structures and transitions—to develop coherent paragraphs. In fact, all of the basic patterns of writing discussed in this book work just as well for organizing paragraphs as they do for organizing entire essays. Here are some examples, with explanations of how they draw on the various modes of writing.

### Narration

One of the oldest and most common ways of developing a paragraph on almost any subject is by narrating a story about it. When you construct a NARRATIVE (Chapter 6), you focus on events: you tell what happened. In the following paragraph, a writer tells what happened on the day she returned to her hometown in Kentucky soon after publishing her first novel:

In November 1988, bookstoreless though it was, my hometown hosted a big event. Paper banners announced it, and stores closed in honor of it. A crowd assembled in the town's largest public space—the railroad depot. The line went out the door and away down the tracks. At the front of the line they were plunking down $16.95 for copies of a certain book.
—BARBARA KINGSOLVER, "In Case You Ever Want to Go Home Again"

Narratives are organized by time, and they usually present events in chronological order. In this narrative, the time is a particular day in 1988 when the triumphant young author returns to her hometown for a booksigning. The events of the day ("banners announced," "stores closed," "crowd assembled," "line went out the door") are presented in chronological order—all leading up to the climactic event ("plunking down" the money to buy the book) at the end of the paragraph.

> Joan Didion tells a classic story on this theme in "On Going Home" (p. 763).

## Description

A common way of developing a paragraph, especially when you're writing about a physical object or place, is to give a detailed **DESCRIPTION** (Chapter 7) of your subject. When you describe something, you show the reader how it looks, sounds, feels, smells, or tastes, as in the following description of her grandmother's house (or *casa*) in Puerto Rico as the author remembers it:

> I remember how in my childhood it sat on stilts; this was before it had a downstairs. It rested on its perch like a great blue bird, not a flying sort of bird, more like a nesting hen, but with spread wings. Grandfather had built it soon after their marriage. He was a painter and housebuilder by trade, a poet and meditative man by nature. As each of their eight children were born, new rooms were added. After a few years, the paint did not exactly match, nor the materials, so that there was a chronology to it, like the rings of a tree, and Mamá could tell you the history of each room in her casa, and thus the genealogy of the family along with it.        —JUDITH ORTIZ COFER, "More Room"

Descriptions of physical objects are often organized by the configuration of the object. Here the object is a house, and the writer develops this descriptive paragraph by moving from one part of the house to another (stilts, new rooms, mismatched paint and materials), ending up with an overall sense of the family's history as chronicled in the physical attributes of the house.

> Paul Crenshaw organizes his description around common weather patterns (p. 203).

## Example

When you use **EXAMPLES** (Chapter 8) to develop a paragraph, you give specific instances of the point you're making. In the following tongue-in-cheek paragraph, a linguist uses multiple examples to show how "unreliable" the English language can be:

> In this unreliable English tongue, greyhounds aren't always grey (or gray); panda bears and koala bears aren't bears (they're marsupials); a woodchuck is a groundhog, which is not a hog; a horned toad is a lizard; glowworms are fireflies, but fireflies are not flies (they're beetles); ladybugs and lightning

bugs are also beetles (and to propagate, a significant proportion of ladybugs must be male); a guinea pig is neither a pig nor from Guinea (it's a South American rodent); and a titmouse is neither mammal nor mammaried.

—RICHARD LEDERER, "English Is a Crazy Language"

Although the language and punctuation of this paragraph are playfully complex, the organization is simple: it is a series, or list, of brief examples in more or less random order.

In addition to using multiple examples to develop a paragraph, you can also focus on a single example, as in this paragraph from an essay on the limits of dictionary definitions:

> Definitions are especially unhelpful to children. There's an oft-cited 1987 study in which fifth graders were given dictionary definitions and asked to write their own sentences using the words defined. The results were discouraging. One child, given the word *erode*, wrote, "Our family erodes a lot," because the definition given was "eat out, eat away."
>
> —ERIN MCKEAN, "Redefining Definition"

Here the writer states the point to be exemplified, identifies the source of the example she is going to use, comments on the significance of that source, and then gives the example: an exemplary use of example to develop a paragraph.

## Process Analysis

When you use **PROCESS ANALYSIS** (Chapter 9) to a develop a paragraph, you tell the reader how to do something—or how something works or is made—by breaking the process into steps. In the following paragraph, a young writer explains what she sees as the first steps in learning to be a writer:

> To begin, don't write about yourself. I'm not saying you're uninteresting. I realize that your life has been so crazy no one could make this stuff up. But if you want to be a writer, start by writing about other people. Observe their faces, and the way they wave their hands around. Listen to the way they talk. Replay conversations in your mind—not just the words, but the silences as well. Imagine the lives of others. If you want to be a writer, you need to get over yourself. This is not just an artistic choice; it's a moral choice. A writer attempts to understand others from the inside.
>
> —ALLEGRA GOODMAN, "So, You Want to Be a Writer? Here's How."

In a process analysis, the steps of the process are usually presented in the order in which they occur in time. Here the first step ("To begin") is something not to do: "don't write about yourself"; it is followed by five more steps in order: start, observe, listen, replay, imagine. At the end of the paragraph comes the end result of the process: (you will) "understand others from the inside."

## Comparison and Contrast

With a COMPARISON (Chapter 10) of two or more subjects, you point out their similarities and differences. In the following paragraph, a historian compares two Civil War generals, Ulysses S. Grant and Robert E. Lee:

> So Grant and Lee were in complete contrast, representing two diametrically opposed elements in American life. Grant was the modern man emerging; beyond him, ready to come on the stage, was the great age of steel and machinery, of crowded cities and a restless burgeoning vitality. Lee might have ridden down from the old age of chivalry, lance in hand, silken banner fluttering over his head. Each man was the perfect champion of his cause, drawing both his strengths and his weaknesses from the people he led.
>
> —BRUCE CATTON, "Grant and Lee"

Here the writer examines both of the subjects he is comparing in a single paragraph, moving systematically from the characteristics of one to those of the other.

Often, when comparing or contrasting two subjects, you will focus first on one of them, in one paragraph; and then on the other, in another paragraph, as in this comparison of two monkeys, Canto and Owen, who are being fed different diets in order to see which one will live the longer (if not happier) life:

> Canto looks drawn, weary, ashen and miserable in his thinness, mouth slightly agape, features pinched, eyes blank, his expression screaming, "Please, no, not another plateful of seeds!"
>
> Well-fed Owen, by contrast, is a happy camper with a wry smile, every inch the laid-back simian, plump, eyes twinkling, full mouth relaxed, skin glowing, exuding wisdom as if he's just read Kierkegaard and concluded that "Life must be lived forward, but can only be understood backward."
>
> —ROGER COHEN, "The Meaning of Life"

The author of this comparison doesn't really believe that monkeys can read philosophy, but he fancifully assigns that power to the second monkey in order to sharpen the contrast between the two simians. Owen's wisdom is in opposition to

Canto's despair ("not another plateful of seeds!"). So are the two monkeys' other traits, presented one by one in the same order from paragraph to paragraph.

## Classification

With **CLASSIFICATION** (Chapter 11), you divide your subject into categories. In the following passage, a writer classifies the different kinds of English she uses:

> Fortunately, for reasons I won't get into today, I later decided I should envision a reader for the stories I would write. And the reader I decided upon was my mother, because these were stories about mothers. So with this reader in mind—and in fact she did read my early drafts—I began to write stories using all the Englishes I grew up with: the English I spoke to my mother, which for lack of a better term might be described as "simple"; the English she used with me, which for lack of a better term might be described as "broken"; my translation of her Chinese, which could certainly be described as "watered down"; and what I imagined to be her translation of her Chinese if she could speak in perfect English, her internal language, and for that I sought to preserve the essence, but neither an English nor a Chinese structure. I wanted to capture what language ability tests can never reveal: her intent, her passion, her imagery, the rhythms of her speech and the nature of her thought.                 —AMY TAN, "Mother Tongue"

Gloria Anzaldúa builds paragraphs around different types of Spanish (p. 773).

This is a complex paragraph, obviously; but the heart of it is the author's classification of her various "Englishes" into four specific types. The opening statements in the paragraph explain how this classification system came about, and the closing statement explains the purpose it serves.

## Definition

A **DEFINITION** (Chapter 12) explains what something is—or is not. Is a good waitress, or other skilled blue-collar worker, merely physically competent; or is she intellectually smart as well? According to the author of this paragraph from an essay on the "brilliance" of blue-collar workers, how we define intelligence depends on a number of factors:

> I couldn't have put it in words when I was growing up, but what I observed in my mother's restaurant defined the world of adults, a place where competence

was synonymous with physical work. I've since studied the working habits of blue-collar workers and have come to understand how much my mother's kind of work demands of both body and brain. A waitress acquires knowledge and intuition about the ways and the rhythms of the restaurant business. Waiting on seven to nine tables, each with two to six customers, Rosie devised memory strategies so that she could remember who ordered what. And because she knew the average time it took to prepare different dishes, she could monitor an order that was taking too long at the service station.

—MIKE ROSE, "Blue-Collar Brilliance"

In this paragraph, the writer first presents an overly simplified definition of "competence" among "blue-collar workers" as the ability to do physical labor. He then redefines this key term to include a mental component ("knowledge and intuition"), concluding the paragraph by observing how his mother's work as a waitress demonstrates these defining traits.

For more paragraphs defining "Blue-Collar Brilliance," see p. 497.

## Cause and Effect

One of the most fundamental ways of developing a paragraph is to examine what CAUSED your subject, or what EFFECTS it may have (Chapter 13). In the following paragraph, a science writer analyzes why young boys are more often diagnosed with behavioral disorders than girls are:

> Lest males of all ages feel unfairly picked upon, researchers point out that boys may be diagnosed with behavioral syndromes and disorders more often than girls for a very good reason: their brains may be more vulnerable. As a boy is developing in the womb, the male hormones released by his tiny testes accelerate the maturation of his brain, locking a lot of the wiring in place early on; a girl's hormonal bath keeps her brain supple far longer. The result is that the infant male brain is a bit less flexible, less able to repair itself after slight injury that might come, for example, during the arduous trek down the birth canal. Hence, boys may well suffer disproportionately from behavioral disorders for reasons unrelated to cultural expectations.
>
> —NATALIE ANGIER, "Intolerance of Boyish Behavior"

Here Natalie Angier begins with an effect (a frequent medical diagnosis in boys); she then introduces a possible immediate cause of this effect (a physical vulnerability), followed by a more remote cause (hormonal differences between boys and girls).

## *Argument*

When you ARGUE a point (Chapter 14), you make a claim and give evidence to support it. In the following paragraph, a conservationist takes exception to some of the best efforts in his field:

> There are, as nearly as I can make out, three kinds of conservation currently operating. The first is the preservation of places that are grandly wild or "scenic" or in some other way spectacular. The second is what is called "conservation of natural resources"—that is, of the things of nature that we intend to use: soil, water, timber, and minerals. The third is what you might call industrial troubleshooting: the attempt to limit or stop or remedy the most flagrant abuses of the industrial system. All three kinds of conservation are inadequate, both separately and together.
>
> —WENDELL BERRY, "Conservation Is Good Work"

The point Berry is arguing here is that even the most common forms of conservation in practice today are (in his view) "inadequate." Before stating that point at the end of the paragraph, however, he must first identify the different kinds of conservation and then devote a sentence to each one.

## Introductory Paragraphs

As noted in Chapter 4, a well-constructed essay has a beginning, middle, and ending. Every paragraph plays an important role within this basic structure, but introductory and concluding paragraphs are particularly important because they represent your first and last chance to engage the reader.

In an introductory paragraph, you tell the reader what your essay is about—and otherwise seek to earn the reader's interest. The following famous introductory paragraph to an important document is as clear and stirring today as it was in 1776:

> When in the Course of human events, it becomes necessary for one people to dissolve the political bands which have connected them with another, and to assume among the powers of the earth, the separate and equal station to which the Laws of Nature and of Nature's God entitle them, a decent respect to the opinions of mankind requires that they should declare the causes which impel them to the separation.
>
> —THOMAS JEFFERSON, *The Declaration of Independence*

This paragraph tells the reader exactly what's coming in the text to follow: an inventory of the reasons for the colonies' rebellion. It also seeks to justify the writer's cause and win the sympathy of the reader by invoking a higher authority: the "Laws" of God and nature trump those of Britain's King George III. Here are a few other ways to construct an introductory paragraph that may entice the reader to read on.

**Use an anecdote to lead into what you have to say.** This introductory paragraph, from a report about research on technology and literacy, begins with a story (actually two of them) about how today's students read and write:

> Two stories about young people, and especially college-age students, are circulating widely today. One script sees a generation of twitterers and texters, awash in self-indulgence and narcissistic twaddle, most of it riddled with errors. The other script doesn't diminish the effects of technology, but it presents young people as running a rat race that is fueled by the Internet and its toys, anxious kids who are inundated with mountains of indigestible information yet obsessed with making the grade, with success, with coming up with the "next big thing" but who lack the writing and speaking skills they need to do so.    —ANDREA LUNSFORD, "Our Semi-literate Youth? Not So Fast"

The author of this paragraph considers both of the stories she is reporting to be inaccurate; so after introducing them here, she goes on in the rest of the essay to construct "alternative narratives" that are based upon her own research.

See p. 715 for a cluster of stories on the effects of digital culture.

**Ask a question—or questions.** This strategy should be used sparingly, but it works especially well when you want to begin with a touch of humor—or otherwise suggest that you don't have all the answers. In this opening paragraph, a food critic explores new territory:

> I've always wondered about dog food. Is a Gaines-burger really like a hamburger? Can you fry it? Does dog food "cheese" taste like real cheese"? Does Gravy Train actually make gravy in the dog's bowl, or is that brown liquid just dissolved crumbs? And exactly what *are* by-products?
> —ANN HODGMAN, "No Wonder They Call Me a Bitch"

Sound appetizing? Even if your subject doesn't exactly appeal to everyone, a strong opening paragraph like this can leave readers eager for more—or at least willing to hear you out.

*Start with a quotation or dialogue.* In this example from *Outside* magazine, the author opens with an intriguing bit of dialogue, words that get the reader's interest and make a point about the beauty of nature:

> "The thing is, there's this red dot," says Beau Turner, standing quietly in a longleaf-pine forest on his Avalon Plantation, 25,000 red-clay acres half an hour south of Tallahassee. It's 6:30 on a late-spring morning, and the humidity is rolling in like a fog; already I regret the hot coffee in my hand. One of our chores today is to band some new woodpecker chicks with Avalon identification, but then the red dot came up and I was anxious to see it. Not much bigger than the head of a pin, the red dot is a nearly Zen idea of nature's beauty. It sits behind the ear of the male red-cockaded woodpecker, an endangered species that Turner has spent the last four years trying to reintroduce to this land.
>
> —Jack Hitt, "One Nation, Under Ted"

*Place your subject in a historical context.* In the essay from which this introduction is taken, an economist makes the point that the climate may be changing faster than originally estimated; but first he puts the issue in historical perspective:

> The 1995 consensus was convincing enough for Europe and Japan: the report's scientific findings were the basis for the Kyoto negotiations and the treaty they produced; those same findings also led most of the developed world to produce ambitious plans for reductions in carbon emissions. But the consensus didn't extend to Washington, and hence everyone else's efforts were deeply compromised by the American unwillingness to increase the price of energy. Our emissions continued to soar, and the plans of many of the Kyoto countries in Western Europe to reduce emissions sputtered.
>
> —William McKibben, "Warning on Warming"

*Shock or provoke the reader—mildly.* You don't want to alarm your reader needlessly, but sometimes you may want to say "listen here" by being mildly provocative or controversial:

> Let's use the F word here. People say it's inappropriate, offensive, that it puts people off. But it seems to me it's the best way to begin, when it's simultaneously devalued and invaluable.
>
> Feminist. Feminist, feminist, feminist.          —Anna Quindlen,
> "Still Needing the F Word"

## Choose a Method (or Methods) of Development That Sets Up the Rest of Your Essay

The following paragraph is about the organizing power of paragraphs:

> I can remember picking up my father's books before I could read. The words themselves were mostly foreign, but I still remember the exact moment when I first understood, with a sudden clarity, the purpose of a paragraph. I didn't have the vocabulary to say "paragraph," but I realized that a paragraph was a fence that held words. The words inside a paragraph worked together for a common purpose. They had some specific reason for being inside the same fence. This knowledge delighted me. I began to think of everything in terms of paragraphs. Our reservation was a small paragraph within the United States. My family's house was a paragraph, distinct from the other paragraphs of the LeBrets to the north, the Fords to our south and the Tribal School to the west. Inside our house, each family member existed as a separate paragraph but still had genetics and common experiences to link us. Now, using this logic, I can see my changed family as an essay of seven paragraphs: mother, father, older brother, the deceased sister, my younger twin sisters and our adopted little brother.
>
> —Sherman Alexie, "Superman and Me"

Alexie uses several methods of development in this paragraph. First, he narrates the story of "the exact moment" he learned what a paragraph was. He then defines what he means by "a paragraph" ("a fence that held words"). And, finally, he uses this definition to classify people and places into "distinct" paragraphs that lead to an entire "essay of seven paragraphs."

## Body Paragraphs

The body of your essay supports and develops your thesis; it is where you give the evidence for the main point you're making. Suppose you're making the point that avoiding left turns while driving is good for the environment because it cuts down on carbon emissions. The various kinds of evidence you cite to support this thesis can provide useful ways of developing body paragraphs in your argument.

**Facts and figures.** According to their website, United Parcel Service used to plan truck routes "by hand"; now they use computers to minimize left-turns because, they say, that saves energy. The following paragraph in support of this point is built around related facts and figures:

Since the deployment of this route planning technology in 2004, UPS has eliminated millions of miles off delivery routes, taking already-expedient routes and giving them razor edge efficiency. As a result, UPS has saved ten million gallons of gas and reduced carbon dioxide emissions by 100,000 metric tons, the equivalent of taking 5,300 passenger cars off the road for an entire year.                                                         —UPS, "Saving Fuel"

**Expert testimony.** Why do you still see UPS drivers occasionally making left turns? In this body paragraph from a recent post on *priceonomics*, the author builds up to a quotation from a company executive:

Since UPS uses software to map out routes, it can send drivers on right-turn heavy routes while making exceptions when a left turn is easier and faster. As an amicable senior VP of the company said in an interview about the rule, "That's why I love the engineers, they just love to continue to figure out how to make it better."                                                  —ALEX MAYYASI,
"Why UPS Trucks Don't Turn Left"

**Personal experience.** Making left turns wastes time as well as energy. To develop this related point in the body of an essay about avoiding left turns, you might include a body paragraph based on personal experience: "First I made the trip through the Chicago Loop taking nothing but right turns. I travelled down Columbus Drive, took a right on Congress Parkway, and then took another right turn to my destination, the Dirksen Federal Building at Dearborn and Adams streets. Then I made the trip through the Loop to the Dirksen Building taking mostly left turns. The traffic was the same, but the left-turn trip took me three minutes and thirty seconds longer than the right-turn trip."

## How Much Evidence Is Enough?

That depends in part on the scope of your topic. UPS's claim that avoiding left turns saves gas can be substantiated with a few facts and figures. A broader discussion on the need and means for combating climate change in general, however, might require more evidence. Ultimately, it's the reader who determines how much evidence is enough. If the reader is convinced, the evidence is sufficient. If the reader is still wavering, more (or different) evidence may be in order.

## QUESTIONS ABOUT SUPPORTING EVIDENCE

**Is your evidence concrete and specific?** Have you provided details that will make your point clear and interesting to the reader?

**Is your evidence relevant to the case?** Will the reader understand immediately why you're citing particular facts, figures, personal experience, and other evidence? Do you need to explain further? Or choose other evidence?

**Is your evidence sufficient to prove the case?** Have you cited enough evidence, or is the reader likely to require additional—or better—support before becoming convinced?

**Are your sources fully and adequately documented?** Have you represented your sources fairly and accurately? Can readers locate them easily if they want to check your facts or interpretation? Have you scrupulously avoided representing the words or ideas of other writers as your own? (For more information on using and citing sources, see the Appendix.)

## Concluding Paragraphs

The final paragraph of an essay should be just as satisfying as the opening paragraph. The conclusion of your essay is your last chance to drive home your point and to leave the reader with a sense of closure. Here are a few ways this is commonly done.

*Restate your main point.* But don't just repeat it; add a little something new. A recent government report about climate change, for example, adds the following:

> What is new over the last decade is that we know with increasing certainty that climate change is happening now. . . . Global climate is projected to continue to change over this century and beyond, but there is still time to act to limit the amount of change and the extent of damaging impacts.
> —U.S. Global Change Research Program,
> *Climate Change Impacts in the United States: Highlights*

Sometimes a grim conclusion has no hopeful sequel: "World ends tomorrow; get ready." When there is one, however, you're always well advised to end a negative conclusion on a positive note.

***Show the broader significance of your subject.*** In an essay about protecting wolves, an advocate for one of nature's most fearsome predators ends her appeal with the following:

> Many biologists have warned that we are approaching another mass extinction. The wolf is still endangered and should be protected in its own right. But we should also recognize that bringing all the planet's threatened and endangered species back to healthy numbers—as well as mitigating the effects of climate change—means keeping top predators around.
>
> —MARY ELLEN HANNIBAL,
> "Why the Beaver Should Thank the Wolf"

Hannibal is aware that not everyone wants wolves in the backyard; but by linking this single threatened species to the mass extinction of other species and to climate change, she broadens a wooly subject into territory that even sheep farmers might be willing to consider.

***End with a recommendation.*** This strategy is especially appropriate when you're winding up an argument. Before coming to the conclusion stated in the following paragraph, the author, a sportswriter, has made the claim that student athletes should be paid for their "work":

> The republic will survive. Fans will still watch the NCAA tournament. Double-reverses will still be thrilling. Alabama will still hate Auburn. Everybody will still hate Duke. Let's do what's right and re-examine what we think is wrong.
>
> —MICHAEL ROSENBERG, "Let Stars Get Paid"

Not only is he recommending pay for college athletes, the author of this paragraph asks the reader to rethink, and totally revise, the conventional wisdom that says paying them is morally wrong.

# CHAPTER 6

# Narration

Narrative is the oldest and most compelling method of holding someone's attention; everyone wants to be told a story. —WILLIAM ZINSSER

Narration is the storytelling mode of writing. The minute you say to someone, "You won't believe what happened to me this morning," you have launched into a narrative. To understand how narration works, let's have a look at the story of a young man's arrival, after an arduous journey, in the city of Philadelphia:

> I walked up the street, gazing about till near the market-house I met a boy with bread. I had made many a meal on bread, and, inquiring where he got it, I went immediately to the baker's he directed me to, in Second-street, and ask'd for bisket, intending such as we had in Boston; but they, it seems, were not made in Philadelphia. Then I asked for a three-penny loaf, and was told they had none such. So not considering or knowing the difference of money, and the greater cheapness nor the names of his bread, I bade him give me three-penny worth of any sort. He gave me, accordingly, three great puffy rolls. I was surpriz'd at the quantity, but took it, and, having no room in my pockets, walk'd off with a roll under each arm, and eating the other. Thus I went up Market-street as far as Fourth-street, passing by the door of Mr. Read, my future wife's father; when she, standing at the door, saw me, and thought I made, as I certainly did, a most awkward, ridiculous appearance. Then I turned and went down Chestnut-street and part of Walnut-street, eating my roll all the way, and, coming round, found myself again at Market-street wharf, near the boat I came in, to which I went for a draught of the river water; and, being filled with one of my rolls, gave the other two to a woman and her child that came down the river in the boat with us, and were waiting to go farther.                              —BENJAMIN FRANKLIN, *Autobiography*

## Telling What Happened

What makes Franklin's text a narrative? Like all narratives, the story of his arrival in Philadelphia is an account of events. It answers the question "What happened?"— to a particular person in a particular place and time. Young Franklin arrived in the city, shopped for bread, ate, gazed and strolled about, saw a young woman, performed an act of charity.

Annie Dillard builds a narrative around the ordinary events of kids at play (p. 141).

Narratives focus on events, but you do not have to live a life of high adventure or witness extraordinary acts in order to write a compelling narrative. The events in Franklin's story, you'll notice, are all perfectly ordinary; they could have happened to anybody. The interest, even the drama, that we all enjoy in a well-told story often comes not so much from the nature of the events themselves as from how they are presented.

"Thus I went up Market-street as far as Fourth-street, passing by the door of Mr. Read, my future wife's father; when she, standing at the door, saw me, and thought I made, as I certainly did, a most awkward, ridiculous appearance."

In this chapter, we will examine how to come up with the raw materials for a story, how to select details from those raw materials to suit your purpose and audience, and how to organize those details as a narrative—by the use of chronology, transitions, verb tenses, and plot. We will also review the critical points to watch for as you read over a narrative, as well as common errors to avoid when you edit. But first, let's consider *why* we write narratives at all—and how they can help us to make a point.

## Why Do We Write Narratives?

Everybody likes a good story, and we tell stories for many reasons: to connect with other people, to entertain, to record what people said and did, to explain the significance of events, to persuade others to act in a certain way, or to accept our point of view on an issue. Ben Franklin, for example, tells his famous story at the beginning of his *Autobiography* in order to capture the reader's attention right off the bat—and to set the scene for the rest of his life story.

Brief illustrative narratives, or **ANECDOTES**, appear in all kinds of writing, often at the beginning. Writers typically use them to grab the reader's interest and then lead into their main points, much as a graduation speaker opens with a humorous story or poignant tale before getting down to the serious business of talking about life after college.

Franklin's great point in his *Autobiography* is to show readers how he succeeded in life, and so he begins with the story of his humble arrival in Philadelphia as a young man from out of town. That way, says Franklin, "you may in your mind compare such unlikely beginnings with the figure I have since made."

Although a good story can be an end in itself, this chapter focuses on narratives that are written to make a point or support an argument. Such a narrative can be a brief part of a longer work, or it can be used to structure an entire essay.

> Marjane Satrapi's point in "Kim Wilde" (p. 129) is to show how her family resisted political oppression.

Suppose you are a geneticist, and you are writing about mitochondrial DNA and how it can be used to study human evolution. (Mitochondrial DNA is passed down, unaltered, from generation to generation on the mother's side.) Suppose, further, that you have isolated seven strains of mitochondrial DNA and traced them back to the seven prehistoric female ancestors of all persons presently alive. How would you convey your exciting conclusions to a general audience?

# THE SUCCESS STORY

One common narrative pattern, which Ben Franklin practically invented in his famous *Autobiography*, is the success story. As in many fairy tales, the central event of such a narrative is the transformation of the hero or heroine. One reading in this chapter that uses a variation on this pattern is Kurt Streeter's "Have a Caltastic Day!" (p. 119), which tells how a minority student from a tough neighborhood succeeded (or at least didn't fail) in his first year at college.

> Kashawn Campbell sat inside a cramped room on a dorm floor that Cal reserves for black students. It was early January, and he stared nervously at his first college transcript.
>
> There wasn't much good to see.
>
> He had barely passed an introductory science course. In College Writing 1A, his essays—pockmarked with misplaced words and odd phrases—were so weak that he would have to take the class again. . . .
>
> He tried to stay calm. He promised himself he would beat back the depression that had come in waves those first months of school. He would work harder, be better organized, be more like his roommate and new best friend, Spencer Simpson, who was making college look easy.
>
> On a nearby desk lay a small diary he recently filled with affirmations and goals. He thumbed through it.
>
> "I can do this! I can do this!" he had written. "Let the studying begin! . . . It's time for Kashawn's Comeback!"

To see how you can use the success-story pattern in your own writing—and how narratives differ from the actual events on which they are based—think of a successful person you might write about and make a list of key events in that person's life. Then identify a "turning point"—a particular event or series of events that changed the fortunes of your hero or heroine forever. Divide the rest of the events on your list into "before" and "after." Imagine the story you might construct around this outline.

Now take the same person and life events and consider how you would arrange them according to some other pattern, such as a journey or a fall from grace. This time, instead of dividing your narrative into before and after, imagine a different story line—a meandering path or a downward spiral. As you can see, you would end up telling a different story about the same person.

Bryan Sykes, a professor of genetics at the Institute of Molecular Medicine at Oxford University, recently had to solve this problem because his research team had isolated those seven separate lines of human descent. He decided to convey the findings by recreating the story of each of these "seven daughters of Eve," whose DNA can be identified by modern research methods.

Here is how he concludes his narrative about one of them, a woman who lived forty-five thousand years ago:

> Ursula had no idea, of course, that both her daughters would give rise, through their children and grandchildren, to a continuous maternal line stretching to the present day. She had no idea she was to become the clan mother, the only woman of that time who could make that claim. Every single member of her clan can trace a direct and unbroken line back to Ursula. Her clan were the first modern humans successfully to colonize Europe. Within a comparatively short space of time they had spread across the whole continent, edging the Neanderthals into extinction. Today about 11 percent of modern Europeans are the direct maternal descendants of Ursula. They come from all parts of Europe, but the clan is particularly well represented in western Britain and Scandinavia. —BRYAN SYKES, *The Seven Daughters of Eve*

Sykes's story about Ursula efficiently explains a number of complicated points about genetic studies and human descent. By giving each of the maternal ancestors a story, Sykes makes his findings much easier to understand—and to remember. Sometimes there's no better way to make a point than by telling a good story—*if* it really fits the subject you are writing about and doesn't go off on a tangent.

## Composing a Narrative

Let's go back to the adventures of Ben Franklin for a moment. How did Franklin know, on his initial stroll around the city, that the young woman he saw standing at Mr. Read's door would one day be his wife? Obviously, he couldn't know this when he first saw her. Franklin's reference to his future wife shows us not that young Franklin was psychic but that his narrative has been carefully composed— after the fact, as all narratives are.

As the author of a narrative, you know everything that is going to happen, so you can present events in any order you please. However, if you want anyone else to understand the point you are trying to make, you need to compose your narrative carefully. Consider, first of all, your AUDIENCE and your PURPOSE for writing. Then think about which details to include and how to organize those details so that readers can follow your story and see your point in telling it. To make your story a compelling one, be sure to give it a **PLOT** and tell it from a consistent **POINT OF VIEW**.

## Thinking about Purpose and Audience

The first thing to do as you compose a narrative is to think hard about the audience you want to reach and the purpose your narrative is intended to serve. Suppose you are emailing a friend about a visit to a computer store, and your purpose is simply to say what you did yesterday. In this case, your narrative can ramble on about how you got to the store, discovered it was much larger than you expected, went into the monitor section and looked around, then wandered over to the printers and couldn't get a salesperson's attention but eventually spoke to a very helpful manager, and so on. The story might end with your emerging triumphantly from the store with a good printer at a good price. It wouldn't matter much that your story goes on and on because you're writing to a friendly reader who is interested in everything you do and has time to listen.

Now suppose you are writing an advertisement, the purpose of which is to sell printers to the general public. You could still write about your visit to a computer store, but you would tell your story differently because you now have a different purpose and audience: "When I walked into ComputerDaze, I couldn't believe my eyes. Printers everywhere! And the cheap prices! Plus they give you a ream of paper absolutely free! I went home with a printer under each arm." Or suppose you are writing a column in a computer magazine, and your purpose is to show readers how to shop for a printer by telling them about the problems you dealt with as you shopped. You might write, "The first hurdle I encountered was the numbing variety of brands and models."

Whatever your purpose, you will want to think about how much your audience is likely to know about your subject—computers, for instance—so you can judge how much background information you need to give, how much technical language you can use, what terms you may need to define, and so on. If you are writing for an audience that knows nothing about computers and peripherals, for instance, you might even have to explain what an external hard drive is before you tell your readers how to buy or use one.

> Don't know where U.S. Marines keep their dog tags? Anne Bernays fills you in, p. 153.

## Generating Ideas:
## Asking What Happened—and Who, Where, When, How, and Why

Before you can tell a good story, you have to have a story to tell. How do you come up with the raw materials for a narrative in the first place? **BRAINSTORMING, CLUSTERING**, and other methods can help you generate ideas. But a narrative is not just a kind of writing; it is also a way of thinking, one that can help you find ideas to write about. How do you get started? Let's look at an example.

Consider the following passage in which Annie Dillard tells about what happened one Saturday afternoon when her father was preparing to leave for a trip:

> Getting ready for the trip one Saturday, he roamed around our big brick house snapping his fingers. He had put a record on: Sharkey Bonano, "Li'l Liza Jane." I was reading Robert Louis Stevenson on the sunporch: *Kidnapped*. I looked up from my book and saw him outside; he had wandered out to the lawn and was standing in the wind between the buckeye trees and looking up at what must have been a small patch of wild sky. Old Low-Pockets. He six feet four, all lanky and leggy; he had thick brown hair and shaggy brows, and a mild and dreamy expression in his blue eyes.
>
> —ANNIE DILLARD, *An American Childhood*

We can only imagine the exact process by which a superb writer like Dillard brought to light the vivid details of her past to form a passage like this. However, we do know that she wrote it many years after the fact, and so she must have probed her memory to find the details for her narrative.

As she prepared to write about her past experience, Dillard may well have asked herself the questions that journalists typically ask when developing a story: who, what, where, when, how, and why? Certainly her narrative answers most of those questions: *who* (she and her father), *what* (reading and listening to music), *where* (on the sunporch), *when* (one Saturday), *why* (to get ready for a trip).

If Dillard had stopped her questioning here, though, she would have turned up only the skeleton of a narrative, one that might read something like this:

> Getting ready for his trip, Father roamed around the house listening to music while I read on the sunporch. He wandered outside and looked up at the sky. He was tall with thick hair and blue eyes.

This is the beginning of a narrative, but only the beginning, because it lacks the vivid details by which Dillard brings the past to life.

When you are planning a narrative, then, keep asking *who, what, where, when, how,* and *why.* Look for lots of particular details, both visual and auditory. "Just take a period," the writer John Steinbeck once advised a friend who was trying to write his life story. "Then try to remember it so clearly that you can see things: what colors and how warm or cold and how you got there. . . . It is important to tell what people looked like, how they walked, what they wore, what they ate." That way, instead of a generic girl with a nameless book and an anonymous man listening to unidentified music, your readers will see and hear Old Low-Pockets snapping his fingers as "Li'l Liza Jane" plays in the background and you pore over *Kidnapped*.

You will also want your readers to know *why* you're telling this particular story. In Dillard's case, the who, what, where, and when are vividly presented. We can see the scene, and everything that happens in it, clearly. But the *why*—Why is her father preparing for a trip? Why is she telling the story?— is not so obvious.

As it happens, Dillard's father is about to leave his family in Pittsburgh and his job at the American Standard Company and take off down the Ohio River, heading, ultimately, to New Orleans, birthplace of jazz. Dillard could have simply told us that her father was an impractical man who suffered from wanderlust and a romantic notion of the cool life far away from the familiar world of manufacturing and plumbing fixtures. However, by constructing a narrative in which her father snaps his fingers to a jazz tune with a "dreamy expression" in his eyes, Dillard not only makes her point, she gives evidence in support of it at the same time. Every detail in her narrative is carefully selected to make that point.

> Even the title of Dillard's memoir suggests why she is telling her story (p. 141).

## Organizing and Drafting a Narrative

Once you've figured out what's going to happen in your narrative, it's time to get down to the business of organizing your material and writing a draft. As you draft a narrative, your task is to turn the *facts* of what happened into a *story* of what happened. To do this, you will need to put the events in CHRONOLOGICAL ORDER, connect them with appropriate TRANSITIONS and verb tenses, give your narrative a PLOT—and somehow indicate the point you are making. The templates on p. 102 can help you get started.

### STATING YOUR POINT

Most of the narrative writing you do as a student will be for the purpose of making some kind of point, and sometimes you'll want to state that point explicitly. If you are writing about information technology for an economics class, for example, you might tell your story about going to a computer store; and you would probably want to explain why you were telling about the experience in a THESIS statement like this: "Go into any computer store today, and you will discover that information technology is the main product of American business."

# TEMPLATES FOR DRAFTING

When you begin to draft a narrative, you need to say who or what the narrative is about, where it takes place, and what's happening as the story opens—moves fundamental to any narrative. See how Annie Dillard makes such moves in the beginning of her essay in this chapter:

> We were standing up to our boot tops in snow in a front yard on trafficked Reynolds Street, waiting for cars.
> —ANNIE DILLARD, "An American Childhood"

Dillard says who her narrative is about ("we"), where it takes place ("a front yard on trafficked Reynolds Street"), and what is happening as the story opens (she and her friends are "waiting for cars," as it turns out, to throw snowballs at). Here are two more examples from this chapter:

> This is the true story of a dyed-in-the-wool pacifist Jewish woman who recently spent two days at the Marine Corps Base at Quantico, Virginia, and survived, almost intact. —ANNE BERNAYS, "Warrior Day"

> I closed the door to the sterile white examination room to face a thin, pale young boy, fourteen years old and sitting on the exam table with his knees pulled to his chest. —JEFF GREMMELS, "The Clinic"

The following templates can help you make some of these basic moves in your own writing. But don't take these as formulas where you just have to fill in the blanks. There are no shortcuts to good writing, but these templates can serve as starting points.

▶ This is a story about _____.
▶ The time and place of my story are _____ and _____.C As the narrative opens, X is in the act of _____.
▶ What happened next was _____, followed by _____ and _____.
▶ At this point, _____.
▶ The climax of these events was _____.
▶ When X understood what had happened, he / she said "_____."
▶ The last thing that happened to X was _____.
▶ My point in telling this story is to show that _____.

## FOLLOWING CHRONOLOGICAL ORDER

In his arrival narrative, Ben Franklin's point is to show how far he's going to go from his humble beginnings. To this end, he arranges events in chronological order. First his arrival; then breakfast, followed by a stroll around the town; next comes the encounter with Miss Read; and, finally, the return to the wharf and the dispensing of the bread—all in the order in which they occurred *in time*. There is no law that says events in a narrative have to follow chronological order, and there are times when you will want to deviate from it. As a general rule, though, arrange events chronologically so your reader doesn't have to figure out what happened when.

## DEVELOPING A PLOT

Connecting events in chronological order is always better than presenting them haphazardly. Chronology alone, however, no matter how faithfully followed, is insufficient for organizing a good narrative. A narrative, yes; a good narrative, no.

Suppose Ben Franklin returned for a visit to modern-day Philadelphia and filed the following account:

> I took 76 East (the Schuylkill Expressway) to 676 East, exited at Broad Street (the first exit) and continued straight on Vine Street to 12th Street. Then I turned right and proceeded two blocks to the Convention Center. There I paused for lunch (a Caesar salad with three great puffy rolls), afterward continuing my journey down 12th and back to Vine. Proceeding east for some distance, I then rounded Franklin Square, crossed the Franklin Bridge, and entered into New Jersey.

This account is, technically, a narrative, and it follows chronological order. By comparison with the original, however, it is pretty dull. If it went on like this for another paragraph or two, most readers would give up long before Franklin got back to Boston. Little more than an itinerary, this narrative moves steadfastly from place to place, but it doesn't really get anywhere because it has no plot.

Whether we read about pirates on the high seas or hobbits and rings of power, one of the most important elements that can make or break the story is how well it is plotted. It is no different when you write narratives of your own—events need to be related in such a way that one leads directly to, or causes, another. Taken together, the events in your narrative should have a beginning, a middle, and an end. Then your narrative will form a complete action: a plot.

One of the best ways to plot a narrative is to set up a situation; introduce a conflict; build up the dramatic tension until it reaches a high point, or CLIMAX; then release the tension and resolve the conflict. Consider the following little horror story, replete with a giant insect. First we set up the situation:

> Little Miss Muffet sat on a tuffet
> Eating her curdos and whey.

Now comes the conflict:

> Along came a spider*

Then the climax:

> Who sat down beside her

And finally the resolution:

> And frightened Miss Muffet away.

You knew all along how it was going to end; but it's still a satisfying story because it's tightly plotted with a keen sense of completion at the close.

Back to Ben Franklin's narrative. One reason this story of starting out in Philadelphia is among the most famous personal narratives in American literature, even though it's just one paragraph, is that it has a carefully organized plot—a *beginning* action (the hero's arrival); a *middle* (the stroll), in which a complication is introduced and the tension rises as the young hero sees his future wife and appears ridiculous; and an *ending* (the return to the wharf), in which the narrative tension is resolved as the hero comes back to his starting point and dispenses bounty in the form of the bread.

## ADDING TRANSITIONS

Notice the many direct references to time in Ben Franklin's narrative: *then, immediately, when, again.* No doubt, you can think of countless others: *first, last, not long after, next, while, thereafter, once upon a time.* Such direct references to the order of time can be boring in a narrative if they become too predictable, as in *first, second, third.* But used judiciously, such transitions provide smooth links from one event to

*Recognizing a good plot twist when he saw one, best-selling novelist James Patterson—whose thrillers have sold more copies than those of Stephen King, John Grisham, and Dan Brown combined—chose this line for the title of his first blockbuster, *Along Came a Spider* (1993).

another, as do other connecting words and phrases like *thus, therefore, consequently, what happened next, before I knew it, as he came back to the dock.*

## USING APPROPRIATE VERB TENSES

In addition to clear transition words, your verb tenses, especially the sequence of tenses, can help you to connect events in time. To review for a moment: An action in the past perfect tense (he *had arrived*) occurs before an action in the past tense (he *arrived*), which occurs before an action in the present tense (he *arrives*), which occurs before an action in the future tense (he *will arrive*). Actions in the present perfect (he *has arrived*) may start in the past and continue in the present.

Many of the verbs in Franklin's narrative are in the simple past tense: *walked, went, ask'd, thought, found, gave.* "I had made many a meal on bread," however, is in the past perfect tense because the action had already occurred many times *before* young Franklin asked for directions to the bakery.

Tense sequences mark the time of actions in relation to one another. Thus, all actions that happen more or less at the same time in your narrative should be in the same tense: "The young man got off the boat, went to the bakery, and walked around the town." Don't shift tenses needlessly; but when you *do* need to indicate that one action happened before another in time, be sure to change tenses accordingly—and accurately. Sometimes you may need to shift out of chronological order altogether. (It's called a FLASHBACK if you shift back in time, a FLASH-FORWARD if you shift into the future.) Most of the time, however, stick to chronology.

Notice how often Franklin uses *-ing* forms of verbs: *gazing, inquiring, intending, considering, knowing, having, eating, passing, standing, eating* (again), *coming, being, waiting.* Putting *-ing* on the end of a verb makes the verb progressive. If Franklin's writing seems especially vivid, part of his secret lies in those progressive verb forms, which show past actions as if they are still going on as we read about them more than two centuries later.

## MAINTAINING A CONSISTENT POINT OF VIEW

Such is the difference between life and a *narrative* of life: life happens, often in disorderly fashion; a narrative, by contrast, must be carefully composed—from a particular point of view. Why do you think Annie Dillard wrote that her father looked up "at what must have been a small patch of wild sky"? Why didn't she just come out and say that the sky *was* wild? The reason is that, as the NARRATOR, or teller of her story, Dillard is speaking from the vantage point of herself as a child sitting on the sunporch. From that point of view, she could not logically have seen the sky as her father saw it.

As you construct a narrative, you need to maintain a logical and consistent point of view. Don't attribute perceptions to yourself or your narrator that are physically impossible ("I lay inside on the sofa while Old Low-Pockets wandered out to the lawn. His back to the house, he stared dreamily in the direction of his impending journey. A tear came into his eye"). If you do claim to see (or know) more than you reasonably can from where you sit, your credibility with the reader will soon be strained.

In a narrative written in the grammatical **FIRST PERSON** (*I* or *we*), like Dillard's, the speaker can be both an observer of the scene ("I looked up from my book and saw him outside") *and* a participant in the action ("I was reading Robert Louis Stevenson on the sunporch"). In a narrative written in the grammatical **THIRD PERSON** (*he, she, it,* or *they*), as is the case in most articles and history books (and in Bryan Sykes' narrative about Ursula), however, the narrator is often merely an observer, though sometimes an all-knowing one.

> A writer uses *she* instead of *I* to give a nuanced view of the Marine Corps on p. 153.

## ADDING DIALOGUE

In contrast to narratives told in the third person—which can have unlimited points of view—first-person narratives are *always* limited to telling us only what the narrator knows or imagines. There is a means, however, by which even first-person narrators can introduce the points of view of other people into a story. That is by the use of dialogue, or quoting their direct speech. "Lie on your back," her mother tells young Dillard elsewhere in her narrative. "Look at the clouds and figure out what they look like."

As a first-person narrator, Dillard might have written, "My mother told me to look at the clouds and figure out what they look like." But these words would be filtered through Dillard's point of view. They would be a step removed from the person who said them and so would lack the immediacy of direct dialogue.

Suppose you are a witness to an accident in which a pedestrian is hit by a turning car, and you want to tell what happened—in a police report, say. Your narrative might begin with an account of how you noticed a car stopped at a red light and then saw another car approach suddenly from the right and pause. After the light changed, the first car went straight ahead; then the second car turned left. At the same time, a pedestrian, who had been trying to cross behind the first car, moved into the middle of the street and was hit by the turning car.

Why did the pedestrian cross the street against traffic? Your narrative can't say for sure because you don't know what was going on in the pedestrian's mind. If, however, you (or the police) approached the man and started asking him questions as he pulled himself to his feet, his point of view might be revealed in the ensuing dialogue.

Then, if you incorporated that dialogue into your narrative, you would not only capture another person's motives and point of view, but your narrative would be more interesting and lively:

"Why did you cross the street?"

"The stoplight was red and the little man on the pedestrian sign was on."

"Did you see the car turning in your direction as you crossed?"

"No, the stopped car was blocking my view."

"After it started up, did you see the other car?"

"Yes."

"Why did you cross anyway?"

"The little man told me to."

You can *tell* the reader of your narrative that someone is delusional or means well or would never hurt a fly. But if you let people in your narrative speak for themselves and *show* what they are thinking, the reader can draw his or her own conclusions. Then your story will seem more credible, your characters will come to life, and your whole narrative will have a greater dramatic impact.

## USING OTHER METHODS

Narratives don't take place in a vacuum. As you tell what happens in your narrative, you'll likely need to draw on other methods of writing as well. For example, to show why your characters (the people in your narrative) do what they do, you may need to analyze the CAUSES AND EFFECTS of their actions. Or you may want to COMPARE AND CONTRAST one character with another. Almost certainly, you will want to DESCRIBE the characters and the physical setting of your narrative in some detail.

Drew Hansen analyzes the effect a singer had on a speech (p. 147).

In Franklin's case, for instance, the description of his "awkward, ridiculous appearance" as he walks around the streets of Philadelphia "with a roll under each arm" is important to the story. The tattered young man may look foolish now—but not for long. This is an American success story, and already the new arrival is staking out his territory.

# EDITING FOR COMMON ERRORS IN NARRATIVES

As with other kinds of writing, narration calls for distinctive patterns of language and punctuation—and thus invites certain kinds of errors. The following tips will help you check your writing for errors that often appear in narratives.

## Check verb tenses to make sure they accurately indicate when actions occur

Because narrative writing focuses on actions or events—what happens or happened—it relies mightily on verbs. Some writers get confused about when to use the simple past tense (Ben *arrived*), the present perfect (Ben *has arrived*), and the past perfect (Ben *had arrived*).

Use the simple past to indicate actions completed at a specified time in the past.

▶ He ~~has~~ completed the assignment this morning.

Use the present perfect to indicate actions begun and completed at some unspecified time in the past, or actions begun in the past and continuing into the present.

▶ The war in the north ~~goes~~ has gone on for five years now.

▶ For five years now, the insurgents have fought in the north.

Use the past perfect to indicate actions completed *by* a specific time in the past or before another past action occurred.

▶ The bobcats arrived next, but by then the muskrats had moved out.

## Check dialogue to be sure it's punctuated correctly

Narrative writing often includes the direct quotation of what people say. Punctuating dialogue can be challenging because you have to deal with the punctuation in the dialogue itself and also with any punctuation necessary to integrate the dialogue into the text.

Commas and periods always go inside the quotation marks.

▶ "Perspective in painting is hard to define," my art history professor said.

▶ She then noted that in Western painting, "perspective means one thing."

Semicolons and colons always go outside the quotation marks.

▶ But "in Asian painting, it means quite another"; then she went on to clarify.

▶ Asian painting presents the landscape "in layers": from the tops of mountains to the undersides of leaves in the same picture.

Question marks, exclamation points, and dashes go *inside* the quotation marks if they are part of the quoted text but *outside* if they are not part of the quoted text.

▶ The teacher asked, "Sam, how would you define perspective in art?"

▶ Did you say, "Divine perspective"?

Go to wwnorton.com/write/back-to-the-lake for quizzes on these common errors.

## Reading a Narrative with a Critical Eye

Once you have drafted a narrative, it's always a good idea to ask someone else to read it. And, of course, you yourself will want to review what you have written from the standpoint of a critical reader. Here are some questions to keep in mind when checking a narrative.

**PURPOSE AND AUDIENCE.**  Does the narrative serve the purpose it is intended to serve? Is it appropriate for its intended audience? Does it need any additional background information or definitions?

**THE STORY.**  Does it consist mainly of actions and events? Do they constitute a plot, with a clear beginning, middle, and end? Is every action in the narrative necessary to the plot? Have any essential actions been left out?

**THE POINT.**  Does the narrative have a clear point to make? What is it? Is it stated explicitly in a thesis? If not, should it be?

**ORGANIZATION.**  Is the story line easy to follow? Are the events in chronological order? Are there any unintentional lapses in chronology or verb tense? Are intentional deviations from chronology, such as flashbacks, clearly indicated?

**TRANSITIONS.** Are there clear transitions to help readers follow the sequence of events? Have you checked over each transition to see that it logically connects the adjoining parts of the narrative?

**DIALOGUE AND POINT OF VIEW.** If there is no dialogue in the narrative, would some direct speech help bring it to life? If there is dialogue, does it sound like real people talking? Is the narrative told from a consistent, plausible point of view?

**DETAILS.** Does the narrative include lots of concrete details, especially visual and auditory ones? Does it show as well as tell?

**THE BEGINNING.** Will the beginning of the narrative get the reader's attention? How? How well does it set up what follows? How else might the narrative begin?

**THE ENDING.** How satisfying is it? What does it leave the reader thinking or feeling? How else might the narrative end?

**OTHER METHODS.** Look again at the people and places in your narrative. Are the motives of the people clearly explained? Are the physical attributes of the setting clearly delineated? If not, use CAUSE AND EFFECT, DESCRIPTION, and other methods of development to fill in these gaps.

**COMMON ERRORS.** Are any verb tenses in the narrative needlessly complicated? For example, does the narrative use the past perfect (*had been*) when the simple past (*was*) will do? If so, change to the simpler form.

## Student Example

Jeff Gremmels was a medical student at the University of Illinois College of Medicine at Rockford when he wrote "The Clinic." As part of his training, Gremmels saw patients weekly at one of the university's primary care centers. This selection centers on a particularly difficult case—one in which the novice doctor needs to look beyond physical explanations.

"The Clinic" won first prize in an essay competition sponsored by the University of Illinois College of Medicine. Why would a college of medicine promote a writing contest? "Because writing is a good way to clarify our thoughts and feelings," said Margaret Maynard, the microbiologist in charge of the contest. Also, she notes, the college "wanted to foster a compassionate, humanitarian approach to the practice of medicine . . . to graduate caring, concerned doctors, not just technically gifted ones." "The Clinic" suggests that the author, now a practicing radiologist in Illinois and Missouri, was well on his way to becoming just such a physician. First published in the *Rockford Register Star* in 1998, this essay has also appeared in *Becoming Doctors*, an anthology of essays by medical students.

## The Clinic

Every Wednesday, as part of my second-year medical student experience in Rockford, I travel north to see patients at the UIC University Primary Care Clinic at Rockton. Early this past winter, I was handed the chart of a new patient and I was told I was seeing him for "stomachaches." I closed the door to the sterile white examination room to face a thin, pale young boy, fourteen years old and sitting on the exam table with his knees pulled to his chest. His head jumped as the exam door snapped briskly shut. I introduced myself and crouched at eye-level next to him. He tightened the grip on his knees. "What's wrong?" Silence filled the bleach-tinged air, and his eyes stared at me, unblinking.

"He's not eating anything, says his stomach hurts." The voice came from the mother in the corner of the room. I hadn't even noticed her as I entered, all my attention focused immediately on the tensed figure on the bed. "For the past two weeks, it's been nothing but cereal, and only a handful of that." I listened to the mother sketch a history of nausea, stomachaches, and absent stares. It gave the impression of more than the typical stomachache, and I plied ahead, waiting to finally ask the key question that slipped the knot on this mystery and sent the bacteria or virus or swallowed garden flower culprit plummeting into my lap. The knot refused to give.

"Where did he get the bruises?" I ventured, hoping to unearth some bleeding disorder with a forgotten manifestation of gastrointestinal symptoms. The mother looked at the scattered marks around the red-head's temples through her friendly librarian glasses, then up at me.

"He's very active, normally, and <u>gets</u> into all sorts of spots. He <u>comes</u> in from the woods with new cuts and scrapes every night.

**Marginal annotations:**

1 — FIRST-PERSON point of view

— DESCRIPTIVE details set the scene and focus on the patient

2 — DIALOGUE provides information narrator did not know

— Narrator introduces a key conflict into the PLOT

3 — Mother uses present and past perfect tenses to refer to earlier actions by her son; narrator uses past tense to describe mother's actions in the exam room

4

You <u>should have seen</u> him after the big rains, all mud and torn jeans." With this she <u>looked</u> back at the alabaster boy huddling on the bed and <u>smiled</u> with the memory of his past spirit.

A professor teaching our physical diagnosis class told us we should know 80 percent of the cases coming before us by hearing the history alone. This case was quickly proving itself the undesired 20 percent. I moved to the physical exam. The boy was not keen on the concept of my examining him, and made his desires very clear as he refused every request to look up at me or to open his clamped mouth. I wanted to solve this puzzle and began to insist more forcefully until finally, with his surprisingly strong mother, I managed to pull his loose shirt over his head. Beneath that shirt lay pale doughy skin, its spongy texture belying the taut musculature beneath. On the surface of the skin was a continuation of the light bruising around his temples. As the mother sat down and the boy resumed his curled-ball posture, my eyes picked out almost one-dozen small, red "U"s, with two small bars between the uprights like a German umlaut.[1] Raised and bright, more like a rash or burn than a bruise, I hoped these would be the clues I needed to solve my mystery of the afternoon. Further examination revealed nothing more than a continuation of the pattern down to his ankles.

I combed my cloudy memories of past lectures for anything reminiscent of this strange mark <u>as</u> I walked up the hall to find a doctor. The search failed to exhume any diseases with ties to Germanic vowels.

<u>As</u> I explained my cryptic findings to the attending physician, I saw her eyes quickly open, contradicting my belief that she was actually asleep. Pushing insurance papers towards me, she quickly stated, "I'm going to look at him. I want you to have the mother fill these out in the waiting room." I followed her white lab coat to the exam room and completed my assigned mission. I returned from the waiting room—despite the mother's distant protests of having

5

6

7

Events in exam room presented in CHRONOLOGICAL ORDER

TRANSITIONS increase suspense, then lead to CLIMAX of plot

1. *Umlaut:* A two-dot diacritical mark that appears over certain vowels in German (in this instance, Ü).

already completed the same forms—to find the attending physician on the phone and admitting my patient directly to hospital care.

Twenty-five minutes later, I again sat in her office, listening to the diagnosis. "The wheels of a lighter, a disposable lighter, leave those two umlaut marks—nothing else looks like it. It's almost always abuse in his age group." I couldn't think of any reply, and we spent several minutes gazing into the carpet, silent and introspective. I left the clinic alone and went directly to my apartment, missing the evening lecture on "Insulin and Diabetic Control." 8

Four days later, I went to the hospital to see the boy who was once my patient. I read the psychiatrist's chart notes slowly, rereading the passages describing the boy's abuse by his stepfather and his three-year history of self-mutilation and depression. It never entered my mind, so avid for a solution, to ask for a history of hospitalizations or illness, and I felt the cavernous shadows of my own missing knowledge hinting at their depth. My focus had always been on the disease, the physiologic atrocity accosting the patient's unsuspecting organs and cells. This was my first glimpse into an arena I had utterly neglected—the patient's psyche—quietly present in everyone and in every disease. 9

*More transitions lead to narrator's final understanding of events*

Entering the boy's room, I found him asleep, an IV pole standing sentry over his frail visage. I picked up a crumpled note from the floor, smoothing it to reveal the young patient's shaky handwriting: 10

> I wish I were a paper airplane,
> Soaked in gas, shooting red flames,
> burning with an orange glow, over
> all the people below.
> I could fall through the sky
> like a comet or a meteorite.
> I could become a UFO,
> become someone I did not know.

Years of lectures, labs, and research could not match the education I received in five days with this single boy. 11

*Narrator's main point in telling the story*

## *Analyzing a Student Narrative*

In "The Clinic," Jeff Gremmels draws upon rhetorical strategies and techniques that good writers use all the time when they write a narrative. The following questions, in addition to focusing on particular aspects of Gremmels' text, will help you to identify those common strategies and techniques so you can adapt them to your own writing. These questions will also help to prepare you for the analytical questions—on content, structure, and language—that you'll find after all the other selections in this chapter, along with suggestions for writing on related topics.

### FOR CLOSE READING

1. A key question to ask about any narrative is "Whose story is it?" Would you say "The Clinic" is the boy's story or the medical student's? Or both? Why?

2. Why is Jeff Gremmels unable, on his own, to determine what is wrong with his patient? How does the attending physician figure it out?

3. When the attending physician explains the strange marks on the patient's body, Gremmels says he "couldn't think of any reply" (8). Why is the student doctor left speechless?

### Strategies and Structures

1. What is Gremmels' PURPOSE in writing about this particular experience? How do you know?

2. "The Clinic" is told as a medical detective story. Why do you think Gremmels chose that genre?

3. Make a list of the main clues in this case. How does Gremmels reveal them to the reader, and how do these clues advance the narrative?

4. The last sentence of his essay, Gremmels says, "was put there because I suspected the medical school judges would like it. I, personally, think the story should end with the poem" (11). What do you think? Why?

5. *Other Methods.* As a rule, mystery stories present EFFECTS, and the detective has to figure out CAUSES. Is this true of "The Clinic"? Explain.

### Thinking about Language

1. Why does Gremmels introduce the METAPHOR of the knot in paragraph 2?

2. The DENOTATION of "exhume" is "to find or uncover" (6). What are the CONNOTATIONS of the word here, and what does the word contribute to the narrative?

3. In paragraph 9, the second-year medical student mentions the "cavernous shadows of my own missing knowledge." Is this phrase appropriate, in your opinion? Why or why not? How does it affect the TONE of the essay? Explain.

## FOR WRITING

1. Write a paragraph or two narrating from your perspective a visit to a doctor—or a teacher, counselor, or someone else you've gone to for help. Put the events of the visit in chronological order, and use transitions as needed to lead your reader through the story. Pay particular attention to the first sentence; see if you can make it introduce your main point. Then, switch perspectives, and rewrite your narrative from the POINT OF VIEW of the other person. Keep in mind how he or she might see both you and the visit differently than you do.

2. Write a narrative essay about some problem you had to diagnose and solve. The problem can be about anything—a car or computer, for example, or a friend or family member. Try to develop a PLOT that will get and hold readers' interest.

3. In your journal, jot down the notable events of your day in chronological order. Then write a brief narrative recounting those events—for yourself, a friend, or family member (as in a letter or an extended text message), or for a more general audience. Carefully select and arrange each event that you include so as to give your narrative a beginning, middle, and end.

4. Write a collaborative narrative about something significant that happened to a friend, teacher, or other person of interest. Begin with an interview, either in person or online. Then, based on your notes or correspondence, draft a narrative of this slice of the person's life. Submit your draft to your collaborator for comments, corrections, and additions. Based on these responses, rework your narrative and ask the other person to critique (or even rewrite) the "final" version.

5. Write a brief RHETORICAL ANALYSIS of the poem at the end of Gremmels's narrative. Be sure to comment on what it apparently reveals about the author.

You'll find quizzes on the readings at wwnorton.com/write/back-to-the-lake.

# A Vanity License Plate

In only two words, the license plate of this sports car tells a story. It may not tell the whole story of the courtship and marriage *before* the divorce, but we know how the story ended: she got the Porsche. Narratives tell what happened (however briefly). To construct a compelling narrative, as this ad does, you need to set up a situation (such as a troubled marriage) in a particular time (the recent past) and place (a tree-shaded, urban neighborhood of elegant townhouses); then introduce a conflict (divorce proceedings would qualify); build up the tension (she wants his car); and resolve the conflict (she gets it). More than just a tale of conflict and revenge, however, this story has a point to make. The law firm of Sanders, Lyn & Ragonetti wants the reader's business, and it knows that narratives are a good way to attract the attention of potential clients—particularly women seeking a divorce who want to ride off into the sunset in style.

[ **FOR WRITING** ]····························································································

Research and write an illustrated advertisement that "tells the story" of a law firm, hospital, bank, shop, theater, or other service or sales establishment (or a new product or service it represents). Using *Google Images* and other resources, find a photo or other image that illustrates the story you have to tell. Write an appropriate caption for that image. Include a general slogan for the enterprise, if appropriate.

Sanders, Lyn & Ragonetti Associates, Trial Lawyers

202-195 County Court Blvd. Brampton, Ontario L6W-4P7 Tel:(905)450-1711 Fax:(905)450-7066 www.slra.com

# SUGGESTIONS FOR WRITING

1. In "Have a Caltastic Day!" (p. 119), Kurt Streeter writes about a student who barely survives his first writing course at the University of California, Berkeley, with the help of a dedicated teacher. Read Streeter's narrative, and write a LITERACY NARRATIVE telling about your success (or difficulty) in coming to grips with the written word. Your narrative could focus, for example, on an early memory of reading a favorite childhood story. Or it might deal with a later experience, such as writing assignment in school that you found particularly challenging or enlightening.

2. Write a RHETORICAL ANALYSIS of the role of the narrator (the person who tells the story) in "Kim Wilde" (p. 129), a chapter from Marjane Satrapi's graphic narrative *Persepolis*. Be sure to consider how the narrator is related to young Marjane and why the narrator's words appear mostly in boxes set off from the other images, like a voiceover in a movie.

3. "If you had a choice between spending a summer in Nepal and spending a summer in the library," Annie Dillard advises, "go to the library." Read Dillard's "An American Childhood" (p. 141), and write a POSITION PAPER of approximately 400 words explaining why you think this is (or is not) good advice for a young writer. Refer to specific details in Dillard's narrative (and/or other narratives) to support your point.

4. In "Tell Them About the Dream, Martin!" (p. 147), Drew Hansen tells about the day the singer Mahalia Jackson, who was sitting nearby, shouted out to Martin Luther King Jr. to put the dream into his famous "I Have a Dream" speech. Read Hansen's narrative and King's speech (see wwnorton.com/back-to-the-lake for links to a couple of versions) and write a RHETORICAL ANALYSIS comparing the speech as delivered with the speech as it might have been without the dream reference.

5. Unlike the other narratives in this chapter, which are all true stories, Richard Russo's "Dog" (p. 157) is a work of fiction. Nonetheless, the true stories and the fiction use many of the same strategies and techniques of narrative. What are some of them? Choose one of the other narratives in this chapter and COMPARE AND CONTRAST it with Russo's short story as related forms of storytelling. Give lots of specific EXAMPLES from the texts indicating where they are similar (and different).

# Have a Caltastic Day!

Kurt Streeter (b. 1966) is a reporter for the *Los Angeles Times* where he writes about "religion, regular people, and cities." A former tennis pro, Streeter is also a sportswriter. His chronicle of the career of a young female boxer from East Los Angeles—and her relationship with her struggling father, an ex-gangster—was included, along with a tale of an elderly boxing timekeeper, in *Best American Sportswriting* (2006). Streeter attended the University of California, Berkeley, graduating with a degree in political science in 1989, the same year he led the Berkeley tennis team to the NCAA Indoor Championships. In 2013, Streeter won an award for "Best Feature" writing from the California Newspaper Publishers Association for a series of articles about life and death in a hospice for prison inmates.

"Have a Caltastic Day!" (editor's title) tells the story of Kashawn Campbell, a freshman at UC Berkeley from a tough neighborhood in South L.A. Raised by a single mother, Campbell was a straight-A student in high school. At Berkeley, however, he found a different world, struggling to keep his GPA above a 2.0, the cutoff for staying in school. Streeter's narrative of Campbell's first year in college is a variation on the success-story genre—with a cliffhanger ending; it first appeared in the *Los Angeles Times* in August 2013.

S CHOOL HAD ALWAYS BEEN his safe harbor.    1

Growing up in one of South Los Angeles' bleakest, most violent neighbor-    2
hoods, he learned about the world by watching *Jeopardy* and willed himself to become a straight-A student.

His teachers and his classmates at Jefferson High all rooted for the slight and    3
hopeful African American teenager. He was named the prom king, the
most likely to succeed, the senior class salutatorian. He was accepted to
UC Berkeley, one of the nation's most renowned public universities.

P. 106 gives tips on writing a narrative in the third person.

A semester later, Kashawn Campbell sat inside a cramped room on a dorm floor    4
that Cal reserves for black students. It was early January, and he stared nervously at his first college transcript.

MLA CITATION: Streeter, Kurt. "Have a Caltastic Day!" 2013. *Back to the Lake.* Ed. Thomas Cooley. 3rd ed. New York: Norton, 2015. 119–26. Print.

There wasn't much good to see.                                                           5

He had barely passed an introductory science course. In College Writing 1A, his    6
essays—pockmarked with misplaced words and odd phrases—were so weak that
he would have to take the class again.

He had never felt this kind of failure, nor felt this insecure. The second term    7
was just days away and he had a 1.7 GPA. If he didn't improve his grades by school
year's end, he would flunk out.

He tried to stay calm. He promised himself he would beat back the depression     8
that had come in waves those first months of school. He would work harder, be
better organized, be more like his roommate and new best friend, Spencer
Simpson, who was making college look easy.

On a nearby desk lay a small diary he recently filled with affirmations and goals.  9
He thumbed through it.

"I can do this! I can do this!" he had written. "Let the studying begin! . . . It's  10
time for Kashawn's Comeback!"

This is the story of Kashawn Campbell's freshman year.                            11

Nothing had ever been easy for Kashawn.                                          12

"When I delivered him, I thought he was dead," said his mother, Lillie, recalling  13
the umbilical cord tight around his neck. "He was still as stone but eventually he
came to. Proved he was a survivor. Ever since, I've called him my miracle child."

A single mom, she often worked two jobs to make ends meet, at times as a        14
graveyard shift security guard. Someone needed to care for her baby, so she paid an
elderly neighbor named Sylvia to house, feed and care for Kashawn.

"Me and Kashawn always had a strong connection," Lillie said. "But Sylvia        15
raised my boy, yes she did."

Sylvia didn't read many magazines, newspapers or books. Only rarely did she      16
take Kashawn outside their neighborhood. Still, she was kind and loving, and he
loved her in turn, as if she were his grandmother.

"I used what she taught me and expanded it," Kashawn said. That meant decid-     17
ing early on that the life he was surrounded by wasn't what he wanted his future to
be. "I had to be the one to push myself to do beyond well. . . . If I didn't do that,
nothing was going to ever change."

Jefferson, made up almost entirely of Latinos and blacks, had a woeful reputa-   18
tion. His freshman year, just under 13% of its students were judged to be proficient
in English, less than 1% in math.

"It was so rare to have a kid like Kashawn, especially an African American male,  19
wanting that badly to go to college," said Jeremy McDavid, a former Jefferson vice
principal. "We got together as a staff and decided that this kid, we cannot let him
down."

By the end of his senior year, Kashawn's 4.06 grade point average was second best 20 in the senior class. Because of a statewide program to attract top students from every public California high school, a spot at a UC system campus waited for him.

But when he got his acceptance letter from Berkeley, he couldn't celebrate like 21 he always thought he would. It was Sylvia. She was losing a battle with cancer.

He sat near her hospice bed on a muggy day to give her the news. "I'm going to 22 Cal, grandma," he said. She could barely open her eyes. "I'm going up there and I'm going to keep working hard and doing great. Nothing's going to change."

Sylvia died later that day. 23

A month later, when his mother drove him to Berkeley and dropped him off at his 24 dormitory, Kashawn still crumbled into tears at the thought of Sylvia.

Yet he did everything he could to fit in. He lived at the African-American Theme 25 Program—two floors in Christian Hall housing roughly 50 black freshmen, an effort to build bonds among a community whose numbers have dwindled over the last two decades.

He filled his dorm room with Cal posters, and wore clothes emblazoned with 26 the school's name. Each morning the gawky, bone-thin teen energetically reminded his dorm mates to "have a Caltastic day!"

Kashawn Campbell

"It was clear that Kashawn was someone who didn't know about, or maybe care 27
about, social norms," said one of his friends. "A lot of people would laugh at first.
They didn't understand how someone could be that enthusiastic."

But as the semester got going, he began to stumble. The first essay for the writ- 28
ing class that accounted for half of his course load was so bad his teacher gave him
a "No Pass." Same for the second essay.

"It's like a different planet here," he said one day, walking down Telegraph Ave- 29
nue through a mash of humanity he'd never been exposed to before: white kids,
Asian kids, rich kids, bearded hipsters and burnt-out hippies. Many of them
jaywalked. Not Kashawn. Just as he'd been taught, he only used crosswalks, only
stepped onto the street when the coast was clear or a light flashed green. His shoulders slumped.

"I'm not used to the people. Not used to the type of buildings. Definitely not 30
used to the pressure I feel."

**How and
when to
change verb
tenses is
explained on
p. 105.**

Part of the pressure came from race. After peaking at 7% in the late 31
1980s and early '90s, the undergraduate African American population at
Cal had been declining for years, especially since Proposition 209 had
banned affirmative action in admissions to California public colleges. When
Kashawn arrived, 3% of Berkeley undergraduates were African American.

The low numbers were the source of constant talk on the theme program floors, 32
the symbolic center of black life for Cal freshmen.

"Sometimes we feel like we're not wanted on campus," Kashawn said, sur- 33
rounded at a dinner table by several of his dorm mates, all of them nodding in
agreement. "It's usually subtle things, glances or not being invited to study groups.
Little, constant aggressions."

He also felt a more personal burden. 34

He couldn't let his mother down. She kept a box stuffed with each of his perfect 35
report cards. She swore that he was going to be a lawyer, maybe even the president.
Back home her bank account was running low, and he sent some of his scholarship
money home to keep her going.

He'd never been depressed. Now clouds of sadness descended every few weeks. 36
When they did he was barely able to speak, even to Spencer, his roommate.

The biggest of his burdens was schoolwork. At Jefferson, a long essay took a page 37
and perfect grades came after an hour of study a night.

At Cal, he was among the hardest workers in the dorm, but he could barely keep 38
afloat.

Seeking help, he went at least once a week to the office of his writing instructor, 39
Verda Delp.

The more she saw him, the more she worried. His writing often didn't make   40
sense. He struggled to comprehend the readings for her class and think critically
about the text.

"It took a while for him to understand there was a problem," Delp said. "He   41
could not believe that he needed more skills. He would revise his papers and each
time he would turn his work back in having complicated it. The paper would be
full of words he thought were academic, writing the way he thought a college student should write, using big words he didn't have command of."

At the end of the first semester, after he turned in a final portfolio of revised   42
essays, Delp asked Kashawn to come to her office. She told him this last batch of
work was better. After reviewing his writing, though, it was clear to her that he
had received far too much help from someone else.

Both remember the meeting, recalling Kashawn's shock, his admission that   43
friends and a tutor had offered suggestions and made edits, his insistence that the
bulk of the writing was his own.

Delp reviewed his record: None of his essays had been good enough to receive   44
passing grades. Still, instead of failing him, she gave a reprieve: His report card
would show an "In Progress." The course wouldn't count against his grade point
average, but he would have to take it again.

Before the start of the second term, hoping for a head start, Kashawn moved back   45
into the dorm before anyone else on his floor. He imagined how different things
were going to be from his first semester.

He couldn't wait to see Spencer. "We're both going to do very well this semes-   46
ter," he said. "I believe I can follow his lead and ace all my classes."

They hadn't known each other before the year began. Now they were like brothers,   47
partly because they shared so much. Spencer was raised in a tough L.A. neighborhood by a single mom who had sometimes worked two jobs to pay the
rent. Spencer had gone to struggling public schools, receiving straight A's at
Inglewood High. Spencer didn't curse, didn't party, didn't try to act tough and
was shy around girls.

> COMPARISON (Ch. 10) can be especially useful in a narrative for presenting people.

As much as they had in common, they were also different. Spencer's mother, a   48
medical administrator, had graduated from UCLA and exposed her only child to art,
politics, literature and the world beyond Inglewood. If a bookstore was going out of
business, she'd drive Spencer to the closeout sale and they would buy discounted novels. She pushed him to participate in a mostly white Boy Scout troop in Westchester.

To Spencer, Berkeley was the first place he could feel fully comfortable being   49
intellectual and black, the first place he could openly admit he liked folk music and
punk rock.

Spencer Simpson and Kashawn Campbell talk before their African American Studies class.

He was cruising through Cal, finishing the first semester with a 3.8 GPA despite  50
a raft of hard classes. "I can easily see him being a professor one day," said his
political theory instructor, noting that Spencer was one of the sharpest students in
a lecture packed with nearly 200 undergraduates.

In the second term, Kashawn and Spencer volunteered for the same student  51
organizations, and walked each Friday night to a job washing dishes at a nearby
residence hall.

They even took a class together, African American Studies 5A, a survey of black  52
culture and race relations. It was key for Kashawn: A top grade could ensure he
would be invited back to Cal.

They sat together in the front row. One teacher noticed that Kashawn subcon-  53
sciously seemed to mime his roommate: casually cocking his head and leaning
back slightly as he pondered questions, just like Spencer.

Kashawn reveled in the class in a way he hadn't since high school. He would  54
often be the first one to speak up in discussions, even though his points weren't
always the most sophisticated, said Gabrielle Williams, a doctoral student who
helped teach the class.

He still had gaps in his knowledge of history. But, Williams said, "You could see  55
how engaged he was, how much he loved being there. . . . You could also see that
he was struggling with his confidence, partly because this whole experience was so
overwhelming."

Although the African American Studies class was a bright spot—Kashawn had  56
received an A on an essay and a B on a midterm, the best grades of his freshman
year—the writing course he'd been forced to repeat wasn't going well.

He knew that another failing effort in the class could doom his chances to return  57
to Cal, so he worked as closely with his new instructor as he had with Delp.

There was little to show for the effort. On yet another failing essay, the instructor  58
wrote how surprised she was at his lack of progress, especially, she noted, given the
hours they'd spent going over his "extremely long, awkward and unclear sentences."

He told only Spencer and a few dorm mates how devastating this kind of failure  59
felt, each poor grade another stinging punch bringing him closer to flunking out.
None of the adults in his life knew the depth of his pain: not his professors, his
counselors, any of the teachers at his old high school. He spoke vaguely about
depression to his mother. She told him to read the Bible.

Spencer looked out for Kashawn; he was the first person Kashawn would turn to  60
when depression came. Sometimes in the dorm room, Spencer would look over at
Kashawn and see him sitting in front of his computer, body frozen and face expressionless, JVC headphones wrapped over his ears, but no music playing.

One night Kashawn walked briskly from his room, ending up alone in a quiet,  61
beige-walled lounge at Christian Hall. His mind raced. He chastised himself for his
college grades, for being too sensitive, too trusting, too naive.

"Why was I even born?" he wondered. It felt like he was outside his body, look-  62
ing at himself from above. "Is life really worth living under these conditions?"

He tried to calm down. "The way I was stressing myself out, it wasn't good, it  63
wasn't healthy at all," he would recall later. "I just had to find my way out of that
lounge. Had to get help, because this was a monster I needed to tame."

It wasn't long before he found himself sitting for the first time in a campus psy-  64
chologist's office. The counselor urged him to put his life in better perspective.
Maybe he didn't have to be the straight-A kid he'd been in high school anymore.
Maybe all that mattered was giving his best. The visit seemed to change him. His
dorm mates had been so worried about his dark moods that some had called their
parents, asking advice on how best to help their friend. As weeks passed and his
smile returned, everyone breathed a little easier.

"I've learned the hard way that academics are not who you are," Kashawn said  65
as he walked through Sproul Plaza, heading back to the dorm one day in May.
"They are something you need to learn to get to the next level of life, but they can't
define me. My grades at Cal are not Kashawn Campbell."

Finals week. The school year was nearly over. After staying up all night to finish,  66
Kashawn turned in the final portfolio for his writing course.

"I'm proud of you," his instructor said, as he handed her the essays in a black  67
folder. "You've tried as hard as anyone I've ever seen."

Soon he'd taken his last test, turned in his last report. He stood on a sidewalk  68
outside the dorm, saying goodbye to Spencer, stifling tears. Then he was on a
Greyhound bus, heading home to Los Angeles, where he slept on the floor in his
mother's apartment and waited for his grades.

Would he flunk out?    69

"All I can do is pray," he said.    70

One morning this summer he walked slowly to the kitchen table, sat in a black  71
chair and cracked open his laptop. Cal's website had just posted grades.

He scrolled down the page and saw the results for College Writing. His teacher  72
said he'd improved slightly, but not enough. She gave him an incomplete. To get a
grade he'd have to turn in two more essays, if he came back to school.

His heart raced. He saw that he'd passed a three-unit seminar. He scanned fur-  73
ther, his eyes resting finally on a line that said African American Studies 5A. There
was his grade.

A-.    74

"Yes!" he exclaimed. An A- lifted his GPA above a 2.0.    75

He wasn't a freshman anymore. He would return to Cal for his sophomore  76
year. ◆

## FOR CLOSE READING

1. According to Kurt Streeter, why is the "hero" of his narrative, Kashawn Campbell, so determined to succeed at the University of California, Berkeley? Where and how does Streeter reveal Campbell's motives most fully? For example, what part does "grandma" Sylvia play in the story (22)?

2. To the extent that Campbell's story is one of self-enlightenment and growing up, what does he learn about himself? What brings about this moment of enlightenment (or *epiphany*) in the narrative?

3. Campbell's friend Spencer Simpson works hard in school, too; but his success seems to come easier—or at least with less personal stress. Why? What particular details does Kerry cite to explain, in part, this key difference between the two friends?

4. Kashawn Campbell barely passes most of his courses at Berkeley and has to take beginning writing over again, yet Streeter casts his story as a version of the success story. Is this rendering of events justified? Why or why not?

5. According to his writing instructor, Verda Delp, what common mistakes does Campbell make, at first, in the writing and revising he does for her course? What advice would you give Campbell for correcting these problems? In general, how and how well do Campbell's teachers deal with their student's difficulties?

## Strategies and Structures

1. When and where does Streeter's narrative break with chronology and go back to his subject's childhood? What is the purpose of this FLASHBACK?

2. "It's time for Kashawn's Comeback!" (10). Streeter's choice of this bit of DIALOGUE—particularly the word *comeback*—helps to set up the PLOT of the narrative that follows. How? Point to particular events and other specific details that fit a come-from-behind pattern in "the story of Kashawn Campbell's freshman year" as Streeter tells it (11).

3. Campbell visits the office of a campus psychologist. "The visit," said Streeter, "seemed to change him" (64). How does this critical event serve Streeter as a turning point for the rest of his narrative?

4. Streeter divides his narrative into six distinct sections: paragraphs 1–11, 12–23, 24–44, 45–55, 56–66, and 66–76. The last section he identifies as "Finals week" (66). How would you label the other sections, and why?

5. Streeter's narrative takes place in several different settings. What are some of the main places in the story, and how does he describe them? What kind of scene is the "beige-walled lounge" (61)? Why does Campbell say, "I just had to find my way out of that lounge" (63)?

6. *Other Methods.* "As much as they had in common," says Streeter of Campbell and his friend Spencer Simpson, "they were also different" (48). How and where does Streeter use COMPARISON AND CONTRAST—of the two friends, their backgrounds and families—to advance his narrative? Point to specific passages in the text.

## Thinking about Language

1. Before he came to Berkeley, says Streeter, school was Campbell's "safe harbor" (1). What are the implications of this METAPHOR, and how does Streeter use them in his narrative?

2. Of her student's revisions, Campbell's writing instructor says that "each time he would turn his work back in having complicated it" (41). In what sense is she using the term *complicated*? In what more positive sense might the word be applied to Streeter's narrative as it goes from section to section?

3. Campbell is given a "reprieve" at the end of his first semester (44). To whom and under what circumstances is this term usually applied? How appropriate is Streeter's use of it here?

4. What "monster" is Campbell referring to in paragraph 63? Why does Campbell need to "tame" the monster instead of slaying it (63)?

5. Unlike most of the other pedestrians around the Berkeley campus, Campbell never "jaywalked" (29). In American slang at the beginning of the automobile era when the word *jaywalk* was coined, a *jay* was a silly or inexperienced person.

What is Streeter telling us about his main character by citing this detail about Campbell's safety habits?

## FOR WRITING

1. Retell the story of Kashawn Campbell's first year at college from his own point of view—or that of Spencer Simpson, Verna Delp, or some other person in the story.

2. "Have a Caltastic Day!" is composed in the short paragraphs common to newspaper feature writing. Suppose you were editing Streeter's narrative for inclusion in a more literary or scholarly publication. Choose a section and explain which paragraphs you would advise the author to combine or otherwise revise, and why.

3. Streeter tells what is basically a success story—of springing from humble beginnings, overcoming difficult obstacles, and advancing one's place in the world. Rewrite the story of Kashawn Campbell—or someone you know who has had difficulty making the transition from high school to college—as a coming-of-age story, a psychological or sociological case history, or in some other genre that relies heavily on narrative.

4. Keep a journal of your difficulties, successes, and ordinary experiences as a student during the school year. At the end of the year, write a narrative (either in the first-person or more detached third-person) about your academic and other, related adventures; be sure to give your narrative a clear beginning, middle, and end.

5. Collaborate with a classmate or friend—your equivalent of Spencer Simpson—on a narrative of your joint adventures during your first year in college or first year away from home. You can proceed by each writing a separate draft and then exchanging drafts; or you can take turns writing (and critiquing) installments in serial fashion.

You'll find quizzes on the readings at
wwnorton.com/write/back-to-the-lake.

# Kim Wilde

Marjane Satrapi (b. 1969) is a graphic novelist, film director, and author of children's books. Satrapi grew up in Teheran, the daughter of politically active parents who opposed the Iranian monarchy in favor of more democratic policies. After the Shah of Iran was deposed in 1979, however, Satrapi's parents grew even more alarmed by the repressive regime of the fundamentalists. (Satrapi later chronicled this period in her graphic narrative *Persepolis*, which was published in the United States in 2004.) As a teenager, Satrapi was sent to live and study at a French speaking school in Austria. After high school, she returned to Iran and ultimately earned a master's degree in visual communication from Islamic Azad University in Tehran. In 2008, the film version of *Persepolis* won a César Award for Best First Film.

"Kim Wilde," a chapter from *Persepolis*, is named after the British pop singer who, along with Michael Jackson, was one of young Satrapi's cultural heroes as she and her family lived under the strictures, both personal and political, of a rigid society whose arbitrary rules and restrictions are captured in the stark blacks and whites of Satrapi's graphic style. Graphic narratives use the same elements and conventions—such as point of view, chronology and, especially, dialogue—as any other kind of narrative; they just add pictures to the words.

As graphic narratives move from panel to panel, they are following chronological order (p. 103).

MLA CITATION: Satrapi, Marjane. "Kim Wilde." 2004. *Back to the Lake*. Ed. Thomas Cooley. 3rd ed. New York: Norton, 2015. 130–38. Print.

A YEAR AFTER MY UNCLE DIED, THE BORDERS WERE REOPENED. MY PARENTS RAN TO GET PASSPORTS.

LOOK AT THE LAST PAGE: "IT IS STRICTLY FORBIDDEN TO TRAVEL IN OCCUPIED PALESTINE WITH THIS DOCUMENT."

MY GOD. JUST LOOK AT ME IN THIS PICTURE, WITH THE SCARF ON MY HEAD.

CAN I SEE?

SHE SURE DIDN'T LOOK VERY HAPPY. IN FACT, SHE WAS UNRECOGNIZABLE.

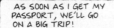

AS SOON AS I GET MY PASSPORT, WE'LL GO ON A BIG TRIP!

WELL, ACTUALLY...

WE WANT TO SPEND SOME TIME TOGETHER, JUST THE TWO OF US, FOR A FEW DAYS.

WHERE?

TURKEY.

BAH...TURKEY'S FOR THE BIRDS. ONLY UNCOOL PEOPLE GO TO TURKEY. IF YOU'RE TAKING A TRIP, WHY NOT GO TO EUROPE OR THE UNITED STATES?!...

IF YOU WANT US TO BRING YOU BACK SOME PRESENTS, JUST ASK.

WHAT CAN YOU BRING ME BACK FROM TURKEY? SHISH-KEBABS?

LISTEN MARJI, WHERE DO YOU THINK ALL THE HIP STUFF YOU LIKE COMES FROM?

DURING THE WAR, THERE WERE NO IMPORTS FROM THE WEST.

A DENIM JACKET, CHOCOLATE, A POSTER, NO, TWO POSTERS. ONE OF KIM WILDE AND ONE OF IRON MAIDEN.

IRON MAIDEN? THOSE FOUR BRUTES?

THEY'RE NOT BRUTES. I REALLY LIKE WHAT THEY DO.

YOU LIKE THAT?

I LOVE IT.

SEE, MOM?

FIRST THING AFTER THEY GOT TO ISTANBUL, THEY WENT TO BUY THE POSTERS.

I'M GLAD WE FOUND JUST WHAT SHE WANTED!

ABSOLUTELY! IT'S SO HARD FOR KIDS IN IRAN. THE POOR THINGS.

TELL ME THE TRUTH, YOU REALLY LIKE IRON MAIDEN?

ABSOLUTELY!

YOU HYPOCRITE!

I WONDER HOW WE'RE GOING TO GET THEM PAST CUSTOMS!

I'VE BEEN WONDERING MYSELF. THEY'RE ENORMOUS.

AS SOON AS THEY WERE IN THE HOTEL, THEY SET TO FINDING A WAY.

WE COULD FOLD THEM AND HIDE THEM IN THE LINING OF THE SUITCASE!

FOLD THEM? THAT WILL LEAVE MARKS. SHE'LL BE DISAPPOINTED.

WE COULD JUST CARRY THEM UNDER OUR ARMS AND ACT NATURAL.

UNDER OUR ARMS? COME ON!

AND THEN MY MOTHER HAD A GREAT IDEA...

TAKE OFF YOUR COAT.

SHE TORE OUT THE LINING.

THEN, SHE PLACED THE TWO POSTERS BEHIND IT...

...AND THEN SEWED IT BACK IN.

I PUT MY POSTERS UP IN MY ROOM.

IRON MAIDEN

KIM WILDE

I PUT MY 1983 NIKES ON...

...AND MY DENIM JACKET WITH THE MICHAEL JACKSON BUTTON, AND OF COURSE, MY HEADSCARF.

SO WHAT DO YOU THINK?

NICE! VERY CUTE!

OK, I'M GOING OUT.

WHERE?

TO BUY SOME TAPES.

WHERE?

NOT FAR. ON GANDHI AVENUE.

BE BACK IN AN HOUR!

I'LL BE BACK IN TWO HOURS.

FOR AN IRANIAN MOTHER, MY MOM WAS VERY PERMISSIVE. I ONLY KNEW TWO OR THREE OTHER GIRLS WHO COULD GO OUT ALONE AT THIRTEEN.

FOR A YEAR NOW, THE FOOD SHORTAGE HAD BEEN RESOLVED BY THE GROWTH OF THE BLACK MARKET. HOWEVER, FINDING TAPES WAS A LITTLE MORE COMPLICATED. ON GANDHI AVENUE YOU COULD FIND THEM SOMETIMES.

ESTEVIE VONDER

ABBA, BEE GEES

YAZOO

JULIO IGLESIAS

PINK FLOYD

JIKAEL MACKSON

VIDEOS, MUSIC, CARDS, LIPSTICK, NAIL POLISH, CHESS SET, PANTYHOSE, CHOCOLATE, ...,...

I BOUGHT TWO TAPES: KIM WILDE AND CAMEL.

HOW MUCH?

110 TUMANS.

♪WE'RE THE KIDS IN AMERICA ♪WHOA...

YOU! STOP!

THEY WERE GUARDIANS OF THE REVOLUTION, THE WOMEN'S BRANCH. THIS GROUP HAD BEEN ADDED IN 1982, TO ARREST WOMEN WHO WERE IMPROPERLY VEILED. (LIKE ME, FOR EXAMPLE.)

THEIR JOB WAS TO PUT US BACK ON THE STRAIGHT AND NARROW BY EXPLAINING THE DUTIES OF MUSLIM WOMEN.

WHY ARE YOU WEARING THOSE "PUNK" SHOES?

WHAT PUNK SHOES?

THOSE!

SHUT UP! THEY'RE PUNK.

BUT THESE ARE SNEAKERS!

IT WAS OBVIOUS THAT SHE HAD NO IDEA WHAT PUNK WAS.

THERE WAS NO ALTERNATIVE. I HAD TO LIE.

I WEAR THESE BECAUSE I PLAY BASKETBALL.

I'M ON MY SCHOOL'S TEAM.

OH SURE. I CAN TELL BY YOUR HEIGHT!

AND YOU WEAR THIS JACKET FOR BASKETBALL TOO??

WHAT DO I SEE HERE? MICHAEL JACKSON! THAT SYMBOL OF DECADENCE?

NO, IT'S MALCOLM X, THE LEADER OF BLACK MUSLIMS IN AMERICA.

DON'T GIVE ME THAT! IT'S MICHAEL JACKSON!

WHO? I DON'T KNOW HIM.

BACK THEN, MICHAEL JACKSON WAS STILL BLACK.

LOWER YOUR SCARF, YOU LITTLE WHORE!

AREN'T YOU ASHAMED TO WEAR TIGHT JEANS LIKE THESE??

THEY SHRANK!!

GO ON, GET IN THE CAR. WE'RE TAKING YOU DOWN TO THE COMMITTEE.

THE COMMITTEE WAS THE HQ OF THE GUARDIANS OF THE REVOLUTION.

AT THE COMMITTEE, THEY DIDN'T HAVE TO INFORM MY PARENTS. THEY COULD DETAIN ME FOR HOURS, OR FOR DAYS. I COULD BE WHIPPED. IN SHORT, ANYTHING COULD HAPPEN TO ME. IT WAS TIME FOR ACTION.

I'M SORRY MA'AM! I'LL NEVER DO IT AGAIN...

GET IN THE CAR!

MA'AM, MY MOTHER'S DEAD. MY STEPMOTHER IS REALLY CRUEL AND IF I DON'T GO HOME RIGHT AWAY, SHE'LL KILL ME...

SHE'LL BURN ME WITH THE CLOTHES IRON!

SHE'LL MAKE MY FATHER PUT ME IN AN ORPHANAGE

MAYBE SHE BELIEVED ME, MAYBE SHE JUST PRETENDED TO. BUT, MIRACULOUSLY, SHE LET ME GO.

BACK HOME...

MARJI! WHAT HAPPENED? HAVE YOU BEEN CRYING?

NO MOM. I'M JUST TIRED. I'M GOING TO MY ROOM.

THERE WAS NO WAY I COULD TELL THE TRUTH. SHE NEVER WOULD HAVE LET ME GO OUT ALONE AGAIN.

I GOT OFF PRETTY EASY, CONSIDERING. THE GUARDIANS OF THE REVOLUTION DIDN'T FIND MY TAPES.

♫ WE'RE THE KIDS IN AMERICA WHOAO ♫

TO EACH HIS OWN WAY OF CALMING DOWN.

## FOR CLOSE READING

1. Why are Marjane Satrapi's parents in such a hurry to get passports and go on a trip to Turkey? Why don't they take her with them?

2. What kind of "contraband" does Satrapi ask her parents to bring back to her? What do her requests suggest about society and popular culture in Iran—and America?

3. Given the dangers of getting caught, why don't Satrapi's parents refuse to bring back the things she wants? Are they justified in taking such risks to satisfy their daughter's demands? Why or why not?

4. On the streets of Teheran, Satrapi has no trouble buying Kim Wilde audiotapes and Camel cigarettes. Why does Satrapi include this incident in her narrative? What does it tell the reader about the complexity of the city and its culture?

5. Why doesn't Satrapi confess to her mother that she has been stopped by the "Guardians of the Revolution, Women's Branch"? Should she have? Why or why not?

## Strategies and Structures

1. Satrapi's aim in "Kim Wilde," as in the rest of *Persepolis*, is to depict what life was like for her and her family and friends under an authoritarian political and religious regime. How and how well does "Kim Wilde" accomplish this purpose? Support your answer by pointing to specific events in the narrative.

2. In a narrative, events unfold one after another in linear fashion. Why? How does the sequence of panels in Satrapi's graphic narrative illustrate this linear principle of narrative in general? Explain by referring to several specific panels.

3. In "Kim Wilde," the beginning action of the PLOT takes place in five panels on the first page. What is the nature of that action and where is it set? How do the plot and setting of Satrapi's narrative change on the next page?

4. After her parents purchase the forbidden items in Istanbul, the plot of Satrapi's narrative takes yet another turn, also depicted on a single page. What happens in *this* sequence of events? What other distinct twists and turns does the narrative take before ending in the last three panels with Satrapi safe at home and "calming down" in her room?

5. A common element in narrative writing is suspense, which comes from the reader's not knowing what is going to happen next. How does Satrapi create suspense in her narrative? How and where does she temper that suspense with humor?

6. *Other Methods.* In addition to CHRONOLOGY, Satrapi uses CAUSE AND EFFECT to organize the events of her narrative. Having purchased the posters, for example, her parents must then hide them. Point out other examples of actions in the story that are linked by cause and effect; explain what they contribute to the plot and motivation of the characters.

## Thinking about Language

1. In "We're the Kids in America," Kim Wilde sings, "Outside a new day is dawning" and "There's a new wave coming, I warn ya." How does Satrapi's ALLUSION to this song help to thicken the plot and enhance the significance of her narrative?

2. *Graphic narratives* are often called *comics*. Both terms denote a story told in words and pictures. How, if at all, do the two terms differ in their CONNOTATIONS?

3. Some key terms in the nomenclature of graphic narratives are *panels, gutters, dialogue balloons, thought balloons, captions,* and *sound effects.* Point to several examples of Satrapi's use of these devices in "Kim Wilde."

4. What is the significance of the light bulb in panel 15? Would the meaning of this figure be apparent in a graphic narrative written in some language other than English? Why or why not?

5. Graphic narratives are very popular in Japan, where they're called "Manga." What is the literal translation of this word, and how does it compare in meaning with that of the English word *comics*?

## FOR WRITING

1. In a graphic narrative, words and images work together to carry the story line. Choose a panel (or sequence of panels) in "Kim Wilde" that you find particularly appealing. Then, in a paragraph or two, describe these images in some detail; explain how they complement what is being said—and vice versa.

2. Most of the time, Satrapi and her parents wear dark clothes. Only in private, or when defying convention, are they depicted in lighter garb. Write an essay analyzing Satrapi's use of black and white as both a visual and a thematic element in "Kim Wilde." Be sure to say why such a stark color scheme is (or is not) more appropriate to her story than the full color range used by some graphic artists.

3. In collaboration with several of your classmates, look for examples of graphic narratives intended to be read in non-Western fashion, such as from right to left and back to front rather than left to right and front to back. (Japanese *manga*, in particular, can be found in English translation both on the internet and in print.) Have each member of the group report briefly in writing on his or her experience with reading at least one such text.

4. Write a joint LITERACY NARRATIVE based on your and your classmates' reports of reading non-Western narratives "backwards." Does this difference mean that Japanese and other non-Western writers tell their stories backwards?

5. Write an EVALUATION of "Kim Wilde" (or some other chapter in *Persepolis*). What is the apparent purpose of the narrative besides showing us how and where the characters live? How and how well does Satrapi accomplish this larger purpose? For what kind of audience is her narrative intended? How successfully does she speak to that audience? Cite lots of evidence from the text to support your view.

You'll find quizzes on the readings at
wwnorton.com/write/back-to-the-lake.

# ANNIE DILLARD

## An American Childhood

Annie Dillard (b. 1945) grew up in Pittsburgh with a book in her hand. Her master's thesis at Hollins College was on Thoreau's *Walden,* to which her work has been compared. Dillard is known for her meditative essays on nature, collected in *A Pilgrim at Tinker Creek* (1974), which won the Pulitzer Prize for nonfiction, and *Teaching a Stone to Talk* (1982). She has published a novel, *The Maytrees* (2007), and two memoirs, *A Writing Life* (1989) and *An American Childhood* (1987), from which the following is taken.

This selection is a narrative of childhood, an adventure through Dillard's old neighborhood—and her imagination. Her inspiration? Classic narratives of adventure, such as Robert Louis Stevenson's *Kidnapped.* According to Dillard, "you have enough experience by the time you're five years old" to create your own adventure narrative. "What you need is the library. . . . What you have to learn is the best of what is being thought and said. If you [have] a choice between spending a summer in Nepal and spending a summer in the library, go to the library."

S OME BOYS TAUGHT ME TO PLAY FOOTBALL. This was fine sport. You thought    1
up a new strategy for every play and whispered it to the others. You went out for a pass, fooling everyone. Best, you got to throw yourself mightily at someone's running legs. Either you brought him down or you hit the ground flat on your chin, with your arms empty before you. It was all or nothing. If you hesitated in fear, you would miss and get hurt: you would take a hard fall while the kid got away, or you would get kicked in the face while the kid got away. But if you flung yourself wholeheartedly at the back of his knees—if you gathered and joined body and soul and pointed them diving fearlessly—then you likely wouldn't get hurt, and you'd stop the ball. Your fate, and your team's score, depended on your concentration and courage. Nothing girls did could compare with it.

> Part of telling a good story is telling why you're telling it. See "Stating Your Point," p. 101.

Boys welcomed me at baseball, too, for I had, through enthusiastic practice,    2
what was weirdly known as a boy's arm. In winter, in the snow, there was neither baseball nor football, so the boys and I threw snowballs at passing cars. I got in trouble throwing snowballs, and have seldom been happier since.

MLA CITATION: Dillard, Annie. "An American Childhood." 1987. *Back to the Lake.* Ed. Thomas Cooley. 3rd ed. New York: Norton, 2015. 141-45. Print.

On one weekday morning after Christmas, six inches of new snow had just fallen. We were standing up to our boot tops in snow on a front yard on trafficked Reynolds Street, waiting for cars. The cars traveled Reynolds Street slowly and evenly; they were targets all but wrapped in red ribbons, cream puffs. We couldn't miss.

I was seven; the boys were eight, nine, and ten. The oldest two Fahey boys were there—Mikey and Peter—polite blond boys who lived near me on Lloyd Street, and who already had four brothers and sisters. My parents approved of Mikey and Peter Fahey. Chickie McBride was there, a tough kid, and Billy Paul and Mackie Kean too, from across Reynolds, where the boys grew up dark and furious, grew up skinny, knowing, and skilled. We had all drifted from our houses that morning looking for action, and had found it here on Reynolds Street.

It was cloudy but cold. The cars' tires laid behind them on the snowy street a complex trail of beige chunks like crenellated castle walls. I had stepped on some earlier; they squeaked. We could have wished for more traffic. When a car came, we all popped it one. In the intervals between cars we reverted to the natural solitude of children.

I started making an iceball—a perfect iceball, from perfectly white snow, perfectly spherical, and squeezed perfectly translucent so no snow remained all the way through. (The Fahey boys and I considered it unfair actually to throw an iceball at somebody, but it had been known to happen.)

I had just embarked on the iceball project when we heard tire chains come clanking from afar. A black Buick was moving toward us down the street. We all spread out, banged together some regular snowballs, took aim, and, when the Buick drew nigh, fired.

A soft snowball hit the driver's windshield right before the driver's face. It made a smashed star with a hump in the middle.

Often, of course, we hit our target, but this time, the only time in all of life, the car pulled over and stopped. Its wide black door opened; a man got out of it, running. He didn't even close the car door.

He ran after us, and we ran away from him, up the snowy Reynolds sidewalk. At the corner, I looked back; incredibly, he was still after us. He was in city clothes: a suit and tie, street shoes. Any normal adult would have quit, having sprung us into flight and made his point. This man was gaining on us. He was a thin man, all action. All of a sudden, we were running for our lives.

Wordless, we split up. We were on our turf; we could lose ourselves in the neighborhood backyards, everyone for himself. I paused and considered. Everyone had vanished except Mikey Fahey, who was just rounding the corner of a yellow brick house. Poor Mikey, I trailed him. The driver of the Buick sensibly picked the two of us to follow. The man apparently had all day.

With this transition paragraph (p. 104), Dillard introduces the particular day she is telling about.

"He chased us silently, block after block. He chased us silently over picket fences, through thorny hedges, between houses, around garbage cans, and across streets."

He chased Mikey and me around the yellow house and up a backyard path we knew by heart: under a low tree, up a bank, through a hedge, down some snowy steps, and across the grocery store's delivery driveway. We smashed through a gap in another hedge, entered a scruffy backyard and ran around its back porch and tight between houses to Edgerton Avenue; we ran across Edgerton to an alley and up our own sliding woodpile to the Halls' front yard; he kept coming. We ran up Lloyd Street and wound through mazy backyards toward the steep hilltop at Willard and Lang.

12

He chased us silently, block after block. He chased us silently over picket fences, 13
through thorny hedges, between houses, around garbage cans, and across streets.
Every time I glanced back, choking for breath, I expected he would have quit. He
must have been as breathless as we were. His jacket strained over his body. It was
an immense discovery, pounding into my hot head with every sliding, joyous step,
that this ordinary adult evidently knew what I thought only children who trained
at football knew: that you have to fling yourself at what you're doing, you have to
point yourself, forget yourself, aim, dive.

Mikey and I had nowhere to go, in our own neighborhood or out of it, but away 14
from this man who was chasing us. He impelled us forward; we compelled him to
follow our route. The air was cold; every breath tore my throat. We kept running,
block after block; we kept improvising, backyard after backyard, running a frantic
course and choosing it simultaneously, failing always to find small places or hard
places to slow him down, and discovering always, exhilarated, dismayed, that only
bare speed could save us—for he would never give up, this man—and we were losing speed.

He chased us through the backyard labyrinths of ten blocks before he caught us 15
by our jackets. He caught us and we all stopped.

We three stood staggering, half blinded, coughing, in an obscure hilltop back- 16
yard: a man in his twenties, a boy, a girl. He had released our jackets, our pursuer,
our captor, our hero: He knew we weren't going anywhere. We all played by the
rules. Mikey and I unzipped our jackets. I pulled off my sopping mittens. Our
tracks multiplied in the backyard's new snow. We had been breaking new snow all
morning. We didn't look at each other. I was cherishing my excitement. The man's
lower pants legs were wet; his cuffs were full of snow, and there was a prow of
snow beneath them on his shoes and socks. Some trees bordered the little flat backyard, some messy winter trees. There was no one around: a clearing in a grove, and
we the only players.

It was a long time before he could speak. I had some difficulty at first recalling 17
why we were there. My lips felt swollen; I couldn't see out of the sides of my eyes; I
kept coughing.

"You stupid kids," he began perfunctorily. 18

We listened perfunctorily indeed, if we listened at all, for the chewing out was 19
redundant, a mere formality, and beside the point. The point was that he had
chased us passionately without giving up, and so he had caught us. Now he came
down to earth. I wanted the glory to last forever.

But how could the glory have lasted forever? We could have run through every 20
backyard in North America until we got to Panama. But when he trapped us at the
lip of the Panama Canal, what precisely could he have done to prolong the drama
of the chase and cap its glory? I brooded about this for the next few years. He could

only have fried Mikey Fahey and me in boiling oil, say, or dismembered us piece-meal, or staked us to anthills. None of which I really wanted, and none of which any adult was likely to do, even in the spirit of fun. He could only chew us out there in the Panamanian jungle, after months or years of exalting pursuit. He could only begin, "You stupid kids," and continue in his ordinary Pittsburgh accent with his normal righteous anger and the usual common sense.

If in that snowy backyard the driver of the black Buick had cut off our heads, 21 Mikey's and mine, I would have died happy, for nothing has required so much of me since as being chased all over Pittsburgh in the middle of winter—running terrified, exhausted—by this sainted, skinny, furious red-headed man who wished to have a word with us. I don't know how he found his way back to his car. ◆

As indicated on p. 94, you can make an exciting narra-tive out of ordi-nary, everyday events.

## FOR CLOSE READING

1. When she was growing up in Pittsburgh, says Annie Dillard, nothing that girls nor-mally did "could compare with" playing football (1). What was so special to her about this "boys'" sport?

2. How old is Dillard at the time of the big chase? Does it matter that she is the youngest in the game—and the only girl? Why or why not?

3. As the chase goes on, Dillard's pursuer becomes her "hero" (16). Why? How, according to Dillard, is true "glory" to be achieved in any pursuit (19)?

4. What do the man's appearance and behavior tell us about the America of Dillard's childhood?

## Strategies and Structures

1. Dillard begins her narrative with an account of learning to play football and other boys' games. Why is this introduction necessary to the PLOT of the story?

2. As the chase unfolds, Dillard steadily increases the tension between the adversar-ies. How? Give examples from the text.

3. Dillard gives only the beginning of the victor's lecture, "You stupid kids" (18). Why doesn't she quote his whole speech?

4. What does the young Dillard learn by imagining different outcomes to the chase? What does this lesson reveal about her PURPOSE for writing?

5. *Other Methods.* Dillard's narrative includes vivid DESCRIPTION. Imagine the chase scene without the descriptive detail—of a perfect iceball, for instance, or of what the man was wearing. How does such description contribute to the point Dillard is making in this essay? What do you think that point is?

## Thinking about Language

1. What is "righteous anger" (20)? How does it differ from other kinds? Why is such anger "normal" in the time and place that Dillard is describing (20)?

2. What is the meaning of "perfunctorily" (18, 19)? Why is the word appropriate?

3. They were "the only players," says Dillard, when the chase comes to an end (16). In what sense(s) is she using the word *players* here? How is she using "grove" (16)?

## FOR WRITING

1. Did you ever get in trouble while playing a childhood sport or game? Write a paragraph about what happened.

2. Write a narrative about an early childhood encounter in which adults did not behave as you expected them to. Be careful to establish a consistent **POINT OF VIEW**, whether that of a child or of an adult looking back—or both, as Dillard does.

3. Write a narrative in which the setting is your old neighborhood. Show and tell the reader about something that you and your friends typically did there. Write as an adult looking back, but try to capture your point of view as a child as well.

4. In a **RHETORICAL ANALYSIS** of 400–500 words, compare and contrast young Annie Dillard with young Marjane Satrapi in "Kim Wilde" (pp. 130–38). Discuss them both as people and as characters in a narrative.

5. Collaborate with a friend or classmate in writing and comparing narratives of growing up in different places. Consider focusing on similar events, such as a trip to the beach or a family meal. Share your narratives and, in writing, compare the differences.

You'll find quizzes on the readings at
wwnorton.com/write/back-to-the-lake.

DREW HANSEN

# "Tell Them about the Dream, Martin!"

Drew Hansen (b. 1972) is a lawyer practicing in Seattle; in 2012, he was elected to the Washington State House of Representatives. A graduate of Harvard, Hansen studied theology as a Rhodes Scholar at Oxford (England), later earning his law degree from Yale. He is the author of *The Dream: Martin Luther King, Jr., and the Speech That Inspired a Nation* (2003).

Martin Luther King Jr. delivered his famous "I Have a Dream" speech at the Lincoln Memorial in Washington, D.C., on August 28, 1963, before a crowd of about 250,000 people. It was one of the first mass demonstrations to be covered by television; and by late afternoon, according to Hansen, some speakers thought "the TV crews would leave to process their film for the evening news." This is why, vying for the spotlight, organizers of the event pushed King's speech to the end of a long day. In the version given to the press, King did not even include the "I have a dream" language; and before his time came to speak, the tired audience was packing up to go home. According to Hansen's narrative of the lesser known events of that day, these circumstances were altered—and history made—by the timely intervention of the great gospel singer Mahalia Jackson, who also had a late slot on the program. "Tell Them about the Dream, Martin!" (editor's title) appeared as an Op-Ed in the *New York Times* in August 2013.

T HE REV. DR. MARTIN LUTHER KING JR.'S SPEECH at the March on Washington   1
for Jobs and Freedom in 1963 was unusual among great American speeches in that its most famous words—"I have a dream"—were improvised.

King had certainly thought about using the "dream" refrain in Washington. He   2
had been fine-tuning it earlier that year. In April, in Birmingham, Alabama, deputies of the public safety commissioner, Eugene Connor, known as Bull, attended a mass meeting at the 16th Street Baptist Church, where they reported that King "said that he had a dream of seeing little Negro boys and girls walking to school with little white boys and girls, playing in the parks together and going swimming together."

When you go back in time in a narrative, be sure to use appropriate verb tenses, p. 105.

MLA CITATION: Hansen, Drew. "Tell Them about the Dream, Martin!" 2013. *Back to the Lake*. Ed. Thomas Cooley. 3rd ed. New York: Norton, 2015. 147–50. Print.

And in June, King electrified an audience at Cobo Hall in Detroit, saying: "I   3
have a dream this afternoon that one day, right here in Detroit, Negroes will be
able to buy a house or rent a house anywhere that their money will carry them and
they will be able to get a job."

But King thought he wouldn't have time to use the "dream" language at the   4
March. He had asked his advisers to prepare drafts—an unusual move, as King
typically didn't do more than jot down a few notes on the back of a church bulletin
before speaking—and he liked a "bad check" metaphor in one of the drafts, which
would support an argument that America had failed to fulfill its promises of liberty
and equality to black citizens. He didn't think he could fit both that and the
"dream" refrains into the five minutes allotted to each speaker. Walter E. Fauntroy,
one of King's advisers, counseled him not to worry about the time limits. "Look,
Martin," he said, "you do what the spirit say do."

When King arrived at the Willard Hotel in Washington the night before the   5
march, he still didn't have a complete draft. King called his aides together in the
lobby, and they started arguing about what should go in the speech. One wanted
King to talk about jobs, another wanted him to talk about housing discrimination.
Finally King said: "My brothers, I understand. I appreciate all the suggestions. Now
let me go and counsel with the Lord."

King went up to his room and spent the night writing the speech in longhand.   6
Andrew Young stopped by and saw that King had crossed out words three and four
times, trying to find the right rhythm, as if he were writing poetry. King finished at
about 4 in the morning and handed the manuscript to his aides so it could be typed
up and distributed to the press. The speech did not include the words "I have a
dream."

King awoke the next morning to the disappointing news that the crowds at the   7
March were smaller than expected. "About 25,000," the television reporters were
saying, as King left the hotel. Bayard Rustin, the march's chief organizer, was standing at the Washington Monument, where reporters pressed him about why so few
people had shown up. Rustin looked intently at a yellow legal pad in his hand. "Gentlemen," he said, "everything is going exactly according to plan." One of Rustin's
aides looked over his shoulder and saw that the pad Rustin was looking at was blank.

But at Union Station, buses and trains were coming in regularly, swelling crowds   8
that some onlookers compared to those that had gathered at the end of World War
II. Train No. 42 of the Southern Railroad, which had carried Medgar Evers's body
to Washington two months earlier, arrived full of marchers. A "Freedom Special,"
chartered from Florida, pulled in and discharged nearly 800 young people singing
a massed chorus of "We Shall Overcome."

By late morning, the lawns around the Washington Monument were packed   9
with people, many of whom opened up the box lunches they had prepared (no may-

onnaise, the march organizers had warned—it might spoil) and started to picnic. Then, around 11 a.m., some people began walking to the Lincoln Memorial, more followed, and soon most of the crowd was on its way. This surprised Rustin, who had planned for the leaders of the major civil rights groups to lead the way to the Memorial. "My God, they're going!" he shouted. "We're supposed to be leading them!" He hustled the leaders together, and they joined hands at a break in the middle of the crowd, with most of the marchers already far ahead.

There was a long afternoon program of songs and speeches at the Lincoln Memo- 10 rial. King had the last speaking slot—not just because he was a hard act to follow, but because some other speakers thought they might get better coverage if they spoke earlier in the day. (By late afternoon, some leaders believed, the TV crews would leave to process their film for the evening news.) As the program went on, people packed up and started to walk away. Many had spent several days and nights on buses and trains to Washington, and they were tired and ready to head home.

Then A. Philip Randolph, the 74-year-old initiator of the march, who had secured 11 an executive order on nondiscrimination in defense-industry employment and contracts by pressuring President Franklin D. Roosevelt with a threat of a march on Washington in 1941, introduced the gospel singer Mahalia Jackson. She sang two

Mahalia Jackson sings on the steps of the Lincoln Memorial during the March on Washington. (Martin Luther King Jr. is at the lower-right-hand corner.)

spirituals, "I Been 'Buked and I Been Scorned" and "How I Got Over." King was seated nearby, clapping his hands on his knees and calling out to her as she sang. Roger Mudd, covering the event for CBS News, said after the first song: "Mahalia Jackson. And all the speeches in the world couldn't have brought the response that just came from the hymns she sang. Miss Mahalia Jackson." Then, after a speech by Rabbi Joachim Prinz, from the American Jewish Congress, it was King's turn to speak.

King read from his prepared text for most of his speech, which relied on the 12 Bible, the Constitution and the Declaration of Independence—just as President John F. Kennedy had a few months earlier, when he called for civil rights legislation in a nationally televised address: "We are confronted primarily with a moral issue. It is as old as the Scriptures and is as clear as the American Constitution."

As King neared the end, he came to a sentence that wasn't quite right. He had 13 planned to introduce his conclusion with a call to "go back to our communities as members of the international association for the advancement of creative dissatisfaction." He skipped that, read a few more lines, and then improvised: "Go back to Mississippi; go back to Alabama; go back to South Carolina; go back to Georgia; go back to Louisiana; go back to the slums and ghettos of our Northern cities, knowing that somehow this situation can and will be changed."

See p. 106 for tips on adding dialogue to a narrative.

Nearby, off to one side, Mahalia Jackson shouted: "Tell them about the 14 dream, Martin!" King looked out over the crowd. As he later explained in an interview, "all of a sudden this thing came to me that I have used—I'd used many times before, that thing about 'I have a dream'—and I just felt that I wanted to use it here." He said, "I say to you today, my friends, so even though we face the difficulties of today and tomorrow, I still have a dream." And he was off, delivering some of the most beloved lines in American history, a speech that he never intended to give and that some of the other civil rights leaders believed no one but the marchers would ever remember. ◆

## FOR CLOSE READING

1. What was "unusual," according to Drew Hansen, about the composition of Martin Luther King's "I Have a Dream" speech as he delivered it in Washington in 1963 (1)? In what ways was the process simply normal procedure for King himself?

2. Why would a singer, especially of blues and spirituals, be a likely collaborator for an orator on such an occasion as Hansen reconstructs in "Tell Them about the Dream, Martin!"?

3. In Hansen's account, Jackson urges King forward in his performance by reminding him of "the dream" (14). Where and how did King support Jackson in *her* performance?

4. On the day that Hansen tells about, King's speech came last in the order events, after people were getting "tired and ready to head home" (10). How else, besides reminding him of the dream, did Mahalia Jackson help to save the day for the reception of King's speech?

5. The 1963 marchers on Washington were advised not to use mayonnaise on their sandwiches because it might spoil (9). Is Hansen justified in reporting such a minor detail in his narrative of such an important historical event? Why or why not?

## Strategies and Structures

1. What is Hansen's main purpose in retelling the story of the day King delivered his famous speech? What point is he making about the speech that can't be gleaned from simply watching a video of the event on *YouTube*? Where and how does he make that point most effectively?

2. King's usual method of composing a speech, according to Hansen, was to "jot down a few notes on the back of a church bulletin before speaking" (4). What are some of the advantages and disadvantages of this method of composition?

3. "Tell them about the dream, Martin!" is not the only direct quotation in Hansen's essay. Where else does Hansen incorporate bits of dialogue, and what do they contribute to his narrative?

4. The March on Washington occurred on a single day in 1963. How and where does Hansen depart from the CHRONOLOGY of that day to bring ideas and events into his narrative from other times and places? Where and why does he stick closely to the order of events on August 28?

5. *Other Methods.* How, and how well, does Hansen DESCRIBE the physical setting and the people in his narrative? Point to specific details in the text that help to capture the look and feel of the particular time and place he is writing about.

## Thinking about Language

1. In an earlier speech in Detroit, King's "dream" may have gotten the attention of his audience; but they were not literally "electrified" by it (3). Why are such metaphors nonetheless common in descriptions of speeches and other performances? Under what circumstances might a critic say that a performer "electrocuted" the audience?

2. Why does Hansen refer to the theme of racial equality in King's speeches as a "refrain" (2)? Where does the term come from, and how does it apply to writing speeches, especially when the writer "crosses out words three and four times" (6).

3. Why do you think King liked the "bad check" METAPHOR to which Hansen refers in paragraph 4? What does his including it in the speech suggest about King's sense of his audience?

4. Where and how does Hansen himself use the repetition and rhythms of music or poetry in the language of his narrative? Cite several specific examples from the text.

## FOR WRITING

1. Videos of King's delivery of his speech on August 28, 1963, are all over the internet. Watch the one on the links page at wwnorton.com/write/back-to-the-lake, and write an objective, third-person narrative of the event as if you were reporting it for a newspaper. Cite specific words and phrases (such as "I have a dream") in your report—as well as the speaker's key points and ideas.

2. In a brainstorming session with several of your classmates, enumerate and discuss some of the differences—including the possibilities for improvisation—between *hearing* a text (as in a presented speech, lecture, or sermon) and *reading* a text. In a paragraph or two, present the conclusions of your discussion, perhaps using oral and written versions of King's (or someone else's) speech as an example.

3. In a journal or notebook, record your experiences, over time, in listening to a particular lecturer, speaker, or commentator—whether on campus or in the media—whom you find to be particularly effective (or ineffective). Write a narrative illustrating and commenting on that person's characteristic use of specific verbal techniques and devices.

4. Write an EVALUATION of King's "I Have a Dream" speech in which you explain what makes it one of "the great American speeches" (1)—or, alternatively, why you think the speech is overrated.

5. Write a review of Drew Hansen's book, *Martin Luther King, Jr., and the Speech That Inspired a Nation* (2003). Your review should focus on how and how well Hansen tells the story of King's speech—and argues the case for its historic and literary significance.

........................................................................

You'll find quizzes on the readings at
wwnorton.com/write/back-to-the-lake.

ANNE BERNAYS

# Warrior Day

Anne Bernays (b. 1930) is a novelist and teacher of writing at Harvard. She is married to Justin Kaplan, the editor mentioned in her essay, who is the author of several biographies of major figures in American literature. Grandniece of Sigmund Freud, the father of psychoanalysis, Bernays attended Wellesley and graduated from Barnard College in 1952. Her novels include *Professor Romeo* (1989) and *Trophy House* (2005).

In "Warrior Day," which appeared in the "Lives" feature of the *New York Times Magazine* in 2009, Bernays tells the story of attending her grandson's graduation from the Basic School for young Marine officers at Quantico, Virginia. Narrating her experience in the third person, Bernays captures both the events of the visit, such as her firing an M-16 on the rifle range, and her conflicting emotions toward those events.

T HIS IS THE TRUE STORY of a dyed-in-the-wool pacifist Jewish woman who recently spent two days at the Marine Corps Base at Quantico, Virginia, and survived, almost intact.

Years earlier she was a sure-footed young New Yorker with liberal convictions. She married an introverted editor, moved to Cambridge, Massachusetts, and began raising three daughters. What a delightful life they led. The "best schools." No money worries. The Vietnam War was raging, and the woman roiled in opposition to it, but she didn't feel she could leave her children to protest.

Skip ahead more than a decade—during which the life of this family ran as smoothly as a Rolls Royce. The oldest daughter married a man who renovated houses, and they bought their own near Boston. Within five years they had two sons. David, the oldest, was a solid, handsome athlete who also excelled academically. He went to a college in Maine, where he did well in his studies and played on the football team. After school, Dave took a management-track job with a construction company. Then one day he announced he was joining the Marines.

Use a flash-forward (p. 105) when you need to skip ahead.

This was a blow to the first woman (now referred to as "the grandmother"). She couldn't conceive of anyone wanting to do this; it seemed as exotic and unsettling as if he had joined a monastery.

MLA CITATION: Bernays, Anne. "Warrior Day." 2009. *Back to the Lake*. Ed. Thomas Cooley. 3rd ed. New York: Norton, 2015. 153–55. Print.

Dave's graduation from the Basic School at Quantico (which the grandmother   5
referred to silently as Guantánamo) took place this spring. His mother and
grandparents flew down together on a Tuesday. The grandmother was filled with
trepidation. The schedule: Wednesday, Warrior Day; Thursday, graduation.

Greeting them, Dave peppered his language with initials: P.O.V.; I.O.C.[1] They   6
passed through a checkpoint, and an enlisted man saluted Dave, whose new lieutenant's bars shone. They walked along a corridor with posters and legends—
reminders that marines always act in exemplary ways. Dave's "bedroom" was the
size of a walk-in closet: there were bunk beds and a sink. Another room held desks
and a small refrigerator. His roommates were ordinary, bright twenty-somethings,
only more polite.

No time for breakfast. In a filled auditorium, a colonel welcomed them. He   7
referred to himself as a teacher and the trainees as students. Quantico was a "campus." The course was divided into segments: leadership; academics; military skills.
The men were being trained not to be soldiers or marines but "warfighters."

Next on the agenda: the firing range. Sitting on bleachers, the visitors were   8
instructed in how to "employ the weapon system," meaning how to shoot an M-16
rifle. The grandmother was issued a flak jacket, a Kevlar helmet and two little
things she first thought were candies but turned out to be earplugs. A warrior
helped her hold up her M-16. She pulled the trigger and hit the target five times.
She felt a rush of excitement that embarrassed her. Later they saw an amphibious
tank, an "up-armored" Humvee and a captured Iraqi tank, all beat up. Someone
asked Dave why his dog tag was on the tongue of his boot, under the laces. He said,
"You don't want to know."

Graduation Day. At 6:30 a.m. they drove to Dave's barracks, but then he phoned   9
his mother to say that he was delayed by an unspecified snafu. Waiting for him, the
family saw one marine drop the white dress pants he was carrying onto the wet
pavement. Another, in his dress uniform, dragged a vacuum cleaner. The grandmother found this almost unbearably poignant. Finally Dave appeared, smiling. It
took him 45 minutes to put on his dress uniform. "There are lots of suspenders and
straps and things that hold the thing together," he explained. The grandmother
recaptured a moment when, as a girl, she had a brief romance with a West Point
cadet; his uniform was irresistible.

P.O.I.; A.A.V.; P.A.O. The graduation ceremony was S.R.O.[2] Dave came in 11th in   10
a class of 282, making him an honor graduate. He would be a platoon commander.

---

1. *I.O.C.*: Infantry officer candidate. *P.O.V.*: Privately owned vehicle. Both acronyms are used in processing visitors through the checkpoint.

2. *S.R.O.*: Standing-room only; a nonmilitary acronym. *P.A.O.*: Public affairs officer. *A.A.V.*: Amphibious
assault vehicle. *P.O.I.*: Program of instruction at Basic School.

How could the grandmother's heart not swell with pride? Conflicting emotions swirled within. The speeches were crisp and to the point. Marines possessed the warrior spirit; had character and integrity; upheld the highest standards.

Each new second lieutenant, six platoons of them, walked straight-backed across the stage to receive his or her diploma. The women, more than a sprinkling, looked smart and self-conscious. The Marine brass band played beautifully. Dispersal. Picture-taking.                                                                                    11

"You know," Dave told his grandmother, "I'm responsible for the lives of 40 men." ◆                                                                                         12

## FOR CLOSE READING

1. Anne Bernays begins her narrative by announcing that she is a "pacifist" (1). What bearing does this information have upon her story?

2. Why is the grandmother embarrassed by the "rush of excitement" she feels when she hits the target with an M-16 rifle (8)? Where else in her narrative does Bernays exhibit conflicting emotions? What are some of them?

3. What causes the grandmother to recall her youthful romance with a West Point cadet (9)?

4. To what extent, if any, do the grandmother's attitudes toward the military and her grandson's career choice change or develop as a result of the experience she writes about here?

## Strategies and Structures

1. Whose story is this? The grandmother's? Her grandson Dave's? The Marine Corps'? Explain.

2. Throughout her narrative, Bernays speaks of herself in the THIRD PERSON as "the grandmother." Why do you think she uses this POINT OF VIEW instead for the more conventional FIRST-PERSON "I"?

3. Most of the events in Bernays' narrative are presented in CHRONOLOGICAL ORDER. Point out several examples, and note the time tags she uses—such as "next on the agenda" (8).

4. Bernays composes her narrative mostly in short sentences and phrases—like notations in a diary. What effect does this brisk style have on the pace of events in her story and on her presentation of herself as a participant in those events?

5. Bernays focuses on the two days she spent with her family at Quantico. Where and why does she use a FLASHBACK to widen the time frame of her narrative?

6. Bernays ends her narrative with a line of DIALOGUE spoken by her grandson, a new Marine Corps second lieutenant. Why do you think she gives him the last word in the story?

7. *Other Methods.* How and where does Bernays COMPARE her actual experience of military life with what she had expected it to be like?

## Thinking about Language

1. Why does Bernays pepper her narrative with acronyms like "P.O.V." and "S.R.O." (6, 10)? Should she have explained what they stand for? Why or why not?

2. Bernays, a novelist, finds the pre-graduation scene in Dave's barracks to be "unbearably poignant" (9). Why? What are the implications of this phrase?

3. As a pacifist during the Vietnam War era, Bernays says she "roiled in opposition" to the conflict (2). Why might Bernays have chosen this phrase to describe her feelings instead of simply saying that she was opposed to the war?

4. Bernays compares the course of her family life to the running of a Rolls Royce (3). What are the implications of this SIMILE?

## FOR WRITING

1. Make a list, in chronological order, of the principal events leading up to a graduation or other formal ceremony that you participated in. Group the events on your list into "scenes."

2. Recount a "true story" about a ceremonial occasion—such as a graduation, wedding, or memorial service—that you witnessed or took part in. Show how and where the actual events of the experience met (or conflicted with) your expectations.

3. Write a RHETORICAL ANALYSIS explaining how Bernays's narrative would have been different if it were written in the more conventional first person; speculate on why she might have chosen a third-person point of view for a personal narrative.

You'll find quizzes on the readings at wwnorton.com/write/back-to-the-lake.

Richard Russo (b. 1949) is a novelist and the author of, among other works, *Nobody's Fool* (1993); *Empire Falls* (2001), which received the Pulitzer Prize in fiction; and *Elsewhere: A Memoir* (2012). His latest novel is *That Old Cape Magic* (2009). Before he turned exclusively to writing, Russo taught fiction writing at Southern Illinois University and Colby College.

Out of this experience came his academic novel, *Straight Man* (1997), about William Henry Devereaux Jr., the son of two English professors and himself the chair of the English department at the mythical West Central Pennsylvania University. "Dog," which first appeared as a short story in the *New Yorker* in 1996, is the prologue to that novel. In "Dog" we return to the narrator's childhood. His parents are in the process of splitting up, though their son doesn't know it yet. All he wants is a dog, and he sets out relentlessly to get one. As you'll see, though, this is far more than a boy-meets-dog narrative.

They're nice to have. A dog. —F. Scott Fitzgerald, *The Great Gatsby*

TRUTH BE TOLD, I'm not an easy man. I can be an entertaining one, though it's 1 been my experience that most people don't want to be entertained. They want to be comforted. And, of course, my idea of entertaining might not be yours. I'm in complete agreement with all those people who say, regarding movies, "I just want to be entertained." This populist position is much derided by my academic colleagues as simpleminded and unsophisticated, evidence of questionable analytical and critical acuity. But I agree with the premise, and I too just want to be entertained. That I am almost never entertained by what entertains *other* people who just want to be entertained doesn't make us philosophically incompatible. It just means we shouldn't go to movies together.

> Always consider your purpose and audience (p. 99) when you start a narrative.

The kind of man I am, according to those who know me best, is exasperating. 2 According to my parents, I was an exasperating child as well. They divorced when I was in junior high school, and they agree on little except that I was an impossible

MLA CITATION: Russo, Richard. "Dog." 1996. *Back to the Lake.* Ed. Thomas Cooley. 3rd ed. New York: Norton, 2015. 157-62. Print.

child. The story they tell of young William Henry Devereaux, Jr., and his first dog is eerily similar in its facts, its conclusions, even the style of its telling, no matter which of them is telling it. Here's the story they tell.

I was nine, and the house we were living in, which belonged to the university, was my fourth. My parents were academic nomads, my father, then and now, an academic opportunist, always in the vanguard of whatever was trendy and chic in literary criticism. This was the fifties, and for him, New Criticism[1] was already old. In early middle age he was already a full professor with several published books, all of them "hot," the subject of intense debate at English department cocktail parties. The academic position he favored was the "distinguished visiting professor" variety, usually created for him, duration of visit a year or two at most, perhaps because it's hard to remain distinguished among people who know you. Usually his teaching responsibilities were light, a course or two a year. Otherwise, he was expected to read and think and write and publish and acknowledge in the preface of his next book the generosity of the institution that provided him the academic good life. My mother, also an English professor, was hired as part of the package deal, to teach a full load and thereby help balance the books.

The houses we lived in were elegant, old, high-ceilinged, drafty, either on or close to campus. They had hardwood floors and smoky fireplaces with fires in them only when my father held court, which he did either on Friday afternoons, our large rooms filling up with obsequious junior faculty and nervous grad students, or Saturday evenings, when my mother gave dinner parties for the chair of the department, or the dean, or a visiting poet. In all situations I was the only child, and I must have been a lonely one, because what I wanted more than anything in the world was a dog.

Predictably, my parents did not. Probably the terms of living in these university houses were specific regarding pets. By the time I was nine I'd been lobbying hard for a dog for a year or two. My father and mother were hoping I would outgrow this longing, given enough time. I could see this hope in their eyes and it steeled my resolve, intensified my desire. What did I want for Christmas? A dog. What did I want for my birthday? A dog. What did I want on my ham sandwich? A dog. It was a deeply satisfying look of pure exasperation they shared at such moments, and if I couldn't have a dog, this was the next best thing.

Life continued in this fashion until finally my mother made a mistake, a doozy of a blunder born of emotional exhaustion and despair. She, far more than my father, would have preferred a happy child. One spring day after I'd been badgering her pretty relentlessly she sat me down and said, "You know, a dog is something

1. *New Criticism*: A twentieth-century literary theory in America and Britain that stressed the close reading of texts.

you earn." My father heard this, got up, and left the room, grim acknowledgment that my mother had just conceded the war. Her idea was to make the dog conditional. The conditions to be imposed would be numerous and severe, and I would be incapable of fulfilling them, so when I didn't get the dog it'd be my own fault. This was her logic, and the fact that she thought such a plan might work illustrates that some people should never be parents and that she was one of them.

I immediately put into practice a plan of my own to wear my mother down. 7 Unlike hers, my plan was simple and flawless. Mornings I woke up talking about dogs and nights I fell asleep talking about them. When my mother and father changed the subject, I changed it back. "Speaking of dogs," I would say, a forkful of my mother's roast poised at my lips, and I'd be off again. Maybe no one *had* been speaking of dogs, but never mind, we were speaking of them now. At the library I checked out a half dozen books on dogs every two weeks and left them lying open around the house. I pointed out dogs we passed on the street, dogs on television, dogs in the magazines my mother subscribed to. I discussed the relative merits of various breeds at every meal. My father seldom listened to anything I said, but I began to see signs that the underpinnings of my mother's personality were beginning to corrode in the salt water of my tidal persistence, and when I judged that she was nigh to complete collapse, I took every penny of the allowance money I'd been saving and spent it on a dazzling, bejeweled dog collar and leash set at the overpriced pet store around the corner.

During this period when we were constantly "speaking of dogs," I was not a 8 model boy. I was supposed to be "earning a dog," and I was constantly checking with my mother to see how I was doing, just how much of a dog I'd earned, but I doubt my behavior had changed a jot. I wasn't really a bad boy. Just a noisy, busy, constantly needy boy. Mr. In and Out, my mother called me, because I was in and out of rooms, in and out of doors, in and out of the refrigerator. "Henry," my mother would plead with me. "Light somewhere." One of the things I often needed was information, and I constantly interrupted my mother's reading and paper grading to get it. My father, partly to avoid having to answer my questions, spent most of his time in his book-lined office on campus, joining my mother and me only at mealtimes, so that we could speak of dogs as a family. Then he was gone again, blissfully unaware, I thought at the time, that my mother continued to glare homicidally, for long minutes after his departure, at the chair he'd so recently occupied. But he claimed to be close to finishing the book he was working on, and this was a powerful excuse to offer a woman with as much abstract respect for books and learning as my mother possessed.

Gradually, she came to understand that she was fighting a battle she couldn't 9 win and that she was fighting it alone. I now know that this was part of a larger cluster of bitter marital realizations, but at the time I sniffed nothing in the air but victory. In late August, during what people refer to as "the dog days," when she made one last, weak condition, final evidence that I had earned a dog, I relented and truly tried to reform my behavior. It was literally the least I could do.

What my mother wanted of me was to stop slamming the screen door. The 10 house we were living in, it must be said, was an acoustic marvel akin to the Whispering Gallery in St. Paul's, where muted voices travel across a great open space and arrive, clear and intact, at the other side of the great dome. In our house the screen door swung shut on a tight spring, the straight wooden edge of the door encountering the doorframe like a gunshot played through a guitar amplifier set on stun, the crack transmitting perfectly, with equal force and clarity, to every room in the house, upstairs and down. That summer I was in and out that door dozens of times a day, and my mother said it was like living in a shooting gallery. It made her wish the door wasn't shooting blanks. If I could just remember not to slam the door, then she'd see about a dog. Soon.

I did better, remembering about half the time not to let the door slam. When I 11 forgot, I came back in to apologize, sometimes forgetting then too. Still, that I was trying, together with the fact that I carried the expensive dog collar and leash with me everywhere I went, apparently moved my mother, because at the end of that first week of diminished door slamming, my father went somewhere on Saturday morning, refusing to reveal where, and so of course I knew. "What *kind*?" I pleaded with my mother when he was gone. But she claimed not to know. "Your father's doing this," she said, and I thought I saw a trace of misgiving in her expression.

When he returned, I saw why. He'd put it in the backseat, and when my father 12 pulled the car in and parked along the side of the house, I saw from the kitchen window its chin resting on the back of the rear seat. I think it saw me too, but if so it did not react. Neither did it seem to notice that the car had stopped, that my father had gotten out and was holding the front seat forward. He had to reach in, take the dog by the collar, and pull.

As the animal unfolded its long legs and stepped tentatively, arthritically, out of 13 the car, I saw that I had been both betrayed and outsmarted. In all the time we had been "speaking of dogs," what I'd been seeing in my mind's eye was puppies. Collie puppies, beagle puppies, Lab puppies, shepherd puppies, but none of that had been inked anywhere, I now realized. If not a puppy, a young dog. A rascal, full of spirit and possibility, a dog with new tricks to learn. *This* dog was barely ambulatory. It stood, head down, as if ashamed at something done long ago in its puppydom, and I thought I detected a shiver run through its frame when my father closed the car door behind it.

The animal was, I suppose, what might have been called a handsome dog. A 14 purebred, rust-colored Irish setter, meticulously groomed, wonderfully mannered, the kind of dog you could safely bring into a house owned by the university, the sort of dog that wouldn't really violate the no pets clause, the kind of dog, I saw clearly, you'd get if you really didn't want a dog or to be bothered with a dog. It'd belonged, I later learned, to a professor emeritus of the university who'd been put into a nursing home earlier in the week, leaving the animal an orphan. It was like a painting of a dog, or a dog you'd hire to pose for a portrait, a dog you could be sure wouldn't move.

Both my father and the animal came into the kitchen reluctantly, my father closing the screen door behind them with great care. I like to think that on the way home he'd suffered a misgiving, though I could tell that it was his intention to play the hand out boldly. My mother, who'd taken in my devastation at a glance, studied me for a moment and then my father. 15

"What?" he said. 16

My mother just shook her head. 17

My father looked at me, then back at her. A violent shiver palsied the dog's limbs. The animal seemed to want to lie down on the cool linoleum, but to have forgotten how. It offered a deep sigh that seemed to speak for all of us. 18

"He's a good dog," my father said, rather pointedly, to my mother. "A little high-strung, but that's the way with purebred setters. They're all nervous." 19

This was not the sort of thing my father knew. Clearly he was repeating the explanation he'd just been given when he picked up the dog. 20

"What's his name?" my mother said, apparently for something to say. 21

My father had neglected to ask. He checked the dog's collar for clues. 22

"Lord," my mother said. "Lord, lord." 23

"It's not like we can't name him ourselves," my father said, irritated now. "I think it's something we can manage, don't you?" 24

"You could name him after a passé school of literary criticism," my mother suggested. 25

"It's a she," I said, because it was.

It seemed to cheer my father, at least a little, that I'd allowed myself to be drawn into the conversation. "What do you say, Henry?" he wanted to know. "What'll we name him?" 26 27

This second faulty pronoun reference was too much for me. "I want to go out and play now," I said, and I bolted for the screen door before an objection could be registered. It slammed behind me, hard, its gunshot report even louder than usual. As I cleared the steps in a single leap, I thought I heard a thud back in the kitchen, a dull, muffled echo of the door, and then I heard my father say, "What the hell?" I went back up the steps, cautiously now, meaning to apologize for the door. Through the screen I could see my mother and father standing together in the middle of the kitchen, looking down at the dog, which seemed to be napping. My father nudged a haunch with the toe of his cordovan loafer.[2] 28

---

2. *Cordovan loafer:* A style of casual but expensive men's shoes made from fine horse leather.

He dug the grave in the backyard with a shovel borrowed from a neighbor. My   29
father had soft hands and they blistered easily. I offered to help, but he just looked
at me. When he was standing, midthigh, in the hole he'd dug, he shook his head
one last time in disbelief. "Dead," he said. "Before we could even name him."

I knew better than to correct the pronoun again, so I just stood there thinking   30
about what he'd said while he climbed out of the hole and went over to the back
porch to collect the dog where it lay under an old sheet. I could tell by the careful
way he tucked that sheet under the animal that he didn't want to touch anything
dead, even newly dead. He lowered the dog into the hole by means of the
sheet, but he had to drop it the last foot or so. When the animal thudded
on the earth and lay still, my father looked over at me and shook his head.
Then he picked up the shovel and leaned on it before he started filling in
the hole. He seemed to be waiting for me to say something, so I said, "Red."

**A well-plotted story needs to give a clear sense of an ending (p. 104). Thud.**

My father's eyes narrowed, as if I'd spoken in a foreign tongue. "What?" he said.   31

"We'll name her Red," I explained.   32

In the years after he left us, my father became even more famous. He is some-   33
times credited, if credit is the word, with being the Father of American Literary
Theory. In addition to his many books of scholarship, he's also written a literary
memoir that was short-listed for a major award and that offers insight into the personalities of several major literary figures of the twentieth century, now deceased.
His photograph often graces the pages of the literary reviews. He went through a
phase where he wore crewneck sweaters and gold chains beneath his tweed coat,[3]
but now he's mostly photographed in an oxford button-down shirt, tie, and jacket,
in his book-lined office at the university. But to me, his son, William Henry
Devereaux, Sr., is most real standing in his ruined cordovan loafers, leaning on the
handle of a borrowed shovel, examining his dirty, blistered hands, and receiving
my suggestion of what to name a dead dog. I suspect that digging our dog's grave
was one of relatively few experiences of his life (excepting carnal ones) that did not
originate on the printed page. And when I suggested we name the dead dog Red,
he looked at me as if I myself had just stepped from the pages of a book he'd started
to read years ago and then put down when something else caught his interest.
"What?" he said, letting go of the shovel, so that its handle hit the earth between
my feet. "What?"

It's not an easy time for any parent, this moment when the realization dawns   34
that you've given birth to something that will never see things the way you do,
despite the fact that it is your living legacy, that it bears your name.  ◆

---

3. *Crewneck sweaters ... tweed coat:* Tweed coats are stereotypical clothing for professors and other
academics. Crewneck sweaters worn with heavy gold chains were a macho style of the 1970s.

## FOR CLOSE READING

1. Why does Henry want a dog?

2. How and why does young Henry earn the nickname "Mr. In and Out" (8)? How appropriate is the name?

3. What plan does Henry set into motion in paragraph 7? How well does it work?

4. Henry relents from his plan and tries hard not to slam the screen door. What does this change of heart show the reader about his character and personality? What can we make of his final screen-door slam (28)?

## Strategies and Structures

1. Richard Russo's story of a boy and his dog doesn't actually begin until paragraph 4. What is the PURPOSE of the first two paragraphs of the narrative?

2. Where and why does Russo's story engage in a FLASH-FORWARD to a time in the future? How does he bring the story back to the present?

3. Besides telling a boy-meets-dog story, Russo's narrator is also telling the story of how he became "the kind of man I am" (2). What kind of man is he, and what are some of the CAUSES?

4. Russo does not introduce extensive DIALOGUE into his story until paragraph 16. Why do you think he waits until this particular point before letting his characters speak?

5. *Other Methods.* Russo DESCRIBES in detail the "acoustic marvel" of a house in which the Devereaux family is living (10). Why does he pay so much attention to the screen door in particular? Point out other places where Russo's descriptions support the actions of the story.

## Thinking about Language

1. Russo uses the following academic language in paragraph 1: "populist position," "much derided," "questionable analytical and critical acuity," "premise," "philosophically incompatible." Why does he use such language so early in his story?

2. Why does Henry's father refer to the new dog as "he" (19)? What does the boy's reaction to this "faulty pronoun reference" tell you about his upbringing and future (28)? Give examples of other times when Henry challenges his father.

3. When his parents tell the story of him and his first dog, says Henry, the story is "eerily similar in . . . its telling" (2). Why does he consider their mutual agreement about the story to be "eerie"?

## FOR WRITING

1. Write a paragraph or two narrating your efforts to convince your family to acquire a pet or something else you've wanted.

2. Write a narrative essay about something that mattered a lot to you when you were a child—a dog, a doll, a game, etc. Your essay should tell about some memorable incident. Make sure the essay has a beginning, middle, and ending, and choose details that will bring the incident alive for the reader. Be sure to indicate why the incident was significant to you.

3. The writer Annie Proulx has praised Russo for creating characters "as real as we are," ones readers can see "coming out of doorways, lurching through life." Write a narrative essay about some real person you know. Focus on an incident (to be sure you write a narrative, not just a description). Choose details that will give readers a sense of who the person is, and arrange actions carefully to lead readers through the story.

4. "Redemption is always the prize in a Russo story," writes a reviewer in the *Washington Post*. "Nowhere do we see that more clearly than in *Elsewhere*," his memoir of childhood published in 2012. Write a RHETORICAL ANALYSIS of "Dog" (or, alternatively, of *Elsewhere*) as a story of redemption.

5. Read Russo's (or some other person's) MEMOIR and make notes in your journal of your observations and reactions. Consider the author's strategies and techniques of narration as well as those of the memoir as a genre.

· · · · · · · · · · · · · · · · · · · · · · · · · · · · · · · · · · · · · · · · · · · · · · ·

You'll find quizzes on the readings at
wwnorton.com/write/back-to-the-lake.

# CHAPTER 7

# Description

We went fishing the first morning. I felt the same damp moss covering the worms in the bait can, and saw the dragonfly alight on the tip of my rod as it hovered a few inches from the surface of the water.    —E. B. White

In his classic essay "Once More to the Lake," E. B. White writes about going out early one morning in a rowboat with his young son:

> We went fishing the first morning. I felt the same damp moss covering the worms in the bait can, and saw the dragonfly alight on the tip of my rod as it hovered a few inches from the surface of the water. It was the arrival of the fly that convinced me beyond any doubt that everything was as it always had been, that the years were a mirage and that there had been no years. The small waves were the same, chucking the rowboat under the chin as we fished at anchor, and the boat was the same boat, the same color green and the ribs broken in the same places, and under the floorboards the same fresh-water leavings and débris—the dead helgramite, the wisps of moss, the rusty discarded fishhook, the dried blood from yesterday's catch. We stared silently at the tips of our rods, at the dragonflies that came and went. I lowered the tip of mine into the water, tentatively, pensively dislodging the fly, which darted two feet away, poised, darted two feet back, and came to rest again a little farther up the rod.

You can picture the tranquil scene because this passage is a little masterpiece of descriptive writing with every detail carefully chosen to create the illusion of time standing still.

## Telling How Something Looks, Sounds, Feels, Smells, or Tastes

Description appeals to the senses: it gives the reader something to look at (the green boat, the rusty fishhook, the hovering dragonfly); to feel (the damp moss); to hear (the small waves); and to smell (the drying fish blood). As for taste, White appeals more directly to that sense later in his essay, when he and his young son go to a nearby farmhouse for dinner (fried chicken, apple pie). What does a subject look, sound, feel, smell, or taste like? These are the fundamental questions that descriptive writing addresses.

In this chapter we will see where to fish for the specific physical details you need for building a good description. We will examine how to select ones that best suit your PURPOSE and AUDIENCE and how to organize and present those details so they contribute directly to the DOMINANT IMPRESSION you want your description to make.

Then we will review the critical points to watch for as you read back over and revise your description, as well as common errors to avoid as you edit.

## Why Do We Describe?

Description is a means of showing rather than telling. We describe something—a person, a lake, a memory, a chemical reaction—so that the reader can experience it directly as we do. Description makes anything we write less ABSTRACT, or general, and more CONCRETE, referring to specific characteristics we can perceive directly with the senses. White, for example, could simply tell us that time seemed to stand still on the lake, but he makes the abstract idea of timelessness much easier to grasp by showing us such specific details as the dragonfly hovering (like time) at the end of his fishing rod.

## Composing a Description

Your reader will find almost anything you write easier to comprehend if you describe your subject in vivid detail. However, in a personal essay about your grandmother's cooking, you will probably describe things differently than in a lab report on dissecting a shark.

For a journalist's objective description of an unusual star athlete, see p. 209.

There are basically two ways of describing something—objectively or subjectively. An *objective description* presents its subject impartially. Its purpose is to provide the reader with information, as in this description of a watershed in southern Alaska:

> Duck Creek is a small anadromous [running upriver from the sea] fish stream located in an old outwash channel of the Mendenhall Glacier in the center of the most populated residential area of Alaska's capital, Juneau. Duck Creek supports a large over-wintering population of coho salmon juveniles that migrate into the stream each fall from the estuarine wetlands.
>
> —ENVIRONMENTAL PROTECTION AGENCY,
> "Make Way for Salmon in Duck Creek"

The EPA's description is objective not only because it uses precise scientific terms ("anadromous," "estuarine") but because it is made up entirely of factual information about its subject—the size and age of the creek, where it is located, the type of fish that inhabit it, and so on.

# USING DESCRIPTION IN AN ABSTRACT

The following is an abstract (or précis) that accompanied an article on the physical properties of tension springs in the *American Journal of Physics*. It uses description extensively:

A slinky is an example of a tension spring: in an un-stretched state a slinky is collapsed, with turns touching; and a finite tension is required to separate the turns from this state. If a slinky is suspended from its top and stretched under gravity and then released, the bottom of the slinky does not begin to fall until the top section of the slinky, which collapses turn by turn from the top, collides with the bottom. The total collapse time $tc$ (typically ~0:3s for real slinkies) corresponds to the time required for a wave front to propagate down the slinky to communicate the release of the top end. We present a modification to an existing model for a falling tension spring [Calkin, Am. J. Phys. 61, 261–264 (1993)] and apply it to data from filmed drops of two real slinkies. The modification of the model is the inclusion of a finite time for collapse of the turns of the slinky behind the collapse front propagating down the Slinky during the fall.

—R. C. Cross and M. S. Wheatland, "Modeling a Falling Slinky"

*Description of a slinky in an "un-stretched state"*

*Description of a slinky in a "stretched" state*

*Description of a falling slinky released "under gravity"*

*Description of a falling (or fallen) slinky in its final state*

Description is so basic to report writing that one type of summary, the *descriptive abstract*, attempts to capture an entire experiment or project in a single phrase. (The other two types are the *informative abstract*, like the one above, and the *proposal abstract*, which describes what a study, is going to do.) Here, for example, are some brief descriptive abstracts that appeared along with the Slinky study:

Video-based spatial portraits of a nonlinear vibrating string [Am. J. Phys. 80, 862 (2012)]

Exact non-Hookean scaling of cylindrically bent elastic sheets and the large-amplitude pendulum [Am. J. Phys. 79, 657 (2011)]

Strain in layered zinc blende and wurtzite semiconductor structures grown along arbitrary crystallographic directions [Am. J. Phys. 78, 589 (2010)]

Brief (and fascinating) as they are, descriptive abstracts like these can be boiled down even further to a specific category (*portraits, scaling, strain*) followed by an even-more-descriptive phrase.

A *subjective description* provides information, too. But it also conveys the writer's personal response to the subject being described, as in this piece from an article about a visit to the Iowa State Fair:

And then I wound up at an open-air brick pavilion for the llama judging. Llamas are gentle, dignified beasts, and here were four of them being shown by teenagers. The animals' military bearing, heads high, their stately gait, their dark soulful eyes—they looked as if they'd walked straight out of *Dr. Doolittle*. . . . According to a poster, they are raised for "fiber, showing, carting, guardians and companionship." One girl stood by her llama and blew gently on its nose, and he looked lovingly into her eyes. A sort of conversation. If every teenager had his or her own llama, this would be a very different country.        —GARRISON KEILLOR, "A Sunday at the State Fair"

This is a subjective description: the author feels or imagines that the llamas are dignified and loving—and that one is having a "conversation" with his keeper.

However, many of the other details in Keillor's description—including the physical location, the number of llamas on display, who the exhibitors are, and the exact words of the poster explaining what llamas are raised for—are rendered objectively. Most descriptions include a combination of subjective and objective elements. And even the most subjective description should be grounded in the concrete physical features of the person, place, or thing it describes—which is why E. B. White's description of the lake is so effective.

Paul Crenshaw (p. 203) combines both subjective and objective descriptions of the weather.

Not all subjective descriptions are so successful, however. Consider the following passage, which refers to the same lake described by White. According to the region's official website, the area around that lake is "famous for its sparkling scenic streams and chain of seven lakes, its panoramic views of fields, hills and woodlands, its inviting towns and villages."

Sparkling streams, panoramic views. Sounds like a nice place. The same could be said, however, of a large car wash with a picture window in the waiting room. This subjective description offers no definite impression of the lakes because it merely names abstract qualities. So does the rest of the site, which says that the region is "picturesque and welcoming," providing "a retreat for peace and tranquility."

Picturesqueness and tranquility are difficult to smell or taste. The problem with this tourist-brochure prose is that it tells the reader what to think *about* the place; it doesn't capture the place itself. The fundamental purpose of descriptive writing, whether subjective or objective, is to recreate the characteristics of its subject so vividly that readers perceive it with their own eyes and ears—and mind.

Good descriptive writing is built on concrete particulars rather than abstract qualities. So don't just write, "It was a dark and stormy night"; try to make your reader see, hear, and feel the wind and rain.

## Thinking about Purpose and Audience

Your purpose in describing something—whether to picture your subject as objectively as possible, capture it in a certain light or mood, express your feelings about it, persuade the reader to visit (or avoid) it, or merely to amuse the reader—will determine the details you'll want to include in your description. For example, the official Belgrade Lakes website promotes family vacations; like E. B. White, it dwells on the beauty, peace, and tranquility of the place, as well as the fishing and boating. Its slogan—"Where Memories Last a Lifetime"—might almost have been drawn from White's description. The website, however, aims to persuade the general public to visit the area and thus emphasizes "wholesome family fun" and "activities for all ages"—and leaves out the storm clouds that gather in White's description.

PINE ISLAND, BELGRADE LAKES, ME.                                       51807

A postcard of Belgrade Lakes, Maine, c. 1914.

Suppose you were describing Belgrade Lakes to friends who were thinking of going there and wanted information about the area. You might express your feelings toward the region, but your main purpose would be to inform your friends about it—as objectively as possible—so they could decide for themselves whether or not to go. You would talk about the peace and quiet, of course; but you would also include other aspects of the scene, such as the pebble beaches, touristy shops, and local restaurants—not to mention the night crawlers at the Pickled Trout Saloon. Instead of selecting details that presented only one aspect of the place, you would choose representative details that painted a fair and accurate picture of what it was like as a whole.

Whatever your purpose, you need to take into account how much your audience already knows (or does not know) about the subject you are describing. For example, if you want to describe to someone who has never been on your campus the mad rush that takes place there when classes change, you're going to have to fill in the background for them: the main quadrangle with its sun worshipers in bathing suits, the brick-and-stone classroom buildings on either side, the library looming at one end. On the other hand, if you were to describe this same scene to fellow students who already know the territory well, you could skip the background description and go directly to the mob scene.

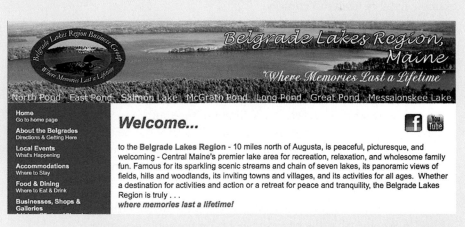

*Three ways of looking at a lake.* This website—like the old postcard on p. 170 and E. B. White's classic essay "Once More to the Lake" on p. 219—describes the Belgrade Lakes region of central Maine. All three capture the peace and tranquility of the place; but the two earlier "views" emphasize its remote, timeless qualities, while the website, which can be updated at any time, presents the region as an easily accessible tourist destination.

## Generating Ideas:
## Asking How Something Looks, Sounds, Feels, Smells, or Tastes

Good descriptive writing begins and ends with the concrete physical characteristics of whatever you are describing. To gather those details, you need to ask what your subject looks, sounds, feels, smells, or tastes like. Methods like BRAINSTORMING and LISTING can help you probe for ideas as you run through each of the five senses.

Another resource for answering these questions is direct experience and observation. Even if you are describing a familiar subject—a lake you've often visited, your old neighborhood, a person from your hometown—go back to the source. Try to see your subject objectively as well as subjectively; take notes—much like a reporter on assignment, or a traveler in a strange land.

Judith Ortiz Cofer (p. 197) draws on memories of her grandmother's house in Puerto Rico.

One of your richest sources of ideas for a description, especially if you are describing something from the past, is memory. Ask others—friends, parents—to help you remember things accurately and truthfully. Let's assume you're describing your hometown. Pick a spot, maybe the main shopping street or town square. Ask yourself what it looked like, and in your mind's eye, try to see specific details: colors, landmarks, signs on the buildings. Then try to recall sounds, smells, textures—and what you did there. As sensations stand out in your memory, let them dominate your description. This example recalls a town in Kentucky:

> Food was better in town, we thought. It wasn't plain and everyday. The centers of pleasure were there—the hamburger and barbecue places, the movie shows, all the places to buy things. Woolworth's, with the pneumatic tubes overhead rushing money along a metallic mole tunnel up to a balcony; Lochridge & Ridgway, with an engraved sign on the third-story cornice: STOVES, APPLIANCES, PLOWS. . . . A circuit of the courthouse square took you past the grand furniture stores, the two dime stores, the shoe stores, the men's stores, the ladies' stores, the banks, the drugstores. You'd walk past the poolroom and an exhaust fan would blow the intoxicating smell of hamburgers in your face. —BOBBIE ANN MASON, "Being Country"

What makes this description so vivid is the specific details—the pneumatic tubes in Woolworth's, the engraved words on the appliance store.

For a photograph of the courthouse square at the period Mason describes, see p. 511.

How did the writer generate such details? As she searched her memory, we can imagine Mason asking herself, "What *did* the place look like exactly? What did it sound like? What did it smell and taste like?" Many writers find that tastes and smells are particularly evocative. In fact, it is the "intoxicating" smell of hamburgers from the poolroom that provides the high point of Mason's description—and that may have brought the place to life for her as she searched her memory for ideas.

The pond of memory is a rich reservoir of sensations for the writer of description. The process of recovering its treasures is a little like fishing: think back to the spots you knew well; bait the hook by asking the key sensory questions; weigh and measure everything you pull up. As you revise, you can always throw back the ones you can't use. Just the right details for capturing your subject on paper *are* lurking there, often in plain sight—or just below the surface. Your job as a writer is to bring those details to light, with the life still in them.

## Organizing and Drafting a Description

Once you've gathered the specific details that capture your subject, you're ready to begin organizing and drafting. As you write, let those details speak for themselves. Give enough of them so that readers can picture your subject clearly, but select and arrange particular details so they contribute to the dominant impression you want your description to make. Maintain a consistent vantage point throughout and, of course, let readers know the point of your description. The templates on p. 175 can help you get started with your draft.

### STATING YOUR POINT

Description is seldom an end in itself. Ordinarily, we describe something to someone for a reason. Why are you describing a particular fishing trip, or a woman hanging out laundry, or bloody footprints in the snow? You need to let the reader know. It can be by way of an explicit THESIS statement: "This description of Washington's ragged army at Yorktown shows that the American general faced many of the same challenges as Napoleon in the winter battle for Moscow, but Washington turned them to his advantage."

Or your reasons can be stated less formally. Consider the following description of the streets of Havana, Cuba:

> Everywhere I went, there were men and women waiting in lines. There were lines to get water, lines to have cheap cigarette lighters repaired, lines to get into the city's lone merchandise store in Miramar where a simple sledgehammer cost fifty-six dollars. At the nationalized health care clinics, the lines wrapped away for blocks; the somber aged, the ill, the expectant young mothers, all waiting, patiently enduring.
>
> —RANDY WAYNE WHITE, *Last Flight Out*

The point of this description is to show that everyday life is difficult in a Communist system where everything is centrally controlled, including simple consumer goods and services. Randy Wayne White is writing a descriptive travel essay, however, not a political treatise. So he states his point informally, as a personal observation: "A few weeks of living like that, and I myself—not the bravest of men—would consider worming into an inner tube and paddling north."

See how E. B. White does this with a single chilling phrase (p. 224, ¶13).

You don't always have to make a formal statement of your thesis—"Communism failed as a social system because it failed as an economic system"—when you write a description. But you *should* include a clear statement, however informal, of why you're writing the description.

## BEGINNING WITH DETAILS

One way *not* to begin a description is to leap immediately into a general statement of the impression your subject is supposed to make. Instead, you should begin with specific descriptive details, and let your readers form that impression for themselves. The following statement, for example, would not be the best way to begin a description of the Grand Canyon: "As the abyss yawned at my feet, I was swept away by the beauty and majesty of the scene."

Few writers have taught us this lesson better than Ernest Hemingway, whose stories and newspaper correspondence are full of powerful descriptions that show us a place or object long before telling us what to think of it. Here's Hemingway's rendition of a father and son fishing on a lake early in the morning:

> They were seated in the boat, Nick in the stern, his father rowing. The sun was coming up over the hills. A bass jumped, making a circle in the water. Nick trailed his hand in the water. It felt warm in the sharp chill of the morning.                          —ERNEST HEMINGWAY, "Indian Camp"

The boy in the story, Nick Adams, has just witnessed a grisly suicide. As Nick and his father row home, the boy is soothed by the morning sun, the leaping bass, and the warm water. Nature seems kind, and the story ends with a direct statement of what the boy thinks about the scene: "In the early morning on the lake sitting in the stern of the boat with his father rowing, he felt quite sure that he would never die."

The purpose of Hemingway's description is to show us the boy's naïveté. However, Hemingway does not deliver the punch line—the boy's stated feeling about the scene—until he has given us the physical details on which that feeling is based. You could organize an entire descriptive essay on this model: detail (early morning), detail (lake), detail (boat), detail (boy sitting in the stern), detail (father rowing)—dominant impression (boy feeling "quite sure he would never die").

# TEMPLATES FOR DRAFTING

When you begin to draft a description, you need to identify who or what you're describing, say what your subject looks or feels like, and indicate the traits you plan to focus on—moves fundamental to any description. See how Judith Ortiz Cofer makes such moves in the beginning of her essay in this chapter:

> My grandmother's house is like a chambered nautilus; it has many rooms, yet is not a mansion. Its proportions are small and its design simple. —JUDITH ORTIZ COFER, "More Room"

Ortiz Cofer identifies what she's describing ("my grandmother's house"); says something about what her subject looks like ("a chambered nautilus"); and indicates some of the physical characteristics (the proportions and design of the house) that she plans to discuss. Here is one more example from this chapter:

> I stood on the steps with my father as he pointed in the distance, where a dark funnel coiled downward from the black clouds, like smoke, or wind taking shape and color. At the base of the tornado dust and debris hovered, circling slowly, and I heard the sound of storm for the first time. It grew out of air, out of wind. It seemed as silent as noise can be, a faint howling that reached us over the rain, almost peaceful from a distance. —PAUL CRENSHAW, "Storm Country"

The following templates can help you make some of these basic moves in your own writing. But don't take these as formulas where you just fill in the blanks. There are no shortcuts to good writing, but these templates can serve as starting points.

▶ X is like a _____; it has _____, _____, and _____.

▶ He / she looked a lot like _____, except for _____, which _____.

▶ From the perspective of _____, however, X could be described as _____.

▶ In some ways, namely _____, X resembles _____; but in other ways, X is more like _____.

▶ X is not at all like _____ because _____.

▶ Mainly because of _____ and _____, X gives the impression of being _____.

▶ From this description of X, you can see that _____.

## CREATING A DOMINANT IMPRESSION

Some descriptions, such as Hemingway's, appeal to several different senses—the sight of the rising sun, the sound of the jumping bass, the touch of the warm water in the chilled air. Don't feel that you have to give equal attention to all five senses when you write a description; but whether you appeal to a single sense or several, make sure they all contribute to the dominant impression you want your description to make upon the reader.

The dominant impression conveyed by Hemingway's description of fishing on the lake, for example, is that of peace and calm—the soothing tranquility of nature. Now, suppose you were to describe a similar morning scene on a freshwater lake in a rowboat. But instead of bass and sunrise, you call the reader's attention to an ominous dark cloud in the distance, drawing nearer. The wind rises. The reader hears a nasty grating sound as the little boat scrapes over a sunken log in the fast-flowing current. Instead of gently chucking the boat under the chin, the waves, now grown to white caps, flip it over with a crash, throwing you into the icy water. Nature, the reader concludes as you disappear beneath the surface, is not kind. The reader is left with the dominant impression of danger because you have chosen to build your description on particular details (mostly sounds) that contribute to a sense of danger and foreboding.

## ARRANGING THE DETAILS

While the events in a **NARRATIVE** are usually organized chronologically, the physical elements of a description are often organized according to their location.

So as you begin to get your description down on paper, the physical configuration of whatever you're describing will often suggest a pattern of organization to you. Bobbie Ann Mason's description on p. 511 of the sights and smells of her hometown in Kentucky, for example, follows the "circuit" of the courthouse square. In Mason's description, we get the furniture stores, then the dime stores, then the men's and ladies' stores and the banks, and, finally, the poolroom, because that is the order in which young Mason would have seen them all, starting where she did and walking around the main square of the town.

Descriptions of places are often organized, like Mason's, by physical direction—around the block, north to south, front to back, left to right, inside to outside, near to far, top to bottom. If you were describing a room, for example, you might use an outside-to-inside order, starting with the door (don't forget the knob and other details). Next you could present the main physical features of the room as they might appear to someone just crossing the threshold (oak floors, high ceilings, ancient fireplace). Then would come the grand piano, the candle on a stand, the

old lady mending a tapestry—just as these objects might appear to a person entering the room and adjusting his or her eyes to the light.

A particular object can suggest an order of arrangement as well as a
place can. For instance, in the following description of a tarpon, addressed
to a blind boy who has just caught it, the order of the details follows the
anatomy of the fish.

"More Room" (p. 197) traces several generations of a family by describing home renovations.

> He's mostly silver, but the silver is somehow made up of *all* the colors. . . . He
> has all these big scales, like armor all over his body. They're silver, too, and
> when he moves they sparkle. He has a strong body and a large powerful tail.
> He has big round eyes, bigger than a quarter, and a lower jaw that sticks out
> past the upper one and is very tough. His belly is almost white and his back is
> a gunmetal gray. When he jumped he came out of the water about six feet,
> and his scales caught the sun and flashed it all over the place.
> —CHEROKEE PAUL McDONALD, "A View from the Bridge"

McDonald's description begins and ends with the colors of the fish, its most noticeable feature (to a sighted person) in the glinting sun. Most of his description, however, is organized according to the parts of the subject itself, moving from the body
of the tarpon as a whole to the tail, eyes, belly, and back. From whole to parts, or
parts to whole: you can go either way when constructing a description. Or you can
describe the most important or unusual features of your subject first, then the least
important or most familiar ones (or vice versa). Or you can go from the largest to
smallest, or from specific to general, or from concrete to abstract—or vice versa—
so long as you maintain a consistent vantage point.

## MAINTAINING A VANTAGE POINT

In McDonald's essay, as the title suggests, the vantage point is from the bridge.
Here's the beginning of the essay, before the boy catches the tarpon:

> I was coming up on the little bridge in the Rio Vista neighborhood of Fort
> Lauderdale, deepening my stride and breathing to negotiate the slight incline
> without altering my pace. And then, as I neared the crest, I saw the kid.
>
> He was a lumpy little guy with baggy shorts, a faded T-shirt and heavy
> sweat socks falling down over old sneakers.
>
> Partially covering his shaggy blond hair was one of those blue baseball
> caps with gold braid on the bill and a sailfish patch sewn onto the peak. Cov-
> ering his eyes and part of his face was a pair of those stupid-looking '50s-style
> wrap-around sunglasses.

Like his description of the tarpon, McDonald's description of the boy moves from the whole (lumpy little guy in shorts and T-shirt) to the parts (hair, cap, patch, eyes, face, glasses). It also presents those details in the order in which the observer perceives them from his vantage point. That is, the reader of McDonald's essay sees only what the runner sees as he comes over the bridge. For example, at this point in his description, the runner does not yet know that the boy is blind, which is why he's wearing "stupid-looking" sunglasses. As you compose a description, be careful to maintain a consistent vantage point, as McDonald does.

## USING FIGURATIVE LANGUAGE

Because descriptive writing presents the reader with images of the physical world, it lends itself to the use of figurative language. The three figures of speech you are most likely to use in composing a description are similes, metaphors, and personification.

*Similes* tell the reader what something looks, sounds, or feels like, using *like* or *as*:

> She was like a pretty kite that floated above my head.     —MAYA ANGELOU

> Suspicion climbed all over her face like a kitten, but not so playfully.
> —RAYMOND CHANDLER

> Two policemen . . . were leaning into a third woman as if she were a stalled car.
> —T. C. BOYLE, *Talk, Talk*

*Metaphors* make implicit comparisons, without *like* or *as*:

> All the world's a stage.

> You are my sunshine.

> Papa was a rolling stone.

Metaphors have two parts: the subject of the description (*world*, *you*, *Papa*); and the thing (*stage*, *sunshine*, *rolling stone*) to which that subject is being implicitly compared.

*Personification* assigns human qualities to inanimate objects, as in this poetic description of a mirror:

> I am silver and exact.
> I have no preconceptions.
> Whatever I see I swallow immediately
> Just as it is, unmisted by love or dislike.     —SYLVIA PLATH, "Mirror"

## USING OTHER METHODS

When you describe something, you will often have reason to use other methods as well—to DEFINE it, analyze what CAUSED it, and so on. Especially if you are describing something that is unfamiliar to the reader—as in this description of a cemetery in rural El Salvador—consider COMPARING it with something the reader already knows about:

> Plunged like daggers to the ground are the crosses, mainly a fabulous aqua color, though some are bleached white and some are unpainted. . . . It looks like the aftermath of a piñata party, with crepe-paper chains strewn like leis about the necks of the gravestone markers, plastic red roses wreathed at the feet, errant scraps of yellow paper and transparent cellophane trapped between the blades of grass.      —BETH KEPHART, *Still Love in Strange Places*

"Daggers" imply violence, of course; but the cemetery in this colorful description is far from somber. The dominant impression is a sense of festive disorder, as Kephart compares this strange scene to a more familiar one in which children have just left after hammering a piñata to release the candy and toys inside.

## EDITING FOR COMMON ERRORS IN DESCRIPTIONS

Descriptive writing is often marred by qualifiers that are overly abstract, empty, or out of sequence. The following guidelines will help you check your description for these common problems and correct them.

### Check your details to see if you can make them more concrete

▶ Great Pond is so ~~amazing and incredible~~ <u>clear and deep</u> that floating on it in a boat seems like floating on air.

*Amazing* and *incredible* are abstract terms; *clear* and *deep* describe the water in more concrete terms.

▶ The Belgrade region is famous for its ~~charming views~~ <u>panoramic views of fields, hills, and woodlands</u>.

The corrected sentence says more precisely what makes the views charming.

### Check for filler words like *very, quite, really,* and *truly*

▶ The lake was ~~very much secluded~~ fifteen miles from the nearest village.

### If you've used several adjectives together, be sure they are in the right order

Subjective adjectives (those that reflect the writer's own opinion) go before objective adjectives (those that are strictly factual): write "fabulous four-door Chevrolet" rather than "four-door fabulous Chevrolet." Beyond that, adjectives usually go in the following order: number, size, shape, age, color, nationality.

▶ The streets of Havana were lined with many ~~old big~~ big old American cars.

### Check for common usage errors

#### *Unique, perfect*

Don't use *more* or *most, less* or *least,* or *very* before words like *unique, equal, perfect,* or *infinite.* Either something is unique or it isn't.

▶ Their house at the lake was a ~~very~~ unique place.

#### *Awesome, cool*

Not only are these modifiers too abstract, they're overused. You probably should delete them or replace them with fresher words no matter how grand the scene you're describing.

▶ The Mississippi is ~~an awesome river~~ the largest river system in the United States.

Go to wwnorton.com/write/back-to-the-lake for quizzes on these common errors.

# Reading a Description with a Critical Eye

Once you have drafted a description, try it out on someone else to get a sense of what's working and what needs revision. Then read it over yourself with a critical eye. Here are some questions to keep in mind when reviewing descriptive writing.

**PURPOSE AND AUDIENCE.** Who is the intended audience, and why will they be reading this description? Does it tell them everything they'll need to know, or will they need more background information?

**THE POINT.** Does the description have a clear point? Is that point set out in a thesis statement? If not, should it be?

**SPECIFIC DETAILS.** Are there enough details to give the reader a vivid impression of the subject? To which senses in particular does the description appeal—sight? sound? smell? touch? taste?

**OBJECTIVE OR SUBJECTIVE?** Are the details of the description presented objectively, subjectively, or does it contain elements of both? Is the degree of objectivity appropriate for the overall purpose and audience of the description? If not, how can it be made more informative and less emotional (or vice versa)?

**DOMINANT IMPRESSION.** What overall impression does the description give? Does every detail contribute directly to that impression? What additional details would make the dominant impression clearer or stronger? Do any details detract from that impression?

**ORGANIZATION.** How are the details of the description presented—by moving from part to whole? Whole to part? North to south? Most important to least important? Some other way?

**VANTAGE POINT.** From what perspective are the various aspects of the subject described? Near and intimate? Far and detached? Somewhere in between? Is that perspective maintained consistently throughout the description?

**FIGURATIVE LANGUAGE.** What figures of speech, such as metaphors, similes, or personification, does the description use? Are they appropriate for this purpose and audience?

**OTHER METHODS.** Has the description been expanded to include other methods of development—for example, by analyzing what caused something, or by comparing its attributes to those of other things with which the reader may already be familiar?

**COMMON ERRORS.** Check the adjective phrases in the description (*very beautiful, quite tall, really awesome*). Eliminate empty qualifiers like *very, quite,* and *really;* and substitute concrete terms for abstract ones. Instead of *awesome,* for example, use the physical quality that inspired the awe (*clear, bright, deep*).

## Student Example

Melissa Hicks spent her teenage years in rural Maine on a small farm with a make-shift house, a barn with a tree in the middle, and a cow named Francis Mary who gave the family milk for making butter. All this and more, past and present, are described in detail in "The High Price of Butter," which Hicks wrote for an introductory writing course at Lane Community College in Eugene, Oregon. Hicks's essay was runner-up for the 2010 Norton Writer's Prize.

The High Price of Butter

*In my house we have butter and margarine. The butter is for cooking. The margarine is for macaroni and cheese. I swear that it's the butter that makes everything taste so good. My favorite foods that remind me of my mother and my own childhood. In the grocery store aisle, I stand under the harsh white lights of the dairy case, margarine in one hand and butter in the other. I weigh them in my hand and compare the price; I weigh them in my mind, thinking of the high cost of butter. No matter how long I stand and weigh, I always put the butter in my cart. I remember the times when I was a girl—the taste of sweet, fresh butter melting on my tongue. I remember the work it took, and I know the price is more than fair.*  1

For my fourteenth birthday, I got a cow. I did not ask for a cow. I had very clearly asked for a horse. While every girl-child wants a horse, I felt that I had earned mine. I had worked at a farm down the road for the last two summers. I rode my bike to the stables. I would shovel the manure, feed the horses, ride for hours, and then pedal home exhausted. I knew how to take care of a horse. The life my family had worked and sweated for, clearing our own little spot in the Maine woods, was as well suited to horse-raising as any of our other pursuits. Even more, my father had dropped hints here and  2

Introduction uses the taste of butter to link present and past

there. While he would not definitively say it was a horse, he did say I could ride it. The fact was, I didn't know beans about cows.

We had a small farm in rural Maine. We cleared the land to put our trailer there. We hauled the brush and burned it. We pulled stumps, sometimes with the help of a tractor or a friendly neighbor with access to dynamite. We had a well and a septic tank dug. Onto the trailer we built a two-room addition with clean lumber and tongue-and-groove walls. My father's handmade bookshelves separated it into halves, one half being my parents' bedroom. A door led into the trailer, where my sisters and I slept.

We had to apply to the town office to put up new cedar poles for the power lines to our lot. On our two acres we raised chickens, rabbits, and sometimes a pig. We had room for so many animals that turned into dinner, but in all the years I'd begged, we had never had room for a horse.

Down the hill from our house sat our barn. Like everything else we'd worked so hard on during the summer leading up to my fourteenth birthday, it was a sure sign of horses to come. The barn had one stall. It was built so that the back door opened into the rabbits' shed, and as soon as you entered, you could see their red eyes through the black doorway in the rear. It smelled like clean hay and fresh ammonia, and when the days were cold (as they were in September), the smells seemed to bite my cheeks with the cold.

The barn was built around a huge cedar tree with white-ringed wounds where my father's chainsaw had slid through thick branches. Nailed to its furry brown bark were sections of two-by-fours, rising parallel to the loft. Its roots gripped the floor tightly, still growing. One side of the square hole that framed the loft entrance was nailed to the tree with thick spikes. We avoided picturing the consequences of its either growing or dying, but it was sure to do both eventually.

The main door into the barn was aligned diagonally with the door to the rabbits' shed on the opposite wall. To the right was the stall, and to the left a large open window of the kind that horses stick their heads through. On the floor below it was a massive water

3

4

5

6

7

Describes the general setting where the remembered events took place

Specific details like this capture the particulars of life on Hicks's family farm

tank, more than bathtub size; above it was a recently installed spigot. In a corner were a stack of green poles and pegs, and loops of wire to install an electric fence. These were all signs of impending horses.

The cow actually arrived about a week before my birthday. She was a small, brown cow—a Guernsey. She was a heifer that would soon birth a calf, and we would get to milk her. My father had gotten her from a farmers' co-operative program. After the calf was weaned, we would donate it back to them. We would have butter and cheese and fresh milk from my cow.

School had just started. Despite the farm, my parents both had day jobs, like everyone else I knew. This was making ends meet. It was another reason to get up early in the morning, and another chore to be done when I got home. The most bitter part though, was that the heifer was still not a horse.

*This is not the butter I knew as a girl. I hear the crinkle as I pull it from its plastic shopping bag and place it, still in its perfect slick cardboard packaging, on the counter to soften. I bang through the kitchen, leaving a trail of open cabinets in my wake as I thrust goodies onto shelves. I pull out my cutting board before I twirl around to twist the knobs on my stove. I set my oven to 425° and bend low to grab my casserole dish from under the sink. I plunk it on the cutting board before whirling again to dig through the cupboards for filling.*

*I think to myself, it's a shame to use canned filling with the real butter, but even my mother couldn't do scratch every time. The oven is not yet heated, and I am thinking of my cobbler. I pull out a mixing bowl and measuring cup. I think of my mother and how she prepared everything in advance so she could just add and mix when the right time came. I break the seal on the butter's box, setting two sticks inside the blue Pyrex dish. The remaining two are sent to the fridge.*

I named her Francis Mary. It suited her. She had large brown eyes that always seemed sadly pensive, with soft cream-colored hair rimming them. The fur around her eyes ended abruptly in the deep reddish-brown of her fur. For spite and for pretend, I decided I

Focus is on the cow, an important part of making butter

"Making ends meet" sums up the economic scene that Hicks is describing

Descriptive details of the present are just as specific as those pertaining to the past

All-important cow gets a name and a full physical description

8

9

10

11

12

would ride her. I sat on her after milking-time one day. My sneakers bumped the rough wood planks on either side of the stall when she shifted. Our breaths blew mightily, visibly—twin streams in autumn air. The milk steamed quietly in its bucket. On a shelf sat my tape player. I sang "Faith" with George Michael and whispered encouragement to Francis Mary while I tugged on the rope I'd tied to her halter. When the tape ended, I picked up the milk and headed up to our house.

The back steps crossed over a muddy trench. Our main trailer sat up on a little ledge. The steps were wooden and rickety, with sticky, abrasive tar paper stapled to the wooden planks; the handrails were sturdy two-by-fours and there were no fronts or sides (fig. 1). Between the holes, you saw the muddy gully, unless you saw cold white snow and muddy footprints.

13 · · · · · · These physical details show harsher aspects of life on the farm

Fig. 1. Me and my sister Angela (right) in an old photograph taken at our home in Maine, where I learned to make butter from my parents and received a cow as a present on my fourteenth birthday.

Dirty barn clothes meant using these steps. We left our dirty 14
boots outside the door. Here were windows of plastic sheeting,
empty seed pots and trays, old watering dishes, and big plastic
outdoor toys, outgrown and overused, left dirty in various corners.
It was a greenhouse in the spring, and a den for hairy spiders all
year long.

After dinner, usually twilight—sometimes in the dark—I'd 15
lift heavy buckets of milk up the stairs into the warmth of the
kitchen. A wooden sign says "Willkommen" above the stove. I step
outside to take off my rubber-toed boots; jacket and gloves were
hung in the barn. My cheeks pink, I step back inside in wool socks
and hang my hat on the peg.

My father is standing by the sink. He takes the aluminum 16
buckets and pours them through a large metal sieve into precooled
pitchers, waiting in the sink. In the clear plastic we can see the
cream as it cools and separates from the milk. My father covers the
pitchers and puts them in the fridge. My mother watches the news
as I start my homework. My sisters disappear, whispering about
Barbies and coloring books. I draw pictures of princesses and
half-heartedly pretend to do my algebra. If we weren't making butter,
I could disappear into my room. I could wrap myself in jackets and
blankets, and put on thick gloves. I could pull curls from the kitchen
phone-cord and run it under the back door, huddling and whispering
to girlfriends, or worse even, boys.

*Thanks to my mother, I don't need a recipe for anything. But for* 17
*cobbler, one must measure. I pull the waxy paper off the butter, letting*
*the sticks fall whole into my pan. Sturdy long rectangles of solidified*
*cream bounce sullenly as they hit. They leave a mark as they tumble, a*
*visible trail of clean grease and flavor. These go into the oven. I melt them*
*whole and let them bubble and simmer until the butter turns brown.*

*"No matter how long you cook it, margarine will never brown,"* 18
*my mother said while preparing some supper or other. "That's how you*
*know the difference." It seemed awfully silly to me at the time. I couldn't*

> Switches to
> present tense
> for immediacy

*imagine why I would want butter brown, or even how brown was any different from burnt. I remember the words, and wonder if anyone else gets such a thrill from waiting for their butter to bubble.*

Hours later, the milk is cold. It is quiet as we gather around the kitchen table, a last task before bedtime—not every day, but often. Washcloths lie on warm wood, wet and ready for the occasional drop. My parents have put the pitchers of milk back on the table and are skimming with clean, cold, metal ladles. They are large and gleaming. They look medicinal against the whiteness of the milk. They are cold next to the pictures of fruit in happy bowls, the small glories hanging from refrigerator magnets, and the homey dark wood of the table.

19    Describes in detail the key scene of making butter in the old kitchen

The cream sings and tinkles as it rushes into waiting Ball jars. It is thick and deep-sounding for a liquid. A white line runs around the top of each pitcher, a line of fat where the cream has bubbled up from the depths of the comparatively thin milk. Each jar is filled about halfway before being topped with a rubber ring, copper top, and screw ring by my mother.

20    Gives sounds as well as sights in the kitchen

She hands me a jar. I feel the coldness as the milk sloshes inside the glass, cooling the tips of my fingers and palms. I raise it about level with my head and begin shaking. My arms and shoulders warm as I shake the jar. Time seems to slow down, and it's no time before my arms start to burn. By this time, a second jar is ready, handed to the next eldest, Emily. Her hair is brown like mine, but thicker. Sometimes there is a third jar—often not.

21    Sounds are followed by sensations of touch

As my arms tire, I alter the motion. Instead of shaking the jar up and down, I go side to side. My youngest sister has the darkest hair, in long braids. She asks for the jar. My mother, setting the milk back in the fridge, tells her to wait her turn.

22

I shake, and I shake. My face feels red and there is always a greasy strand of hair in my eyes. Everything is stupid and embarrassing, especially cows and shit-kicker boots. I don't want to make my own butter or weed gardens. I don't want meat from little

23

white packages, made of the animals I fed all last year. I want some food with a price tag. I feel self-conscious; my fat shakes with the jar. I worry about my bra. I know that soon I will sweat, and I feel like that would make me shrivel and die. My father is heading down to the barn one more time, to check on the water and the rabbits. He tells us to switch jars.

I give mine to my mother, and Emily passes hers to Angela, the youngest. I link my fingers, stretch out my arms and push. We giggle and talk as the constant sloshing grows thicker, audible lumps under the warm yellow lightbulbs in the kitchen. In the mirror, we are reflected, dark heads bent as we shake and talk. When the second team tires, we alternate rolling and shaking the jars. Emily rolls her jar back and forth across the table to my mother. A yellow lump rolls in whitish liquid, slowly growing larger; waxen and heavy, it thuds and rolls inside the Ball jar, one beat behind.   24

I shake, slower now. A dull golden lump is heavy in my jar too. Up and down three times: Shake, shake, shake. Side to side again. I pass it to my sister. Soon we will roll our jar, too. My mother rolls the jar to Emily who picks it up and shakes. Now the table is empty; Angela and I begin to roll our jar automatically to each other over the smooth wood. We see brown whirls of wood flash by under the speeding, tumbling butter.   25

My mother is putting store-bought rolls into the preheated oven. She takes the jar from Emily, after washing her hands, and scrapes the butter with a spatula into cold, heavy, cast-iron molds from the fridge. They are cold even on the counter in the daytime. The molds are shaped like ripened ears of corn with their husks spread out behind them. We will sell this butter.   26

She puts the molds back into the refrigerator and takes the last jar from me. She scrapes that into a large ball with her hands on a cutting board, and cuts it square with a knife. She collects the scraps into a longer oval with her hands again, and cuts away a stick.   27

She cuts the larger block in pieces twice as my sisters and I wipe the table. Finally, my mother wraps the butter in white wax paper.

Now the kitchen is quiet, without the rolling and thudding. I silently fantasize about flaky biscuits melting on my tongue. My sisters and I are yawning, but our stomachs growl at the smell. On the cutting board are the scraps from the last block of butter. They are not grocery-store squares, but long strips, thick and round on one side. The image of a delightfully buttery slug comes to mind, slithering onto a hot roll before leaving a slick buttery trail down my throat. The best part of the butter is that there was plenty.     28

*The butter melts, forming first a slowly oozing lump, then a golden liquid coating, bubbling delicately inside the stove. I know this because my nose tells me. I could look inside the oven, but there is no need. I open the lids on my counter bins: Two cups flour (into the measuring cup out to the bowl), two cups sugar; I get two cups of milk, which I pour before closing the door. Last I grab a spoon, and dip it twice into the baking powder. Now I whisk, smoothing the lumpy ooze into a thick, creamy batter.*     29

*I run my can opener across two cans of filling and smile.*     30

*"It's two of everything, so you can't ever forget!" I can see my mother smiling through the phone as she guides me.*     31

*By this time the butter is bubbling quicker, brown crispy bunches collecting on the top of the hot yellow liquid. I pull it out of the oven and put it on the stovetop. I turn back to the counter to take off my oven mitts and pour half of the batter from the bowl, straight into the boiling butter. It sizzles, and the batter rises immediately. The butter rushes up around the edges of the pan, and rises over the batter, to settle in yellow pools in its center.*     32

*I spoon out the filling, amber apples smelling of cinnamon, sitting on a fluffy bed of clouds and sweet molten butter. The other half of the batter goes on top, and quickly I put the pan back into the oven. I smile, leaning on the counter, and wait. Soon I will have my cobbler. My*     33

The climactic sensation is taste—eating the butter

*tongue prepares for the first bite of sweet dough and apple, and the little rush of butter in every bite, that will drip, softly onto its buds. Like every time before and every time to come, I will pull it from the oven and*

Passing the family tradition on to the new generation

·····• *proudly say to my son,*

"*Look Cy, I made it from scratch. And I used real butter, too.*"   34

To me the cost of butter is more than a price tag. The cost of   35
butter reminds me of my childhood, and how my family struggled

Conclusion returns to the economic cost of butter, but it's outweighed by the value of connecting with the past

to be pioneers in the twentieth century. The cost of butter reminds
·····• me of the value of hard work, and how that work brought my family
together. I always think of Francis Mary, who never was a horse, but
allowed me to ride her anyway. I think of cold fingers, frozen noses,
and sloshing warm milk on my pants. Yet the cost of butter is more
than a symbol of hard work and quality. The fact that I buy it is an
affirmation of my own choices in life. Because of my childhood, I
know the cost in sweat of butter. As an adult, I choose to pay that
price in cash.

## Analyzing a Student Description

In "The High Price of Butter," Melissa Hicks draws upon rhetorical strategies and techniques that good writers use all the time when they write a description. The following questions, in addition to focusing on particular aspects of Hicks's text, will help you to identify those common strategies and techniques so you can adapt them to your own writing. These questions will also help to prepare you for the analytical questions—on content, structure, and language—that you'll find after all the other selections in this chapter, along with suggestions for writing on related topics.

## FOR CLOSE READING

1. In the bulk of her essay, Melissa Hicks describes her teenage years as a member of a tight-knit family living on a small farm in Maine. What period of her life is she describing in the italicized paragraphs of her essay?

2. As an adult, Hicks buys her butter in a store. Why didn't she and her family do this when she was living on the family farm? Aside from making their own butter, what else did Hicks and her family do to improve their economic condition?

3. According to Hicks, "every girl-child wants a horse" (2). Instead of a horse for her fourteenth birthday, however, she gets a cow. Hicks is disappointed, but she soon accepts the situation and makes do. How and why did she learn to deal with disappointment in this way?

4. For Hicks as an adult, good butter and the price she pays for it are "more than a symbol of hard work and quality" (35). What else do they symbolize for her? Why does she nevertheless "pay that price in cash" (35)?

## Strategies and Structures

1. When Hicks describes, for example, the door of the barn on her family's farm, she doesn't just say that it "opened into the rabbits' shed." She lets the reader see what she saw through it: "as soon as you entered, you could see their red eyes through the black doorway in the rear" (5). Point out other passages in which Hicks lets you see, in vivid detail, the people, animals, and objects that she is remembering.

2. Although sight is an important sense in Hicks's description of family life, she appeals to all the other senses as well. Point out places in her essay where she effectively invokes taste, touch, sound, and smell—for example, when she recalls the "slug" of homemade butter that leaves a "slick buttery trail down my throat" (28).

3. Is Hicks's descriptive essay primarily **OBJECTIVE** or **SUBJECTIVE**? Or a combination of the two? Give specific examples to explain your judgment.

4. Hicks's extended description of her home and family, both past and present, gives the **DOMINANT IMPRESSION** of strength achieved "in sweat" (34). How does Hicks strike this particular balance among the many details, both physical and emotional, that she cites, as, for example, in the butter-making scene (19–28)? Point to other passages in Hicks's description that contribute to this dominant impression.

5. A good way to organize any description of a place or object is to structure it around the layout or design of the place or object being described. How and where does Hicks do this with her description of the house, barn, and other parts of the family farm in Maine? Of her own kitchen later in Oregon?

6. *Other Methods.* Hicks's description has many elements of **NARRATIVE**. What are some of them, and how does she use different narrative plot lines to connect the parts, past and present, of her description?

7. Hicks uses **PROCESS ANALYSIS** to explain how she makes a cobbler like her mother's. Where else in her essay does she use this method? For what purposes?

## Thinking about Language

1. How is the *cost* of a commodity, such as a pound of butter, different from its *price*? Why does Hicks conclude her essay by referring to the high cost of butter rather than its high price?

2. For Hicks, butter is a "symbol," among other things, of "hard work and quality" (35). How, and how well, does she establish this symbolic aspect of butter and butter-making in her description?

3. "I didn't know beans about cows" (2). Why do speakers of English say this but not, for example, "I didn't know cows about beans"? What's so special, linguistically speaking, about knowing beans?

4. The Hicks family's cow, Francis Mary, was a "Guernsey" (8). Where does this designation come from, and why is it frequently applied to cows?

## FOR WRITING

1. In a paragraph or two, write a description of tasting, seeing, smelling, hearing, or feeling something that always reminds you of childhood. Describe what you recall as well as the act of recalling it.

2. Write out one of your favorite recipes for making a dish (or building something). In addition, describe where the recipe (or other set of instructions) came from, and how you learned to follow it.

3. In 150-200 words, write a description of a product or service you think is not worth the price. Explain why you are willing to pay that much anyway—or why you refuse to do so.

4. Drawing on notes in your journal, conversations with your family, old photographs, or other memory jogs—including, of course, eating or other sensations—write an essay-length **MEMOIR** of a distinct period in your earlier life. Be sure to describe what people and places looked and smelled like, how food tasted, what music or other sounds you heard, and otherwise how it felt to you back then as you remember that particular time now.

5. By some estimates, the average price of a cheeseburger is $4.49. This figure does not include such "externalities" as the carbon generated by growing beef or medical treatment for people who eat too many cheeseburgers, which, along with many other factors, can drive up the actual cost of a burger considerably. In collaboration with several classmates, do some research on the collateral costs of producing a cheeseburger (or other commodity or item of food), and describe your findings, including the total cost, in detail in a REPORT.

You'll find quizzes on the readings at wwnorton.com/write/back-to-the-lake.

# A *Facebook* Post

Whether on *Facebook* or elsewhere, when you describe something, such as a house you once lived in, you tell what it looks (or looked) like and what characteristics distinguish it from other, similar objects. When the photographer and writer Tony Mendoza returned to his family's beach house in Cuba, it was "in perfect condition, just as I remembered it when I left in 1960"—unlike the house next door, which "had disappeared." The porch of the house overlooked the ocean, and there Mendoza found a young woman playing a saxophone, a "scene" he describes, along with a photo of the view from the porch, in a recent posting on his *Facebook* page. Like any form of memoir, Mendoza's posting is a means of capturing the past in writing (and images) in present consciousness: "I tried to remember those days when I was young and full of energy and very happy to be spending summers in our house by the sea."

[ **FOR WRITING** ]··········································································

Write a 150-word description of the scene pictured in the photograph on the facing page. Consider which senses the photo appeals to and the dominant impression it creates. Also describe how the composition of the photo contributes to the dominant impression.

**Tony Mendoza**
April 24

I went back to Cuba in 1996. One of the first places I wanted to see was my family's house in Varadero Beach. As I got closer to the house, I expected to see a ruin, since all the houses I was walking by were gutted. I was pleasantly surprised—the house was in perfect condition, just as I remembered it when I left in 1960. It was a government guest house, impeccably maintained. The front door was open. I walked in and found a young woman, her eyes closed, playing a saxophone on the porch which overlooked the ocean. I liked the scene, it reminded me of a movie I had seen, and I liked the melody. When she opened her eyes, she found me there. We talked. I told her I grew up in the house, and she offered to give me a tour. Afterward, I went down to the water, put all my clothes in a pile with the camera on top, and went in. I was in the water for a while, looking towards the house. The house next to ours, the del Valle house, had disappeared. In its place there was a large pile of sand. I tried to remember those days when I was young and full of energy and very happy to be spending summers in our house by the sea.

# SUGGESTIONS FOR WRITING

1. Go to the website of Belgrade Lakes, Maine, or some other resort that you have never actually visited. Based on the information you find on the website, write a description of the place that you could email to a friend or relative in order to persuade him or her to join you there.

2. Old photographs can bring the past to life in present consciousness at the same time that they remind us of the gulf between past and present. In 150–200 words, describe what you see in the scene pictured on the old postcard on p. 170—or in some other old photo that you can find or remember. Be sure to describe the photo itself in some detail as well as the **DOMINANT IMPRESSION**—such as familiarity or nostalgia—that it conveys. If it reminds you of another place or time, or a visit you once made, describe that scene as well.

3. Using the Slinky abstract as a model, write an **ABSTRACT** of an experiment you've worked on or read about. Or, alternatively, write a **PROPOSAL** of an experiment that you would like to see conducted.

4. Write a description of these video frames illustrating the physicists' methodology as expressed in the abstract on p. 168. Be sure to explain how what you see in the frame corresponds to what the physicists report in their written description of the experiment.

5. "It seemed to me, as I kept remembering all this," writes E. B. White in "Once More to the Lake," "that those times and those summers had been infinitely precious and worth saving" (p. 222). Using description as your basic method, write a **POSITION PAPER** about the value (or lack thereof) of remembering and writing about the past, whether in the form of a personal memoir or as more general history.

# More Room

Judith Ortiz Cofer (b. 1952) is a native of Puerto Rico but moved to Paterson, New Jersey, as a small child. Though Ortiz Cofer grew up and went to school on the "mainland," she often returned for extended visits to her grandmother's home in Puerto Rico, the *casa de Mamá* described in "More Room." This bicultural experience is the basis of much of Ortiz Cofer's writing, including her novel *The Meaning of Consuelo* (2003), which won the Americas Award; *The Latin Deli* (1993), a collection of essays and poems that won the Anisfield-Wolf Book Award; and *Into the Cruel Country: Notes for an Elegy* (2015), a memoir. Ortiz Cofer is the Regents' and Franklin Professor of English and Creative Writing, Emerita, at the University of Georgia.

"More Room" is from *Silent Dancing* (1990), a memoir of Ortiz Cofer's childhood in Puerto Rico and New Jersey. In this description, Ortiz Cofer shows how a few remembered details can bring back an entire scene and the people in it.

M Y GRANDMOTHER'S HOUSE is like a chambered nautilus; it has many rooms, 1
yet it is not a mansion. Its proportions are small and its design simple. It is a house that has grown organically, according to the needs of its inhabitants. To all of us in the family it is known as *la casa de Mamá*. It is the place of our origin; the stage for our memories and dreams of Island life.

I remember how in my childhood it sat on stilts; this was before it had a down- 2
stairs. It rested on its perch like a great blue bird, not a flying sort of bird, more like a nesting hen, but with spread wings. Grandfather had built it soon after their marriage. He was a painter and housebuilder by trade, a poet and meditative man by nature. As each of their eight children were born, new rooms were added. After a few years, the paint did not exactly match, nor the materials, so that there was a chronology to it, like the rings of a tree, and Mamá could tell you the history of each room in her *casa*, and thus the genealogy of the family along with it.

Descriptive writing often includes figures of speech (p. 178).

3

Her room is the heart of the house. Though I have seen it recently, and both woman and room have diminished in size, changed by the new perspective of my

MLA CITATION: Ortiz Cofer, Judith. "More Room." 1990. *Back to the Lake.* Ed. Thomas Cooley. 3rd ed. New York: Norton, 2015. 197–200. Print.

eyes, now capable of looking over countertops and tall beds, it is not this picture I carry in my memory of Mamá's *casa*. Instead, I see her room as a queen's chamber where a small woman loomed large, a throne-room with a massive four-poster bed in its center which stood taller than a child's head. It was on this bed where her own children had been born that the smallest grandchildren were allowed to take naps in the afternoons; here too was where Mamá secluded herself to dispense private advice to her daughters, sitting on the edge of the bed, looking down at whoever sat on the rocker where generations of babies had been sung to sleep. To me she looked like a wise empress right out of the fairy tales I was addicted to reading.

Though the room was dominated by the mahogany four-poster, it also contained ⁴ all of Mamá's symbols of power. On her dresser instead of cosmetics there were jars filled with herbs: *yerba buena, yerba mala*,[1] the making of purgatives and teas to which we were all subjected during childhood crises. She had a steaming cup for anyone who could not, or would not, get up to face life on any given day. If the acrid aftertaste of her cures for malingering did not get you out of bed, then it was time to call *el doctor*.

And there was the monstrous chifforobe she kept locked with a little golden key ⁵ she did not hide. This was a test of her dominion over us; though my cousins and I wanted a look inside that massive wardrobe more than anything, we never reached for that little key lying on top of her Bible on the dresser. This was also where she placed her earrings and rosary at night. God's word was her security system. This chifforobe was the place where I imagined she kept jewels, satin slippers, and elegant sequined, silk gowns of heartbreaking fineness. I lusted after those imaginary costumes. I had heard that Mamá had been a great beauty in her youth, and the belle of many balls. My cousins had other ideas as to what she kept in that wooden vault: its secret could be money (Mamá did not hand cash to strangers, banks were out of the question, so there were stories that her mattress was stuffed with dollar bills, and that she buried coins in jars in her garden under rosebushes, or kept them in her inviolate chifforobe); there might be that legendary gun salvaged from the Spanish-American conflict over the Island. We went wild over suspected treasures that we made up simply because children have to fill locked trunks with something wonderful.

On the wall above the bed hung a heavy silver crucifix. Christ's agonized head ⁶ hung directly over Mamá's pillow. I avoided looking at this weapon suspended over where her head would lay; and on the rare occasions when I was allowed to sleep on that bed, I scooted down to the safe middle of the mattress, where her body's impression took me in like a mother's lap. Having taken care of the obligatory

---

1. *Yerba buena, yerba mala*: Literally "good herb, bad herb." *Yerba buena* usually refers to a species of mint. *Yerba mala* could be almost any "bad herb."

religious decoration with a crucifix, Mamá covered the other walls with objects sent to her over the years by her children in the States. *Los Nueva Yores*[2] were represented by, among other things, a postcard of Niagara Falls from her son Hernán, postmarked, Buffalo, N.Y. In a conspicuous gold frame hung a large color photograph of her daughter Nena, her husband and their five children at the entrance to Disneyland in California. From us she had gotten a black lace fan. Father had brought it to her from a tour of duty with the Navy in Europe (on Sundays she would remove it from its hook on the wall to fan herself at mass). Each year more items were added as the family grew and dispersed, and every object in the room had a story attached to it, a *cuento* which Mamá would bestow on anyone who received the privilege of a day alone with her. It was almost worth pretending to be sick, though the bitter herb purgatives of the body were a big price to pay for the spirit revivals of her story-telling.

Mamá slept alone on her large bed, except for the times when a sick grandchild warranted the privilege, or when a heartbroken daughter came home in need of more than herbal teas. In the family there is a story about how this came to be. 7

When one of the daughters, my mother or one of her sisters, tells the *cuento* of how Mamá came to own her nights, it is usually preceded by the qualifications that Papá's exile from his wife's room was not a result of animosity between the couple, but that the act had been Mamá's famous bloodless coup for her personal freedom. Papá was the benevolent dictator of her body and her life who had had to be banished from her bed so that Mamá could better serve her family. Before the telling, we had to agree that the old man was not to blame. We all recognized that in the family Papá was as an *alma de Dios*, a saintly, soft-spoken presence whose main pleasures in life, such as writing poetry and reading the Spanish large-type editions of *Reader's Digest*, always took place outside the vortex of Mamá's crowded realm. It was not his fault, after all, that every year or so he planted a baby-seed in Mamá's fertile body, keeping her from leading the active life she needed and desired. He loved her and the babies. Papá composed odes and lyrics to celebrate births and anniversaries and hired musicians to accompany him in singing them to his family and friends at extravagant pig-roasts he threw yearly. Mamá and the oldest girls worked for days preparing the food. Papá sat for hours in his painter's shed, also his study and library, composing the songs. At these celebrations he was also known to give long speeches in praise of God, his fecund wife, and his beloved island. As a middle child, my mother remembers these occasions as a time when the women sat in the kitchen and lamented their burdens, while the men feasted out in the patio, their rum-thickened voices rising in song and praise for each other, *compañeros* all. 8

2. *Los Nueva Yores*: The New Yorkers.

It was after the birth of her eighth child, after she had lost three at birth or in ₉ infancy, that Mamá made her decision. They say that Mamá had had a special way of letting her husband know that they were expecting, one that had begun when, at the beginning of their marriage, he had built her a house too confining for her taste. So, when she discovered her first pregnancy, she supposedly drew plans for another room, which he dutifully executed. Every time a child was due, she would demand, *more space, more space.* Papá acceded to her wishes, child after child, since he had learned early that Mamá's renowned temper was a thing that grew like a monster along with a new belly. In this way Mamá got the house that she wanted, but with each child she lost in heart and energy. She had knowledge of her body and perceived that if she had any more children, her dreams and her plans would have to be permanently forgotten, because she would be a chronically ill woman, like Flora with her twelve children: asthma, no teeth, in bed more than on her feet.

And so, after my youngest uncle was born, she asked Papá to build a large room ₁₀ at the back of the house. He did so in joyful anticipation. Mamá had asked him special things this time: shelves on the walls, a private entrance. He thought that she meant this room to be a nursery where several children could sleep. He thought it was a wonderful idea. He painted it his favorite color, sky blue, and made large windows looking out over a green hill and the church spires beyond. But nothing happened. Mamá's belly did not grow, yet she seemed in a frenzy of activity over the house. Finally, an anxious Papá approached his wife to tell her that the new room was finished and ready to be occupied. And Mamá, they say, replied: "Good, it's for *you.*"

And so it was that Mamá discovered the only means of birth control available to ₁₁ a Catholic woman of her time: sacrifice. She gave up the comfort of Papá's sexual love for something she deemed greater: the right to own and control her body, so that she might live to meet her grandchildren—me among them—so that she could give more of herself to the ones already there, so that she could be more than a channel for other lives, so that even now that time has robbed her of the elasticity of her body and of her amazing reservoir of energy, she still emanates the kind of joy that can only be achieved by living according to the dictates of one's own heart. ◆

## FOR CLOSE READING

1. Mamá's house in Puerto Rico was originally built on stilts to avoid high water, but the lower level got filled in when the family needed more room. How are these old additions different from the new room with shelves and a private entrance?

2. Mamá exercises "dominion" over all her house and family (5). Her grandchildren ascribe her power to the exotic items in her room, but what is the true source of her power?

3. If Mamá is the "queen" (3) of the house and household that Judith Ortiz Cofer describes, what are some of Papá's other roles (besides that of prince consort)?

4. When Papá is preparing birthday odes and patriotic hymns to be sung at annual feasts, what are the women in the family doing? Why? What is Ortiz Cofer suggesting about the culture she is describing?

5. Ortiz Cofer describes the outside of her grandmother's house before moving to the inside. What specific details does she focus upon?

## Strategies and Structures

1. Why does Mamá need more room? What point is Ortiz Cofer making about women and families by describing her grandmother's home?

2. Once she moves inside the house, which room does Ortiz Cofer single out? Why? What does it contribute to her description of Mamá?

3. Ortiz Cofer is not so much describing her grandmother's house as it is today as the house as it exists in her memory. How is this "picture" different from present-day reality (3)? How does she capture the place from the viewpoint of a child?

4. Mamá's house is full of her "symbols of power" (4). What DOMINANT IMPRESSION of the place and of her do they help convey to the reader?

5. *Other Methods.* In addition to describing her grandmother's house and its contents, "More Room" tells the story of a "bloodless coup" (8). What coup? How does this NARRATIVE relate to Ortiz Cofer's description of the house?

## Thinking about Language

1. "Build three more stately mansions, O my soul. / As the swift seasons roll!" So begins the final stanza of "The Chambered Nautilus" (1858) by Oliver Wendell Holmes. How does Ortiz Cofer make use of this ALLUSION?

2. *Cuento* (6, 8) is the Spanish word for story. Why does Ortiz Cofer mention the telling of stories in her description?

3. Mamá's room, says Ortiz Cofer, is the "heart" of the house (3). What are the implications of this METAPHOR?

## FOR WRITING

1. Write a paragraph or two in which you COMPARE the present-day aspects of a house, room, or other place with those of the place as you picture it in memory.

2. Write a description of a house or other place that captures the tension (or harmony) among its inhabitants by describing the physical features of the place.

3. "More Room" is from Ortiz Cofer's memoir *Silent Dancing*. Read more from—or even better, all of—this richly descriptive exploration of growing up in two worlds. Keep notes of your reading in a reading journal.

4. Along with several others in your writing class, divide *Silent Dancing* into sections and assign each person in the group a different section to read and take notes on. Discuss the book together as a group and share all notes.

5. In collaboration with several others in your class, do some research on the work of a famous architect, such as Frank Lloyd Wright or Frank Gehry. Choose a particular building or project designed by that person and, using description extensively, write a critical evaluation of that structure or design. Be sure to say how the major components fit together (or don't) to serve their intended purpose.

You'll find quizzes on the readings at wwnorton.com/write/back-to-the-lake.

# PAUL CRENSHAW

# Storm Country

Paul Crenshaw (b. 1972) grew up in Logan County, Arkansas, in the heart of "Tornado Alley," the region of spectacularly violent weather stretching from North Dakota to southern Texas and Louisiana that he describes in "Storm Country." Crenshaw's sense of geography—and of his entire childhood—was formed, he says, through late-night "radio reports of tornado warnings or sightings . . . in a storm cellar." A graduate of the MFA Writing Program at the University of North Carolina at Greensboro, Crenshaw teaches writing and literature at Elon University in North Carolina. His essays and stories have appeared in *Shenandoah, North American Review, Antioch Review, Hayden's Ferry Review,* and other publications.

In the following two complete sections of "Storm Country," which was first published in the *Southern Humanities Review* in 2004, Crenshaw describes a place and its people in rich physical and emotional detail—both as he observed them and as they linger "in my mind."

M Y GRANDFATHER COULD TELL by the way leaves hung on the trees if it would  1
rain that day or not—an old-time meteorologist who watched the seasons and the sky simply because they were there.

"See there?" he said once. We were standing outside the cellar as the first storms  2
began to fire up in the heat of late afternoon. Low green clouds hung silent in the distance, and I have since learned that when clouds turn green, one should take cover. A point hung from the cloud, a barb that looked ominous as the clouds passed on and we watched them go, and always after I have looked for low barbs hanging from dark green clouds, for silent formations that might spawn destruction. He knew, standing on the cellar stairs watching through the little window, when a tornado might drop from the clouds. He knew the feel of the air, the presence that announces a heavy storm.

Sometimes it will stop raining when the funnel falls. Sometimes the wind stops  3
and the trees go still and the air settles on you as everything goes quiet. Then, faint

MLA CITATION: Crenshaw, Paul. "Storm Country." 2004. *Back to the Lake.* Ed. Thomas Cooley. 3rd ed. New York: Norton, 2015. 203–06. Print.

A good
description
appeals to the
physical senses;
turn to p. 166
to learn how.

at first as the storm gathers speed, you can hear the force as it spins itself into existence, touching earth, whirling out into the day or night. It sounds like rusted sirens, howling dogs, the call of a freight train on a long trip across the plains somewhere in the western night, pushing speed and sound before it, lonely and forlorn on its midnight ride.

I've seen tornadoes drop from a clear blue sky. I've seen barns and houses and fields wiped out, cattle thrown for a distance to lie in the rain bawling with broken legs. Once I watched as a three- or four-hundred-pound cut of sheet metal floated across the highway, touched down once, then lifted off again, light as air. I've seen towns wrecked by tornadoes in November, houses swept away, all that was left of a church roof lying on the ground, unscathed but for a few shingles missing at one corner. One time I was almost struck by a bullet of hail the size of my fist. It crashed through the window and landed on our living-room floor. We all looked at it for a moment. My mother tried to protect the curtains as the rain came in, but my father herded us toward the cellar up the hill at my grandfather's house.

I know the sound of storms, the low growl of thunder that means storms in the distance, the loud quick clap that means storms overhead. I've blinked in the afterglow of forked lightning, watched flash lightning light the hills as night turns into day. I've seen the remains of exploded houses, nothing left of the house but kindling, from when the tornado drops and the air pressure changes and the air inside the house has to get out.

I've seen storms come with no warning, boiling up out of a western sky rimmed with the red rays of the last sun, lightning flickering in the twilight, the air gone heavy and still. I've seen them sweep through with hardly a ripple but the wind in your hair, passing to other places and other times. I've huddled in hallways and bathtubs and cellars listening to tornadoes pass overhead, and when I see on television the remnants of a town destroyed by the force of storms, I always offer, however briefly, a thanks that it was not my people, or my town.

The first tornado I can remember was when I was eight. The storm came in the afternoon, as many storms do. It was early in March—a month that, as the saying goes in Arkansas, enters like a lion, leaves like a lion. My father was watching a basketball game on TV when the sound disappeared, followed by the steady beep that means an announcement is coming. Thunderstorms are moving through the area, the announcement ran at the bottom of the screen. Tornadoes possible. Take shelter. When the announcement disappeared the state of Arkansas appeared on the screen, the western counties lit like radiation. My father went out to study the sky and came back in at a run.

"Let's go," he said.

The trees were dancing as we ran to the truck, leaves and small branches   9
swirling in the wind and falling all around. At the road up the hill to my
grandfather's house a dust devil[1] danced before my father ran his truck through
it, dispersing the dust. A line of rain moved toward us through the fields. The
clouds in the distance were green.

By the time we reached the top of the hill the wind was rocking the truck and   10
the first drops of rain were hitting the hood, big and loud and hard. The curtain of
rain reached us, going from a few drops to a downpour in an instant. The wind
ripped the truck door from my father's hand. My grandfather ran out from the
cellar door, where he'd been watching for us, waiting. He took my brother, my
father took me. We couldn't see the cellar in the rain. Thunder rumbled the hills,
and lightning stabbed down, sharp and quick, splitting the rain, everything quiet
for an instant before the thunder struck.

We splashed through the rain and into the cellar. I was wet, plastered to my   11
father's chest. My mother took us down the stairs. My father and grandfather
stood, peering through the window at the rain. The day had gone dark.

Downstairs, my grandmother was telling stories to my two younger cousins,   12
who were flinching in the sharp crashes of each thunder. The room smelled of
kerosene, of earth and wind and rain. My skin was wet, hair cold as my mother
wrapped me in a quilt. In the brief silences between thunderclaps, we could hear
the rain and my father and grandfather on the stairs. I peered through the door
and heard my father say, "There it is."

He turned and saw me standing at the bottom of the stairs and motioned me up.   13
The rain had slowed and was falling lightly now, the wind settled down in the
trees. I stood on the steps with my father as he pointed in the distance, where a
dark funnel coiled downward from the black clouds, like smoke, or wind taking
shape and color. At the base of the tornado dust and debris hovered, circling slowly,
and I heard the sound of storm for the first time. It grew out of air, out of wind. It
seemed as silent as noise can be, a faint howling that reached us over the rain,
almost peaceful from a distance. But then it would hit a line of trees, or a fence,
shooting trees and fence posts and barbed wire into the air. It crossed over a pond
and water turned it almost white for an instant. It hit an old barn like a fist,
smashing boards and metal, slinging the debris about.

We watched, not speaking, as the tornado moved over the empty fields in the   14
distance, leaving a swath of devastation in its wake. After a time it folded itself

---

1. *Dust devil:* A small, high-velocity swirl of wind made visible by the sand or dust that turns within it.

back into the underbelly of the clouds, rising silently, dispersing like smoke in the wind, the sound gone and the air still once again.

"It's over," my father said, but I could still see in my mind the black funnel  15 dropping from the clouds, twisting across the landscape, throwing trees and dirt and anything in its path, tearing tracts of land as it went on its way. Before me was the result, the path of the tornado, cut through the hills. And, for no reason it seemed, it faded away, gone as surely as it had come.

We stood there for a long time after it was over, silent, watching the clouds roll  16 on through, speeding swiftly toward night. After a time—an hour or three or four—the clouds peeled back, revealing bright stars flung across the sky.

My father, and my grandfather, had watched other tornadoes before, just like  17 that one, had seen them and knew what they could do. I had thought that they were standing guard through the night, watching until it was safe for us to come out, putting themselves between us and the danger that lurked outside. But as we turned and went down the stairs together I realized they watched from the window to see the terrible beauty of the storm rolling across the hills, hail falling from the sky, streaks of lightning in the jagged edges of the storm, the twisting funnel of clouds that held such power.  ◆

## FOR CLOSE READING

1. How did Paul Crenshaw learn so much about the weather conditions that generate storms, particularly ones with tornadoes? Who taught him to be such a skilled "meteorologist" (1)?

2. Generation after generation, Crenshaw's family passes on its expert knowledge of storms. Why do the family members need to do this?

3. Crenshaw believed as a child that his parents and grandparents were simply "standing guard" when they kept a close lookout for brewing storms (17). He discovered later that they kept watch for other reasons as well. What were they?

4. Crenshaw ascribes no significance, beyond the natural and human, to the phenomena he is describing. Should he have mentioned the supernatural as well? Why or why not?

## Strategies and Structures

1. Is Crenshaw's description mostly OBJECTIVE or SUBJECTIVE? Explain your reading by referring to specific passages in the text.

2. Crenshaw's description is made up mostly of sights and sounds. Point out places in the text where he emphasizes these physical sensations. Why do you think he relies on these two senses in particular?

3. Point out passages in which Crenshaw describes his family's feelings and emotions during a storm. How does the scene in the storm cellar (11–16) contribute directly to the picture?

4. What DOMINANT IMPRESSION (awe and wonder at the power of nature; fear and trembling at the helplessness of the people; faith in the security of home and family; some combination of these or other emotions) is Crenshaw's description likely to leave upon the reader? Explain why you think so.

5. *Other Methods.* Crenshaw uses a FLASHBACK ("when I was eight") to recall the first time he remembers witnessing a tornado (7). Where else in his description does he use strategies of NARRATIVE like this?

6. According to Crenshaw, why do houses and other structures sometimes "explode" in a tornado (5)? Throughout his essay, how and how well does Crenshaw analyze the CAUSES and EFFECTS of the physical phenomena he is describing?

## Thinking about Language

1. Observers of oncoming tornadoes often describe them as sounding like a "freight train" (3). Does Crenshaw expand effectively on this common comparison? Or does he lapse into CLICHÉ? Explain.

2. Where else in his description does Crenshaw use SIMILES to describe what he and his family see, hear, and feel? What do these FIGURES OF SPEECH contribute to his description?

3. Why isn't a *meteorologist* someone who just studies meteors (1)? Look up the root meaning of the word in your dictionary and explain why the term is not a misnomer.

4. "Sometimes," says Crenshaw, "it will stop raining when the funnel falls" (3). Why does he switch to the future tense here?

## FOR WRITING

1. In a paragraph or two, describe an impressive storm, fire, waterfall, rainbow, or other natural phenomenon that you have witnessed. Be sure to include your feelings and emotions as well as the physical conditions that prompted them.

2. Write an essay describing how some particular knowledge or skill—reading weather (or other) patterns in nature, hunting and fishing, cooking and cleaning, playing a game or sport—was passed on to you by family members or friends. Set your description in a specific time and place.

3. A weather report is a form of information gathering and reporting. In a paragraph or two, define and describe the genre as you understand it from watching the weather report on television or the internet, or reading about it in your local newspaper. (For example, a weather report typically predicts future effects based on present causes.) How does a typical weather report compare with an academic research report?

4. Keep a weather diary for some period of time, preferably several weeks or months. Take special note of particularly dramatic events, such as storms, by describing them in detail; but include the mundane details of everyday meteorology as well.

• • • • • • • • • • • • • • • • • • • • • • • • • • • • • • • • • • • • • • • • • • •

You'll find quizzes on the readings at
wwnorton.com/write/back-to-the-lake.

MICHAEL J. MOONEY

# The Most Amazing Bowling Story Ever

Michael J. Mooney is a staff writer at *D Magazine* and a regular contributor of sports and crime stories to *GQ, Outside, Grantland,* and other magazines and blogs. A graduate of the University of Texas at Austin, Mooney
was a student at the Mayborn School of Journalism in Denton, Texas,
when two of his profiles—"The Day Kennedy Died" and "Royal Flushed"—
were selected to appear in the 2009 annual collections of *Best American
Crime Reporting* and *Best American Sports Writing.* Whether in sports,
crime, or other fields, a *profile* is a biographical sketch of a person (the
surgeon who tried to save President Kennedy) or a group (the colorful
players who introduced Mooney to the world of professional poker).

In "The Most Amazing Bowling Story Ever," which appeared in the July
2012 issue of *D Magazine,* Mooney profiles a fellow Texan, Bill Fong, whose
Chinese mother pushed him to excel in school. Fong himself, who "hasn't
had a lot of success in life," preferred the alleys (bowling, that is) of Chicago and, later, Plano, Texas, north of Dallas. Because it shows people
doing what they do best (or worse), a profile typically includes elements of
narrative. Mooney's profile of Ron Washington, manager of the Texas
Rangers baseball team, for example, appeared in the 2012 edition of *Best
American Sports Writing* under the title, "He Do What He Do." As a *picture
in words,* however, a profile is also a detailed description, both physical
and psychological, of its key subject, such as a bowler who one night bowls
a near-perfect game—and almost dies.

W HEN BILL FONG APPROACHES THE LANE, fifteen-pound bowling ball in hand, 1
he tries not to breathe. He tries not to think about not breathing. He wants
his body to perform a series of complex movements that his muscles themselves
have memorized. In short, he wants to become a robot.

Fong, forty-eight years old, six feet tall with broad shoulders, pulls the ball into 2
his chest and does a quick shimmy with his hips. He swings the ball first backward,
then forward, his arm a pendulum of kinetic energy, as he takes five measured

MLA CITATION: Mooney, Michael J. "The Most Amazing Bowling Story Ever." 2012. *Back to the Lake.* Ed.
Thomas Cooley. 3rd ed. New York: Norton, 2015. 209–16. Print.

steps toward the foul line. He releases the ball, and it glides across the oiled wooden planks like it's floating, hydroplaning, spinning counterclockwise along a trajectory that seems to be taking it straight for the right-hand gutter. But as the ball nears the edge of the lane, it veers back toward the center, as if guided by remote control. The hook carries the ball back just in time. In a heartbeat, what was a wide, sneering mouth of pins is now—nothing.

He comes back to the table where his teammates are seated—they always sit 3 and bowl in the same order—and they congratulate him the same way they have thousands of times over the last decade. But Fong looks displeased. His strike wasn't good enough.

"I got pretty lucky that time," he says in his distinctly Chicago accent. "The 4 seven was hanging there before it fell. I've got to make adjustments." With a pencil, he jots down notes on a folded piece of blue paper.

His teammates aren't interested in talking about what he can do to make his 5 strikes more solid, though, or even tonight's mildly competitive league game. They're still discussing a night two years ago. They mention it every week, without fail. In fact, all you have to do is say the words "That Night" and everyone at the Plano Super Bowl knows what you're talking about. They also refer to it as "The Incident" or "That Incredible Series." It's the only time anyone can remember a local recreational bowler making the sports section of the Dallas Morning News. One man, an opponent of Fong's that evening, calls it "the most amazing thing I've ever seen in a bowling alley."

Bill Fong needs no reminders, of course. He thinks about that moment—those 6 hours—every single day of his life.

Mooney is DEFINING *perfection* here; see p. 179 for using other methods in a description.

Most people think perfection in bowling is a 300 game, but it isn't. Any 7 reasonably good recreational bowler can get lucky one night and roll twelve consecutive strikes. If you count all the bowling alleys all over America, somebody somewhere bowls a 300 every night. But only a human robot can roll three 300s in a row—thirty-six straight strikes—for what's called a "perfect series." More than 95 million Americans go bowling, but, according to the United States Bowling Congress, there have been only twenty-one certified 900s since anyone started keeping track.

Bill Fong's run at perfection started as most of his nights do, with practice at 8 around 5:30 p.m. He bowls in four active leagues and he rolls at least twenty games a week, every week. That night, January 18, 2010, he wanted to focus on his timing.

Timing is everything. When your timing is right, when your arms, legs, and 9 torso all move in rhythm toward the lane, you have better balance. When you're balanced, you're also more accurate. And when you're accurate, your decision-making also improves. By contrast, if your timing is off, your balance is off, and

"He releases the ball, and it glides across the oiled wooden planks like it's floating, hydroplaning, spinning counterclockwise along a trajectory that seems to be taking it straight for the right-hand gutter."

you don't hit your targets. There are too many variables to assess, too many elements to gauge, and you can't possibly make the best decisions. Fong knows a hot streak is all about timing. So in practice that night, he breathed, he tried to erase all thoughts, and he tried to make his approach with each body part functioning as programmed.

That night, he didn't roll many strikes in practice. There was nothing to make him think this night would be anything special. 10

Fong's team, the Crazy Eights (he picked the name because eights are lucky in Chinese culture), was assigned lanes twenty-seven and twenty-eight, one of Fong's favorite pairs. The left lane, twenty-seven, hooks more, he says. The right lane, twenty-eight, tends to be more direct. 11

Frame one was on the left lane. As always, he was last in the bowling order, the anchor position. He watched his teammates roll and noticed each one throw a ball that hooked early and missed the pocket, the sweet spot between the head pin and the three pin on the right, the place that gives you the best chance of getting a strike. So when it was Fong's turn, he opted to roll a deeper hook, to stay outside and ride the edge of the gutter a little longer. 12

The result was a loud, powerful strike. His ball slammed into the pocket with a ₁₃ vengeance, obliterating all ten pins. His next roll, on twenty-eight, was another violent strike. All four of the first frames were robust strikes, actually. But his teammates barely took notice.

"To tell you the truth, that wasn't that unusual," says JoAnn Gibson, a sweet ₁₄ Southern woman who enjoys the company more than she does the actual bowling.

"Bowlers like Bill can roll off mini-streaks like that all the time," says Tom ₁₅ Dunn, a more serious bowler who sometimes flirts innocently with JoAnn.

Both Gibson and Dunn have bowled with or against Fong in this league since ₁₆ the Clinton administration. They've been teammates for nine years. James Race, who, with his perpetual smile and polite demeanor, reminds the other teammates of Mister Rogers, came a few years later. They don't really hang out much outside the bowling alley, but no matter what's going on in life, they go to Plano Super Bowl for a few hours on Monday nights.

Fong's fifth roll of the night wasn't so beautiful. His approach and release ₁₇ seemed the same—he was becoming the robot—and the ball hit the pocket, but the pins didn't go down quickly. The ten pin was wobbling upright, teetering, when Fong got what is called a "messenger." From the left, one of the pins he'd just sent bouncing came back across the lane, clipping the ten just enough to knock it off balance. When he got back to the table, his teammates congratulated him, but Fong called it what it was: a lucky strike.

In the sixth frame, he had another loud, devastating strike. Then another. Then ₁₈ another. With each throw, he could tell it was a strike from the moment it left his hand. He'd watch as the pins were there one second, then gone the next. "It felt like driving and catching a green light, then the next one, then the next, then turning, and still catching every green light everywhere you go," Fong says.

Before he knew it, it was the tenth frame. Back on the right lane, he again tried ₁₉ to swing the ball wide, let it run along the outside of the lane, next to the gutter. The first two rolls of the tenth frame both tucked into the pocket just as Fong hoped, and both were solid strikes.

On the last roll, though, something happened. He could tell from the sound of ₂₀ the pins. As the clutter at the end of the lane cleared, he could see the nine pin (the second from the right on the last row) still standing. He watched the chaos of the flying pins, each rotating right past the upright nine. Fong craned his neck, watching, hoping. Until one of the pins popped up from its side and swiped the nine down.

"The best way to describe the first 300 was just 'powerful,'" Race says. ₂₁

P. 176 explains when to use an abstraction like "powerful" in a description.

One of the Super Bowl employees announced Fong's name and score ₂₂ over the loudspeaker, something Fong is a particular fan of. There was a round of applause.

"Sometimes, when you have a lot of 300s, or if you get more than one in a week, 23 they won't announce it," he says.

The night was just beginning. 24

Aside from bowling, Bill Fong hasn't had a lot of success in life. His Chinese 25 mother demanded perfection, but he was a C student. He never finished college, he divorced young, and he never made a lot of money. By his own account, his parents didn't like him much. As a bowler, his average in the high 230s means he's probably better than anyone you know. But he's still only tied as the fifteenth best bowler in Plano's most competitive league. Almost nothing in life has gone according to plan.

He likes to say he got his approach to bowling from the hard-hitting alleys in his 26 native Chicago, where he went to high school with Michelle Obama. He was one of the few kids from Chinatown interested in bowling at the time. Despite his strict mother and the fact that his friends were all on the honor roll, little William preferred sports. He dreamed of being a professional athlete one day. He wasn't big— too short for basketball, too slender for football—but he'd run up and down the block as a boy, racing imaginary friends.

When Fong was young, his parents divorced. He remembers the man who would 27 become his stepdad taking his mom out on dates to a local bowling alley, where they could bring the kids. He noticed that when he was bowling, he wasn't thinking about whatever was going on behind him. His mind could focus on the ball, the lane, the pins—and the rest of the world would disappear. He had never been captivated by anything like that.

. . .

"Looking back," Fong says, "I guess bowling just always filled whatever emp- 28 tiness I had."

. . . Throughout the second game, Fong continued using his more aggressive ball on 29 the left lane, and the more polished, less aggressive ball on the right lane. And the strikes kept coming.

It seemed like even members of the other team were smiling when Fong was up 30 to roll. Fong himself was laughing and smiling, pointing and calling out to friends at other lanes. He remembers shrugging a lot. "I felt loose as a goose," he says.

As he sent strike after strike down the lanes, he began to feel magical. Literally, 31 the way he was commanding the balls to turn and burrow into the unsuspecting pins, it felt a little like he was moving heavy objects with only the power of his mind. In the fourth frame, both the seven and the ten pins stayed up just a bit longer than he wanted. As he gestured with both arms, they fell. Something similar happened in the eighth frame.

"It was like Moses parting the sea," he says. "I'd move my hands and everything would get out of the way." 32

Soon the other bowlers began stepping back when he was up, taking extra precaution not to get in his way. "Nobody wants to mess up a streak like that," Dunn says. 33

By the tenth frame, Fong found that most people around him wouldn't make eye contact for fear they would be the last thing he would see before rolling a dud. On the first roll of the last frame, he had what he calls a "happy accident." For the first time that night, one of his powerful throws missed its mark ever so slightly. But because the oil was now evaporating on the left lane, too, the ball found the pocket for a perfect strike. Noticing what happened on the first roll, he adjusted his position and finished the game with two more powerful strikes, numbers twenty-three and twenty-four of the night. 34

Once again, Fong got to hear his name called from the speakers. And again he took a moment to shake hands with the line of people waiting to congratulate him. A few were embarrassed that they hadn't come over after the first 300. People were delightfully confused, shaking their heads as they patted Fong on the back. 35

"Never seen anything like it," they said. "Back-to-back 300s." 36

And Fong shook his own head. "Me neither," he said. 37

There's almost never a time when every decision you make is correct and every step is in the right direction. Life, like bowling, is full of complicating factors, unpredictable variables, plenty of times when there is no right answer. But Bill Fong had some experience with near-perfection prior to the night. He'd had another amazing run two years before that. He'd bowled a 297, then a 300. Someone mentioned to him that with another great game he could beat the Texas state series record, which was 890. Fong can admit it now: he choked in that third game. He could feel himself thinking too much, slipping out of the zone. Soon he was out of rhythm and his balance was off. That night he shot a 169 in the last game; he didn't even break 800 for the series. It was exactly what he was trying to avoid after his two straight 300s. 38

So this time, before game three, he approached a friend who was bowling a few lanes down. Fong mentioned that he was thinking about switching balls again, using the less aggressive ball on both lanes in the final game. His friend, who had plenty of 300s under his own belt, was surprised but gave him simple advice: "Trust your instinct." 39

When that first roll of the third game produced another strike—another risky decision rewarded—Fong felt like he was floating. He wasn't drinking, but he felt a little drunk. Both his teammates and his opponents bowled as fast as they could to get out of his way. By the time he struck in the fifth frame, he realized he would almost certainly break the coveted 800 mark. He was relieved. 40

By the sixth frame, a large crowd had formed behind Fong. Dozens of people 41 had stopped bowling to watch. Texts were sent and statuses posted to Facebook, and the audience grew.

"We were more nervous than he was at the time," Gibson says. "It was almost 42 like he was putting on a show up there."

Each time he approached the lane, the entire bowling alley went silent. Every 43 time he let fly another roll, there were audible moans from strangers and shouts from the crowd: "That's it, baby!" Each time he struck, the room erupted with applause. In all his life, Bill Fong had never heard anyone cheering him like that.

He had thirty-three straight strikes entering the tenth frame of the third game. 44 Out came the cell phone cameras. There were whispers, but as soon as Fong picked up his ball, it was dead quiet. He turned to look at the crowd behind him, now well over one hundred people, densely packed from the end of the snack bar to the vending machines eighty feet away.

That's when the magic left him. Fong began to feel nervous, like the world was 45 watching him pee. He felt the buzz—whatever it had been—leave his body. As he stood in front of lane twenty-eight, he felt numb. He tried to push through it.

He lined up and threw a ball without much hook on it. As soon as it left his 46 hand, Fong began waving at it, trying to will the ball left. It connected with the pocket but without the usual force. As the other pins dropped, the nine pin stayed up for what seemed like ages. But just as the gasp of the crowd reached a crescendo, one of the pins rolling meekly across the lane bumped the nine just enough to tip it. The room exploded with cheers and whistles. The sound was enough to shake one of the cameras now capturing the moment.

Fong looked dizzy as he walked back to the ball exchange. For the first time that 47 night, he began sweating profusely. But he realized the mistake he'd made on his last throw, and the second roll was much cleaner. Again there were shouts from the audience as the ball blazed down the lane, zipping back in time to smash the pins apart in a powerful, driving strike. And there was even more cheering as all ten pins fell. Thirty-five strikes down, one to go.

Before his final roll, Fong wiped his ball with his towel. He heard a woman's 48 voice behind him, a stranger, saying, "We are having fun, aren't we?" He lifted the ball to his chest and stood calmly for a moment. Then he took five steps and released the ball toward perfection.

It looked good from his hand, arcing out the way so many of his great strikes 49 that night had, cutting back to the pocket just in time. Several people started applauding before the ball even reached the end of the lane—that's how good it looked. But this time, as the pins scrambled, something unimaginable happened. The ten pin, farthest to the right, wobbled. But it didn't fall.

Some of the people in the room couldn't process what they'd just witnessed. 50
How could the last roll, like the thirty-five before it, not be a strike?

Strangers fell to their knees. It was hard for anyone to breathe. 51

Fong turned and walked to his right. He was empty. Blank. 52

His friends, the ones who were prepared seconds ago to tackle him in celebration, 53
grabbed him and held him still. As he stood there, Fong wanted to say something—
anything—but he couldn't make a sound.

. . . It turns out Bill Fong was having a stroke. With the stress, the tension of the 54
night, his already high blood pressure had surpassed dangerous levels. Not long
after, he had another stroke. When the doctor saw the scar tissue and heard about
the night of dizziness, he explained to Fong that he had suffered what could very
easily have been a fatal stroke. That night at the bowling alley, had things gone differently, he could have died.

It also means that with the sweating and dizziness he was feeling in the third 55
game, it's likely that Fong bowled the last few frames through the beginning of that
stroke—which makes the accomplishment that much more amazing.

When he had his heart surgery, he was in the hospital for a week. Not many 56
family members visited him. Nobody came from his haircutting days. But he
didn't lack for visitors. Plenty of people from the bowling alley took the time to
see him, not just teammates but also some longtime opponents. They asked him
how he felt and encouraged him to get well quickly. And, one by one, they each
mentioned that incredible night in January, when Bill Fong fell just one pin short
of perfect.

Rehab was hard at first. The strokes took a lot of his strength. But within a few 57
months—earlier than doctors recommend—Fong was back to his usual form, back
to rolling five days a week. More recently, he's been sharper than ever. Since that
night, Fong has rolled ten more 300s and four series of at least 800.

As they're talking about that night, one of his teammates poses the question: 58
wouldn't Fong rather be alive with an 899 than dead with a 900? It's really a
rhetorical question, but Fong takes a moment to consider it seriously. It takes him
awhile, but eventually Fong says he'd rather be alive.

"Well," says Race, the Mister Rogers of the group, "we're sure happy to have you 59
still here and bowling with us."

Tonight, Fong struggles through the first few games. But in the final game of the 60
night, he starts with three straight strikes. Then a fourth. Then a fifth. In the sixth
frame, he throws it well but leaves the ten pin standing, taunting him.

After picking up the spare, Fong comes back to the table, shaking his head and 61
looking at his teammates.

"I've got to make adjustments," he says, and he begins making notes. ◆ 62

## FOR CLOSE READING

1. In what ways was Bill Fong different from most of the other kids he grew up with in Chicago? Why did he take up bowling? Was it a good life decision for him? Why or why not?

2. What's so extraordinary about bowling 899 in a three-game series? Why was it even more extraordinary that Fong did so on "That Night" (5)?

3. When asked whether he would "rather be alive with an 899 than dead with a 900," why does Fong hesitate before answering in the affirmative (58)?

4. Michael Mooney says Fong's achievement that night was "amazing." Is he right, or is this just sportswriter's hype? Explain your view.

5. "I've got to make adjustments," Fong says (4, 62). What do these words, quoted at the beginning of Mooney's essay and then again at the end, tell us about Fong as a bowler? as a person?

## Strategies and Structures

1. Mooney begins his description with a detailed physical portrait of Fong and his bowling style. Point to specific visual details that you find particularly effective, and explain what they contribute to the picture.

2. How and where does Mooney use the *sounds* and *tactile* sensations of the Plano Super Bowl to flesh out his description? Why are these particular details appropriate for describing what goes on in a bowling alley?

3. Mooney writes in the present tense (*approaches, swings*) in the first five paragraphs of his description. Why does he switch to past tense (*started, wanted*) in paragraph 8? When and why does he switch back to the present tense?

4. In bowling, says Mooney, "perfection" is reserved for human robots (7). Fong is not a robot but a human and, therefore, imperfect by definition. How and where does Mooney create the DOMINANT IMPRESSION of someone striving toward an elusive goal in both sport and life? Point to specific details in the text.

5. *Other Methods.* Mooney's description of Fong and the Plano Super Bowl is interwoven with a NARRATIVE of what happened there. Point out places in the text where Mooney effectively works in such elements of narrative as CHRONOLOGY, PLOT, and DIALOGUE.

## Thinking about Language

1. Why does Mooney use quotation marks and capital letters for "That Night," "The Incident," and "That Incredible Series" (5)?

2. A bowl is a vessel for holding water and food. Since there is no such bowl (or pitcher) in the game, where does *bowling* get its name?

3. Mooney frequently pairs the words *robot* and *perfection* in his profile of Fong. What are the implications of using these terms together in a description of a skilled athlete? Of this athlete in particular?

4. Fong and his teammates think of James Race as "the Mister Rogers of the group" (16, 59). Explain this ALLUSION. How does it illuminate Race's comment that "we're sure happy to have you still here and bowling with us" (59)?

5. According to Mooney, the existential question that Fong's teammates pose to him in the end is "really a rhetorical question" (58)? What's *rhetorical* about it?

## FOR WRITING

1. Observe a talented athlete who is deeply engaged in his or her sport. In a paragraph or two, describe how he or she looks and sounds (and smells?) when making characteristic moves or plays.

2. Write a descriptive essay about an athlete, musician, or other performing artist who exhibits "near-perfection" in some demanding form of physical or intellectual endeavor (38). (A chess player would be a good example of the latter.) Make every detail in your description contribute directly to that dominant impression as you focus on a particular game or performance.

3. "Crazy Eights" is the name of a traditional card game as well as a bowling team in Texas. Look up several accounts of how the game is played, synthesize them, and write a brief description of the game. Be sure to cite your sources.

4. Along with several other people, visit the "Lake Links" page at wwnorton.com/back-to-the-lake and watch a video of the moments that robbed Bill Fong of a perfect bowling score. Discuss the video among yourselves and make note of everyone's comments. Based on those notes and comments, write your own description of Fong and his big night.

5. Through an entire season or playoff series in a sport that interests you, keep a journal focusing on a single team or player. Include not only your own observations about characteristic games and plays but specific details of what people said and did and how particular places looked sounded and otherwise appealed to your senses.

6. Write a profile of someone—such as a member of your family, a teacher, a professional or semiprofessional athlete, a public figure—who has achieved success in his or her walk of life despite having to make adjustments to obstacles along the way. Describe the person and what he or she does (or did) in copious physical detail, but also give a sense of who and what that person has made of himself or herself over time.

You'll find quizzes on the readings at wwnorton.com/write/back-to-the-lake.

# E. B. WHITE

# Once More to the Lake

Elwyn Brooks White (1899–1985) was born in Mount Vernon, New York. He graduated from Cornell University in 1921 and worked as a journalist and advertising copywriter before joining the staff of the *New Yorker* in 1926. From 1938 to 1943, he also wrote a regular column for *Harper's Magazine*. White's numerous books include the children's classic *Charlotte's Web* (1952) and his updating of William Strunk's 1918 *Elements of Style* (1959), a guide to writing.

Written in August 1941 on the eve of World War II, "Once More to the Lake" originally appeared in *Harper's* and helped to establish White's reputation as a leading essayist of his day. The lake described here is Great Pond in south-central Maine. As White returns to this familiar scene, it seems unchanged—at first.

O NE SUMMER, along about 1904, my father rented a camp on a lake in Maine   1
and took us all there for the month of August. We all got ringworm from some kittens and had to rub Pond's Extract on our arms and legs night and morning, and my father rolled over in a canoe with all his clothes on; but outside of that the vacation was a success and from then on none of us ever thought there was any place in the world like that lake in Maine. We returned summer after summer—always on August 1 for one month. I have since become a salt-water man, but sometimes in summer there are days when the restlessness of the tides and the fearful cold of the sea water and the incessant wind that blows across the afternoon and into the evening make me wish for the placidity of a lake in the woods. A few weeks ago this feeling got so strong I bought myself a couple of bass hooks and a spinner and returned to the lake where we used to go, for a week's fishing and to revisit old haunts.

I took along my son, who had never had any fresh water up his nose and who   2
had seen lily pads only from train windows. On the journey over to the lake I began to wonder what it would be like. I wondered how the time would have marred this unique, this holy spot—the coves and streams, the hills that the sun set behind, the camps and the paths behind the camps. I was sure that the tarred road would have

MLA CITATION: White, E. B. "Once More to the Lake." 1941. *Back to the Lake*. Ed. Thomas Cooley. 3rd ed. New York: Norton, 2015. 219-24. Print.

found it out, and I wondered in what other ways it would be desolated. It is strange how much you can remember about places like that once you allow your mind to return into the grooves that lead back. You remember one thing, and that suddenly reminds you of another thing. I guess I remembered clearest of all the early mornings, when the lake was cool and motionless, remembered how the bedroom smelled of the lumber it was made of and of the wet woods whose scent entered through the screen. The partitions in the camp were thin and did not extend clear to the top of the rooms, and as I was always the first up I would dress softly so as not to wake the others, and sneak out into the sweet outdoors and start out in the canoe, keeping close along the shore in the long shadows of the pines. I remembered being very careful never to rub my paddle against the gunwale for fear of disturbing the stillness of the cathedral.

The lake had never been what you would call a wild lake. There were cottages 3 sprinkled around the shores, and it was in farming country although the shores of the lake were quite heavily wooded. Some of the cottages were owned by nearby farmers, and you would live at the shore and eat your meals at the farmhouse. That's what our family did. But although it wasn't wild, it was a fairly large and undisturbed lake and there were places in it that, to a child at least, seemed infinitely remote and primeval.

I was right about the tar: it led to within half a mile of the shore. But when I got 4 back there, with my boy, and we settled into a camp near a farmhouse and into the kind of summertime I had known, I could tell that it was going to be pretty much the same as it had been before—I knew it, lying in bed the first morning, smelling the bedroom and hearing the boy sneak quietly out and go off along the shore in a boat. I began to sustain the illusion that he was I, and therefore, by simple transposition, that I was my father. This sensation persisted, kept cropping up all the time we were there. It was not an entirely new feeling, but in this setting, it grew much stronger. I seemed to be living a dual existence. I would be in the middle of some simple act, I would be picking up a bait box or laying down a table fork, or I would be saying something, and suddenly it would be not I but my father who was saying the words or making the gesture. It gave me a creepy sensation.

We went fishing the first morning. I felt the same damp moss covering the 5 worms in the bait can, and saw the dragonfly alight on the tip of my rod as it hovered a few inches from the surface of the water. It was the arrival of this fly that convinced me beyond any doubt that everything was as it always had been, that the years were a mirage and that there had been no years. The small waves were the same, chucking the rowboat under the chin as we fished at anchor, and the boat was the same boat, the same color green and the ribs broken in the same places, and under the floorboards the same freshwater leavings and débris—the dead helgramite, the wisps of moss, the rusty discarded fishhook, the dried blood from yesterday's catch. We stared silently at the tips of our rods, at the dragonflies that came and went. I lowered the tip of mine into the water, tentatively, pensively dislodging the fly, which darted two feet away, poised, darted two feet back, and came to rest again a little farther up the rod. There had been no years between the ducking of this dragonfly and the other one—the one that was part of memory. I looked at the boy, who was silently watching his fly, and it was my hands that held his rod, my eyes watching. I felt dizzy and didn't know which rod I was at the end of.

We caught two bass, hauling them in briskly as though they were mackerel, 6 pulling them over the side of the boat in a businesslike manner without any landing net, and stunning them with a blow on the back of the head. When we got back for a swim before lunch, the lake was exactly where we had left it, the same number of inches from the dock, and there was only the merest suggestion of a breeze. This seemed an utterly enchanted sea, this lake you could leave to its own devices for a few hours and come back to, and find that it had not stirred, this constant and trustworthy body of water. In the shallows, the dark, water-soaked sticks and twigs, smooth and old, were undulating in clusters on the bottom against the clean ribbed sand, and the track of the mussel was plain. A school of minnows swam by, each minnow with its small individual shadow, doubling the attendance, so clear and sharp in the sunlight. Some of the other campers were in swimming, along the shore, one of them with a cake of soap, and the water felt thin and clear and unsubstantial. Over the years there had been this person with the cake of soap, this cultist, and here he was. There had been no years.

Up to the farmhouse to dinner through the teeming, dusty field, the road under 7 our sneakers was only a two-track road. The middle track was missing, the one with the marks of the hooves and the splotches of dried, flaky manure. There had always been three tracks to choose from in choosing which track to walk in; now the choice was narrowed down to two. For a moment I missed terribly the middle alternative. But the way led past the tennis court, and something about the way it lay there in the sun reassured me; the tape had loosened along the backline, the alleys were green with plantains and other weeds, and the net (installed in June and removed in September) sagged in the dry noon, and the whole place steamed with midday heat and hunger and emptiness. There was a choice of pie for dessert, and one was blueberry and one was apple, and the waitresses were the same country girls, there having been no passage of time, only the illusion of it as in a dropped curtain—the waitresses were still fifteen; their hair had been washed, that was the only difference—they had been to the movies and seen the pretty girls with the clean hair.

Summertime, oh, summertime, pattern of life indelible, the fade-proof lake, the 8 woods unshatterable, the pasture with the sweetfern and the juniper forever and ever, summer without end; this was the background, and the life along the shore was the design, the cottages with their innocent and tranquil design, their tiny docks with the flagpole and the American flag floating against the white clouds in the blue sky, the little paths over the roots of the trees leading from camp to camp and the paths leading back to the outhouses and the can of lime for sprinkling, and at the souvenir counters at the store the miniature birch-bark canoes and the postcards that showed things looking a little better than they looked. This was the American family at play, escaping the city heat, wondering whether the newcomers in the camp at the head of the cove were "common" or "nice," wondering whether it was true that the people who drove up for Sunday dinner at the farmhouse were turned away because there wasn't enough chicken.

Don't forget to tell the reader why (p. 173) you're describing "all this."

It seemed to me, as I kept remembering all this, that those times and those summers had been infinitely precious and worth saving. There had been jollity and peace and goodness. The arriving (at the beginning of August) had been so big a business in itself, at the railway station the farm wagon drawn up, the first smell of the pine-laden air, the first glimpse of the smiling farmer, and the great importance of the trunks and your father's enormous authority in such matters, and the feel of the wagon under you for the long ten-mile haul, and at the top of the last long hill catching the first view of the lake after eleven months of not seeing this cherished body of water. The shouts and cries of the other campers when they saw you, and the trunks to be unpacked, to give up their rich burden. (Arriving was less exciting nowadays, when you sneaked up in your car and parked it under a tree near the camp and took out the bags and in five minutes it was all over, no fuss, no loud wonderful fuss about trunks.)

Peace and goodness and jollity. The only thing that was wrong now, really, was the sound of the place, an unfamiliar nervous sound of the outboard motors. This was the note that jarred, the one thing that would sometimes break the illusion and set the years moving. In those other summertimes all motors were inboard; and when they were at a little distance, the noise they made was a sedative, an ingredient of summer sleep. They were one-cylinder and two-cylinder engines, and some were make-and-break and some were jump-spark, but they all made a sleepy sound across the lake. The one-lungers throbbed and fluttered, and the twin-cylinder ones purred, and purred, and that was a quiet sound, too. But now the campers all had outboards. In the daytime, in the hot mornings, these motors made a petulant, irritable sound; at night, in the still evening when the afterglow lit the water, they whined about one's ears like mosquitoes. My boy loved our rented outboard, and his great desire was to achieve single-handed mastery over it, and authority, and he soon learned the trick of choking it a little (but not too much), and the adjustment of the needle valve. Watching him I would remember the things you could do with the old one-cylinder engine with the heavy flywheel, how you could have it eating out of your hand if you got really close to it spiritually. Motorboats in those days didn't have clutches, and you would make a landing by shutting off the motor at the proper time and coasting in with a dead rudder. But there was a way of reversing them, if you learned the trick, by cutting the switch and putting it on again exactly

9

10

on the final dying revolution of the flywheel, so that it would kick back against compression and begin reversing. Approaching a dock in a strong following breeze, it was difficult to slow up sufficiently by the ordinary coasting method, and if a boy felt he had complete mastery over his motor, he was tempted to keep it running beyond its time and then reverse it a few feet from the dock. It took a cool nerve, because if you threw the switch a twentieth of a second too soon you would catch the flywheel when it still had speed enough to go up past center, and the boat would leap ahead, charging bull-fashion at the dock.

We had a good week at the camp. The bass were biting well and the sun shone endlessly, day after day. We would be tired at night and lie down in the accumulated heat of the little bedrooms after the long hot day and the breeze would stir almost imperceptibly outside and the smell of the swamp drift in through the rusty screens. Sleep would come easily and in the morning the red squirrel would be on the roof, tapping out his gay routine. I kept remembering everything, lying in bed in the mornings—the small steamboat that had a long rounded stern like the lip of a Ubangi, and how quietly she ran on the moonlight sails, when the older boys played their mandolins and the girls sang and we ate doughnuts dipped in sugar, and how sweet the music was on the water in the shining night, and what it had felt like to think about girls then. After breakfast, we would go up to the store and the things were in the same place—the minnows in a bottle, the plugs and spinners[1] disarranged and pawed over by the youngsters from the boys' camp, the Fig Newtons and the Beeman's gum. Outside, the road was tarred and cars stood in front of the store. Inside, all was just as it had always been, except there was more Coca-Cola and not so much Moxie and root beer and birch beer and sarsaparilla. We would walk out with the bottle of pop apiece and sometimes the pop would backfire up our noses and hurt. We explored the streams, quietly, where the turtles slid off logs and dug their way into the soft bottom; and we lay on the town wharf and fed worms to the tame bass. Everywhere we went I had trouble making out which was I, the one walking at my side, the one walking in my pants.

One afternoon while we were there at that lake a thunderstorm came up. It was like the revival of an old melodrama that I had seen long ago with childish awe. The second-act climax of the drama of the electrical disturbance over a lake in America has not changed in any important respect. This was the big scene, still the big scene. The whole thing was so familiar, the first feeling of oppression and heat and a general air around camp of not wanting to go very far away. In midafternoon (it was all the same) a curious darkening of the sky, and a lull in everything that had made life tick; and then the way the boats suddenly swung the other way at their moorings with the coming of a breeze out of the new quarter, and the premonitory rumble. Then the kettle drum, then the snare, then the bass drum

11

12

---

1. *Plugs and spinners*: Types of fishing lures.

and cymbals, then crackling light against the dark, and the gods grinning and licking their chops in the hills. Afterward the calm, the rain steadily rustling in the calm lake, the return of light and hope and spirits, and the campers running out in joy and relief to go swimming in the rain, their bright cries perpetuating the deathless joke about how they were getting simply drenched, and the children screaming with delight at the new sensation of bathing in the rain, and the joke about getting drenched linking the generations in a strong indestructible chain. And the comedian who waded in carrying an umbrella.

When the others went swimming, my son said he was going in, too. He pulled    13
his dripping trunks from the line where they had hung all through the shower and wrung them out. Languidly, and with no thought of going in, I watched him, his hard little body, skinny and bare, saw him wince slightly as he pulled up around his vitals the small, soggy, icy garment. As he buckled the swollen belt, suddenly my groin felt the chill of death. ◆

## FOR CLOSE READING

1. When and with whom did E. B. White first visit the lake he describes so palpably? With whom—and in approximately what time period—does he return to the lake, as described in his essay?

2. What **DOMINANT IMPRESSION** of the lake and its surrounding do you take away from White's description? Explain.

3. In paragraph 2, is White describing the lake as it was in the past, or as it is in the present time of his essay? How about in paragraphs 4–6? And in paragraph 11? Explain.

4. In addition to his own adventures on the lake, White is also describing those of "the American family at play" (8). What sentiments and behaviors does he identify as particularly American?

5. Do American families still take summer vacations "at the lake"? How has the pattern of family play—on a lake or elsewhere—changed since White wrote his essay? How has it remained the same?

### Strategies and Structures

1. In his description of the "primeval" lake, White stresses its qualities of calm and timelessness (3). What particular details contribute most effectively to this impression? What is his point in making it?

2. When he returned to the lake with his young son, the two of them went fishing, says White, "the first morning" (5). Point out other direct references to time in White's essay. How does he use CHRONOLOGY and the passing of time to organize his entire description?

3. One way in which the lake of his childhood has definitely changed, says White, is in its sounds. What new sounds does he describe? How does he incorporate this change into his description of the lake as a timeless place?

4. How would White's essay have been different without the last paragraph, in which he watches his young son get ready to go swimming?

5. *Other Methods.* As White describes the lake, he also tells a story about it. What's the plot of that story? How does White's NARRATIVE fit in with and support his description?

## Thinking about Language

1. What is the difference between an illusion and a "mirage" (5)? How and where do White's physical descriptions of the lake lead him to willful misinterpretations of the scene?

2. When he describes the lake as not only "constant" but "trustworthy" (6), White has PERSONIFIED the natural scene. When and where does it seem to take on a mind of its own in sharp contrast to his desires?

3. Why does White repeat the word *same* in paragraph 5?

4. When out in the boat alone as a boy, White did not want to disturb the "stillness of the cathedral" (2). What are the implications of this phrase? In what ways is White's son depicted as a chip off the old block?

5. The lake that White describes might be said to reside as much in memory as in the state of Maine. Why might fishing in a pond or lake provide an especially apt METAPHOR for probing memory—and writing about it?

## FOR WRITING

1. Briefly describe a memorable family vacation or other outing. What do you remember most about it, and why? Try to recall the details that led you to this memory.

2. Recall a place that seemed "unique" or "holy" to you when you first visited it. Write an essay describing how it has changed since then, and how it has remained the same. In choosing details to include, think about what dominant impression you want to give.

3. Write an essay describing how a familiar sight, taste, or sound triggers your remembrance of things past. Try to tie what you find back in with the present.

4. Write an essay-length memoir recalling a place you once lived in or visited frequently. Describe the physical characteristics of the place in detail, but also capture the act of remembering it by describing how the sight of a particular object—or a particular taste, sound, smell, or texture—triggers your remembrance.

5. Time seems to stand still on the lake in White's essay. Study how he achieves this sensation—for example, note his use of the image of the dragonfly—and write an essay about a place (such as the interior of an old house, a museum, or a natural setting) that seems timeless or out of time. Be sure to explain why it gives this impression.

6. One of White's sources for "Once More to the Lake" is Henry David Thoreau's *Walden: Or Life in the Woods*. Do some research on *Walden*, particularly Thoreau's depiction of the pond itself; and write a REPORT on White and Thoreau as nature writers.

You'll find quizzes on the readings at wwnorton.com/write/back-to-the-lake.

# American Smooth

Rita Dove (b. 1952) was the Poet Laureate of the United States from 1993 to 1995. A native of Akron, Ohio, where she played the cello from a young age, she attended Miami University in Oxford, Ohio, and the Writer's Workshop at the University of Iowa. Dove is currently Commonwealth Professor of English at the University of Virginia at Charlottesville. Her poetry collections include *On the Bus with Rosa Parks* (1999), *American Smooth* (2004), and *Sonata Mulattica* (2009). Dove is married to the German writer Fred Viebahn, her partner in the ballroom dances described in *American Smooth*.

Her method in these poems, Dove told an interviewer, was "to provide a humble description of the dance technique—what each part of the body should be doing . . . in the hopes of finding the poem's true desire, to achieve flight of consciousness, a lifting of the spirit as well as of the human form." In the title poem of *American Smooth*, however, the speaker focuses her description on the sensation (and appearance) of weightlessness, which she considers the "goal" of any dance.

We were dancing—it must have
been a foxtrot or a waltz,
something romantic but
requiring restraint,
rise and fall, precise                                    5
execution as we moved
into the next song without
stopping, two chests heaving
above a seven-league
stride—such perfect agony                                 10
one learns to smile through,
ecstatic mimicry
being the *sine qua non*
of American Smooth.
And because I was distracted                               15
by the effort of

MLA CITATION: Dove, Rita. "American Smooth." 2004. *Back to the Lake.* Ed. Thomas Cooley. 3rd ed. New York: Norton, 2015. 227-28. Print.

keeping my frame
(the leftward lean, head turned
just enough to gaze out                                    20
past your ear and always
smiling, smiling),
I didn't notice
how still you'd become until
we had done it                                             25
(for two measures?
four?)—achieved flight,
that swift and serene
magnificence,
before the earth                                           30
remembered who we were
and brought us down. ◆

## FOR CLOSE READING

1. In "American Smooth" is Rita Dove describing the particular moves of two people dancing, or how those moves felt to one of them at the time? Or both of these? Explain.

2. According to Dove, the essential ingredient or quality that DEFINES American Smooth is "ecstatic mimicry" (12). What do you think she means by this phrase?

3. Why is the speaker in Dove's poem always "smiling, smiling" (21)?

## Strategies and Structures

1. From whose perspective does Dove describe the dancing couple in her poem? Why do you think she chooses this POINT OF VIEW?

2. Is the description of the dancers more SUBJECTIVE or OBJECTIVE? Where does the speaker in Dove's poem reach the heights, so to speak, of subjectivity? Where is he or she most objective in describing the physical scene?

3. What DOMINANT IMPRESSION of the dancers and the dance does Dove give the reader in "American Smooth"? Which particular details in her description do you think contribute most directly to this impression?

4. Dove renders her entire poem in two long, flowing sentences. Why do you think she choose this structure for her theme?

5. *Other Methods.* Dove describes a dance step that she and her partner executed so well that they seemed, for a moment, to be flying. What does the dance step EXEMPLIFY in American culture generally? What else is she describing?

## Thinking about Language

1. In "Puss in Boots" and other folk and fairy tales, "seven-league boots" allow the wearer to cover great distances—a league is often defined as approximately three miles—in a single stride. Explain the ALLUSION to this magical footwear in line 9 of Dove's poem.

2. "Perfect agony" is a contradiction in terms (10). Is the OXYMORON justified here? Why or why not?

3. *Sine qua non* is Latin for "without which none" (13). How appropriate is the phrase as Dove uses it here? Explain.

4. What's so "American," according to Dove, about the smooth style of dancing (and more?) that she is describing?

## FOR WRITING

1. In a paragraph or two, explain how to execute a particular dance step—such as the dosado, enchufla, gancho, grapevine, heel pull, or moonwalk—by describing what skilled dancers do when they execute that step.

2. Write an essay describing a time on the dance floor, or basketball or tennis court, or in the gym or swimming pool, or on a skateboard or bicycle when you felt as if you were achieving flight. Be sure to describe not only how you felt but the exact moves that made you feel that way.

3. Read Dove's poem on at least three different days and make notes of each reading in your journal. Read the poem again, go over your journal notes, and write a 400-word TEXTUAL ANALYSIS of the poem based on this in-depth reading. Use description extensively to capture specific details in the text that you want to analyze.

4. Read and discuss "American Smooth" with several of your classmates. Write a collaborative analysis of the poem that focuses on the *differences* in the ways each person in the group reads some aspect of the text.

You'll find quizzes on the readings at
wwnorton.com/write/back-to-the-lake.

# CHAPTER 8

# Example

An art dealer knows at a glance that a supposedly ancient statue is a fake. After five minutes in a new course, a student accurately predicts that the professor is going to be a brilliant teacher—or a bore. Listening to a husband and wife bicker in his office, a trained psychologist can tell, with 90 percent accuracy, whether the couple will still be together in fifteen years. These are all examples that journalist Malcolm Gladwell uses to illustrate "thin-slicing," the idea that human beings can make accurate judgments based on "the very thinnest slice" of information.

Examples help us to understand such concepts by giving us a slice of information that is typical of the whole pie. Because a single good example is often worth a dozen lengthy explanations, we use examples all the time to support or explain what we have to say. The use of examples—exemplification—is so basic to human communication, in fact, that it is hard to imagine writing without them.

## Giving a "For Instance"

When you define something, such as thin-slicing or the law of supply and demand, you say what it is. When you exemplify something, you give an instance or illustration. To show us what he means by thin-slicing, Gladwell cites the example of an apparently happy couple who were recorded in the "love lab" while having the following conversation about their new dog:

> Sue: Sweetie! She's not smelly. . .
> Bill: Did you smell her today?
> Sue: I smelled her. She smelled good. I petted her, and my hands didn't stink or feel oily. Your hands have never smelled oily.
> Bill: Yes, sir.
> Sue: I've never let my dog get oily.
> Bill: Yes, sir. She's a dog.
> Sue: My dog has never gotten oily. You'd better be careful.
> Bill: No, you'd better be careful.
> Sue: No, you'd better be careful. . . . Don't call my dog oily, boy.
> —Malcolm Gladwell, *Blink*

Is this couple's marriage in jeopardy? According to the experts whom Gladwell consulted, it is if this "slice" (or example) is representative of their relationship as a whole. To the researcher who knows what to look for, says Gladwell, "The truth of a marriage can be understood in a much shorter time than anyone imagined."

This is, as Gladwell goes on to say, "a beautiful example" of the complicated psychological process he is explaining. Examples are particular items or instances—a couple playfully bickering about their dog, a crispy taco with guacamole, "The

Raven"—that can be taken to represent a whole group: psychological thin-slicing, Tex-Mex food, the poems of Edgar Allan Poe.

In this chapter, we will see how to choose examples that truly represent—or exemplify—your subject. We'll consider how many and what kinds of examples are sufficient to make your point about that subject, and then discuss how to organize an entire essay around those examples. Finally, we'll review critical points to watch for as you read over an exemplification essay, as well as common errors to avoid when you edit.

## Why Do We Cite Examples?

For most of us, it is easier to digest a piece of pie than the whole pie at once. The same goes for examples: They make general concepts easier to grasp (and swallow), and they give the flavor of the whole in a single bite. As writers, we cite examples to explain ABSTRACT ideas or support general statements by making them more CONCRETE and specific.

Suppose we were writing about a street bazaar and wanted to make the point that it offered a wide range of goods. This may sound like a straightforward statement, but it could refer to everything from livestock to homemade bread. To clarify what we mean exactly, we would need to give specific examples, as in the following:

> Everything was for sale—flowers, bolts of cloth, candles, fruits and vegetables, shoes, coffee beans, toys, cheap jewelry, canned goods, religious articles, books, kerosene, candy, nylons, towels—all of it spilling onto the street in colorful profusion.
> —FRANK CONROY, *Stop-Time*

Using examples like this helps us (and our readers) to narrow down the universe from "everything" to something a little more specific. It shows just what corner of the great bazaar we're talking about, and it gives the reader a more definite sense of the bazaar's "colorful profusion." Even more important, by using concrete examples like bolts of cloth and kerosene, Conroy explains exactly what was for sale, making his statement clearer and more interesting.

## Composing an Essay That Uses Examples

An essay built around examples has basically two parts: a statement about a general category of things or ideas ("everything was for sale") and specific items from that category that illustrate the statement ("bolts of cloth, candles, fruits and vegetables, shoes, coffee beans, toys, cheap jewelry," and so on). What if Conroy had

## USING EXAMPLES IN A RÉSUMÉ

When you write a résumé—whether for a school or job application, as part of a website or blog, or for some other purpose—you present yourself and your accomplishments in a short form that can be readily reviewed by the intended audience. The conventional way of doing this is by breaking your career into categories and giving specific examples, in each category, of your education, skills, experience, and other attributes. The categories may vary, depending on your work experience and the level of the position you're looking for, but should include your personal data, goal, work history, skills, and hobbies. Anyone can set up a set of impressive categories like this on a résumé, but only you can fill in appropriate examples that show who you really are.

Let's say you're a senior executive of dubious repute, though not on Wall Street, and you're looking for a job at the master-of-the-universe level. You'd want to craft your résumé to highlight your unique strengths and accomplishments:

**Tell potential employers up front whom they're dealing with.**

### DARTH VADER
Death Star, in a Galaxy Far, Far Away
DVader@galacticempire.gov

**Let them know what you're going to do for (or to!) them.**

**Goal:** To serve the Emperor and bring all rebel galaxies to the dark side.

**Work History:**

**Emphasize scope, don't forget to include dates.**

Commander, Galactic Empire armed forces, overseeing
    construction of two Death Stars    19BBY to present
Chancellor Palpatine's Jedi representative    20BBY–19BBY
Battle Commander, Army of the Republic    22BBY–19BBY
Mentor to Padawan Ahsoka Tano    22BBY–19BBY

**List pertinent skills.**

**Skills:** Mastery of the Force, experienced battle strategist, imposing physical appearance, lightsaber duel expertise

**Show you're a normal person.**

**Hobbies:** Levitating underlings remotely by the throat, building protocol droids and lightsabers

illustrated his statement about the profusion of items on sale in the marketplace with the following examples instead: boxes and boxes of ladies' gloves, stall after stall of ladies' hats, piles and piles of ladies' shoes?

While these examples would illustrate the large numbers of items on offer in the marketplace, they lack variety and, consequently, don't fully support Conroy's statement that "everything" was on sale. When you compose an essay based on examples, consider which particular aspects of your subject you want to emphasize and look for examples that illustrate all of those qualities or characteristics.

As you come up with representative examples, you will also need to decide just how many examples to use and how best to organize them and present them to your readers. The exact number and kinds of examples you cite, however, will depend upon your AUDIENCE and PURPOSE, as well as the main point you're illustrating.

## Thinking about Purpose and Audience

The purpose of "All Seven Deadly Sins Committed at Church Bake Sale," the satirical piece from the *Onion* included in this chapter, is to entertain readers who have some idea of what happens at church bake sales and who will be amused by an "exposé" of such a (normally) innocent event. For this purpose and audience, the writer chooses humorous, exaggerated examples of "sinful" behavior at the sale. In total, says the *Onion*, "347 acts of sin were committed at the bake sale."

But suppose you wanted to write a straightforward, informative report about a bake sale for the church bulletin. In that case, you would focus on actual examples of the people staffing the booths and the kinds of baked goods sold. Or if you were writing about the bake sale in order to persuade others to participate next time, you might offer examples of the money earned at various booths, how much fun participants had, and what good causes the money will be used for. In each case, your purpose shapes the kinds of examples you use.

So does your audience. No matter what your subject, you need to take into account how much your audience already knows (or does not know) about your subject—the *Onion* piece is careful to define "deadly" sins for readers who might be in doubt—and how sympathetic they are likely to be to your position. Suppose you are writing a paper for a course in health and nutrition, and your purpose is to argue that the health of Americans in general has declined over the last decade. If you were writing for your teacher alone—or for an audience of doctors or nutritionists—a few key examples would probably suffice to make your point.

Your paper, however, is intended for a more general audience, such as your classmates. So you will need to give more background information and cite more (and more basic) examples than you would if you were addressing an audience of specialists. If your readers are unfamiliar with your subject or not likely to see it as you do, you are going to have to work even harder to come up with sufficient examples. For instance, you may have to give extra examples to remind the athletes in your audience that their physical condition is not necessarily representative of the general state of health among all Americans.

## Generating Ideas: Finding Good Examples

Techniques like LISTING, BRAINSTORMING, and CLUSTERING can help you come up with examples on almost any subject. As you select examples, look for ones that display as many of the typical characteristics of your subject as possible.

Suppose you were writing an essay about the seven deadly sins, and you decided to focus on the sin of gluttony. One characteristic of gluttony is overeating. As you looked around for good examples of this characteristic, you might be tempted to choose someone like the international speed-eating champion Sonya Thomas, who holds world records for devouring chicken wings (183 in twelve minutes), tacos (40 in ten minutes), and oysters (444 in eight minutes). She would seem to be a prime example of gluttony. Thomas, however, weighs only about a hundred pounds; and though she eats a lot, Thomas has many other characteristics, such as discipline and endurance, that we typically associate with great athletes. Perhaps she isn't such a good example of a glutton after all.

So as you look for examples, search for ones that exemplify *all* the essential traits of the subject you're examining. Gluttons, for instance, not only eat a lot; they are often lazy. To exemplify the concept of gluttony more accurately and completely, therefore, we need to look for something or someone who exhibits both of these essential traits. How about Jabba the Hutt, the obese alien of *Star Wars* fame? Would he, perhaps, make a better example of gluttony than Sonya Thomas?

Jabba eats a lot—that's why he is so grossly overweight. Also, when not eating, he is forever tugging at his water pipe, another sign of overindulgence. What about lethargy, a prime characteristic of the glutton? Jabba can hardly rise from his cushions, much less dart around the galaxy participating in eating contests. And when he does attempt to move, he waddles heavily from side to side. Since Jabba embodies most of the chief characteristics of a glutton—he is both fat *and* lazy—he would make a better example of gluttony than the trim and energetic Thomas.

## Organizing and Drafting an Exemplification Essay

Once you have a number of examples that exhibit the chief characteristics of your subject, you're ready to organize them and put them in a draft. The simplest way to organize an essay based on examples is to state your THESIS at the beginning and then give your best examples to support it. You could also present your examples in order of increasing importance or interest, perhaps saving the best for last. Or, if you plan to use a large number of examples, you might organize them into categories.

However you organize your essay, you'll need to state your point clearly, provide sufficient and representative examples, and use transitions to help readers follow your text. The templates on p. 238 can help you with your draft.

## STATING YOUR POINT

Usually, in an essay based on examples, you will state your point directly in a thesis statement in your introduction. For example:

College teams depend more on teamwork than on star athletes for success.

In general, the health of Americans has declined over the last ten years.

Mitt Romney's 2012 presidential campaign made a number of tactical errors.

From a close reading of almost any major scene in *The Great Gatsby*, we can conclude that Fitzgerald's narrator, Nick Carraway, is not to be trusted.

As observed on the popular websites devoted to harmful campus gossip, online anonymity poses serious ethical problems.

Each of these thesis statements cries out for specific examples to support it. How many specific examples would you need to do the job sufficiently—and what kinds?

## PROVIDING SUFFICIENT EXAMPLES

Sufficiency isn't strictly a matter of numbers. Ultimately, whether or not your examples are sufficient to prove your point will depend on your audience. If your readers are inclined to agree with you, one or two well-chosen examples may suffice, which is what sufficiency implies: enough to do the job and no more. So consider your intended audience, and choose examples you think they will find interesting and convincing.

> "This Little Piggy Didn't Go to Market," p. 253, focuses on a single fortunate example.

Also, consider how broad or narrow your subject is. As you select examples to support a thesis, you have basically two choices: you can use multiple brief examples or one or two extended examples.

Multiple examples work well when you are dealing with different aspects of a large subject (a presidential campaign strategy) or exemplifying trends involving large numbers of people (Americans whose health has declined, college athletes). Extended examples, on the other hand, work better when you are talking about the implications of a particular case (a single scene in a novel; a particular website).

> To illustrate a linguistic trend, Molly Hennessy-Fiske uses multiple examples of Texas speech (p. 261).

Take the proposition that the health of Americans, on average, has declined over the last ten years. To support a sweeping general statement like this, which applies to millions of people, you would probably need to use multiple examples rather than one or two extended ones.

# TEMPLATES FOR DRAFTING

When you begin to draft an essay based on examples, you need to identify the subject, say what its main characteristics are, and indicate specific examples that exhibit those characteristics—moves fundamental to exemplification. See how Molly Hennessy-Fiske makes such moves in her essay in this chapter:

> There are many aspects to "talking Texan": pronunciation, cadence, syntax, not to mention vocabulary. And, technically, there are several Texas accents—the drawl of East Texans like Matthew McConaughey, say, or the nasal West Texas twang of Laura Bush.
> —MOLLY HENNESSY-FISKE, "Texas Talk Is Losing Its Twang"

Hennessy-Fiske identifies her dual subject (dialectical components of "talking Texan," various Texas dialects), says what the main characteristics of that subject are (pronunciation, cadence, syntax, vocabulary; drawl, twang), and then gives examples of people whose speech illustrates those characteristics (McConaughey and Bush). Here's one more example taken from this chapter; the writer gives her example first and then the subject it exemplifies:

> This little piggy found wandering this summer along a bustling Queens boulevard is among hundreds of animals—including cows, sheep, goats, and chickens—that apparently managed to flee in recent years from New York City's growing number of urban slaughter markets.
> —VERENA DOBNIK, "This Little Piggy Didn't Go to Market"

The following templates can help you make some of these basic moves in your own writing. But don't take these as formulas where you just fill in the blanks. There are no shortcuts to good writing, but these templates can serve as starting points.

▶ About X, it can generally be said that _____; a good example would be _____.

▶ The main characteristics of X are _____ and _____, as exemplified by _____, _____ and _____.

▶ For the best example(s) of X, we can turn to _____.

▶ _____ is a particularly representative example of X because _____.

▶ Additional examples of X include _____, _____, and _____.

▶ From these examples of X, we can conclude that _____.

On its website, the Institute of Medicine of the National Academies, lists eighteen indicators of the nation's health. If you were drawing on this data to make your point  about the decline in health among Americans in recent years, you would not likely focus on only one or two of these indicators, since health is a broad topic that encompasses many factors. Instead, you would want to cite multiple examples—low birth weights in infants, tobacco use, obesity, reduced access to health insurance, shorter average life expectancies, and decreased spending on health care—of the many different factors that contribute to the general decline you are illustrating.

Now let's consider how a reviewer of video games uses a single, extended example to support his thesis about their artistic and social potential:

> One of the finest games of 2013, and undoubtedly the most important, was *Gone Home*, which had no combat or killing but used the perspective of the first-person shooter genre, as well as some of the same narrative techniques, to tell a story about two teenage girls in love. *Gone Home*, however, was not universally beloved. Some players resented the idea that the game didn't involve much conventional challenge, in the sense of puzzles to solve or buttons to mash. —CHRIS SULLENTROP, "CAN VIDEO GAMES SURVIVE?"

Limiting video games to puzzles and buttons would be a mistake, Sullentrop argues. His thesis—that the possibilities of video games are almost "limitless"—might be supported by multiple examples of different games, such as *Grand Theft Auto* and *Call of Duty*. However, his thesis has to do with the potential quality (not quantity) of video games as a broad form of communication, so he chooses to focus on a single extended example of a particularly fine game, *Gone Home*.

## USING A RANGE OF REPRESENTATIVE EXAMPLES

Be sure that your examples fairly and accurately support the point you're making. For instance, if you were trying to convince readers that a particular political candidate failed to get elected because of errors in campaign tactics, you would need to cite a number of mistakes from different points in the campaign. Or if you were writing about how the best college athletic teams depend on teamwork for success, you would want to choose examples from several different teams.

Those examples should be as representative as possible. If you are writing, say, about the health benefits of swimming every day, Olympic gold medalist Michael Phelps is probably not a good example. Even though Phelps is a great swimmer, he is not representative (or typical) of swimmers in general, the subject you're exemplifying.

How do women make history? Mae West, though "bad," was a good example, p. 267.

## USING TRANSITIONS BETWEEN EXAMPLES

To make a point with exemplification, you need to do more than state your claim and then give examples, no matter how effective they may be. You need to relate those examples to each other and to the point you're making by using clear TRANSI-TIONS and other connecting words and phrases.

You can always use the phrases "for example" and "for instance": "The sloth, for example, is one of many animals that survive because of their protective coloration. Other animals—for instance, wolves and wild dogs—do so by going around in packs." But consider using other transitions and connecting phrases as well, such as: *more specifically, exactly, precisely, thus, namely, indeed, that is, in other words, in fact, in particular.* ("The sloth, in particular, survives by blending in with its surroundings.") Or try using a RHETORICAL QUESTION, which you then go on to answer: "So what strategy of survival does the sloth exemplify?"

Stephanie Cawley locates new examples in a text by saying "early in the comic" and "much later" (pp. 245–46).

## USING OTHER METHODS

The purpose of examples is to give concrete and specific illustrations of a general topic. Consequently, the examples themselves should be presented in ways that are as concrete and specific as you can make them. Let's say you're writing on the topic of common survival strategies among mammals. As an example, you've chosen the three-toed sloth, a tree-inhabiting eater of insects and plants from Central and South America. You can pre-sent such an example in a number of ways.

For instance, you can DESCRIBE it in some detail: "covered with unkempt fur that looks like the trunk of the tree it hides in." Or you can NARRATE what it does: "nothing at all, even when approached by the most dangerous of predators." Or you can analyze the CAUSES AND EFFECTS of its distinctive behavior: "such passivity fools predators into looking elsewhere for live food." And so on.

## EDITING FOR COMMON ERRORS IN EXAMPLES

Exemplification invites certain kinds of errors, particularly with lists or a series of examples. The following tips will help you check your writing for errors that often turn up when you use examples.

**If you list a series of examples, be sure they are parallel in structure**

▶ Animals avoid predators in many ways. They travel in groups, move fast, blend~~ing~~ in with their surroundings, and look~~ing~~ threatening.

**Edit out *etc.*, *and so forth*, or *and so on* when they don't add materially to your sentence**

▶ Animals typically avoid predators by traveling in groups, moving fast, ~~and~~ blending in with their surroundings~~, etc.~~

**Check your use of *i.e.* and *e.g.***

These abbreviations of Latin phrases are often used interchangeably to introduce examples, but they do not mean the same thing: *i.e.* means "that is" and *e.g.* means "for example." Since most of your readers do not likely speak Latin, it is a good idea to use the English equivalents.

▶ The chameleon is an animal that uses protective coloration—~~i.e.~~ that is, it changes color to blend in with its surroundings.

▶ Some animals change colors to blend in with their surroundings—~~e.g.~~ for example, the chameleon.

Go to wwnorton.com/write/back-to-the-lake for quizzes on these common errors.

# Reading an Essay Based on Examples with a Critical Eye

Once you've drafted your essay, ask someone else to read it and tell you which examples they find especially effective and which ones, if any, they think should be replaced or developed more sharply. Here are questions to keep in mind when checking your use of examples in an essay.

**PURPOSE AND AUDIENCE.** What is the overall purpose of the essay—to inform? entertain? persuade? How well does the text achieve that purpose? How familiar is the intended audience likely to be with the subject of the essay? What additional information might they find useful? What terms might they need to have defined or further explained?

**THE POINT.** What is the main point of the essay? Is it stated in a thesis? If not, should it be? How and how well do the examples support the thesis?

**ORGANIZATION.** Does the essay use multiple shorter examples, a few extended examples, or a combination of the two? Is this arrangement appropriate to the thesis of the essay—using multiple examples, for instance, to support a generalization that applies in many instances and extended examples to illustrate particular cases?

**SUFFICIENT EXAMPLES.** Are the examples presented in the essay sufficient to illustrate its key point or points? If not, how could the examples be made more persuasive? Would more examples be more convincing? Or do some examples need to be developed more fully? Which ones?

**CONCRETE AND SPECIFIC EXAMPLES.** Do the examples explain the topic in ways that are concrete (perceptible to the senses) and specific (narrowed down)? If not, how might they be sharpened and clarified?

**REPRESENTATIVE EXAMPLES.** Do the examples fairly and accurately represent the group they claim to represent? If the essay is based on one or two extended examples, do they represent *all* the important characteristics of the subject?

**TRANSITIONS.** Check all the transition words and phrases in the essay. How effectively do they introduce and link the examples? Do they explicitly connect the examples to the ideas they are illustrating? Where might transitions be added or strengthened?

**OTHER METHODS.** Does the essay incorporate any other methods of development? Would it be improved by including some DESCRIPTION or NARRATION, for example?

**COMMON ERRORS.** Does the paper include examples in a series? If so, does the form of any item in the series need to be changed to make it grammatically parallel with the others?

## Student Example

For a complete chapter from *Persepolis*, see p. 129. Stephanie Cawley wrote "The Veil in *Persepolis*" as a student at Stockton College in New Jersey. Focusing on a chapter from a graphic memoir by the Iranian artist and author Marjane Satrapi, it is part of Cawley's longer study on "Hybridity in Comics" that first appeared on her school's *Postcolonial*

*Studies* website in 2011. As indicated by the marginal annotations of Cawley's text, this essay reveals a lot about how to use examples to write a TEXTUAL ANALYSIS, a genre of academic writing that typically uses multiple examples from a written or visual text to make a key point about the text as a whole.

### The Veil in *Persepolis*

The representation of the veiled woman has become an important issue for postcolonial feminists who want to emphasize the importance of understanding localized meanings and knowledges rather than accepting the outside, Western viewpoint as the dominant truth. Although in *Persepolis* Marjane Satrapi represents the veil in a way that is consistent with a Western viewpoint of its being part of a systematic oppression of women, she also counters the representation of Middle Eastern women as passive, oppressed and monolithic by illustrating acts of overt and subtle resistance to the veil and the regime and by emphasizing the individual identities of women beneath the veil.

States the THESIS of Cawley's analysis.

The very first page of *Persepolis* establishes the comic's resistance to the Western image of the veiled woman. The first panel shows a ten-year-old Marjane, seated, the black veil surrounding her cartoonish face (Satrapi 3). The second panel shows a group of Marjane's classmates similarly veiled, with Marjane just out of the frame to the left (3). Monica Chiu, in "Sequencing and Contingent Individualism in the Graphic, Postcolonial Spaces of Satrapi's *Persepolis* and Okubo's *Citizen 13660*" reads these panels as "representing Marji as both an individual girl and a member of her class" (102). Far from the stereotypical, homogenizing representations of veiled women common to the western media, the simplified cartoonish style of Satrapi's artwork forces the viewer to notice the subtle variations Satrapi has given each of the girls—differences in hair texture, eye shape, and expression (Satrapi 3)—affirming them, as Chiu says, as individuals, but also as part of a shared experience. At the bottom of the page, in perhaps one of the most iconic images from *Persepolis*,

Uses examples from the text to show that the girls have "individual identities."

Presents the text itself (both graphic and verbal) as evidence to support the author's thesis.

(Satrapi 3)

the group of girls is shown refusing to wear their veils—some complaining it is too hot, others using their veils to play-act political or fantastical games, and others jumping rope with them (3). This image of even the youngest women resisting wearing the veil in a

Uses examples from the text to show that the girls offer "resistance to the veil."

variety of creative ways runs counter to the images presented in the Western media of passive, victimized women who are oppressed and flattened into a monolithic group by wearing the veil.

Examples of other forms of resistance.

(Satrapi 75)

This trope of resistance to the veil continues even after the regime has become increasingly powerful and all women are required and forced to wear the veil. Emma Tarlo, in her "Sartorial Review" of *Persepolis* notes that "more subtle indicators" (349) become the way to distinguish between the fundamentalist and more secular men and women. Satrapi represents this with a drawing showing the slight changes in stylings that people adopt to make visible their resistance to the regime (Satrapi 75).

3

(Satrapi 132–133)

Early in the comic, <u>some acts of resistance to the imposed clothing are even more bold</u>; while still relatively young, Marjane is

4

In these examples, the resistance is "more bold."

stopped by the Guardians of the Revolution for stepping into the street wearing a denim jacket and Nike sneakers with her veil in an attempt to align herself with the forbidden Western youth culture she adores (133). An embrace of Western appearance through clothing is shown to be an act of resistance for Iranians, particularly Iranians who, like Marjane at this point, have not been to the West and experienced alienation or isolation there.

Much later, when Marjane returns to Iran after spending time in Vienna, she discovers that her friends have adopted what Marjane initially sees as a superficial interest in Western standards of beauty—"They all looked like the heroines of American TV series" (259). Marjane later realizes that wearing makeup and adopting Western beauty standards is "an act of resistance on their part" (259). Marjane herself is easily identified as having been an outsider for some time due to her inability to wear the veil in the sneakily fashionable way that the other women do (293). While on the surface this expression of resistance through an embrace of Western culture appears to support western liberal feminist ideology, the fact that these women demonstrate agency and independence, not relying on outside forces to enact political change, problematizes this simple reading.

Subtle markers of resistance to the universalizing nature of the veil become increasingly important over the course of *Persepolis* as a way to visibly communicate political ideologies and also individual identities. Instead of the passive women accepting the enforced veil-wearing usually represented in the Western media, Satrapi represents women resisting the authority of the regime through their clothing and their bodies, and also represents them as individuals while still wearing their veils. The acts of resistance to the regime are perhaps so subtle—having to do with slight reconfigurations and small details such as wearing red socks—that they may not even be noticeable or understandable by an outsider without Marjane as a guide. This representation complicates, if not outright displaces, the Western stereotype of the veiled Muslim woman being passively oppressed.

As Marjane learns to read the signs, so does the reader.

Restates the thesis as a conclusion proven by the foregoing examples.

5

6

Works Cited

Chiu, Monica. "Sequencing and Contingent Individualism in the Graphic, Postcolonial Spaces of Satrapi's *Persepolis* and Okubo's *Citizen 13660*." *English Language Notes* 46.2 (2008): 99–114. Print.

Satrapi, Marjane. *The Complete Persepolis*. New York: Pantheon, 2007. Print.

Tarlo, Emma. "Marjane Satrapi's *Persepolis*: A Sartorial Review." *Fashion Theory* 11.2/3 (2007): 347–356. Print.

## Analyzing a Student Exemplification Essay

In "The Veil in *Persepolis*," Stephanie Cawley draws upon rhetorical strategies and techniques that good writers use all the time when they exemplify a subject. The following questions, in addition to focusing on particular aspects of Cawley's text, will help you to identify those common strategies and techniques so you can adapt them to your own writing. These questions will also help to prepare you for the analytical questions—on content, structure, and language—that you'll find after all the other selections in this chapter, along with suggestions for writing on related topics.

### FOR CLOSE READING

1. In *Persepolis*, says Stephanie Cawley, young Marjane, the central character, serves the reader "as a guide" (6). A guide to what? Why does the "Western" reader need a guide in Satrapi's book?

2. According to Cawley, what is "the Western image of the veiled woman" (2)? In what ways does she find this image to be inaccurate?

3. Under a repressive political regime, says Cawley (and, of course, Satrapi herself), how people dress or wear their hair can be meaningful. How so? Why does it matter, for example, that the women in Satrapi's autobiographical comic wear their veils in "sneakily fashionable" ways (5)?

4. According to Cawley, what *is* the basic function or role of the veil in Satrapi's work? Point to specific passages in her textual analysis that most clearly define this reading of the veil.

## Strategies and Structures

1. Cawley's basic point is that the veil is an image of "resistance" throughout *Persepolis*, but she is also arguing that the reader has to learn how to interpret those images properly. Point out examples in the text that support this point.

2. Early in her TEXTUAL ANALYSIS, Cawley locates a particular place ("the very first page") in the text she is writing about; she then DESCRIBES that part of the text in some detail (2). Point out several other places in Cawley's essay where she follows this fundamental step in analyzing any text.

3. In addition to locating and describing specific pieces of Satrapi's text, Cawley also DEFINES what each piece means or signifies. Point out several examples of *this* step in her analysis.

4. Having broken down the text she is analyzing into its constituent parts—and having indicated what the parts mean individually—how and where does Cawley put the pieces back together to explain their overall significance? Locate and describe particular places in her essay where Cawley takes this key *synthesizing* step, typical of textual analysis as a form of academic writing.

5. *Other Methods.* Citing the work of other readers, such as Monica Chiu and Emma Tarlo, Cawley ARGUES that Satrapi's use of the veil in *Persepolis* "complicates, if not displaces" Western views of the veiled woman (6). How, and how well, does this external evidence support Cawley's claim?

## Thinking about Language

1. Look up the root meaning of *iconic* in your dictionary (2). How does this meaning account for the use of the word with such different referents as a face in a religious painting, an object in a comic, and a graphic on a computer screen?

2. What is a *trope*, and why does Cawley use the term for the veil in *Persepolis* (3)?

3. What does Cawley mean by *problematizes* in paragraph 5? by *agency* and *ideology* (5)? Is her use of these terms literary, political, or both? Explain.

4. In what sense might Cawley's own analysis of *Persepolis* be called a "sartorial" review (3)?

## FOR WRITING

1. From Cawley's essay, or Satrapi's "Kim Wilde" (p. 129), or a complete version of *Persepolis*, choose a panel or page and, in a few paragraphs, describe what you see there. Don't forget to mention the words as well as the images.

2. Clothes are important throughout *Persepolis*. Write a 4–6 page textual analysis of clothes as a trope of political submission and resistance in "Kim Wilde" (p. 129) or in some other chapter of Satrapi's graphic memoir.

3. In 250–300 words, write a critical EVALUATION of Cawley's essay, or of one of the other essays mentioned in her Works Cited. Is the claim or thesis of the essay clear and substantial? How and how well is that claim or thesis supported in the text?

4. Mine Okubo's *Citizen 13660*, to which Cawley refers, is a graphic memoir by a Japanese-American of her life in relocation centers in California and Utah during World War II. Images and text from various editions of Okubo's narrative are readily available on the internet and in print. Examine a number of them; and in separate entries in a journal—preferably over a period of time—describe representative examples of Okubo's drawings and note your reactions to them.

5. In collaboration with several of your classmates, discuss the role and character of the hero or heroine in your (and their) favorite comics. (Douglas Wolk's "Superhero Smackdown," p. 361, may give you some ideas.) COMPARE AND CONTRAST different figures as you consider—and take notes on—the cultural, social, or political values they embody. Choose one or two figures, and write a collaborative essay analyzing how and why those figures exemplify important values or norms in the culture they represent or resist. Refer to specific scenes and adventures.

You'll find quizzes on the readings at wwnorton.com/write/back-to-the-lake.

# BBQ Menu and Escaped Piglet

Examples are individual specimens (a plate of Uncle Willie's BBQ, a happy piglet) taken from a larger group, whether of physical items (food, sheltered animals) or ideas (styles of cooking, animal rights) that exhibit the basic characteristics of the group ("Wood Smoked on Site," "rooting in the dirt and mud"). In writing, we use examples all the time to give the flavor of the whole in a single bite, as on a restaurant menu telling readers what particular dishes are on offer. The items on a restaurant menu also give examples of classes or categories of food (pork, poultry, beef, seafood) and ways of preparing it ("Real Down Home" at Uncle Willie's).

Because of increased numbers of immigrant populations, with their own food rules and requirements, more and more meat is being produced in smaller urban slaughterhouses and live markets. Most animals—pigs, chickens, sheep, cows, goats—that enter those slaughterhouses or markets end up on menus like this one from Uncle Willie's BBQ in Connecticut. An example of one that didn't is Winston the piglet, pictured here in a photo provided by Farm Sanctuary in Watkins Glen, where he ended up after escaping from a live market in New York City. The full story of Winston's escape and early retirement can be found on p. 253.

[ **FOR WRITING** ] ···········································································

Using a section of Uncle Willie's fare as a model, create a menu, with copious examples, to fit the tastes of one of the following: Winston the piglet, a member of your family, a vegetarian, a fast-food junkie, a celebrity chef, some other food-conscious person (or animal).

Menu from Uncle Willie's Barbecue

Winston takes early retirement at Farm Sanctuary

# SUGGESTIONS FOR WRITING

1. In "The Veil in *Persepolis*" (p. 243), Stephanie Cawley says the typical Western view of the veiled woman in Islamic cultures is that she is systematically "passive, oppressed, monolithic." Write a **POSITION PAPER** outlining what you consider to be an accurate view of the veiled woman. Use the evidence Cawley cites, plus additional examples gathered from your own research.

2. Although it's a parody, "All Seven Deadly Sins Committed at Church Bake Sale" (p. 257) correctly notes that the seven deadly sins as identified "by Gregory the Great in the fifth century" are avarice, sloth, envy, lust, gluttony, pride, and wrath. Do some additional research into the history of the seven deadlies, and write an essay that gives traditional examples of each sin.

3. In "Texas Talk Is Losing Its Twang" (p. 261), Molly Hennessy-Fiske gives numerous examples of how regional speech in Texas is changing as a result of "urbanization, pop culture and an influx of newcomers." Texas is not the only state where such changes are taking place. Write a **REPORT** of approximately 600 words giving examples of how speech patterns are changing in your region (or some other locality you're familiar with).

4. "A first-year student at a California university told me," writes Laurel Thatcher Ulrich in "Well-Behaved Women Seldom Make History" (p. 267), "that to make history, people need to do the unexpected. She offered the example of the civil rights activist Rosa Parks who 'would not leave her seat.'" Write a brief profile of a person you find interesting who made history by doing the unexpected.

5. Alan Lightman's "14 May 1905" (p. 277) is a chapter from *Einstein's Dreams*, Lightman's fictional foray into the mind of Albert Einstein at the time he was conceiving his theory of relativity. Do some research into Einstein's theory, and write a **REPORT** explaining an important aspect—for example, the scientist's ideas about time—by giving specifics of physical phenomena, such as the notion that clocks would run slower under deep gravity.

# This Little Piggy Didn't Go to Market

Verena Dobnik is a reporter for the Associated Press news service. She is based in New York City, where she has covered stories ranging from fatal train wrecks to the controversy over whether to outlaw horse-drawn carriage rides in Central Park. Born in Slovenia, Dobnik was educated at Harvard University and Boston University. In addition to Texas and New York, she has lived in Switzerland, Canada, Italy, and Iceland.

In "This Little Piggy Didn't Go to Market" (editor's title), first published on the Associated Press website in August 2013, Dobnik writes about the growing trend, especially in urban areas, to process and sell meat at storefront slaughterhouses and live markets. Occasionally, a prospective dinner escapes while still on the hoof or wing. Dobnik cites numerous examples of pigs, cows, sheep, goats, chickens, ducks, and other fortunate animal escapees, but her chief example is Winston the piglet (photo on p. 251), who successfully broke out of a facility in Queens. Winston, says Dobnik, "is now a five-hour drive and a world away, on a 175-acre farm in Watkins Glen."

WINSTON ESCAPED DEATH to find a piglet's paradise.   1

The little piggy found wandering this summer along a bustling Queens   2 boulevard is among hundreds of animals—including cows, sheep, goats and chickens—that apparently managed to flee in recent years from New York City's growing number of urban slaughter markets.

Escaping to the streets amid honking cars and busy pedestrians comes with a   3 beautiful reward for those lucky enough to survive: a trip to an animal sanctuary in the wide open spaces north of the city where they can live out their days without fear of becoming someone's dinner.

"None of them come to us friendly," says Susie Coston, director of the Farm   4 Sanctuary, which has taken in more than 500 farm animals from the city in the last decade. "They know what blood smells like and they're very scared and high-strung, running to get away."

The case of Winston, so named by newspaper readers who followed his fate, is hardly unusual. The little porker had apparently been on the lam

A good example is an individual case (p. 239) that represents an entire group.

MLA CITATION: Dobnik, Verena. "This Little Piggy Didn't Go to Market." 2013. *Back to the Lake*. Ed. Thomas Cooley. 3rd ed. New York: Norton, 2015. 253–54. Print.

for days in an area with many storefront slaughterhouses before he was caught by city animal-control officers. They turned him over to the sanctuary, and his home now is a five-hour drive and a world away, on a 175-acre farm in Watkins Glen, where he is free to frolic.

"Winston is doing magnificently well," Coston says, adding that he "spends his    6 nights rooting in the dirt and mud and spinning and playing with his best friend Ruby, a piglet who recently fell off a transport truck."

Other residents there include Maxine, a cow caught in Queens six years ago    7 after a police chase. A tag on Maxine's back with numbers and bar codes indicated she was headed for slaughter, as were a lamb found hoofing it through the South Bronx and a goat rescued from a busy Brooklyn intersection.

More than one hundred chickens were on the loose at various times in    8

For tips on using multiple examples like this, see p. 237. the last year alone, along with twenty-seven ducks, three goats and a pig, according to the city's animal control agency. Officials say escaped animals are sometimes claimed by the slaughterhouses or urban farms from which they fled, but that is rare.

New York City is home to nearly ninety storefront slaughter markets, a number    9 that has nearly doubled in the last two decades because of an influx of immigrants accustomed to cooking with freshly butchered meats.

Reading signs and prices often written in Arabic, Hebrew or Spanish, customers    10 typically choose their dinner from birds fluttering in cages or goats and sheep staring from pens. In separate spaces, animals are slaughtered and eviscerated at lightning-fast speed following the halal Islamic practice or kosher Jewish tradition.

"Halal to me means more than just the slaughter; it starts on the farm, and we    11 make sure animals are properly fed and cared for," says Imran Uddin, owner of the Madani Halal live market in Queens' Ozone Park neighborhood. As he speaks, a young goat pokes its nose through a chain-link fence and playfully nibbles at his shirt.

A retail menu scribbled on a blackboard one day included a young roasting    12 chicken at $1.65 a pound, pigeon—also called squab—for $8 apiece, and a water duck for $13.

None of Uddin's animals has ever escaped, but he says some from live markets    13 in the surrounding residential neighborhood have gotten away in the past.

New Yorkers who catch sight of an animal on the run call police or city officials    14 who drive it to a temporary shelter where it's cared for until it goes to one of about a half-dozen privately funded sanctuaries in the state.

"We work very hard to get the animals placed, to get them the care where they    15 can live out their life," says Richard Gentles, spokesman for Animal Care & Control of NYC. ♦

## FOR CLOSE READING

1. The example of Winston the free piglet, says Verena Dobnik, is "hardly unusual" (4). Why are more and more animals escaping from urban slaughterhouses and live markets these days?

2. How did Winston's companions Maxine and Ruby become members of Farm Sanctuary in Watkins Glen?

3. Slaughterhouses do occasionally reclaim their lost property, says Dobnik, but returning animals are "rare" (7). Why would that likely be the case?

4. Escaped animals in urban settings, as Dobnik notes, are often rounded up by the police and other public officers. Who funds and organizes the effort to take care of these escapees once they are captured?

## Strategies and Structures

1. Is Winston the piglet a clear and appealing example of his kind? Why or why not?

2. Winston's case is heart-warming rather than pan-warming. How does Dobnik nonetheless avoid (if she does) becoming overly sentimental in her REPORT? What else do Winston and his friends exemplify besides being lucky survivors?

3. In addition to following the adventures of a few animals, fortunate and otherwise, Dobnik has done considerable field research, including gathering statistics about the meat industry and interviewing people at New York's Animal Care & Control and elsewhere. If we see her essay as a research report on animal control and changes in the meat industry, what are her main findings, and how does she use examples to support those conclusions?

4. *Other Methods.* Winston finds a home at a place called Farm Sanctuary (11). How and where might Dobnik's account of Winston's fate, and that of his friends, be seen as an ARGUMENT in support of privately funded animal sanctuaries? Point to specific passages in the text where she seems particularly sympathetic to such a cause.

## Thinking about Language

1. At Farm Sanctuary, Winston is said to "frolic" (4). Why might Dobnik have chosen this term to describe the pig's activities instead of simply *play* or *relax*?

2. What kind of slang is "on the lam" (4)? Why does Dobnik use it to describe Winston the piglet?

3. In Jewish tradition, what is meant by keeping "kosher" (9)?

4. Comment on the IRONY of the young goat's nibbling "playfully" on Imran Uddin's shirt (10).

## FOR WRITING

1. Write a paragraph giving examples of the facilities at a perfect retirement place for farm or other animals.

2. Using examples of specific companies or dealers, write a brief research report on immigration and changes in the meat, clothing, or some other industry or business—or in education.

3. In Islamic law, most aspects of daily life, including food and drink, are divided into five categories: compulsory (*fard*), recommended (*mustahabb*), allowed (*hallal*), disliked (*makruh*), forbidden (*haram*). Do some research, including interviews with friends or classmates, and write an essay of approximately 500 words explaining the role and function of this system and giving examples of each kind.

4. Winston has a number of cousins in literature, including Wilbur the pig in E. B. White's classic book for children, *Charlotte's Web* (1952). Read (or re-reread) White's book—or another sophisticated story about animals that you remember from childhood—and write a TEXTUAL ANALYSIS, using examples, of the roles of some of the animals in the story. (In *Charlotte's Web*, for example, the spider is a writer.) Be sure to consider the extent to which the story appeals to adult readers as well as children.

You'll find quizzes on the readings at wwnorton.com/write/back-to-the-lake.

# All Seven Deadly Sins Committed at Church Bake Sale

The *Onion* was founded as a satirical weekly newspaper in 1988 by two juniors at the University of Wisconsin, Tim Keck and Christopher Johnson, who distributed a handful of copies to their friends around the Madison area. Today, the *Onion* website receives approximately 11 million unique visits per month. (The print edition ceased publication in 2013.) The *Onion* has long attributed its success to "fearless reporting and scathing commentary." Consider, for instance, these *Onion* headlines: "Cases of Glitter Lung on the Rise among Elementary-School Art Teachers," "Study Reveals Pittsburgh Unprepared for Full-Scale Zombie Attack," "Supreme Court Mistakenly Used Belgium's Constitution for Last 3 Rulings." Such satire has won the *Onion* a Thurber Prize for American Humor and a handful of Webby Awards. Several collections of its articles have made the *New York Times* best-seller list, including *Ad Nauseam* (2003) and *Our Dumb World* (2007).

The *Onion's* brand of satire is marked by its pitch-perfect mimicry of the reporting styles that many papers routinely use to inflate the banal into the newsworthy. In the following article, an *Onion* investigative reporter sniffs out numerous concrete and specific examples of the "deadly sins" committed at a church bake sale.

G ADSDEN, AL—The seven deadly sins—avarice, sloth, envy, lust, gluttony, pride, and wrath—were all committed Sunday during the twice-annual bake sale at St. Mary's of the Immaculate Conception Church. 1

In total, 347 individual acts of sin were committed at the bake sale, with nearly every attendee committing at least one of the seven deadly sins as outlined by Gregory the Great in the fifth century.

See p. 237 for what makes a "sufficient" number of examples. You don't have to cite all 347.

"My cookies, cakes, and brownies are always the highlight of our church bake sales, and everyone says so," said parishioner Connie Barrett, 49, openly committing the sin of pride. "Sometimes, even I'm amazed by how well my goodies turn out."

Fellow parishioner Betty Wicks agreed. 4

MLA CITATION: The Onion. "All Seven Deadly Sins Committed at Church Bake Sale." 2007. *Back to the Lake.* Ed. Thomas Cooley. 3rd ed. New York: Norton, 2015. 257-59. Print.

"Every time I go past Connie's table, I just have to buy something," said the 245-pound Wicks, who commits the sin of gluttony at every St. Mary's bake sale, as well as most Friday nights at Old Country Buffet. "I simply can't help myself—it's all so delicious." 5

The popularity of Barrett's mouth-watering wares elicited the sin of envy in many of her fellow vendors. 6

"Connie has this fantastic book of recipes her grandmother gave her, and she won't share them with anyone," church organist Georgia Brandt said. "This year, I made white-chocolate blondies and thought they'd be a big hit. But most people just went straight to Connie's table, got what they wanted, and left. All the while, Connie just stood there with this look of smug satisfaction on her face. It took every ounce of strength in my body to keep from going over there and really telling her off." 7

While the sins of wrath and avarice were each committed dozens of times at the event, Barrett and longtime bake-sale rival Penny Cox brought them together in full force. 8

"Penny said she wanted to make a bet over whose table would make the most money," said Barrett, exhibiting avarice. "Whoever lost would have to sit in the dunk tank at the St. Mary's Summer Fun Festival. I figured it's for such a good cause, a little wager couldn't hurt. Besides, I always bring the church more money anyway, so I couldn't possibly lose." 9

Moments after agreeing to the wager, Cox became wrathful when Barrett, the bake sale's co-chair, grabbed the best table location under the pretense of having to 10

Patti George (far right) commits the sin of envy as she eyes fellow parishioner Mary Hoechst's superior strawberry pie.

keep the coffee machine full. Cox attempted to exact revenge by reporting an alleged Barrett misdeed to the church's priest.

"I mentioned to Father Mark [O'Connor] that I've seen candles at Connie's 11 house that I wouldn't be surprised one bit if she stole from the church's storage closet," said Cox, who also committed the sin of sloth by forcing her daughter to set up and man her booth while she gossiped with friends. "Perhaps if he investigates this, by this time next year, Connie won't be co-chair of the bake sale and in her place we'll have someone who's willing to rotate the choice table spots."

The sin of lust also reared its ugly head at the bake sale, largely due to the pres- 12 ence of Melissa Wyckoff, a shapely 20-year-old redhead whose family recently joined the church. While male attendees ogled Wyckoff, the primary object of lust for females was the personable, boyish Father Mark.

Though attendees' feelings of lust for Wyckoff and O'Connor were never acted 13 on, they did not go unnoticed.

"There's something not right about that Melissa Wyckoff," said envious and 14 wrathful bake-sale participant Jilly Brandon, after her husband Craig offered Wyckoff one of her Rice Krispie treats to "welcome her to the parish." "She might have just moved here from California, but that red dress of hers should get her kicked out of the church."

According to St. Mary's treasurer Beth Ellen Coyle, informal church sponsored 15 events are a notorious breeding ground for the seven deadly sins.

"Bake sales, haunted houses, pancake breakfasts . . . such church events are rife 16 with potential for sin," Coyle said. "This year, we had to eliminate the 'Guess Your Weight' booth from the annual church carnival because the envy and pride had gotten so out of hand. Church events are about glorifying God, not violating His word. If you want to do that, you're no better than that cheap strumpet Melissa Wyckoff." ◆

## FOR CLOSE READING

1.  Who established the names and number of the seven deadly sins as we know them today?

2.  How "deadly" do you find the sins reported here? That is, how well do the reporter's examples represent the general concept he says he is exemplifying?

3.  The *Onion* reporter records "347 individual acts of sin" at the church bake sale (2). Is anything suspicious about these statistics? How do you suppose the reporter came up with this number?

4.  Which sins does parishioner Connie Barrett commit? How does her bake-sale success encourage the sins of others?

5.  Which single sin among the seven do the patrons of the bake sale only contemplate, rather than act upon? Who inspires it?

## Strategies and Structures

1. A spoof is a gentle PARODY or mildly satirical imitation. What general PURPOSE does a spoof or parody usually serve? What is the writer's specific purpose here, and who is the intended AUDIENCE?

2. Pride, avarice, and the other "deadly sins" are ABSTRACT concepts. How do the reporter's examples make them more CONCRETE and specific? Are the examples sufficient, or should there be more? Explain.

3. The reporter gives numerous examples of what people say at the church bake sale. Why? What purpose do these verbal examples serve?

4. *Other Methods.* To bolster the examples, the reporter uses elements of NARRATIVE. What are some of them?

## Thinking about Language

1. What, exactly, is a "strumpet," and why do you think the reporter uses this rather than a stronger word to describe Melissa Wyckoff (16)?

2. Deadly (or mortal) sins can be distinguished from venial sins. According to your dictionary, what is the difference between the two kinds? Give examples.

3. Give a SYNONYM for each of the following words: "avarice," "sloth," "gluttony," and "wrath" (1).

4. Another word for "pride" is *hubris*. What is the difference between the two, according to your dictionary?

## FOR WRITING

1. Write a paragraph about one sin you would add to the traditional list.

2. Write an exemplification essay illustrating how the seven deadly sins are routinely committed in the library, in your classes, or in some other place at your school.

3. Have a look at the *Onion* website; read a few examples of the "reporting" and what the editors have to say about style and content; then compose an *Onion*-like news report of your own. If you can't think of a subject that fits the genre, look back at the first selection in this chapter on Winston the escaped piglet.

4. Humor writing has its own demands and conventions. Do some research on the subject, and write a 400–500-word analysis of humor as a distinctive type of writing. Give lots of examples—and cite your sources.

⋯⋯⋯⋯⋯⋯⋯⋯⋯⋯⋯⋯⋯⋯⋯⋯•

You'll find quizzes on the readings at
wwnorton.com/write/back-to-the-lake.

## MOLLY HENNESSY-FISKE

# Texas Talk Is Losing Its Twang

Molly Hennessy-Fiske is the Houston bureau chief for the *Los Angeles Times*. A native of upstate New York, Hennessy-Fiske attended Harvard University and worked as a reporter in Boston, Miami, and Washington, among other cities, before joining the *Times*. She has completed journalism fellowships in Lebanon and Mexico—and won a number of awards for her reporting in such places as Afghanistan, Egypt, and Iraq.

"Fewer Texans are speaking in the traditional dialect," says Hennessy-Fiske, "as urbanization, pop culture and an influx of newcomers have conspired to displace the local language." This observation is borne out by the many examples she cites in "Texas Talk Is Losing Its Twang," which first appeared in the *Los Angeles Times* in January 2013. Hennessy-Fiske's sources range from students and professors at the University of Texas at Austin to actors Matthew McConaughey and Larry Hagman and former First Lady Laura Bush.

D ON GRAHAM, AN ENGLISH PROFESSOR at the University of Texas at Austin, 1
likes to tell the story of a student who once worked as a cowboy. "Wore hat and boots," Graham says. "He was the real deal."

At the end of the academic year, the student told Graham, "You were the only 2
professor at UT I ever had who spoke English."

"What he meant," Graham says, "was I was the only one who spoke his language." 3

And by language, the student meant talking Texan—the distinctive twang and 4
drawl that becomes almost an attitude, from the first "howdy" to the last "thank you, kindly." Conversation can be as extreme as the landscape in Texas, where locals will tell you it gets hotter than a stolen tamale and the wind blows like perfume through a prom.

The former cowboy had noticed what Graham, a Texas native who grew up out- 5
side Dallas, had also detected over the years. "Texas has always had its own almost national identity," Graham says. "Language was one of the commonalities that bound people together. More and more, I hear fewer people that I talk to who sound like myself."

MLA CITATION: Hennessy-Fiske, Molly. "Texas Talk Is Losing Its Twang." 2013. *Back to the Lake*. Ed. Thomas Cooley. 3rd ed. New York: Norton, 2015. 261–65. Print.

Research bears out his suspicion: Urbanization, pop culture and an influx of 6 newcomers—including Californians, with a Valley Girl dialect that has wormed its way into American speech since the 1970s—are all eroding the iconic Texas twang.

Back in the 1980s, about 80 percent of Texans interviewed by researchers at UT 7 Austin, including many students, had traditional Texas accents. Now that's down to a third.

The uniquely Texas manner of speech is being displaced and modified by 8 General American English, the generic, Midwestern dialect often heard on television. That's surprising, given the Texas accent's enduring nature.

The Texas accent "has great symbolic value. It has a local identity versus, say, 9 Arizona English. That makes Texas English more resilient," said Lars Hinrichs, an English language and linguistics professor at UT Austin.

There are many aspects to "talking Texan": pronunciation, cadence, syntax, not 10 to mention vocabulary. And, technically, there are several Texas accents—the drawl of East Texans like Matthew McConaughey, say, or the nasal West Texas twang of Laura Bush.

By interviewing and monitoring scores of Texas speakers, then measuring sound 11 waves when they speak, Hinrichs and a team of researchers at UT Austin's five-year-old Texas English Project hope to gauge the degree to which Texas accents and dialects have changed.

Texas accents are traditionally considered variants of Southern American 12 English, spoken from southern Maryland to eastern New Mexico, noticeable in words like pie (pah) and my (mah).

But in Texas that pronunciation varies, especially when the vowel is followed by 13 a consonant, which some Texans pronounce as a diphthong, or two-part sound. Examples of Texified diphthongs: "TRAY-up" (trap), "FAH-ees" (face) and "KAY-ut" (cat).

Many younger Texans are abandoning the diphthongs, and can no longer dif- 14 ferentiate the vowels in cot and caught (CAW-ut)—just like Yankee counterparts, according to UT Austin researchers.

A similar transition is taking place with the "oo" vowel sound. 15

"For instance," Hinrichs says one day at his office as he pulls up graphs of sound 16 waves on his office computer. "What does a Texas ghost say?"

That would be "boo," with the vowel sounding like the "oo" in "goose." At least 17 if the ghost talks like an old-time Texan.

A modern Texas ghost might say "beeew." The new pronunciation is a variation 18 of the monophthong that sounds more like a diphthong, more typical of both Northern and Midwest speakers.

Hinrichs' graphs showed that change, or "dialect leveling," as divergent lines, 19 most apparent among younger speakers. It appears to have spread from Dallas to Houston and into central Texas. One of his graduate students, Axel Bohmann, 28,

Technically, there are several Texas accents—the drawl of East Texans like Matthew McConaughey (left) and Lady Bird Johnson (middle), say, or the nasal West Texas twang of Laura Bush (right).

speculates that the change was due in part to younger people "style shifting," speaking with different accents in different settings—say, at home and at work—or adopting aspects of accents they hear in mass media.

"Young women are generally more attuned to the prestige of things: clothes, makeup and language. So they play around with that," Hinrichs says.    20

He and Bohmann are both from Germany, drawn to central Texas by its mix of dialects and accents, the legacy of Southern, Mexican and German immigrants.    21

"It's one of the most vibrant places to study language change and dialects," Hinrichs says. "Dialects used to be a simple function of place. Now they're a more complex function of identity."    22

Another doctoral student working with Hinrichs, Kate Shaw Points, is a 32-year-old Boston native who has lived in Texas for almost a decade. In that time she's learned to talk Texan, but deploys it strategically.    23

"When I'm at the mechanic, I talk like a Texan because I don't want them to cheat me," she says, but when she's watching a Red Sox game, she reverts.    24

She researched people who, depending on the setting, changed the way they said the "i" in "time." They might give it a Southern "ah" sound among fellow Texans, then switch to the clipped standard English "eye" in other settings.    25

In many ways, talking Texan is about belonging and regional pride. "That's another reason you're never going to see the Texas accent go away," Points said.    26

That's true. But the way of talking is changing.                                                                                    27

Deborah Darnell, 51, a substitute teacher from Austin interviewed by the Texas          28
English Project, says students are sometimes surprised by her pronounced accent.

"Where are you from?" they ask. "Do you live in the country?"                                        29

Sometimes she jokes with them: "Oh yeah, I've been up since dawn, milking the          30
cows and roping the horses."

Darnell doesn't even consider her accent that strong, certainly not compared          31
with her grandmother "from San Antone" or her mother.

"My mom—she's got a strong accent! She's 75 and she'll say, 'Oh my heavens, I          32
sound like Lady Bird Johnson!'" Darnell said. "There's not as many Texans, true
Texans, anymore, because there's a lot of people moving here from all over."

The state is full of new arrivals, and they are probably having an impact on          33
Texas speech, Hinrichs said. Texas led the nation in migration from other states as
of the last census with 486,558 newcomers—the majority, nearly 69,000, from
California.

The late Larry Hagman of *Dallas* fame noticed the change as well.                          34

"Now people are from Milwaukee or New York—someplace else. Dallas has just          35
exploded," Hagman, 81, said while filming in Dallas a few months before he died in
November.

Hagman, a native of Weatherford, outside Fort Worth, had lived all over the          36
world—including Malibu and London. But when in Texas, he talked like his oil
baron character, J. R. Ewing—for instance, "It was so hot you could fry eggs on the
cement." And that's pronounced SEE-ment.

"And I still say ice box," he said. "When you're down here, you try to fit in. It          37
makes people more comfortable."

Another of Hinrichs' students, Gina Forsythe, 22, is among the vanguard of young          38
Texas speakers. Her mother is of Mexican and Puerto Rican descent, her father
white. She definitely sounds Southern but doesn't consider her accent truly Texan.

"Whenever I hear the true Texas accent, I think it sounds so funny," Forsythe          39
said. "I don't know if it's because me and my peers are not using it as much, or if
we're subconsciously choosing not to."

Among Forsythe's set, there's a stigma attached to talking too traditionally          40
Texan.

**Use other meth-ods (p. 240), such as CAUSE AND EFFECT, to help explain your examples.**   "So much of what's driving the new vocabulary is Internet culture—          41
Facebook and Twitter and shortening words," she said. "I still hear Valley
Girl lingo constantly, and of course I'm a part of it—like, like, like, every
other word."

Two key indicators that Forsythe speaks with a new Texas accent: She          42
pronounces "pin" and "pen" differently (in traditional Texan, both sound like "pin")

and "cot" and "caught" the same, like someone outside the Lone Star State. She also avoids phrases like "might could," "fixin' to" or "down yonder."

But there are certain shifts even Forsythe is unwilling to make. Her boyfriend is from Connecticut, and instead of "y'all" says "you guys." 43

"It sounds so outdated and gender-unfriendly," she said. 44

And then there's "yous guys," a Sopranos staple Forsythe heard during a trip to New York City—and won't be repeating. 45

"That doesn't even make grammatical sense!" ◆ 46

## FOR CLOSE READING

1. Texas speech is losing more than just its drawl (DRAW-al) and twang (TWA-ang). What are some of the other qualities of "traditional Texas accents" that, according to Molly Hennessy-Fiske, have changed in recent years (7)?

2. According to Hennessy-Fiske and the people she interviewed, what are the major reasons for this "dialect leveling" in Texas (19)?

3. Ghosts are not real and, therefore, do not speak. So why does Hennessy-Fiske quote a ghost in paragraphs 16–18? How is the speech of an old-fashioned Texas ghost different from that of a "modern Texas ghost" (18)?

4. Two of the researchers interviewed by Hennessy-Fiske hail from Germany. What inspired them to come to Texas to do their work?

5. Hennessy-Fiske "might could" have addressed in detail the issue of whether Texans should conserve their old speech patterns, but she doesn't (42). Should she have? Why or why not?

### Strategies and Structures

1. What is the role of the "former cowboy" in the introductory paragraphs of Hennessy-Fiske's essay (5)?

2. To help define the linguistic concept of "a diphthong, or two-part" vowel sound, Hennessy-Fiske gives several examples (13). What are some of them? Are they helpful for understanding the concept? Why or why not?

3. What is Hennessy-Fiske's purpose in citing the example of the late *Dallas* actor Larry Hagman in paragraphs 34–37? Is Hagman a good example? Why or why not?

4. "Texas Talk Is Losing Its Twang" is a report of Hennessy-Fiske's (and others') research into the subject of linguistic change in regional Texas dialects. How and how well does giving examples serve her as a method of development in her research report?

5. *Other Methods.* Throughout her report, Hennessy-Fiske COMPARES AND CONTRASTS traditional Texas speech with newer ways of "talking Texan" (26). Is this an effective strategy? Why or why not?

## Thinking about Language

1. In the phrase "hotter than a stolen tamale," why would the tamale retain its heat despite the lapse of time necessary to steal it (4)?

2. What is "General American" (GA) speech (8)? Hennessy-Fiske defines it as "the generic, Midwestern dialect often heard on television" (8). What are some of the typical characteristics of this dialect? Give several examples.

3. Using "like, like, like, every other word," says one researcher interviewed by Hennessy-Fiske, is a characteristic of "Valley Girl lingo" (41). What dialect is she referring to, and what are some other "indicators" of "Valley Girl" speech (42)?

4. What are the implications of attaching the word "stigma" to the practice of "talking too traditionally Texan" (40)?

## FOR WRITING

1. In a paragraph or two, give several examples of the pronunciation of particular words that you consider to be indicators of Texan or other Southern regional speech. Spell them out phonetically, as Hennessy-Fiske does.

2. In a paragraph or two, give several examples of lexicon (vocabulary, word choice), such as "ice box" for refrigerator, that you think of as markers of these dialects.

3. The three words *merry, marry,* and *Mary* are frequently used in dialect studies as markers of regional speech. Do a little internet (or other) research on the subject and, in approximately 500 words, explain, with the use of examples, the common role of these three terms as dialect indicators.

4. Keep a linguistic journal in which you note, over time, interesting variations in pronunciation, vocabulary, and grammar that you hear and use in talking to others in different social and regional situations.

5. Compare your pronunciation of the following words with that of several of your classmates, preferably ones from different regions from yours: *cement, pecan, cot, caught, pen, pin, merry, marry,* and *Mary.* On the basis of this comparison, identify and describe your dialect in 150–250 words.

You'll find quizzes on the readings at
wwnorton.com/write/back-to-the-lake.

# Well-Behaved Women Seldom Make History

Laurel Thatcher Ulrich (b. 1938) is a professor of history at Harvard University and a former president of the American Historical Association. She is the author of books and articles on the women of colonial America, including *A Midwife's Tale* (1990), a biography that won a Pulitzer Prize and that Ulrich helped adapt into a documentary for the PBS series *American Experience*. Ulrich grew up in Idaho and attended the University of Utah, Simmons College, and the University of New Hampshire. She identifies herself as a Mormon feminist and has co-edited a collection of essays about the lives of Mormon women called *All God's Critters Got a Place in the Choir* (1995).

In 1976, Ulrich wrote a scholarly article that included the following phrase in the opening paragraph: "Well-behaved women seldom make history." Not long after her article was published, this line, often slightly altered, began appearing on bumper stickers and T-shirts across the country. In the following selection, which comprises the introductory chapter to her 2007 book with the same title, Ulrich uses her now-famous phrase as an example not only of the fragility of fame and popular culture, but of how history itself gets made—and written.

S OME TIME AGO a former student e-mailed me from California: "You'll be delighted to know that you are quoted frequently on bumpers in Berkeley." Through a strange stroke of fate I've gotten used to seeing my name on bumpers. And on T-shirts, tote bags, coffee mugs, magnets, buttons, greeting cards, and websites.

When you cite examples in a series, try to use the same grammatical form (p. 240).

I owe this curious fame to a single line from a scholarly article I published 2 in 1976. In the opening paragraph, I wrote: "Well-behaved women seldom make history." That sentence, slightly altered, escaped into popular culture in 1995, when journalist Kay Mills used it as an epigraph for her informal history of American women, *From Pocahontas to Power Suits*. Perhaps by accident, she changed the word *seldom* to *rarely*. Little matter. According to my dictionary, *seldom* and *rarely* mean the same thing: "Well-behaved women *infrequently*, or on *few occasions*, make history." This may be one of those occasions. My original article was a study of the well-behaved women celebrated in Puritan funeral sermons.

MLA CITATION: Ulrich, Laurel Thatcher. "Well-Behaved Women Seldom Make History." 2007. *Back to the Lake*. Ed. Thomas Cooley. 3rd ed. New York: Norton, 2015. 267–75. Print.

In 1996, a young woman named Jill Portugal found the "rarely" version of the quote in her roommate's copy of *The New Beacon Book of Quotations by Women*. She wrote me from Oregon asking permission to print it on T-shirts. I was amused by her request and told her to go ahead; all I asked was that she send me a T-shirt. The success of her enterprise surprised both of us. A plain white shirt with the words "Well-behaved women rarely make history" printed in black roman type became a best-selling item. Portugal calls her company "one angry girl designs." Committed to "taking over the world, one shirt at a time," she fights sexual harassment, rape, pornography, and what she calls "fascist beauty standards." [3]

Her success inspired imitators, only a few of whom bothered to ask permission. My runaway sentence now keeps company with anarchists, hedonists, would-be witches, political activists of many descriptions, and quite a few well-behaved women. It has been featured in *CosmoGirl*, the *Christian Science Monitor*, and *Creative Keepsake Scrapbooking Magazine*. According to news reports, it was a favorite of the pioneering computer scientist Anita Borg. The Sweet Potato Queens of Jackson, Mississippi, have adopted it as an "official maxim," selling their own pink-and-green T-shirt alongside another that reads "Never Wear Panties to a Party." [4]

See p. 239 to make sure you choose a range of examples that fit the situation.

My accidental fame has given me a new perspective on American popular culture. While some women contemplate the demise of feminism, others seem to have only just discovered it. A clerk in the Amtrak ticket office in D.C.'s Union Station told a fellow historian that all the women in her office wore the button. "I couldn't resist telling her that I was acquainted with you, and she just lit right up, and made me promise to tell you that the women at the Amtrak office thank you for all your 'words of wisdom.'" [5]

. . .

The "well-behaved women" quote works because it plays into longstanding stereotypes about the invisibility and the innate decorum of the female sex. Many people think women are less visible in history than men because their bodies impel them to nurture. Their job is to bind the wounds, stir the soup, and bear the children of those whose mission it is to fight wars, rule nations, and define the cosmos. Not all those who make this argument consider women unimportant—on the contrary, they often revere the contributions of women as wives, mothers, and caregivers—or at least they say so. But they also assume that domestic roles haven't changed much over the centuries, and that women who perform them have no history. A New Hampshire pastor captured this notion when he wrote in his commonplace book in 1650, "Woman's the center & lines are men." If women occupy the fixed center of life, and if history is seen as a linear progression of public events, a changing panorama of wars and kingdoms, then only those who through outrageous behavior, divine intervention, or sheer genius step into the stream of public consequence have a history. [6]

The problem with this argument is not only that it limits women. It also limits      7
history. Good historians are concerned not only with famous people and public
events but with broad transformations in human behavior, things like falling death
rates or transatlantic migration. Here seemingly small actions by large numbers of
people can bring about profound change. But this approach runs up against another
imperative of history—its reliance on written sources. Until recent times most
women (and a great many men) were illiterate. As a consequence their activities
were recorded, if at all, in other people's writing. People who caused trouble might
show up in court records, newspapers, or their masters' diaries. Those who quietly
went about their lives were either forgotten, seen at a distance, or idealized into
anonymity. Even today, publicity favors those who make—or break—laws.

But the difficulty is bigger than that. History is an account of the past based on      8
surviving sources, but it is also a way of making sense out of the present. In the
heat and confusion of events, people on all sides of an issue mine old stories for
inspiration, enlightenment, or confirmation. Their efforts add to the layers of
understanding attached to the original events, shaping what later generations
know and care about. Scholars sometimes call these popular reconstructions of the
past "memory" to distinguish them from formal history. But serious history is also
forged in the tumult of change. History is not just what happened in the past. It is
what later generations choose to remember.

· · ·

Historians don't own history. But we do have a lot of experience sifting through      9
competing evidence. Historical research is a bit like detective work. We re-create
past events from fragments of information, trying hard to distinguish credible
accounts from wishful thinking. One of our jobs is to explore the things that get
left out when a person becomes an icon. Recent scholarship on the Sweet Potato
Queens' heroine, Mae West, is a good example. There is no question about West's
reputation for misbehavior. She said it herself: "When I'm bad, I'm better." Beginning her stage career at the age of six, she moved from playing the saintly Little Eva
in *Uncle Tom's Cabin* to shimmying her way to fame. In uptight Boston, theater
owners cut off the lights "with West's first ripple." But in New York she was the
darling of urban sophisticates who wanted to explore the seamy side of life without
leaving their theater seats. When she moved to Hollywood in the 1930s, censors
tried to clean up her scripts, but she knew how to fill even the blandest lines with
sexual innuendo. *Variety* complained that "Mae couldn't sing a lullaby without
making it sexy."

That is how Mae West made history. But what sort of history did she make?      10
Some recent studies focus on her debts to the male homosexuals whose outrageous
impersonations defined *camp* in the 1920s. Others claim that her largest debt was
to African American entertainers. West's shimmy, for example, ultimately derived
from West African traditions adapted in rural dance halls, or "jooks." Her ballad

Mae West, photographed in the 1930s.

"Honey let yo' drawers hang down low" (which may have inspired the Sweet Potato Queens' "Never Wear Panties to a Party") was a favorite in southern jooks. In the early twentieth century, West, the sexually active, streetwise girl from Brooklyn, gave middle-class audiences a glimpse of worlds that both fascinated and repelled. Like the legendary Godiva,[1] she allowed people to imagine the unimaginable. Because she was also a savvy businesswoman, she was able to live off other people's fantasies.

A first-year student at a California university told me that to make history, people need to do the unexpected. She offered the example of civil rights activist Rosa Parks, "who would not leave her seat." I like her emphasis on the unexpected. It not only captures the sense of history as the study of how things change, it offers a somewhat more complex way of understanding the contribution of a woman like Parks.

Was Parks a well-behaved woman? The Montgomery, Alabama, bus company did not think so. As the student from California recognized, Parks made history precisely because she dared to challenge both social norms and the law. Her refusal to obey the statute that required her to give up her seat to a white passenger sparked the 361-day-long boycott that thrust Martin Luther King into the public

1. *Godiva:* Lady Godiva, an eleventh-century Anglo-Saxon noblewoman who reportedly rode naked through the streets of Coventry to protest taxes imposed by her husband.

eye and led to a historic Supreme Court decision outlawing segregation on public transportation. Yet Parks became an icon for the civil rights movement not only for her courage but because the media identified her as a hard-working seamstress who simply got tired of moving to the back of the bus. Few people outside Montgomery knew her as the politically conscious secretary of the local NAACP, nor understood how many years she and her husband had been working for social justice before that fateful day on the bus. In 1954 and 1955, Parks had attended workshops on desegregation sponsored by the radical Highlander Folk School in Tennessee, a public education project that Mississippi's Senator James Eastland excoriated as a "front for a conspiracy to overthrow this country."

Nor has popular history recorded the names of other Montgomery women—    13
teenagers—whose arrests that year for refusing to give up their seats failed to ignite a movement. Years later, E. D. Nixon, president of the Montgomery NAACP, explained why he hadn't chosen any of these other women to make a historic stand against segregation. "OK, the case of Louise Smith. I found her daddy in front of his shack, barefoot, drunk. Always drunk. Couldn't use her. In that year's second case, the girl, very brilliant but she'd had an illegitimate baby. Couldn't use her. The last case before Rosa was the daughter of a preacher who headed a reform school for years. My interview of her convinced me that she wouldn't stand up to pressure. She were even afraid of me. When Rosa Parks was arrested, I thought, 'This is it!' 'Cause she's morally clean, she's reliable, nobody had nothing on her, she had the courage of her convictions." Parks's publicly acknowledged good behavior helped to justify her rebellion and win support for her cause. As one friend recalled, she "was too sweet to even say 'damn' in anger."

After Parks's death in the fall of 2005, the airways were filled with tributes cele-    14
brating the life of the "humble seamstress," the "simple woman" who sparked a revolution because her feet were tired. Reviewing these eulogies, syndicated columnist Ellen Goodman asked, "Is it possible we prefer our heroes to be humble? Or is it just our heroines?" She wondered if it wasn't time Americans got over the notion that women are "accidental heroines," unassuming creatures thrust into the public eye by circumstances beyond their control. Goodman noted that Parks and her compatriots spent years preparing for just such an opportunity. She concluded: "Rosa Parks was 'unassuming'—except that she rejected all the assumptions about her place in the world. Rosa Parks was a 'simple woman'—except for a mind made up and fed up. She was 'quiet'—except, of course, for one thing. Her willingness to say 'no' changed the world."

The California student said that in contrast to Parks a "well-behaved woman" is    15
"a quiet, subservient, polite, indoors, cooking, cleaning type of girl who would never risk shame by voicing her own opinion." There is a delicious irony in this part of her definition. Notice that it associates a particular kind of work—cooking

Rosa Parks's mug shot, taken shortly after her arrest on December 1, 1955, for refusing to obey a bus driver's order to give up her seat to a white passenger.

and cleaning—with subservience and passivity. Yet the boycott that made Parks famous was sustained by hundreds of African American domestic servants—cooks and maids—who walked to work rather than ride segregated buses. They too did the unexpected.*

Serious history talks back to slogans. But in the contest for public attention, slogans usually win. Consider my simple sentence. It sat quietly for years in the folds of a scholarly journal. Now it honks its ambiguous wisdom from coffee mugs and tailgates. 16

. . .

In my scholarly work, my form of misbehavior has been to care about things that other people find predictable or boring. My second book is a case in point. At a distance, the life of Martha Moore Ballard was the stuff from which funeral sermons were made. She was a "good wife" in every sense of the word, indistinguishable from all the self-sacrificing and pious women celebrated in Puritan eulogies. In conventional terms, she did not make history. She cherished social order, respected authority, and abhorred violence. As a midwife and healer, she relied on home-grown medicines little different from those found in English herbals a century before her birth. Her religious sentiments were conventional; her reading was limited to the Bible, edifying pamphlets, and newspapers. Although she lived through the American Revolution, she had little interest in politics. She was a caregiver and a sustainer rather than a mover and shaker. 17

Ballard made history by performing a methodical and seemingly ordinary act— writing a few words in her diary every day. Through the diary we know her as a pious herbalist whose curiosity about the human body led her to observe and record autopsies as well as nurse the sick, whose integrity allowed her to testify in a sensational rape trial against a local judge who was her husband's employer, and whose sense of duty took her out of bed at night not only to deliver babies but to care for the bodies of a wife and children murdered by their own husband and father. The power of the diary is not only in its sensational stories, however, but in its patient, daily recording of seemingly inconsequential events, struggles with fatigue and discouragement, conflicts with her son, 18

For tips on keeping a diary, see p. 55.

---

* Awele Makeba's powerful one-woman show, "Rage Is Not a 1-Day Thing," dramatizes the lives of sixteen little-known participants, male and female, black and white. For details see her website, http://www.awele.com/programs.htm. For a list of resources prepared for the fiftieth anniversary of the boycott in 2005, see http://www.teachingforchange.org/busboycott/busboycott.htm. Additional documents can be found in Stewart Burns, ed., *Daybreak of Freedom: The Montgomery Bus Boycott* (Chapel Hill and London: University of North Carolina Press, 1997). Herbert Kohl, *She Would Not Be Moved: How We Tell the Story of Rosa Parks and the Montgomery Bus Boycott* (New York and London: The New Press, 2005), urges teachers to move from the theme "Rosa Was Tired" to the more historically accurate concept "Rosa Was Ready." [Author's note]

and little things—like the smell of a room where a dead body lay. In Ballard's case, the drama really was in the humdrum. The steadiness of the diary provided the frame for everything else that happened.

. . .

Although I have received mail addressed to Martha Ballard and have been identified on at least one college campus as a midwife, I am only a little bit like my eighteenth-century subject. Like her, I was raised to be an industrious housewife and a self-sacrificing and charitable neighbor, but sometime in my thirties I discovered that writing about women's work was a lot more fun than doing it. I remember thinking one winter day how ironic it was that I was wrapped in a bathrobe with the heat of a wood stove rising toward my loft as I wrote about a courageous woman who braved snowstorms and crossed a frozen river on a cake of ice to care for mothers in labor. I felt selfish, pampered, and decadent. But I did not stop what I was doing. I did not know why I needed to write Martha's story, and I could not imagine that anybody else would ever want to follow me through my meandering glosses on her diary. I was astonished at the reception of the book. Even more important than the prizes was the discovery of how important this long-dead midwife's story was to nurses, midwives, and anonymous caregivers dealing with quite different circumstances today. These readers helped me to see that history is more than an engaging enterprise. It is a primary way of creating meaning. The meaning I found in Martha Ballard's life had something to do with my own life experience, but perhaps a lot more to do with the collective experiences of a generation of Americans coping with dramatic changes in their own lives. [19]

When I wrote that "well-behaved women seldom make history," I was making a commitment to help recover the lives of otherwise obscure women. I had no idea that thirty years later, my own words would come back to me transformed. While I like some of the uses of the slogan more than others, I wouldn't call it back even if I could. I applaud the fact that so many people—students, teachers, quilters, nurses, newspaper columnists, old ladies in nursing homes, and mayors of western towns—think they have the right to make history. [20]

Some history-making is intentional; much of it is accidental. People make history when they scale a mountain, ignite a bomb, or refuse to move to the back of the bus. But they also make history by keeping diaries, writing letters, or embroidering initials on linen sheets. History is a conversation and sometimes a shouting match between present and past, though often the voices we most want to hear are barely audible. People make history by passing on gossip, saving old records, and by naming rivers, mountains, and children. Some people leave only their bones, though bones too make history when someone notices. [21]

Historian Gerda Lerner has written: "All human beings are practicing historians. . . . We live our lives; we tell our stories. It is as natural as breathing." [22]

But if no one cares about these stories, they do not survive. People do not only make history by living their lives, but by creating records and by turning other people's lives into books or slogans. ◆

## FOR CLOSE READING

1. According to Laurel Thatcher Ulrich, what accounts for the near-viral popularity of her slogan about well-behaved women and history? Do you think this is a good explanation? Why or why not?

2. Throughout history, says Ulrich, "well-behaved" women have rarely left their mark on the public record. Why not?

3. Historically, according to Ulrich, how has "good behavior" in women been **DEFINED**? By whom and for what purpose or purposes?

4. In her essay, Ulrich gives numerous examples of women who have made history. How "well-behaved" were they? Explain by referring to several of the particular instances she cites.

## Strategies and Structures

1. Ulrich's essay was written as an introduction to a book in which she explores the circumstances under which women have made history. How, and how well, do you think her essay serves such a **PURPOSE**? Does it make you want to read her book? Why or why not?

2. A professional historian, Ulrich is not writing strictly for other scholars here. Who *is* her **AUDIENCE**? Why do you think so? Point to specific clues in her text.

3. Ulrich begins her essay by giving the history of her slogan about women who make history. How, and how well, does this account exemplify what Ulrich goes on to say about what history is and how it gets made?

4. Among the many examples in Ulrich's essay of women who did make history, which ones do you find particularly compelling? Why?

5. Where and how does Ulrich use herself and her own career as examples? Are they fitting examples? Explain.

6. *Other Methods.* "The problem with this argument," writes Ulrich, "is not only that it limits women. It also limits history" (7). What limited **DEFINITION** of history is Ulrich referring to here? How does she define history? What **ARGUMENT** is *she* making?

## Thinking about Language

1. Ulrich says that her original slogan was probably altered "by accident" (2). Was the accidental change also an editorial improvement? Why or why not?

2. Why is Ulrich so careful to point out that *seldom* and *rarely* "mean the same thing" (2)?

3. Some phrases are inherently ambiguous. Is "well-behaved" a good example, especially when applied to women (or men or children) in general? Why or why not?

4. What "delicious irony" is Ulrich referring to in paragraph 15? Why does she find this particular example of IRONY to be so "delicious"?

## FOR WRITING

1. Make a list of slogans you have seen—on car bumpers, T-shirts, or wherever—that you think are particularly good (or bad) examples of the argument they are intended to support. Choose one, and write a paragraph or two using that slogan to make a point.

2. Write a PROFILE of a relatively obscure person—whether well- or ill-behaved—whom you think should be better known than she or he is. Be sure to explain how you came to know or know about this person, why you think she or he should be more famous, and why this person failed to make history—or why history failed to take this person sufficiently into account.

3. Do some research on the Rosa Parks case, and write a REPORT about its significance for the American Civil Rights movement. Include examples of Parks's typical behavior off the bus as well as on.

4. With several of your classmates, read more by and about Laurel Thatcher Ulrich, and write a collaborative PROFILE of Ulrich as a feminist scholar and writer.

..............................................................•

You'll find quizzes on the readings at
wwnorton.com/write/back-to-the-lake.

Alan Lightman (b. 1948) is a physicist who is also a writer of fiction and poetry. Lightman grew up in Memphis and graduated from Princeton University and the California Institute of Technology. Now at the Massachusetts Institute of Technology, where he is a leading authority on the theory of astrophysical processes under extreme temperatures and densities, Lightman was the first M.I.T. professor to receive a joint appointment in both humanities and the sciences. He is the author of novels, including *Einstein's Dreams* (1993); the book-length narrative poem, *Song of Two Worlds* (2009); and dozens of essays and short stories in publications ranging from *The Atlantic to Salon*. In 2003, Lightman started the nonprofit Harpswell Foundation, which seeks to create a new generation of women leaders in Cambodia and elsewhere through programs offering housing, education, and leadership training.

In *Einstein's Dreams*, which has been translated into thirty languages and adapted into numerous musical and theater works, Lightman imagines a series of dreams about time that disturb the sleep of the great physicist in 1905 as he was working on his theory of relativity. Conceiving of time as waves emanating from a still center, "14 May 1905," a sample dream from the series, takes representative time travelers to the center where time stops. From there, Lightman exemplifies a human dilemma that is as old as time.

1 THERE IS A PLACE WHERE TIME STANDS STILL. Raindrops hang motionless in air. Pendulums of clocks float mid-swing. Dogs raise their muzzles in silent howls. Pedestrians are frozen on the dusty streets, their legs cocked as if held by strings. The aromas of dates, mangoes, coriander, cumin are suspended in space.

2 As a traveler approaches this place from any direction, he moves more and more slowly. His heartbeats grow farther apart, his breathing slackens, his temperature drops, his thoughts diminish, until he reaches dead center and stops. For this is the center of time. From this place, time travels outward in concentric circles—at rest at the center, slowly picking up speed at greater diameters.

MLA CITATION: Lightman, Alan. "14 May 1905." 1993. *Back to the Lake*. Ed. Thomas Cooley. 3rd ed. New York: Norton, 2015. 277–78. Print.

Examples replace *abstract* terms, p. 233, with more concrete ones (*parents, lovers*).

Who would make pilgrimage to the center of time? Parents with children, and lovers.

And so, at the place where time stands still, one sees parents clutching their children, in a frozen embrace that will never let go. The beautiful young daughter with blue eyes and blond hair will never stop smiling the smile she smiles now, will never lose this soft pink glow on her cheeks, will never grow wrinkled or tired, will never get injured, will never unlearn what her parents have taught her, will never think thoughts that her parents don't know, will never know evil, will never tell her parents that she does not love them, will never leave her room with the view of the ocean, will never stop touching her parents as she does now.

And at the place where time stands still, one sees lovers kissing in the shadows of buildings, in a frozen embrace that will never let go. The loved one will never take his arms from where they are now, will never give back the bracelet of memories, will never journey far from his lover, will never place himself in danger in self-sacrifice, will never fail to show his love, will never become jealous, will never fall in love with someone else, will never lose the passion of this instant in time.

One must consider that these statues are illuminated by only the most feeble red light, for light is diminished almost to nothing at the center of time, its vibrations slowed to echoes in vast canyons, its intensity reduced to the faint glow of fireflies.

Those not quite at dead center do indeed move, but at the pace of glaciers. A brush of the hair might take a year, a kiss might take a thousand. While a smile is returned, seasons pass in the outer world. While a child is hugged, bridges rise. While a goodbye is said, cities crumble and are forgotten.

And those who return to the outer world . . . Children grow rapidly, forget the centuries-long embrace from their parents, which to them lasted but seconds. Children become adults, live far from their parents, live in their own houses, learn ways of their own, suffer pain, grow old. Children curse their parents for trying to hold them forever, curse time for their own wrinkled skin and hoarse voices. These now old children also want to stop time, but at another time. They want to freeze their own children at the center of time.

Lovers who return find their friends are long gone. After all, lifetimes have passed. They move in a world they do not recognize. Lovers who return still embrace in the shadows of buildings, but now their embraces seem empty and alone. Soon they forget the centuries-long promises, which to them lasted only seconds. They become jealous even among strangers, say hateful things to each other, lose passion, drift apart, grow old and alone in a world they do not know.

Some say it is best not to go near the center of time. Life is a vessel of sadness, but it is noble to live life, and without time there is no life. Others disagree. They would rather have an eternity of contentment, even if that eternity were fixed and frozen, like a butterfly mounted in a case. ◆

## FOR CLOSE READING

1.  If time consists of waves radiating out from the center, why, according to Lightman, would a traveler to the center of time gradually grow motionless?

2.  Lightman imagines a number of advantages to living at the center of time. What are some of them?

3.  What advantages does Lightman imagine to living in time as we normally do? And the disadvantages?

4.  What sort of relationship does Lightman (and Einstein) imagine between time and light in "14 May 1905"? How would this relationship fit in with the theory that time flows in waves like a slinky toy?

## Strategies and Structures

1.  The first examples that come to mind (Lightman's, Einstein's) of people who might want to travel to "the place where time stands still" are parents and lovers (3). Why these two groups? What specific human desires do they exhibit by going there?

2.  Lightman gives several examples of people not quite at the "dead center" of time (7)? What does their behavior exemplify? Are the examples well chosen? Why or why not?

3.  Lightman gives numerous examples of what life is like for "those who return to the outer world" (8). What qualities of life do they represent? How and how well?

4.  What are the implications of Lightman's example of "a butterfly mounted in a case" (10)?

5.  *Other Methods.* "Some say. . . . Others disagree" (10). The conclusion of Lightman's piece takes the form of a debate or ARGUMENT. What is at issue in the argument? Which side, if either, does Lightman take? Why end a meditation on time and life in this fashion?

## Thinking about Language

1.  Why does Lightman say that the time travelers are making a "pilgrimage" (3)? What do pilgrims typically seek?

2.  What kind of bracelet is Lightman referring to when he a mentions a "bracelet of memories" (5)? What is he comparing the bracelet to? How apt is the comparison?

3.  Lightman refers to the people in paragraph 6 as "statues." What are the implications of this METAPHOR?

4.  Most of paragraph 4 in Lightman's meditation is a single sentence about a "beautiful young daughter with blue eyes." How does the rhythm and flow of the sentence exemplify what the writer is saying?

## FOR WRITING

1.  Besides lovers and parents, who else might be tempted to live in state of timelessness like that imagined in "14 May 1905"? Write a paragraph or two imagining examples of other kinds of people and what they might do (or not do) at the center of time.

2.  In 400–600 words, write your own dream of time, perhaps using some alternative to the theory that time is relative. Use plenty of examples to explain what you mean.

3.  In 400–600 words, write an essay exemplifying the following theme: "Without time there is no life" (10).

4.  Keep a dream journal. Write in it dreams that you remember, preferably soon after dreaming them. Also, write down dreams that you imagine having.

5.  In a textual analysis of approximately 800 words, COMPARE AND CONTRAST Lightman's "14 May 1905" with "Ode on a Grecian Urn" (1819) by the British Romantic poet John Keats (1795–1821). Give plenty of examples from both texts to support your reading.

........................................................•

You'll find quizzes on the readings at
wwnorton.com/write/back-to-the-lake.

CHAPTER 9

# Process Analysis

Writing is a multistage process. . . . The stages are interactive and frequently occur simultaneously. The writing process consists of prewriting, drafting, revising, editing, and publishing.

—Nora M. Kneebone,
West Iron County Middle School

B y some accounts, Stephen (Steph) Curry of the Golden State Warriors is the greatest shotmaker in NBA history. How does he do it? It's a simple process, as analyzed in the profile of Curry on p. 284: *Step 1:* bring the ball into the pocket just below your chest; *Step 2:* using your middle finger and forefinger as a "shooting fork," find the seam at the center of the ball; *Step 3:* bring the ball up while bending your right palm back "like a waiter holding a tray of dishes"; *Step 4:* release ball, flashing "love never fails" message tattooed in Hebrew on the inside of your shooting wrist.

Go to wwnorton.com/write/back-to-the-lake for a diagram of Curry's process.

## Telling How or How To

A process is a series of actions, such as preparing to shoot a basketball, that produces an end result, such as putting the ball through the hoop from far out on the floor. When you *analyze* a process, you break it down into a number of steps, as we did above with Steph Curry's "elevation-type" basketball shot. (Go ahead, kids; try this at home.)

On p. 317, Dave Barry tells (inaccurately) "How to Jump-start Your Car When the Battery Is Dead."

There are two basic kinds of process analysis, directive and explanatory. A directive process analysis tells the reader how to do something—shoot a basketball, throw a boomerang, administer CPR, or avoid being eaten by an alligator. An explanatory process analysis tells the reader how something works or is made—the U.S. Senate, cloning, a key lime pie.

In this chapter, we will explore how to analyze a process, including how to break it into a sequence of steps, how to select the specific details that best suit your purpose and audience, and how to organize and present those details effectively. We will also review the critical points to watch for as you read over and revise a process analysis, as well as common errors to avoid when you edit.

## Why Do We Analyze Processes?

The human mind is naturally analytical, inclined to take things apart to see how the pieces fit together. There are many reasons for analyzing a process. Sometimes we simply want to understand how something works, as when we analyze how wind flowing over a curved wing creates a difference in pressure that lifts an airplane. Other times we want to know how to do something, such as fly a plane. If the process produces an undesirable result, as with the spread of a disease, our purpose in analyzing it may be to prevent it from occurring again.

Step 4 of Steph Curry's shotmaking process.

# USING PROCESS ANALYSIS IN A PROFILE

In a recent article for *ESPN Magazine*, sportswriter David Fleming makes the claim that the "elevation-type" shot of Golden State's Steph Curry is "reinventing" how professional basketball players shoot the ball. Here is Fleming's analysis of making the shot:

> The ball rises up Curry's body into the ideal shooting pocket just below his chest, while his middle finger and forefinger—his shooting fork—search instinctively for a seam at the center of the ball. As the ball continues its ascent, his right palm bends back flat until the skin of his wrist begins to wrinkle. The last thing . . . any defender wants to see in this situation are the 16 Hebrew characters that Curry, in June, had tattooed on the inside of his shooting wrist. By the time that message from *Corinthians* (love never fails) flashes, it's too late.
>
> —DAVID FLEMING,
> "How Stephen Curry Is Reinventing Shooting Before Our Eyes"

When you write a process analysis like this, your purpose is often to explain to the reader how to replicate the process, such as making a cake. Fleming, of course, does not really expect his readers to replicate a process that took a gifted and disciplined athlete many years to perfect. Process analysis is not necessarily an end in itself. As with all the other methods of development discussed in this book, you can use it to a larger purpose. Fleming's larger purpose in writing is to **PROFILE** Curry as a person and a player. In other words, he uses process analysis as a basis for a type of writing (the profile) that sports writers—not to mention historians and students writing about history or literature or the history of science—use all the time.

How did Curry become Curry? "As a kid," says Fleming, "Curry mastered tight-elbow discipline by lying in bed and throwing a balled-up sock as close to the ceiling as he could, without touching it, hundreds of times a night." Here's a glimpse, from Fleming's profile, of where Curry went next:

> Shooting touch is a bit of a misnomer. It isn't bestowed, it's built, through ungodly, torturous repetition—shot by shot, day by day, year by year, until the complex kinetic chain of movements is burned into the muscles. Curry has never lacked the motivation for that kind of solitary lab work. Barely six feet and 150 pounds as a senior at Charlotte Christian School, he received no scholarship offers from major schools and instead chose tiny Davidson College, north of his hometown of Charlotte. Two years later, still unable to grow a mustache, Curry single-handedly led the Wildcats to the [championship of the] Elite Eight.

## Composing a Process Analysis

When you compose a process analysis, your first task is to break down the process into its main steps. If you are analyzing how to take down a Christmas tree using the Bombeck method, the process is simple and the steps are few: grab a rope of tinsel by one end, give it a jerk, and catch the ornaments as they spin off. Even in this simple case, you'll notice, the steps of the process must be presented to the reader in a particular order, usually CHRONOLOGICAL. With a multistage process—such as writing an essay or playing a video game—figuring out that order can be challenging, especially if the process has more than one possible outcome.

Removing the decorations from a Christmas tree is a process that *could* be accomplished in a single step. (All you really have to do is shake the tree.) Let's take a more challenging example, such as that of a complicated natural process, one we can analyze but not necessarily control—the spread of the bubonic plague.

> For tips on analyzing undesirable processes that *can* be controlled, see "How to Create New Habits" (p. 321).

The spread of the plague is an excellent example of a natural process we'd like to eradicate. A carrier, usually a flea, bites an infected animal, usually a rat. The flea picks up infected blood and transfers the bacilli that cause the plague to the human victim, again by biting. Having entered the bloodstream, the bacilli travel to the lymph nodes, where they begin to replicate. Eventually the lymph nodes swell, creating what Wendy Orent describes in *Plague* as "the huge, boggy, exquisitely painful mass we know as a bubo." The order is always the same—up to a point. The buboes never appear before the victim is infected. And the victim is never infected before the flea bites. What happens after the buboes appear, however—whether the victim lives or dies—is not fixed.

The order of events in natural disasters can also be difficult to determine with certainty. In an earthquake or hurricane, for example, it is true that the ground trembles or the wind blows first; but then many things start to happen all at once. In other words, the actions and events of many processes are, as Nora Kneebone observed, "interactive and frequently occur simultaneously." When you write about a process, however, you must present events in an orderly sequence. Whatever it turns out to be, the sequence in which you choose to relate those events will provide the main principle for organizing your written analysis.

### Thinking about Purpose and Audience

One purpose for writing a process analysis is to tell your readers how to do something. For this purpose, a basic set of instructions or directions will usually do the job, as when you give someone the recipe for your Aunt Mary's famous pound cake.

When, however, you want your audience to understand, not duplicate, a complicated process—such as the spread of a disease, the cloning of a sheep, or the chemistry that makes a cake rise—your analysis should be more explanatory than directive. So instead of giving instructions ("add the sugar to the butter"), you would go over the inner workings of the process in some detail, telling readers, for example, *what happens* when they add baking powder to the cake mixture.

Here's a chef's analysis of the baking process:

> The first step in making a pound cake is to take a fat, such as butter or shortening, or a combination of the two, and beat it with an electric mixer. This incorporates air bubbles. Then, sugar is sprinkled slowly into the butter. As the sharp sugar crystals cut into the butter, tiny pockets are formed and fill with air as the mixer blades pull more butter over the top of the hole to close it. This makes the butter double in volume and become creamy in texture, which is why this procedure is called "creaming." . . . Then, the eggs are usually added, which adds more volume and allows the mixture to hold even more air. The dry ingredients, including the baking soda or powder, are then added, usually alternating with liquid. When the baking soda or powder comes into contact with liquid, carbon dioxide is released. As the batter heats up, bubbles form and the batter rises.
>
> —RICK MCDANIEL, "Chemistry 101 for Pound Cakes"

This is much more information than your readers will need if you are just giving them a recipe for pound cake. However, if you are writing for a food magazine and you want readers to understand why their cakes may fall if they open the oven door during the baking process—it's because the bubbles collapse before the batter sets up—then such explanatory details are appropriate.

The nature of your audience, too, will affect the information you include in your analysis. How much does your intended reader already know about the process you're analyzing? Why might he or she want to know more, or less? If you are giving a set of instructions, will the reader require any special tools or equipment? What problems or glitches is the reader likely to encounter? Will you need to indicate where he or she can look for more information on your topic? Ask questions like these, and select the steps and details you present accordingly.

## Generating Ideas: Asking How Something Works

BRAINSTORMING, LISTING, and other methods of discovery can help you generate ideas for your process analysis. When you analyze a process, the essential question to ask yourself is *how*. How does a cake rise? How do I make chicken salad? How does an engine work? How do I back out of the garage?

When you're thinking about writing a process analysis, ask yourself a *how* question about your topic, research the answer, and write down all of the steps involved. These will form the foundation of your process analysis. For instance, "How do I back out of the garage?" might result in a list like this:

> step on the gas
> turn the key in the ignition
> put the car in reverse
> cut the steering wheel to the right
> back out of the garage

This list includes all the essential steps for backing a car out of a garage, but you wouldn't want your reader to try to follow them in this order. Once you have a list of all the steps in your process, you need to begin thinking about how to present them to your reader.

## Organizing and Drafting a Process Analysis

First you'll need to put the steps in a certain order with appropriate transitions between them. Then choose pronouns and verb forms that fit the type of analysis you're writing, whether directive or explanatory. Think about the main point you want your analysis to make and state it clearly. Finally, consider whether you should demonstrate the process visually. The templates on p. 289 can help you get started.

### PUTTING THE STEPS IN ORDER

Many processes, especially those linked by CAUSE AND EFFECT, follow a prescribed order. For example, before the bacillus that causes bubonic plague can enter a victim's bloodstream, a flea must first bite an infected rat, then bite the human. The process of infection won't work if the steps that make up the process unfold in any other order.

But sometimes the steps that make up a process can take place in almost any order. Consider the following tongue-in-cheek analysis of manly behavior:

> The Wild Man process involves five basic phases: Sweating, Yelling, Crying, Drum-Beating, and Ripping Your Shirt Off Even If It's Expensive.
> —JOE BOB BRIGGS, "Get in Touch with Your Ancient Spear"

A man in the process of reverting to his "wild" self would not necessarily go through the phases of the process in the exact order indicated here. For example, he might tear his shirt off first, before sweating or yelling. (Yelling first might even help to induce the sweating phase.)

Another process that can take place in almost any order is pulling an all-nighter, p. 307.

When you write about the wild man (or any other) process, however, you must organize and present the main steps of the process in *some* order. If the process is a linear one, such as driving to a particular address in Dallas, you simply start at the earliest point in time and move forward, step by step, to the end result. If the process is cyclical, such as what's happening in your car engine as you drive, you will have to pick a logical point in the process and then proceed through the rest of the cycle. If, however, the process you are analyzing does not naturally follow chronology, try arranging the steps of your analysis from most important to least important, or the other way around.

## USING TRANSITIONS

As you recount the main steps in the process one by one, let the reader know when you are moving from one step to another by including clear TRANSITIONS, such as *next, from there, after five minutes, then.* The actions and events that make up a process are repeatable—unlike those in a narrative, which happen only *once* upon a time. So you will frequently use such expressions as *usually, normally, in most cases, whenever.* But also note any deviations from the normal order that might occur by using transitions like *sometimes, rarely, in one instance.*

## USING APPROPRIATE PRONOUNS

In an explanatory process analysis, you need to focus on the things (fleas and rats, engines, oranges) and activities (infection, compression and combustion, culling and scrubbing) that make up the process. Thus you will write about the process most of the time in the THIRD PERSON (*he, she, it,* and *they*):

> Moving up a conveyer belt, oranges are scrubbed with detergent before they roll on into the juicing machines.                    —JOHN MCPHEE, *Oranges*

The *you* may be implied, as in "Find Another Brother" (p. 314).

In a directive process analysis, by contrast, you are telling the reader directly how to do something. So you should typically use the second person (*you*): "When making orange juice, first you need to cut the oranges in half."

## USING APPROPRIATE VERB FORMS

In an explanatory process analysis, you indicate how something works or is made, so your verbs should be in the indicative mood:

# TEMPLATES FOR DRAFTING

When you begin to draft a process analysis, you need to say what process you're analyzing and identify some of the most important steps in the process—moves fundamental to any process analysis. See how nature writer Diane Ackerman makes such moves in the following example:

> But how do the colored leaves fall? As a leaf ages, the growth hormone, auxin, fades, and cells at the base of the petiole divide. Two or three rows of small cells, lying at right angles to the axis of the petiole, react with water, then come apart, leaving the petioles hanging on by only a few threads of xylem. A light breeze, and the leaves are airborne.
> —DIANE ACKERMAN, "Why Leaves Turn Color in the Fall"

Ackerman identifies the process she's analyzing (the falling of leaves) and indicates some important steps in the process (leaf ages; growth hormone fades; stem cells divide, react with water, and come apart; leaf drops). Here is an example on how to jump-start a car, taken from this chapter:

> Connect one end of the *red* jumper cable to the *positive* terminal (also called the ignition or carburetor) on your car's battery. Then connect the other end of the red cable to an electronic part such as the radio of the opposing car.　　—DAVE BARRY, "How to Jump-start Your Car
> When the Battery Is Dead"

The following templates can help you make some of these basic moves in your own writing. But don't take these as formulas where you just fill in the blanks. There are no shortcuts to good writing, but these templates can serve as starting points.

▶ In order to understand how *X* works, we can divide it into the following steps: _____, _____, _____, and _____.

▶ The various steps that make up *X* can be grouped into the following stages: _____, _____, and _____.

▶ The end result of *X* is _____.

▶ In order to repeat *X*, you must first _____; then _____ and _____; and finally _____.

▶ The tools and materials you will need to replicate *X* include _____, _____, and _____.

▶ The most important reasons for understanding / repeating *X* are _____, _____, and _____.

As the rotor <u>moves</u> around the chamber, each of the three volumes of gas alternately <u>expands</u> and <u>contracts</u>. It is this expansion and contraction that <u>draws</u> air and fuel into the engine, <u>compresses</u> it, and <u>makes</u> useful power.

—KARIM NICE, "How Rotary Engines Work"

In a directive process analysis, on the other hand, you are telling the reader how to do something, so your verbs should be in the imperative mood, as in these instructions for reviewing for exams:

<u>Start</u> preparing for your exams the first day of class. . . . <u>Plan</u> reviews as part of your regular weekly study schedule. . . . <u>Read</u> over your lecture notes and <u>ask</u> yourself questions on the material you don't know well. . . . <u>Review</u> for several short periods rather than one long period.

—*University of Minnesota Duluth Student Handbook*

Notice that the verbs in these two examples are both in the present tense. That is because they express habitual actions. Instructions are always written in the present tense because they tell how something is (or should be) habitually done: "As you place the oranges on the conveyor belt, keep hair and fingers clear of the rollers."

Explanations, on the other hand, are written in the present tense when they tell how a process is habitually performed:

At low tide, researchers collect the algae by the handful and place it in plastic baggies. Back at the lab, they separate out the different strains and examine each type under a microscope.

But explanations are written in the *past* tense when they explain how a process was performed on a particular occasion, even though the process itself is repeatable:

At low tide, researchers collected the algae by the handful and placed it in plastic baggies. Back at the lab, they separated out the different strains and examined each type under a microscope.

Be careful not to switch between past tense and present tense in your analysis, unless you're intentionally switching from explaining how a process is usually performed (present) to how it was performed on a particular occasion (past).

## STATING YOUR POINT

A good process analysis should have a point to make—a THESIS. That point should be clearly expressed in a thesis statement so the reader will know why you're

# EXPLAINING A PROCESS VISUALLY

Sometimes a process is best explained by *showing* how it works. (Just try writing a paragraph telling readers how to tie their shoes, for example.) If that's the case with some part of the process you're analyzing, you may want to include a diagram or drawing, such as the one below.

Notice that words accompany each step in this visual explanation. When you use a visual, make sure it is clearly labeled for the reader, whether that means describing what the visual shows and indicating the sequence of events, as here, or labeling parts of a diagram (for instance, the parts of an engine).

## How To Tie a Half Windsor

1. Place the necktie around your collar and arrange the tie so that the wider end (A) is longer than the narrow end (B), then cross A over B.

2. Twist A around and behind B.

3. Bring A up.

4. Pull A down through the loop.

5. Bring A around front, crossing over B from left to right.

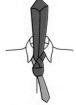

6. Again thread A up and through the loop.

7. Pull A down through the front of the knot.

8. Tighten the knot: hold B with one hand and pull the knot up toward the collar with the other hand.

analyzing the process and what to expect. In addition, your thesis statement should in some way identify the process and indicate its end result. For example:

> You cannot understand how the Florida citrus industry works without understanding how fresh orange juice gets processed into "concentrate."
>
> —JOHN MCPHEE, *Oranges*

Caitlin Ghegan's point in analyzing how to play Quidditch (p. 296) is to promote the "sport."

This thesis statement clearly tells the reader what process the writer is analyzing (making concentrate from fresh orange juice), why he's analyzing it (as a foundation for understanding the Florida citrus industry), and what the end result of the process is (orange juice concentrate). As you draft a process analysis, make sure your thesis statement includes all of this information, so that your reader knows just what to expect from your analysis.

## CONCLUDING A PROCESS ANALYSIS

A process is not complete until it yields a final result. Likewise, a process analysis is not complete until it explains how the process ends—and what this result means for the reader.

The process of turning orange juice into concentrate, for example, does not end when the juice is extracted from the fruit. The extracted juice must be further refined and then shipped to the consumer, as John McPhee explains in the conclusion of his analysis: "From the extractor the orange concentrate flows into holding tanks from which it is later tapped, packaged, frozen, and shipped to grocery stores all over the country." And that, he might have added, is how you get your "fresh" o.j. in the morning.

Even this is not the end of the story, however. If you were writing a directive analysis of the process of making orange juice from concentrate, your conclusion would need to remind readers to add cold water to the concentrate before serving.

## USING OTHER METHODS

Analyzing the likely outcomes of a process and the steps leading to it may not always tell your readers everything they want or need to know. To explain a complicated process fully and completely, you may need to draw on other methods besides process analysis. Take, for instance, the process by which teenagers become addicted to tobacco. A teenager, let's call her Courtney, crosses the threshold from casual smoking to addiction. (Already we are expanding our analysis by giving an EXAMPLE.) Courtney now smokes half a dozen cigarettes every day. The process goes on—and on.

Over the next five years, Courtney gradually increases her intake of nicotine, a few cigarettes at a time, until one day she is a confirmed pack-a-day-plus smoker.

Why? Why does Courtney become addicted while her sister, Brittany, never goes beyond a few cigarettes a day? Merely knowing *how* the process of addiction occurs—that it takes place in phases, from nonsmoking to experimentation to addiction—isn't necessarily going to tell us *why* it occurs, though that's an important question to consider.

For the answer—and to make our analysis more meaningful—we could draw on the other methods discussed in this book. For example, we could CLASSIFY and DIVIDE teenage smokers into types: quitters (those who experiment with smoking but soon give it up); chippers (those who continue to smoke but never get addicted to tobacco); and addicts (those who regularly smoke six or more cigarettes a day).

Analyzing what categories teenage smokers fall into still doesn't tell us why some chippers become addicts while others never do. To learn why individual smokers cross the line, we also need to analyze the CAUSES of nicotine addiction.

It turns out that as long as Courtney smokes about five cigarettes a day and no more, she can go on for years without becoming addicted. Once she starts smoking more than that, however, the residual level of nicotine in her body reaches what Malcolm Gladwell calls a "tipping point," and Courtney slowly sides into addiction. Having analyzed the causes of Courtney's addiction, we might then ARGUE that she and her peers should never start smoking in the first place.

## EDITING FOR COMMON ERRORS IN A PROCESS ANALYSIS

Process analysis invites certain types of errors, particularly in the choice of pronouns and verb forms. The following tips will help you check your writing for these two common problems.

### Check your pronouns

Remember to use third-person pronouns (*he, she, it, they*) when you're explaining how something works or is done—and to use the second-person pronoun (*you*) when you're telling someone how to do something.

▶ When trees are harvested, ~~you have to~~ they are cut down ~~each one~~ by hand.

The reader is not actually harvesting the trees.

▶ To harvest trees properly, ~~they~~ you must ~~be~~ cut them down by hand.

Here the reader is the one harvesting the trees.

**Check your verbs to make sure you haven't switched needlessly between the indicative and the imperative**

▶ According to the recipe, we should stir in the nuts. ~~Then~~ and then sprinkle cinnamon on top.

Or

▶ ~~According to the recipe, we should stir~~ Stir in the nuts. ~~Then~~ and then sprinkle cinnamon on top.

Go to wwnorton.com/write/back-to-the-lake for quizzes on these common errors.

## Reading a Process Analysis with a Critical Eye

One complex process that doesn't proceed in linear fashion is writing. Although the phases of the writing process are sequential—that is, you have to organize and draft an essay before you can revise and edit it—they are also repeatable, unlike the steps in most strictly linear processes. (You wouldn't want to bake a cake, for example, and then take it out of the oven and stir it again.) So once you've "completed" your draft, go back, check it over thoroughly, and revise what you've written. Repeat as necessary.

Since the heart of your analysis is the process itself, you need to make sure, first of all, that your reader will be able to follow every step. So ask a friend or classmate to review your draft and tell you whether he or she has any questions about how the process works—or any suggestions for making it clearer. Here are some questions to keep in mind when checking a process analysis.

**PURPOSE AND AUDIENCE.** Is the purpose of the analysis to tell the audience how to do something, or is it to explain how something works or is made? How likely is the intended audience to want or need this information? What additional information, if any, should the analysis provide? For example, is there any special equipment that readers might need to know about? Any terms that need to be defined?

**ORGANIZATION.** Are all of the important steps of the process included? Are they arranged chronologically, or in some other order that makes sense—such as from most important to least important?

**TRANSITIONS.** Are there clear transitions between each step? Are the transitions overly predictable (*first, second, third*)? If so, consider changing them for variety.

**PRONOUNS.** Is the analysis primarily directive or explanatory? If it's directing the reader to do something, is it written mostly in the second person, referring to the reader as *you*? If the analysis is primarily explanatory, is it written mostly in the third person (*he, she, it,* and *they*)?

**VERBS.** If the analysis is directive, are the verbs in the imperative (or commanding) mood? If it's explanatory, are they in the indicative (or stating) mood? Is there any needless switching between the two moods? With verbs in the imperative mood, remember, the pronoun *you* is often understood rather than explicitly stated: "(You) Check over every aspect of the draft carefully."

**THE POINT.** What is the point of the analysis? Is there a thesis statement at the beginning that tells the reader why this particular process is being analyzed and what to look for in the rest of the essay? Is the significance or end result of the process clearly indicated?

**VISUALS.** Are charts, drawings, or other illustrations included to help explain the process? If not, should there be? Are the visuals labeled and anchored appropriately in the text?

**CONCLUSION.** Does the analysis end with a clear indication of the outcome of the process? If there are several possible outcomes, does it indicate what they are and which results are most likely?

**OTHER METHODS.** Does the analysis include other methods of development? For instance, does it give **EXAMPLES** of the process? Does it analyze what **CAUSED** key actions or events in the process and what **EFFECTS** they might have? Does it **CLASSIFY** or **DIVIDE** part of the process? Does it offer an **ARGUMENT** about the process?

**COMMON ERRORS.** Does the analysis consistently use either the indicative or the imperative voice? If it switches needlessly between the two, choose one and stick with it.

## Student Example

Caitlin Ghegan is a marketing assistant at a publishing company in Boston and a 2013 graduate of Ithaca College in Ithaca, New York, where she majored in writing, with a minor in web programming. "In Defense of Quidditch," which Ghegan wrote in her senior year, won her college's annual writing contest in the category of feature and magazine writing.

As conceived by J. K. Rowling in the Harry Potter books, Quidditch was originally played by young wizards on flying broomsticks following ancient rules and rivalries. Nonwizards can also ride their brooms and chase the snitch in tournaments from Australia to Canada and the United States, but they must play by the more down-to-earth rules of the International Quidditch Association. As Caitlin Ghegan analyzes the nonmagical play of the game here, "not too much has been changed from Rowling's text"—except, of course, that the players cannot fly. Such details prompt critics to consider nonmagical Quidditch "something of a joke." So in addition to analyzing the game, Ghegan also defends it—on the grounds that "Quidditch fans are a force to be reckoned with."

In Defense of Quidditch:
Will the Game Ever Be Taken Seriously as a Sport?

The seventeenth of November was a cold one in Newport, 1
Rhode Island. At Fort Adams State Park, centuries-old stone walls could not keep the harbor wind from biting at visitors' noses. Tents clustered near the fort's wide entrance rippled visibly from

NARRATIVE introduction tells about a particular match

across the courtyard. Several gathered teams had bedecked their flimsy shelters with signs and team colors; it was easy to recognize Vassar's hot pink regalia and the swarm of purple shirts from NYU, among many others.

Spectators huddled on plastic fold-up chairs, each perched 2
on the edge of his or her seat, watching the referee drift back and forth between the two sides of the field, conversing with both teams: Stony Brook University and Middlebury College. Across the courtyard, twenty other northeast teams drifted between the five marked fields, clutching brooms and Styrofoam cups of hot butterbeer (a steaming butterscotch drink), waiting anxiously for the tournament to start.

Yes, a Quidditch tournament.

The 2012 Northeast Regionals tournament in Newport was one of a series of meets, all hosted by the International Quidditch Association, to occur across the globe. As most people understand, the game was taken from J. K. Rowling's Harry Potter series, but this event wasn't just a "play date" for fantasy lovers. Though each served as a sectional championship, there was much more at stake: a spot in the World Cup bracket, among teams from Australia, France, and Canada. Regardless of the brooms, the capes, and the obscure fantasy references, this was a competition.

You might laugh or raise an eyebrow, but Quidditch fans are a force to be reckoned with. At last count in November 2012, there were 833 collegiate and community Quidditch teams registered in the United States alone. Sixty-one come from Canada. There are groups everywhere from Britain to Brazil, South Africa to Russia. This isn't just a fad for the wizard-minded. In fact, this wide-ranged community can agree that the sport is just getting started.

Quidditch, as the character Oliver Wood so astutely claimed in *Harry Potter and the Sorcerer's Stone*, "is easy enough to understand." Apart from the obvious fact that players cannot fly in the non-magical world, not too much has been changed from Rowling's text. The sport's structure has often been compared to that of ice hockey. On each side, three "chasers" act as center and wings; they pass a Quaffle ball up and down the field to score on one of three upright hoops. Two "beaters" act as defensemen, tossing a slightly deflated kickball, known as a Bludger, at opposing players. These beaters colloquially state their job is to "annoy people"; every hit from a Bludger means an opposing player must drop whatever ball he or she may be holding and run back to touch the hoops on his or her team's respective side. A "keeper" is a goaltender. A "seeker" effectively ends a match when he catches the golden snitch . . . a runner.

The snitch runner adds a distinct element of silliness to the game of Quidditch. He or she wears all-yellow clothing and a "tail" known as the snitchball at the back of a pair of shorts. A snitch

3
4

Identifies the subject to be analyzed

5

Uses process analysis to ARGUE a CLAIM about the status of Quidditch

6

Explanatory analysis of players' roles and special equipment

7

runner dances, cartwheels, and flips people over to avoid capture. He comes and goes, not always staying near the field. At last year's World Cup in New York City, the final match's snitch dressed in street clothes and hid in the stadium at Randall's Island, watching as the seekers confusedly tried to find him.

Though J. K. Rowling conceived of the sport, twenty-six-year-old Xander Manshel crafted it for the "muggle," or non-magical, world. As a student at Middlebury College in Vermont (graduating in 2009), Manshel pitched the idea to his group of friends. Among the group was current International Quidditch Association Commissioner Alex Benepe.                                                                                           8

Benepe, also a 2009 graduate of Middlebury College, is a fixture at most tournaments held throughout the Northeast. Players can always find the chairman of the IQA board strolling across the pitches with his trademark black cane, top hat, and maroon-and-gold Gryffindor scarf. He enthusiastically asserts that Quidditch has "something for everyone."                                                                                           9

"I think people come to the sport for many different reasons," Benepe says. "Some people come and take it very, very seriously as a sport and don't want to do any of the wacky, fun stuff—and then you get the people that are here pure for the Harry Potter stuff. So you get all different people from different walks of life."                                                              10

Its unique characteristics, he believes, give strength to the game. There are aspects of Quidditch that neither spectators nor players will find in other sports. All teams, regardless of level (elementary-school-age to adult community teams), are co-ed; a rule asserts that all official matches must have at least two people of the opposite gender. Quidditch is also one of the very few competitively played games with more than one ball, an element that adds an intense and exciting sense of chaos. Most of all, the community believes that players of any level of athletic ability, shape, or size can excel.                                                                          11

And yet in spite of its appeal, most of the public considers Quidditch something of a joke.                                                                       12

Introduces unique elements of the game

Fig. 1. "Some people come and take it very, very seriously as a sport," says Alex Benepe, commissioner of the International Quidditch Association. Photograph courtesy of Erik Jaworski.

Common skepticism and mockery stem from stigma; spectators and sports enthusiasts cannot overlook that the game came from a children's book. Players are mocked for carrying brooms, given their inability to fly. Chris Bucholz, blogger for Cracked.com, asks his readers, "Could one of these horribly, horribly mentally ill people have cottoned on to the fact that the published rules for the game make no sense?"

Some state that Quidditch players cannot even be considered as athletes. Blogger Kenneth Diaz, who writes for USAToday.com sports commentary site Bareknucks.com, asserts that Quidditch

13

14

Anticipates a major objection to Ghegan's position

enthusiasts are nothing more than overly zealous role-players. "These quidditch enthusiasts (I will not refer to these people as quidditch 'players.' Ever.) grow ever more bold in their public displays of unfunny stupidity—the worst kind of stupidity," he declared in an entry from November 2010. "They've even deluded themselves into taking it seriously."

*Identifies a potential problem with replicating the process*

Aside from the sociocultural reaction that Quidditch garners   15
from outsiders, sports professionals consider Quidditch far too dangerous. At World Cup V, where over eighty teams competed in several matches, the IQA reported 136 injuries ranging in severity from small scratches to some that required hospital transport.

And several colleges and universities refuse to support the   16
game due to its "dangerous" nature. Administrators at Boston's Emerson College, one of the oldest and best-ranked teams in the country, barred its Quidditch group from becoming an official club. In November, the community team at Ithaca College, located in Ithaca, New York, was rejected for a second time on the grounds that the sport was not developed with safety in mind.

Dr. Craig Paiement, associate professor of sports management   17
at Ithaca College, says that the main concern is the broom that players run around with in between their legs, which creates "unnecessary danger." Though he doesn't know much about the sport, he says its future progress at the college seems unlikely.

*A key element of play poses another problem*

"I would say that it is unlikely that general public will ever   18
give it a 'real sport' status because of its start in a fiction movie," Paiement adds. "The issue with the broom leaves it steeped in 'fantasy' and that will hold it back."

Benepe argues that the stigma itself is the real reason that   19
sports authorities consider the sport dangerous.

"I don't think that Quidditch is more dangerous than other   20
sports; I just think that because it's less socially engrained than other sports, people are more shocked by it," Benepe says. "You know, people die playing football every year, but it's okay because it's football. It's held up on a pillar in society. . . . I think Quidditch, in order to get to the point where people are okay that it's a sport where

people get hurt, [needs to become] professional—as in people can make a living playing it and get hurt doing it."

Having been a head referee at more than eleven regional and national tournaments, Chris McCormick, a sophomore Quidditch player at Metropolitan State College of Denver, has closely regulated more than forty official matches. McCormick sees the "newness" of the sport as the cause of underdeveloped or "unsafe" regulations and rules.

21

"I would say our tackling levels and our rules level needs to be upped," he says. "There's very few ways to do a one-handed tackle with the brooms safely. On the other hand, there are ways to do it. But most people who come to Quidditch come from a non-sporting background. . . . [Injuries are] going to happen with any contact sport, but if people know how to tackle safely and take a tackle safely, injuries will be reduced."

22

Regardless of whether or not the sport is dangerous, McCormick says that those arguing the game is more about role-playing than an athletic activity clearly have never seen it played.

23

"People who are the most defensive about Quidditch invading the sports world are those wannabe jocks," he claims. "They're the kind of people who would root for a team but never actually play the sport themselves because they know they're incapable."

24

Though it faces many barriers to its further development, the International Quidditch Association continues to spread its influences across the globe. This past summer, the IQA created an Olympic Summer Games series in Oxford, hosted by an official London 2012 affiliate at the Olympic torch festival in South Park. The event, where all-star representatives from the United States, United Kingdom, France, and Australia met to compete, lasted two full days. At the 2013 World Cup in Kissimmee, Florida, which will be held in April, thirty-three teams from the United States, Canada, France, and Australia will compete.

25

Critics will laugh, but the sport will thrive, supported by an intensely devoted player base.

26

Restates author's claim as a conclusion

At the end of tournament matches, opponents line up not to 27
passively shake hands but to excitedly offer embraces and invites to
upcoming meets.

"There's no other sport where teams are as friendly as they 28
are, hugging and being friends off the pitch," McCormick says. "In
most other sports I've seen, you are enemies. You are out for their
blood. With Quidditch, that's over as soon as the match ends. You're
respectful, you're friends. That is what makes Quidditch special."

## Analyzing a Student Process Analysis

"In Defense of Quidditch" draws upon rhetorical strategies and techniques that
good writers use all the time when they analyze a process. The following questions,
in addition to focusing on particular aspects of Caitlin Ghegan's text, will help you
to identify those common strategies and techniques so you can adapt them to your
own writing. These questions will also help to prepare you for the analytical
questions—on content, structure, and language—that you'll find after all the other
selections in this chapter, along with suggestions for writing on related topics.

### FOR CLOSE READING

1. According to Caitlin Ghegan, what makes Quidditch unlike other sports? Which
   differences does she find particularly important?

2. For what reason, according to the game's critics, do Quidditch players join in a
   sport where they cannot fly but ride brooms anyway? Is this skeptical view of the
   players' motives justified? Why or why not?

3. Quidditch was invented, of course, by J. K. Rowling, author of the Harry Potter
   books. How did it get adapted for use in non-magical circles?

4. According to Ghegan, why do some sports professionals, including practitioners of
   sports medicine, consider the game unlikely to become a standard sport?

### Strategies and Structures

1. Instead of explaining right off the bat how Quidditch is played, Ghegan begins her
   essay as a news story about a sports tournament. Is this a wise strategy? Why or
   why not?

2. Where does Ghegan shift from **NARRATIVE** to **PROCESS ANALYSIS**? After explaining
   how to play Quidditch, what process does she analyze next?

3. As indicated by her title, Ghegan's ultimate purpose is to support the spread of Quidditch and to defend it from detractors. Where does her "defense" begin? What reasons does she give in support of her claim that "critics will laugh, but the sport will survive" (26)?

4. *Other Methods.* How and where does Ghegan use COMPARISON AND CONTRAST— particularly of Quidditch to other sports—to support her analysis of both the play of the game and the rise of Quidditch as a "sociocultural" phenomenon (15)?

## Thinking about Language

1. Throughout her essay, Ghegan refers to Quidditch as a "sport." Is this designation accurate? What's the difference between a *sport* and a *game*?

2. Look up the root meaning of *tournament* in your dictionary (3). Why is this term especially appropriate for a sporting event that includes tents "clustered" amid "centuries-old stone walls" (1)?

3. Stated "colloquially," the role of the beater in Quidditch is "to annoy people" (6). What is meant here by "colloquial," and why might Ghegan choose such a qualifier to describe such a significant element in her analysis?

4. The phrase "in defense of" usually signifies an *attempt* at justifying or vindicating something. Why did Ghegan likely choose it for the title of her of essay instead of, say, "The Triumph of Quidditch"?

## FOR WRITING

1. When he claims that the game "is easy enough to understand," Oliver Wood, the fictional character cited by Ghegan, is speaking of Quidditch as played by young wizards with magical powers (6). Do some Harry Potter research and, in a paragraph or two, explain how to play the original version of Quidditch as conceived by J. K. Rowling.

2. Look up the rules of play for nonmagical Quidditch on *usquidditch.org* or some other web site. In a paragraph or two, analyze and explain the "official" play of the game to readers who might be unfamiliar with it. Cite your sources.

3. Write a process analysis explaining how to play an imaginary game that resembles one or more of the following: chess, ping pong, tennis, crew, archery, blind man's buff. Be sure to give an interesting name to your game.

4. You and several of your classmates join in a "circle game" such as *One Frog, Pass the Banana, Sausage, I'm Going on a Picnic, Human Pinball,* or *Pterodactyl*. After a suitable period of play, each player should write his or her own account of what happened. Read and critique each other's papers.

You'll find quizzes on the readings at wwnorton.com/write/back-to-the-lake.

# How to Cross the Street

A process analysis tells how to do something by breaking it down into steps. Recipes are common examples, as is the set of instructions on a gasoline pump or ATM machine. On this street-crossing sign, the process of crossing the street is broken down into three fundamental steps: (1) Start Crossing; (2) Watch for Vehicles; (3) Finish Crossing. In addition to instructions for crossing the street, this sign also explains the meanings of the various lights at the intersection. When you write a process analysis, you may want to include illustrations along with your text—or text along with your visuals. The visuals should actually help to explain the process, however, and not merely serve as decoration. For most readers, the lights at an intersection are self-explanatory—a walking figure means Go; an unblinking red hand means Stop. For those who need extra instruction, the traffic engineers who designed this sign have provided it; however, they've left out one critical step: "Read this sign *before* crossing the street."

[ **FOR WRITING** ]······················································································

What's wrong with this picture? In a paragraph or two, analyze and evaluate the street-crossing sign on p. 305. How would you change it (if at all) to make it more effective?

# SUGGESTIONS FOR WRITING

1. Read "In Defense of Quidditch" on p. 296, and write a **POSITION PAPER** defending (or attacking) its status as a true sport. Be sure to include an analysis of how the game is played.

2. "Popular culture," says Alex Horton in his advice to college-bound veterans on p. 313, "is replete with images of the maladjusted veteran, from Rambo to Travis Bickle to Red Forman." Starting with the **EXAMPLES** Horton gives, do some research on the image of the maladjusted veteran in popular culture, especially in film and television, and write a **REPORT** explaining how and why that image has come about.

3. "Do this next part VERY, VERY CAREFULLY OR YOU WILL DIE," says Dave Barry in "How to Jump-Start a Car When the Battery Is Dead" (p. 317). Actually, this is the likely result of following his instructions at all. Rewrite Barry's analysis of the jump-starting process so that the reader won't be in danger—and might actually get the job done.

4. In "How to Create New Habits" (p. 321), Charles Duhigg uses the example of a Procter & Gamble campaign to get customers to buy a new product. Read Duhigg's analysis, do some research on recent discoveries about habit formation, and write a **CULTURAL ANALYSIS** of approximately 400 words about a person, organization, or other group that permanently changed its habitual behavior—and how they did it.

5. Billy Collins was poet laureate of the United States from 2001 to 2003. "Fishing on the Susquehanna in July," p. 331, is a representative example of his work, which is generally considered to be both sophisticated and accessible. Read "Fishing" and as much of Collins's other poetry as you can; do some research on his life and career; and write a 400-word **PROFILE** of the poet and his work.

## JOSHUA PIVEN, DAVID BORGENICHT, AND JENNIFER WORICK

# How to Pull an All-Nighter

Joshua Piven (b. 1971) and David Borgenicht have made an industry out of teaching people how to deal with unlikely situations. In 1998, while watching a movie in which a man without piloting experience was forced to land a plane, Borgenicht concluded that life is filled with "worst-case scenarios" for which the average person is utterly unprepared. He recruited Piven, a fellow University of Pennsylvania graduate, to help him research and write a manual for such situations—*The Worst-Case Scenario Survival Handbook* (1999). Addressing situations that range from the merely improbable (delivering a baby in a taxicab) to the barely imaginable (a sword fight), the book was so popular that there are now *Worst-Case Scenario Survival* handbooks for everything from holidays and golfing to weddings and dating, as well as calendars, cards, and a reality television series.

The *Worst-Case Scenario Survival Handbook: College* (2004), co-authored by Jennifer Worick, brings the *Worst-Case* outlook to college life. "How to Pull an All-Nighter" is from that collection and deals with a process that some students might actually engage in—staying up all night to study. As with the authors' instructions for surviving a stadium riot or shark attack, however, readers of this point-by-point analysis might be better advised to avoid the situation in the first place.

**Eat a light dinner.** Do not skip a meal, but do not eat to the point of drowsiness 1 or sluggishness. Select foods with protein, like chicken breast, and complex carbohydrates, such as whole-wheat bread, brown rice, or beans, to provide you with energy and stamina for a long night. Later, when you feel your energy ebb, eat an energy bar.

**Consume peppermint.** Peppermint is a stimulant; even a whiff of it will make 2 you more alert and awake. Eat peppermint candy, chew peppermint gum, or drink peppermint-flavored herbal tea. Rub peppermint oil on your temples or wrists.

MLA CITATION: Piven, Joshua, David Borgenicht, and Jennifer Worick. "How to Pull an All-Nighter." 2004. *Back to the Lake.* Ed. Thomas Cooley. 3rd ed. New York: Norton, 2015. 307–09. Print.

**Turn on the radio or television.** A bit of white noise in the background will 3 engage your senses. Select a classical or jazz station on the radio. If you turn on the television, turn to an infomercial or shopping channel. Keep the volume low. Do not select a rerun of your favorite situation comedy or anything you might otherwise be interested in.

**Turn on a strong overhead light.** A bright light will help you see what you are 4 reading as well as prevent you from falling into a deep sleep. Close the curtains and put clocks out of sight; your body will become confused as to what time of night it is.

**Turn down the thermostat.** The cold temperature will help keep you awake. 5 Make sure the temperature does not dip below 50°F, at which you are susceptible to hypothermia, especially if you have wet hair or skin. A high temperature slows your pulse and makes you drowsy.

**Do not lie down.** Pinch yourself or wear tight shoes and constricting under- 6 wear. Physical discomfort will keep you distracted and awake.

**Consume caffeine.** Drink caffeinated beverages or eat a few caffeinated mints, but 7 proceed with caution: Too much caffeine can leave you distracted and wired. Three hundred milligrams is considered a safe daily amount of caffeine for adults, which translates into a six-pack of soda or three to four cups of brewed coffee.

**Breathe deeply.** Go to an open window or step outside for a few minutes. Stand 8 up straight, close your eyes, and inhale deeply through your nose. Hold the breath for as long as you can. Exhale slowly through your nose or mouth. Repeat several times. Deep breathing will clear your mind and give you a shot of energy.

**Stretch.** Stretch your limbs by taking a walk or doing a few yoga poses. This will 9 work out any tension you are holding in your muscles.

Give the steps in the right order if you want your reader to replicate a process (p. 287).

- Lift your arms over your head and reach for the sky, alternating arms.
- Lean over to each side and then lean forward from the waist, bringing your arms out in front of you and down to the ground.
- Let your arms dangle; swing them from side to side.

**Do a headstand.** Increase your circulation by standing on your head.

10

- Find an area of clear floor space next to a wall.
- Kneel on the floor, facing the wall.
- Place your head on the floor a few inches from the wall.
- Place your forearms on the floor on either side of your head.
- Raise your body and legs slowly up the wall. Keep your body weight on your arms, not your head. Lean against the wall as needed.

**Raise your heart rate.** If you find yourself nodding off, do a few calisthenics to raise your heart rate. Do 25 jumping jacks, or skip rope or jog in place for 5 minutes.   11

**Get a study partner.** Even if he is not cramming for the same exam, you and your partner can quiz each other and talk as you start to get drowsy. Do not stay up with someone you know will distract you with either idle chatter or sexual tension.   12

**Be Aware**

Even if you don't plan on going to sleep, set your alarm clock. To make sure that you are awake when you need to be, set every alarm you can find—watches, computers, cell phones, and hand-held electronic devices often have built-in alarms. Arrange for a friend or your roommate to back up the alarms with a wake-up call. ◆   13

## FOR CLOSE READING

1. What are the main steps into which Joshua Piven, David Borgenicht, and Jennifer Worick divide the process of pulling an all-nighter?
2. Which steps do you think would be most effective? Least effective? Why?
3. What steps would you add to (or remove from) this process analysis?

## Strategies and Structures

1. Who might care about the process that the authors of this selection are explaining? What particular AUDIENCE do they have in mind? How can you tell?

2. The authors of this selection do not say why they are explaining how to pull an all-nighter. What might their PURPOSE be, and should they state it more directly? Why or why not?

3. The instructions in this selection could be followed in almost any order. Why? On the other hand, why do individual directives—such as those for breathing deeply, stretching, and doing a headstand—actually require the reader to follow a particular sequence?

4. An essay has an introduction, a body, and a conclusion. What parts of the essay form are missing from "How to Pull an All-Nighter"? If this selection is not really an essay, what it is? Explain.

5. How, and how well, does the illustration in this selection take the place of verbal explanations?

6. *Other Methods.* As Piven, Borgenicht, and Worick analyze the process of staying awake all night, they give a number of specific EXAMPLES. Which ones do you think contribute most to the analysis? Why?

## Thinking about Language

1. The verbs in the headings that introduce each section of this text are all in the imperative mood. Why?

2. What pronoun is understood in each heading? What grammatical "person" is it in? Why?

3. In what sense are the authors of the selection using the word "translates" (7)?

## FOR WRITING

1. Write a paragraph or two telling someone how to pull an all-nighter.

2. Write an essay explaining how to study so as to avoid all-nighters and other educational pitfalls.

3. Collect all-nighter stories and advice from several of your classmates, and together write a process analysis explaining how to pull (or avoid pulling) an all-nighter, based on your collective wisdom.

4. Take hour-by-hour notes in your journal of your thoughts and condition during an all-nighter or other studying marathon. At the end, explain whether the note-taking was helpful—or just another headache.

You'll find quizzes on the readings at
wwnorton.com/write/back-to-the-lake.

ALEX HORTON

# On Getting By: Advice for College-Bound Vets

Alex Horton (b. 1985) is a U.S. Army veteran of the war in Iraq and a free-lance writer on military and entertainment topics. Among the publications in which his work has appeared are the *New York Times, Stars & Stripes, Foreign Policy,* the *Atlantic,* and the *Guardian.* A native of Texas and a graduate of Georgetown University, he now lives in Washington, D.C. Previously he was a staff writer for *VAntage Point,* a website hosted by the Department of Veterans Affairs to help vets navigate the federal bureaucracy and obtain their benefits. In 2006, Horton started a blog, *Army of Dude,* from his barracks; it was originally intended simply as a way to keep in touch with his family and to tell them about Army life. He had disliked writing in high school; but in the military, he says, "writing became my only creative outlet, a way to relay thoughts and experiences that I would never dare speak out loud. . . . This blog was a closely guarded secret."

"On Getting By" is a post from January 2010, written after Horton was back in school under the GI Bill. It outlines a behavioral system based on Horton's firsthand analysis of adapting to the "unfamiliar, unpredictable and strange environment on campus." In the original version, Horton linked to other posts, both within and outside his blog; these links have been replaced here with footnotes.

IN MY PREVIOUS POST, I outlined some basic principles* needed to successfully [1] navigate the murky waters of education under the GI Bill. The challenges in dealing with the VA for education benefits are considerable, yet veterans new to college face an unfamiliar, unpredictable and strange environment on campus. If taken all at once, these hurdles can quickly overwhelm a student veteran and distract from the overall goal: to finish a degree on time with benefits to spare. Next week I will be in class for my fifth semester of higher education, and in my time I have tinkered with a system of how to bring up my veteran status, discussing Iraq and Afghanistan in the classroom and dealing with the myriad reactions fellow students have had. The system cannot be expected to work for everyone, but as

* "Here To There: Tips and Tricks for the Student Veteran," December 29, 2009. [Author's link]

MLA CITATION: Horton, Alex. "On Getting By: Advice for College-Bound Vets." 2010. *Back to the Lake.* Ed. Thomas Cooley. 3rd ed. New York: Norton, 2015. 311–15. Print.

veterans file into classrooms for the first time this spring, these tips could help in the development of a coping system better tailored for you. These should simply help to get you started.

### Modesty Is the Best Policy

For tips on using other methods, such as CLASSIFICA- TION, with a process analy- sis, see p. 292.

There are only two kinds of veterans in school: those who prattle on about their time in the military and overseas, and those who do not. The former will find any opportunity to bring up their time in Afghanistan or Iraq, even if it is not relevant to class discussion. They forget one of the tenets of military experience—the role of the consummate professional. Joining the military and serving in a time of war are sacred acts and carry a certain degree of respect and modesty. We owe it to our injured buddies and fallen friends not to brag about our exploits overseas. We have done our fair share of things that set us apart from others in the classroom, and that is exactly why it is best to retain an understated presence among others.

This is a difficult situation as it applies to reintegration, as the chasm between veterans and civilians has never been wider. From World War II to Vietnam, it would have been a difficult task to know someone that neither served overseas nor had a family member or friend who did. Now there are whole classrooms filled with those people. As Matthew McConaughey spoke prophetically in *Dazed and Confused*, "I get older, they stay the same age." An 18-year-old in college this year would have been nine years old during the invasion of Afghanistan and eleven years old during the invasion of Iraq. They have grown up with war to the point of it becoming a mind numbingly prosaic concept. It would be a frustrating battle to try and close the rift with those who don't see a rift at all. The best thing to do is use your judgment when bringing up your veteran status in the classroom. I've done it just a few times and felt uncomfortable enough to think twice about the next time. Now I tend to mention it in private conversation, not when I have the floor in public, and even then it is a casual touch on the subject. When you are ready to talk . . .

### . . . Prepare for a Question Salvo

No matter how much you try to keep it stashed away from students and coworkers, your military experience will come out sooner or later. There are things you simply cannot hide forever, like going to prison or reading *Twilight*.[1] Once you begin to move past casual conversation, it's only a matter of time before that period of your

---

1. *Twilight:* Published in 2005, the first book in a quartet of vampire romance novels for young adults by Stephenie Meyer.

life is visited. It usually begins with a discussion of age. When I tell people I'm twenty-four, the follow-up questions are almost always, "What have you done since high school?" or, "Why did you wait so long to go to school?" People tend to catch on if you mention extended vacations in the Middle East or recite monologues, so at that point it is best to come clean. However, be prepared for the questions they are more than willing to hurl your way. They might not know anyone who has deployed, but our hyperviolent culture has removed any restraint left in the world and enables them to ask any question that comes to mind. Here is what you can expect, in order of the most frequently asked:

1. What's it like?
2. Was it really hot?
3. Did you kill anyone?
4. How hot was it? Like, really hot?
5. Do you regret it?
6. Did you see any camel spiders?
7. Were you in Iran?

It's hard to get upset at some of those questions, as I find it difficult to think of   5
what I'd ask if the roles were switched. #3 can be blamed on ignorance and apathy, but #5 is the most troubling I've heard. It suggests that there is something shameful about service, duty and sacrifice. Both questions trivialize an important part of our lives. The best answer to #3 I've heard comes from the The Kitchen Dispatch* comment section: "I will forgive you for asking that question if you forgive me for not answering it." Something that personal should never be asked, only told.

The flip side to some of those cavalier probes are questions that handle the topic   6
with kid gloves. Once a coworker found out I was in the Army, she asked, "Did you go to . . . one of those places they send people?" It was uncomfortable for her just to utter those dirty "I" and "A" words, like we were speaking about some subversive topic. The kind of questions you will get will be all over the map, spanning from a place of genuine interest to the depths of sheer morbidity. Be prepared to answer anything, or politely let them know the subject isn't appropriate for casual banter.

## Let the Right Ones In

Popular culture is replete with images of the maladjusted veteran, from Rambo   7
to Travis Bickle to Red Forman. These characters are ingrained in our national conscious and typically become placeholders in the event someone doesn't personally know a veteran. When these sources are taken at face value, war veterans

---

* Kanani Fong, "Seven Things Never to Say to a Veteran," January 3, 2010. [Author's link]

are invariably crazy, depressive, easily startled, quick to anger and alcoholics. We come from broken homes, trying to escape jail time and were too dumb or poor to go to college after high school. The best way to combat these silly notions is to let people get to know you, the person, before you, the veteran. Those stereotypes aren't going anywhere soon, so the best idea is to take the concept of guarding your veteran status in the classroom and carry it over to blossoming relationships. That way your service and overseas experience complement your personality and don't define it. Revealing too much at one time can damage a friendship before it takes off. Just like in the classroom, take it slow. If they are worth keeping around, they'll understand why. We have met our lifelong friends already; we can afford to be picky.

### Try to Keep a Straight Face

There's a huge disparity between what you have been asked to do in the service and 8 what you will be asked to do in school. At the very basic level you were asked to maintain a clean weapon and uniform. Many of you were tasked with watching the back of your fellow soldiers while in imminent danger or operating complex machinery and vehicles. At school, you'll be held responsible for showing up and turning in work before deadlines. That's it. Like I mentioned in the earlier post, college seems like an insurmountable gauntlet of crushed dreams when you're in the military. Once you transition to civilian life and take a few classes, you'll be astounded at the lack of discipline and drive in some of your classmates. It's a big joke, but try to maintain composure. I'm not saying it's easy the whole way through, but I guarantee you've done something harder than a five-page essay. As they say, the rest is downhill.

### Find Another Brother

If you were in active duty, the friends you met along the way are now scattered 9 across the country. Perhaps I've always been an introvert, but I don't make friends as easy as some people. I've met just two people in fourteen classes that I consider friends, and one of them is an Afghanistan veteran. It's easy to understand why we get along. Do your best to find other veterans in your class and say hello. Talking to them will come easier than the eighteen-year-old hipster next to you, with his passion for ironic hats.[2] Find out if there is a veteran's organization on campus, but be wary of their motives. While some will join to find support and befriend fellow veterans, others will use it for recognition. . . .

---

2. *Ironic hats:* Hats and caps displaying humorous or ironic messages (such as "Ironic Hat") or indicating a trade or profession that the wearer clearly does not belong to.

**Enjoy the Ride**

Besides getting a degree or learning new skills, people go to college to meet new 10 people and to experience a different life. If you've served since September 12, 2001, you've already had a bit of each. But don't let that stop you from enjoying everything school has to offer. It's the last time very little will be expected of you, unless you get another government job. Then you're golden.

If you are recently out of the military and on your way to college, these tenets, 11 coupled with the GI Bill pointers, should help you get started in academia. Like most things, your experience may vary, and I would hope you don't safeguard your veteran status like it's a dark secret or the true location of Jimmy Hoffa's body. It's something to be proud of, but not flaunted. It's something to share with your friends who genuinely want to know about the world you lived in, but not with the people who have twisted notions of what you have done overseas. The last thing you want people to know you as is the guy who went to Iraq. You want them to say "Hey, that's Alex, he's good people," and not "I wonder how many ear necklaces he has. I'm betting two." Hopefully these tips will help even just a tiny bit in that regard. ◆

> One of the last steps in analyzing a process is to say what the end result should be (p. 292).

## FOR CLOSE READING

1. What process is Alex Horton analyzing? Do you think his "system" is likely to serve its intended purpose (1)? Why or why not?

2. Horton thinks veterans should not "hide" their military service from their class-mates (4). How does he think they should deal with the subject? Do you think this is good advice? Why or why not?

3. How appropriate do you consider Horton's proposed answer to the question, "Did you kill anyone?" (5). Explain.

4. According to Horton, how are military veterans usually **DEFINED** in "popular cul-ture" (7)? How accurate is his assessment? How and where should it be changed?

## Strategies and Structures

1. Who is the intended **AUDIENCE** for Horton's blog post? Who else might find his advice to be useful? For what **PURPOSE**?

2. Horton divides veterans into two categories. What are they, and how does this **CLASSIFICATION** system help to explain how student veterans can best adapt to their new circumstances?

3. How (and how well) does the first step in Horton's analysis prepare the way for the later steps?

4. When Horton presents his list of questions in step two, he wonders what questions he would ask "if the roles were switched" (5). What does asking himself this suggest about his character and credibility as a writer?

5. What point is Horton making when he uses the EXAMPLE of "the five-page essay" (8)? Is it a good example? Why or why not?

6. *Other Methods.* Where else does Horton COMPARE AND CONTRAST being in the military with being in school? How (and how well) does the comparison support his analysis of how veterans can get by in their new circumstances?

## Thinking about Language

1. What is Horton's (humorous) point in putting "going to prison" in the same phrase with "reading *Twilight*" (4)?

2. Horton describes the culture he and other veterans are returning to as "hyperviolent" (4). Is there any IRONY here? Explain.

3. Horton uses the word *conscious* when what he means is *consciousness* (7). Are such verbal slips more acceptable in a blog than in more formal academic writing? Why or why not?

4. In a blog, how appropriate are such slang terms as "come clean" and "you're golden" (4, 10)? Explain.

## FOR WRITING

1. Write a paragraph or two telling veterans what questions you think they will need to be ready to answer—and why—when they enter college.

2. What advice would you give high-school students to help them "get started in academia" (11)? Write an analysis of the process based on your experience.

3. "Joining the military and serving in a time of war," says Horton, "are sacred acts and carry a certain degree of respect and modesty" (2). In approximately 600 words, write a POSITION PAPER supporting (or challenging) this statement. Use process analysis where appropriate, but also be sure to give substantial reasons for your position.

4. If you are just getting started in college, or in a new school, keep a journal for a term or two of the process of adaptation you're going through. Using your journal as a basis, write a process analysis telling arriving students how to get by in their new environment.

5. Interview a veteran at your school about his or her experiences there and elsewhere after returning from military service. Write a PROFILE of that person, including some analysis of how he or she has adapted to civilian life.

You'll find quizzes on the readings at
wwnorton.com/write/back-to-the-lake.

DAVE BARRY

# How to Jump-start Your Car When the Battery Is Dead

Dave Barry (b. 1947) is the author of more than thirty books of humor. A graduate of Haverford College, Barry taught writing for a consulting firm before joining the *Miami Herald* as a humor columnist in 1983. (When you write a business letter, Barry advised his students, do not say things like, "Enclosed, please find the enclosed enclosures.") Barry's columns—collected in such volumes as *Dave Barry: Boogers Are My Beat* (2003)—earned him a Pulitzer Prize for commentary in 1988 and appeared weekly until 2005. In *I'll Mature When I'm Dead* (2010), Barry covered various aspects of adulthood—surprising many people, including his publisher, who claims that Barry "struggled hard against growing up his entire life."

*You Can Date Boys When You're Forty* (2014), in which this selection first appeared, takes the next illogical step—into "Parenting and Other Topics He Knows Very Little About." These would include jump-starting a car, which Barry nonetheless manages to analyze into a fourteen-step process with humorous, if alarming, results at every turn.

1. Obtain a working car from somewhere and park it next to your car.

2. Or, if the owner isn't around, you could just take off in the working car.

3. No, that would be wrong.

4. On both cars, locate the hood, which is a big flat piece of metal in the front with bird poop on it.

5. Open both hoods. There will be a button or lever inside the car on the driver's side that you need to push or pull, and then a latch somewhere under the front of the hood that you need to reach in and release. So your best bet is to use a crowbar.

6. Locate your car's battery. It will be a black box partly covered with a whitish-greenish fuzz. This is car leprosy. *Do not touch it.*

7. Obtain some jumper cables from somewhere.

8. Call 911 and let them know there might be an emergency soon.

9. Do this next part VERY, VERY CAREFULLY OR YOU WILL DIE.

A process analysis should always specify when special equipment (p. 286) is needed.

MLA CITATION: Barry, Dave. "How to Jump-start Your Car When the Battery Is Dead." 2014. *Back to the Lake*. Ed. Thomas Cooley. 3rd ed. New York: Norton, 2015. 317–18. Print.

10. Connect one end of the *red* jumper cable to the *positive* terminal (also called the ignition or carburetor) on your car's battery. Then connect the other end of the red cable to an electronic part such as the radio of the opposing car. Repeat this process *in the opposite order* with the *black* jumper cable, taking care to reverse the polarity.

11. Try to start your car. If the engine explodes in a giant fireball, something is wrong.

12. Maybe you should have somebody else try to start your car while you go get coffee a minimum of 150 yards away.

13. If by some miracle your car actually starts, *do not turn it off ever again.*

14. When you drive, be alert for further signs of trouble, such as a flickering of your headlights, which is an indication of a problem in your electrical system; or a collision with a building, which is an indication that you forgot to put the hood back down. ◆

## FOR CLOSE READING

1. Dave Barry says it would be wrong to "just take off" in a replacement car "if the owner isn't around" (2). Why does (even) Barry, who is giving advice as a parent, concede that this shouldn't be done?

2. In step 5, Barry recommends using a crowbar, presumably because he assumes that finding and activating the hood release is likely to be tricky. From your experience, is this a valid assumption? Why or why not?

3. Barry notes that step number 10 (connecting the cables) in the jump-starting process is VERY IMPORTANT. However, his instructions here seem . . . flawed. What's wrong with them?

4. Once the car miraculously starts, Barry jumps ahead to the be-alert-for-further-signs-of-trouble step. What steps in between does he leave out?

## Strategies and Structures

1. Assuming the role of know-it-all father who is giving sage counsel to a young daughter, Barry attenuates the process he's analyzing into fourteen steps. In a less humorous (but more accurate) analysis, the process of jump-starting a car can be accomplished in about half-a-dozen essential steps. If you begin with "obtain car" and "open hood," what would the other steps be?

2. Among the six-or-so essential steps in jump-starting a car, which one is the most complicated? What smaller steps could you break it down into for clarity—and safety?

3. When connecting the jumper cables, says Barry, take special care "to reverse the polarity" (10). Where else in his analysis do we get signs like this that Barry's persona has virtually no idea what he's doing but that Barry himself does (maybe)?

4. *Other Methods*. Barry frequently uses comic (not to mention unnecessary) DEFINITIONS, as in step 4 where he tells the reader what the hood of a car is. What do these contribute to his humor? Point out several examples in the text.

5. Explain Barry's use of CAUSE AND EFFECT in step 14.

## Thinking about Language

1. "This is car leprosy. *Do not touch it*" (6). This is good advice but imperfect use of technical terminology. Point to other places in the text where Barry demonstrates his skill at using terms that are precise but incorrect (or vice versa).

2. Barry frequently over-reacts to the situation, leading to OVERSTATEMENT. Point out several examples.

3. "If the engine explodes in a giant fireball, something is wrong" (11). Is this UNDERSTATEMENT? Explain.

## FOR WRITING

1. Write a brief analysis of one of the following processes: jump-starting a car, changing a tire, bathing a cat, painting a room, decorating and undecorating a Christmas tree.

2. Write a **PARODY** of useful advice to a son, daughter, or a parent on one of the following topics: grocery shopping, using the internet, driving a car, succeeding in school, using proper grammar, being a humorist.

3. Write a **RHETORICAL ANALYSIS** of a how-to book. It can be one of Barry's, but almost any bookstore has a section devoted to instruction and advice, particularly self-help. And, of course, *Amazon* offers how-to "lists." (Be sure to include the hyphen when searching.) In your analysis, don't forget to explain how and how well the book uses process analysis to develop its subject.

You'll find quizzes on the readings at
wwnorton.com/write/back-to-the-lake.

# How to Create New Habits

Charles Duhigg (b. 1974) is a reporter for the business section of the *New York Times*, where he was part of a team of reporters who wrote "The iEconomy," a series of articles about Apple and its international influence, that won the 2013 Pulitzer Prize for explanatory journalism. Duhigg, a native of New Mexico, is a graduate of Yale University and Harvard Business School. Before joining the *Times*, he worked in private equity and as a reporter for the *Los Angeles Times*.

"How to Create New Habits" (editor's title) is from Duhigg's best-selling book about the science of habit formation, *The Power of Habit: Why We Do What We Do in Life and Business* (2012). The cue-response-reward process for establishing new habits (and selling consumer products) was the brain-child of the early advertising theorist Claude C. Hopkins (1866–1932), whose *Scientific Advertising* was first published in 1923 and is sometimes still taught in business school. The selling process is not always so cut and dried, as Duhigg demonstrates by analyzing how Procter & Gamble almost botched the marketing of one of its (later) most successful consumer products.

THE SCIENTISTS AND MARKETING EXECUTIVES at Procter & Gamble were gath- 1
ered around a beat-up table in a small, windowless room, reading the transcript of an interview with a woman who owned nine cats, when one of them finally said what everyone was thinking.

"If we get fired, what exactly happens?" she asked. "Do security guards show up 2
and walk us out, or do we get some kind of warning beforehand?"

The team's leader, a onetime rising star within the company named Drake Stimson, 3
stared at her.

"I don't know," he said. His hair was a mess. His eyes were tired. "I never thought 4
things would get this bad. They told me running this project was a promotion."

It was 1996, and the group at the table was finding out . . . how utterly unsci- 5
entific the process of selling something could become. They all worked for one of the largest consumer goods firms on earth, the company behind Pringles potato chips, Oil of Olay, Bounty paper towels, Cover Girl cosmetics, Dawn, Downy, and

MLA CITATION: Duhigg, Charles. "How to Create New Habits." 2012. *Back to the Lake*. Ed. Thomas Cooley. 3rd ed. New York: Norton, 2015. 321–29. Print.

Duracell, as well as dozens of other brands. P&G collected more data than almost any other merchant on earth and relied on complex statistical methods to craft their marketing campaigns. The firm was incredibly good at figuring out how to sell things. In the clothes-washing market alone, P&G's products cleaned one out of every two laundry loads in America. Its revenues topped $35 billion per year.

However, Stimson's team, which had been entrusted with designing the ad cam- 6 paign for one of P&G's most promising new products, was on the brink of failure. The company had spent millions of dollars developing a spray that could remove bad smells from almost any fabric. And the researchers in that tiny, windowless room had no idea how to get people to buy it.

The spray had been created about three years earlier, when one of P&G's chem- 7 ists was working with a substance called hydroxypropyl beta cyclodextrin, or HPBCD, in a laboratory. The chemist was a smoker. His clothes usually smelled like an ashtray. One day, after working with HPBCD, his wife greeted him at the door when he got home.

"Did you quit smoking?" she asked him.                                                8

"No," he said. He was suspicious. She had been harassing him to give up ciga- 9 rettes for years. This seemed like some kind of reverse psychology trickery.

"You don't smell like smoke, is all," she said.                                      10

The next day, he went back to the lab and started experimenting with HPBCD 11 and various scents. Soon, he had hundreds of vials containing fabrics that smelled like wet dogs, cigars, sweaty socks, Chinese food, musty shirts, and dirty towels. When he put HPBCD in water and sprayed it on the samples, the scents were drawn into the chemical's molecules. After the mist dried, the smell was gone.

When the chemist explained his findings to P&G's executives, they were ecstatic. 12 For years, market research had said that consumers were clamoring for something that could get rid of bad smells—not mask them, but eradicate them altogether. When one team of researchers had interviewed customers, they found that many of them left their blouses or slacks outside after a night at a bar or party. "My clothes smell like cigarettes when I get home, but I don't want pay for dry cleaning every time I go out," one woman said.

P&G, sensing an opportunity, launched a top-secret project to turn HPBCD into 13 a viable product. They spent millions perfecting the formula, finally producing a colorless, odorless liquid that could wipe out almost any foul odor. The science behind the spray was so advanced that NASA would eventually use it to clean the interiors of shuttles after they returned from space. The best part was that it was cheap to manufacture, didn't leave stains, and could make any stinky couch, old jacket, or stained car interior smell, well, scentless. The project had been a major gamble, but P&G was now poised to earn billions-if they could come up with the right marketing campaign.

They decided to call it Febreze, and asked Stimson, a thirty-one-year-old 14 wunderkind with a background in math and psychology, to lead the marketing team. Stimson was tall and handsome, with a strong chin, a gentle voice, and a taste for high-end meals. . . . Before joining P&G, he had spent five years on Wall Street building mathematical models for choosing stocks. When he relocated to Cincinnati, where P&G was headquartered, he was tapped to help run important business lines, including Bounce fabric softener and Downy dryer sheets. But Febreze was different. It was a chance to launch an entirely new category of product—to add something to a consumer's shopping cart that had never been there before. All Stimson needed to do was figure out how to make Febreze into a habit, and the product would fly off the shelves. How tough could that be?

Stimson and his colleagues decided to introduce Febreze in a few test markets— 15 Phoenix, Salt Lake City, and Boise. They flew in and handed out samples, and then asked people if they could come by their homes. Over the course of two months, they visited hundreds of households. Their first big breakthrough came when they visited a park ranger in Phoenix. She was in her late twenties and lived by herself. Her job was to trap animals that wandered out of the desert. She caught coyotes, raccoons, the occasional mountain lion. And skunks. Lots and lots of skunks. Which often sprayed her when they were caught.

"I'm single, and I'd like to find someone to have kids with," the ranger told 16 Stimson and his colleagues while they sat in her living room. "I go on a lot of dates. I mean, I think I'm attractive, you know? I'm smart and I feel like I'm a good catch."

But her love life was crippled, she explained, because everything in her life 17 smelled like skunk. Her house, her truck, her clothing, her boots, her hands, her curtains. Even her bed. She had tried all sorts of cures. She bought special soaps and shampoos. She burned candles and used expensive carpet shampooing machines. None of it worked.

"When I'm on a date, I'll get a whiff of something that smells like skunk and I'll 18 start obsessing about it," she told them. "I'll start wondering, does he smell it? What if I bring him home and he wants to leave?

"I went on four dates last year with a really nice guy, a guy I really liked, and I 19 waited forever to invite him to my place. Eventually, he came over, and I thought everything was going really well. Then the next day, he said he wanted to 'take a break.' He was really polite about it, but I keep wondering, was it the smell?"

"Well, I'm glad you got a chance to try Febreze," Stimson said. "How'd you like it?" 20

She looked at him. She was crying. 21

"I want to thank you," she said. "This spray has changed my life." 22

After she had received samples of Febreze, she had gone home and sprayed her 23 couch. She sprayed the curtains, the rug, the bed spread, her jeans, her uniform, the interior of her car. The bottle ran out, so she got another one, and sprayed everything else.

"I've asked all of my friends to come over," the woman said. "They can't smell it anymore. The skunk is gone." 24

By now, she was crying so hard that one of Stimson's colleagues was patting her on the shoulder. "Thank you so much," the woman said. "I feel so free. Thank you. This product is so important." 25

Stimson sniffed the air inside her living room. He couldn't smell anything. *We're going to make a fortune with this stuff,* he thought. 26

Stimson and his team went back to P&G headquarters and started reviewing the marketing campaign they were about to roll out. The key to selling Febreze, they decided, was conveying that sense of relief the park ranger felt. They had to position Febreze as something that would allow people to rid themselves of embarrassing smells. . . . They wanted to keep the ads simple: Find an obvious cue and clearly define the reward. 27

Don't forget to define your audience, p. 285, and their specific needs.

They designed two television commercials. The first showed a woman talking about the smoking section of a restaurant. Whenever she eats there, her jacket smells like smoke. A friend tells her if she uses Febreze, it will eliminate the odor. The cue: the smell of cigarettes. The reward: odor eliminated from clothes. The second ad featured a woman worrying about her dog, Sophie, who always sits on the couch. "Sophie will always smell like Sophie," she says, but with Febreze, "now my furniture doesn't have to." The cue: pet smells, which are familiar to the seventy million households with animals. The reward: a house that doesn't smell like a kennel. 28

Stimson and his colleagues began airing the advertisements in 1996 in the same test cities. They gave away samples, put advertisements in mailboxes, and paid grocers to build mountains of Febreze near cash registers. Then they sat back, anticipating how they would spend their bonuses. 29

A week passed. Then two. A month. Two months. Sales started small—and got smaller. Panicked, the company sent researchers into stores to see what was happening. Shelves were filled with Febreze bottles that had never been touched. They started visiting housewives who had received free samples. 30

"Oh, yes!" one of them told a P&G researcher. "The spray! I remember it. Let's see." The woman got down on her knees in the kitchen and started rooting through the cabinet underneath the sink. "I used it for a while, but then I forgot about it. I think it's back here somewhere." She stood up. "Maybe it's in the closet?" She walked over and pushed aside some brooms. "Yes! Here it is! In the back! See? It's still almost full. Did you want it back?" 31

Febreze was a dud. 32

For Stimson, this was a disaster. Rival executives in other divisions sensed an 33 opportunity in his failure. He heard whispers that some people were lobbying to kill Febreze and get him reassigned to Nicky Clarke hair products, the consumer goods equivalent of Siberia.

One of P&G's divisional presidents called an emergency meeting and announced 34 they had to cut their losses on Febreze before board members started asking questions. Stimson's boss stood up and made an impassioned plea. "There's still a chance to turn everything around," he said. "At the very least, let's ask the PhDs to figure out what's going on." P&G had recently snapped up scientists from Stanford, Carnegie Mellon, and elsewhere who were supposed experts in consumer psychology. The division's president agreed to give the product a little more time.

So a new group of researchers joined Stimson's team and started conducting 35 more interviews. Their first inkling of why Febreze was failing came when they visited a woman's home outside Phoenix. They could smell her nine cats before they went inside. The house's interior, however, was clean and organized. She was somewhat of a neat freak, the woman explained. She vacuumed every day and didnt like to open her windows, since the wind blew in dust. When Stimson and the scientists walked into her living room, where the cats lived, the scent was so overpowering that one of them gagged.

"What do you do about the cat smell?" a scientist asked the woman. 36

"It's usually not a problem," she said. 37

"How often do you notice a smell?" 38

"Oh, about once a month," the woman replied. 39

The researchers looked at one another. 40

"Do you smell it now?" a scientist asked. 41

"No," she said. 42

The same pattern played out in dozens of other smelly homes the researchers 43 visited. People couldn't detect most of the bad smells in their lives. If you live with nine cats, you become desensitized to their scent. If you smoke cigarettes, it damages your olfactory capacities so much that you can't smell smoke anymore. Scents are strange; even the strongest fade with constant exposure. That's why no one was using Febreze, Stimson realized. The product's cue—the thing that was supposed to trigger daily use—was hidden from the people who needed it most. Bad scents simply weren't noticed frequently enough to trigger a regular habit. As a result, Febreze ended up in the back of a closet. The people with the greatest proclivity to use the spray never smelled the odors that should have reminded them the living room needed a spritz.

A process, by definition, is repeatable (p. 288).

Stimson's team went back to headquarters and gathered in the windowless 44 conference room, rereading the transcript of the woman with nine cats. The psychologist asked what happens if you get fired. Stimson put his head in his hands.

If he couldn't sell Febreze to a woman with nine cats, he wondered, who *could* he sell it to? How do you build a new habit when there's no cue to trigger usage, and when the consumers who most need it don't appreciate the reward?

. . .

After their disastrous interview with the cat woman, Drake Stimson's team at P&G 45 started looking outside the usual channels for help. They began reading up on experiments. . . . They asked a Harvard Business School professor to conduct psychological tests of Febreze's ad campaigns. They interviewed customer after customer, looking for something that would give them a clue how to make Febreze a regular part of consumers' lives.

One day, they went to speak with a woman in a suburb near Scottsdale. She was 46 in her forties with four kids. Her house was clean, but not compulsively tidy. To the surprise of the researchers, she loved Febreze.

"I use it every day," she told them. 47

"You do?" Stimson said. The house didn't seem like the kind of place with smelly 48 problems. There weren't any pets. No one smoked. "How? What smells are you trying to get rid of?"

"I don't really use it for specific smells," the woman said. "I mean, you know, I've 49 got boys. They're going through puberty, and if I don't clean their rooms, it smells like a locker. But I don't really use it that way. I use it for normal cleaning—a couple of sprays when I'm done in a room. It's a nice way to make everything smell good as a final touch."

They asked if they could watch her clean the house. In the bedroom, she made 50 her bed, plumped the pillows, tightened the sheet's corners, and then took a Febreze bottle and sprayed the smoothed comforter. In the living room, she vacuumed, picked up the kids' shoes, straightened the coffee table, and sprayed Febreze on the freshly cleaned carpet. "It's nice, you know?" she said. "Spraying feels like a little mini-celebration when I'm done with a room." At the rate she was using Febreze, Stimson estimated, she would empty a bottle every two weeks.

P&G had collected thousands of hours of videotapes of people cleaning their 51 homes over the years. When the researchers got back to Cincinnati, some of them spent an evening looking through the tapes. The next morning, one of the scientists asked the Febreze team to join him in the conference room. He cued up the tape of one woman—a twenty-six-year-old with three children—making a bed. She smoothed the sheets and adjusted a pillow. Then, she smiled and left the room.

"Did you see that?" the researcher asked excitedly. 52

He put on another clip. A younger, brunette woman spread out a colorful bed- 53 spread, straightened a pillow, and then smiled at her handiwork. "There it is again!" the researcher said. The next clip showed a woman in workout clothes tidying her kitchen and wiping the counter before easing into a relaxing stretch.

Each ad was calibrated to elicit a craving, with Febreze positioned as the reward.

The researcher looked at his colleagues.                                    54

"Do you see it?" he asked.                                                  55

"Each of them is doing something relaxing or happy when they finish cleaning,"  56
he said. "We can build off that! What if Febreze was something that happened at
the end of the cleaning routine, rather than the beginning? What if it was the fun
part of making something cleaner?"

Stimson's team ran one more test. Previously, the product's advertising had  57
focused on eliminating bad smells. The company printed up new labels that showed
open windows and gusts of fresh air. More perfume was added to the recipe, so
that instead of merely neutralizing odors, Febreze had its own distinct scent. Television commercials were filmed of women spraying freshly made beds and spritz-
ing just-laundered clothing. The tagline had been "Gets bad smells out of fabrics." It
was rewritten as "Cleans life's smells."

Each change was designed to appeal to a specific, daily cue: Cleaning a room.  58
Making a bed. Vacuuming a rug. In each one, Febreze was positioned as the reward:
the nice smell that occurs at the end of a cleaning routine. Most important, each ad
was calibrated to elicit a craving: that things will smell as nice as they look
when the cleaning ritual is done. The irony is that a product manufactured
to destroy odors was transformed into the opposite. Instead of eliminating
scents on dirty fabrics, it became an air freshener used as the finishing
touch, once things are already clean.

See p. 292 for
tips on deter-
mining how a
process analysis
should end.

When the researchers went back into consumers' homes after the new ads aired  59
and the redesigned bottles were given away, they found that some housewives in the
test market had started expecting—craving—the Febreze scent. One woman said
that when her bottle ran dry, she squirted diluted perfume on her laundry. "If I don't
smell something nice at the end, it doesn't really seem clean now," she told them.

"The park ranger with the skunk problem sent us in the wrong direction,"  60
Stimson told me. "She made us think that Febreze would succeed by providing a
solution to a problem. But who wants to admit their house stinks?

"We were looking at it all wrong. No one craves scentlessness. On the other  61
hand, lots of people crave a nice smell after they've spent thirty minutes cleaning."

The Febreze relaunch took place in the summer of 1998. Within two months,  62
sales doubled. Within a year, customers had spent more than $230 million on the
product. Since then, Febreze has spawned dozens of spin-offs—air fresheners,
candles, laundry detergents, and kitchen sprays—that, all told, now account for
sales of more than $1 billion per year. Eventually, P&G began mentioning to
customers that, in addition to smelling good, Febreze can also kill bad odors.

Stimson was promoted and his team received their bonuses. The formula had  63
worked. They had found simple and obvious cues. They had clearly defined the
reward.

But only once they created a sense of craving—the desire to make everything   64
smell and nice as it looked—did Febreze become a hit. ◆

## FOR CLOSE READING

1. According to Charles Duhigg, how did Procter & Gamble invent or, more accurately, discover the spray for removing bad smells from clothes that they would eventually market under the brand name Febreze?

2. Ultimately, Febreze and related products would put more than a billion dollars a year into P&G's coffers. Why was the product such a flop when it was first test-marketed in Phoenix, Salt Lake City, and Boise?

3. In the research team's initial failure to market Febreze successfully, what was the role of the "park ranger with the skunk problem" (60)? of "the woman with nine cats" (43)?

4. At first, the whole idea behind Febreze was to make bad smells scentless. Why did the scientists at P&G eventually have to change the Febreze formula and put some scent back into it?

5. In the re-formulation of Febreze—and its ultimate success as a consumer product—what was the role of the woman in Scottsdale with four kids whose "house was clean, but not compulsively tidy" (46)?

## Strategies and Structures

1. In business school, the marketing researchers at P&G had been taught that forming new habits in their customer base was a three-step process. According to Duhigg, what are those three steps and how does he use them to help organize his essay?

2. If noticing a bad smell—of tobacco, skunk, or cat, say, on clothes and in the house—proved to be a false cue for creating the habit of using Febreze, what did the researchers at P&G find to be the real cue? How did they change the other steps in the habit-forming process—and why did they need to?

3. In addition to a scientifically determined process for forming new habits, Duhigg is writing about "the process of selling something" and how "utterly unscientific" it could become (5). How and where does Duhigg analyze the selling process as one of repeated trial and error in his account of the marketing campaign for Febreze?

4. Although he is not writing a traditional research report, Duhigg is reporting on the research of others. How and how well does he use process analysis to explain the methodology of the researchers at Procter & Gamble?

5. *Other Methods.* Duhigg uses the example of Febreze to EXEMPLIFY both how new habits are formed (or not formed) and how the researchers and managers at Procter & Gamble developed a wildly successful new product. Is it a good example? Why or why not?

## Thinking about Language

1. "They decided to call it Febreze" (14). Was this a good choice for the name of a product that eliminates odors in fabrics? Why or why not?

2. Given their research results, why did the marketing people at P&G conclude that "Cleans life's smells" was a better slogan for their new product than "Gets bad smells out of fabrics" (57)? Were they right?

3. Why does Duhigg replace "expecting" with "craving" in paragraph 59?

4. Why is it IRONIC, as Duhigg says, "that a product manufactured to destroy odors was transformed into the opposite" (58)?

## FOR WRITING

1. Write a paragraph explaining how and why you use a common household product.

2. Do you sometimes use a product for a purpose for which it is not intended, such as Coca-Cola to clean your windshield? Write a brief essay analyzing how you do so and what results, beneficial or otherwise, you obtain.

3. Along with several of your classmates, do some research on the history and development of some familiar products or services, assigning a different one to each member of the group. Compare notes, and choose one of the products or services to write about. Using process analysis as the main method of development, collaborate on a final REPORT that analyzes the research—scientific and not so scientific—that went into the development and marketing of your subject.

4. The habit-forming process as analyzed by Duhigg (and P&G) is based on the idea of a "habit loop" as formulated by Claude C. Hopkins, a pioneer in the field of advertising. Do some research into Hopkins's theories, and write a paper of approximately 500 words on the process of habit formation as Hopkins understood it.

5. Keep a habit-forming journal in which you record, on a regular basis, your efforts at losing weight, gaining weight, stopping smoking, organizing your time, improving your finances, or some other change in habitual action. Analyze the process as you go, and try to break it down into steps that actually work (or not).

You'll find quizzes on the readings at
wwnorton.com/write/back-to-the-lake.

# Fishing on the Susquehanna in July

Billy Collins (b. 1941) grew up in New York, the son of an electrician and a nurse. He studied at the College of the Holy Cross and the University of California, Riverside, where he earned a PhD in romantic poetry. The poet laureate of the United States from 2001 to 2003, Collins teaches English at Lehman College of the City University of New York and at Southampton Stony Brook, a campus of the State University of New York.

"Fishing on the Susquehanna in July" is from Collins's poetry collection *Picnic, Lightning* (1998). The poem is a description of "American scenes"—particularly of a man fishing on a river in Maryland—as depicted in paintings that Collins once viewed in a Philadelphia art gallery. As Collins looks at the fisherman, however, he goes beyond merely describing the tranquil scene to demonstrate how art, including the art of writing, "manufactures" experience.

I have never been fishing on the Susquehanna          1
or on any river for that matter
to be perfectly honest.

Not in July or any month
have I had the pleasure—if it is a pleasure—          5
of fishing on the Susquehanna.

I am more likely to be found
in a quiet room like this one—
a painting of a woman on the wall,

a bowl of tangerines on the table—          10
trying to manufacture the sensation
of fishing on the Susquehanna.

MLA CITATION: Collins, Billy. "Fishing on the Susquehanna in July." 1998. *Back to the Lake.* Ed. Thomas Cooley. 3rd ed. New York: Norton, 2015. 331-32. Print.

There is little doubt
that others have been fishing
on the Susquehanna,                                                    15

rowing upstream in a wooden boat,
sliding the oars under the water
then raising them to drip in the light.

But the nearest I have ever come to
fishing on the Susquehanna                                             20
was one afternoon in a museum in Philadelphia,

when I balanced a little egg of time
in front of a painting
in which that river curled around a bend

under a blue cloud-ruffled sky,                                        25
dense trees along the banks,
and a fellow with a red bandana

sitting in a small, green
flat-bottom boat
holding the thin whip of a pole.                                       30

That is something I am unlikely
ever to do, I remember
saying to myself and the person next to me.

Then I blinked and moved on
to other American scenes                                               35
of haystacks, water whitening over rocks,

even one of a brown hare
who seemed so wired with alertness
I imagined him springing right out of the frame.  ◆

# FOR CLOSE READING

1. Billy Collins says he has never been fishing on the Susquehanna in July, so what gives him the authority to write about it in this poem?

2. Collins is not in a boat when he writes the poem. Where is he? Why isn't he somewhere else, such as in a boat fishing on a river?

3. When was Collins in an art museum in Philadelphia, and why does he bring that experience into the picture?

## Strategies and Structure

1. Which of the following most accurately describes Collins's poem? Choose one. Explain why you think so by referring to details in the text.

   a. Collins is telling the reader how to fish.

   b. Collins is telling the reader how to look at pictures in a gallery.

   c. Collins is telling the reader how to write a poem.

   d. Collins is showing how he writes poetry.

   e. All of the above.

2. Though Collins himself has not, he is sure "that others have been fishing / on the Susquehanna" (14-15). Where and how does Collins briefly analyze this process?

3. What process is Collins analyzing in lines 19-39? What did he call it earlier, and where is it best accomplished?

4. When analyzing a process, you should tell readers what the key ingredients are and what special equipment is required. Where and how does Collins do this (if he does)?

5. *Other Methods.* This poem is a carefully crafted DESCRIPTION of "American scenes" (35). Which of the five senses—sight, sound, touch, smell, and taste—does Collins emphasize in capturing them? What DOMINANT IMPRESSION does he create in the reader?

## Thinking about Language

1. Collins says he is trying to "manufacture" sensations (11)? What are the implications of his use of this term instead of, say, *imitate* or *capture* or *explore*?

2. You've heard of egg timers, but "a little egg of time" (22)? What is Collins talking about here? Explain the METAPHOR.

3. How is Collins defining the word "scenes" (35)? How do you know?

4. "The picture was so alive it seemed to spring from the frame" is a familiar statement about viewing art. How does Collins's poem take the reader beyond it? Point to specific passages in the text to support your reading.

## FOR WRITING

1.  Write a paragraph or two analyzing what seems to be going on in a painting or photograph that presents people (or animals) engaged in some process.

2.  In a brief essay, analyze what seems to be going on in an interesting painting or photograph—and also try to capture how looking at the painting or photograph makes you think or feel. Cite specific details to illustrate your sensations.

3.  In an essay or poem, show what you think it would feel like to experience something you have never experienced, such as sky diving, climbing the Eiffel Tower, eating ants, fishing for tarpon, writing a song.

4.  In approximately 500 words, write a RHETORICAL ANALYSIS of "Fishing on the Susquehanna in July" or of some other poem by Billy Collins. Be sure to analyze not only what the poem has to say but how the poem says it.

You'll find quizzes on the readings at
wwnorton.com/write/back-to-the-lake.

# CHAPTER 10

# Comparison and Contrast

In close combat, and with no preparation, Iron Man would make mincemeat out of the Dark Knight with his superior strength. But Batman knows this and would not only then know Stark's weaknesses, but would have a contingency plan to take him down. . . . One-on-one, it's not really close: Batman in a landslide.

—SHAWN ADLER, "Iron Man vs. Batman"

When we compare and contrast things—red apples and golden apples, theories of history, superheroes—we look at both the similarities and the differences between them. Whether we emphasize the similarities (comparison) or the differences (contrast), however, will depend not only on who or what we're comparing but on our *basis* of comparison.

## Finding Similarities and Differences

If we compare two superheroes—Iron Man and Batman, for example—on the basis of their *strengths*, we are likely to emphasize their similarities. To begin with, both are extraordinarily wealthy. According to *Forbes* magazine, Batman has roughly $6.8 billion from the Wayne Corp. and his inheritance; Iron Man has approximately $3 billion from Stark Industries. Also, both are intelligent and cunning in the pursuit of evildoers; and both possess great physical strength, although Iron Man's high-tech armor gives him an edge here—when he is wearing it. Furthermore, both have faithful sidekicks (Jim Rhodes and Robin), and their adventures are underwritten by two of the most potent companies in the entertainment business, Marvel and DC comics, respectively.

For a comparison of DC and Marvel, see "Superhero Smackdown," p. 361.

On the basis of their strengths—they *are* superheroes after all—Iron Man and Batman would seem to be alike in many ways. If, however, we compare the two characters on the basis of their *weaknesses*, we are likely to come up with a cape-full of differences. Here is *MTV News's* assessment of the most "glaring weakness" they find when comparing (or rather contrasting) Tony Stark and Bruce Wayne (aka Iron Man and Batman):

> Stark has been known to hit the bottle every once in a while, making him vulnerable at best and unavailable at worst. . . . Due to his upbringing and strict moral code, Wayne is unable to trust people and, oftentimes, isn't able to see any good in them at all. . . . Batman's biggest weakness may turn out to be his greatest strength. Because he was unable to trust the Justice League, for instance, he kept dossiers on all the members, learning their secret identities and weaknesses should he ever need to take them down. He investigated Superman. Do we think he wouldn't also have a file on that goody-goody Tony Stark? Stark's weakness, meanwhile, just makes him incorrigible.
> —SHAWN ADLER, "Iron Man vs. Batman: Who Would Come Out on Top?
> We Compare the Epic Superheroes Side-by-Side"

## COMPARING WAYS TO SAY "THANK YOU"

Sometimes the purpose of a comparison is to point out similarities where the reader might normally expect differences. And *vice versa*.

Reimagining the thank-you note in contrasting ways.

For example, we might normally expect men and women to say "thank you" for more or less the same reason—to acknowledge a gift or service. This is not always the case, according to the sociolinguist Deborah Tannen:

> Many women use "thanks" as an automatic conversation starter and closer; there's nothing literally to say thank you for. Like many rituals typical of women's conversation, it depends on the goodwill of the other to restore the balance. When the other speaker doesn't recipro-cate, a woman may feel like someone on a seesaw whose partner aban-doned his end.  —DEBORAH TANNEN, "But What Do You Mean?"

The partner who abandoned his end of the conversation, says Tannen, is the man who says "You're welcome" to the woman's ritual "thank you": she is starting or ending a conversation; he is taking credit. (Read the rest of Tannen's essay on p. 437.)

This passage is mostly contrast; that is, it stresses the differences between the two figures being compared. They *are* still being compared, however: comparisons are about relationships, whether of sameness or difference. In this chapter, therefore, we will use the word *comparison* both for drawing similarities between two related subjects *and* for pointing out their differences. (We'll reserve *contrast* for occasional use when describing differences only.) In this chapter we will also look more deeply into when and why we compare things, how to make effective comparisons, and how to compose and organize an essay that uses common strategies of comparison and contrast. Finally, we'll review the critical points to watch for as you read over and revise your essay, as well as common errors to avoid when you edit.

## Why Do We Compare?

For most ordinary mortals, one form of comparison that frequently comes out on top of all others is comparison shopping. The reason you compare before you buy, of course, is so you can select the best product for your needs at the best price. For this purpose you may consult a buying guide, such as *Consumer Reports*.

In a recent issue, the professional comparers at *Consumer Reports* compared similar makes, models, and brands of tablet computers, dishwashing soap, online florists, stain remover, barbecue sauce, 3D TVs, and food processors—all so consumers can be aware of the differences among them.

Bruce Catton does this with two very different Civil War generals on p. 377.
One of the main reasons we compare things—and not just consumer products—is to discover differences between two subjects that we would otherwise expect to be similar. For example, on a botany exam you might compare the leaf structure of two related species of ferns. Or, in literature, you might compare two Shakespearean sonnets.

We also make comparisons in order to find similarities between subjects that we might otherwise consider to be entirely different, as in this opening paragraph from a book on what happens to the human body after death:

> The way I see it, being dead is not terribly far off from being on a cruise ship. Most of your time is spent lying on your back. The brain has shut down. The flesh begins to soften. Nothing much new happens, and nothing is expected of you. —MARY ROACH, *Stiff*

We don't normally think of being dead and taking a cruise as being very much alike. By pointing out similarities between the two that we may not have noticed, however, Roach enables us to see both of these subjects—particularly the grimmer one—in a new light. This particular kind of comparison between two seemingly unrelated subjects is called an **ANALOGY**: it explains a less-familiar subject by comparing it to something we are likely to know more about.

## Composing an Essay That Compares and Contrasts

The root meaning of the word *compare* is "to put with equals," and so the first thing you need to do when composing an essay that compares and contrasts is to choose subjects that are truly comparable—apples to apples, oranges to oranges.

If two subjects are different in every way, there is little point in comparing them. The same is true if they are entirely alike. Your subjects should have enough in common to provide a solid basis of comparison. A train and a jetliner, for instance, are very different machines; but both are modes of transportation, and that shared characteristic can become the basis for comparing them.

When you look for shared characteristics in your subjects, don't stretch your comparison too far, however. You don't want to make the logical blunder that the Duchess commits in Lewis Carroll's *Alice in Wonderland*:

> "Very true," said the Duchess: "flamingos and mustard both bite. And the moral of that is—'Birds of a feather flock together.'"
>
> "Only mustard isn't a bird," Alice remarked.
>
> "Right as usual," said the Duchess: "what a clear way you have of putting things."

Flamingos and mustard both bite, but not in ways that are similar enough to make them truly comparable. So beware what you compare. Before you bring two subjects together as equals in an essay, make sure they are "birds of a feather" by looking carefully at the characteristics that make them different from others but similar to one another. Those characteristics should be significant enough to form a solid basis of comparison. In Wonderland, you might compare turtles and tanks, for example, on the grounds that both move relatively slowly and have hard outer coverings. In the real world, however, don't bring two subjects together when the differences between them are far more significant than the similarities. Better to compare mustard and ketchup, or flamingos and roseate spoonbills—unless, of course, you plan to show just how much two apparently dissimilar subjects (being dead and going on a cruise, skyscrapers and airplanes) actually have in common.

## Thinking about Purpose and Audience

Suppose that you are comparing running shoes for the simple purpose of buying a new pair to replace your old ones. In this case, you are comparing them in order to evaluate them—to decide which shoe fits your needs best, so you can choose the right one at the right price. However, if you were writing a comparison of several kinds of running shoes for *Consumer Reports*, you would be comparing your subjects in order to inform readers about them. Instead of evaluating the shoes and choosing a pair to fit your needs, your purpose would be to give readers the information they need to choose for themselves.

With comparisons, as with shoes, one size does not fit all. Whether you're writing a comparison to inform, evaluate, or for some other purpose, always keep the specific needs of your audience in mind. How much do your readers already know about your topic? Why should they want or need to know more? What distinctions can you make that they haven't already thought of?

If you are comparing running shoes for a runner's magazine or a shoe catalogue, for example, your readers are probably running enthusiasts who already know a good bit about your subject; so you should distinguish carefully among the different brands or models you're discussing. Thus you might point out that New Balance models 901 and 816 are both durable, lightweight training shoes. The 901, however, is meant for the runner who is (in the words of the manufacturer) "looking for greater stability from heel to toe," while the 816 offers "a deeper toe box for runners needing more space in the forefoot."

A comparison like this is geared toward readers who are experienced runners and have highly specialized needs. Such fine distinctions would be lost on readers who are simply looking for the cheapest running shoe available, or the highest quality one, or the most stylish. So before you compare, size up your readers, and tailor your comparison to fit their specific needs.

## Generating Ideas: Asking How Two Things Are Alike or Different

BRAINSTORMING and LISTING can help as you think about your comparison. Once you have a clear basis for comparing two subjects—flamingos and roseate spoonbills are both large pink birds; trains and jetliners are modes of mass transportation; NB 901s and 816s are medium-priced running shoes—the next step is to look for specific points of comparison between them. So ask yourself the key questions that any comparison raises: How, specifically, are your two subjects alike? How do they differ?

As you probe for similarities and differences between your subjects, make a point-by-point list like the following one pertaining to bathing customs in the United States and Japan:

**DIFFERENCES**

| *American bath* | *Japanese bath* |
|---|---|
| fast and efficient | slow and contemplative |
| usually solitary | often communal, even public |
| bather scrubs own back | family members scrub one another's backs |
| about getting clean | about family and community |
| mundane | ritualistic |
| stare at ceramic tile | watch the moon rise |
| concerned with the body | concerned with the soul |

**SIMILARITIES**

| *American bath* | *Japanese bath* |
|---|---|
| cleanliness is important | cleanliness is important |

Listing the main ways in which two subjects are alike or different will help you to determine whether they're actually worth comparing—and will also help you to get the similarities and differences straight in your own mind before attempting to explain them to an audience.

Notice that in the lists above, each point on the American side matches the point on the Japanese side. If the point on the American side is "stare at ceramic tile," the point on the Japanese side is also about what you look at while bathing: "watch the moon rise." When you draw up your list, make sure you look at the same elements in both subjects. If you talk about the communal aspect of the Japanese bath, you need to mention whether American baths are communal or solitary—or your comparison will be incomplete.

## Organizing and Drafting a Comparison

Once you have a list of the specific ways in which your two subjects are alike or different, you're ready to organize, and then to begin drafting, your comparison. Make sure, however, that your main points of comparison deal with significant characteristics of your two subjects and that you draw a sufficient number of them. The templates on p. 345 can help you get started.

## CHOOSING A METHOD OF ORGANIZATION

There are fundamentally two ways of organizing a comparison: you can go point by point or subject by subject. Let's look at the POINT-BY-POINT method at work in a comparison of the career patterns of two ambitious women:

> Both Cleo and Alice are hard-driving workers; both are achievers; both spend so much time working that they have very little left for traditional leisure pursuits. The fundamental difference between Alice and Cleo is that they define work differently. Cleo is working *for* her company. Alice works *through* her company while working for herself. Cleo is a stabilizer. Alice is a scrambler. Most of us fall into one of these two camps. To make the most of your own career and psych out the people around you, it's essential to be able to tell them apart. —ELWOOD CHAPMAN, *Working Woman*

With a point-by-point organization like this, you discuss each point of comparison (or contrast) between your two subjects before going on to the next point. Here's an informal outline of Chapman's point-by-point comparison:

1. Kind of workers
   Cleo is hard-driving, an achiever
   Alice is hard-driving, an achiever
2. Time spent working
   Cleo spends all her time working
   Alice spends all her time working
3. How they define work
   Cleo works for her company
   Alice works for herself
4. How they affect their coworkers
   Cleo is a stabilizer
   Alice is a scrambler

After using the point-by-point method to compare the two workers in the first paragraph of his essay, Chapman switches to the SUBJECT-BY-SUBJECT method in the next two paragraphs:

> Cleo is a classic workaholic. She works from dawn till dusk (more than five days a week as necessary) with a major utility. She earns a good salary, is highly esteemed by her bosses for her loyalty and reliability, and enjoys extraordinary job security (it probably would cost her employer at least 20 percent more than she earns to replace her).

Alice, a mid-management person in a financial institution, also works overtime, though she rarely spends more than 35 to 40 hours a week on actual work assignments. The rest of her time is given over to company information-gathering, checking out opportunities with competing firms, image building and similar activities.

This method discusses each subject individually, making a number of points about one subject and then covering more or less the same points about the other subject. Here is another informal outline of Chapman's subject-by-subject comparison:

Jamie Gullen uses this method to compare two cultures, p. 350.

1. Cleo
   workaholic
   earns a good salary
   respected for her loyalty and reliability
   enjoys extraordinary job security
2. Alice
   workaholic
   rarely spends all her time on work assignments
   rest of time spent on career building

Which method of organization should you use? Any method that presents your points of comparison and contrast clearly and simply to the reader is a good method of organization. However, you will probably find that the point-by-point method works best for beginning and ending an essay, while the subject-by-subject method serves you well for longer stretches in the main body of your essay.

One reason for using the subject-by-subject method to organize most of your essay is that the point-by-point method, when relentlessly applied, can make the reader a little seasick: stabilizers give time, scramblers steal time; stabilizers avoid stress, scramblers seek it; stabilizers hate change, scramblers use it; stabilizers want job security, scramblers switch jobs with every opportunity; stabilizers are humble, scramblers trust themselves to the brink of disaster. And so on.

With the point-by-point method, you make more or less the same number of points for both subjects. With the subject-by-subject method, on the other hand, you can make as many points as you like on each subject. You do not have to give equal weight to both. The subject-by-subject method is, thus, indispensable for treating a subject in depth, whereas the point-by-point method is an efficient way of presenting a balanced comparison. Because it touches on both subjects more or less equally, the point-by-point method can also help you convince readers that two subjects are, indeed, fundamentally alike (or dissimilar).

The point-by-point method, in other words, is particularly useful for establishing a basis of comparison at the beginning of an essay, for reminding readers along the way why two subjects are being compared, and for summing up. Thus, after treating Cleo and Alice separately throughout most of his article, Chapman comes back to the point-by-point method in the final paragraph:

> Alice is already ahead of Cleo in income and career status. Alice also receives a very genuine if different sort of esteem—the sort of wary respect the fox gets from the rabbit. And although Alice does not have the traditional job security that Cleo clings to, she has a different and far more valuable kind: she knows that whatever may happen in her current job, she can find another easily.

As used by David Sedaris (p. 369), this method is also great for purposes of humor.

Like the fox and the rabbit, says Chapman, scramblers usually get ahead in their careers, while stabilizers tend to lag a little behind. Chapman is not recommending Alice over Cleo as a career model, however. He's simply highlighting the differences between them because his main point in comparing the two women is to argue that most workers fall into the two camps they represent.

## STATING YOUR POINT

Your main point in drawing a comparison will determine whether you emphasize the similarities or the differences between your subjects. If you are comparing coaches you had in high school, for instance, you might focus on their differences in order to show the reader what constitutes a good (or bad) coach. If you're comparing two good blind dates to explain what makes for a successful one, however, you would focus on the similarities.

Whatever the main point of your comparison might be, make it clear right away in the form of an explicit THESIS statement, and tell the reader which you are going to emphasize—the similarities or the differences between your subjects. Then, in the body of your essay, draw a sufficient number of specific points of comparison to prove your main point.

## PROVIDING SUFFICIENT POINTS OF COMPARISON

How many points of comparison are enough to do the job? Sufficiency isn't strictly a matter of numbers. It depends, in part, on just how inclined your audience is to accept (or reject) the main point your comparison is intended to make.

If you are comparing subjects that your readers are not familiar with, you may have to give more reasons for drawing the parallel than you would if your readers

# TEMPLATES FOR DRAFTING

When you begin to draft a comparison, you need to identify your subjects, state the basis on which you're comparing them, and indicate whether you plan to emphasize their similarities or their differences—moves fundamental to any comparison. See how David Sedaris makes such moves near the beginning of his essay in this chapter:

> Certain events are parallel, but compared with Hugh's, my childhood was unspeakably dull. When I was seven years old, my family moved to North Carolina. When he was seven years old, Hugh's family moved to the Congo. We had a collie and a house cat. They had a monkey and two horses named Charlie Brown and Satan. —DAVID SEDARIS,
> "Remembering My Childhood on the Continent of Africa"

Sedaris identifies his two subjects ("Hugh's, my childhood"), states the basis on which he is comparing them ("certain events are parallel"), and indicates that he is planning to emphasize the differences ("my child was unspeakably dull"). Here is one more example from this chapter:

> They were two strong men, these oddly different generals, and they represented the strengths of two conflicting currents that, through them, had come into final collision.
> —BRUCE CATTON, "Grant and Lee: A Study in Contrasts"

The following templates can help you make some of these basic moves in your own writing. But don't take these as formulas where you just fill in the blanks. There are no shortcuts to good writing, but these templates can serve as starting points.

- ▸ X and Y can be compared on the grounds that both are _____.
- ▸ Like X, Y is also _____, _____, and _____.
- ▸ Although X and Y are both _____, the differences between them far outweigh the similarities. For example, X is _____, _____, and _____, while Y is _____, _____, and _____.
- ▸ Unlike X, Y is _____.
- ▸ Despite their obvious differences, X and Y are basically alike in that _____.
- ▸ At first glance, X and Y seem _____; however, a closer look reveals _____.
- ▸ In comparing X and Y, we can clearly see that _____.

already know a lot about your subjects. In comparing dying to going on a cruise, for example, Mary Roach compares the two on the humorous basis that they are both forms of leisure, and she draws five points of comparison between them: (1) much of the time is spent lying on your back; (2) the brain shuts down; (3) the flesh begins to soften; (4) nothing new happens; (5) not much is expected of you. Roach might have gone on to make additional points of comparison, such as (6) you don't go anywhere in particular and (7) there's not much room in the cabin. Five points, however, are probably enough to persuade the reader that the two subjects are worth comparing, and any more than that would be going overboard.

Patricia Park, cites just two points of comparison (p. 357) when contrasting her speech with that of native Koreans.
   To determine how many points of comparison you need to make, follow Roach's example: give a sufficient number to get your larger point across, but not so many that you run the comparison into the ground. In other words, whether your points of comparison are sufficient to support your thesis is not determined so much by how many you give as by how persuasive they seem to the reader. So consider your intended readers, and choose points of comparison you think they will find useful, interesting, or otherwise convincing.

## USING OTHER METHODS

Comparison deals with subjects that have something significant in common, so CLASSIFICATION and DEFINITION can be useful in writing that compares. The following paragraph, for example, uses both methods to establish a firm basis for comparing writing to other ways of using language:

> Traditionally, the four language processes of listening, talking, reading, and writing are paired in either of two ways. The more informative seems to be the division many linguists make between first-order and second-order processes with talking and listening characterized as first-order processes; reading and writing, as second-order.
>
>    —JANET EMIG, "Writing as a Mode of Learning"

The author of this passage from a formal academic paper in linguistics and language acquisition is comparing writing to other "language processes," particularly talking. Her main point in making the comparison is to argue that, among all the ways in which humans learn to use language, writing is unique.

   To support this point and develop her comparison, Emig uses a number of other methods besides comparison and contrast. First, she classifies writing as a "second-order" use of language, and the more natural process of talking as a "first-order" use. Then, elsewhere in her introduction, Emig defines these two basic kinds of language activities: first-order language skills, such as talking, are learned *without* formal instruction, whereas second-order language skills, such as writing, are learned only *with* formal instruction.

Not every linguist would agree that writing is unique among human language activities. But it would be difficult to contest Emig's point that learning to write well takes a special, perhaps unique, form of language instruction by knowledgeable teachers who are dedicated to a difficult task. How else, but through highly specialized training, could we learn to draw formal written comparisons and contrasts in such academic disciplines as history, geography, sociology—and linguistics?

## EDITING FOR COMMON ERRORS IN COMPARISONS

As with other kinds of writing, comparisons use distinctive patterns of language and punctuation—and thus invite some common mistakes. The following tips will help you check your writing for errors that often crop up in comparisons.

### Check that all comparisons are complete

Remember that all comparisons examine at least two items; check to see that both are mentioned. Readers need to understand what is being compared.

▶ When you take a bath, it is always better to relax <u>than to hurry</u>.

▶ Most hot tubs are not as hot <u>as typical Japanese baths</u>.

### Be sure that all comparisons are grammatically consistent

Check to see that the items you're comparing are parallel in grammatical form. The original version of this sentence unintentionally compares a bath with a place.

▶ U.S. baths tend to be much less ritualistic than <u>those</u> in Japan.

### Clarify comparisons that can be taken more than one way

▶ Fumio taught me more than Sam <u>did</u>.

Or

▶ Fumio taught me more than <u>he taught</u> Sam.

**Check for common usage errors**

*Good, well, better*

*Good* is an adjective; *well* is the adverb form. *Better* is both adjective and adverb.

▶ Hilary is a *good* musician; she plays the violin as *well* as Tom does and *better* than I do.

*Between, among*

Use *between* when you're comparing two items; use *among* when you're comparing three or more.

▶ *Between* Britain and France, France has the better health-care system.

▶ *Among* all the countries of Europe, France has the best health-care system.

Go to wwnorton.com/write/back-to-the-lake for quizzes on these common errors.

## Reading a Comparison with a Critical Eye

Once you've drafted an essay that uses comparison, ask someone else to look over your draft and tell you how effective he or she finds your basic comparison—and why. Then read it over yourself, too, with a critical eye. Here are some questions to keep in mind when checking a comparison.

**SUBJECTS OF COMPARISON.** What specific subjects does this essay compare? Are those subjects similar enough to justify the comparison? On what basis are they compared? Does the text emphasize the similarities or the differences between them? Or does it give equal weight to both?

**PURPOSE AND AUDIENCE.** Who are the intended readers, and what is the general purpose of the comparison—to inform? to evaluate? some other purpose? Does the comparison achieve this purpose? If not, what changes might help? What background information is included, and is it sufficient for the intended readers to fully understand the text? Are there any key terms that readers might need to have defined?

**THE POINT.** What is the main point of the essay? Has it been made clear to the reader? Is there an explicit thesis statement? If not, should there be?

**ORGANIZATION.** How is the comparison organized? Where does it use the point-by-point method of organization? The subject-by-subject method? When comparing subjects point by point, does the essay give more or less equal weight to each subject? When treating first one subject and then the other, does the essay follow more or less the same order in laying out the points of comparison for each subject?

**POINTS OF COMPARISON.** What are the specific points of comparison in the essay? Are they sufficient to convince the reader that the comparison is valid? Do they cover the same elements in both subjects? Have any important points been omitted—and if so, what are they?

**OTHER METHODS.** What other methods are used besides comparison and contrast? Does the essay CLASSIFY subjects? DEFINE them? Make an ARGUMENT about them? What other methods might support the comparison?

**COMMON ERRORS.** Have all of the direct comparisons in the essay been fully completed? Do they all answer the question, *Compared to what?* If they don't, fill in the missing term to complete the comparison.

## Student Example

Jamie Gullen is a native of New York City. While an undergraduate at Cornell University, she spent several months in Copenhagen as a participant in the Danish Institute for Study Abroad (DIS). At first, Gullen expected her host country to be "culturally similar" to the one she had left behind. Comparing the two cultures during her months abroad, however, Gullen soon realized how much she had to learn—about herself as well as her hosts. The following essay is the result of that comparative process. It won a prize in the DIS student essay contest in the spring of 2006 under its original title, "Self-Discovery and the Danish Way of Life."

## The Danish Way of Life

As my final weeks in Copenhagen began drawing to a close, 1
I was surprised to find myself waiting patiently at a red light even
though there were no cars or bikes in the near vicinity. As a New
York City native, this observation was cause for a significant pause
and some serious self-reflection. My thoughts settled on my first
month in Copenhagen when I was having a discussion with a
fellow DIS student. She was saying she had expected to feel some
significant change in who she was from being abroad, but so far
she felt like the same person she had always been. This got me
thinking about whether or not I had experienced a significant
change of self from being abroad in a culture totally different from
the one in which I grew up. At that time, I did not have a good
response to that question, but as I stood waiting for the green light
on a spring night in Copenhagen, I found I had stumbled upon some
important insights.

The answer I came to is that the very core of who I am and 2
the things that matter most to me have remained very much the
same. But rather than viewing this in a negative light as some kind
of stagnation or lack of personal growth, I realized it was exactly
the opposite. Study abroad doesn't change who you are; it helps
you discover who you are. By removing the immediate cultural
environment in which I was immersed from the day I was born,
I was able to discern which values and habits were really central
to who I am as a person and which were merely the results of the
influences of my family, friends, school, city, country, and cultural
surroundings.

Before I came to Denmark, I expected it to be fairly culturally 3
similar to the United States. It is a democratic Western country
where English is widely spoken and where American culture
pervades television and movies, and the Danish government is very
closely aligned with the American government. I was shocked to
find out that the Danish way of life couldn't be more different from
what I was expecting. The biggest difference I experienced originates

Gullen uses
NARRATION to
set up her
comparison

The essay will
emphasize
differences
between the
two cultures

Gullen's
PURPOSE in
making the
comparison is
self-evaluation

Shared charac-
teristics estab-
lish a basis for
the comparison

with the Danish word *hygge*. This word has no direct translation into English, and when I asked a Danish person to define it for me, it took her five minutes just to begin to touch upon what the word signifies. That is because it is much more than a word; it is a way of life. What she told me was that *hygge* is most closely translated as the English word *cozy* and that it is experienced socially. It is a closeness and intimacy between friends, enjoyment of food and wine; it is dinner that lasts for four hours because of good conversation; and it is décor with dim lighting and candles everywhere. While I have experienced *hygge* during my stay in Denmark both with Danes and my fellow DIS students, it took some time for me to process the true significance of the word.

DEFINING a key term captures the differences between the two countries

The <u>turning point</u>, in my understanding of both *hygge* and myself, was on my program's short study tour in western Denmark. As I discussed everything from Danish politics to local Danish soccer teams with some natives in the small town of Kolding, the conversation casually turned to <u>differences</u> between the Danish and the American way of life. I was noting that many Danish people I have met view their careers as a way to provide for themselves financially and to engage in fields that interest them intellectually, but their conception of self-worth is not tied up in the prestige of their jobs or the number of hours worked each week or the amount of the paycheck they bring home in comparison to their peers. It was through this observation that I realized the true importance of *hygge*; it recognizes the humanness of life and the individuality of the person. It is an appreciation of what really matters: friends, family, love, intimacy, and happiness.

4

Turning point allows for a comparison of her mindset before and after the trip

Subject-by-subject method gives; Danish characteristics first, then American ones

Growing up, I lived in a fast-paced city, attended a rigorous high school and college, was surrounded by career-driven highly motivated peers, and was encouraged by my parents to put academics first. Coming to Denmark and experiencing *hygge* and the Danish way of life and learning served as a jolt to the immediate cultural world that had shaped me. I was forced to consider life from another angle. What I found is that deep down I have always held the *hygge* values to be of importance, and I have always wanted to be

5

engaged in helping other people find a happy and peaceful way of life. It is just easier now to see how my external cultural evironment has impacted and shaped these values and my sense of DIS, Danish, and my international self.

When I arrive home in New York City, it will no doubt take    6
very little time for me to join in with the throngs of jaywalkers marching defiantly across Madison Avenue, but what I have learned from being abroad in Denmark about who I am and what matters most to me will be knowledge that stays with me forever.

Conclusion returns to opening narrative

## Analyzing a Student Comparison

In "The Danish Way of Life," Jamie Gullen draws upon rhetorical strategies and techniques that good writers use all the time when they make a comparison. The following questions, in addition to focusing on particular aspects of Gullen's text, will help you to identify those common strategies and techniques so you can adapt them to your own writing. These questions will also help to prepare you for the analytical questions—on content, structure, and language—that you'll find after all the other selections in this chapter, along with suggestions for writing on related topics.

### FOR CLOSE READING

1. What was the biggest difference between Danish and American culture that Jamie Gullen experienced while studying abroad in Denmark?

2. According to Gullen, how do the Danes approach their jobs and careers as compared with their American counterparts?

3. Gullen says that "study abroad doesn't change who you are" (2). What does it do, in her view? How?

4. What important lesson did Gullen learn from her period of study abroad?

### Strategies and Structures

1. How does Gullen use the NARRATIVE device of waiting for a traffic light to help structure her entire essay?

2. In her introduction, Gullen says she "stumbled upon some important insights" as an American studying in Denmark (1). Gullen does not specify what those insights are, however, until after she compares the two countries in the main body of her essay. Should she have done so earlier? Why or why not?

3. How did the act of making comparisons lead Gullen to a "turning point" in her understanding of both her host country and herself (4)? Does her comparison emphasize the similarities between the two cultures, or their differences, or both? Explain.

4. Gullen sums up what she learned from her Danish experience in paragraph 5. Why doesn't she end there? What does paragraph 6 add to her comparison?

5. *Other Methods.* The "biggest difference" between Denmark and America that she encountered during her study abroad, says Gullen, can be summed up in the Danish word *hygge* (3). How does Gullen use an extended DEFINITION of this term to support her comparison of the two countries?

## Thinking about Language

1. The Danes, says Gullen, usually translate *hygge* as the English word *cozy* (3). Judging from Gullen's definition of the term, how would you translate it?

2. What are the CONNOTATIONS of "stumbled" and "natives" (1, 4)?

3. A "turning point" implies an irreversible change (4). What, if anything, is irreversible about Gullen's experience as a student in Denmark?

## FOR WRITING

1. Write a paragraph contrasting what you see as a key difference between the culture of mainstream America with that of some other country or group.

2. Think of another country you would like to visit (or have already visited). Write an essay that compares that culture and your own. What do you expect (or what did you find) to be the main similarities and differences between them?

3. Write a POSITION PAPER on the purpose of traveling to new places with a culture different from your own. Be sure to consider Gullen's suggestion that travel brings about "a significant change of self" (1).

4. Do some research on the place, and write an imaginary travel journal about your travels in Denmark or some other country you'd like to visit ("My first night in Copenhagen, I . . .").

You'll find quizzes on the readings at wwnorton.com/write/back-to-the-lake.

# A Souvenir Coffee Mug

In the inscription on this coffee mug, purchased in a bookstore on the Kenyon campus in Gambier, Ohio, the novelist E. L Doctorow compares two institutions of higher learning. One is his alma mater, a private college known for its liberal arts program, particularly the study of poetry. The other is a large state institution known for its . . . football team. When you make comparisons like this, choose two subjects (Kenyon, Ohio State) from the same general category (schools in Ohio) that are nevertheless different enough in some details (poetry, football) to make the comparison worthwhile. The details you choose will depend on your purpose for drawing the comparison. The Kenyon coffee mug, for instance, is intended to promote the liberal arts: "We grapple with metaphors," said one Kenyon administrator; "they clinch in the mud." Down the road at Ohio State, university officials would call this poetic license. To promote the range of academic programs offered by a large public university, their competing coffee mugs might read: "The way they do poetry at Kenyon, we do football at Ohio State—and medieval literature, law, medicine, business, and engineering."

[ **FOR WRITING** ]··················································································

Write or find a slogan, motto, or quotation comparing and
contrasting two schools, towns, or celebrities that you would
like to see inscribed on a coffee mug. Feel free to include an
appropriate visual with the words. If you quote someone, don't
forget the quotation marks and the attribution.

"Poetry was
what we did at
Kenyon,
the way at
Ohio State
they played football."

—E.L. Doctorow

# SUGGESTIONS FOR WRITING

1. Both "The Danish Way of Life" (p. 350) and "Where Are You From?" (p. 357) compare what the authors expected to find in foreign lands with the realities they encounter there—and back home. Read both essays carefully and write a RHETORICAL ANALYSIS in which, among other points, you compare and contrast how the two writers present cultural differences.

2. In addition to "Superhero Smackdown," p. 361, Douglas Wolk is also the author of *Reading Comics: How Graphic Novels Work and What They Mean* (2007). On *Amazon* and elsewhere, read several reviews of this award-winning study and write an ABSTRACT (or summary) of what Wolk has to say. Cite your sources, of course. (Or, alternatively, read the book itself and do your own critical EVALUATION of it.)

3. Write a research REPORT on the history and career of Wonder Woman. Include a detailed comparison of her powers (and weaknesses) with those of her male counterparts. In the course of your report, respond to Douglas Wolk's assertion (p. 363, ¶9) that the owners of the Wonder Woman franchise have never been able to successfully get her "off the ground as either a movie or a TV show."

4. "Remembering My Childhood on the Continent of Africa" (p. 369) is a perennial favorite among fans of the humor writer David Sedaris. The author, of course, did not grow up in Africa but in North Carolina. As background for understanding this essay and Sedaris's other work, do some research on his life and career and write a brief PROFILE of the man and his humor. Be sure to compare Sedaris's work with that of other humor writers, such as Mindy Kaling ("Types of Women in Romantic Comedies Who Are Not Real," p. 427).

5. In "Grant and Lee: A Study in Contrasts" (p. 377), the historian Bruce Catton associates General Ulysses S. Grant, commander of the Northern armies during the American Civil War, with the future. "Grant was the modern man emerging," he writes; "beyond him, ready to come on the stage, was the great age of steel and machinery, of crowded cities and a restless burgeoning vitality." The period to which Catton refers is 1865–1915. Do some research on this time in American history and write a REPORT explaining why it is often called "the age of energy." Be sure to compare it briefly with other periods in American history, either before or after.

# Where Are You From?

Patricia Park is a native of New York City and the daughter of Korean immigrants. Park attended the Bronx High School of Science but majored in English at Swarthmore College. After earning an M.F.A. at Boston University, she taught English and writing there, at Queens College of the City University of New York, and at Ewha Women's University in Seoul, South Korea. Her first novel, *Re Jane*, which Park describes as "a Korean-American re-telling of *Jane Eyre* by Charlotte Brontë," is scheduled for publication in 2015. Park's essays—on topics ranging from the challenges of being single to "The Reason My Korean Family Is Actually Jewish on Paper"—have appeared in the *New York Times*, the *Guardian*, and *Slice Magazine*.

"Where Are You From?," which appeared in the *Guardian* in April 2013, asks her "least favorite question," says Park, because she and other "hyphenated Americans" are always facing such "subtle rhetorical reminders of our out-group status." The reminders get even less subtle, however, when she visits modern Korea and is forced to compare it with the "motherland" of family myth.

A S A NON-WHITE AMERICAN, I'm often asked where I'm from and whether I've been "back home." And people don't mean New York City, where I was born and raised. They look at me, and my ethnic face, and they mean South Korea.

That was how I used to answer, too. Even though I had never lived in South Korea until I was almost 30. Even though my parents were born in what is now North Korea, fled to the South as wartime refugees, then took the slow boat to Argentina, before becoming naturalized Americans. Despite the fact that I recited the pledge of allegiance at school each morning, despite my blue U.S. passport, I never self-identified as American while growing up; it had never occurred to me that I was.

What I describe is hardly a new phenomenon: scores of fellow ethnic "others" have long felt similarly un-American growing up in the United States, facing subtle rhetorical reminders of our out-group status. It's well-trodden territory, treated in

MLA CITATION: Park, Patricia. "Where Are You From?" 2013. *Back to the Lake*. Ed. Thomas Cooley. 3rd ed. New York: Norton, 2015. 357–59. Print.

*My Big Fat Greek Wedding, The Joy Luck Club,* and the works of Chang-Rae Lee. As "hyphenated Americans," our identities are qualified—our Americanness is made subordinate, and secondary, to all the ethnic matter that precedes it. We are constantly told to look to that other home, our "real" home, as the place where we truly belong.

But what we have failed to address is the reverse phenomenon: what exactly 4 awaits us when we "return" to the quote-unquote motherland. As a society we carry romantic notions of stepping off the plane—or boat—and being met with open arms, perpetuated by the likes of Olive Garden commercials ("When you're here, you're family!") and even *Jersey Shore,* where Snooki et al. set off for Italy to search for their roots under every pizza box and carafe of Chianti. Conan O'Brien famously parodied this romanticized attachment to the "old country" when he traveled to Ireland and pressed his giant orange head into the bosom of each and every startled passerby, claiming kinship.

It is wrong to assume that hyphenated-Americans can simply "return" to the 5 "motherland" and automatically fit in. I, too, was once guilty of the same misguided notion, when I traveled to Seoul as a Fulbright scholar to reconnect with my ethnic identity. My parents left the Korean peninsula shortly after electricity came into vogue; as such, my cultural knowledge was at least forty years out of date. Weaned on stories of my parents' war-torn childhood, I pictured straw-thatched houses dotting the fields of rice paddies, and villagers gathering in the town square to kick around the old pigskin (a pig's bladder blown up like a soccer ball). I clung fiercely to this quaint, rustic (read: naïve) image of the old country.

When I touched down in Korea, I was shocked to find the place that I thought I 6 knew so intimately—the place I was supposed to hail from—was so foreign. Gray skyscrapers towered over the paved streets. Neon storefronts blinked advertisements for cell phones and fried chicken. My "kinsmen"—bedecked in suits and heels—jostled past me without a word, let alone greeting.

Whenever I communicated in our "native" tongue, the South Koreans laughed 7 at my antiquated vocabulary (I peddled words like apothecary, outhouse) and my distinctly American cadence (I spoke in iambic pentameter). They said I was a "foreigner"; not one of "our country's people," the term they used to refer to themselves. Never did they call me Korean. Once again I felt like the other—except this time, I was otherized by the ethnic group I was told my whole life I was a part of.

There is a real danger in spending your whole life thinking you belong to some 8 other place that's anywhere but here. My time abroad might have been less culturally wrought if I had never tried to assume an automatic entitlement to Korea. What my experience in South Korea affirmed for me was that you can't go (back) home again—that home was never yours to lay claim to in the first place. I have since returned home, to New York City, with a new-found sense of orientation, and belonging.

Read Joan Didion's "On Going Home" (p. 763) for a different take on this theme.

But it's an uphill battle. I don't always feel American, especially on days when people insist on asking, "No, where are you from from?" or compliment my accent-free English. But we must challenge our views on hyphenated-Americans and their place of belonging. You might even say it's time we collectively weaned ourselves off the proverbial teat of the motherland.

See p. 344 for tips on stating your main point when drawing a comparison.

Change is slow, and hard. But if we take even the smallest, simplest steps—like 10 revising the rhetoric we use to talk about where we come from—the sooner Americans like myself might stop looking for acceptance over there, and start to feel we, too, have a claim to our real homeland here in the United States. ◆

## FOR CLOSE READING

1. Patricia Park says she "never self-identified as American while growing up" in New York City (2). Should she have? Why or why not?

2. Park claims that many "ethnic" Americans feel "un-American" even though they were born and raised in the United States (3). Is this a valid observation? Explain.

3. What made Park change her mind about where home really is for her? Why couldn't she just "go (back) home again" to Korea (8)?

4. "There is a real danger in spending your whole life thinking you belong to some other place that's anywhere but here" (8), says Park. What "danger" is Park referring to? How does she attempt to avoid it in her own life?

## Strategies and Structures

1. Before describing her "return" to Korea, Park explains how she used to feel as a "hyphenated American" (3, 5). What specific characteristics and attitudes does she cite?

2. In paragraphs 5-7, Park contrasts what she expects to find in the Korean "motherland" with what she actually finds when she visits there for the first time. What are some of the more striking differences, and how does she use her own "naïve" attitudes toward "the old country" to heighten the contrast (5)?

3. Once Park returns from her "time abroad," how do her views of America and being an American compare with the views she held before she left (8)? Point to specific details in the text that capture the change.

4. *Other Methods.* In addition to comparing her different views of who she is and where she belongs, Park is also making a point about the need to identify with the place one actually comes from. How and how well does the comparison support her **ARGUMENT**?

5. To illustrate her point about how the use of language, or "rhetoric," can shape cultural identity, Park cites the recurring question, "Where are you from?" (10). Is this a good **EXAMPLE**? Why or why not?

### Thinking about Language

1. What does Park mean exactly by "hyphenated Americans" (3, 5)? How does her use of this term fit in with what she says about the power of language?

2. Park says she was "weaned" on stories of war-time Korea (5). Where and how does this METAPHOR come up again in her essay?

3. Why did the modern Koreans she talked to in the old country find Park's use of "words like apothecary, outhouse" to be somewhat "foreign" (6)?

4. Why does Park put "kinsmen" in quotation marks (6)?

5. Explain the meaning and derivation of "otherized" (7).

## FOR WRITING

1. In a paragraph or two, explain how you would answer the question "Where are you from?"

2. Write an essay of about 500 words that compares and contrasts your views of home and your native country with those of your parents or other relatives.

3. In a short POSITION PAPER, attack or defend (rhetorically, that is) the proposition that "there is a real danger in spending your whole life thinking you belong to some other place" (8). Be sure to identify and compare different views of "belonging."

4. Keep a "language journal" in which you record examples of how people define you by the way you speak or write. Try to capture their exact words. Also, record instances of your defining others by *their* language use.

5. In collaboration with several of your classmates, compare experiences, do some research, and write a REPORT on language and cultural identity. You can focus on the experience of "hyphenated Americans" as Park does, or on some other aspect of the topic, such as the language of a particular group or region. Be sure to address the question of how language contributes to a sense of belonging (or of not belonging).

You'll find quizzes on the readings at
wwnorton.com/write/back-to-the-lake.

DOUGLAS WOLK

# Superhero Smackdown

Douglas Wolk lives in Portland, Oregon, where he produces records under the label *Dark Beloved Cloud*. A graduate of Harvard and the Columbia School of Journalism—and the former host of a radio program in Jersey City, New Jersey—Wolk writes about comics, popular music, technology, social networks, and copyright issues for publications ranging from *Spin* and *Rolling Stone* to the *New York Times* and the *Huffington Post*. He is also the author of *Live at the Apollo* (2004), a book about music albums, and *Reading Comics: How Graphic Novels Work and What They Mean* (2007), which won an Eisner Award, the comics industry's equivalent of an Oscar.

In "Superhero Smackdown," which appeared in *Slate* in August 2013, Wolk compares Iron Man and Batman—and the entertainment giants who stand behind them. "Who would win in a fight," he asks, "Marvel or DC?"

A T A TENDER AGE, most fans of superhero comics start honing their arguments in an ancient debate: "Which is better—Marvel or DC?" They may not yet realize that the fight has long been waged not just on the page, but also in boardrooms and on the NYSE.[1] To understand the battle between the two major American mainstream comic book companies, we can go straight to the source material, because each is very much like one of its biggest franchise players. Marvel, it's fair to say, is Iron Man; DC is Batman.

As with those two crime fighters, DC and Marvel are both colorful public fronts with staggering amounts of corporate cash and power behind them: DC Entertainment is owned by Time Warner, and Marvel Entertainment is part of the Walt Disney Company. That's where the similarities end. DC, like Batman, is fantastically regimented, a little bit irrational, and hesitant to reach out beyond its home turf; like Bruce Wayne, its relationships with its extended family are fraught with resentment of its imperious ways. Marvel, like Iron Man, adapts to circumstances, makes endless duplicates of its biggest successes, and always seems to be a bit ahead of the curve; like Tony Stark, it can be slovenly about the details when they

1

2

---

1. *NYSE*: New York Stock Exchange.

MLA CITATION: Wolk, Douglas. "Superhero Smackdown." 2013. *Back to the Lake*. Ed. Thomas Cooley. 3rd ed. New York: Norton, 2015. 361–66. Print.

count. (Marvel's book publishing program, for instance, has a longstanding reputation as a total mess, with popular titles falling out of print for years on end.)

Most superheroes' goals are not to destroy their rivals, but to overtake and con-   3
tain them. (Batman puts them in Arkham Asylum; Iron Man in Negative Zone
Prison Alpha.) That's how Marvel and DC generally interact with each other, and
the rest of the comics business, at this point. The Big Two, which both date back to
the 1930s, have been uncomfortably bonded to one another for decades. They collectively control about 70 percent of the comics retail market; if either of them
were to stop publishing, it would likely destroy the fragile ecosystem of American
comics stores. In the 1960s, when DC's parent company controlled Marvel's distribution and limited the number of titles they could publish, Stan Lee's editorials in
Marvel's comics sniped gently at the "Distinguished Competition." Once Marvel
started publishing a *Captain Marvel* series in 1968, DC acquired the rights to the
'40s-era Captain Marvel character, who appeared on the TV show *Shazam!* (After
several decades of not being able to print the name of their own Captain Marvel on
comic book covers for trademark reasons, DC started referring to him simply as
Shazam, more or less as a gesture of defeat.)

Still, they used to be more cooperative rivals. After a string of parodic storylines   4
in the '60s and '70s (in which Marvel's Avengers fought the Squadron Sinister—a
thinly disguised version of DC's Justice League—and the Justice League returned
the favor by battling the Champions of Angor, who were the Avengers in all but
name), the two publishers reached a sort of détente. Between 1976 and 2003, there
were a string of co-published DC/Marvel crossover comics, in which Superman
would meet Spider-Man, or the X-Men would fight the New Teen Titans; Iron Man
and Batman even encountered one another in *JLA/Avengers*. These days, each company makes a great show of pretending the other doesn't exist, aside from the occasional sideswipe. Once DC got into the habit of referring to its fictional universe as
the DCU, for instance, Marvel named its all-you-can-read digital initiative Digital
Comics Unlimited.

As you'd expect from colorful characters, both publishers have weak-   5
nesses that can be turned against them. Marvel publishes more iterations
of its biggest titles than Iron Man has built models of his armor, which
can make it nearly impossible for casual fans to figure out what to read.
So, wait, if I want to check out the series of books where Spider-Man is
an African-American/Latino kid named Miles Morales, is that *Amazing
Spider-Man, Superior Spider-Man, Essential Spider-Man, Ultimate Spider-Man, Ultimate Comics Spider-Man, Marvel Universe Ultimate Spider-Man* or *Spider-Man 2099*?

Wolk switches
here to the
subject-by-
subject method
of comparison,
p. 342.

(The answer, by the way, is *Ultimate Comics Spider-Man*, starting with Volume 1.   6
Naturally, Marvel has recently published two *different* books called *Ultimate Comics
Spider-Man*, Volume 1. Miles is in one of them and not the other.)

DC, likewise, has a Batman-ish tendency to alienate its allies and collaborators. 7
Artists and writers have complained of constant editorial second-guessing over the
past few years, as sales of most of its superhero titles have spiraled downward. The
company burned some bridges with *Before Watchmen*—a set of prequels to Alan
Moore and Dave Gibbons' perennially best-selling graphic novel *Watchmen*, produced over Moore's vociferous objections. And the adventurous, creator-driven DC
imprint Vertigo was gutted with the departure of its executive editor Karen Berger
early this year.

So enough wind-up—who wins the Iron Man–Batman showdown? It turns out 8
that there's an *Iron Man 3*–like twist: The rivalry that counts is between the real-
world equivalents of Stark Industries and Wayne Enterprises. Within the past few
years, Marvel and DC have changed their names, from "comics" to "entertainment" companies, to reflect where the real money is: in film, TV, and games.
Marvel will sell, perhaps, a few million dollars' worth of *Iron Man* comic books this
year, while the worldwide gross of *Iron Man 3* so far is $1.2 billion and counting. If
every monthly issue of *Batman* sold as well as this June's (they usually don't), the
series would gross about $6.8 million this year, or roughly 1/150 of what *The Dark
Knight Rises* has made so far. So both companies now effectively treat their comics
divisions as research-and-development arms, since, on the economic scale of film
studios, it's astonishingly cheap to commission material from even top-tier comics
writers and artists, print it up, and see how the fans respond.

DC hasn't been doing badly in theaters, especially if you can wipe *Jonah Hex* and 9
*Green Lantern* out of your mind. *The Dark Knight* and *The Dark Knight Rises* were
huge hits, and this summer's *Man of Steel* performed decently, too. But there's not
much on the other side of "To Be Continued" at the moment. DC announced a
*Superman/Batman* movie at Comic-Con last month, but the long-rumored *Justice
League* film is a distant dream, especially since they haven't been able to get
*Wonder Woman* off the ground as either a movie or a TV show.

Meanwhile, there are seven forthcoming movies about Marvel characters that 10
are far enough into production to have announced release dates. The snag is that
Marvel Entertainment doesn't actually control the movie rights to all of their characters, thanks to deals cut long ago. (The *Arrested Development*[2] gag about a *Fantastic Four* movie made in six days for legal reasons isn't far off from what really
happened in 1992.) Sony's got Spider-Man, and plans to release three more *Amazing
Spider-Man* movies between now and 2018; Fox has the film rights to the X-Men
(including Wolverine), Daredevil, and the Fantastic Four.

---

2. *Arrested Development:* A sitcom that aired on Fox from 2003 to 2006; the gag referenced here is from
a delayed fourth season that was released by Netflix in 2013.

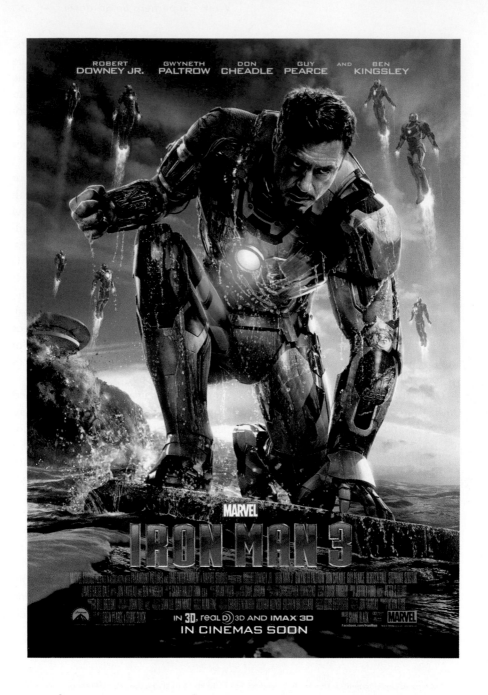

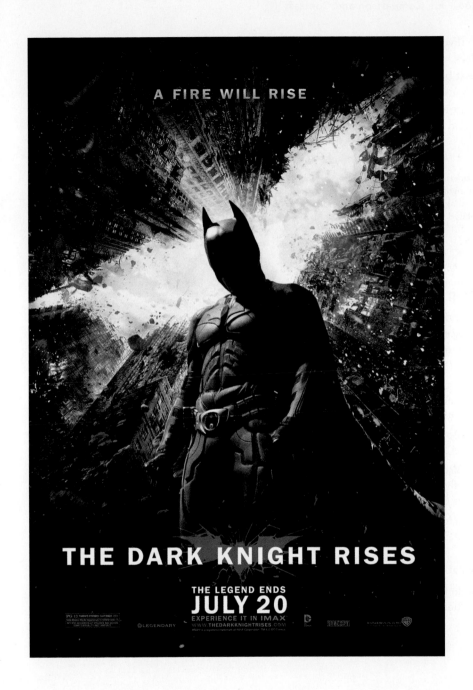

Even so, what Marvel Studios has been doing with the characters the company    11
*does* control—fitting their stories together into the "Marvel Cinematic Universe"
that began with the first Iron Man movie in 2008, reached fruition with last year's
*Avengers* movie, and continues with the upcoming *S.H.I.E.L.D.* TV show[3]—is a brilliant idea (and, naturally, borrowed from comics). Right now, DC's Batarangs don't
stand a chance against Marvel's repulsor rays.  ◆

3. *Upcoming . . . show: Marvel's Agents of S.H.I.E.L.D.* aired on ABC in 2013 and was renewed for 2014.

## FOR CLOSE READING

1.  What does Douglas Wolk mean when he says, "Right now, DC's Batarangs don't
    stand a chance against Marvel's repulsor rays" (10)? Why does he think Marvel is
    currently winning the "smackdown" between the two rival companies? Is he right?
    Why or why not?

2.  According to Wolk, why are Marvel and DC so "uncomfortably bonded to one
    another" by comparison with the rest of the players in the action-heroes
    industry (3)?

3.  Both companies, says Wolk, have "weaknesses that can be turned against them"
    (5). What are some of those weaknesses on either side of the corporate battle?

4.  Why does Wolk say that "both companies now effectively treat their comics
    divisions as research-and-development arms" (7)? Based on the evidence he cites,
    is this an accurate assessment?

5.  Wolk begins his essay with a searching question: "Which is better—Marvel or DC"
    (1)? Which position would you defend in this "ancient debate" (1). Why?

## Strategies and Structures

1.  In his comparison of Marvel and DC, does Wolk cite mostly differences or similari-
    ties? Explain by pointing to specific places in the text.

2. Corporations have a way of being faceless. How does Wolk address this problem in his comparison and contrast of Marvel and DC? Is it a good solution? Why or why not?

3. In paragraph 2, Wolk uses the subject-by-subject method to compare DC and Marvel. What specific traits and characteristics does he identify on the two sides. Is the comparison well balanced? Explain.

4. Wolk is using comparison and contrast as a handy way of developing a critical EVALUATION. What is the subject of that analysis, and how does Wolk use this method to make his point?

5. *Other Methods.* Wolk choses Ironman and Batman as representative EXAMPLES of the two companies they belong to. Are they good examples? Why or why not?

## Thinking about Language

1. *Smackdown* is a term from entertainment wrestling. Why does Wolk use it here? How appropriate is the term to his subject?

2. Explain the METAPHORICAL implications of Wolk's use of the phrase *fragile ecosystem* (3).

3. "Squadron Sinister" reverses the usual order of modifier-noun in English. What effect do you think Marvel was shooting for when the company did this in its battle with DC (4)?

4. Wolk is not comparing baseball players, so what "wind-up" is he referring to (8)?

5. Why does the Marvel Entertainment division of the Walt Disney Company refer to its film business as "Marvel Cinematic Universe" rather than, say, "Marvel Movies" or "Marvel Cinema" (2)?

## FOR WRITING

1. Make a list of the traits you would cite in comparing and contrasting your two favorite superheroes.

2. For all their strengths, superheroes have their characteristic weaknesses as well. Write an essay comparing two or more superheroes, but pay as much attention to their shortcomings as their powers—and how those imperfections might or might not make them appeal more directly to readers or viewers.

3. In a fight, Wolk claims, Marvel Entertainment would thrash its DC rival. Is he right? Do some additional research on the economic and creative positions of

the two companies, and write your own "smackdown" comparison of these entertainment giants. Be sure to say what the loser needs to do to improve its game.

4. Write a **LITERACY NARRATIVE** based on your (and your friends') recollections of reading comic books as a kid. Refer to particular characters and episodes, and explain not only what they taught you about reading and storytelling but about life and fantasy.

You'll find quizzes on the readings at wwnorton.com/write/back-to-the-lake.

DAVID SEDARIS

# Remembering My Childhood
# on the Continent of Africa

David Sedaris (b. 1956) made a name for himself as an elf in "Santaland," the story about working with the Santas at Macy's that he told on National Public Radio's *Morning Edition* in 1992. His hilarious autobiographical tales have been a public radio staple ever since, and his numerous book-length collections, from *Barrel Fever (1994)* to *Squirrel Seeks Chipmunk* (2010), have all been best sellers. In 2001 Sedaris won the Thurber Prize for American Humor and was named "Humorist of the Year" by *Time* magazine. His latest collection is *Let's Explore Diabetes with Owls* (2013).

Lopsided comparisons have always been a rich source of comedy. In "Remembering My Childhood on the Continent of Africa," taken from his collection *Me Talk Pretty One Day* (2000), Sedaris juxtaposes his own "unspeakably dull" childhood in Raleigh, North Carolina, with the African childhood of his partner, Hugh Hamrick, a diplomat's son.

WHEN HUGH WAS IN THE FIFTH GRADE, his class took a field trip to an Ethio- 1 pian slaughterhouse. He was living in Addis Ababa at the time, and the slaughterhouse was chosen because, he says, "it was convenient."

This was a school system in which the matter of proximity outweighed such 2 petty concerns as what may or may not be appropriate for a busload of eleven-year-olds. "What?" I asked. "Were there no autopsies scheduled at the local morgue? Was the federal prison just a bit too far out of the way?"

Hugh defends his former school, saying, "Well, isn't that the whole point of a 3 field trip? To see something new?"

"Technically yes, but . . ." 4

"All right then," he says. "So we saw some new things." 5

One of his field trips was literally a trip to a field where the class watched a 6 wrinkled man fill his mouth with rotten goat meat and feed it to a pack of waiting hyenas. On another occasion they were taken to examine the bloodied bedroom curtains hanging in the palace of the former dictator. There were tamer trips, to textile factories and sugar refineries, but my favorite is always the slaughterhouse.

MLA CITATION: Sedaris, David. "Remembering My Childhood on the Continent of Africa." 2000. *Back to the Lake*. Ed. Thomas Cooley. 3rd ed. New York: Norton, 2015. 369-75. Print.

A typical field trip for Hugh: a small, rural slaughterhouse.

To compare two subjects in depth like this, use the subject-by-subject method (p. 342). It wasn't a big company, just a small rural enterprise run by a couple of brothers operating out of a low-ceilinged concrete building. Following a brief lecture on the importance of proper sanitation, a small white piglet was herded into the room, its dainty hooves clicking against the concrete floor. The class gathered in a circle to get a better look at the animal, who seemed delighted with the attention he was getting. He turned from face to face and was looking up at Hugh when one of the brothers drew a pistol from his back pocket, held it against the animal's temple, and shot the piglet, execution-style. Blood spattered, frightened children wept, and the man with the gun offered the teacher and bus driver some meat from a freshly slaughtered goat.

When I'm told such stories, it's all I can do to hold back my feelings of jealousy. 7 An Ethiopian slaughterhouse. Some people have all the luck. When I was in elementary school, the best we ever got was a trip to Old Salem or Colonial Williamsburg, one of those preserved brick villages where time supposedly stands still and someone earns his living as a town crier. There was always a blacksmith, a group of wandering patriots, and a collection of bonneted women hawking corn bread or gingersnaps made "the ol'-fashioned way." Every now and then you might come across a doer of bad deeds serving time in the stocks, but that was generally as exciting as it got.

A typical field trip for David: Colonial Williamsburg.

Certain events are parallel, but compared with Hugh's, my childhood was 8 unspeakably dull. When I was seven years old, my family moved to North Carolina. When he was seven years old, Hugh's family moved to the Congo. We had a collie and a house cat. They had a monkey and two horses named Charlie Brown and Satan. I threw stones at stop signs. Hugh threw stones at crocodiles. The verbs are the same, but he definitely wins the prize when it comes to nouns and objects. An eventful day for my mother might have involved a trip to the dry cleaner or a conversation with the potato-chip deliveryman. Asked one ordinary Congo afternoon what she'd done with her day, Hugh's mother answered that she and a fellow member of the Ladies' Club had visited a leper colony on the outskirts of Kinshasa. No reason was given for the expedition, though chances are she was staking it out for a future field trip.

Due to his upbringing, Hugh sits through inane movies never realizing that 9 they're often based on inane television shows. There were no poker-faced sitcom martians in his part of Africa, no oil-rich hillbillies or aproned brides trying to wean themselves from the practice of witchcraft.[1] From time to time a movie would arrive packed in a dented canister, the film scratched and faded from its slow trip

---

1. *Martians . . . practice of witchcraft*: References to *My Favorite Martian, The Beverly Hillbillies,* and *Bewitched,* popular U.S. TV shows in the 1960s.

around the world. The theater consisted of a few dozen folding chairs arranged before a bedsheet or the blank wall of a vacant hangar out near the airstrip. Occasionally a man would sell warm soft drinks out of a cardboard box, but that was it in terms of concessions.

When I was young, I went to the theater at the nearby shopping center and 10 watched a movie about a talking Volkswagen. I believe the little car had a taste for mischief but I can't be certain, as both the movie and the afternoon proved unremarkable and have faded from my memory. Hugh saw the same movie a few years after it was released. His family had left the Congo by this time and were living in Ethiopia. Like me, Hugh saw the movie by himself on a weekend afternoon. Unlike me, he left the theater two hours later, to find a dead man hanging from a telephone pole at the far end of the unpaved parking lot. None of the people who'd seen the movie seemed to care about the dead man. They stared at him for a moment or two and then headed home, saying they'd never seen anything as crazy as that talking Volkswagen. His father was late picking him up, so Hugh just stood there for an hour, watching the dead man dangle and turn in the breeze. The death was not reported in the newspaper, and when Hugh related the story to his friends, they said, "You saw the movie about the talking car?"

I could have done without the flies and the primitive theaters, but I wouldn't 11 have minded growing up with a houseful of servants. In North Carolina it wasn't unusual to have a once-a-week maid, but Hugh's family had houseboys, a word that never fails to charge my imagination. They had cooks and drivers, and guards who occupied a gatehouse, armed with machetes. Seeing as I had regularly petitioned my parents for an electric fence, the business with the guards strikes me as the last word in quiet sophistication. Having protection suggests that you are important. Having that protection paid for by the government is even better, as it suggests your safety is of interest to someone other than yourself.

Hugh's father was a career officer with the U.S. State Department, and every 12 morning a black sedan carried him off to the embassy. I'm told it's not as glamorous as it sounds, but in terms of fun for the entire family, I'm fairly confident that it beats the sack race at the annual IBM picnic. By the age of three, Hugh was already carrying a diplomatic passport. The rules that applied to others did not apply to him. No tickets, no arrests, no luggage search: he was officially licensed to act like a brat. Being an American, it was expected of him, and who was he to deny the world an occasional tantrum?

They weren't rich, but what Hugh's family lacked financially they more than 13 made up for with the sort of exoticism that works wonders at cocktail parties, leading always to the remark "That sounds fascinating." It's a compliment one rarely receives when describing an adolescence spent drinking Icees at the North Hills Mall. No fifteen-foot python ever wandered onto my school's basketball court. I begged, I prayed nightly, but it just never happened. Neither did I get to witness a military coup in which forces sympathetic to the colonel arrived late at night to assassinate my next-door neighbor. Hugh had been at the Addis Ababa teen club when the electricity was cut off and soldiers arrived to evacuate the building. He and his friends had to hide in the back of a jeep and cover themselves with blankets during the ride home. It's something that sticks in his mind for one reason or another.

Among my personal highlights is the memory of having my picture taken with Uncle Paul, the legally blind host of a Raleigh children's television show. Among Hugh's is the memory of having his picture taken with Buzz Aldrin on the last leg of the astronaut's world tour. The man who had walked on the moon placed his hand on Hugh's shoulder and offered to sign his autograph book. The man who led Wake County schoolchildren in afternoon song turned at the sound of my voice and asked, "So what's your name, princess?"   14

When I was fourteen years old, I was sent to spend ten days with my maternal grandmother in western New York State. She was a small and private woman named Billie, and though she never came right out and asked, I had the distinct impression she had no idea who I was. It was the way she looked at me, squinting through her glasses while chewing on her lower lip. That, coupled with the fact that she never once called me by name. "Oh," she'd say, "are you still here?" She was just beginning her long struggle with Alzheimer's disease, and each time I entered the room, I felt the need to reintroduce myself and set her at ease. "Hi, it's me. Sharon's boy, David. I was just in the kitchen admiring your collection of ceramic toads." Aside from a few trips to summer camp, this was the longest I'd ever been away from home, and I like to think I was toughened by the experience.   15

About the same time I was frightening my grandmother, Hugh and his family were packing their belongings for a move to Somalia. There were no English-speaking schools in Mogadishu, so, after a few months spent lying around the family compound with his pet monkey, Hugh was sent back to Ethiopia to live with a beer enthusiast his father had met at a cocktail party. Mr. Hoyt installed security systems in foreign embassies. He and his family gave Hugh a room. They invited him to join them at the table, but that was as far as they extended themselves. No one ever asked him when his birthday was, so when the day came, he kept it to himself. There was no telephone service between Ethiopia and Somalia, and letters to his parents were sent to Washington and then forwarded on to Mogadishu, meaning that his news was more than a month old by the time they got it. I suppose it wasn't much different than living as a foreign-exchange student. Young people do it all the   16 time, but to me it sounds awful. The Hoyts had two sons about Hugh's age who were always saying things like "Hey that's *our* sofa you're sitting on" and "Hands off that ornamental stein. It doesn't belong to you."

He'd been living with these people for a year when he overheard Mr. Hoyt tell a    17
friend that he and his family would soon be moving to Munich, Germany, the beer capital of the world.

"And that worried me," Hugh said, "because it meant I'd have to find some other    18
place to live."

Where I come from, finding shelter is a problem the average teenager might    19
confidently leave to his parents. It was just something that came with having a mom and a dad. Worried that he might be sent to live with his grandparents in Kentucky, Hugh turned to the school's guidance counselor, who knew of a family whose son had recently left for college. And so he spent another year living with strangers and not mentioning his birthday. While I wouldn't have wanted to do it myself, I can't help but envy the sense of fortitude he gained from the experience. After graduating from college, he moved to France knowing only the phrase "Do you speak French?"—a question guaranteed to get you nowhere unless you also speak the language.

While living in Africa, Hugh and his family took frequent vacations, often in the    20
company of their monkey. The Nairobi Hilton, some suite of high-ceilinged rooms in Cairo or Khartoum: these are the places his people recall when gathered at a common table. "Was that the summer we spent in Beirut or, no, I'm thinking of the time we sailed from Cyprus and took the *Orient Express* to Istanbul."

Theirs was the life I dreamt about during my vacations in eastern North    21
Carolina. Hugh's family was hobnobbing with chiefs and sultans while I ate hush puppies at the Sanitary Fish Market in Morehead City, a beach towel wrapped like a hijab around my head.[2] Someone unknown to me was very likely standing in a muddy ditch and dreaming of an evening spent sitting in a clean family restaurant, drinking iced tea and working his way through an extra-large seaman's platter, but that did not concern me, as it meant I should have been happy with what I had. Rather than surrender to my bitterness, I have learned to take satisfaction in the life that Hugh has led. His stories have, over time, become my own. I say this with no trace of a kumbaya.[3] There is no spiritual symbiosis; I'm just a petty thief who lifts his memories the same way I'll take a handful of change left on his dresser. When my own experiences fall short of the mark, I just go out and spend some of

---

2. *Hijab:* A veil worn by Muslim women. *Hush puppies:* Small, deep-fried balls of cornmeal dough.

3. *Kumbaya:* The title and refrain of an African American folk song that originated as a slave spiritual. The song was a popular hit in the 1960s and is sung by many youth organizations; the word has come to be associated with unity and closeness.

his. It is with pleasure that I sometimes recall the dead man's purpled face or the report of the handgun ringing in my ears as I studied the blood pooling beneath the dead white piglet. On the way back from the slaughterhouse, we stopped for Cokes in the village of Mojo, where the gas-station owner had arranged a few tables and chairs beneath a dying canopy of vines. It was late afternoon by the time we returned to school, where a second bus carried me to the foot of Coffeeboard Road. Once there, I walked through a grove of eucalyptus trees and alongside a bald pasture of starving cattle, past the guard napping in his gatehouse, and into the waiting arms of my monkey. ◆

## FOR CLOSE READING

1. As children in school, both David Sedaris and Hugh Hamrick took occasional field trips. What is Sedaris's point in comparing their experiences? Broadly speaking, how do they compare?

2. Why did Sedaris find the movie about a talking Volkswagen to be "unremarkable" (10)? How did Hugh react to it, and why was his experience so different?

3. Instead of surrendering to his "bitterness," Sedaris has learned "to take satisfaction" from Hugh's account of his childhood (21). Why does Sedaris claim to be bitter, and how seriously are we supposed to take his claim?

4. Besides satisfaction and loose change, what else has Sedaris learned to "take" from Hugh's life?

5. Whose childhood would you prefer to remember having lived, Sedaris's or Hugh's? Why?

### Strategies and Structures

1. In comparing the early lives of himself and his partner, Sedaris emphasizes the differences. On what basis does he compare their experiences nevertheless? What did their childhoods have in common?

2. In paragraph 8, Sedaris uses the point-by-point method to organize his comparison. What would have been the result if he had kept on alternating like this between his two subjects throughout the rest of the essay? Explain.

3. How sufficient do you find Sedaris's main points of comparison for explaining his jealousy of Hugh's childhood (7)? How and how well do they prepare us for the ending, in which Sedaris takes over his friend's memories?

4. *Other Methods.* Sedaris's comparison includes many elements of personal NARRA-TIVE. What are some of them? (Cite specific examples from the text.) How would the essay be different without any narrative?

## Thinking about Language

1. His life and Hugh's shared the same verbs, says Sedaris, but different nouns and objects (8). What does Sedaris mean by this, and why is he comparing the lives of two boys to grammatical parts of speech?

2. Among the "personal highlights" of his childhood, says Sedaris, is "the memory of having my picture taken with Uncle Paul, the legally blind host of a Raleigh children's television show" (14). How is Sedaris using IRONY here?

3. A "hijab" is a veil (21). What sort of hijab does Sedaris wear in the Sanitary Fish Market in Morehead City?

4. Sedaris describes himself as a "petty thief" (21). What is he stealing in this essay, and what has caused him to sink to this level?

## FOR WRITING

1. Ask a friend or family member to write down his or her recollections of an important event that you have both experienced. You do the same. Then, in a paragraph or so, compare and contrast the two versions.

2. In an essay, compare your childhood with that of someone whose early experience was very different from your own. Your counterpart can be someone you know personally or someone you don't know, as long as you're familiar with details of his or her childhood.

3. Write a critical EVALUATION of one of Sedaris's essays or books. In addition to explaining why you liked (or didn't like) the essay or book, compare and contrast representative passages or events in the text, and use them as examples to help explain what the text is about and how it works, including what makes it humorous (or not).

4. Discuss this or some other Sedaris essay (or essays) with several of your classmates. Take notes on each other's readings and reactions, and give an oral report comparing and contrasting the different views.

...........................................................•

You'll find quizzes on the readings at
wwnorton.com/write/back-to-the-lake.

BRUCE CATTON

# Grant and Lee: A Study in Contrasts

Bruce Catton (1899–1978), grew up in Benzonia, Michigan, listening to the stories told by Union army veterans and reenacting the battles of the Civil War. After serving briefly in the U.S. Navy during World War I, Catton worked as a reporter until the outbreak of World War II, during which he served as director of information for the War Production Board. A founding editor of *American Heritage* magazine, he wrote many volumes about the Civil War, including *A Stillness at Appomattox* (1954), which won a Pulitzer Prize and a National Book Award. In 1976 Catton was honored with a Presidential Medal of Freedom as America's foremost historian of the Civil War.

"Grant and Lee: A Study in Contrasts" was first published in *The American Story* (1955), a collection of essays by leading historians. Catton compares the U.S. Civil War generals Ulysses S. Grant, who led the Union army, and Robert E. Lee, who led the forces of the Confederacy.

W HEN ULYSSES S. GRANT and Robert E. Lee met in the parlor of a modest   1
house at Appomattox Court House, Virginia, on April 9, 1865, to work out the terms for the surrender of Lee's Army of Northern Virginia, a great chapter in American life came to a close, and a great new chapter began.

These men were bringing the Civil War[1] to its virtual finish. To be sure, other   2
armies had yet to surrender, and for a few days the fugitive Confederate government would struggle desperately and vainly, trying to find some way to go on living now that its chief support was gone. But in effect it was all over when Grant and Lee signed the papers. And the little room where they wrote out the terms was the scene of one of the poignant, dramatic contrasts in American history.

They were two strong men, these oddly different generals, and they represented   3
the strengths of two conflicting currents that, through them, had come into final collision.

---

1. *Civil War* (1861–1865): The war fought between those states and territories of the United States that remained loyal to the federal government in Washington under President Abraham Lincoln ("the Union") and the slave-holding Southern states that formed a separate government led by Jefferson Davis ("the Confederacy").

MLA CITATION: Catton, Bruce. "Grant and Lee: A Study in Contrasts." 1955. *Back to the Lake.* Ed. Thomas Cooley. 3rd ed. New York: Norton, 2015. 377–81. Print.

Back of Robert E. Lee was the notion that the old aristocratic concept might [4] somehow survive and be dominant in American life.

Lee was tidewater Virginia,[2] and in his background were family, culture, and [5] tradition . . . the age of chivalry transplanted to a New World which was making its own legends and its own myths. He embodied a way of life that had come down through the age of knighthood and the English country squire. America was a land that was beginning all over again, dedicated to nothing much more complicated than the rather hazy belief that all men had equal rights and should have an equal chance in the world. In such a land Lee stood for the feeling that it was somehow of advantage to human society to have a pronounced inequality in the social structure. There should be a leisure class, backed by ownership of land; in turn, society itself should be keyed to the land as the chief source of wealth and influence. It would bring forth (according to this ideal) a class of men with a strong sense of obligation to the community; men who lived not to gain advantage for themselves, but to meet the solemn obligations which had been laid on them by the very fact that they were privileged. From them the country would get its leadership; to them it could look for the higher values—of thought, of conduct, of personal deportment— to give it strength and virtue.

Lee embodied the noblest elements of this aristocratic ideal. Through him, the [6] landed nobility justified itself. For four years, the Southern states had fought a desperate war to uphold the ideals for which Lee stood. In the end, it almost seemed as if the Confederacy fought for Lee; as if he himself was the Confederacy . . . the best thing that the way of life for which the Confederacy stood could ever have to offer. He had passed into legend before Appomattox. Thousands of tired, underfed, poorly clothed Confederate soldiers, long since past the simple enthusiasm of the early days of the struggle, somehow considered Lee the symbol of everything for which they had been willing to die. But they could not quite put this feeling into words. If the Lost Cause, sanctified by so much heroism and so many deaths, had a living justification, its justification was General Lee.

Grant, the son of a tanner on the Western frontier, was everything Lee was not. [7] He had come up the hard way and embodied nothing in particular except the eternal toughness and sinewy fiber of the men who grew up beyond the mountains. He was one of a body of men who owed reverence and obeisance to no one, who were self-reliant to a fault, who cared hardly anything for the past but who had a sharp eye for the future.

---

2. *Tidewater Virginia*: The coastal plain region of eastern Virginia, where rivers receive tidal inflow from the Chesapeake Bay, which is traditionally associated with aristocracy and old families. The first English colony in North America, Jamestown, settled in 1607, is in the Tidewater area.

Lee's surrender to Grant at Appomattox Court House, Virginia, on April 9, 1865, as depicted in a Currier and Ives lithograph.

These frontier men were the precise opposites of the tidewater aristocrats. Back 8 of them, in the great surge that had taken people over the Alleghenies[3] and into the opening Western country, there was a deep, implicit dissatisfaction with a past that had settled into grooves. They stood for democracy, not from any reasoned conclusion about the proper ordering of human society, but simply because they had grown up in the middle of democracy and knew how it worked. Their society might have privileges, but they would be privileges each man had won for himself. Forms and patterns meant nothing. No man was born to anything, except perhaps to a chance to show how far he could rise. Life was competition.

Yet along with this feeling had come a deep sense of belonging to a national 9 community. The Westerner who developed a farm, opened a shop, or set up in business as a trader, could hope to prosper only as his own community prospered—and his community ran from the Atlantic to the Pacific and from Canada down to Mexico. If the land was settled, with towns and highways and accessible markets, he could better himself. He saw his fate in terms of the nation's own destiny. As its horizons expanded, so did his. He had, in other words, an acute dollars-and-cents stake in the continued growth and development of his country.

And that, perhaps, is where the contrast between Grant and Lee becomes most 10 striking. The Virginia aristocrat, inevitably, saw himself in relation to his own region. He lived in a static society which could endure almost anything except change. Instinctively, his first loyalty would go to the locality in which that society existed. He would fight to the limit of endurance to defend it, because in defending it he was defending everything that gave his own life its deepest meaning.

The Westerner, on the other hand, would fight with an equal tenacity for the 11 broader concept of society. He fought so because everything he lived by was tied to growth, expansion, and a constantly widening horizon. What he lived by would survive or fall with the nation itself. He could not possibly stand by unmoved in the face of an attempt to destroy the Union. He would combat it with everything he had, because he could only see it as an effort to cut the ground out from under his feet.

So Grant and Lee were in complete contrast, representing two diametrically 12 opposed elements in American life. Grant was the modern man emerging; beyond him, ready to come on the stage, was the great age of steel and machinery, of crowded cities and a restless burgeoning vitality. Lee might have ridden down from the old age of chivalry, lance in hand, silken banner fluttering over his head. Each man was the perfect champion of his cause, drawing both his strengths and his weaknesses from the people he led.

---

3. *Alleghenies:* The Allegheny Mountains, which run from northern Pennsylvania to southwestern Virginia.

Yet it was not all contrast, after all. Different as they were—in background, in 13 personality, in underlying aspiration—these two great soldiers had much in common. Under everything else, they were marvelous fighters. Furthermore, their fighting qualities were really very much alike.

Each man had, to begin with, the great virtue of utter tenacity and fidelity. 14 Grant fought his way down the Mississippi Valley in spite of acute personal discouragement and profound military handicaps. Lee hung on in the trenches at Petersburg after hope itself had died. In each man there was an indomitable quality . . . the born fighter's refusal to give up as long as he can still remain on his feet and lift his two fists.

For winding up a comparison, the point-by-point method (p. 342) can be especially useful.

Daring and resourcefulness they had, too; the ability to think faster and move 15 faster than the enemy. These were the qualities which gave Lee the dazzling campaigns of Second Manassas and Chancellorsville and won Vicksburg for Grant.

Lastly, and perhaps greatest of all, there was the ability, at the end, to turn 16 quickly from war to peace once the fighting was over. Out of the way these two men behaved at Appomattox came the possibility of a peace of reconciliation. It was a possibility not wholly realized, in the years to come, but which did, in the end, help the two sections to become one nation again . . . after a war whose bitterness might have seemed to make such a reunion wholly impossible. No part of either man's life became him more than the part he played in this brief meeting in the McLean house at Appomattox. Their behavior there put all succeeding generations of Americans in their debt. Two great Americans, Grant and Lee—very different, yet under everything very much alike. Their encounter at Appomattox was one of the great moments of American history. ◆

## FOR CLOSE READING

1. According to Bruce Catton, Grant and Lee represented two distinct "currents" in American life and history (3). What were those currents, and what contrasting qualities and ideals does Catton associate with each man?

2. Even though they were "in complete contrast," says Catton, Grant and Lee also "had much in common" (12, 13). In what ways were the two men alike?

3. Although Grant and Lee were both "great Americans" (16), as Catton says, they were deadly enemies. Why did each man take the side he did?

4. Why, according to Catton, are all future generations of Americans "in their debt" (16)? Do you agree? Why or why not?

## Strategies and Structures

1. On what basis is Catton comparing his two subjects? Where does he tell the reader what that basis of comparison is?

2. Why does Catton emphasize the differences between the two men he is comparing? For what audience and purpose is he drawing such a strong contrast?

3. Catton uses the subject-by-subject method through most of his essay. When and why does he switch to the point-by-point method?

4. *Other Methods.* Besides comparing and contrasting the two generals, Catton's study also analyzes the CAUSES AND EFFECTS of the American Civil War. How does this analysis support and clarify his comparison?

## Thinking about Language

1. What view of history—and Grant's and Lee's roles in it—is suggested by Catton's use of METAPHORS from the theater in paragraphs 2 and 16?

2. Why do you think Catton capitalizes "Lost Cause" in paragraph 6?

3. "Obeisance" (7) means homage of the sort paid to a king. Why might Catton choose this term instead of *obedience* when describing General Grant?

4. What are the CONNOTATIONS of "sinewy fiber" (7), and how does Catton's general DESCRIPTION of Grant justify the use of this phrase?

## FOR WRITING

1. Make an outline of the key points you would make in a comparison and contrast of two famous generals, great athletes, favorite aunts, or other people.

2. Write an essay comparing and contrasting two present-day public figures—for example, two U.S. presidents—whose actions, you feel, will put all succeeding generations of Americans in their debt.

3. Do a RHETORICAL ANALYSIS of the portrait of Lee surrendering to Grant on p. 379. Compare it with other Currier and Ives lithographs of the period and also with what Catton says about the two men in the picture.

4. Write a 500–600-word research REPORT on one of the following: Lee after Appomattox, Grant's years in the White House. Don't forget to compare the postwar figure with the wartime hero. Cite your sources.

5. *The Personal Memoirs of U. S. Grant* was published by Grant's friend Mark Twain in 1885–86. Do some research on the history of the book—and the relationship between the two men—and write a REPORT comparing them as friends and writers.

You'll find quizzes on the readings at wwnorton.com/write/back-to-the-lake.

# WILLIAM SHAKESPEARE

## Sonnet 130

William Shakespeare (1554–1616) is not only English literature's greatest dramatist but also one of its greatest poets. Plays performed on the Elizabethan stage were rich with poetry for both practical reasons (there were few elaborate sets or special effects, so a play's setting had to be conjured almost entirely through words) and reasons of convention (audiences expected poetry, not realistic dialogue). Shakespeare's reputation as a great poet would be assured even if he had written nothing but dramas.

In 1592, however, an outbreak of plague led authorities to close the theaters for two years, and the playwright turned to the composition of verse narratives. In 1609 the first edition of Shakespeare's sonnets was published. These sonnets were immediately recognized—and have been regarded ever since—as supreme expressions of the sonnet form. Sonnet 130 is about two ways of drawing comparisons.

> My mistress' eyes are nothing like the sun;                    1
> Coral is far more red, than her lips red:
> If snow be white, why then her breasts are dun;
> If hairs be wires, black wires grow on her head.
> I have seen roses damasked, red and white,                    5
> But no such roses see I in her cheeks;
> And in some perfumes is there more delight
> Than in the breath that from my mistress reeks.
> I love to hear her speak, yet well I know
> That music hath a far more pleasing sound:                    10
> I grant I never saw a goddess go,
> My mistress, when she walks, treads on the ground:
> And yet by heaven, I think my love as rare,
> As any she belied with false compare. ◆

MLA CITATION: Shakespeare, William. "Sonnet 130." 1609. *Back to the Lake*. Ed. Thomas Cooley. 3rd ed. New York: Norton, 2015. 383. Print.

## FOR CLOSE READING

1.  The speaker of Shakespeare's poem can find no similarities between the brightness of his lady's eyes and that of the sun, or the color of her cheeks and the pink (damask), white, or red of the rose. Why not?

2.  What kind of lover *would* make such comparisons?

3.  What is Shakespeare's speaker assuming about the character of his "mistress" and what will please her (1)? Explain.

## Strategies and Structures

1.  Who, do you suppose, is the intended AUDIENCE for Shakespeare's love poem: a particular lady, ladies in general, or readers of traditional love poetry, whether male or female? Some combination of these? Why do you think so?

2.  Shakespeare's poem emphasizes the differences between the lady and the lovely things to which he compares her. What is his purpose in avoiding the extravagant praise found in so many love poems of the period?

3.  The English (or Shakespearean) sonnet consists of three quatrains followed by a couplet. Each group of four lines presents a different aspect of a subject, and the final two lines tie the whole together in some way. If the first four lines of Sonnet 130 deal with various sights, what is compared in lines 5–8? Lines 9–12?

4.  How (and how well) do the final two lines of Shakespeare's poem resolve the tension generated by the rest of the comparison? Explain.

5.  *Other Methods.* The woman in Sonnet 130 appears in many other Shakespearean sonnets, where she is known as "the dark lady." How does the DESCRIPTION of her in this poem fit this general characterization?

## Thinking about Language

1.  Besides signifying general drabness, "dun" (3) is a mousey brown color. Is Shakespeare saying that the lady's skin is this color, or is he countering one HYPERBOLE with another? Explain.

2.  To the reader of Shakespeare's day, "wires" (4) would have called to mind fine threads of beaten gold used in jewelry or embroidery. What is supposed to be shocking here is the color of the lady's hair. Why?

3.  The meaning of "reeks" has changed since Shakespeare's time (8). Originally, the word meant "to emit smoke" rather than "to stink." How does this meaning fit in with Shakespeare's description, especially in line 12, of the lady as a down-to-earth creature?

## FOR WRITING

1. In line 14, "any she" may mean "any woman." With this in mind, translate the last two lines of Shakespeare's poem into modern English.

2. Write a paragraph summarizing the main points of comparison that Shakespeare makes in Sonnet 130.

3. Write a TEXTUAL ANALYSIS of Shakespeare's Sonnet 130 as a critique of making comparisons in love and love poetry.

4. Do some research on the biographical details that are actually known about William Shakespeare, and write a 400-word PROFILE of the man as a historical figure. Be sure to say how it compares with the myth.

You'll find quizzes on the readings at wwnorton.com/write/back-to-the-lake.

# CHAPTER 11

# Classification

You can divide your whole life into two basic categories. You're either staying in or going out.
—JERRY SEINFELD, *Seinlanguage*

Let's say you live near the coast of Florida or Louisiana or the Carolinas, and you have just survived a hurricane. The power is back on; so is the water. The roof, however, is not. What kind of roof did you have? Which kinds held up well in the storm? What kind should you put back on your house? These are all questions of classification.

## Breaking a Subject into Categories

When you DESCRIBE something, you say what its characteristics are: "My old roof was a tasteful gray with green ridge caps." Classification is concerned with characteristics, too: "This is not my roof in your front yard. This is a metal roof, the kind they have across the lake. My roof was tile." When you classify something (a roof, an aquatic mammal, someone's personality), however, you say what category it belongs to—metal, asphalt, tile; dolphin, manatee, whale; introverted, extroverted—based on the characteristics of each category. There are basically two ways to classify.

When we classify individuals, we sort them into groups: this dog is a hound, that one is a terrier. When we classify groups—dogs, bicycles—we divide them into subgroups—hounds, terriers, retrievers; street bikes, mountain bikes, racing bikes. In this chapter, we will learn what constitutes a category (or significant group), how to devise a valid classification system, and how to use that system when you compose an essay. We'll also review the critical points to watch for as you read over and revise your essay, as well as common errors to avoid as you edit. We will use the term *classification* to refer to both sorting and dividing, since, in either case, we are always going to be organizing a subject into categories.

## Why Do We Classify?

We classify things in order to choose the kinds that best meet our needs. The hurricane was a direct hit, and neither tile nor asphalt roofs stood up well. What other kinds are there, and which kind is most likely to survive the next high wind?

Choosing among similar kinds of objects or ideas is only one reason for using classification in our thinking and writing, however. We classify people and things for many purposes: to evaluate (good dog, bad dog); to determine causes (mechanical failure, weather, or pilot error?); to conduct experiments (test group, control group), and to measure results (winners, losers, and runners-up).

# USING CLASSIFICATION IN A REVIEW

Reviewing a restaurant is much like doing a critical EVALUATION of anything else—a story, book, musical performance, consumer product, television show, or film. You analyze (or break apart) the subject into its components, describe those individual pieces in some detail, and then make a judgment or recommendation based on the sum of the parts. In this review, the writer uses classification to evaluate the food and ambience in one type of restaurant in relation to those of other types:

> As a type of eating place, the bistro falls somewhere between a brasserie and a full-fledged restaurant. Bistros are usually smaller than either, but this place was spacious and had a nice collection of old wood tables with some heft and character. The walls displayed lots of framed black-and-white photographs, featuring an eclectic assortment of athletes; but you wouldn't call the bar a sports bar, either, because there were also photos of other celebrities and of urban skylines at night. An old upright piano added to the ambiance. The total effect was one of warmth and effortless, sincere old-fashioned charm—the comfort of an established restaurant and the informality of a brasserie combined.
>
> When the bill came, we got one of the great benefits of eating at a bistro. For about the same price as the plate of the day and a beer at a brasserie we got individually prepared dishes that would have cost two or three times as much at a standard restaurant. Long live the bistro!—one of my favorite types of French eateries, especially when it's as good as this one.

Dessert at the Bistro d'en Face: chocolate soufflé and vanilla ice cream.

—BARBARA JOY WHITE, *Paris Journal*

We also classify in order to make sense of the world, grouping individuals according to the common traits that tell us the most about them. Consider the duckbill platypus. Even though it has a bill and lays eggs, biologists classify the platypus as a mammal with birdlike characteristics rather than a bird with mammalian ones. Why?

It's not simply that the platypus has mostly mammalian traits, such as hair, milk glands, and a neocortex region in the brain. Among all living mammals, only the platypus and the spiny anteater retain a few of the birdlike characteristics once common to many mammals. That these creatures are in a class by themselves tells us that, far from being a bird, the platypus simply branched off early from the family tree, before other mammals lost those traits in the course of evolution.

So if you're ever inclined to think of classification systems as mere catalogues, remember the platypus. By accurately classifying this strange mammal and other apparent anomalies, we can discover not only where each one belongs in the scheme of things, we can learn more about the basis of the natural order itself.

## Composing an Essay That Uses Classification

Classification is a way of understanding and ordering the world—and of organizing your thoughts in almost any kind of writing, from a shopping list to a formal essay or even a whole book. Whether you are writing about animals, people, machines, movies, or political movements, the first step is to divide your subject into appropriate categories. Those categories will be determined by the various attributes of your subject, of course; but they will also depend on your PRINCIPLE OF CLASSIFICATION—the basis on which you are classifying your subject. Dogs, for example, are usually classified on the basis of breed or size. If you're classifying dogs by size, your categories might be standard, miniature, and toy. But if breed is your principle of classification, then your categories would be golden retriever, greyhound, poodle, Irish setter, and so on.

### Thinking about Purpose and Audience

In order to classify anything accurately, you have to examine all its important attributes. The specific traits you focus on and the categories you divide your subject into, however, will be determined largely by your purpose and audience. Consider the example of the roof that blew off in a hurricane. If your purpose is to determine—and write an article for your neighborhood newsletter explaining—

what kind of roof will stay on best in the next hurricane, you're going to look closely at such traits as weight and wind resistance. And you are going to pay less attention to other traits, such as color or energy efficiency or even cost, that you might consider more closely if you had a different purpose in mind.

Once you've determined which kind of roof has the highest wind rating, you probably are not going to have a hard time convincing these readers (many of whom also lost their roofs) that this is the kind to buy. They may expect you to prove that the kind you are recommending does in fact have the characteristics you claim for it (superior resistance to wind), but they are not likely to question the importance of those characteristics or the validity of focusing on them in your article. However, since your audience of homeowners may not be experts in roofing materials, you'll want to make sure you define any technical terms and use language they'll be familiar with. You won't always be able to assume that your readers will appreciate the way you choose to classify a subject, however. So be prepared to explain why your audience should accept the criteria you use to classify your subject and the weight you place on particular attributes.

> Amy Tan (p. 419) found this out, she says, when her reader was her mother.

## Generating Ideas: Considering What Kinds There Are

Classifying can be intellectually demanding work, as it was for the man who was hired by the hour to sort a bushel of apples into green, ripe, and rotten. After an hour and a half went by and the man had only two puny piles to show for his labor, his employer asked why he was so slow. The man shook his head and replied, "It's the decisions."

There are many techniques you can use—CLUSTERING, LOOPING, LISTING, and more—to help you decide what subject you want to classify and why. Once you have a subject in mind and a reason for classifying it—you're in an apple orchard and you're hungry—the next decision you need to consider is what kinds there are. Then you can choose the ones that best suit your PURPOSE and AUDIENCE.

> Why tell a bald-faced lie when there are so many other kinds to choose from (p. 409)?

Let's say your subject is movies. Movies can be classified by genre—drama, comedy, romance, horror, thriller, musical. This might be a good classification system to use if you are analyzing movies for a film course. For the purpose of reviewing movies for a campus audience, however, a different set of categories would be more appropriate.

If you are reviewing movies in the school newspaper, your principle of classification would be their quality, and you would divide them into, say, five categories: "must see," "excellent," "good," "mediocre," and "to be avoided at all costs." If you were reviewing some of those same movies for a parenting magazine, however, you might use different categories: "good for all ages," "preschool," "six and up," and "not suitable for children."

When you're coming up with categories for an essay that classifies, make sure your categories are appropriate to your purpose and audience.

## Organizing and Drafting an Essay That Uses Classification

The backbone of an essay that uses classification is the system you create by dividing your subject into categories that interest your readers and that are directly relevant to the point you're making. Those categories should deal with significant aspects of your subject and should be inclusive without overlapping. Also think about including visuals, and about other methods of development you might want to use in addition to classification. The templates on p. 393 can help you get started.

### ORGANIZING A CLASSIFICATION

In the opening paragraphs of your essay, tell the reader what you're classifying and why, and explain your classification system, because much of the rest of your essay will be organized around that system. If you were writing an essay classifying bicycles, for example, something like this might make a good introduction:

> If you are buying or renting a bicycle, you need to know which features to look for in order to meet your needs. Bikes can best be divided into the following categories: mountain bikes, racing bikes, messenger bikes, touring bikes, and stunt bikes. If you understand these six basic types and the differences among them, you can make an informed decision, whether you're choosing a bicycle for a lifetime or just for the afternoon.

Not only does an introduction like this tell the reader what you're classifying and why, it provides a solid outline for organizing the rest of your essay.

Typically, the body of an essay that uses classification is devoted to a point-by-point discussion of each of the categories that make up your classification system. Thus if you are classifying bicycles into mountain bikes, racing bikes, messenger bikes, touring bikes, and stunt bikes, you would spend a paragraph, or at least several sentences, explaining the most important characteristics of each type. Depending upon the complexity of your subject, there will be more or fewer categories to explain; but remember that you must have at least two categories—vertebrates and invertebrates, good movies and bad movies—if you are to have a viable classification system.

# TEMPLATES FOR DRAFTING

When you begin to draft an essay that uses classification, you need to identify your subject and explain the basis on which you're classifying it—moves fundamental to any classification. See how Deborah Tannen makes such moves in the beginning of her essay in this chapter:

> Unfortunately, men and women often have different ideas about what's appropriate, different ways of speaking. . . . Here [are] the biggest areas of miscommunication.
> —DEBORAH TANNEN, "But What Do You Mean?"

Tannen identifies her subject ("areas of miscommunication") and explains the basis on which she's classifying them (differences between men and women). Here is one more example from this chapter:

> Language is the tool of my trade. And I use them all—all the Englishes I grew up with.
> —AMY TAN, "Mother Tongue"

The following templates can help you make some of these basic moves in your own writing. But don't take these as formulas where you just fill in the blanks. There are no shortcuts to good writing, but these templates can serve as starting points.

▶ X can be classified on the basis of _____.

▶ Classified on the basis of _____, some of the most common types of X are _____, _____, and _____.

▶ X can be divided into two basic types, _____ or _____.

▶ Experts in the field typically divide X into _____, _____, and _____.

▶ Some other, less common types of X are _____, _____, and _____.

▶ This particular X clearly belongs in the _____ categeory, since it is _____, _____, and _____.

▶ _____, _____, and _____ are examples of this type of X.

▶ By classifying X in this way, we can see _____.

Once you've laid out, in some detail, the categories that make up your classification system, remind the reader what your principle of classification is, and what point you are making by classifying your subject this way. The point of classifying bicycles by function, for example, is to inform the reader what categories of bicycles exist and which type is best suited to the reader's needs—climbing mountains, racing, delivering packages, doing tricks, or just cruising around.

## STATING YOUR POINT

Classification isn't an end in itself, but a way of relating objects and ideas to each other within an orderly framework. So when you compose an essay that uses classification, ask yourself not only what categories your subject can be divided into, but also what you can learn about that subject by classifying it in that way. Then tell the reader in a THESIS statement what your main point is and why you're dividing up your subject as you do. Usually, you'll want to state your main point in the introduction of your essay as you explain your classification system. Occasionally, your thesis statement may not come until the end, after you've thoroughly explained how your classification system works.

Let's look at an essay in which the point of the classification is not obvious. Here is the main introductory paragraph:

> I have moved more often than I care to remember. However, one thing always stays the same no matter where I have been. There is always a house next door, and that house contains neighbors. Over time, I have begun putting my neighbors into one of four categories: too friendly, unsociable, irritable, and just right.    —Jonathan R. Gould Jr., "The People Next Door"

Having introduced his subject and outlined his four-part classification system at the beginning of his essay, Gould devotes a paragraph to each of the four categories, taking them in order and looking at particular neighbors who fit each one—the "overly friendly" neighbor who had to be told that his house was on fire "in an attempt to make him leave," the "unsociable" neighbor who looked at the fresh-baked apple pie offered by Gould's wife "as if she intended to poison them," and so on. But what is Gould's point in classifying his neighbors according to this scheme?

In addition to making us smile, Gould's point is to make an observation about human nature. Here's the last paragraph of his essay:

> I have always felt it was important to identify the types of neighbors that were around me. Then I am better able to maintain a clear perspective on our relationship and understand their needs. After all, people do not really change; we just learn how to live with both the good and the bad aspects of their behavior.

Gould could have explained his point at the beginning of his essay, but he chose to build up to it instead. In a humorous essay, this can be an effective strategy—part of the fun is wondering where the game is headed and how it's going to end. When you have a more serious purpose in mind, however, you're better off making your main point clear in the beginning of your essay and then, in the conclusion, saying how what you've just written proves that point.

## CHOOSING SIGNIFICANT CHARACTERISTICS

Whatever your purpose is, base your categories on the most significant characteristics of your subject—ones that explain something important about it. All neighbors, for example, have at least one thing in common: they are people who live nearby. This trait, however, doesn't tell us much about them. Proximity may be an essential trait in DEFINING neighbors, but it is not a very useful characteristic for classifying them. For the same reason, you probably would not discuss such attributes as color or decoration when classifying bicycles. Whether a bicycle is blue with red racing stripes or red with blue stripes may be important aesthetically, but these attributes do not tell the reader what kind it is, since all different kinds of bicycles come in all different colors. Color, in other words, while important for classifying wine and laundry, isn't significant when it comes to bicycles. So as you choose your categories, make sure they're based on significant characteristics that actually help the reader to distinguish one type from another.

With bicycles, these would be such attributes as weight, strength, configuration of the handlebars, and thickness of the tires. Thick, knobby tires, heavy frames, and strong cross-braced handlebars that protect the rider from sudden jolts are significant characteristics of mountain bikes. Thin, smooth tires, lightweight frames, and dropped handlebars that put the rider in a more streamlined position are typical of racing bikes. Wide but relatively smooth tires, raised (but not cross-braced) handlebars, and sturdy, medium-weight frames—not to mention large padded seats—indicate touring bikes. And so on.

Citing significant characteristics is even more essential when you have a two-part classification system, also called a binary system. A binary system has the advantage of being very inclusive. All people can be divided into the living and the dead, for instance. Binary classification systems, however, potentially sacrifice depth for breadth. That is, you can use a binary system to classify a lot of people or things, but it may not necessarily tell the reader much about them. Pointing out that Shakespeare, for example, belongs in the "dead" category doesn't tell readers nearly as much about him as explaining that he was a playwright, a poet, and an actor.

Deborah Tannen (p. 437) uses a binary system: male and female.

## USING VISUALS IN CLASSIFICATION

If you are dealing with multiple categories, consider including illustrations in your essay. Statistical graphics, such as bar graphs, allow readers to grasp complex classification systems at a glance. The one below, based on data from the Bureau of Labor Statistics, classifies ten different occupations according to their projected rates of growth over a ten-year period. Which occupations will grow the fastest between 2012 and 2022? By what percentages will their numbers increase? Which occupations will grow at a lesser rate? How much will a particular occupation—home health aides, for example—grow in relation to other occupations? Sometimes, questions like these are best answered by presenting your data visually.

**Fastest-Growing Occupations (projected), 2012–2022**

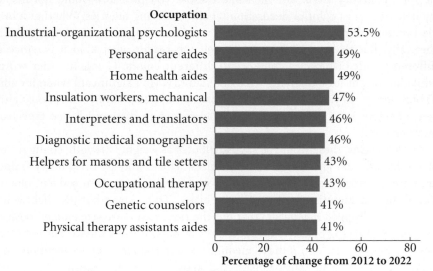

Data from Bureau of Labor Statistics, U.S. Department of Labor, 2013.

## CHOOSING CATEGORIES THAT ARE INCLUSIVE AND DON'T OVERLAP

Not only must you divide your subject into categories that are truly distinctive, those categories must be inclusive enough to cover most cases. And they must not overlap.

Classifying ice cream into chocolate and vanilla alone isn't very useful because this system leaves out several other important kinds, such as strawberry, pistachio, and rum raisin. The categories in a good classification system include all kinds: for instance, no-fat, low-fat, and full-fat ice cream. And they should not overlap. Thus, chocolate, vanilla, homemade, and Ben and Jerry's do not make a good classification system because the same scoop of ice cream could fit into more than one category.

## BREAKING CATEGORIES INTO SUBCATEGORIES

The categories in an essay that uses classification should be broadly inclusive; but if your categories start to become too broad to be useful, try dividing them into narrower subcategories. Suppose you were drafting an essay on the Great Depression of the 1930s for a history class, and you were focusing on "tramps," the itinerant men (and occasionally women) who took to the road—especially the railroads—in search of food and work. In the lingo of the day, those tramps who begged, you would point out, were classified as "dings," and those who worked for a living were called "working stiffs." A third kind, who neither begged nor worked, were called "nose divers."

"Nose divers" designated a relatively narrow category of tramp—those who attended church and worshipped or prayed ("nose dived") in order to partake of meals and beds provided by the church. "Working stiffs," on the other hand, could get their living by almost any means; and to classify them accurately, you would need to divide this broad, general kind into subtypes—harvest tramp, tramp miner, fruit tramp, construction tramp, and sea tramp. Your essay would then go on to specify the chief characteristics of each of these narrower categories.

## USING OTHER METHODS

DEFINITION can be especially useful when you classify something because you will need to define your categories (and any subcategories) according to their distinguishing characteristics. You will also need to DESCRIBE those characteristics. Sometimes you may have reason to analyze the CAUSES of certain characteristics, or what EFFECTS they may have. The author of the following passage uses all three methods (and more) to classify the ailments of horses confined to their stalls:

> In his natural state the horse is a range animal. If he cannot roam a reasonable territory, he may express his frustration by developing some unpleasant or even health-threatening habits. Chewing on fences or stall boards may be followed by cribbing and wind-sucking, vices in which the horse bites down on a hard surface and swallows air at the same time, to the accompaniment of little grunts. (Some will argue that cribbing is a genetically acquired habit, but it is rarely seen in a horse at liberty.)

Further, a continually stabled horse may become a weaver, swaying from side to side in a restless, compulsive pattern. To me, this is as sad a scenario as watching a caged tiger pace back and forth behind bars. Cribbers and weavers, for obvious reasons, frequently develop digestive problems. The message is clear, then: as much turnout for as many hours as possible.　　　—MAXINE KUMIN, *Women, Animals, and Vegetables*

In this passage, Kumin classifies overly confined horses as cribbers and weavers. Defining the behaviors of both kinds as "unpleasant or even health-threatening habits," she then describes the characteristics that distinguish each kind: the cribber "bites down on a hard surface and swallows air at the same time," whereas the weaver sways "from side to side in a restless, compulsive pattern."

Kumin is so concerned about the welfare of overly confined horses, however, that she does more than simply classify, define, and describe their ailments. She analyzes the cause of those ailments and ARGUES for a particular remedy. Cribbing and weaving are not genetic conditions, says Kumin; they are acquired behaviors caused by the confinement itself. Her point, therefore, is clear: horse owners should let their animals range more freely, instead of confining them to the stable.

## EDITING FOR COMMON ERRORS IN A CLASSIFICATION

Classification invites problems with listing groups or attributes. Here are some tips for checking your writing for these errors—and editing any that you find.

**If you've listed categories in a single sentence, make sure they are parallel in form**

▶ A horse can be nervous, aggressive, or calm~~ly accept a saddle~~.

▶ Some say work can be divided into two categories. We're either working too hard or ~~it's a waste of~~ wasting time.

**Check that adjectives are in the following order: size, age, color**

Adjectives identify characteristics, so you'll probably use at least some adjectives when you write an essay that uses classification.

▶ big old brown ~~big~~ boots

Go to wwnorton.com/write/back-to-the-lake for quizzes on these common errors.

# Reading a Classification with a Critical Eye

The most important part of any essay that uses classification is the classification system itself. Does yours have one? How many categories does it include? What are they? Once you've drafted your essay, ask someone else to read your draft and tell you how well your classification system supports your point—and how it might be improved. Should any categories be redefined or omitted? Should any new ones be added? Here are some questions to keep in mind when checking a classification.

**PURPOSE AND AUDIENCE.** Is there a good reason for classifying this particular subject this way? Who is the intended audience of the essay? Does the essay give sufficient background information for the audience to understand (and accept) the proposed classification? Are key terms defined, especially ones that might be unfamiliar to some readers?

**THE POINT.** Is the main point of the essay clearly laid out in a THESIS statement? How and how well does the classification itself support the main point?

**THE CLASSIFICATION SYSTEM AND THE CATEGORIES.** Is the classification system appropriate for the subject and purpose of the essay? What is the PRINCIPLE OF CLASSIFICATION? Should that principle be revised in any way? If so, how? Do the categories suit the essay's purpose and audience?

**SIGNIFICANT CHARACTERISTICS.** Do the characteristics that make up the categories tell the reader something important about the subject? Does the essay demonstrate that the things being classified actually have these characteristics?

**INCLUSIVE CATEGORIES.** Do the categories include most cases? If not, what new categories need to be added in order to make the classification system complete?

**OVERLAPPING CATEGORIES.** Can any individual item fit into more than one of the categories that make up the classification system? If so, how might the principle of classification be revised so they don't overlap?

**SUBCATEGORIES.** Would any of the basic categories that make up the classification system be clearer or easier to explain if they were divided into subgroups?

**VISUALS.** Would a graph, diagram, or other illustration make the categories easier to understand?

**OTHER METHODS.** Does the essay use other methods of development? For instance, does it clearly DEFINE all the basic categories and subcategories? Does it fully DESCRIBE the distinctive attributes of each category? Does it analyze what CAUSED those attributes, or what EFFECTS they might have? Does it make an ARGUMENT?

**COMMON ERRORS.** Look for lists of categories and traits in series. Do all the items have approximately the same grammatical form? If they don't, change them so each one is grammatically parallel to the other.

## Student Example

Michelle Watson was a student at Roane State Community College in eastern Tennessee when she wrote this essay for an English class. "Shades of Character" is based on Watson's research in child psychology and education, particularly her study of typical childhood personalities. Watson's instructor, Jennifer Jordan-Henley, chose the essay for publication on the website of the college's Online Writing Lab.

Citing the work of several experts, Watson classifies children's personalities according to commonly recognized types. This classification system provides a framework for organizing the entire report, which discusses each type in turn, paying close attention to the significant attributes that distinguish one "shade" of behavior from another. Watson documents her sources using the MLA style.

Shades of Character

Anyone who has spent time around children will notice that   1
each one has a special personality all his or her own. Children, like
adults, have different traits that make up their personalities. Experts
have researched these traits in detail, and they classify children

Classification
system is made
up of three per-   ......•
sonality types
determined by
experts

into different categories. Some experts have named more than
three categories, but Dr. Peter L. Mangione[1] has chosen three that

1. *Dr. Peter L. Mangione:* A child psychologist and codirector of the Center for Child and Family Studies in Sausalito, California. He is the content developer and writer of the video *Flexible, Fearful, or Feisty: The Different Temperaments of Infants and Toddlers* (1990), produced by the California Department of Education. All quotations from Dr. Mangione are from this video.

most experts agree with. These categories are "flexible," "fearful," and "feisty." Children generally may have similar interests, <u>but the way they interact and deal with these interests</u> displays their personality types.

Explains the PRINCIPLE OF CLASSIFICATION for the categories

The flexible personality is the most common of the three types. About "forty percent of all children fall into the flexible or easy group" (Mangione). These children usually handle feelings of anger and disappointment by becoming only mildly upset. This does not mean that they do not feel mad or disappointed, they just choose to react mildly. These actions mean the flexible child is easy to take care of and be around. According to Mangione, such children usually "adapt to new situations and activities quickly, are toilet-trained easily, and are generally cheerful." Flexible children are subtle in their need for attention. Instead of yelling and demanding it, they will slowly and politely let their caregivers know about the need. If they do not get the attention right away, they "seldom make a fuss." They patiently wait, but they still make it known that they need the attention. These children also are easygoing, so routines like feeding and napping are regular (Mangione).

2

Watson devotes two paragraphs to each category; ¶2 & 3 explain the significant characteristics of "flexible" children

Flexible children may be referred to as "good as gold" because of their cheerful attitudes. Since these are well-behaved children, the caregiver needs to make sure the child is getting the attention he or she needs. The caregiver should "check in with the flexible child from time to time" (Mangione). By checking in with the child regularly, the caregiver will be more knowledgeable about when the child needs attention and when he or she does not.

3

Suggests the PURPOSE for classifying children (to aid in their care)

The next temperament is the fearful type. These are the more quiet and shy children. This kind makes up about 15 percent of all children, according to Mangione. They adapt slowly to new environments and take longer than flexible children when warming up to things. When presented with a new environment, fearful children often cling to something or someone familiar, whether it be the main caregiver or a material object such as a blanket. The

4

Significant characteristics of "fearful" children explained in ¶4 & 5

fearful child will cling until he or she feels comfortable with the new situation. This can result in a deep attachment of the child to a particular caregiver or object. Fearful children may also withdraw when pushed into a new situation too quickly (Mangione). They may also withdraw when other children are jumping into a new project or situation they are not comfortable with. These children may tend to play alone rather than with a group.

In dealing with fearful children, caregivers find they need more attention than flexible children. A good technique for helping these children is having "a sequence of being with, talking to, stepping back, remaining available, and moving on" (Mangione). The caregiver can also help fearful children by giving them "extra soothing combined with an inch-by-inch fostering of independence and assertiveness" (Viorst 174). One of the most effective techniques is just taking everything slowly and helping the child to become more comfortable with his or her surroundings.

The third temperament type is called feisty. About "ten percent" of children fit into this category (Mangione). Feisty children express their opinions in a very intense way. Whether they are happy or mad, everyone around them will know how they feel. These children remain active most of the time, and this causes them to be very aggressive. Feisty children often have a tendency toward "negative persistence" and will go "on and on nagging, whining and negotiating" if there is something they particularly want ("Facts About Temperament"). Unlike flexible children, feisty children are irregular in their napping and feeding times, but they do not adapt well to changes in their routines. They get "used to things and won't give them up" ("Facts About Temperament"). Anything out of the ordinary can send them into a fit. If these children are not warned of a change, they may react very negatively (Mangione). Feisty children also tend to be very sensitive to their surrounding environment. As a result, they may have strong reactions to their surroundings.

5

6

By including percentages, Watson shows how little her categories overlap and how inclusive they are, since the categories cover in total about 65% of the population

Significant characteristics of "feisty" children explained in ¶6 & 7

When dealing with feisty children, the caregiver should know strategies that receive positive results when different situations arise. Mangione supports the "redirection technique" to calm feisty children. This method helps when the child is reacting very negatively to a situation. According to Mangione, to properly implement the redirection technique, the caregiver should

> begin by recognizing and empathizing with the feelings of the feisty child and placing firm limits on any unacceptable behavior. This response lets the child know that both his or her desire for the toy and feelings of anger when denied the toy are acceptable to the caregiver. At the same time, the caregiver should clearly communicate to the child that expressing anger through hurtful or disruptive behavior is not acceptable. The child will probably need time to experience his or her emotions and settle down. Then offer an alternative toy or activity that may interest the child, who is then given time to consider the new choice and to accept or reject it.

Caregivers should consider that these children generally do not have regular feeding and napping times. The caregiver should be flexible when working with these children and should try to conform more to the desires of the child (Mangione). If there is going to be a change in a child's routine, the caregiver has an easier time when the child has been warned of the change.

Generally speaking, children can be divided into three groups, but caregivers must not forget that each child is an individual. Children may have the traits of all three of the personality groups, but they are categorized into the one they are most like. Whatever their temperament, children need to be treated according to their individual needs. When these needs are met appropriately the child will be happier, and those around the child will feel better also. Knowing the general personality types and how to react to them will help to make the caregiver's job much easier and aid in the relief of unnecessary stress.

7

8

Conclusion reiterates the categories and ends with a THESIS statement explaining why it's helpful to classify children this way

Works Cited

"Facts About Temperament." Australian *Temperament Project*.
    Australian Temperament Project, n.d. Web. 25 Oct. 2000.

Mangione, Peter L., cont. dev./writ. *Flexible, Fearful, or Feisty: The*
    *Different Temperaments of Infants and Toddlers*. Prod. J. Ronald
    Lally. Cont. dev. S. Signer and J. Ronald Lally. Dir. Janet
    Poole. Media Services Unit, California Dept. of Education,
    1990. Videocassette.

Viorst, Judith. "Is Your Child's Personality Set at Birth?" *Redbook*
    Nov. 1995: 174+. *Academic OneFile*. Web. 23 Oct. 2000.

## Analyzing a Student Classification

In "Shades of Character," Michele Watson draws upon rhetorical strategies and techniques that good writers use all the time when they classify things. The following questions, in addition to focusing on particular aspects of Watson's text, will help you to identify those common strategies and techniques so you can adapt them to your own writing. These questions will also help to prepare you for the analytical questions—on content, structure, and language—that you'll find after all the other selections in this chapter, along with suggestions for writing on related topics.

### FOR CLOSE READING

1. According to Michelle Watson, experts in child psychology agree on at least three basic types when classifying the personalities of young children: "flexible," "fearful," and "feisty" (1). What are the main characteristics of each type?

2. If every child has "a special personality all his or her own," how is it that Watson and the experts she cites can group them into personality types (1)? Explain.

3. "Feisty children," says Watson, "express their opinions in a very intense way" (6). What specific techniques does she offer for dealing with such children?

### Strategies and Structures

1. Watson not only identifies "the general personality types" of young children; she explains "how to react to them" (8). Why? Who is her intended audience, and what is her main point in classifying infants and toddlers as she does?

2. Watson lays out her classification system in the opening paragraph of her essay. What is her principle of classification? Why does she use this principle instead of classifying by sex, height, weight, or some other physical characteristic?

3. In what order does Watson present the personality types in her classification system? Is this arrangement logical? Why or why not?

4. How significant are the characteristics that Watson uses to define her three personality types? Does she always describe the same kind of behavior, such as how a child reacts to objects, when defining each type? Should she? Explain.

5. *Other Methods.* In the conclusion of her essay, Watson reminds the reader that "children can be divided into three groups" (8). What ARGUMENT is she also making here? How and how well does her classification of children support that argument?

### Thinking about Language

1. What are the CONNOTATIONS of "feisty" (1)? What other terms might experts have chosen for this personality type, and why do you think they settled on this one?
2. Watson speaks of *caregivers* throughout her essay. Why do you think she uses this term instead of *parents* or *family members*?
3. How would you DEFINE "negative persistence" (6)?

### FOR WRITING

1. Which of Watson's three personality types were you as a child? Write a paragraph using your early behavior as an EXAMPLE of the type.

2. Using the three-part system that Watson discusses, write an essay classifying you and your siblings, or several other children you have known, into each of the various types. Be sure to explain your purpose in classifying them this way.

3. Peter L. Mangione and his colleagues have initiated a social campaign called "For Our Babies." Visit their website, *forourbabies.org*, and write a critical EVALUATION of the organization's "Call to Action" (a PDF on the "Who We Are" section of the site) or some other aspect of their campaign.

4. Write a PROFILE of a child: your subject can be a sibling; a child you have worked with, for example at a summer camp; or just a youngster you know or know about. Describe the child's personality and temperament, using the three-part classification system that Michelle Watson advocates if it helps you to understand your subject. But focus mostly on your subject as a person with distinctive traits and characteristics.

5. In collaboration with several classmates, discuss what each of you was like as a child. Each person should write out his or her story and share it with the group. Edit the stories together, and collect them into an "album."

You'll find quizzes on the readings at wwnorton.com/write/back-to-the-lake.

# A Classic Movie Poster

When we classify things or people, we divide them into different categories based on their distinguishing characteristics. Take movies, for example. Some of the most common types (or genres) are horror movies, musicals, westerns, romantic comedies, drama, action, and fantasy films—all categories based largely on plot and setting. As indicated by this classic movie poster, one familiar subtype of popular film—the high school movie—can be identified on the basis of its characters, and they are almost always types and stereotypes, at least at the beginning of the film. A brain, a beauty, a jock, a rebel, and a recluse: the types depicted in John Hughes's *The Breakfast Club* (1985), the definitive high school movie of the 1980s, have nothing in common, apparently, until they spend a Saturday together in detention at Shermer High. Baring their souls to each other is not the only thing that turns "five total strangers" into a tight-knit group of real people, at least for a day. They have a common enemy: "Alright, people," says Mr. Vernon, the assistant principal, "we're going to try something different today. I want you to write an essay, of no less than a thousand words, describing to me who you think you are." Of course one student in the group, Brian Johnson ("the brain"), does all the work in what is supposed to be a collaborative assignment—"You see us as a brain, an athlete, a basket case, a princess, and a criminal. Correct?"—but he signs the essay for one and all as: "The Breakfast Club." Such is the transformative nature of high school—and of a well-designed writing prompt using classification.

[ **FOR WRITING** ] ··································································

"A brain, a beauty, a jock, a rebel, and a recluse": do some
research on *The Breakfast Club*, and write a paragraph or
two identifying the characters in the poster according to
the category each one belongs to. Indicate how the actors
in the film fulfill the demands of their respective roles.

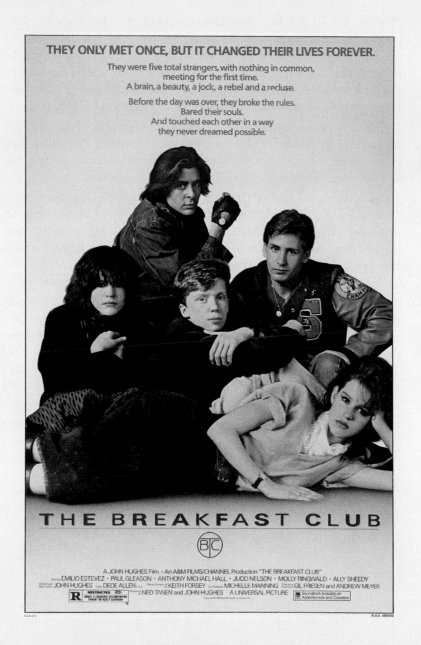

# SUGGESTIONS FOR WRITING

1. "We lie. We all do" says Stephanie Ericsson in "The Ways We Lie," p. 409. Read Ericsson's classification of lies into the types she thinks we use most often, and write a **POSITION PAPER** supporting or contesting the premise that we all lie at least some of the time. If you agree with Ericsson, you might want to identify some additional types of your own. If not, you might question some of the specific types of lies she mentions.

2. Do a critical **EVALUATION** of one of the essays, stories, or books by Amy Tan indicated in the headnote on p. 419. Be sure to mention Tan's use of language, particularly the various forms of English that her characters speak, as a way of establishing their ethnic and cultural identities.

3. As an American writer of Chinese ancestry, Amy Tan has been asked "Why there are not more Asian Americans represented in American literature. . . . Why do so many Chinese students go into engineering?" Read her tentative explanation on p. 424, and write a research **REPORT** or **POSITION PAPER** giving your own "broad sociological" answer to this question. Include plenty of evidence for your conclusions, and cite your sources.

4. "Many of the conversational rituals common among women," according to the sociolinguist Deborah Tannen, "are designed to take the other person's feelings into account, while many of the conversational rituals common among men are designed to maintain the one-up position." Read Tannen's "But What Do You Mean?" on p. 437, and write a **PROPOSAL** for a study or experiment you would conduct to confirm (or contest) what she says about the "different ways of speaking" between men and women.

5. In 400–500 words, write a **RHETORICAL ANALYSIS** of one of Anne Sexton's poems. Some of her major collections of poetry are listed in the headnote on p. 445.

# The Ways We Lie

Stephanie Ericsson (b. 1953) was two months pregnant with her first child when her husband suddenly died. Already an author of screenplays and two books about addiction, Ericsson poured her grief into her journals, which were excerpted in the *Utne Reader* and then collected in a volume of essays, *Companion Through the Darkness: Inner Dialogues on Grief* (1993). The book struck a chord with both critics and readers.

"There are many ways to lie," writes Ericsson in this essay from the *Utne Reader*. Beginning with a broad definition of *lie*, "The Ways We Lie" identifies some of the most common kinds, including the falsehoods we tell ourselves as well as those we inflict upon other people.

THE BANK CALLED TODAY and I told them my deposit was in the mail, even though I hadn't written a check yet. It'd been a rough day. The baby I'm pregnant with decided to do aerobics on my lungs for two hours, our three-year-old daughter painted the living-room couch with lipstick, the IRS put me on hold for an hour, and I was late to a business meeting because I was tired.

I told my client the traffic had been bad. When my partner came home, his haggard face told me his day hadn't gone any better than mine, so when he asked, "How was your day?" I said, "Oh, fine," knowing that one more straw might break his back. A friend called and wanted to take me to lunch. I said I was busy. Four lies in the course of a day, none of which I felt the least bit guilty about.

We lie. We all do. We exaggerate, we minimize, we avoid confrontation, we spare people's feelings, we conveniently forget, we keep secrets, we justify lying to the big-guy institutions. Like most people, I indulge in small falsehoods and still think of myself as an honest person. Sure I lie, but it doesn't hurt anything. Or does it?

I once tried going a whole week without telling a lie, and it was paralyzing. I discovered that telling the truth all the time is nearly impossible. It means living with some serious consequences: The bank charges me $60 in overdraft fees, my partner keels over when I tell him about my travails, my client fires me for telling her I didn't feel like being on time, and my friend takes it personally when I say I'm not hungry. There must be some merit to lying.

MLA CITATION: Ericsson, Stephanie. "The Ways We Lie." 1993. *Back to the Lake*. Ed. Thomas Cooley. 3rd ed. New York: Norton, 2015. 409–16. Print.

But if I justify lying, what makes me any different from slick politicians or the corporate robbers who raided the S&L industry?[1] Saying it's okay to lie one way and not another is hedging. I cannot seem to escape the voice deep inside me that tells me: When someone lies, someone loses.

See p. 396 for more about using definition along with classification. What far-reaching consequences will I, or others, pay as a result of my lie? Will someone's trust be destroyed? Will someone else pay *my* penance because I ducked out? We must consider the *meaning of our actions*. Deception, lies, capital crimes, and misdemeanors all carry meanings. *Webster's* definition of *lie* is specific:

1. a false statement or action especially made with the intent to deceive;
2. anything that gives or is meant to give a false impression.

A definition like this implies that there are many, many ways to tell a lie. Here are just a few.

## The White Lie

A man who won't lie to a woman has very little consideration for her feelings.
—BERGEN EVANS

The white lie assumes that the truth will cause more damage than a simple, harmless untruth. Telling a friend he looks great when he looks like hell can be based on a decision that the friend needs a compliment more than a frank opinion. But, in effect, it is the liar deciding what is best for the lied to. Ultimately, it is a vote of no confidence. It is an act of subtle arrogance for anyone to decide what is best for someone else.

Yet not all circumstances are quite so cut-and-dried. Take, for instance, the sergeant in Vietnam who knew one of his men was killed in action but listed him as missing so that the man's family would receive indefinite compensation instead of the lump-sum pittance the military gives widows and children. His intent was honorable. Yet for twenty years this family kept their hopes alive, unable to move on to a new life.

## Facades

Et tu, Brute?
—CAESAR

We all put up facades to one degree or another. When I put on a suit to go to see a client, I feel as though I am putting on another face, obeying the expectation that

---

1. *S&L industry:* Savings and loan (S&L) associations accept savings deposits from consumers and issue home mortgage loans. In the S&L crisis of the 1980s, more than a thousand independent savings and loan institutions in America collapsed, costing the U.S. government an estimated $125 billion and probably contributing to the economic recession of the early 1990s.

serious businesspeople wear suits rather than sweatpants. But I'm a writer. Normally, I get up, get the kid off to school, and sit at my computer in my pajamas until four in the afternoon. When I answer the phone, the caller thinks I'm wearing a suit (though the UPS man knows better).

But facades can be destructive because they are used to seduce others into an illusion. For instance, I recently realized that a former friend was a liar. He presented himself with all the right looks and the right words and offered lots of new consciousness theories, fabulous books to read, and fascinating insights. Then I did some business with him, and the time came for him to pay me. He turned out to be all talk and no walk. I heard a plethora of reasonable excuses, including in-depth descriptions of the big break around the corner. In six months of work, I saw less than a hundred bucks. When I confronted him, he raised both eyebrows and tried to convince me that I'd heard him wrong, that he'd made no commitment to me. A simple investigation into his past revealed a crowded graveyard of disenchanted former friends. 10

## Ignoring the Plain Facts

> Well, you must understand that Father Porter is only human. . . .
>
> —A MASSACHUSETTS PRIEST

In the '60s, the Catholic Church in Massachusetts began hearing complaints that Father James Porter was sexually molesting children. Rather than relieving him of his duties, the ecclesiastical authorities simply moved him from one parish to another between 1960 and 1967, actually providing him with a fresh supply of unsuspecting families and innocent children to abuse. After treatment in 1967 for pedophilia, he went back to work, this time in Minnesota. The new diocese was aware of Father Porter's obsession with children, but they needed priests and recklessly believed treatment had cured him. More children were abused until he was relieved of his duties a year later. By his own admission, Porter may have abused as many as a hundred children. 11

Ignoring the facts may not in and of itself be a form of lying, but consider the context of this situation. If a lie is *a false action done with the intent to deceive*, then the Catholic Church's conscious covering for Porter created irreparable consequences. The church became a co-perpetrator with Porter. 12

## Deflecting

> When you have no basis for an argument, abuse the plaintiff.      —CICERO

I've discovered that I can keep anyone from seeing the true me by being selectively blatant. I set a precedent of being up-front about intimate issues, but I never bring 13 up the things I truly want to hide; I just let people assume I'm revealing everything. It's an effective way of hiding.

Any good liar knows that the way to perpetuate an untruth is to deflect attention from it. When Clarence Thomas[2] exploded with accusations that the Senate hearings were a "high-tech lynching," he simply switched the focus from a highly charged subject to a radioactive subject. Rather than defending himself, he took the offensive and accused the country of racism. It was a brilliant maneuver. Racism is now politically incorrect in official circles—unlike sexual harassment, which still rewards those who can get away with it.

Some of the most skillful deflectors are passive-aggressive people who, when accused of inappropriate behavior, refuse to respond to the accusations. This you-don't-exist stance infuriates the accuser, who, understandably, screams something obscene out of frustration. The trap is sprung and the act of deflection successful, because now the passive-aggressive person can indignantly say, "Who can talk to someone as unreasonable as you?" The real issue is forgotten and the sins of the original victim become the focus. Feeling guilty of name-calling, the victim is fully tamed and crawls into a hole, ashamed. I have watched this fighting technique work thousands of times in disputes between men and women, and what I've learned is that the real culprit is not necessarily the one who swears the loudest.

## Omission

The cruelest lies are often told in silence.            —R. L. STEVENSON

Omission involves telling most of the truth minus one or two key facts whose absence changes the story completely. You break a pair of glasses that are guaranteed under normal use and get a new pair, without mentioning that the first pair broke during a rowdy game of basketball. Who hasn't tried something like that? But what about omission of information that could make a difference in how a person lives his or her life?

For instance, one day I found out that rabbinical legends tell of another woman in the Garden of Eden before Eve. I was stunned. The omission of the Sumerian goddess Lilith from Genesis—as well as her demonization by ancient misogynists as an embodiment of female evil—felt like spiritual robbery. I felt like I'd just found out my mother was really my stepmother. To take seriously the tradition that Adam was created out of the same mud as his equal counterpart, Lilith, redefines all of Judeo-Christian history.

2. *Clarence Thomas*: U.S. Supreme Court justice who was accused of sexual harassment during his 1991 Senate confirmation hearings.

Some renegade Catholic feminists introduced me to a view of Lilith that had 18
been suppressed during the many centuries when this strong goddess was seen
only as a spirit of evil. Lilith was a proud goddess who defied Adam's need to control her, attempted negotiations, and when this failed, said adios and left the Garden of Eden.

This omission of Lilith from the Bible was a patriarchal strategy to keep women 19
weak. Omitting the strong-woman archetype of Lilith from Western religions and
starting the story with Eve the Rib has helped keep Christian and Jewish women
believing they were the lesser sex for thousands of years.

## Stereotypes and Clichés

> Where opinion does not exist, the status quo becomes stereotyped and all
> originality is discouraged. —BERTRAND RUSSELL

Stereotype and cliché serve a purpose as a form of shorthand. Our need for vast 20
amounts of information in nanoseconds has made the stereotype vital to modern
communication. Unfortunately, it often shuts down original thinking, giving those
hungry for the truth a candy bar of misinformation instead of a balanced meal. The
stereotype explains a situation with just enough truth to seem unquestionable.

All the "isms"—racism, sexism, ageism, et al.—are founded on and fueled by the 21
stereotype and the cliché, which are lies of exaggeration, omission, and ignorance.
They are always dangerous. They take a single tree and make it a landscape. They
destroy curiosity. They close minds and separate people. The single mother on welfare is assumed to be cheating. Any black male could tell you how much of his
identity is obliterated daily by stereotypes. Fat people, ugly people, beautiful people, old people, large-breasted women, short men, the mentally ill, and the homeless all could tell you how much more they are like us than we want to think. I
once admitted to a group of people that I had a mouth like a truck driver. Much to
my surprise, a man stood up and said, "I'm a truck driver, and I never cuss." Needless to say, I was humbled.

## Groupthink

> Who is more foolish, the child afraid of the dark, or the man afraid of
> the light? —MAURICE FREEHILL

Irving Janis, in *Victims of GroupThink*, defines this sort of lie as a psychological phe- 22
nomenon within decision-making groups in which loyalty to the group has become
more important than any other value, with the result that dissent and the appraisal
of alternatives are suppressed. If you've ever worked on a committee or in a
corporation, you've encountered groupthink. It requires a combination of other

forms of lying—ignoring facts, selective memory, omission, and denial, to name a few.

The textbook example of groupthink came on December 7, 1941. From as early as the fall of 1941, the warnings came in, one after another, that Japan was preparing for a massive military operation. The Navy command in Hawaii assumed Pearl Harbor was invulnerable—the Japanese weren't stupid enough to attack the United States' most important base. On the other hand, racist stereotypes said the Japanese weren't smart enough to invent a torpedo effective in less than 60 feet of water (the fleet was docked in 30 feet); after all, U.S. technology hadn't been able to do it. 23

On Friday, December 5, normal weekend leave was granted to all the commanders at Pearl Harbor, even though the Japanese consulate in Hawaii was busy burning papers. Within the tight, good-ole-boy cohesiveness of the U.S. command in Hawaii, the myth of invulnerability stayed well entrenched. No one in the group considered the alternatives. The rest is history. 24

### Out-and-Out Lies

The only form of lying that is beyond reproach is lying for its own sake.

—OSCAR WILDE

Of all the ways to lie, I like this one the best, probably because I get tired of trying to figure out the real meanings behind things. At least I can trust the bald-faced lie. I once asked my five-year-old nephew, "Who broke the fence?" (I had seen him do it.) He answered, "The murderers." Who could argue? 25

At least when this sort of lie is told it can be easily confronted. As the person who is lied to, I know where I stand. The bald-faced lie doesn't toy with my perceptions—it argues with them. It doesn't try to refashion reality, it tries to refute it. *Read my lips.*[3] . . . No sleight of hand. No guessing. If this were the only form of lying, there would be no such thing as floating anxiety or the adult-children-of-alcoholics movement. 26

### Dismissal

Pay no attention to that man behind the curtain! I am the Great Oz!

—THE WIZARD OF OZ

Dismissal is perhaps the slipperiest of all lies. Dismissing feelings, perceptions, or even the raw facts of a situation ranks as a kind of lie that can do as much damage to a person as any other kind of lie. 27

---

3. *Read my lips*: A phrase made especially famous during President George H. W. Bush's 1988 election campaign. He emphatically said, "Read my lips: no new taxes." Once in office, he did raise taxes.

The roots of many mental disorders can be traced back to the dismissal of real- 28
ity. Imagine that a person is told from the time she is a tot that her perceptions are
inaccurate. *"Mommy, I'm scared."* "No, you're not, darling." *"I don't like that man next
door, he makes me feel icky."* "Johnny, that's a terrible thing to say, of course you like
him. You go over there right now and be nice to him."

I've often mused over the idea that madness is actually a sane reaction to an 29
insane world. Psychologist R. D. Laing supports this hypothesis in *Sanity, Madness
& the Family*, an account of his investigations into families of schizophrenics. The
common thread that ran through all of the families he studied was a deliberate,
staunch dismissal of the patient's perceptions from a very early age. Each of the
patients started out with an accurate grasp of reality, which, through meticulous
and methodical dismissal, was demolished until the only reality the patient could
trust was catatonia.

Dismissal runs the gamut. Mild dismissal can be quite handy for forgiving the 30
foibles of others in our day-to-day lives. Toddlers who have just learned to manip-
ulate their parents' attention sometimes are dismissed out of necessity. Absolute
attention from the parents would require so much energy that no one would get
to eat dinner. But we must be careful and attentive about how far we take our
"necessary" dismissals. Dismissal is a dangerous tool, because it's nothing less
than a lie.

## Delusion

> We lie loudest when we lie to ourselves.               —ERIC HOFFER

I could write the book on this one. Delusion, a cousin of dismissal, is the tendency 31
to see excuses as facts. It's a powerful lying tool because it filters out information
that contradicts what we want to believe. Alcoholics who believe that the problems
in their lives are legitimate reasons for drinking rather than results of the drinking
offer the classic example of deluded thinking. Delusion uses the mind's ability to
see things in myriad ways to support what it wants to be the truth.

But delusion is also a survival mechanism we all use. If we were to fully contem- 32
plate the consequences of our stockpiles of nuclear weapons or global warming, we
could hardly function on a day-to-day level. We don't want to incorporate that
much reality into our lives because to do so would be paralyzing.

Delusion acts as an adhesive to keep the status quo intact. It shamelessly employs 33
dismissal, omission, and amnesia, among other sorts of lies. Its most cunning
defense is that it cannot see itself.

> The liar's punishment . . . is that he cannot believe anyone else.
>                                    —GEORGE BERNARD SHAW

These are only a few of the ways we lie. Or are lied to. As I said earlier, it's not easy  34
to entirely eliminate lies from our lives. No matter how pious we may try to be, we
will still embellish, hedge, and omit to lubricate the daily machinery of living. But
there is a world of difference between telling functional lies and living a lie. Martin
Buber once said, "The lie is the spirit committing treason against itself." Our acceptance of lies becomes a cultural cancer that eventually shrouds and reorders reality
until moral garbage becomes as invisible to us as water is to a fish.

How much do we tolerate before we become sick and tired of being sick and  35
tired? When will we stand up and declare our *right* to trust? When do we stop
accepting that the real truth is in the fine print? Whose lips do we read this year
when we vote for president? When will we stop being so reticent about making
judgments? When do we stop turning over our personal power and responsibility
to liars?

Maybe if I don't tell the bank the check's in the mail I'll be less tolerant of the  36
lies told me every day. A country song I once heard said it all for me: "You've got to
stand for something or you'll fall for anything." ◆

## FOR CLOSE READING

1. According to Ericsson, what basic characteristics do all lies have in common? How,
   and how well, do the kinds of lies she lists fit this basic **DEFINITION**?

2. Ericsson classifies lies into ten different categories. Which kinds of lies does she
   herself admit to committing? Who does she say commits the other kinds?

3. Some kinds of lies, says Ericsson, are more serious than others. Which kinds does
   she find least harmful? Which kinds do the most damage? How?

4. Why doesn't Ericsson get more worked up about "out-and-out" (or "bald-faced")
   lies (25–26)?

5. "We lie," says Ericsson. "We all do" (3). Do you agree? Why or why not?

6. "We must consider the *meaning of our actions*," says Ericsson (6). Why? What reasons does she give for taking responsibility for our lies? Do you agree with Ericsson's
   **ARGUMENT**, especially with what she says about "trust" (25, 35)? Why or why not?

## Strategies and Structures

1. Throughout her essay, Ericsson admits that she tells lies. Why do you think she
   adopts this confessional strategy? How effective do you find it? Why?

2. Why is Ericsson classifying lies in this essay? Where does she state her main point in doing so most directly?

3. Ericsson identifies the main characteristics, as she sees them, of each category of lie that she discusses. How significant do you find these characteristics?

4. Ericsson says that some kinds of lies, such as "groupthink," are made up of "a combination of other forms of lying" (22). Does this sort of overlapping invalidate her system? Why or why not?

5. Ericsson warns against stereotyping in paragraphs 20–21. On what basis does she object to stereotypes? Can she be accused of engaging in this practice at any point in her essay? Explain your answer by referring to specific kinds of lies and their characteristics.

6. *Other Methods.* Ericsson gives EXAMPLES of each of the different categories of lies. Which examples do you find most effective? Least effective? Explain.

## Thinking about Language

1. What are the differences between a white lie (7–8) and an out-and-out lie (25–26)? What are the CONNOTATIONS of each expression?

2. Ericsson quotes R. L. Stevenson as saying, "The cruelest lies are often told in silence." How can lying be committed in silence?

3. Ericsson writes that "our acceptance of lies becomes a cultural cancer" (34). Why do you think she uses the expression "cultural cancer"?

## FOR WRITING

1. Have you ever lied in one or more of the ways that Ericsson cites? Write a paragraph or two on each kind of lie you've told, giving examples from your own experience but classifying them according to Ericsson's categories.

2. Using classification, write an essay on the ways people do one of the following: tell the truth, avoid work, make friends, break with friends, find a job, quit a job, or delude themselves.

3. Ericsson begins her characterization of each type of lie with an epigraph—a quotation appropriate to the text that follows. In collaboration with several classmates, compile a list of alternate epigraphs to replace some of the ones Ericsson has supplied.

4. In your journal, keep a record of the lies you hear, tell, or are tempted to tell. Take note of the context of each lie and what you actually did and said in that situation. Reflect upon the different types of lies, the occasions and reasons for them, and the results of telling them (or not).

5. "A man who won't lie to a woman," Ericsson quotes the writer and editor Bergan Evans as saying, "has very little consideration for her feelings" (7). Do you agree, or is this misogynistic nonsense—or humor, ill-advised or otherwise? Using this provocative statement as a starting point, write a brief essay arguing a POSITION on the issue of the value of white lies in general and the white lie by men to women—or the reverse—in particular.

You'll find quizzes on the readings at
wwnorton.com/write/back-to-the-lake.

# Mother Tongue

Amy Tan (b. 1952), a daughter of Chinese immigrants, was born in Oakland, California. She earned an MA in linguistics from San Jose State University and worked on programs for disabled children before becoming a free-lance business writer. In 1987 she visited China for the first time. On returning to the United States, she set to work on a collection of intercon-nected stories about Chinese American mothers and daughters. *The Joy Luck Club* (1989) was an international success, and was translated into sev-enteen languages (including Chinese). Since then Tan has published sev-eral novels, including *The Kitchen God's Wife* (1991), *The Bonesetter's Daughter* (2001), and *The Valley of Amazement* (2013)—in addition to two children's books and a book of nonfiction, *The Opposite of Fate: A Book of Musings* (2003), which explores lucky accidents, choice, and memory.

In her essay "Mother Tongue," which first appeared in the literary magazine *Threepenny Review* in 1990, Tan classifies various forms of the English language, from her mother's "broken English" (a term she dislikes) to the complex prose of academia. "And I use them all," she writes "all the Englishes I grew up with."

I AM NOT A SCHOLAR OF ENGLISH or literature. I cannot give you much more    1
than personal opinions on the English language and its variations in this country or others.

I am a writer. And by that definition, I am someone who has always loved lan-    2
guage. I am fascinated by language in daily life. I spend a great deal of my time
thinking about the power of language—the way it can evoke an emotion, a visual
image, a complex idea, or a simple truth. Language is the tool of my trade. And I
use them all—all the Englishes I grew up with.

Recently, I was made keenly aware of the different Englishes I do use. I was giv-    3
ing a talk to a large group of people, the same talk I had already given to half a
dozen other groups. The nature of the talk was about my writing, my life, and my
book, *The Joy Luck Club*. The talk was going along well enough, until I remembered
one major difference that made the whole talk sound wrong. My mother was in the
room. And it was perhaps the first time she had heard me give a lengthy speech,

MLA CITATION: Tan, Amy. "Mother Tongue." 1990. *Back to the Lake*. Ed. Thomas Cooley. 3rd ed. New York: Norton, 2015. 419–24. Print.

using the kind of English I have never used with her. I was saying things like, "The intersection of memory upon imagination" and "There is an aspect of my fiction that relates to thus-and-thus"—a speech filled with carefully wrought grammatical phrases, burdened, it suddenly seemed to me, with nominalized forms, past perfect tenses, conditional phrases, all the forms of standard English that I had learned in school and through books, the forms of English I did not use at home with my mother.

Just last week, I was walking down the street with my mother, and I again found   4
myself conscious of the English I was using, the English I do use with her. We were talking about the price of new and used furniture and I heard myself saying this: "Not waste money that way." My husband was with us as well, and he didn't notice any switch in my English. And then I realized why. It's because over the twenty years we've been together I've often used the same kind of English with him, and sometimes he even uses it with me. It has become our language of intimacy, a different sort of English that relates to family talk, the language I grew up with.

So you'll have some idea of what this family talk I heard sounds like, I'll quote   5
what my mother said during a recent conversation which I videotaped and then transcribed. During this conversation, my mother was talking about a political gangster in Shanghai who had the same last name as her family's, Du, and how the

gangster in his early years wanted to be adopted by her family, which was rich by comparison. Later, the gangster became more powerful, far richer than my mother's family, and one day showed up at my mother's wedding to pay his respects. Here's what she said in part:

"Du Yusong having business like fruit stand. Like off the street kind. He is Du like Du Zong—but not Tsung-ming Island people. The local people call putong, the river east side, he belong to that side local people. That man want to ask Du Zong father take him in like become own family. Du Zong father wasn't look down on him, but didn't take seriously, until that man big like become a mafia. Now important person, very hard to inviting him. Chinese way, came only to show respect, don't stay for dinner. Respect for making big celebration, he shows up. Mean gives lots of respect. Chinese custom. Chinese social life that way. If too important won't have to stay too long. He come to my wedding. I didn't see, I heard it. I gone to boy's side, they have YMCA dinner. Chinese age I was nineteen." 6

You should know that my mother's expressive command of English belies how much she actually understands. She reads the *Forbes*[1] report, listens to *Wall Street Week*, converses daily with her stockbroker, reads all of Shirley MacLaine's books with ease—all kinds of things I can't begin to understand. Yet some of my friends tell me they understand 50 percent of what my mother says. Some say they understand 80 to 90 percent. Some say they understand none of it, as if she were speaking pure Chinese. But to me, my mother's English is perfectly clear, perfectly natural. It's my mother tongue. Her language, as I hear it, is vivid, direct, full of observation and imagery. That was the language that helped shape the way I saw things, expressed things, made sense of the world. 7

Lately, I've been giving more thought to the kind of English my mother speaks. Like others, I have described it to people as "broken" or "fractured" English. But I wince when I say that. It has always bothered me that I can think of no way to describe it other than "broken," as if it were damaged and needed to be fixed, as if it lacked a certain wholeness and soundness. I've heard other terms used, "limited English," for example. But they seem just as bad, as if everything is limited, including people's perceptions of the limited English speaker. 8

I know this for a fact, because when I was growing up, my mother's "limited" English limited *my* perception of her. I was ashamed of her English. I believed that her English reflected the quality of what she had to say. That is, because she expressed them imperfectly her thoughts were imperfect. And I had plenty of 9

---

1. *Forbes*: A business-oriented periodical that focuses on stocks, bonds, business trends, and other items of interest to investors.

empirical evidence to support me: the fact that people in department stores, at banks, and at restaurants did not take her seriously, did not give her good service, pretended not to understand her, or even acted as if they did not hear her.

My mother has long realized the limitations of her English as well. When I was 10 fifteen, she used to have me call people on the phone to pretend I was she. In this guise, I was forced to ask for information or even to complain and yell at people who had been rude to her. One time it was a call to her stockbroker in New York. She had cashed out her small portfolio and it just so happened we were going to go to New York the next week, our very first trip outside California. I had to get on the phone and say in an adolescent voice that was not very convincing, "This is Mrs. Tan."

And my mother was standing in the back whispering loudly, "Why he don't send 11 me check, already two weeks late. So mad he lie to me, losing me money."

And then I said in perfect English, "Yes, I'm getting rather concerned. You had 12 agreed to send the check two weeks ago, but it hasn't arrived."

Then she began to talk more loudly. "What he want, I come to New York tell 13 him front of his boss, you cheating me?" And I was trying to calm her down, make her be quiet, while telling the stockbroker, "I can't tolerate any more excuses. If I don't receive the check immediately, I am going to have to speak to your manager when I'm in New York next week." And sure enough, the following week there we were in front of this astonished stockbroker, and I was sitting there red-faced and quiet, and my mother, the real Mrs. Tan, was shouting at his boss in her impeccable broken English.

We used a similar routine just five days ago, for a situation that was far less 14 humorous. My mother had gone to the hospital for an appointment, to find out about a benign brain tumor a CAT scan had revealed a month ago. She said she had spoken very good English, her best English, no mistakes. Still, she said, the hospital did not apologize when they said they had lost the CAT scan and she had come for nothing. She said they did not seem to have any sympathy when she told them she was anxious to know the exact diagnosis, since her husband and son had both died of brain tumors. She said they would not give her any more information until the next time and she would have to make another appointment for that. So she said she would not leave until the doctor called her daughter. She wouldn't budge. And when the doctor finally called her daughter, me, who spoke in perfect English—lo and behold—we had assurances the CAT scan would be found, promises that a conference call on Monday would be held, and apologies for any suffering my mother had gone through for a most regrettable mistake.

I think my mother's English almost had an effect on limiting my possibilities in 15 life as well. Sociologists and linguists probably will tell you that a person's developing language skills are more influenced by peers. But I do think that the language spoken in the family, especially in immigrant families which are more insular, plays a large role in shaping the language of the child. And I believe that it affected my results on achievement tests, IQ tests, and the SAT. While my English skills were never judged as poor, compared to math, English could not be considered my strong suit. In grade school I did moderately well, getting perhaps B's, sometimes B-pluses, in English and scoring perhaps in the sixtieth or seventieth percentile on achievement tests. But those scores were not good enough to override the opinion that my true abilities lay in math and science, because in those areas I achieved A's and scored in the ninetieth percentile or higher.

This was understandable. Math is precise; there is only one correct answer. 16 Whereas, for me at least, the answers on English tests were always a judgment call, a matter of opinion and personal experience. Those tests were constructed around items like fill-in-the-blank sentence completion, such as, "Even though Tom was _____, Mary thought he was _____." And the correct answer always seemed to be the most bland combinations of thoughts, for example, "Even though Tom was shy, Mary thought he was charming," with the grammatical structure "even though" limiting the correct answer to some sort of semantic opposites, so you wouldn't get answers like, "Even though Tom was foolish, Mary thought he was ridiculous." Well, according to my mother, there were very few limitations as to what Tom could have been and what Mary might have thought of him. So I never did well on tests like that.

The same was true with word analogies, pairs of words in which you were sup- 17 posed to find some sort of logical, semantic relationship—for example, "*Sunset* is to *nightfall* as _____ is to _____." And here you would be presented with a list of four possible pairs, one of which showed the same kind of relationship: *red* is to *stoplight, bus* is to *arrival, chills* is to *fever, yawn* is to *boring.* Well, I could never think that way. I knew what the tests were asking, but I could not block out of my mind the images already created by the first pair, "*sunset* is to *nightfall*"—and I would see a burst of colors against a darkening sky, the moon rising, the lowering of a curtain of stars. And all the other pairs of words—red, bus, stoplight, boring— just threw up a mass of confusing images, making it impossible for me to sort out something as logical as saying: "A sunset precedes nightfall" is the same as "a chill precedes a fever." The only way I would have gotten that answer right would have been to imagine an associative situation, for example, my being disobedient and staying out past sunset, catching a chill at night, which turns into feverish pneumonia as punishment, which indeed did happen to me.

I have been thinking about all this lately, about my mother's English, about achieve- 18 ment tests. Because lately I've been asked, as a writer, why there are not more Asian Americans represented in American literature. Why are there few Asian Americans enrolled in creative writing programs? Why do so many Chinese students go into engineering? Well, these are broad sociological questions I can't begin to answer. But I have noticed in surveys—in fact, just last week—that Asian students, as a whole, always do significantly better on math achievement tests than in English. And this makes me think that there are other Asian-American students whose English spoken in the home might also be described as "broken" or "limited." And perhaps they also have teachers who are steering them away from writing and into math and science, which is what happened to me.

Fortunately, I happen to be rebellious in nature and enjoy the challenge of disproving assumptions made about me. I became an English major my first year in college, after being enrolled as pre-med. I started writing nonfiction as a freelancer the week after I was told by my former boss that writing was my worst skill and I should hone my talents toward account management.    19

For pointers on using classification to serve a larger purpose, see p. 388.

But it wasn't until 1985 that I finally began to write fiction. And at first I wrote using what I thought to be wittily crafted sentences, sentences that would finally prove I had mastery over the English language. Here's an example from the first draft of a story that later made its way into *The Joy Luck Club*, but without this line: "That was my mental quandary in its nascent state." A terrible line, which I can barely pronounce.    20

Fortunately, for reasons I won't get into today, I later decided I should envision a reader for the stories I would write. And the reader I decided upon was my mother, because these were stories about mothers. So with this reader in mind—and in fact she did read my early drafts—I began to write stories using all the Englishes I grew up with: the English I spoke to my mother, which for lack of a better term might be described as "simple"; the English she used with me, which for lack of a better term might be described as "broken"; my translation of her Chinese, which could certainly be described as "watered down"; and what I imagined to be her translation of her Chinese if she could speak in perfect English, her internal language, and for that I sought to preserve the essence, but neither an English nor a Chinese structure. I wanted to capture what language ability tests can never reveal: her intent, her passion, her imagery, the rhythms of her speech and the nature of her thoughts.    21

Apart from what any critic had to say about my writing, I knew I had succeeded where it counted when my mother finished reading my book and gave me her verdict: "So easy to read." ◆    22

## FOR CLOSE READING

1. Amy Tan classifies the various "Englishes" that she uses into two basic categories. What are they, and what are the main characteristics of each kind?

2. How many different types of English did Tan learn from talking with her mother, a native speaker of Chinese? What are the different attributes of each type?

3. According to Tan, what are the essential attributes of "standard" English (3)? How did she learn to use this kind of English?

4. Which kinds of English does Tan use most often as a writer? Why?

## Strategies and Structures

1. "So you'll have some idea of what this family talk I heard sounds like, I'll quote what my mother said during a recent conversation" (5). Here and elsewhere in her essay Tan addresses the reader directly as "you." Why do you think she does this?

2. Why is Tan classifying the different kinds of English she knows and uses? Is she, for example, conveying information, arguing a point, telling an entertaining story— some other purpose? Explain.

3. Should Tan have laid out her classification system more fully at the beginning of her essay instead of waiting until the end? Why or why not?

4. In paragraphs 15–18, Tan advances an ARGUMENT about IQ and achievement tests. What's her point here, and how does she use classification to support it?

5. *Other Methods.* Tan classifies "all the Englishes" she grew up with in paragraph 21, near the end of her essay. How well does this classification system fit the specific EXAMPLES she has cited earlier? Explain.

## Thinking about Language

1. Explain the PUN in Tan's title. How does it prepare us for the rest of her essay?

2. Tan does not want to use "broken" or "fractured" as names for the kind of English her mother speaks (8). Why not?

3. Tan never gives a name to the kind of English she uses to represent her mother's "internal language" (21). What would you call it? Why?

## FOR WRITING

1. In a paragraph or two, give several examples of "standard" (or "nonstandard") English, and explain why they belong in this category.

2. How many different kinds of English, or other languages, do you use at home, at school, or among friends? Write an essay classifying them, and explaining how and when you use each type.

3. To prove her "mastery" of formal English, says Tan, she wrote sentences like the following: "This was my mental quandary in its nascent state" (20). Analyze this statement (including the rhythm and pronunciation of the words), and write a paragraph explaining why it is (or is not) "a terrible line" (20).

4. In your journal, keep a record of the different kinds of English you hear at school and in the media, including social media. Over time, try to develop a system for classifying the different kinds.

5. Write a **LITERACY NARRATIVE** telling about and analyzing your experience with one of the following: standardized and other language tests; learning a second language; conversing with non-native speakers of English; showing your "mastery" of formal written or spoken English; conversing with speakers of English when English is not your first language.

You'll find quizzes on the readings at
wwnorton.com/write/back-to-the-lake.

MINDY KALING

# Types of Women in Romantic Comedies Who Are Not Real

Mindy Kaling (b. 1979) is an actor, comedian, writer, and producer who has been listed among the "50 Coolest and Most Creative Entertainers" by *Entertainment Weekly*. Kaling was born Vera Mindy Chokalingam in Cambridge, Massachusetts. Her parents, who immigrated from India, picked her "cute American name" from the TV show *Mork & Mindy*. A graduate of Dartmouth College with a degree in playwriting, Kaling has been nominated for several Emmy Awards for her work on the NBC sitcom *The Office* and the Fox sitcom *The Mindy Project*, featuring her character Mindy Lahiri. Kaling has also acted in a number of films, including *The 40-Year-Old Virgin* (2005), *Wreck-It Ralph* (2012), *The Five-Year Engagement* (2012), and *This Is the End* (2013).

"Types of Women in Romantic Comedies Who Are Not Real" is from Kaling's 2011 collection of essays, *Is Everyone Hanging Out Without Me? (And Other Concerns)*. A classification of the types of female characters in a popular form of film and television, it is also a critical analysis of the genre.

WHEN I WAS A KID, Christmas vacation meant renting VHS copies of romantic comedies from Blockbuster and watching them with my parents at home. *Sleepless in Seattle* was big, and so was *When Harry Met Sally*. I laughed along with everyone else at the scene where Meg Ryan fakes an orgasm at the restaurant without even knowing what an orgasm was. In my mind, she was just being kind of loud and silly at a diner, and that was hilarious enough for me.

I love romantic comedies. I feel almost sheepish writing that, because the genre has been so degraded in the past twenty years or so that admitting you like these movies is essentially an admission of mild stupidity. But that has not stopped me from watching them.

I enjoy watching people fall in love on-screen so much that I can suspend my disbelief for the contrived situations that only happen in the heightened world of romantic comedies. I have come to enjoy the moment when the normal lead guy,

MLA CITATION: Kaling, Mindy. "Types of Women in Romantic Comedies Who Are Not Real." 2011. *Back to the Lake*. Ed. Thomas Cooley. 3rd ed. New York: Norton, 2015. 427–30. Print.

say, slips and falls right on top of the hideously expensive wedding cake. I actually feel robbed when the female lead's dress *doesn't* get torn open at a baseball game while the JumboTron is on her. I simply regard romantic comedies as a subgenre of sci-fi, in which the world created therein has different rules than my regular human world. Then I just lap it up. There is no difference between Ripley from *Alien* and any Katherine Heigl character. They're all participating in the same level of made-up awesomeness, and I enjoy every second of it.

For help with less awesome principles of classification, see p. 390.

So it makes sense that in this world there are many specimens of  4
women who I do not think exist in real life, like Vulcans or UFO people or whatever. They are:

### The Klutz

When a beautiful actress is in a movie, executives wrack their brains to find some  5
kind of flaw in her that still allows her to be palatable. She can't be overweight or not perfect-looking, because who would want to see that? A not 100-percent-perfect-looking-in-every-way female? You might as well film a dead squid decaying on a beach somewhere for two hours.

So they make her a Klutz.  6

The 100-percent-perfect-looking female is perfect in every way, except that  7
she constantly falls down. She bonks her head on things. She trips and falls and spills soup on her affable date. (Josh Lucas. Is that his name? I know it's two first names. Josh George? Brad Mike? Fred Tom? Yes, it's Fred Tom.) Our Klutz clangs into Stop signs while riding a bike, and knocks over giant displays of expensive fine china. Despite being five foot nine and weighing 110 pounds, she is basically like a drunk buffalo who has never been a part of human society. But Fred Tom loves her anyway.

### The Ethereal Weirdo

The smart and funny writer Nathan Rabin coined the term *Manic Pixie Dream Girl*  8
to describe a version of this archetype after seeing Kirsten Dunst in the movie *Elizabethtown*. This girl can't be pinned down and may or may not show up when you make concrete plans. She wears gauzy blouses and braids. She decides to dance in the rain and weeps uncontrollably if she sees a sign for a missing dog or cat. She spins a globe, places her finger on a random spot, and decides to move there. This ethereal weirdo abounds in movies, but nowhere else. If she were from real life, people would think she was a homeless woman and would cross the street to avoid her, but she is essential to the male fantasy that even if a guy is boring, he deserves

a woman who will find him fascinating and pull him out of himself by forcing him to go skinny-dipping in a stranger's pool.

## The Woman Who Is Obsessed with Her Career and Is No Fun at All

I, Mindy Kaling, basically have two full-time jobs. I regularly work sixteen hours a  9
day. But like most of the other people I know who are similarly busy, I think I'm a pleasant, pretty normal person. I am slightly offended by the way busy working women my age are presented in film. I'm not, like, always barking orders into my hands-free phone device and telling people constantly, "I have no time for this!" I didn't completely forget how to be nice or feminine because I have a career. Also, since when does having a job necessitate women having their hair pulled back in a severe, tight bun? Often this uptight woman has to "re-learn" how to seduce a man because her estrogen leaked out of her from leading so many board meetings, and she has to do all sorts of crazy, unnecessary crap, like eat a hot dog in a libidinous way or something. Having a challenging job in movies means the compassionate, warm, or sexy side of your brain has fallen out.

## The Forty-Two-Year-Old Mother of the Thirty-Year-Old Male Lead

I am so accustomed to the young mom phenomenon, that when I saw the poster  10
for *The Proposal* I wondered for a second if the proposal in the movie was Ryan Reynolds suggesting he send his mother, Sandra Bullock, to an old-age home.

However, given the popularity of teen moms right now, this could actually be  11
the wave of the future.

## The Sassy Best Friend

You know that really horny and hilarious best friend who is always asking about  12
your relationship and has nothing really going on in her own life? She always wants to meet you in coffee shops or wants to go to Bloomingdale's to sample perfumes? She runs a chic dildo store in the West Village? Nope? Okay, that's this person.

## The Skinny Woman Who Is Beautiful and Toned
## But Also Gluttonous and Disgusting

Again, I am more than willing to suspend my disbelief during a romantic comedy  13
for good set decoration alone. One pristine kitchen from a Nancy Meyers movie

like in *It's Complicated* is worth five Diane Keatons being caught half-clad in a topi-ary or whatever situation her character has found herself in.

But sometimes even my suspended disbelief isn't enough. I am speaking of the 14 gorgeous and skinny heroine who is also a disgusting pig when it comes to food. And everyone in the movie—her parents, her friends, her boss—are all complicit in this huge lie. They are constantly telling her to stop eating and being such a glutton. And this actress, this poor skinny actress who so clearly lost weight to play the likable lead, has to say things like "Shut up you guys! I love cheesecake! If I want to eat an entire cheesecake, I will!" If you look closely, you can see this woman's ribs through the dress she's wearing—that's how skinny she is, this cheesecake-loving cow.

You wonder, as you sit and watch this movie, what the characters would do if 15 they were confronted by an actual average American woman. They would all kill themselves, which would actually be kind of an interesting movie.

### The Woman Who Works in an Art Gallery

How many freakin' art galleries are out there? Are people constantly buying visual 16 art or something? This posh-smart-classy job is a favorite in movies. It's in the same realm as kindergarten teacher in terms of accessibility: guys don't really get it, but the trappings of it are likable and nonthreatening.

> ART GALLERY WOMAN: Dust off the Rothko. We have an important buyer coming into town and this is a really big deal for my career. I have no time for this!

This is one of the rare clichés that actually has a male counterpart. Whenever 17 you meet a handsome, charming, successful man in a romantic comedy, the hero-ine's friend always says the same thing. "He's really successful—he's an . . .
(say it with me)                                                                              18
. . . architect!"                                                                               19
There are like nine people in the entire world who are architects, and one of 20 them is my dad. None of them looks like Patrick Dempsey. ◆

## FOR CLOSE READING

1. Why is Mindy Kaling reluctant to admit that she likes to watch romantic comedies? Why does she do it anyway?

2. "I, Mindy Kaling, basically have two full-time jobs" (9). Why does Kaling make this statement? Is her testimony appropriate here? Why or why not?

3. As depicted by Kaling, what roles do *men* play in romantic comedies? Are they equally "not real" as those of the women in Kaling's classification? Explain.

4. Which type(s) of women in her classification system does Kaling seem to find personally most difficult to accept? Why?

## Strategies and Structures

1. Although Kaling assumes that her readers already know what a romantic comedy is, she still indicates a number of the distinguishing features of the genre (2). What are some of them?

2. Kaling classifies the women in romantic comedies into seven different types. What do they generally have in common? Which categories do you find most valid and informative? Why?

3. Are Kaling's types all-inclusive, or can you think of others? For instance?

4. Kaling classifies romantic comedies as "a subgenre of sci-fi" (3)? Is this a valid way of classifying the form? Why or why not?

5. What is Kaling's PURPOSE in classifying the romantic comedy as a type of fantasy? Choose one of the following: (A) to criticize how the form has been "degraded" (2); (B) to celebrate the "made-up awesomeness" of the form (3); (C) to show she understands the material she is classifying; (D) all of the above? Explain.

## Thinking about Language

1. Kaling speaks twice of being able to "suspend my disbelief" (3, 13). Where did she get this phrase, the original form of which is "that willing suspension of disbelief"?

2. Why does Kaling describe herself as "sheepish"—as opposed to *wolfish* or *bullish*, say—for liking romantic comedies so much (2)?

3. Kaling refers to the types of women in her essay as "specimens" (4). Is this an apt term to use in setting up a classification system? Why or why not?

4. What is an *archetype* (8)? Are archetypes more likely to be found in life or in literature? Explain.

## FOR WRITING

1. Write your own classification of "types of" men or women who are "not real" in a genre of film, television, or video that you like to watch anyway. Be sure to explain what you like (or at least find fascinating) about the genre.

2. The term *romance* in literature and popular culture is usually applied to storylines in which readers or viewers expect to be "watching people fall in love" (3). Write a paragraph or two outlining what you can find out about the broader meaning of the term *romance* as a form of classification in literature. Be sure to include examples (such as *The Scarlet Letter: A Romance*).

3. Keep a viewer's journal as you watch (or rewatch) a favorite television show or type of film or video (including music videos). Give special attention in your notes to the traits and features that distinguish the particular type of show or sound you're watching or hearing.

4. One of the most common binary (or two-part) systems for classifying works of literature is as *comedy* or *tragedy*. (In this context, "comic" doesn't simply mean funny, though Shakespearian comedies, for example, often are.) Do a little research if necessary, and write a RHETORICAL ANALYSIS of 500–600 words in which you explain the traditional classification of works of dramatic literature as *comedies* or *tragedies*. Identify the most common features of the two types (and subtypes), and cite several examples that display them.

You'll find quizzes on the readings at
wwnorton.com/write/back-to-the-lake.

PAUL KRUGMAN

# E Pluribus Unum

Paul Krugman (b. 1953) won the Nobel Prize in economics in 2008 for his work explaining how patterns of international trade and wealth are related to economies of scale in production and to consumer preferences for certain brands in goods and services. He is widely known for his Op-Ed column in the *New York Times* and its accompanying blog, *The Conscience of a Liberal,* which is also the title of one of his more than twenty books. A graduate of MIT and Yale, Krugman has taught at both of those universities as well as Stanford, the London School of Economics, and Princeton. A member of the Council of Economic Advisers in the administration of President Ronald Reagan, he has written several textbooks for economics courses at both introductory and advanced levels. In *End This Depression Now!* (2012), Krugman argues that budget cuts and other austerity measures are contributing to the length and severity of the world-wide recession that began in 2008. Krugman plans to retire from his professorship at Princeton in 2015 in order to teach at the graduate center of the City University of New York.

"E Pluribus Unum" is Krugman's Op-Ed column from the *Times* for the Fourth of July 2013. In addition to classifying hot dogs and potato salad as fundamentally American eats, this essay also identifies the many types of people who make up the single nation with the motto *One out of many.*

I T'S THAT TIME OF YEAR—the long weekend when we gather with friends and 1
family to celebrate hot dogs, potato salad and, yes, the founding of our nation. And it's also a time for some of us to wax a bit philosophical, to wonder what, exactly, we're celebrating. Is America in 2013, in any meaningful sense, the same country that declared independence in 1776?

The answer, I'd suggest, is yes. Despite everything, there is a thread of continu- 2
ity in our national identity—reflected in institutions, ideas and, especially, in attitude—that remains unbroken. Above all, we are still, at root, a nation that believes in democracy, even if we don't always act on that belief.

MLA CITATION: Krugman, Paul. "E Pluribus Unum." 2013. *Back to the Lake.* Ed. Thomas Cooley. 3rd ed. New York: Norton, 2015. 433–35. Print.

And that's a remarkable thing when you bear in mind just how much the country has changed.   3

America in 1776 was a rural land, mainly composed of small farmers and, in the South, somewhat bigger farmers with slaves. And the free population consisted of, well, WASPs: almost all came from northwestern Europe, 65 percent came from Britain, and 98 percent were Protestants.   4

America today is nothing like that, even though some politicians—think Sarah Palin—like to talk as if the "real America" is still white, Protestant, and rural or small-town.   5

*Inclusive categories like rural and urban cover most cases but don't overlap, p. 396.*

But the real America is, in fact, a nation of metropolitan areas, not small towns. Tellingly, even when Ms. Palin made her infamous remarks in 2008 she did so in Greensboro, North Carolina, which may not be in the Northeast Corridor but—with a metropolitan population of more than 700,000— is hardly Mayberry. In fact, two-thirds of Americans live in metro areas with half-a-million or more residents.   6

Nor, by the way, are most of us living in leafy suburbs. America as a whole has only 87 people per square mile, but the average American, according to the Census Bureau, lives in a census tract with more than 5,000 people per square mile. For all the bashing of the Northeast Corridor as being somehow un-American, this means that the typical American lives in an environment that resembles greater Boston or greater Philadelphia more than it resembles Greensboro, let alone true small towns.   7

What do we do in these dense metropolitan areas? Almost none of us are farmers; few of us hunt; by and large, we sit in cubicles on weekdays and visit shopping malls on our days off.   8

And ethnically we are, of course, very different from the founders. Only a minority of today's Americans are descended from the WASPs and slaves of 1776. The rest are the descendants of successive waves of immigration: first from Ireland and Germany, then from Southern and Eastern Europe, now from Latin America and Asia. We're no longer an Anglo-Saxon nation; we're only around half-Protestant; and we're increasingly nonwhite.   9

Yet I would maintain that we are still the same country that declared independence all those years ago.   10

It's not just that we have maintained continuity of legal government, although that's not a small thing. The current government of France is, strictly speaking, the Fifth Republic; we had our anti-monarchical revolution first, yet we're still on Republic No. 1, which actually makes our government one of the oldest in the world.   11

More important, however, is the enduring hold on our nation of the democratic ideal, the notion that "all men are created equal"—all men, not just men from certain ethnic groups or from aristocratic families. And to this day—or so it seems to   12 me, and I've done a lot of traveling in my time—America remains uniquely democratic in its mannerisms, in the way people from different classes interact.

Of course, our democratic ideal has always been accompanied by enormous 13 hypocrisy, starting with the many founding fathers who espoused the rights of man, then went back to enjoying the fruits of slave labor. Today's America is a place where everyone claims to support equality of opportunity, yet we are, objectively, the most class-ridden nation in the Western world—the country where children of the wealthy are most likely to inherit their parents' status. It's also a place where everyone celebrates the right to vote, yet many politicians work hard to disenfranchise the poor and nonwhite.

But that very hypocrisy is, in a way, a good sign. The wealthy may defend their 14 privileges, but given the temper of America, they have to pretend that they're doing no such thing. The block-the-vote people know what they're doing, but they also know that they mustn't say it in so many words. In effect, both groups know that the nation will view them as un-American unless they pay at least lip service to democratic ideals—and in that fact lies the hope of redemption.

So, yes, we are still, in a deep sense, the nation that declared independence and, 15 more important, declared that all men have rights. Let's all raise our hot dogs in salute. ◆

## FOR CLOSE READING

1. Why might Paul Krugman (or any other writer) propose that the Fourth of July is not only a time to celebrate but "to wonder what, exactly, we're celebrating" (1)?

2. The United States has changed immensely since its founding in 1776, says Krugman. What are some of the major changes he cites?

3. Krugman believes that America, despite all the changes, is still essentially the same nation it was almost 250 years ago. Is he right? Why or why not?

4. "Of course our democratic ideal has always been accompanied by enormous hypocrisy" (13), says Krugman. What hypocrisy is he referring to here?

## Strategies and Structures

1. In his THESIS STATEMENT, Krugman says: "Yet I would maintain that we are still the same country that declared independence all those years ago" (10). How, and how well, does he use classes and classification to support it?

2. *E pluribus Unum* is a statement of political philosophy. In the context of Krugman's essay, how might it also be seen as a PRINCIPLE OF CLASSIFICATION?

3. America and Americans used to be classified as largely "white, Protestant, and rural or small-town" (5). According to Krugman, what would those traits and categories be today?

4. When you argue a point in a **POSITION PAPER**, it's a good idea to anticipate opposing views. Where and how does Krugman do that here? Point to specific passages in the text.

5. Fourth of July oratory is usually celebratory. To what extent does Krugman follow that tradition? Where and how does he depart from it?

## Thinking about Language

1. *E pluribus Unum* is often translated as "One out of many." What does that mean, exactly?

2. *Wax* and *wane* usually apply to phases of the moon. What does Krugman mean by "wax a bit philosophical" (1)?

3. What are WASPs (4, 9)? Is the term derogatory or merely descriptive? Explain.

4. *Redemption* usually has religious (or at least moral) overtones (14). Does Krugman use it appropriately in his Fourth of July remarks? Why or why not?

## FOR WRITING

1. "All men are created equal" is, of course, the basis of the political philosophy outlined in the American Declaration of Independence, which classified King George III as a "Tyrant." Review the Declaration (p. 635), and in a paragraph or two explain the specific characteristics attributed by the revolutionaries to the king to justify this classification.

2. Make a list of the characteristics and categories you would cite if you were classifying the population of today's America into its constituent groups.

3. Write a 400–500-word **POSITION PAPER** attacking or defending the proposition that "we are still the same country that declared independence all those years ago" (10).

4. In 400–500 words, write the position paper on the state of the nation and "the democratic ideal" that you would like to see published on the next Fourth of July.

....................................................•

You'll find quizzes on the readings at
wwnorton.com/write/back-to-the-lake.

# DEBORAH TANNEN

# But What Do You Mean?

Deborah Tannen (b. 1945) is a professor of linguistics at Georgetown University. Best known for her studies of how men and women communicate, she is the author of more than twenty books, including *You Just Don't Understand: Men and Women in Conversation* (1990), *You're Wearing That? Understanding Mothers and Daughters in Conversation* (2006), and *You Were Always Mom's Favorite! Sisters in Conversation Throughout Their Lives* (2009).

"But What Do You Mean?" first appeared in Redbook magazine in 1994 and summarizes much of Tannen's best-selling book *Talking from 9 to 5: Women and Men at Work* (1994). In this essay, Tannen classifies the most common ways in which men and women miscommunicate in the workplace.

CONVERSATION IS A RITUAL. We say things that seem obviously the thing to say, without thinking of the literal meaning of our words, any more than we expect the question "How are you?" to call forth a detailed account of aches and pains.   1

Unfortunately, women and men often have different ideas about what's appropriate, different ways of speaking. Many of the conversational rituals common among women are designed to take the other person's feelings into account, while many of the conversational rituals common among men are designed to maintain the one-up position, or at least avoid appearing one-down. As a result, when men and women interact—especially at work—it's often women who are at the disadvantage. Because women are not trying to avoid the one-down position, that is unfortunately where they may end up.   2

> In a binary system, such as male and female, the categories should be especially significant, p. 395.

Here, the biggest areas of miscommunication.   3

## 1. Apologies

Women are often told they apologize too much. The reason they're told to stop doing it is that, to many men, apologizing seems synonymous with putting oneself down. But there are many times when "I'm sorry" isn't self-deprecating, or even an apology; it's an automatic way of keeping both speakers on an equal footing. For example, a well-known columnist once interviewed me and gave me her phone   4

MLA CITATION: Tannen, Deborah. "But What Do You Mean?" 1994. *Back to the Lake*. Ed. Thomas Cooley. 3rd ed. New York: Norton, 2015. 437–42. Print.

number in case I needed to call her back. I misplaced the number and had to go through the newspaper's main switchboard. When our conversation was winding down and we'd both made ending-type remarks, I added, "Oh, I almost forgot—I lost your direct number, can I get it again?" "Oh, I'm sorry," she came back instantly, even though she had done nothing wrong and *I* was the one who'd lost the number. But I understood she wasn't really apologizing; she was just automatically reassuring me she had no intention of denying me her number.

Even when "I'm sorry" *is* an apology, women often assume it will be the first 5 step in a two-step ritual: I say "I'm sorry" and take half the blame, then you take the other half. At work, it might go something like this:

A: When you typed this letter, you missed this phrase I inserted.
B: Oh, I'm sorry. I'll fix it.
A: Well, I wrote it so small it was easy to miss.

When both parties share blame, it's a mutual face-saving device. But if one per- 6 son, usually the woman, utters frequent apologies and the other doesn't, she ends up looking as if she's taking the blame for mishaps that aren't her fault. When she's only partially to blame, she looks entirely in the wrong.

I recently sat in on a meeting at an insurance company where the sole woman, 7 Helen, said "I'm sorry" or "I apologize" repeatedly. At one point she said, "I'm thinking out loud. I apologize." Yet the meeting was intended to be an informal brainstorming session, and *everyone* was thinking out loud.

The reason Helen's apologies stood out was that she was the only person in the 8 room making so many. And the reason I was concerned was that Helen felt the annual bonus she had received was unfair. When I interviewed the colleagues, they said that Helen was one of the best and most productive workers—yet she got one of the smallest bonuses. Although the problem might have been outright sexism, I suspect her speech style, which differs from that of her male colleagues, masks her competence.

Unfortunately, not apologizing can have its price too. Since so many women use 9 ritual apologies, those who don't may be seen as hard-edged. What's important is to be aware of how often you say you're sorry (and why), and to monitor your speech based on the reaction you get.

## 2. Criticism

A woman who cowrote a report with a male colleague was hurt when she read a 10 rough draft to him and he leapt into a critical response—"Oh, that's too dry! You have to make it snappier!" She herself would have been more likely to say, "That's a really good start. Of course, you'll want to make it a little snappier when you revise."

Whether criticism is given straight or softened is often a matter of convention. In general, women use more softeners. I noticed this difference when talking to an editor about an essay I'd written. While going over changes she wanted to make, she said, "There's one more thing. I know you may not agree with me. The reason I noticed the problem is that your other points are so lucid and elegant." She went on hedging for several more sentences until I put her out of her misery: "Do you want to cut that part?" I asked—and of course she did. But I appreciated her tentativeness. In contrast, another editor (a man) I once called summarily rejected my idea for an article by barking, "Call me when you have something new to say."

Those who are used to ways of talking that soften the impact of criticism may find it hard to deal with the right-between-the-eyes style. It has its own logic, however, and neither style is intrinsically better. People who prefer criticism given straight are operating on an assumption that feelings aren't involved: "Here's the dope. I know you're good; you can take it."

## 3. Thank-Yous

A woman manager I know starts meetings by thanking everyone for coming, even though it's clearly their job to do so. Her "thank-you" is simply a ritual.

A novelist received a fax from an assistant in her publisher's office; it contained suggested catalog copy for her book. She immediately faxed him her suggested changes and said, "Thanks for running this by me," even though her contract gave her the right to approve all copy. When she thanked the assistant, she fully expected him to reciprocate: "Thanks for giving me such a quick response." Instead, he said, "You're welcome." Suddenly, rather than an equal exchange of pleasantries, she found herself positioned as the recipient of a favor. This made her feel like responding, "Thanks for nothing!"

Many women use "thanks" as an automatic conversation starter and closer; there's nothing literally to say thank you for. Like many rituals typical of women's conversation, it depends on the goodwill of the other to restore the balance. When the other speaker doesn't reciprocate, a woman may feel like someone on a seesaw whose partner abandoned his end. Instead of balancing in the air, she has plopped to the ground, wondering how she got there.

## 4. Fighting

Many men expect the discussion of ideas to be a ritual fight—explored through verbal opposition. They state their ideas in the strongest possible terms, thinking that if there are weaknesses someone will point them out, and by trying to argue against those objections, they will see how well their ideas hold up.

Those who expect their own ideas to be challenged will respond to another's   17
ideas by trying to poke holes and find weak links—as a way of *helping*. The logic is
that when you are challenged you will rise to the occasion: Adrenaline makes your
mind sharper; you get ideas and insights you would not have thought of without
the spur of battle.

But many women take this approach as a personal attack. Worse, they find it   18
impossible to do their best work in such a contentious environment. If you're not
used to ritual fighting, you begin to hear criticism of your ideas as soon as they are
formed. Rather than making you think more clearly, it makes you doubt what you
know. When you state your ideas, you hedge in order to fend off potential attacks.
Ironically, this is more likely to *invite* attack because it makes you look weak.

Although you may never enjoy verbal sparring, some women find it helpful to   19
learn how to do it. An engineer who was the only woman among four men in a
small company found that as soon as she learned to argue she was accepted and
taken seriously. A doctor attending a hospital staff meeting made a similar discovery. She was becoming more and more angry with a male colleague who'd loudly
disagreed with a point she'd made. Her better judgment told her to hold her tongue,
to avoid making an enemy of this powerful senior colleague. But finally she couldn't
hold it in any longer, and she rose to her feet and delivered an impassioned attack
on his position. She sat down in a panic, certain she had permanently damaged her
relationship with him. To her amazement, he came up to her afterward and said,
"That was a great rebuttal. I'm really impressed. Let's go out for a beer after work
and hash out our approaches to this problem."

## 5. Praise

A manager I'll call Lester had been on his new job six months when he heard that   20
the women reporting to him were deeply dissatisfied. When he talked to them
about it, their feelings erupted; two said they were on the verge of quitting because
he didn't appreciate their work, and they didn't want to wait to be fired. Lester was
dumbfounded: He believed they were doing a fine job. Surely, he thought, he had
said nothing to give them the impression he didn't like their work. And indeed
he hadn't. That was the problem. He had said *nothing*—and the women assumed he
was following the adage "If you can't say something nice, don't say anything." He
thought he was showing confidence in them by leaving them alone.

Men and women have different habits in regard to giving praise. For example,   21
Deirdre and her colleague William both gave presentations at a conference. After-
ward, Deirdre told William, "That was a great talk!" He thanked her. Then she asked,
"What did you think of mine?" and he gave her a lengthy and detailed critique. She

found it uncomfortable to listen to his comments. But she assured herself that he meant well, and that his honesty was a signal that she, too, should be honest when he asked for a critique of his performance. As a matter of fact, she had noticed quite a few ways in which he could have improved his presentation. But she never got a chance to tell him because he never asked—and she felt put down. The worst part was that it seemed she had only herself to blame, since she *had* asked what he thought of her talk.

But had she really asked for his critique? The truth is, when she asked for his 22 opinion, she was expecting a compliment, which she felt was more or less required following anyone's talk. When he responded with criticism, she figured, "Oh, he's playing 'Let's critique each other'"—not a game she'd initiated, but one which she was willing to play. Had she realized he was going to criticize her and not ask her to reciprocate, she would never have asked in the first place.

It would be easy to assume that Deirdre was insecure, whether she was fishing 23 for a compliment or soliciting a critique. But she was simply talking automatically, performing one of the many conversational rituals that allow us to get through the day. William may have sincerely misunderstood Deirdre's intention—or may have been unable to pass up a chance to one-up her when given the opportunity.

## 6. Complaints

"Troubles talk" can be a way to establish rapport with a colleague. You complain 24 about a problem (which shows that you are just folks) and the other person responds with a similar problem (which puts you on equal footing). But while such commiserating is common among women, men are likely to hear it as a request to *solve* the problem.

One woman told me she would frequently initiate what she thought would be 25 pleasant complaint-airing sessions at work. She'd talk about situations that bothered her just to talk about them, maybe to understand them better. But her male office mate would quickly tell her how she could improve the situation. This left her feeling condescended to and frustrated. She was delighted to see this very impasse in a section in my book *You Just Don't Understand*, and showed it to him. "Oh," he said, "I see the problem. How can we solve it?" Then they both laughed, because it had happened again: He short-circuited the detailed discussion she'd hoped for and cut to the chase of finding a solution.

Sometimes the consequences of complaining are more serious: A man might 26 take a woman's lighthearted griping literally, and she can get a reputation as a chronic malcontent. Furthermore, she may be seen as not up to solving the problems that arise on the job.

## 7. Jokes

I heard a man call in to a talk show and say, "I've worked for two women and nei-  27
ther one had a sense of humor. You know, when you work with men, there's a lot of
joking and teasing." The show's host and guest (both women) took his comment at
face value and assumed the women this man worked for were humorless. The guest
said, "Isn't it sad that women don't feel comfortable enough with authority to see
the humor?" The host said, "Maybe when more women are in authority roles,
they'll be more comfortable with power." But although the women this man worked
for *may* have taken themselves too seriously, it's just as likely that they each had a
terrific sense of humor, but maybe the humor wasn't the type he was used to. They
may have been like the woman who wrote to me: "When I'm with men, my wit or
cleverness seems inappropriate (or lost!) so I don't bother. When I'm with my
women friends, however, there's no hold on puns or cracks and my humor is fully
appreciated."

The types of humor women and men tend to prefer differ. Research has shown  28
that the most common form of humor among men is razzing, teasing, and mock-
hostile attacks, while among women it's self-mocking. Women often mistake men's
teasing as genuinely hostile. Men often mistake women's mock self-deprecation as
truly putting themselves down.

Women have told me they were taken more seriously when they learned to  29
joke the way the guys did. For example, a teacher who went to a national conference with seven other teachers (mostly women) and a group of administrators
(mostly men) was annoyed that the administrators always found reasons to leave
boring seminars, while the teachers felt they had to stay and take notes. One
evening, when the group met at a bar in the hotel, the principal asked her how
one such seminar had turned out. She reported, "As soon as you left, it got much
better." He laughed out loud at her response. The playful insult appealed to the
men—but there was a trade-off. The women seemed to back off from her after
this. (Perhaps they were put off by her using joking to align herself with the
bosses.)

There is no "right" way to talk. When problems arise, the culprit may be style  30
differences—and *all* styles will at times fail with others who don't share or understand them, just as English won't do you much good if you try to speak to someone who knows only French. If you want to get your message across, it's not a
question of being "right"; it's a question of using language that's shared—or at least
understood. ♦

# FOR CLOSE READING

1. In this essay, what principle of classification is Deborah Tannen using to classify "different ways of speaking" (2)?

2. In what fundamental way do the "conversational rituals" of men and women differ, according to Tannen (2)? Do you think she's right? Why or why not?

3. Tannen says she is classifying the "different ways" in which men and women speak (2). What else is she classifying?

4. Women, says Tannen, tend to apologize more often than men do. Why? She also finds that women often say "thank-you" when they don't really mean it (13). What *do* they often mean by "thank-you"?

5. In Tannen's view, when women complain, they are often trying to "establish rapport" (24). How does she say most men respond to this technique?

6. Women, says Tannen, often see "verbal opposition" as a direct attack (16). How does she say that men see it?

## Strategies and Structures

1. "Although you may never enjoy verbal sparring, some women find it helpful to learn how to do it" (19). To whom is Tannen speaking here? Can you find other evidence that indicates the identity of her intended AUDIENCE?

2. What is Tannen's underlying purpose in classifying the verbal behavior of men and women in terms of the workplace? How can you tell?

3. Tannen divides her subject into seven main "areas" (3). Are these categories based on significant characteristics? Are they mutually exclusive? Do they cover all kinds of communication? Explain.

4. Tannen breaks "jokes" into the "the types of humor women and men tend to prefer" (28). Why does she use subcategories here and not elsewhere in her classification?

5. How and how well does Tannen use classification to structure her ARGUMENT about women in the workplace?

6. *Other Methods.* Much of Tannen's evidence is ANECDOTAL—that is, she tells brief stories to make her points. How effective do you find these NARRATIVE elements of her essay? Explain.

## Thinking about Language

1. "Conversation," says Tannen, "is a ritual" (1). What is ritual behavior, and why do you think Tannen uses this term?

2. What are the CONNOTATIONS of "hard-edged" when it's applied to women (9)? What are its connotations when applied to men?

3. What is "right-between-the-eyes style" (12)? What two things are being compared in this METAPHOR?

4. Tannen accuses a man of "barking" (11) and several women of allowing their emotions to "erupt" (20). How do these choices of words confirm or contradict her assertions about the way men and women communicate?

## FOR WRITING

1. Can you think of any "areas of miscommunication" (3) between men and women that Tannen has overlooked? Write a paragraph on each kind, providing specific examples.

2. Write an essay about the different ways in which one of the following groups of people communicate (or miscommunicate) with each other: siblings, children and parents, students and teachers, engineers and liberal arts majors, old people and young people, or some other group or groups.

3. In your journal, record instances of miscommunication that you hear or are a party to over time. Note who was involved and what was said. Also, try to analyze the types of miscommunication you experienced and why they occurred.

4. "If you want to get your message across," says Tannen, "it's not a question of being 'right'; it's a question of using language that's shared—or at least understood" (29). In a 400–500-word POSITION PAPER, defend (or contest) this proposition about the value of shared language. Give examples, both negative and positive, from your own experience and from your research.

5. Write a LITERACY NARRATIVE recounting and explaining how you came to understand and deal with gendered conversation rituals and rivalries. Again, be sure to give examples.

You'll find quizzes on the readings at
wwnorton.com/write/back-to-the-lake.

# Her Kind

Anne Sexton (1928–1974) was a poet, playwright, model, and author of children's books. Born in Newton, Massachusetts, she began writing poetry in high school. Sexton did not focus on her writing until 1957, however, when she enrolled in a poetry workshop at the Boston Center for Adult Education. Ten years later she won a Pulitzer Prize in poetry for her collection *Live or Die* (1966). For most of her adult life, Sexton suffered from depression and mental illness. Writing helped Sexton to maintain her sanity, apparently; but on her birthday in 1974, she committed suicide by carbon monoxide poisoning. (Of Sexton's untimely death, her fellow poet, Denise Levetov, wrote that "we who are alive must make clear, as she could not, the distinction between creativity and self-destruction.")

"Her Kind" is the keynote poem in Sexton's first book of poems, *To Bedlam and Part Way Back* (1960). At one point during its composition, Sexton called the poem "Witch" but changed the title when, after much revision, she introduced a second, more detached point of view in the last two lines of each stanza. It is this "I" who classifies the woman she is observing in each stanza and who then affirms that she belongs (or has belonged) to the same "kind."

> I have gone out, a possessed witch,
> haunting the black air, braver at night;
> dreaming evil, I have done my hitch
> over the plain houses, light by light:
> lonely thing, twelve-fingered, out of mind.          5
> A woman like that is not a woman, quite.
> I have been her kind.
>
> I have found the warm caves in the woods,
> filled them with skillets, carvings, shelves,
> closets, silks, innumerable goods;          10
> fixed the suppers for the worms and the elves:
> whining, rearranging the disaligned.

MLA CITATION: Sexton, Anne. "Her Kind." 1960. *Back to the Lake*. Ed. Thomas Cooley. 3rd ed. New York: Norton, 2015. 445–46. Print.

A woman like that is misunderstood.
I have been her kind.

I have ridden in your cart, driver,                                    15
waved my nude arms at villages going by,
learning the last bright routes, survivor
where your flames still bite my thigh
and my ribs crack where your wheels wind.
A woman like that is not ashamed to die.                               20
I have been her kind.   ◆

## FOR CLOSE READING

1. According to Anne Sexton's biographer, Diane Wood Middlebrook, "Her Kind" depicts a different woman in each stanza. In the first is "the witch"; then "the housewife"; and, finally, "the adulteress." Does the poem support this reading? Why or why not?

2. Whether Sexton is writing about three different women or the same woman at different moments in her life, how do they (or she) typically behave? Why? What might be some of the CAUSES?

3. How does the "I" in the first line of each stanza COMPARE AND CONTRAST with the "I" in the last line? Explain.

4. In the last stanza, the woman is riding in a cart. Where is she going?

### Strategies and Structures

1. Sexton identifies three distinguishing characteristics—one in each stanza—of the "kind" of woman she is writing about. What are they?

2. On what basis—age, social status, psychological condition, and so forth—is Sexton constructing her classification system? What other types might there be?

3. Sexton's speaker claims to have been the kind of woman she is imagining. How, and how well, do her DESCRIPTIONS of particular specimens support this claim?

4. *Other Methods.* Each stanza of "Her Kind" tells a story. How, and how well, does Sexton use these NARRATIVES to explain what kind of woman she is writing about?

### Thinking about Language

1. The "I" in Sexton's first stanza says she has done her "hitch" (3). Beside rhyming with "witch," this word suggests a tour of duty, as in the military. Why would Sexton use such a term here?

2. Sexton uses the present perfect tense when her speaker says, "I have been her kind" (7, 14, 21). Why doesn't she use the present tense (*am*)?

3. What does "her kind" often mean in common speech? What alternative "kind" does it assume? How does Sexton build on such assumptions in her poem?

4. The woman in the cart says she is not "ashamed" to die (20). Why is this assertion more startling than if she had simply said she was not "afraid" to die?

## FOR WRITING

1. Sexton's poem consists of three seven-line stanzas, each beginning and ending with "I have." If you had to add a stanza to her poem that began and ended this way, what would happen in those seven lines? Make a list of the actions that would occur.

2. "A woman like that is misunderstood" (13). Choose several of Sexton's poems—or those of some other poet whose work interests you—and write an essay about the kind of woman (or man) the poet presents to the reader as particularly misunderstood. How does the poet help the reader to understand such figures, or block the way to understanding them?

3. Write a **TEXTUAL ANALYSIS** of "Her Kind." Discuss the meaning(s) of the poem but also explain *how* the poem says what it says. Base your comments on frequent references to the text.

4. In collaboration with several classmates, discuss the form and content of "Her Kind." What differences do you and the others observe, if any, between how the poem is read by men and by women in the group? Collaborate on an oral presentation in class on those differences and other significant aspects of your joint reading.

You'll find quizzes on the readings at wwnorton.com/write/back-to-the-lake.

# CHAPTER 12

## Definition

A guy with a twelve-inch arm can
have much more noticeable muscles
than a guy with an eighteen-inch arm
because he has better definition.
—PETE SISCO, *Train Smart*

Y ou know what getting ripped off is. How about getting ripped? According to bodybuilder Pete Sisco, *getting ripped* refers to muscle definition: You build up your muscles so they stick out and are easier to see. Likewise, when you define something—from bodybuilding to high-definition electronics—you make its fundamental nature sharp and clear.

A clear definition tells what something is—"a bodybuilder is an athlete who works for muscle definition"—by assigning the thing being defined (*bodybuilder*) to a specific group or category (*athlete*). It then assigns a defining characteristic to that group or category (*who works for muscle definition*). Let's look at the logic behind this way of defining things.

## Telling What Something Is—and Is Not

A definition explains what something is—and is not—by identifying the characteristics that set it apart from all others like it. Bodybuilders, runners, and swimmers, for example, can all be defined as athletes. Only bodybuilders, however, train specifically for muscle definition and bulk.

In other words, training for muscle definition and bulk is a characteristic that *defines* bodybuilders alone. Runners and swimmers may want and need strong muscles, too, but what *defines* them is their speed on the track and in the pool, not the size or look of their muscles on the beach. Definitions set up boundaries; they say, in effect: "This is the territory occupied by my subject, and everything outside these boundaries is something else." Definition can also be a method of developing a subject in writing, and in this chapter we will see how to use definition when you organize and compose an essay.

Basic dictionary definitions have two parts: the general class to which the term belongs, and the specific characteristics that distinguish the term from other terms in that class. This is the pattern that definitions have followed since Dr. Samuel Johnson compiled the *Dictionary of the English Language* more than 250 years ago. For example, Johnson's famous definition of a "lexicographer," or dictionary maker, as "a harmless drudge" fits this pattern: *drudge* is the general class, and *harmless* is a characteristic that distinguishes the lexicographer from other kinds of drudges.

Here are a few more current examples of basic definitions:

| TERM BEING DEFINED | GENERAL CLASS | DISTINGUISHING CHARACTERISTIC(S) |
| --- | --- | --- |
| writer | user of words | requires peace and quiet |
| muscle | body tissue | fibrous, capable of contracting |
| osprey | hawk | fish-eating |

Because basic definitions like these help to explain the fundamental nature of a subject, they can be useful for beginning almost any kind of essay. When you want to define a subject in depth, however, you will need an *extended definition*. An extended definition includes all the parts of a basic definition—the term you're defining, its general class, and its essential distinguishing characteristics. Unlike a basic definition, however, an extended definition doesn't stop there. It goes on to discuss other important distinguishing characteristics of the subject as well. For instance, if the basic definition of a bodybuilder is "an athlete who trains for muscle definition and bulk," an extended definition of a bodybuilder might look at a bodybuilder's focus and motivation, training regimen, bodybuilding competitions, and so on. Extended definitions also use many of the other methods of development discussed in this book, such as NARRATION, DESCRIPTION, and EXAMPLE.

In this chapter, we will not only see how to write basic definitions that are sharp and clear, we will learn how to construct an extended definition and make it the backbone of an essay. We will consider how to use SYNONYMS and ETYMOLOGIES in a definition, and how to use other methods of development. We'll also review the critical points to watch for as you read over and revise your essay, as well as common errors to avoid when you edit.

## Why Do We Define?

Being naturally curious, human beings define in order to understand the fundamental nature of things. For example, if you were defining *abolitionism* for an exam in U.S. history, you might first consider a brief dictionary definition—"advocacy of the abolishment of slavery in the United States"—but you would move on to discuss the abolition movement before the Civil War and the legal abolishment of slavery by President Lincoln's Emancipation Proclamation. Writing about this term would thus help you make sense of history, in this case the history of an important social and political movement in American culture.

Sometimes, however, understanding a definition can be personally enlightening. The great antislavery orator Frederick Douglass escaped from slavery as a young man. In 1845, he wrote about how he came to learn the meaning of *abolition*:

> If a slave ran away and succeeded in getting clear . . . or did anything very wrong in the mind of a slaveholder, it was spoken of as the fruit of *abolition*. Hearing the word in this connection very often, I set about learning what it meant. The dictionary afforded me little or no help. I found it was "the act of abolishing"; but then I did not know what was to be abolished. Here I was perplexed. I did not dare to ask anyone about the meaning, for I was satisfied that it was something they wanted me to know very little about. After a

patient waiting, I got one of our city papers, containing an account . . . of the slave trade between the States. From this time I understood the words *abolition* and *abolitionist*, and always drew near when that word was spoken, expecting to hear something of importance to myself and fellow-slaves. The light broke in upon me by degrees.    —FREDERICK DOUGLASS, *Narrative*

For a killer example, see "How to Know If You're Dead" (p. 479).

Such is the power and purpose of definitions: without them, we're in the dark about many things of importance to us. Before he could write so powerfully about the concept of *abolition*, young Douglass first had to learn what it meant in common usage. Defining, then, is ultimately a process

## USING DEFINITION IN A POSITION PAPER

"The beginning of wisdom," said the Greek philosopher Socrates, "is the definition of terms." The definition of terms is also the beginning of many a **POSITION PAPER**, because differences of opinion often hinge on different definitions of words—in addition to what is wise, good, or true. The following example is from the introduction to an essay on the reading disability commonly called *dyslexia*:

> I don't care much for the word dyslexia. I generally think of "us" as spatial thinkers and non-dyslexics as linear thinkers, or people who could be most often described as being *dys-spatios*. For spatial thinkers, reading is clearly necessary but over-rated. . . . From the perspective of the linear thinkers, we spatial thinkers seem to "think outside the box," and this accounts for our accomplishments. However, we think outside the box precisely because we have never been in one. Our minds are not clogged up by preconceived ideas acquired through excessive reading. We are, therefore, free to have original thoughts enhanced by personal observations.    —JACK HORNER,
> "The Extraordinary Characteristics of Dyslexia"

Horner is taking the position here that dyslexia, commonly defined as a reading *disability*, isn't really a disability at all. In fact, Horner argues, the term actually connotes a learning *advantage*. Like this one (which you can read in full on p. 493), many position papers hinge on the definition terms. If you accept the writer's definition (or re-definition) of a key term in the debate—*dyslexia* in Horner's case—you are on the verge of accepting the writer's entire position, whether it represents wisdom or folly.

of exploration. We extend our definitions in order to extend our horizons—and those of our readers.

## Composing an Essay That Uses Definition

When you compose a definition essay, your first challenge is to find a topic worth defining. That topic may be complex, like relativity or Marxism or capitalism. Or, sometimes, you may devote an entire essay to a definition because you are arguing that a word or concept means something that others might not have thought of, or might disagree with. For example, if you were defining *intelligent design* in an essay you might want to say, at some length, not only what intelligent design is but why the reader should (or should not) believe in it. Definitions that require a whole essay often deal with terms that are open to debate or controversy. For example: What constitutes *racism* or *sexual harassment*? When does a *fetus* becomes a viable human being? What characterizes *friendship*?

Dictionary definitions will help you begin to think about such questions, but to write an essay that defines something fully—especially if it's something complicated or controversial—you will need to construct an extended definition and probably to call upon other methods of development. That is, you may need to DESCRIBE the subject, give EXAMPLES of it, analyze what CAUSED it or how it works, or COMPARE it with others. Take the concept of *longitude*, for example. Longitude can be defined as "distance measured east and west on the earth's surface." This basic definition doesn't fully define the subject, however. To extend such a definition, you might describe the place from which longitude is measured (the Royal Observatory in Greenwich, England, just outside of London on a steep hill), analyze how it's measured (in minutes and degrees from the prime meridian), and compare it with *latitude* (distance on the earth's surface as measured north and south of the equator).

> To define "Blue-Collar Brilliance," Mike Rose gives the examples of his mother and uncle (p. 497).

### Thinking about Purpose and Audience

When you define something, your general purpose is to say what it is, but you may have any number of specific reasons for doing this. You may be conveying useful information to someone, demonstrating that you understand the meaning of an important term or concept, arguing for a particular definition, or just entertaining the reader. In her essay in this chapter, "How to Know If You're Dead," Mary Roach, for example, defines her subject for most of these reasons combined. "When I tried to explain beating-heart cadavers to my stepdaughter Phoebe yesterday," she writes, "it didn't make sense to her. But if their heart is beating, aren't they still a person? she wanted to know. In the end she decided they were 'a kind of person you could

# USING DEFINITION TO FRAME AN ARGUMENT

"In this world," said Benjamin Franklin, "nothing is certain but death and taxes." No matter what you think of taxes, they won't kill you—literally. By putting taxes and death in the same framework, however, Franklin humorously asserts that the two terms belong in the same general class with the same distinguishing characteristic (both are "certain"). This sort of framing is a clever way of implying that two terms have other characteristics in common as well, in this case negative ones.

Suppose you were the mayor of a small town and you wanted to build a recreation center. How might you convince the citizens of your town that a tax increase (to pay for the new recreation center) was a good thing?

The linguist George Lakoff has pondered such questions. If you consider taxes, for instance, to be a necessary evil, Lakoff suggests, you might present them as "dues." Then you would be defining them as what you pay to live in a civilized society where there are services that have been paid for by previous taxpayers. Defined this way, Lakoff argues, paying taxes becomes an act of patriotism.

Defining a term (*taxes*) by associating it with other terms (*dues*) that carry CONNOTATIONS (patriotism) you want to "rub off" on your key term is a strategy of ARGUMENT that Lakoff and others call "framing." In the following passage, for example, Gretel Ehrlich defines (or redefines) what it means to be a cowboy—normally framed in masculine terms—by framing her subject in feminine terms:

> Cowboys are perhaps the most misunderstood group of workers anywhere. Romanticized in the movies and on billboards as handsome, macho loners always heading off into the sunset, they are more likely to be homebodies or social misfits too shy to work with people. Their work has more to do with mothering and nurturing than with exhibitions of virility. A cowboy can bottle-feed a calf around the clock, forecast weather, use a sewing machine, make anything out of canvas or leather, and serve as midwife to any animal.
>
> —GRETEL EHRLICH, *The Solace of Open Spaces*

Marlboro Man or midwife? The frame of reference in which you define a subject can predispose your readers to accept not only your definition but the larger point your definition is intended to make.

play tricks on but they wouldn't know.'" This, says Roach, "is a pretty good way of summing up" the meaning of a difficult and sometimes controversial term.

Whatever your specific purpose (or purposes) for constructing a definition, you need to consider why your audience might want (or be reluctant) to know more about it and what it means. Also think about how the reader might already define the term. What information can you supply to make it easier for the reader to understand your definition, or be more receptive to it?

Consider the example of longitude again. I you were defining longitude in a manual for would-be sailors, you would compare it with latitude and explain how each measures different directions on the globe. You would also point out that determining longitude requires an accurate timepiece—if not a Global Positioning System—whereas latitude can be estimated just by eyeballing the angle of the sun or stars above the horizon. Since you're defining longitude for navigational purposes, you won't need to point out that, in the days before accurate clocks, measuring (or mismeasuring) longitude posed a grave danger to sailors on the high seas. However, such historical information—though irrelevant in a sailing manual—might be of vital interest if you were constructing a broad definition of longitude for a general audience, as in this passage from an entire book on the subject:

> Here lies the real, hard-core difference between latitude and longitude. . . .
> The zero-degree parallel of latitude [the equator] is fixed by the laws of nature, while the zero-degree meridian of longitude shifts like the sands of time. This difference makes finding latitude child's play, and turns the determination of longitude, especially at sea, into an adult dilemma—one that stumped the wisest minds of the world for the better part of human history.
>
> —DAVA SOBEL, *Longitude*

In *Longitude*, Sobel defines her subject as a scientific, political, and philosophical concept. In an essay, rather than a book, you can't define longitude or any other subject on such a global scale, but you can focus on those aspects of your subject that best suit your purpose and that your audience is most likely to find interesting and useful.

Jack Horner gives his own spatial definition of *dyslexia* on p. 493.

## Generating Ideas: Asking What Something Is—and Is Not

LISTING, CLUSTERING, BRAINSTORMING, and other techniques of discovery can help you generate ideas for a definition. In order to define your subject, you will need to consider what its distinguishing characteristics are—what makes it different from other things in the same general class. How do you know which characteristics are essential to your definition? Start by thinking about the characteristics that tell us the most about it. For instance, suppose we wanted to define what an *engineer* is. We know that engineers often use tools and have specialized knowledge about how things are built. But these characteristics also apply to carpenters and burglars. What characteristics tell us the most about engineers?

According to one expert, these characteristics are all *essential* to engineers:

- They are fascinated with the physical world.
- They value utility over beauty or knowledge.
- They have a thorough understanding of mathematics and science.
- They are trained to apply that knowledge to physical objects and systems.
- Their purpose in doing so is to remake the world by shaping it to practical use.  —MICHAEL DAVIS, "Defining 'Engineer'"

As you come up with a list of essential distinguishing characteristics for your subject, you should also ask what your subject is *not*. Here is how Davis answers that question when defining engineers:

- Engineers are not pure scientists. They may generate knowledge, but that knowledge is not an end in itself, as it can be for a mathematician or physicist.
- Though they may produce beautiful structures, such as bridges or towers, engineers are not artists (in the way that architects are).
- Engineers are not primarily interested in rules (lawyers) or money (accountants) or people (managers).
- Engineers must write reports that are both clear and accurate, but they are not primarily writers either.

The essential distinguishing characteristics that you list—the traits that tell what your subject is and is not—will form the foundation of your definition essay.

## Organizing and Drafting a Definition

When you have a clear idea of your purpose and audience—and a solid list of distinguishing characteristics for your subject—you are ready to start organizing and drafting your essay. First you will need to construct a basic definition of your subject—and then to extend that definition. There are a number of techniques for doing this that can help, including the other methods of development discussed in this book. The templates on p. 458 can also help you get started.

### STATING YOUR POINT

A definition is not an end in itself; you need to say why you're defining your subject. A THESIS statement—usually made in the introduction and perhaps repeated with variations at the end—is a good way to do this. Here is a thesis statement for an extended definition of a *farmer*, written by Craig Schafer, an Ohio State student who grew up on a farm in the Midwest: "By definition, a farmer is someone who tills the soil for a living, but I define a true farmer according to his or her attitudes toward the land." This is a good thesis statement because it gives a clear basic definition of its subject—and then promises to extend it in interesting ways that the reader may or may not agree with at first.

## SPECIFYING ADDITIONAL DISTINGUISHING CHARACTERISTICS

Of all the ways you can extend a basic definition, perhaps the most effective is simply to specify additional characteristics that set your subject apart. Thus, to support his definition of a farmer as a person with certain attitudes toward the land, Schafer goes on to specify what those attitudes are, devoting a paragraph to each:

Bobbie Ann Mason goes into the many characteristics of "being country" on p. 507.

- A farmer is a born optimist. He plants his crops with no assurance that nature will cooperate or that markets will be favorable.
- A farmer is devoted to the soil. He enjoys letting it sift through his fingers or just sniffing the fresh clean aroma of a newly plowed field.
- A farmer is self-denying. His barn is often better planned and sometimes more modern than his house.
- A farmer is independent. Unions have found it impossible to organize him.

By ascribing interesting, even controversial, characteristics like these to your subject, you can take it well beyond the narrow confines of ordinary dictionary definitions. Everybody knows what a farmer is. But a farmer with attitude—or rather, attitudes—is a different story.

## USING SYNONYMS

Another way to extend a definition is by offering SYNONYMS. If you can substitute a more familiar word for the term you are defining, the reader may be more likely to understand and accept your definition. For example, if you were defining a *blog* for readers unfamiliar with the Internet, you might say that it is an electronic journal or diary. You could then go on to say which particular characteristics of journals apply to blogs and which ones don't. Both blogs and journals, you might point out, record the personal thoughts of their authors; but blogs, unlike journals, typically include links to other sites and blogs, and invite response.

Amy Wilentz does this with zombies on p. 487.

# TEMPLATES FOR DRAFTING

When you begin to draft a definition, you need to identify your subject, assign it to a general class, and specify particular characteristics that distinguish it from others in that same class. These moves are fundamental to any definition. See how Amy Wilentz makes them when she defines a zombie in her essay in this chapter:

> The zombie is a dead person who cannot get across to lan guinée. This final rest—in green leafy, heavenly Africa, with no sugarcane to cut and no master to appease or serve—is unavailable to the zombie.
> —AMY WILENTZ, "A Zombie Is a Slave Forever"

Wilentz identifies her subject (*zombie*), assigns it to a general class (*dead person*) and specifies a particular characteristic (*cannot get across to lan guinée*, that is, heaven). Here is one more example from this chapter:

> H. is unique in that she is both a dead person *and* a patient on the way to surgery. She is what's known as a "beating-heart cadaver," alive and well everywhere but her brain.
> —MARY ROACH, "How to Know If You're Dead"

The following templates can help you make some of these basic moves in your own writing. But don't take these as formulas where you just fill in the blanks. There are no shortcuts to good writing, but these templates can serve as starting points.

▶ In general, X can be defined as a kind of _____.

▶ What specifically distinguishes X from others in this category is _____.

▶ X is usually a _____; but it can also be a _____, or even a _____.

▶ X is often used to mean _____, but a better synonym would be _____ or _____.

▶ One way to define X is as the opposite of _____, the distinguishing features of which are _____, _____, and _____.

▶ If we define X as _____, we can then define Y as _____.

▶ By defining X in this way, we can see that _____.

## USING ETYMOLOGIES

Often you can usefully extend the definition of a term by tracing its history, or etymology. This is what an engineer at the University of Houston did when he asked, "Who are we who have been calling ourselves *engineers* since the early nineteenth century?" Here's part of his answer:

> The word *engineering* probably derives from the Latin word *ingeniatorum*. In 1325 a contriver of siege towers was called by the Norman word *engynours*. By 1420 the English were calling a trickster an *yngynore*. By 1592 we find the word *enginer* being given to a designer of phrases—a wordsmith. The *Oxford English Dictionary* gets to the first use of the modern word engineer in 1635, but you might not be crazy about its use. Someone is quoted as calling the devil—"that great engineer, Satan."
>
> —JOHN H. LIENHARD, "The Polytechnic Legacy"

Although few people today would use the word *engineer* to describe Satan, knowing the history of the word and its earlier variations can help us define what an engineer is, namely one who devises things with cleverness and ingenuity, whether it's a siege tower or a carefully crafted piece of writing. You can find the etymology of a word in most dictionaries, alongside the definition.

## USING OTHER METHODS

As you draft a definition, draw on the other methods in this book to round out your definition and support your thesis. Let's say you are defining *cowboy*. You could note that the cowboy is a vital part of the cattle industry and an iconic figure in American culture who is usually thought to be "the rugged silent type." You could ARGUE that this is a misconception, founded on equating him too often with the likes of the Marlboro Man. Then you could go on to describe the attitudes and daily work of the cowboy as you define him.

For more on using argument, see the box on p. 454.

This is what Gretel Ehrlich, a writer who lives on a ranch in Wyoming, does in her extended definition of the American cowboy. Ehrlich's thesis is that "in our hellbent earnestness to romanticize the cowboy we've ironically disesteemed his true character." What is that true character? Ehrlich is going to define it for us, beginning with this basic definition: "A cowboy is someone who loves his work."

Ehrlich might have started with the standard dictionary definition of a cowboy as "a man, usually on horseback, who herds and tends cattle on a ranch, especially in the western U.S." By choosing "loves his work" from among all the other characteristics that might be said to define a cowboy, however, she introduces a distinguishing characteristic of her subject that the reader may not have considered. She then goes on to extend her definition by using a number of other methods of development, as shown in the examples below from her book, *The Solace of Open Spaces*. First she DESCRIBES the work that is the key distinguishing characteristic of her subject.

> A cowboy is someone who loves his work. Since the hours are long—ten to fifteen hours a day—and the pay is $30 he has to. What's required of him is an odd mixture of physical vigor and maternalism. His part of the beef-raising industry is to birth and nurture calves and take care of their mothers. For the most part his work is done on horseback and in a lifetime he sees and comes to know more animals than people.

Next, Ehrlich ANALYZES THE PROCESS of how a cowboy does some of his work:

> If a cow is stuck in a boghole he throws a loop around her neck, takes his dally (a half hitch around the saddle horn), and pulls her out with horsepower. If a calf is born sick, he may take her home, warm her in front of the kitchen fire, and massage her legs until dawn.

Then Ehrlich introduces a little NARRATIVE of a particular cowboy saving a horse:

> One friend, whose favorite horse was trying to swim a lake with hobbles on, dove under water and cut her legs loose with a knife, then swam her to shore, his arm around her neck lifeguard-style, and saved her from drowning.

Because Ehrlich is using her definition to make an argument about the "true character" of the cowboy, an important part of her definition is devoted to COMPARING AND CONTRASTING her idea of a cowboy with that of the cowboy as he is typically (or stereotypically) defined.

> Instead of the macho, trigger-happy man our culture has perversely wanted him to be, the cowboy is more apt to be convivial, quirky, and soft-hearted.

Ehrlich also analyzes the actual CAUSES AND EFFECTS of the cowboy's behavior as she sees them—all in the service of defining what a true cowboy is to her.

> If he's "strong and silent" it's because there is probably no one to talk to. If he "rides away into the sunset" it's because he's been on horseback since four in the morning moving cattle and he's trying, fifteen hours later, to get home to his family. If he's "a rugged individualist" he's also part of a team: ranch work is teamwork and even the glorified open range cowboys of the 1880s rode up and down the Chisholm Trail in the company of twenty or thirty other riders.

This definition does two things: it takes a fresh look at the characteristics usually attributed to the cowboy, and it introduces the author's own, more expansive characteristics. When you construct a new definition or rework an accepted one as Ehrlich does, the new characteristics that you introduce do not have to outlaw the old ones. They just need to open up enough space for the reader to come over to your side of the fence. Thus, the cowboy can still be defined as "strong and silent" when he has to be—like a hero from a Western. But if the American cowboy is to be conceived as more than a cardboard figure, he can also be regarded as "convivial, quirky, and soft-hearted" at times.

## EDITING FOR COMMON ERRORS IN DEFINITIONS

The following tips will help you check your writing for errors that often appear in definitions.

### Check that any word referred to *as a word* is in italics

▶ The term *cowboy* is easy to define, but the life of a cowboy is not so easy to characterize.

▶ Generally referred to as *abolitionism*, the movement to abolish slavery changed the course of U.S. history.

▶ Abolitionism was especially strong in the Northern states, but many Southerners were abolitionists, too.

Where *cowboy* and *abolitionism* are italicized in these sentences, they are being referred to as words. When not italicized, they are referring to concepts.

### Check each basic definition to make sure it includes the class to which the term belongs

▶ Engineering <u>is a professional field that</u> applies science for practical purposes.

▶ A Labrador retriever <u>is a breed of dog that</u> has a friendly disposition and is patient with children.

Without *professional field* and *breed of dog*, the preceding sentences are statements about their subjects rather than definitions of them.

**Check for common usage errors**

*Is where, is when*

*Where* and *when* should not be used to introduce definitions.

▶ Engineering is ~~where you put~~ the practice of putting science to use.

▶ A recession is ~~when~~ the economic condition in which prices go up and sales go down.

*Comprise, compose*

*Comprise* means "to consist of." *Compose* means "to make up." The whole *comprises* the parts; the parts *compose* the whole.

▶ The United States ~~composes~~ comprises fifty states.

▶ Fifty states ~~comprise~~ compose the United States.

Go to wwnorton.com/write/back-to-the-lake for quizzes on these common errors.

# Reading a Definition with a Critical Eye

Once you have a draft of your definition essay, ask a friendly critic to read it and tell you what's working and what isn't. Then read it over yourself with an eye for what can be improved. Here are some questions to keep in mind when checking a definition.

**PURPOSE AND AUDIENCE.** For whom is this definition written? What is its purpose—to define something the reader probably doesn't know much about? to demonstrate your knowledge to an already knowledgeable reader? How is the reader likely to define the subject? Does the definition confirm a standard definition, or challenge or expand it in some way? How?

**THE BASIC DEFINITION.** Does the definition identify the general class to which the subject of the essay belongs, plus the distinguishing characteristics that separate that subject from others in the same class? If not, how might the definition be improved?

**THE POINT.**   What is the main point of the definition? Is it stated as a thesis, preferably in the introduction of the essay? How might the main point be made even clearer to the reader?

**DISTINGUISHING CHARACTERISTICS.**   How does the essay extend the basic definition? Does it introduce essential distinguishing characteristics of the subject? Are the characteristics sufficient to define the subject? Have any essential characteristics been left out? Which characteristics are most informative? Do any need to be sharpened or omitted? Does the definition say what the subject is not? Should it?

**SYNONYMS AND ETYMOLOGIES.**   Are words with similar meanings or word histories used to help define key terms? If not, would either of these devices improve the definition?

**OTHER METHODS.**   What other basic methods of development are used: DESCRIPTION? COMPARISON AND CONTRAST? Something else? If they are not used, how might such methods be incorporated into the definition?

**COMMON ERRORS.**   Do the basic definitions in the essay, for example of the term *cowboy*, include the class or group to which the term belongs? If not, insert that class or group (*man, worker, caretaker*) into the definition.

## Student Example

Gail Babilonia was an undergraduate at Rutgers when she wrote "The Celebrity Chef" as a research paper for an English course. It was one of twelve student essays selected for publication in the 2004 issue of *Dialogues@RU: A Journal of Undergraduate Research*.

"The Celebrity Chef" is a study in communications theory that does more than define a new kind of cook. Using various communications models, this essay also defines a new brand of celebrity whose audience, in turn, can be understood as participants, spectators, or targets.

## The Celebrity Chef

Begins with an
ETYMOLOGY
explaining the
recent history
of *chef*

When we hear the word *chef*, we imagine a nameless    1
Frenchman dressed in an all-white apron and a tall white hat with
ownership rights to a fancy, upscale restaurant. However, today the
chef at a well-known restaurant may no longer be hidden in the
kitchen; well-known chefs can be seen every day on television. The
celebrity chef is a recent addition to both the culinary and media
worlds. Not too long ago, there were only a few: Julia Child was the
most famous, and remains an icon today. Now, however, there are
many more chefs to watch on the Food Network. Emeril Lagasse is
the most popular, and demonstrates the role that celebrity chefs

THESIS statement
explains main
point in defining
a new kind of
chef, followed
by aspects of
the topic
Babilonia plans
to explore

currently play in our lives. Although a recent addition, celebrity
chefs have had a great influence on our culture: they have changed
our ideas about celebrity and about the social status of the chef;
they have redefined the kind of food ordinary people can have, and
transformed the way men feel about cooking. However, the impact
of the celebrity chef is one that most of us barely recognize.

COMPARES the
life and goals of
a student chef
as distinct from
those of the
celebrity chef

Few students in a culinary institute expect to use their    2
certification to become a "celebrity chef" or a Food Network
television personality. There is far too much hard work involved in
becoming a trained chef to have time to think about being a famous
one. Tania Ralli, a student currently enrolled at the French Culinary
Institute in New York City, explains: "[W]e were cooking five hours
a night, three nights a week, after full days at our regular jobs.
The cost, $28,000 in tuition and fees, signaled the depth of our
commitment" (Ralli F4). Because tuition and fees are so high, many
students must work full time and attend school in addition to their
jobs. In their classes, the students cook recipes over and over in
preparation for a final exam in which they cook two recipes
randomly selected from among the hundreds that they have learned.
However, Ralli claims, "cooking school was more than learning
about technique. From developing heat-resistant hands to managing
temperamental personalities, we developed the stamina necessary in
a professional kitchen" (F4). The students are critiqued based on

their efficiency and speed, and on the taste and presentation of their food; they are not trained to be charismatic, friendly, or photogenic. Students focus on surviving in professional kitchens, not on cooking under studio lights. Becoming famous is not a priority for most would-be chefs: students enter the culinary world in hopes of having more practical things like job security, benefits, and decent pay. By and large, they are too sensible to daydream about becoming the next Emeril, which is fortunate because becoming a celebrity chef is beyond their control: becoming a famous chef really depends on the media and the audience.

What makes a chef a "celebrity chef"? According to David Giles, an author who explored the psychology of fame and celebrity, "the defining characteristic of a celebrity is that there is essentially a media production" (2) on television, radio, or in the movies through which a personality is exposed to the public. Actors are celebrities because their media productions are the movies and television shows that they appear in. The celebrity chef receives wide exposure through the media and is well known because of the media; the celebrity chef's own show, and frequent appearances on popular daytime talk shows are his media productions. Without media attention and publicity, a celebrity chef loses the defining characteristic that distinguishes him from a restaurant chef. In connection with celebrity, Giles discusses the differences between two groups of accomplished people, athletes and academics, one exposed to the public more than the other:

> The priorities of the media or the dominant culture determine which spheres of activity are most likely to yield fame to the people within them. In Britain . . . there are huge numbers of footballers [soccer players] who are famous to the general public regardless of our interest in football. . . . Generally speaking, academics are not likely to be as famous as sports people; unless we appear regularly on television, our activities simply aren't visible enough, important enough, or as photogenic as the activities of people working in other fields. (6)

*Margin notes:* 3 — Defines the celebrity aspect of the term *celebrity chef*

Defines celebrity by COMPARING distinguishing features of athletes vs. academics

The celebrity chef, of course, corresponds to the famous                    4
athlete who is recognized even by people who may not follow sports,
and the chef hidden away in a restaurant corresponds to the invisible
and unphotogenic academic who receives little public recognition.
Celebrity chefs have status because they are exposed to the general
public, and are "visible enough" to keep the public's attention
directed toward them (Giles 6). Both a chef in a restaurant and a
celebrity chef have had proper training in fine culinary schools
and have worked for years alongside great chefs as their mentors.

**Main distin-**
**guishing feature**
**of the celebrity** ·····> However, a celebrity chef is exposed to the public through the
**chef is media**        media, especially through television, constantly appearing outside
**exposure**

the restaurant kitchen as a guest on popular talk shows and on
packages of his own line of kitchenware. The public is continuously
exposed to what celebrity chefs have to offer, but we are exposed
to the great restaurant chefs only when we are actually at their
restaurant, or read about them (if we follow the culinary world)
in publications like *Gourmet* and *Food and Wine*. The point is that
celebrity chefs are exposed through mass media—we know of them
because we have no control over when we will stumble upon them
on our favorite morning talk show or at the kitchenware section of
department stores.

The epitome of the celebrity chef is Emeril Lagasse. No other                5
chefs on the Food Network have shows or audiences like he has, and
his show is a true media production. First of all, the set of *Emeril Live*
breaks away from traditional instructive cooking shows: instead of
having Emeril demonstrating and speaking into the camera, the
show has a talk-show format with a live audience and music provided
by Doc Gibbs and the *Emeril Live* Band. The band defines Emeril as
"essentially (part of) a media production" (Giles 2). On no other
cooking show is the chef accompanied by a live band, which
connects *Emeril Live* to entertainment shows like *The Tonight Show*[1]

1. *The Tonight Show/Jay Leno: The Tonight Show*, a television institution, is a one-hour program that is broadcast on the NBC network after the late news. Jay Leno hosted the show from 1992 to the end of May 2009, then resumed hosting duties from January 2010 to February 2014. Bandleader Kevin Eubanks left the show in 2010.

rather than to other cooking shows (Emeril even has conversations with his bandleader, Doc Gibbs, just as Jay Leno does with his band leader, Kevin Eubanks). Moreover, Emeril's show is unique in that it both serves to teach people how to cook and to entertain them, which is what makes him different from any other chef and what makes him a true celebrity.

Aside from the elements of Emeril's show that are a product of set designers, producers, and other creative television production executives, the <u>response of the audience</u> sets Emeril apart. Denis McQuail, a professor emeritus of communication at the University of Amsterdam, Netherlands, describes what he calls an "audience-sender relationship" which can be broken down into three categories: the audience as a target, the audience as participants, and the audience as spectators (40). These categories can help us to understand the rapport that Emeril has with his audience, which makes him a celebrity. Emeril enters from the back of the set, shakes everyone's hands, and makes small-talk with some of the audience members before reaching his place behind the studio's stove. From his entrance, we see how Emeril establishes a relationship with the audience; he could simply start his show by entering from backstage without greeting the audience members, but in doing so, he makes the audience what McQuail calls "participants":

> Communication is defined in terms of sharing and participation, increasing the commonality between sender and receiver, rather than in changing "receivers" in line with the purpose of the "sender"; . . . communication is not instrumental or utilitarian, and the attitude of the audience is likely to be playful or personally . . . committed in one way or another. Audience members are essentially participants. (41)

When he makes contact with the audience, Emeril receives a response that is both "playful" and "personally committed"; he receives this type of feedback because he takes a relaxed and

6

Another distinguishing characteristic of the celebrity chef is audience response

Uses CLASSIFICATION to explain a distinguishing characteristic of celebrity

7

laid-back approach to instructive cooking, constantly including his audience so that they do not feel intimidated by the complicated dishes that he prepares. Furthermore, he gives the audience the opportunity to participate by echoing his notorious sound effect "BAM!" and by being able to taste the food that he has cooked before them. In the way he approaches the audience, he "increases the commonality between the sender [himself] and the receiver [the audience]." He makes himself approachable and down to earth, which makes the audience feel comfortable with him. In addition to being participants, the audience of *Emeril Live* also functions as what McQuail calls the "audience as spectators" (41). Since Emeril has already established the audience as participants, this affects how his audience responds as spectators, which in turn affects Emeril's status as a celebrity:

> The [audience as spectator] arises in a model of communication in which the source . . . simply capture[s] the attention of the audience, regardless of communicative effect. Audience attention is what is measured by ratings and thus cashable in the form of subscriptions, box office receipts, and payments from advertisers. It is also cashable in terms of status and influence within the media and in society generally. Fame and celebrity are more likely to result from sheer amount of public exposure than from measured "effects" or from measures of audience "appreciation." (41–42)

This model can be seen in the way that Emeril "captures" the attention of the audience by entertaining them with funny sound effects and facial expressions while he cooks. Because Emeril has already engaged his audience into his show as participants, he receives this loyalty of his audience as spectators as measured, by his ratings, and by the attendance at his sold-out *Emeril Live* personal appearances. Through these appearances, moreover, Emeril increases his "cashable" status of fame and celebrity through frequent "public exposure."

Uses communications theory to define the audience as "spectator"

8

We have to keep in mind that Emeril's character is a production of the media that is aimed toward a particular audience. McQuail's model of the "audience as a target" explains that "the communication process is considered primarily as the sending of signals or messages over time for the purposes of control or influence. The receiver, and thus the audience, is perceived as a *destination* or *target* for the purposeful transfer or meaning" (41). Emeril's production executives target a specific audience, and control his popularity by giving *Emeril Live* primetime spots on the Food Network, daily at 8 P.M. and 11 P.M., and Emeril's other show *The Essence of Emeril*, at 4 P.M., giving him constant visibility in terms of a specific audience. Emeril's "destination" or "target" seems to be working-class Americans, since the shows air at times when working Americans would be arriving home or settling down to watch television after dinner or at bedtime. This scheduling ensures that Emeril is able to gain the audience's loyalty by making his "media production" available at the times when most of his target audience is watching, and "control" the audience's attention by strategically choosing the most advantageous times to air his shows, which in turn increases his celebrity.

McQuail's audience-response models suggest that Emeril has a great responsibility to his audience in order to maintain his image as a celebrity chef. Although Emeril gains his audience by being charismatic, friendly, and approachable, at the same time, he is creating an illusion by having the audience believe that there is only one way in which he can behave. Richard Dyer, a lecturer in film at the University of Warwick, writing about stars (we can use the terms "stars" and "celebrities" interchangeably since both refer to public figures), claims that

> the roles and/or performance of a star in a film were taken as revealing the personality of the star. . . . What was only sometimes glimpsed and seldom brought out by Hollywood or the stars was that personality was itself a construction known and expressed only through films, stories, publicity. (22–23)

9 ····· Uses communications theory to define the audience as "target"

10

····· Uses *star* as a SYNONYM for celebrity

The public sometimes has a difficult time separating the actor's true character from the character he plays, but is aware of the difference. However, with Emeril there is a different situation because Emeril is part of a media production: there is a constructed public persona that Emeril projects to the audience, and Emeril's funny character is designed to create an illusion that there is only one Emeril. His fans forget that as they watch this chef demonstrate how to prepare food, they are also watching him "cook up" an appealing character, because the audience is unable to differentiate Emeril's persona on television from his identity off camera. Since there is a media production and Emeril is the celebrity-product, the producers have to make sure that Emeril maintains his persona. Convincing the audience that Emeril has only one personality changes the traditional idea of celebrity, since with movie stars, for example, people identify with the characters who are being played rather than with the actors themselves. The audience does not see Emeril "acting" while he is cooking on his television show, and since Emeril projects only one persona, people feel that they are able to identify with him.

Introduces particular characteristics that distinguish Lagasse from other celebrities

As a teacher, Emeril also changes the traditional idea of celebrity. Usually, celebrities are admired for being photogenic or skillful; however, these qualities are not something that people can learn or apply to their own lives. Observing the audience at the show, we see the audience waiting attentively, ready to learn, as if they are waiting for a miracle to happen before their eyes. But that's the thing. Emeril emphasizes how "EASY" it is to prepare these dishes. He constantly uses phrases such as "it's as simple as that" and "it's not rocket science" to encourage the audience to try to cook the dishes themselves. By introducing a recipe as "easy to make," Emeril instills the desire to cook, and the confidence to cook, the kind of food that is usually only served in expensive and intimidating restaurants. Consequently, Emeril's instruction helps to democratize fine food. People may not be able to dine in upscale restaurants because they lack the time or the money, but Emeril changes the

11

idea that fine food is only available at expensive restaurants. By making great food available, Emeril reaches out to those who ordinarily would not experience exquisitely prepared food, and emphasizes that it is not hard for people to cook well themselves. <u>This shows us the difference</u> between a "celebrity" and a "celebrity chef": where celebrities are usually simply entertainers, celebrity chefs are inspirations, teachers, and leaders. The audience is able to connect with the celebrity chef because each show has a lesson that the audience can take home and use. The audiences of movies and television can only watch and admire what the actors do; they can not take home instructions on how to act; however, the celebrity chef can give the audience the knowledge necessary to cook an elaborate meal at home, which ultimately has a greater impact than a movie has on a person's life.

*Distinguishes between celebrities and celebrity chefs*

The celebrity chef also challenges our gender stereotypes. 12 For many years, food in the home has been associated with the women of the household. Traditionally, women have cooked for the family and taken charge of the food served at every meal. Ironically, however, men dominate the culinary world—professional cooking and *haute cuisine* are mostly associated with male chefs and restaurateurs, and industrial kitchens are filled with male chefs. Susan Gregory, a researcher in the sociology of food and the sociology of the family attributes women's dominance of the kitchens at home and the household in general to the nurture factor (Bowlby, Gregory, and McKie 62): cooking at home is part of care and nurturing, and therefore associated with women. That Emeril changes this idea is evident in the people who attend the tapings of *Emeril Live.* Emeril's show attracts men to his audience because in many ways he makes cooking both masculine and possible for them. Recently, when he taped an episode of *Emeril Live* at an Air Force base, the audience was predominately male, and this is, in turn, seen by his television audience. Whenever he sprinkles a spice or garnishes a dish, he utters his notorious sound effect, "BAM!" which seems to appeal to the noisy little boy in the men in his audience.

Introduces the key distinguishing feature of the celebrity chef as a cultural figure

The fact that Emeril is a *male* celebrity chef is what gives him the power to redefine the cooking boundaries in the American household. Emeril is a celebrity, accomplished and qualified, but above all, he helps men feel more comfortable with cooking because he presents himself as someone that guys can relate to, and makes men "participants" in the show.

With the growing popularity of food in the media, celebrity 13 chefs have had an enormous impact on food in our lives. However, not everyone feels that chefs deserve all this media attention. Stephen Bayley, a British media journalist, concludes that it is

> Time, I think, to bury the celebrity chef in all his annoying forms . . . Chefs are artisans who should be confined to their workplace: what they should have in their hands is a spatula and a skillet, not a media schedule. They should be sweating brutally over hot stoves, not perspiring elegantly under the television lights. . . . There he goes, preening and strutting, discommoding the credulous gluttons who pay his salary. (82)

Bayley sums up certain class-based objections to celebrity chefs— that chefs are artisans, not stars, and should stay in the kitchen and serve us, not perform for us. However, as a celebrity chef, Emeril Lagasse has used his status as a chef and a celebrity to encourage his audiences to cook food that is usually reserved for the famous and wealthy, and by instilling in them the confidence to go home and cook his dishes themselves. Most important, Emeril is able to reach out to ordinary men and reassure them that his kind of cooking is not just for the women of the household, or the chefs of the wealthy. By providing entertainment with cooking, Emeril gives the men of his audience the confidence to approach cooking with a different perspective. Moreover, he has changed the culinary and media worlds by fusing them together and adding "BAM!"

Conclusion defines Emeril's distinct contribution

Works Cited

Bayley, Stephen. "The Celebrity Chef." *New Statesman* 17 Dec. 2001: 82. Print.

Bowlby, Sophia, Susan Gregory, and Linda McKie. *Gender, Power and the Household*. New York: St. Martin's Press, 1999. Print.

Dyer, Richard. *Stars*. London: British Film Institute, 1979. Print.

*Emeril Live*. Perf. Emeril Lagasse. Food Network. 8 Nov. 2003. Television.

*Emeril Live*. Perf. Emeril Lagasse. Food Network. 23 Nov. 2003. Television.

*The Essence of Emeril*. Perf. Emeril Lagasse. Food Network. 21 Aug. 2004. Television.

Giles, David. *Illusions of Immortality*. New York: St. Martin's Press, 2000. Print.

Lewis, Robert C. "Restaurant Advertising Appeals and Consumers' Intentions." *Journal of Advertising Research* 21.5 (1981): 69–74. Print.

McQuail, Denis. *Audience Analysis*. Thousand Oaks, CA: Sage Publications, 1997. Print.

Ralli, Tania. "Learning to Sauté in a Melting Pot." *New York Times* 23 Sept. 2003: F-4. Print.

## Analyzing a Student Essay That Uses Definition

In "The Celebrity Chef," Gail Babilonia draws upon rhetorical strategies and techniques that good writers use all the time when they define things. The following questions, in addition to focusing on particular aspects of Babilonia's text, will help you to identify those common strategies and techniques so you can adapt them to your own writing. These questions will also help to prepare you for the analytical questions—on content, structure, and language—that you'll find after all the other selections in this chapter, along with suggestions for writing on related topics.

## FOR CLOSE READING

1. How does Gail Babilonia define a "celebrity chef" (1)?

2. According to Babilonia, what makes Emeril Lagasse a perfect EXAMPLE of a celebrity chef?

3. How has Lagasse made cooking an "acceptable" activity for men (12)?

4. How do chefs like Lagasse use their celebrity status to change our ideas and attitudes about food?

5. What is Babilonia's main point in defining a celebrity chef rather than some other kind of celebrity?

## Strategies and Structures

1. Babilonia's entire essay is built on a single extended example, that of Emeril Lagasse. Is this one case, as she develops it, sufficient to define her subject? Why or why not?

2. What is the purpose of Babilonia's frequent references to the work of David Giles, a professor who has written about the psychology of celebrity (3)? How effective do you find this and Babilonia's other references to experts?

3. Babilonia is defining a celebrity chef. To what extent is she also defining what makes a celebrity? Explain.

4. *Other Methods.* Not only does Babilonia explain how chefs are trained, she analyzes how celebrities are made and how Lagasse, in particular, goes about being a celebrity. How and how well do these forays into PROCESS ANALYSIS serve to support her definition? Point to passages that you find particularly instructive.

## Thinking about Language

1. How does Babilonia use the stereotype of the "nameless Frenchman dressed in an all-white apron" to advance her definition of a celebrity chef (1)?

2. Why do you think cooking schools refer to themselves as "culinary institutes" rather than as "cooking schools" (2)?

3. What is the purpose of Babilonia's ANALOGY between a chef hidden away in the kitchen and an "unphotogenic academic" (4)?

4. Stephen Bayley, a British journalist, thinks its time to "bury" the celebrity chef (13). Why has he chosen such a harsh term?

5. What is "BAM" and how did Lagasse "add" it to both cooking and his show (12–13)? What's his recipe for success?

## FOR WRITING

1. "A celebrity is a person who is famous for being famous." Write a paragraph defining celebrity that *contradicts* this famous definition, attributed to, among others, the artist Andy Warhol and the American historian Daniel J. Boorstin. (Boorstin actually said a celebrity is "a person who is known for his well-knowness," while Warhol spoke of everyone's "fifteen minutes of fame").

2. Write a paragraph defining one of the following: heroism, fame, notoriety, repute, infamy.

3. Write an essay defining what a chef traditionally is and does. Be sure to explain how chefs get to be chefs.

4. Write a PROFILE of a celebrity chef. If you don't already have a favorite chef in mind, consider writing about Julia Child, who introduced French cooking to the American kitchen and was one of the first and most influential celebrity chefs to emerge from the early days of television.

5. Join several of your classmates in planning, shopping for, and cooking a multi-course meal. Afterward, discuss your successes and failures with other members of the group, including whoever cleans up. Then, together, write an EVALUATION of the meal. Feel free to include differences of opinion.

You'll find quizzes on the readings at
wwnorton.com/write/back-to-the-lake.

# An Epitaph

When we define something (or someone), we say what its distinguishing characteristics are. In this cartoon by Roz Chast, a frequent contributor to the *New Yorker*, the deceased's entire life is defined by his verbal and math scores on a standardized test. Chast's purpose in penning the cartoon is to amuse the reader, but she is also making fun of overly narrow definitions. Test scores do not adequately define life—or death. For some people and institutions (such as college admissions offices), narrow definitions can run deep—too deep if they lose sight of the complexities of the person or thing they are defining. Like Mr. Jones' epitaph, good definitions require precision. But when you construct a definition, keep your (and the reader's) eye on the distinguishing features that actually give (or gave) life to your subject.

[ **FOR WRITING** ]·····························································································

Imagine the headstone in Roz Chast's cartoon as a blank slate;
insert a different name (it could be your own), and write an
ideal epitaph for the deceased.

# SUGGESTIONS FOR WRITING

1. In "The Celebrity Chef" (p. 463), Gail Babilonia quotes a journalist who feels that chefs belong in the kitchen and that it's time "to bury the celebrity chef in all his annoying forms." Read Babilonia's essay and write a **POSITION PAPER** supporting or disagreeing with this proposal.

2. In "How to Know If You're Dead" (p. 479), Mary Roach refers to "the specter of live burial that plagued the French and German citizenry in the 1800's." Read Roach's essay, do some historical research, and write a **REPORT** of 400–500 words on the fear of premature burial in Europe and America in the nineteenth century.

3. Jack Horner, in "The Extraordinary Characteristics of Dyslexia" (p. 493), makes the distinction between "linear" and "spatial" thinkers. Check out Horner's definitions of the two types, do some research on the subject ofdyslexia, and write your own **COMPARISON** of the types of thinking he outlines.

4. "There are many reasons the zombie, sprung from the colonial slave economy, is returning now to haunt us" (9), writes Amy Wilentz in "A Zombie Is a Slave Forever" (p. 487). Read Wilentz's essay and other sources about the undead, and write a **POSITION PAPER** defining how zombies are portrayed in popular culture and explaining why they are so numerous today.

5. Read Flannery O'Connor's short story "A Good Man Is Hard to Find" (p. 517); also read as much as you can about her and her other work; and write a **PROFILE** of O'Connor that includes a definition of her place in modern American literature.

MARY ROACH

# How to Know If You're Dead

Mary Roach is a journalist based in Oakland, California, whose first book, *Stiff: The Curious Lives of Human Cadavers* (2003), propelled her to the forefront of popular science writers; one reviewer called her "the funniest science writer in the country." When asked how she came to write a best-seller about a subject most readers would regard as morbid, Roach replied, "Good question. It's possible that I'm a little strange." In fact, a glance at a few of the articles she's written gives one a sense of Roach's wide-ranging, quirky sensibilities: "Don't Jump!" ("Exactly what happens when a person leaps off the Golden Gate Bridge?"); "Turning Orange" ("Raw carrot abuse is nothing to laugh at"); "How to Feel Better about Falling Apart" ("Here's how I cope with my disgusting, sagging middle-aged body"). Roach's book *Spook: Science Tackles the Afterlife* (2005) takes up where *Stiff* leaves off, and her most recent book, *Gulp: Adventures on the Alimentary Canal* (2013), explores the human gastrointestinal tract.

In "How to Know If You're Dead," which first appeared in *Stiff*, Roach explores the meaning of *dead* and finds, surprisingly, that the definition is a subject of disagreement among doctors, lawyers, and would-be spiritualists. Despite the jaunty tone of her prose, Roach is meticulous in her scientific reporting; the meaning of death, she finds, casts more than a little light on the meaning of life.

A PATIENT ON THE WAY TO SURGERY travels at twice the speed of a patient on the way to the morgue. Gurneys that ferry the living through hospital corridors move forward in an aura of purpose and push, flanked by caregivers with long strides and set faces, steadying IVs, pumping ambu bags, barreling into double doors. A gurney with a cadaver commands no urgency. It is wheeled by a single person, calmly and with little notice like a shopping cart. 1

For this reason, I thought I would be able to tell when the dead woman was wheeled past. I have been standing around at the nurses' station on one of the surgery floors of the University of California at San Francisco Medical Center, watching gurneys go by and waiting for Von Peterson, public affairs manager of the 2

MLA CITATION: Roach, Mary. "How to Know If You're Dead." 2003. *Back to the Lake*. Ed. Thomas Cooley. 3rd ed. New York: Norton, 2015. 479–85. Print.

California Transplant Donor Network, and a cadaver I will call H. "There's your patient," says the charge nurse. A commotion of turquoise legs passes with unexpected forward-leaning urgency.

H is unique in that she is both a dead person *and* a patient on the way to surgery. 3 She is what's known as a "beating-heart cadaver," alive and well everywhere but her brain. Up until artificial respiration was developed, there was no such entity; without a functioning brain, a body will not breathe on its own. But hook it up to a respirator and its heart will beat, and the rest of its organs will, for a matter of days, continue to thrive.

H doesn't look or smell or feel dead. If you leaned in close over the gurney, you 4 could see her pulse beating in the arteries of her neck. If you touched her arm, you would find it warm and resilient, like your own. This is perhaps why the nurses and doctors refer to H as a patient, and why she makes her entrance to the OR at the customary presurgery clip.

Since brain death is the legal definition of death in this country, H the person is 5 certifiably dead. But H the organs and tissues is very much alive. These two seemingly contradictory facts afford her an opportunity most corpses do not have: that of extending the lives of two or three dying strangers. Over the next four hours, H will surrender her liver, kidneys, and heart. One at a time, surgeons will come and go, taking an organ and returning in haste to their stricken patients. Until recently, the process was known among transplant professionals as an "organ harvest," which had a joyous, celebratory ring to it, perhaps a little too joyous, as it has been of late replaced by the more businesslike "organ recovery."

How you frame a term (p. 454) can influence how the reader sees it.

In H's case, one surgeon will be traveling from Utah to recover her heart, and 6 another, the one recovering both the liver and the kidneys, will be taking them two floors down. UCSF is a major transplant center, and organs removed here often remain in house. More typically, a transplant patient's surgeon will travel from UCSF to a small town somewhere to retrieve the organ—often from an accident victim, someone young with strong, healthy organs, whose brain took an unexpected hit. The doctor does this because typically there is no doctor in that small town with experience in organ recovery. Contrary to rumors about surgically trained thugs cutting people open in hotel rooms and stealing their kidneys,[1] organ recovery is tricky work. If you want to be sure it's done right, you get on a plane and go do it yourself.

---

1. *Rumors . . . stealing their kidneys*: Reference to a persistent urban legend about people getting drunk at parties, passing out, and waking up in a hotel-room bathtub surrounded in ice and finding that one or both of their kidneys have been removed. These stories are always presented as true and as coming from a reputable but distant source ("it happened to my neighbor's cousin's wife's coworker's son").

Today's abdominal recovery surgeon is named Andy Posselt. He is holding an   7
electric cauterizing wand, which looks like a cheap bank pen on a cord but functions like a scalpel. The wand both cuts and burns, so that as the incision is made,
any vessels that are severed are simultaneously melted shut. The result is that there
is a good deal less bleeding and a good deal more smoke and smell. It's not a bad
smell, but simply a seared-meat sort of smell. I want to ask Dr. Posselt whether he
likes it, but I can't bring myself to, so instead I ask whether he thinks it's bad that I
like the smell, which I don't really, or maybe just a little. He replies that it is neither
bad nor good, just morbid.

I have never before seen major surgery, only its scars. From the length of them,   8
I had imagined surgeons doing their business, taking things out and putting them
in, through an opening maybe eight or nine inches long, like a woman poking
around for her glasses at the bottom of her purse. Dr. Posselt begins just above H's
pubic hair and proceeds a good two feet north, to the base of her neck. He's unzip-
ping her like a parka. Her sternum is sawed lengthwise so that her rib cage can be
parted, and a large retractor is installed to pull the two sides of the incision apart
so that it is now as wide as it is long. To see her this way, held open like a Gladstone
bag,[2] forces a view of the human torso for what it basically is: a large, sturdy container for guts.

On the inside, H looks very much alive. You can see the pulse of her heartbeat in   9
her liver and all the way down her aorta. She bleeds where she is cut and her organs
are plump and slippery-looking. The electronic beat of the heart monitor reinforces
the impression that this is a living, breathing, thriving person. It is strange, almost
impossible, really, to think of her as a corpse. When I tried to explain beating-heart
cadavers to my stepdaughter Phoebe yesterday, it didn't make sense to her. But if their
heart is beating, aren't they still a person? she wanted to know. In the end she decided
they were "a kind of person you could play tricks on but they wouldn't know." Which,
I think, is a pretty good way of summing up most donated cadavers. The things that
happen to the dead in labs and ORs are like gossip passed behind one's back. They are
not felt or known and so they cause no pain.

The contradictions and counterintuitions of the beating-heart cadaver can exact   10
an emotional toll on the intensive care unit (ICU) staff, who must, in the days preceding the harvest, not only think of patients like H as living beings, but treat and
care for them that way as well. The cadaver must be monitored around the clock
and "life-saving" interventions undertaken on its behalf. Since the brain can no
longer regulate blood pressure or the levels of hormones and their release into the
bloodstream, these things must be done by ICU staff, in order to keep the organs

---

2. *Gladstone bag*: An early suitcase, hinged to open in the middle and lie flat.

from degrading. Observed a group of Case Western Reserve University School of Medicine physicians in a *New England Journal of Medicine* article entitled "Psychosocial and Ethical Implications of Organ Retrieval": "Intensive care unit personnel may feel confused about having to perform cardiopulmonary resuscitation on a patient who has been declared dead, whereas a 'do not resuscitate' order has been written for a living patient in the next bed."

. . .

The modern medical community is on the whole quite unequivocal about the brain  11
being the seat of the soul, the chief commander of life and death. It is similarly unequivocal about the fact that people like H are, despite the hoochy-koochy going on behind their sternums, dead. We now know that the heart keeps beating on its own not because the soul is in there, but because it contains its own bioelectric power source, independent of the brain. As soon as H's heart is installed in someone else's chest and that person's blood begins to run through it, it will start beating anew—with no signals from the recipient's brain.

The legal community took a little longer than the physicians to come around to  12
the concept of brain death. It was 1968 when the *Journal of the American Medical Association* published a paper by the Ad Hoc Committee of the Harvard Medical School to Examine the Definition of Brain Death advocating that irreversible coma be the new criterion for death, and clearing the ethical footpath for organ transplantation. It wasn't until 1974 that the law began to catch up. What forced the issue was a bizarre murder trial in Oakland, California.

The killer, Andrew Lyons, shot a man in the head in September 1973 and left  13
him brain-dead. When Lyons's attorneys found out that the victim's family had donated his heart for transplantation, they tried to use this in Lyons's defense: If the heart was still beating at the time of surgery, they maintained, then how could it be that Lyons had killed him the day before? They tried to convince the jury that, technically speaking, Andrew Lyons hadn't murdered the man, the organ recovery surgeon had. According to Stanford University heart transplant pioneer Norman Shumway, who testified in the case, the judge would have none of it. He informed the jury that the accepted criteria for death were those set forth by the Harvard committee, and that that should inform their decision. (Photographs of the victim's brains "oozing from his skull," to quote the *San Francisco Chronicle,* probably didn't help Lyons's case.) In the end, Lyons was convicted of murder. Based on the outcome of the case, California passed legislation making brain death the legal definition of death. Other states quickly followed suit.

Andrew Lyons's defense attorney wasn't the first person to cry murder when a  14
transplant surgeon removed a heart from a brain-dead patient. In the earliest days

of heart transplants, Shumway, the first U.S. surgeon to carry out the procedure, was continually harangued by the coroner in Santa Clara County, where he practiced. The coroner didn't accept the brain-death concept of death and threatened that if Shumway went ahead with his plans to remove a beating heart from a brain-dead person and use it to save another person's life, he would initiate murder charges. Though the coroner had no legal ground to stand on and Shumway went ahead anyway, the press gave it a vigorous chew. New York heart transplant surgeon Mehmet Oz recalls the Brooklyn district attorney around that time making the same threat. "He said he'd indict and arrest any heart transplant surgeon who went into his borough and harvested an organ."

The worry, explained Oz, was that someday someone who wasn't actually brain-dead was going to have his heart cut out. There exist certain rare medical conditions that can look, to the untrained or negligent eye, a lot like brain death, and the legal types didn't trust the medical types to get it right. To a very, very small degree, they had reason to worry. Take, for example, the condition known as "locked-in state." In one form of the disease, the nerves, from eyeballs to toes, suddenly and rather swiftly drop out of commission, with the result that the body is completely paralyzed, while the mind remains normal. The patient can hear what's being said but has no way of communicating that he's still in there, and that no, it's definitely not okay to give his organs away for transplant. In severe cases, even the muscles that contract to change the size of the pupils no longer function. This is bad news, for a common test of brain death is to shine a light in the patient's eyes to check for the reflexive contraction of the pupils. Typically, victims of locked-in state recover fully, provided no one has mistakenly wheeled them off to the OR to take out their heart.

Like the specter of live burial that plagued the French and German citizenry in the 1800s, the fear of live organ harvesting is almost completely without foundation. A simple EEG will prevent misdiagnosis of the locked-in state and conditions like it.

On a rational level, most people are comfortable with the concept of brain death and organ donation. But on an emotional level, they may have a harder time accepting it, particularly when they are being asked to accept it by a transplant counselor who would like them to okay the removal of a family member's beating heart. Fifty-four percent of families asked refuse consent. "They can't deal with the fear, however irrational, that the true end of their loved one will come when the heart is removed," says Oz. That they, in effect, will have killed him.

Even heart transplant surgeons sometimes have trouble accepting the notion that the heart is nothing more than a pump. When I asked Oz where he thought the soul resided, he said, "I'll confide in you that I don't think it's all in the brain. I have to believe that in many ways the core of our existence is in our heart."

Does that mean he thinks the brain-dead patient isn't dead? "There's no question that the heart without a brain is of no value. But life and death is not a binary system." It's a continuum. It makes sense, for many reasons, to draw the legal line at brain death, but that doesn't mean it's really a line. "In between life and death is a state of near-death, or pseudo-life. And most people don't want what's in between."

. . .

The harvesting of H is winding down. The last organs to be taken, the kidneys, are   19
being brought up and separated from the depths of her open torso. Her thorax and abdomen are filled with crushed ice, turned red from blood. "Cherry Sno-Kone," I write in my notepad. It's been almost four hours now, and H has begun to look more like a conventional cadaver, her skin dried and dulled at the edges of the incision.

The kidneys are placed in a blue plastic bowl with ice and perfusion fluid. A   20
relief surgeon arrives for the final step of the recovery, cutting off pieces of veins and arteries to be included, like spare sweater buttons, along with the organs, in case the ones attached to them are too short to work with. A half hour later, the relief surgeon steps aside and the resident comes over to sew H up.

As he talks to Dr. Posselt about the stitching, the resident strokes the bank of fat   21
along H's incision with his gloved hand, then pats it twice, as though comforting her. When he turns back to his work, I ask him if it feels different to be working on a dead patient.

"Oh, yes," he answers. "I mean, I would never use this kind of stitch." He has   22
begun stitching more widely spaced, comparatively crude loops, rather than the tight, hidden stitches used on the living.

I rephrase the question: Does it feel odd to perform surgery on someone who   23
isn't alive?

His answer is surprising. "The patient *was* alive." I suppose surgeons are used to   24
thinking about patients—particularly ones they've never met—as no more than what they see of them: open plots of organs. And as far as that goes, I guess you could say H *was* alive. Because of the cloths covering all but her opened torso, the young man never saw her face, didn't know if she was male or female.

While the resident sews, a nurse picks stray danglies of skin and fat off the oper-   25
ating table with a pair of tongs and drops them inside the body cavity, as though H were a handy wastebasket. The nurse explains that this is done intentionally: "Anything not donated stays with her." The jigsaw puzzle put back in its box.

The incision is complete, and a nurse washes H off and covers her with a blanket   26
for the trip to the morgue. Out of habit or respect, he chooses a fresh one. The transplant coordinator, Von, and the nurse lift H onto a gurney. Von wheels H into an elevator and down a hallway to the morgue. The workers are behind a set of swinging doors, in a back room. "Can we leave this here?" Von shouts. H has

become a "this." We are instructed to wheel the gurney into the cooler, where it joins five others. H appears no different from the corpses already here.*

But H *is* different. She has made three sick people well. She has brought them 27 extra time on earth. To be able, as a dead person, to make a gift of this magnitude is phenomenal. Most people don't manage this sort of thing while they're alive. Cadavers like H are the dead's heros.

It is astounding to me, and achingly sad, that with eighty thousand people on 28 the waiting list for donated hearts and livers and kidneys, with sixteen a day dying there on that list, that more than half of the people in the position H's family was in will say no, will choose to burn those organs or let them rot. We abide the surgeon's scalpel to save our own lives, our loved ones' lives, but not to save a stranger's life. H has no heart, but heartless is the last thing you'd call her. ◆

* Unless H's family is planning a naked open-casket service, no one at her funeral will be able to tell she's had organs removed. Only with tissue harvesting, which often includes leg and arm bones, does the body take on a slightly altered profile, and in this case PVC piping or dowels are inserted to normalize the form and make life easier for mortuary staff and others who need to move the otherwise somewhat noodle-ized body. [Author's note.]

## FOR CLOSE READING

1. A "beating-heart cadaver," says Mary Roach, is "both a dead person *and* a patient on the way to surgery" (3). How is this possible? What are some of the "contradictions and counterintuitions" posed by a beating-heart cadaver (10)?

2. What is the legal definition of death in the United States, according to Roach? What was the role of the Andrew Lyons case in establishing this definition (13)?

3. Define the condition known as "locked-in state" (15). Why do such medical conditions worry some people in regard to organ transplants?

4. How is the legal and medical definition of death complicated by Roach's conversation with Dr. Oz in paragraph 18?

### Strategies and Structures

1. What **ARGUMENT** is Roach making on the basis of her extended definition? What is her main point? Where does she state it?

2. Fifty-four percent of the families whom doctors ask for permission to retrieve the organs of brain-dead patients, says Roach, refuse permission (17). As she notes later, that's "more than half" (28). Do you think such statistics bolster Roach's argument? In what way?

3. Roach uses a number of direct quotations from physicians, nurses, and others. Is this an effective strategy? Support your answer with examples from the selection.

4. *Other Methods.* How does the **EXAMPLE** of patient H contribute to Roach's definition of death? How does it contribute to her **ARGUMENT**?

## Thinking about Language

1. Why, according to Roach, did the medical community change its terminology from "harvesting" organs to "recovering" them (5)? What do you think of the change?

2. Roach uses many nonmedical terms and SIMILES in her essay, such as "like a shopping cart" (1), "hoochy-koochy" (11), and "Cherry Sno-Kone" (19). Point out other examples. Given the seriousness of her subject, do you find such informal language appropriate or inappropriate? Explain your reaction.

3. What cleared "the ethical footpath for organ transplantation," says Roach, was a report published in 1968 in the *Journal of the American Medical Association* (12). What are the implications of this "footpath" METAPHOR?

4. In paragraph 14, while talking about the press coverage of the case, Roach uses the CONCRETE image "vigorous chew" rather than an ABSTRACT phrase such as "good coverage." Which do you prefer, and why?

5. Is Von, the transplant coordinator, right to refer to patient H as "this" (26)? Why or why not?

## FOR WRITING

1. Write a paragraph giving the legal definition of death as doctors and lawyers have come to define it since 1968.

2. Write a paragraph defining death according to some criterion other than "irreversible coma" (12).

3. When Roach asks the transplant surgeon where he thinks the soul resides, Dr. Oz replies that he thinks "the core of our existence is in our heart" (18). Write a brief analysis exploring what such a statement might mean and what its implications might be for medicine and other fields.

4. "It is astounding to me," says Roach, "and achingly sad, that with eighty thousand people on the waiting list for donated hearts and livers and kidneys . . . that more than half" of those who must decide on behalf of a brain-dead person whether to donate his or her organs "will say no" (28). Write a POSITION PAPER agreeing or disagreeing with this statement. Be sure to address what Dr. Oz calls the "irrational" fear "that they, in effect, will have killed him" (17).

5. Write a RHETORICAL ANALYSIS of Edgar Allan Poe's short story "The Premature Burial" (1844). Be sure to evaluate the mental state of Poe's narrator (not Poe himself), especially with regard to the sort of "irrational" fears that Roach discusses with Dr. Oz.

You'll find quizzes on the readings at wwnorton.com/write/back-to-the-lake.

# AMY WILENTZ

# A Zombie Is a Slave Forever

Amy Wilentz (b. 1954) teaches literary journalism in the School of Humanities at the University of California, Irvine. Wilentz grew up in New Jersey and New York City and graduated from Harvard. Her books range in subject matter from the psychology of martyrdom in *Martyrs' Crossing* (2000) to her impressions of moving to the West Coast in *I Feel Earthquakes More Often than They Happen* (2006). A particular focus of Wilentz's reporting over the years is Haiti. For her first book, *The Rainy Season* (1989), about the country's emergence from the longtime dictatorship of the Duvalier family, Wilentz interviewed anyone who would talk to her in Port-au-Prince, "anyone who had anything to say: . . . this priest and that general, . . . this guy I met in the street, and a market lady, and some man who said he was a tailor." Rejecting the nickname that foreign reporters once used for ordinary Haitian citizens, her most recent book, *Farewell, Fred Voodoo: A Letter from Haiti* (2013), is about Haiti as a modern country.

"A Zombie Is a Slave Forever," which appeared in the *New York Times* on October 30, 2012, draws upon Wilentz's years of reporting on the country where the true zombie, by her definition, was born and refuses to die as it colonizes more and more other countries that come to resemble modern Haiti.

Z OMBIES WILL COME TO MY DOOR on Wednesday night—in rags, eye-sockets blackened, pumping devices that make fake blood run down their faces—asking for candies. There seem to be more and more zombies every Halloween, more zombies than princesses, fairies, ninjas or knights. In all probability, none of them knows what a zombie really is. 1

Most people think of them as the walking dead, a being without a soul or someone with no free will. This is true. But the zombie is not an alien enemy who's been CGI-ed by Hollywood. He is a New World phenomenon that arose from the mixture of old African religious beliefs and the pain of slavery, especially the notoriously merciless and coldblooded slavery of French-run, pre-independence Haiti. In Africa, 2

MLA CITATION: Wilentz, Amy. "A Zombie Is a Slave Forever." 2012. *Back to the Lake*. Ed. Thomas Cooley. 3rd ed. New York: Norton, 2015. 487–90. Print.

a dying person's soul might be stolen and stoppered up in a ritual bottle for later use. But the full-blown zombie was a very logical offspring of New World slavery.

For the slave under French rule in Haiti—then Saint-Domingue—in the seventeenth and eighteenth centuries, life was brutal: hunger, extreme overwork and cruel discipline were the rule. Slaves often could not consume enough calories to allow for normal rates of reproduction; what children they did have might easily starve. That was not of great concern to the plantation masters, who felt that children were a waste of resources, since they weren't able to work properly until they reached ten or so. More manpower could always be imported from the Middle Passage. 3

The only escape from the sugar plantations was death, which was seen as a return to Africa, or lan guinée (literally Guinea, or West Africa). This is the phrase in Haitian Creole that even now means heaven. The plantation meant a life in servitude; lan guinée meant freedom. Death was feared but also wished for. Not surprisingly, suicide was a frequent recourse of the slaves, who were handy with poisons and powders. The plantation masters thought of suicide as the worst kind of thievery, since it deprived the master not only of a slave's service, but also of his or her person, which was, after all, the master's property. Suicide was the slave's only way to take control over his or her own body. 4

How to construct a basic definition like this is discussed on p. 453.

And yet, the fear of becoming a zombie might stop them from doing so. The zombie is a dead person who cannot get across to lan guinée. This final rest—in green, leafy, heavenly Africa, with no sugarcane to cut and no master to appease or serve—is unavailable to the zombie. To become a zombie was the slave's worst nightmare: to be dead and still a slave, an eternal field hand. It is thought that slave drivers on the plantations, who were usually slaves themselves and sometimes Voodoo priests, used this fear of zombification to keep recalcitrant slaves in order and to warn those who were despondent not to go too far. 5

In traditional Voodoo belief, in order to get back to lan guinée, one must be transported there by Baron Samedi, the lord of the cemetery and one of the darkest and most complicated of the religion's many complicated gods. Baron is customarily dressed in a business jacket, a top hat and dark glasses; he's foul-mouthed and comic in a low, vicious way. One of Baron's spiritual functions, his most important, is to dig a person's grave and welcome him to the other side. If for some reason a person has thwarted or offended Baron, the god will not allow that person, upon his death, to reach guinée. Then you're a zombie. Some other lucky mortal can control you, it is believed. You'll do the bidding of your master without question. 6

Haiti's notorious dictator François Duvalier, known as Papa Doc, who controlled Haiti with a viselike grip from 1957 until his death in 1971, well understood the Baron's role. He dressed like Baron, in a black fedora, business suit and heavy glasses or sunglasses. Like Baron at a ceremony, when Duvalier spoke publicly, it was often in a near whisper. His secret police, the Tontons Macoutes, behaved with the complete 7

François Duvalier evokes Baron Samedi, in a black fedora, business suit, and heavy glasses.

immorality and obedience of the undead, and were sometimes assumed to be zombies under the dictator's control. I once heard a Haitian radio announcer describe Klaus Barbie, a Nazi known as the Butcher of Lyon, as "youn ansyen Tonton Makout Hitler," or one of Hitler's Tontons Macoutes: a zombie of the Reich.

The only way for a zombie to have his will and soul return is for him to eat 8 salt—a smart boss of a zombie keeps the creature's food tasteless. In the 1980s, with Duvalier's son ousted from power and the moment ripe for reform, the literacy primer put out by the liberation theologians' wing of the Roman Catholic Church in Haiti was called *A Taste of Salt.*

There are many reasons the zombie, sprung from the colonial slave economy, is 9 returning now to haunt us. Of course, the zombie is scary in a primordial way, but in a modern way, too. He's the living dead, but he's also the inanimate animated, the robot of industrial dystopias. He's great for fascism: one recent zombie movie (and there have been many) was called *The Fourth Reich*. The zombie is devoid of consciousness and therefore unable to critique the system that has entrapped him. He's labor without grievance. He works free and never goes on strike. You don't have to feed him much. He's a Foxconn worker in China; a maquiladora seamstress in Guatemala; a citizen of North Korea; he's the man, surely in the throes of psychosis and under the thrall of extreme poverty, who, years ago, during an interview, told me he believed he had once been a zombie himself.

So when kids come to your door this Halloween wearing costumes called Child    10
Zombie Doctor or Shopko's Fun World Zombie, offer them a sprinkling of salt along
with their candy corn. ◆

## FOR CLOSE READING

1. According to Amy Wilentz, "full-blown" zombies are not originally from Africa but are the "offspring of New World slavery" (2). Why was Haiti such fertile ground for zombies to spring from?

2. What role does Baron Samedi, the evil figure in top hat and dark glasses, play in "traditional Voodoo belief" as defined by Wilentz (6)?

3. Why, according to Wilentz, did François "Papa Doc" Duvalier dress and speak like Baron Samedi?

4. Zombies are more numerous than ever, not only in Halloween costumes, but in movies and other forms of popular culture. What explanation does Wilentz give for our undying fascination with zombies? Is it plausible? Why or why not?

5. The next time a zombie appears at your door, why does Wilentz advise offering he/she/it a touch of salt?

## Strategies and Structures

1. "In all probability," says Wilentz of those who dress up like zombies on Halloween, "none of them knows what a zombie really is" (1). Is challenging the usual definitions of your subject in this way a good strategy for beginning a definition? Why or why not?

2. Zombies are usually defined as "the walking dead, a being without a soul or someone with no free will" (2). What additional "personal" traits or characteristics does Wilentz introduce into this standard definition?

3. As further defined by Wilentz, zombies are futuristic, like robots. How and why does she expand her definition of the walking dead of Voodoo tradition to include an economic or political component? Point to specific details in the text that contribute to this part of her definition.

4. *Other Methods.* Zombies are what they are, Wilentz claims, because of certain historical and social conditions. How and where does Wilentz use CAUSE and EFFECT to support this claim and to explain why she defines a zombie as "a slave forever"?

5. How and where can Wilentz's definition of "what a zombie really is" be read as a POSITION PAPER on the use of slave labor in modern industrial societies? Point to specific places in the text where she uses definition to support her argument.

## Thinking about Language

1. Wilentz says zombies were a "logical" product of New World slavery (2). What's "logical" about their birth in the New World?

2. *Samedi* is simply the French word for the day of the week called *Saturday* in English. Why does Baron Samedi have a French name? Why "Saturday" instead of, say, "Sunday"?

3. In Haitian French, *Tonton Macoute* means "Uncle Gunnysack," an embodiment of the devil in Haitian folklore (7). Judging from Wilentz's account of them, how appropriate was the name for a member of "Papa Doc's" secret police?

4. Look up *dystopia* in your dictionary (9). Why might Wilentz have chosen the term to define some aspects of modern industrial society?

5. Look up the meaning and etymology of *fascism* in your dictionary (9). What sort of *group* or *bundle* does the word connote?

## FOR WRITING

1. Write a brief essay defining and distinguishing among the following: *zombies, robots, androids, automatons.* Pay at least as much attention to the differences that define these "creatures" as to their similarities.

2. In 400–500 words, write a definition of Voodoo outlining the origins and traditional beliefs of this religion or cult. (Which is it, by the way? A good definition should explain.)

3. Write a RHETORICAL ANALYSIS of one of the following as a dystopian novel: *Nineteen Eighty-Four* (1949) by George Orwell; *Fahrenheit 451* (1953) by Ray Bradbury; *The Hunger Games* (2008) by Suzanne Collins. As part of your analysis, explain in detail how the author defines a dystopian society.

4. In 500–700 words, write a REPORT on one of the following: some defining aspect of slavery in Haiti (Saint-Domingue) under French rule, 1625–1789; the role of Toussaint Louverture in Haitian history; or the regime of Francois Duvalier and the Tonton Macoutes, 1957–1971.

5. Keep a zombie journal, taking note of zombies you encounter in novels, videos, films, television shows, dance, Halloween costumes, and other forms of popular culture. Your objective, over time, is to define and explain the reasons that "the zombie, sprung from the colonial slave economy, is returning now to haunt us" (9).

You'll find quizzes on the readings at wwnorton.com/write/back-to-the-lake.

JACK HORNER

# The Extraordinary Characteristics of Dyslexia

Jack Horner (b. 1946) grew up in Shelby, Montana, and studied geology and zoology at the University of Montana. He is Regents Professor of Paleontology at the Montana State University and curator of paleontology at the Museum of the Rockies, which has the largest collection of dinosaur remains in the United States. A technical advisor for the *Jurassic Park* movies, Horner was the first person to discover dinosaur eggs in the Western Hemisphere. He is now doing research on the evolution and ecology of dinosaurs and is particularly interested in their growth and behavior.

Although he holds multiple honorary degrees, Horner did not graduate from college because of a common developmental reading disorder often called *dyslexia*. As children, people with dyslexia often have difficulty learning to recognize written words and, thus, the meaning of sentences; and they may have related problems with writing and math. Dyslexia does not indicate a lack of intelligence, however; it is caused by differences in the way the human brain processes symbolic information. In "The Extraordinary Characteristics of Dyslexia" (published in 2008 by the International Dyslexia Association in *Perspectives on Language and Literacy*), Horner bypasses the usual symptoms and defines it as a way of understanding the world that, in some respects, may be superior to more "normal" ways.

EACH OF US can narrate an early experience of failure in schools. Because of 1 it, most of us have known some form of peer persecution. But what most non-dyslexics don't know about us, besides the fact that we simply process information differently, is that our early failures often give us an important edge as we grow older. It is not uncommon that we "dyslexics" go on to succeed at the highest of levels.

I don't care much for the word *dyslexia*. I generally think of "us" as spatial think- 2 ers and non-dyslexics as linear thinkers, or people who could be most often described as being *dys-spatios*. For spatial thinkers, reading is clearly necessary but over-rated. Most of us would rather write about our own adventures than read about someone else's. Most spatial thinkers are extremely visual, highly imaginative, and work in three dimensions, none of which

P. 450 explains how to define a term by saying what it is not.

MLA CITATION: Horner, Jack. "The Extraordinary Characteristics of Dyslexia." 2008. *Back to the Lake*. Ed. Thomas Cooley. 3rd ed. New York: Norton, 2015. 493–95. Print.

have anything to do with time. Linear thinkers (*dys-spatics*) generally operate in a two-dimensional world where time is of the utmost importance. We spatial thinkers fail tests given by linear thinkers because we don't think in terms of time or in terms of written text. Instead, our perception is multidimensional, and we do best when we can touch, observe, and analyze. If we were to give spatial tests to linear thinkers, they would have just as much trouble with our tests as we do with theirs. It is unfortunate that we are the minority and have to deal with the linear-thinkers' exams in order to enter the marketplace to find jobs. Even though we often fail or do miserably on these linear-thinker tests, we often end up in life achieving exceptional accomplishments. From the perspective of the linear thinkers, we spatial thinkers seem to "think outside the box," and this accounts for our accomplishments. However, we think outside the box precisely because we have never been in one. Our minds are not clogged up by preconceived ideas acquired through excessive reading. We are, therefore, free to have original thoughts enhanced by personal observations.

In 1993, I was inducted into the American Academy of Achievement, an organization started in 1964, that annually brings together the highest achievers in America with the brightest American high-school students. The achievers included United States presidents, Nobel Laureates, movie stars, sports figures, and other famous people. The high school students were winners of the best scholarships like the Rhodes, the Westinghouse, the Truman, and so on. In other words, it was supposed to be a meeting of the best of the best according to the linear thinkers who "judge" such things. The idea was that the achievers would somehow, over the course of a three-day meeting, influence the students, and push them on to extraordinary achievement. Interestingly, however, most of us "achievers" admitted that we would never have qualified to be in such a student group. The largest percentage of the achievers were actually people who had difficulties in school and didn't get scholarships, or awards, or other accolades. Most of the achievers were spatial thinkers, while most of the students were linear thinkers. From 1964 until 2000, less than half a dozen students broke the barrier to be inducted at the American Academy of Achievement's annual get-together. How could it be that so many promising students, judged by the linear thinkers themselves, failed to reach the highest levels of achievement?

I think the answer is simple. Linear thinkers are burdened by high expectations from everyone, including themselves. They go out and get good jobs, but they seldom follow their dreams because dream-following is risk-taking, and risk-taking carries the possible burden of failure.

We spatial thinkers have known failure our entire lives and have grown up without expectations, not from our teachers, often not from our parents, and sometimes, not even from ourselves. We don't meet the expectations of linear thinkers and are free to take risks. We are the people who most often follow our dreams, who think differently, spatially, inquisitively.

Personally, I think dyslexia and the consequences of dyslexia—learning to deal 6 with failure—explains my own success. From my failures, I've learned where I need help, such as reading and math. But I've also learned from my accomplishments what I'm better at than the linear thinkers. When I'm teaching linear thinkers here at Montana State University, I know to be patient, as they have just as hard a time with spatial problems as I have with linear ones. We both have learning talents and learning challenges, but I would never think of trading my spatial way of thinking for their linear way of thinking. I think dyslexia is an extraordinary characteristic, and it is certainly not something that needs to be fixed, or cured, or suppressed! Maybe it's time for a revolution! Take us out of classes for special ed, and put us in classes for spatial ed, taught of course, by spatial thinkers! ◆

## FOR CLOSE READING

1. Jack Horner says that "non-dyslexics" are "linear thinkers" (2). What does he mean by this definition? Do you think it's accurate? Why or why not?

2. On the other hand, says Horner, people who are called *dyslexic* are actually "spatial thinkers" (2). Again, what does he mean, and how accurate is *this* definition?

3. Why does Horner think that his spatial perspective has helped him to succeed in his life and career?

4. Why does he think linear thinkers, including "many promising students," even when judged by other linear thinkers, "failed to reach the highest levels of achievement" (3)?

## Strategies and Structures

1. What is Horner's **PURPOSE** in defining dyslexia in positive terms as having "extraordinary characteristics"?

2. In addition to spatial thinkers, what other **AUDIENCE** might Horner and the International Dyslexia Association be interested in reaching? Explain.

3. Nowhere in his essay does Horner cite a standard textbook definition of *dyslexia*. In addition to the extraordinary characteristics, should he have included the ordinary ones in his definition as well? Why or why not?

4. Beside being "spatial thinkers," people with dyslexia have other distinguishing characteristics, according to Horner. What are some of them? Which ones seem particularly effective for extending his basic definition?

5. Horner uses his own life and career as an **EXAMPLE**. How and how well does that example help to explain what it means, in his view, to be dyslexic?

6. *Other Methods.* Horner sees a **CAUSE-AND-EFFECT** relationship between having (or not having) dyslexia and succeeding (or failing) to reach "the highest levels of achievement" (3). What evidence does he offer in support of this analysis? How sufficient is that evidence to prove causality? Explain.

## Thinking about Language

1. New words are often coined by **ANALOGY** with words that already exist (for example, *workaholic* and *alcoholic*). How does Horner derive the word "dys-spatics" (2)?

2. Thinking "outside the box" is a **CLICHÉ** (2). Should Horner have avoided the phrase? Why or why not?

3. What are the implications of *burdened* (4)? Is Horner being **IRONIC** here?

4. Explain the **PUN** in "spatial ed" (6).

## FOR WRITING

1. Write a paragraph or two explaining how "an early experience of failure in schools" or "peer persecution" has "given you an important edge" now (1).

2. Write a definition essay explaining what dyslexia is, what its causes are thought to be, and how it's usually treated. Be sure to cite your sources—and, if appropriate, an interesting case or two, whether "extraordinary" or typical.

3. Horner explains his success and that of other "spatial thinkers" as follows: "Linear thinkers are burdened by high expectations from everyone, including themselves. . . . We spatial thinkers have known failure our entire lives and have grown up without expectations. . . . We don't meet the expectations of linear thinkers and are free to take risks" (4, 5). Write a brief critical **EVALUATION** of Horner's definition of the two types of thinkers and of this explanation for his celebration of the second type.

4. In collaboration with several of your classmates, identify and discuss the different kinds of thinkers among you. Starting with Horner's categories and creating additional ones as needed, write a **COMPARISON** of the strengths and weaknesses of the different ways of thinking represented by individual members of your group.

You'll find quizzes on the readings at wwnorton.com/write/back-to-the-lake.

# Blue-Collar Brilliance

Mike Rose (b. 1944) is a professor of education at the UCLA Graduate School of Education and Information Studies. When he was seven, Rose moved with his parents from Altoona, Pennsylvania, to Los Angeles, where his mother worked as a waitress, and he "watched the cooks and waitresses and listened to what they said." After graduating from Loyola University, Rose earned advanced degrees from the University of Southern California and UCLA. His books on language, literacy, and cognition include *The Mind at Work: Valuing the Intelligence of the American Worker* (2004), *Why School?* (2009), and *Back to School: Why Everyone Deserves a Second Chance at Education* (2012). Rose maintains a blog at mikerosebooks.com.

From his years of teaching and close observation of the workplace, Rose believes that people are smart in many different ways. Consequently, his definition of intelligence in "Blue-Collar Brilliance," from the *American Scholar* (2009), does not separate the mind from the body, as more conventional definitions often do—mistakenly in Rose's view.

M Y MOTHER, ROSE MERAGLIO ROSE (Rosie), shaped her adult identity as a waitress 1 in coffee shops and family restaurants. When I was growing up in Los Angeles during the 1950s, my father and I would occasionally hang out at the restaurant until her shift ended, and then we'd ride the bus home with her. Sometimes she worked the register and the counter, and we sat there; when she waited booths and tables, we found a booth in the back where the waitresses took their breaks.

There wasn't much for a child to do at the restaurants, and so as the hours 2 stretched out, I watched the cooks and waitresses and listened to what they said. At mealtimes, the pace of the kitchen staff and the din from customers picked up. Weaving in and out around the room, waitresses warned *behind you* in impassive but urgent voices. Standing at the service window facing the kitchen, they called out abbreviated orders. *Fry four on two*, my mother would say as she clipped a check onto the metal wheel. Her tables were *deuces*, *four-tops*, or *six-tops* according to

MLA CITATION: Rose, Mike. "Blue-Collar Brilliance." 2009. *Back to the Lake*. Ed. Thomas Cooley. 3rd ed. New York: Norton, 2015. 497–505. Print.

Rosie solved technical and human problems on the fly.

their size; seating areas also were nicknamed. The racetrack, for instance, was the fast-turnover front section. Lingo conferred authority and signaled know-how.

Rosie took customers' orders, pencil poised over pad, while fielding questions 3 about the food. She walked full tilt through the room with plates stretching up her left arm and two cups of coffee somehow cradled in her right hand. She stood at a table or booth and removed a plate for this person, another for that person, then another, remembering who had the hamburger, who had the fried shrimp, almost always getting it right. She would haggle with the cook about a returned order and rush by us, saying, *He gave me lip, but I got him.* She'd take a minute to flop down in the booth next to my father. *I'm all in,* she'd say, and whisper something about a customer. Gripping the outer edge of the table with one hand, she'd watch the room and note, in the flow of our conversation, who needed a refill, whose order was taking longer to prepare than it should, who was finishing up.

I couldn't have put it in words when I was growing up, but what I observed in  4 my mother's restaurant defined the world of adults, a place where competence was synonymous with physical work. I've since studied the working habits of blue-collar workers and have come to understand how much my mother's kind of work demands of both body and brain. A waitress acquires knowledge and intuition about the ways and the rhythms of the restaurant business. Waiting on seven to nine tables, each with two to six customers, Rosie devised memory strategies so that she could remember who ordered what. And because she knew the average time it took to prepare different dishes, she could monitor an order that was taking too long at the service station.

See p. 457 for tips on using synonyms in definitions.

Like anyone who is effective at physical work, my mother learned *to work smart*,  5 as she put it, *to make every move count.* She'd sequence and group tasks: What could she do first, then second, then third as she circled through her station? What tasks could be clustered? She did everything on the fly, and when problems arose—technical or human—she solved them within the flow of work, while taking into account the emotional state of her co-workers. Was the manager in a good mood? Did the cook wake up on the wrong side of the bed? If so, how could she make an extra request or effectively return an order?

And then, of course, there were the customers who entered the restaurant with  6 all sorts of needs, from physiological ones, including the emotions that accompany hunger, to a sometimes complicated desire for human contact. Her tip depended on how well she responded to these needs, and so she became adept at reading social cues and managing feelings, both the customers' and her own. No wonder, then, that Rosie was intrigued by psychology. The restaurant became the place where she studied human behavior, puzzling over the problems of her regular customers and refining her ability to deal with people in a difficult world. She took pride in *being among the public*, she'd say. *There isn't a day that goes by in the restaurant that you don't learn something.*

My mother quit school in the seventh grade to help raise her brothers and sis-  7 ters. Some of those siblings made it through high school, and some dropped out to find work in railroad yards, factories, or restaurants. My father finished a grade or two in primary school in Italy and never darkened the schoolhouse door again. I didn't do well in school either. By high school I had accumulated a spotty academic record and many hours of hazy disaffection. I spent a few years on the vocational track, but in my senior year I was inspired by my English teacher and managed to squeak into a small college on probation.

My freshman year was academically bumpy, but gradually I began to see formal   8
education as a means of fulfillment and as a road toward making a living. I studied
the humanities and later the social and psychological sciences and taught for ten
years in a range of situations—elementary school, adult education courses, tutoring
centers, a program for Vietnam veterans who wanted to go to college. Those students had socioeconomic and educational backgrounds similar to mine. Then I
went back to graduate school to study education and cognitive psychology and
eventually became a faculty member in a school of education.

Intelligence is closely associated with formal education—the type of schooling a per-   9
son has, how much and how long—and most people seem to move comfortably from
that notion to a belief that work requiring less schooling requires less intelligence.
These assumptions run through our cultural history, from the post–Revolutionary
War period, when mechanics were characterized by political rivals as illiterate and
therefore incapable of participating in government, until today. More than once
I've heard a manager label his workers as "a bunch of dummies." Generalizations
about intelligence, work, and social class deeply affect our assumptions about ourselves and each other, guiding the ways we use our minds to learn, build knowledge, solve problems, and make our way through the world.

Although writers and scholars have often looked at the working class, they have   10
generally focused on the values such workers exhibit rather than on the thought
their work requires—a subtle but pervasive omission. Our cultural iconography
promotes the muscled arm, sleeve rolled tight against biceps, but no brightness
behind the eye, no image that links hand and brain.

One of my mother's brothers, Joe Meraglio, left school in the ninth grade to   11
work for the Pennsylvania Railroad. From there he joined the Navy, returned to the
railroad, which was already in decline, and eventually joined his older brother at
General Motors where, over a thirty-three-year career, he moved from working on
the assembly line to supervising the paint-and-body department. When I was a
young man, Joe took me on a tour of the factory. The floor was loud—in some
places deafening—and when I turned a corner or opened a door, the smell of chem-
icals knocked my head back. The work was repetitive and taxing, and the pace was
inhumane.

Still, for Joe the shop floor provided what school did not; it was *like schooling*, he   12
said, a place where *you're constantly learning*. Joe learned the most efficient way to
use his body by acquiring a set of routines that were quick and preserved energy.
Otherwise he would never have survived on the line.

With an eighth-grade education, Joe (hands together) advanced to
supervisor of a G.M. paint-and-body department.

As a foreman, Joe constantly faced new problems and became a consummate   13
multi-tasker, evaluating a flurry of demands quickly, parceling out physical and
mental resources, keeping a number of ongoing events in his mind, returning to
whatever task had been interrupted, and maintaining a cool head under the pressure of grueling production schedules. In the midst of all this, Joe learned more
and more about the auto industry, the technological and social dynamics of the
shop floor, the machinery and production processes, and the basics of paint chemistry and of plating and baking. With further promotions, he not only solved problems but also began to find problems to solve: Joe initiated the redesign of the
nozzle on a paint sprayer, thereby eliminating costly and unhealthy overspray. And
he found a way to reduce energy costs on the baking ovens without affecting the
quality of the paint. He lacked formal knowledge of how the machines under his
supervision worked, but he had direct experience with them, hands-on knowledge,
and was savvy about their quirks and operational capabilities. He could experiment
with them.

In addition, Joe learned about budgets and management. Coming off the line as   14
he did, he had a perspective of workers' needs and management's demands, and
this led him to think of ways to improve efficiency on the line while relieving some

of the stress on the assemblers. He had each worker in a unit learn his or her co-workers' jobs so they could rotate across stations to relieve some of the monotony.

For additional rhetorical education, see "Purpose and Audience," p. 453.

He believed that rotation would allow assemblers to get longer and more frequent breaks. It was an easy sell to the people on the line. The union, however, had to approve any modification in job duties, and the managers were wary of the change. Joe had to argue his case on a number of fronts, providing him a kind of rhetorical education.

Eight years ago I began a study of the thought processes involved in work like that     15
of my mother and uncle. I catalogued the cognitive demands of a range of blue-collar and service jobs, from waitressing and hair styling to plumbing and welding. To gain a sense of how knowledge and skill develop, I observed experts as well as novices. From the details of this close examination, I tried to fashion what I called "cognitive biographies" of blue-collar workers. Biographical accounts of the lives of scientists, lawyers, entrepreneurs, and other professionals are rich with detail about the intellectual dimension of their work. But the life stories of working-class people are few and are typically accounts of hardship and courage or the achievements wrought by hard work.

Our culture—in Cartesian fashion—separates the body from the mind, so that,     16
for example, we assume that the use of a tool does not involve abstraction. We reinforce this notion by defining intelligence solely on grades in school and numbers on IQ tests. And we employ social biases pertaining to a person's place on the occupational ladder. The distinctions among blue, pink, and white collars carry with them attributions of character, motivation, and intelligence. Although we rightly acknowledge and amply compensate the play of mind in white-collar and professional work, we diminish or erase it in considerations about other endeavors—physical and service work particularly. We also often ignore the experience of everyday work in administrative deliberations and policymaking.

But here's what we find when we get in close. The plumber seeking leverage in     17
order to work in tight quarters and the hair stylist adroitly handling scissors and comb manage their bodies strategically. Though work-related actions become routine with experience, they were learned at some point through observation, trial and error, and, often, physical or verbal assistance from a co-worker or trainer. I've frequently observed novices talking to themselves as they take on a task, or shaking their head or hand as if to erase an attempt before trying again. In fact, our traditional notions of routine performance could keep us from appreciating the many instances within routine where quick decisions and adjustments are made. I'm struck by the thinking-in-motion that some work requires, by all the mental activity that can be involved in simply getting from one place to another: the waitress rushing back through her station to the kitchen or the foreman walking the line.

The use of tools requires the studied refinement of stance, grip, balance, and  18
fine-motor skills. But manipulating tools is intimately tied to knowledge of what a
particular instrument can do in a particular situation and do better than other
similar tools. A worker must also know the characteristics of the material one is
engaging—how it reacts to various cutting or compressing devices, to degrees of
heat, or to lines of force. Some of these things demand judgment, the weighing of
options, the consideration of multiple variables, and, occasionally, the creative use
of a tool in an unexpected way.

In manipulating material, the worker becomes attuned to aspects of the envi-  19
ronment, a training or disciplining of perception that both enhances knowledge
and informs perception. Carpenters have an eye for length, line, and angle;
mechanics troubleshoot by listening; hair stylists are attuned to shape, texture, and
motion. Sensory data merge with concept, as when an auto mechanic relies on
sound, vibration, and even smell to understand what cannot be observed.

Planning and problem solving have been studied since the earliest days of mod-  20
ern cognitive psychology and are considered core elements in Western definitions
of intelligence. To work is to solve problems. The big difference between the psychologist's laboratory and the workplace is that in the former the problems are isolated and in the latter they are embedded in the real-time flow of work with all its
messiness and social complexity.

Much of physical work is social and interactive. Movers determining how to get  21
an electric range down a flight of stairs require coordination, negotiation, planning, and the establishing of incremental goals. Words, gestures, and sometimes a
quick pencil sketch are involved, if only to get the rhythm right. How important it
is, then, to consider the social and communicative dimension of physical work, for
it provides the medium for so much of work's intelligence.

Given the ridicule heaped on blue-collar speech, it might seem odd to value its  22
cognitive content. Yet, the flow of talk at work provides the channel for organizing
and distributing tasks, for troubleshooting and problem solving, for learning new
information and revising old. A significant amount of teaching, often informal and
indirect, takes place at work. Joe Meraglio saw that much of his job as a supervisor
involved instruction. In some service occupations, language and communication
are central: observing and interpreting behavior and expression, inferring mood
and motive, taking on the perspective of others, responding appropriately to social
cues, and knowing when you're understood. A good hair stylist, for instance, has
the ability to convert vague requests (*I want something light and summery*) into an
appropriate cut through questions, pictures, and hand gestures.

Verbal and mathematical skills drive measures of intelligence in the Western  23
Hemisphere, and many of the kinds of work I studied are thought to require

relatively little proficiency in either. Compared to certain kinds of white-collar occupations, that's true. But written symbols flow through physical work.

Numbers are rife in most workplaces: on tools and gauges, as measurements, as indicators of pressure or concentration or temperature, as guides to sequence, on ingredient labels, on lists and spreadsheets, as markers of quantity and price. Certain jobs require workers to make, check, and verify calculations, and to collect and interpret data. Basic math can be involved, and some workers develop a good sense of numbers and patterns. Consider, as well, what might be called material mathematics: mathematical functions embodied in materials and actions, as when a carpenter builds a cabinet or a flight of stairs. A simple mathematical act can extend quickly beyond itself. Measuring, for example, can involve more than recording the dimensions of an object. As I watched a cabinetmaker measure a long strip of wood, he read a number off the tape out loud, looked back over his shoulder to the kitchen wall, turned back to his task, took another measurement, and paused for a moment in thought. He was solving a problem involving the molding, and the measurement was important to his deliberation about structure and appearance. 24

In the blue-collar workplace, directions, plans, and reference books rely on illustrations, some representational and others, like blueprints, that require training to interpret. Esoteric symbols—visual jargon—depict switches and receptacles, pipe fittings, or types of welds. Workers themselves often make sketches on the job. I frequently observed them grab a pencil to sketch something on a scrap of paper or on a piece of the material they were installing. 25

Though many kinds of physical work don't require a high literacy level, more reading occurs in the blue-collar workplace than is generally thought, from manuals and catalogues to work orders and invoices, to lists, labels, and forms. With routine tasks, for example, reading is integral to understanding production quotas, learning how to use an instrument, or applying a product. Written notes can initiate action, as in restaurant orders or reports of machine malfunction, or they can serve as memory aids. 26

True, many uses of writing are abbreviated, routine, and repetitive, and they infrequently require interpretation or analysis. But analytic moments can be part of routine activities, and seemingly basic reading and writing can be cognitively rich. Because workplace language is used in the flow of other activities, we can overlook the remarkable coordination of words, numbers, and drawings required to initiate and direct action. 27

If we believe everyday work to be mindless, then that will affect the work we create in the future. When we devalue the full range of everyday cognition, we offer limited educational opportunities and fail to make fresh and meaningful instructional connections among disparate kinds of skill and knowledge. If we 28 think that whole categories of people—identified by class or occupation—are not that bright, then we reinforce social separations and cripple our ability to talk across cultural divides.

Affirmation of diverse intelligence is not a retreat to a softhearted definition of 29 the mind. To acknowledge a broader range of intellectual capacity is to take seriously the concept of cognitive variability, to appreciate in all the Rosies and Joes the thought that drives their accomplishments and defines who they are. This is a model of the mind that is worthy of a democratic society. ◆

## FOR CLOSE READING

1. Mike Rose says that definitions of human intelligence should not be based solely "on grades in school and numbers on IQ tests" (16)? Is he correct? Why or why not?

2. How should intelligence be defined, according to Rose—especially among workers whose tasks are not "closely associated with formal education" (9)? How would he alter more traditional definitions?

3. Rose is opposed to definitions of intelligence that consider "everyday work to be mindless" (28). In his view, what effects are such misguided conceptions likely to have on society "in the future" (28)?

4. What does Rose mean by the "concept of cognitive variability" (29), and where—aside from watching his mother wait tables in a restaurant—did he likely learn about it?

## Strategies and Structures

1. Rose begins his essay with an account of his mother's experience as a waitress (1–6). Is this an effective introduction to his subject? Why or why not?

2. As Rose defines it, what are some of the main traits of "blue-collar brilliance?" Point to specific passages in the text where he identifies those traits most convincingly.

3. How does Rose's childhood role as an observer at his mother's restaurant resemble the adult, scholarly role he adapts throughout this essay? Explain by pointing to specific passages in the text.

4. *Other Methods.* Rose's conclusions about blue-collar intelligence are based on "a model of the mind" that, he claims at the end of his essay, is "worthy of a democratic society" (29). How and how well does Rose's definition support this ARGUMENT?

5. "I couldn't have put it into words," Rose says of this early experience of the workplace (4). How did he learn to put his observations into words? To what extent might his essay be read as a sort of LITERACY NARRATIVE?

## Thinking about Language

1. Point to specific words and phrases in his essay where Rose captures the "lingo" of the workplace (2).

2. What does Rose mean when he says that competence in the workplace was "synonymous" with physical labor (4)?

3. Look up the word *iconography* in your dictionary (10). Before the advent of rock stars and television celebrities, who or what did the term refer to?

4. Rose observed blue-collar workers for the purpose of writing their "cognitive biographies" (15). Point to places in his essay that might be considered examples of this type of writing.

## FOR WRITING

1. Spend an hour or so watching and listening to the workers in a diner, factory, store, hair salon, or other everyday workplace. Take notes on what they say and do, and write a few paragraphs capturing the scene as Rose does in the opening part of his essay.

2. Write an essay of 400–500 words explaining how a group of workers you have observed, blue-collar or otherwise, appeared to understand and define some important aspect of their work. Refer in detail to individual members of the group and what they had to say.

3. In your journal, keep a record of your experience at work. Include not only your own observations of the workplace but those of your co-workers, including what they said and did on specific occasions. Include moments of particular brilliance—and otherwise.

4. Interview several of your classmates about the skills and knowledge they acquired from summer and other jobs. Write a 400–500-word **REPORT** summarizing your findings.

5. Write a **PROFILE** of a worker you have observed and, if possible, talked to at some length. Your subject can be a close friend, a family member, one of your classmates or teachers, or simply someone you have watched perform a task or service. Be sure to include "cognitive" elements of the work being done.

You'll find quizzes on the readings at
wwnorton.com/write/back-to-the-lake.

# Being Country

Bobbie Ann Mason (b. 1940) is a novelist, an essayist, and a short story writer, and the author of a biography, *Elvis Presley* (2002). Mason grew up in western Kentucky on a farm near Mayfield. After graduating from the University of Kentucky, where she later was a writer-in-residence, she received advanced degrees from the State University of New York at Binghamton and the University of Connecticut. Mason writes mostly about the lives of working people in rural Kentucky. Her novels and short story collections include *In Country* (1985), *Zigzagging Down a Wild Trail* (2002), *An Atomic Romance* (2005), *Nancy Culpepper* (2006), and *The Girl in the Blue Beret* (2011).

"Being Country" is a chapter from Mason's *Clear Springs: A Family Story* (2000). In this autobiographical narrative, Mason uses the history and daily life of her extended family to define what it means to be *country*, showing, in rich detail, how she embraced a way of life that, as a teenager, she also dreamed of leaving behind.

F OOD WAS THE CENTER OF OUR LIVES. Everything we did and thought revolved around it. We planted it, grew it, harvested it, peeled it, cooked it, served it, consumed it—endlessly, day after day, season after season. This was life on a farm—as it had been time out of mind.

The area around Clear Springs, on Panther Creek, was one of the first white settlements in the Jackson Purchase. In the spring of 1820, Peyton Washam, his fifteen-year-old son Peter, and a third man whose name has been forgotten came to Panther Creek from Virginia with a plan to build a cabin and plant some corn. Mrs. Washam and the seven other children, whom they had left in a settlement about a hundred miles away, would come along later. Before the men could begin building, they had to slash a clearing from the wilderness. It was tougher than they expected. They had plenty of water, for the place abounded with springs, but they soon ran out of food and supplies. They sent for more, but before these arrived they were reduced to boiling and eating their small treasure (half a bushel) of seed corn—the dried corn that would have let them get out a crop. Then Peyton Washam came down with a fever. He sent for his wife to come quickly. She arrived late at night

MLA CITATION: Mason, Bobbie Ann. "Being Country." 1999. *Back to the Lake*. Ed. Thomas Cooley. 3rd ed. New York: Norton, 2015. 507-14. Print.

and got lost in the canebrake—a thicket of canes growing up to thirty feet high. Frightened in the noisy darkness, she waited, upright and sleepless, beneath an old tree till daylight, according to the accounts. She hurried on then, propelled by worry, but when she reached her husband's camp, she was too late. He had died during the night. Afterwards, she lived out his dream, settling in the vicinity with her children. The area her husband had chosen eventually grew into the community where a dozen branches of my family took root.

This story vexes me. What a bold but pathetic beginning! What careless, untrained pioneers. How could Peyton Washam and his cohorts have run out of food so soon? If they arrived in the spring, they should have planted that seed corn before long (between mid-April and mid-May). Why, in a mild Kentucky spring, did they not get a garden out right away? How could they have run out of supplies before they got their corn in the ground? Of course they had to clear some canebrake, which wasn't easy. But it wasn't as hard as clearing trees. You can even eat cane like a vegetable. In May, there would have been a carpet of wild strawberries. If Peyton Washam was too sick to forage, why didn't the kid and the other guy go pick something? What kind of pioneer eats his seed corn? Why didn't they shoot a squirrel?

Mrs. Washam is the hero of the tale. She survived and her children joined her. She probably could handle a gun. I'm sure she knew how to get out a garden. I picture her coming alone with a basket of cornbread and fried pies, looking for her sick, hungry husband, trying to follow directions scribbled on a piece of paper. Turn left *before* the canebrake. Follow the creek to the large old tree. Or maybe Peyton Washam's handwriting was bad—maybe he meant an *oak* tree.

This was the rough and foolhardy beginning of Clear Springs. The expedition was a man's notion, with a woman coming to the rescue. The men were starving without her. It makes perfect sense to me, in light of everything I know about the rural life that came down to me from that community. When I think of Clear Springs, I think first of the women cooking. Every Christmas we went out to the Mason homeplace for a grand celebration dinner that included at least a dozen cakes. And in the summer we went to big homecoming feasts—called dinner-on-the-ground—at nearby McKendree Methodist Church, which was on Mason land.

One day Mama and Granny were shelling beans and talking about the proper method of drying apples. I was nearly eleven and still entirely absorbed with the March girls in *Little Women*.[1] Drying apples was not in my dreams. Beth's death was weighing darkly on me at that moment, and I threw a little tantrum—what Mama called a hissy fit.

---

1. *Little Women:* Louisa May Alcott's novel about a family of four sisters, published in 1868–1869. The death of Beth, the second-youngest sister, is an especially poignant part of the book that often reduces readers to tears.

"Can't y'all talk about anything but food?" I screamed.     7

There was a shocked silence. "Well, what else is there?" Granny asked.

Granny didn't question a woman's duties, but I did. I didn't want to be hulling beans in a hot kitchen when I was fifty years old. I wanted to *be* somebody, maybe an airline stewardess. Also, I had been listening to the radio. I had notions.

You can always define something by identifying its most important characteristic, p. 455.

Our lives were haunted by the fear of crop failure. We ate as if we didn't know     10
where our next meal might come from. All my life I have had a recurrent food dream: I face a buffet or cafeteria line, laden with beautiful foods. I spend the entire dream choosing the foods I want. My anticipation is deliciously agonizing. I always wake up just as I've made my selections but before I get to eat.

Working with food was fraught with anxiety and desperation. In truth, no one     11
in memory had missed a meal—except Peyton Washam on the banks of Panther Creek wistfully regarding his seed corn. But the rumble of poor Peyton's belly must have survived to trouble our dreams. We were at the mercy of nature, and it wasn't to be trusted. My mother watched the skies at evening for a portent of the morrow. A cloud that went over and then turned around and came back was an especially bad sign. Our livelihood—even our lives—depended on forces outside our control.

I think this dependence on nature was at the core of my rebellion. I hated the     12
constant sense of helplessness before vast forces, the continuous threat of failure. Farmers didn't take initiative, I began to see; they reacted to whatever presented itself. I especially hated women's part in the dependence.

My mother allowed me to get spoiled. She never even tried to teach me to cook.     13
"You didn't want to learn," she says now. "You were a lady of leisure, and you didn't want to help. You had your nose in a book."

I believed progress meant freedom from the field and the range. That meant     14
moving to town, I thought.

Because we lived on the edge of Mayfield, I was acutely conscious of being     15
country. I felt inferior to people in town because we grew our food and made our clothes, while they bought whatever they needed. Although we were self-sufficient and resourceful and held clear title to our land, we lived in a state of psychological poverty. As I grew older, this acute sense of separation from town affected me more deeply. I began to sense that the fine life in town—celebrated in magazines, on radio, in movies—was denied us. Of course we weren't poor at all. Poor people had too many kids, and they weren't landowners; they rented decrepit little houses with plank floors and trash in the yard. "Poor people are wormy and eat wild onions," Mama said. We weren't poor, but we were country.

We had three wardrobes—everyday clothes, school clothes, and Sunday clothes.     16
We didn't wear our school clothes at home, but we could wear them to town. When we got home from church, we had to change back into everyday clothes before we ate Mama's big Sunday dinner.

"All the ingredients except the flour, sugar, and salt came from our farm—the chickens, the hogs, the milk and butter, the Irish potatoes, the beans, peas, corn, cabbage, apples, peaches."

"Don't eat in your good clothes!" Mama always cried. "You'll spill something on them."  17

Mama always preferred outdoor life, but she was a natural cook. At harvest time,  18
after she'd come in from the garden and put out a wash, she would whip out a noon-time dinner for the men in the field—my father and grandfather and maybe some neighbors and a couple of hired hands: fried chicken with milk gravy, ham, mashed potatoes, lima beans, field peas, corn, slaw, sliced tomatoes, fried apples, biscuits, and peach pie. This was not considered a banquet, only plain hearty food, fuel for work. All the ingredients except the flour, sugar, and salt came from our farm—the chickens, the hogs, the milk and butter, the Irish potatoes, the beans, peas, corn, cabbage, apples, peaches. Nothing was processed, except by Mama. She was always butchering and plucking and planting and hoeing and shredding and slicing and creaming (scraping cobs for the creamed corn) and pressure-cooking and canning and freezing and thawing and mixing and shaping and baking and frying.

We would eat our pie right on the same plate as our turnip greens so as not to  19
mess up another dish. The peach cobbler oozed all over the turnip-green juice and the pork grease. "It all goes to the same place," Mama said. It was boarding-house reach, no "Pass the peas, please." Conversation detracted from the sensuous plea-sure of filling yourself. A meal required meat and vegetables and dessert. The bever-ages were milk and iced tea ("ice-tea"). We never used napkins or ate tossed salad. Our salads were Jell-O and slaw. We ate "poke salet" and wilted lettuce. Mama picked tender, young pokeweed in the woods in the spring, before it turned poison, and cooked it a good long time to get the bitterness out. We liked it with vinegar and minced boiled eggs. Wilted lettuce was tender new lettuce, shredded, with sliced radishes and green onions, and blasted with hot bacon grease to blanch the rawness. "Too many fresh vegetables in summer gives people the scours," Daddy said.

Food was better in town, we thought. It wasn't plain and everyday. The centers  20
of pleasure were there—the hamburger and barbecue places, the movie shows, all

South side of Mayfield courthouse square, 1957.

the places to buy things. Woolworth's, with the pneumatic tubes overhead rushing money along a metallic mole tunnel up to a balcony; Lochridge & Ridgway, with an engraved sign on the third-story cornice: STOVES, APPLIANCES, PLOWS. On the mezzanine at that store, I bought my first phonograph records, brittle 78s of big-band music—Woody Herman and Glenn Miller, and Glen Gray and his Casa Loma Orchestra playing "No Name Jive." A circuit of the courthouse square took you past the grand furniture stores, the two dime stores, the shoe stores, the men's stores, the ladies' stores, the banks, the drugstores. You'd walk past the poolroom and an exhaust fan would blow the intoxicating smell of hamburgers in your face. Before she bought a freezer, Mama stored meat in a rented food locker in town, near the ice company. She stored the butchered calf there, and she fetched hunks of him each week to fry. But hamburgers in town were better. They were greasier, and they came in waxed-paper packages.

At the corner drugstore, on the square, Mama and Janice and I sat at filigreed 21 wrought-iron tables on a black-and-white mosaic tile floor, eating peppermint ice cream. It was very cold in there, under the ceiling fans. The ice cream was served elegantly, in paper cones sunk into black plastic holders. We were uptown.

The A&P grocery, a block away, reeked of the rich aroma of ground coffee. 22 Daddy couldn't stand the smell of coffee, but Mama loved it. Daddy retched and scoffed in his exaggerated fashion. "I can't stand that smell!" Granny perked coffee, and Granddaddy told me it would turn a child black. I hated coffee. I wouldn't touch it till I was thirty. We savored store-bought food—coconuts, pineapples, and Vienna sausages and potted meat in little cans that opened with keys. We rarely went to the uptown A&P. We usually traded at a small mom-and-pop grocery, where the proprietors slapped the hands of black children who touched the candy case. I wondered if they were black from coffee.

In the summer of 1954, when I was about to enter high school, my mother got a    23 chance to run a nearby restaurant on the highway across the train track. My parents knew the owner, and one day he stopped by and asked Mama if she'd like to manage the place. She wasn't working at the Merit[2] at that time, and she jumped at the opportunity.

"Why, anybody could cook hamburgers and French fries for the public," Mama    24 said confidently. "That would be easy."

I went with her to inspect the restaurant—a square cinder-block building with a    25 picture-window view of the highway. There were no trees around, just a graveled parking area. It was an informal sort of place, with a simple kitchen, a deep fryer, a grill, some pots and pans. There were five or six tables and a counter with stools. Mama saw potential.

"Catfish platters," she said. "Fish. Hush puppies. Slaw. French fries."    26

I was so excited I couldn't sleep. Running our own little restaurant could mean    27 we wouldn't have to work in the garden. I wanted nothing more to do with okra and beans. Besides, the restaurant had an apartment above it. I wanted to live there, on the highway. Marlene was still running her frozen-custard stand nearby, and now I too would get to meet strangers traveling through. Mama and I inspected the apartment: a living room, a kitchen, and two bedrooms. It was all new and fresh. I loved it.

"Oh, please, let's move here," I begged, wishing desperately for novelty, deliver-    28 ance, and an endless supply of Co'-Colas.

Mama's eyes lit up. "We'll see," she said.    29

A restaurant would be ideal for her. "It's a chance to make big money," she told    30 me. She told the owner she would try it for a while, to see how she liked it. If she became the manager, then she would rent it for a hundred dollars a month.

"If it works out, maybe I could make a hundred dollars a *week*," she said.    31

I tagged along with her when she worked at the restaurant. I felt important    32 waiting on customers—strangers driving along the highway and stopping for a bite to eat right where I was. I wanted to meet somebody from New York. When I drew

2. *Merit*: Kentucky's civil service system.

glasses of foamy Coca-Cola from the fountain, the Coke fizzed over crushed ice. I made grilled-cheese sandwiches in the grilled-cheese machine. I experimented with milk shakes. I was flying.

Most of all, I loved the jukebox. The jukebox man came by to change records and insert new red-rimmed paper strips of titles: Doris Day and Johnnie Ray duets, "Teardrops from My Eyes" by Ruth Brown, and "P.S. I Love You" by a Kentucky vocal group called the Hilltoppers. I listened avidly to everything. I was fourteen and deeply concerned about my suntan, and I was saving pocket money to buy records. 33

The restaurant had a television set, which sat in a corner with something called a television light on top—a prism of soft colors which supposedly kept people from ruining their eyes on TV rays. I had hardly ever watched television, and I was captivated by Sid Caesar's variety show and *I Love Lucy*. When the evening crowd came in, Mama trotted back and forth from the kitchen with her hamburger platters and catfish platters. She would stop and laugh at something Lucy and Ethel were doing on the screen. 34

Mama had to give up the restaurant even before the trial period ended. She didn't do it voluntarily. Granddaddy stepped in and told her she had to. 35

"We need you here at home," he said. "Running a eating place out on the highway ain't fitten work." 36

Daddy didn't stand up for her. "How would you make anything?" he asked her. "By the time you pay out that hundred dollars a month and all the expenses, you won't have nothing left. First thing you know, you'll get behind and then you'll be owing *him*." 37

Granny said, "And who's going to do your cooking here?" 38

That was that. Afterwards, Mama cooked her hamburger platters at home, but they weren't the same without the fountain Cokes and the jukebox and the television. I thought I saw a little fire go out of her then. Much later, her fire would almost die. But my own flame was burning brighter. I had had a glimpse of life outside the farm, and I wanted it. 39

I can still see Mama emerging from that restaurant kitchen, carrying two hamburger platters and gabbing with her customers as if they were old friends who had dropped in to visit and sit a spell. In the glass of the picture window, reflections from the TV set flicker like candles at the church Christmas service. 40

And then the blackberries were ripe. We spent every July and August in the berry patch. The tame berries had spread along the fencerows and creek banks. When they ripened, Mama would exclaim in wonder, "There are *worlds* of berries down there!" She always "engaged" the berries to customers. By June, she would say, "I've already got forty gallons of berries engaged." 41

We strode out at dawn, in the dew, and picked until the mid-morning sun bore    42
down on our heads. To protect her hands from the briars, Mama made gloves from
old bluejeans. Following the berries down the creek bank, we perched on ledges
and tiptoed on unsure footing through thickets. We tunneled. When Mama saw
an  especially large berry just out of reach, she would manage to get it somehow,
even if she had to lean her body against the bush and let it support her while she
plucked the prize. We picked in quart baskets, then poured the berries into red-
and-white Krey lard buckets. The berries settled quickly, and Mama picked an
extra quart to top off the full buckets. By nine o'clock the sun was high, and I
struggled to the house with my four gallons, eager to wash the chiggers off and eat
some cereal.

From picking blackberries, I learned about money. I wouldn't eat the berries,    43
even on my cereal: I wanted the money. One summer I picked eighty gallons and
earned eighty dollars—much more than Mama made in a week when she worked
at the Merit. Granny said food was everything, but I was hungry for something
else—a kind of food that didn't grow in the ground. Yet I couldn't deny that we
were always feasting. We ate sumptuous meals, never missing dessert. Once in a
while, Daddy brought home exotic treats—fried oysters in little goldfish cartons or
hot tamales wrapped in corn shucks. At Christmas, the dairy he drove for produced jugs of boiled custard, and we slurped gallons of it even though it was not
really as good as Granny's, which was naturally yellow from fresh country eggs.
Granny complained that store-bought eggs were pale. When the cows needed feed,
Daddy took a load of corn from the corncrib to the feed mill and had it ground and
mixed with molasses and wheat and oats. He brought it home and filled the feed
bin, a big box with a hinged lid, like a giant coffin. I would chew a mouthful now
and then for the sweetening.

One spring I rode the corn planter behind Daddy on the tractor. He had plowed    44
and disked and harrowed the ground. Sitting in a concave metal seat with holes in
it, I rode the planter, which drilled furrows to receive the seed. At the end of each
row I closed the hoppers so they wouldn't release seed while he turned the tractor
in a wide loop. When he nosed down the next row, I opened the hoppers at his
signal, so that the seed would trickle out again, evenly spaced, behind the drill.
The planter covered the seed behind us. We didn't talk much in our awkward cara-
van. As we rode the long hot rows, rich floods of remembered music accompanied
me as vividly as if I had been wearing a Walkman. Top Ten numbers like "Ruby,"
"The Song from Moulin Rouge," and "Rags to Riches" rolled through my head with
the promise that I would not have to plant corn when I grew up.

As I look back, the men recede into the furrows, into the waves of the ocean,    45
and the women stand erect, churning and frying. ◆

## FOR CLOSE READING

1. According to Bobbie Ann Mason, what it means to be "country" can be defined by what one characteristic in particular? How did this distinguishing feature come to be so important?

2. Mason says her family wasn't poor—they owned their own land, and they always had plenty to eat. So what does she mean when she says "we lived in a state of psychological poverty" (15)?

3. "I was hungry," says Mason, "for something else—a kind of food that didn't grow in the ground" (43). What kind of food is she talking about here?

4. When Mason's mother had to give up running her own restaurant, her daughter thought she "saw a little fire go out of her" (39). What fire? Why did it diminish?

5. As a girl, Mason liked picking blackberries. Why? Why didn't she like riding behind the tractor and planting corn with her father? Why did she dislike farming in general?

6. Mason refers several times to specific songs, musicians, and TV shows. What do these references tell us about her as a teenager growing up in rural America?

## Strategies and Structures

1. In addition to giving a little family background, what is Mason's PURPOSE in beginning her chapter with the NARRATIVE of the settlement of the area in Kentucky where her family's farm was located? Where and why does "seed corn" come up again in her essay (2, 3)?

2. If Mrs. Washam is "the hero" of that opening tale, who is the hero of the rest of the tale Mason is telling (4)? What do the two have in common? Explain.

3. What other characteristics and qualities of "being country"—besides those having to do with producing, preparing, and eating food—does Mason introduce? Where? How do these characteristics help to broaden her basic definition?

4. Mason defines life in the country in part by COMPARING it with life in town. Where does she develop this comparison, and what does it contribute to her definition?

5. *Other Methods.* Mason frequently uses DESCRIPTION to extend her definition and help explain what she means by her key terms. Point out descriptive details in her essay that you find particularly effective for this purpose.

## Thinking about Language

1. Why does Mason refer to herself as "being country" instead of, for example, "being from the country" (15)?

2. Mason says the old settlement story about the family land "vexes" her (3). What are the implications of this word? How does she show her vexation?

3. Why does Mason explain that her family pronounced *iced tea* as "ice-tea" (19)?

4. "I was flying," says Mason of her time as a helper in her mother's restaurant (32). How does this HYPERBOLE tie in with her earlier dreams of becoming an airline stewardess (9)?

5. When describing her memories of her mother at the restaurant, Mason compares the flicker of the TV to the flicker of candles in a church (40). Why? What's the purpose of this ANALOGY?

6. Mason remembers the feed bin on the family farm as looking "like a giant coffin" (43). How does this SIMILE fit in with her other corny memories—or rather memories of corn?

## FOR WRITING

1. In a few paragraphs, describe a group of people doing some kind of particular work that defines who and what they are.

2. Write an essay about growing up that shows how you and your family defined yourselves. Be sure to indicate where and how you didn't fit the mold—or the mold didn't fit you.

3. In approximately 400 words, write a RHETORICAL ANALYSIS of "Being Country" (or some other chapter from Mason's Clear Springs) as a portrait of a young woman who embraces her region and family history but also seems ready to escape what she sees, increasingly, as their shortcomings and limitations.

4. In approximately 400 words, write a RHETORICAL ANALYSIS of "Being Country" as a MEMOIR of a place and family. Define what you mean by the memoir as a type of autobiographical narrative and examine specific descriptive and other passages in the text where you think Mason brings the past to life most vividly.

5. Devote a section of your journal to your family history. Make regular entries as particular scenes and events come back to you and as you visit home and relatives or otherwise learn more about them.

...........................................................•

You'll find quizzes on the readings at
wwnorton.com/write/back-to-the-lake.

# A Good Man Is Hard to Find

Mary Flannery O'Connor (1925–1964) was born in Savannah, Georgia, studied at the Georgia State College for Women, and earned an MFA at the Writer's Workshop of the University of Iowa. Soon afterward, she was diagnosed with lupus, a painful auto-immune disorder that would trouble her for the rest of her brief life. Eight years after she died of the disease, her posthumously collected *Complete Stories* won the 1972 National Book Award. She wrote two novels, *Wise Blood* (1952) and *The Violent Bear It Away* (1960), but she's best known for her witty, sharply observed, darkly ironic, and sometimes shockingly violent short stories—the epitome of what is known as "Southern Gothic."

Above all, O'Connor's fiction is marked by her obsessions with morality and mortality, as well as her unwillingness to accept simplistic explanations for life's mysteries. "A Good Man Is Hard to Find," the title story in her 1955 collection, culminates in a kind of debate over the definition of "goodness"—and the related virtue, *redemption*. Or are there some people in whom no goodness resides, people who are simply irredeemable? O'Connor provides no easy answer.

T HE GRANDMOTHER didn't want to go to Florida. She wanted to visit some of    1
her connections in east Tennessee and she was seizing at every chance to change Bailey's mind. Bailey was the son she lived with, her only boy. He was sitting on the edge of his chair at the table, bent over the orange sports section of the *Journal*. "Now look here, Bailey," she said, "see here, read this," and she stood with one hand on her thin hip and the other rattling the newspaper at his bald head. "Here this fellow that calls himself The Misfit is aloose from the Federal Pen and headed toward Florida and you read here what it says he did to these people. Just you read it. I wouldn't take my children in any direction with a criminal like that aloose in it. I couldn't answer to my conscience if I did."

Bailey didn't look up from his reading so she wheeled around then and faced the    2
children's mother, a young woman in slacks, whose face was as broad and innocent as a cabbage and was tied around with a green head-kerchief that had two points

MLA CITATION: O'Connor, Flannery. "A Good Man Is Hard to Find." 1955. *Back to the Lake.* Ed. Thomas Cooley. 3rd ed. New York: Norton, 2015. 517–30. Print.

on the top like rabbit's ears. She was sitting on the sofa, feeding the baby his apricots out of a jar. "The children have been to Florida before," the old lady said. "You all ought to take them somewhere else for a change so they would see different parts of the world and be broad. They never have been to east Tennessee."

The children's mother didn't seem to hear her but the eight-year-old boy, John  3
Wesley, a stocky child with glasses, said, "If you don't want to go to Florida, why dontcha stay at home?" He and the little girl, June Star, were reading the funny papers on the floor.

"She wouldn't stay at home to be queen for a day," June Star said without raising  4
her yellow head.

"Yes and what would you do if this fellow, The Misfit, caught you?" the grand-  5
mother asked.

"I'd smack his face," John Wesley said.  6

"She wouldn't stay at home for a million bucks," June Star said. "Afraid she'd  7
miss something. She has to go everywhere we go."

"All right, Miss," the grandmother said. "Just remember that the next time you  8
want me to curl your hair."

June Star said her hair was naturally curly.  9

The next morning the grandmother was the first one in the car, ready to go. She  10
had her big black valise that looked like the head of a hippopotamus in one corner, and underneath it she was hiding a basket with Pitty Sing, the cat, in it. She didn't intend for the cat to be left alone in the house for three days because he would miss her too much and she was afraid he might brush against one of the gas burners and accidentally asphyxiate himself. Her son, Bailey, didn't like to arrive at a motel with a cat.

She sat in the middle of the back seat with John Wesley and June Star on either  11
side of her. Bailey and the children's mother and the baby sat in front and they left Atlanta at eight forty-five with the mileage on the car at 55890. The grandmother wrote this down because she thought it would be interesting to say how many miles they had been when they got back. It took them twenty minutes to reach the outskirts of the city.

The old lady settled herself comfortably, removing her white cotton gloves and  12
putting them up with her purse on the shelf in front of the back window. The children's mother still had on slacks and still had her head tied up in a green kerchief, but the grandmother had on a navy blue straw sailor hat with a bunch of white violets on the brim and a navy blue dress with a small white dot in the print. Her collars and cuffs were white organdy trimmed with lace and at her neckline she had pinned a purple spray of cloth violets containing a sachet. In case of an accident, anyone seeing her dead on the highway would know at once that she was a lady.

She said she thought it was going to be a good day for driving, neither too hot 13
nor too cold, and she cautioned Bailey that the speed limit was fifty-five miles an
hour and that the patrolmen hid themselves behind billboards and small clumps of
trees and sped out after you before you had a chance to slow down. She pointed out
interesting details of the scenery: Stone Mountain; the blue granite that in some
places came up to both sides of the highway; the brilliant red clay banks slightly
streaked with purple; and the various crops that made rows of green lace-work on
the ground. The trees were full of silver-white sunlight and the meanest of them
sparkled. The children were reading comic magazines and their mother had gone
back to sleep.

"Let's go through Georgia fast so we won't have to look at it much," John Wesley 14
said.

"If I were a little boy," said the grandmother, "I wouldn't talk about my native 15
state that way. Tennessee has the mountains and Georgia has the hills."

"Tennessee is just a hillbilly dumping ground," John Wesley said, "and Georgia is 16
a lousy state too."

"You said it," June Star said. 17

"In my time," said the grandmother, folding her thin veined fingers, "children 18
were more respectful of their native states and their parents and everything else.
People did right then. Oh look at the cute little pickaninny!" she said and pointed
to a Negro child standing in the door of a shack. "Wouldn't that make a picture,
now?" she asked and they all turned and looked at the little Negro out of the back
window. He waved.

"He didn't have any britches on," June Star said. 19

"He probably didn't have any," the grandmother explained. "Little niggers in the 20
country don't have things like we do. If I could paint, I'd paint that picture," she said.

The children exchanged comic books. 21

The grandmother offered to hold the baby and the children's mother passed him 22
over the front seat to her. She set him on her knee and bounced him and told him
about the things they were passing. She rolled her eyes and screwed up her mouth
and stuck her leathery thin face into his smooth bland one. Occasionally he gave
her a faraway smile. They passed a large cotton field with five or six graves fenced
in the middle of it, like a small island. "Look at the graveyard!" the grandmother
said, pointing it out. "That was the old family burying ground. That belonged to
the plantation."

"Where's the plantation?" John Wesley asked. 23

"Gone With the Wind," said the grandmother. "Ha. Ha." 24

When the children finished all the comic books they had brought, they opened 25
the lunch and ate it. The grandmother ate a peanut butter sandwich and an olive

and would not let the children throw the box and the paper napkins out the window. When there was nothing else to do they played a game by choosing a cloud and making the other two guess what shape it suggested. John Wesley took one the shape of a cow and June Star guessed a cow and John Wesley said, no, an automobile, and June Star said he didn't play fair, and they began to slap each other over the grandmother.

The grandmother said she would tell them a story if they would keep quiet. When she told a story, she rolled her eyes and waved her head and was very dramatic. She said once when she was a maiden lady she had been courted by a Mr. Edgar Atkins Teagarden from Jasper, Georgia. She said he was a very good-looking man and a gentleman and that he brought her a watermelon every Saturday afternoon with his initials cut in it, E. A. T. Well, one Saturday, she said, Mr. Teagarden brought the watermelon and there was nobody at home and he left it on the front porch and returned in his buggy to Jasper, but she never got the watermelon, she said, because a nigger boy ate it when he saw the initials, E. A. T.! This story tickled John Wesley's funny bone and he giggled and giggled but June Star didn't think it was any good. She said she wouldn't marry a man that just brought her a watermelon on Saturday. The grandmother said she would have done well to marry Mr. Teagarden because he was a gentleman and had bought Coca-Cola stock when it first came out and that he had died only a few years ago, a very wealthy man. 26

They stopped at The Tower for barbecued sandwiches. The Tower was a part stucco and part wood filling station and dance hall set in a clearing outside of Timothy. A fat man named Red Sammy Butts ran it and there were signs stuck here and there on the building and for miles up and down the highway saying, TRY RED SAMMY'S FAMOUS BARBECUE. NONE LIKE FAMOUS RED SAMMY'S! RED SAM! THE FAT BOY WITH THE HAPPY LAUGH. A VETERAN! RED SAMMY'S YOUR MAN! 27

Red Sammy was lying on the bare ground outside The Tower with his head under a truck while a gray monkey about a foot high, chained to a small chinaberry tree, chattered nearby. The monkey sprang back into the tree and got on the highest limb as soon as he saw the children jump out of the car and run toward him. 28

Inside, The Tower was a long dark room with a counter at one end and tables at the other and dancing space in the middle. They all sat down at a board table next to the nickelodeon and Red Sam's wife, a tall burnt-brown woman with hair and eyes lighter than her skin, came and took their order. The children's mother put a dime in the machine and played "The Tennessee Waltz," and the grandmother said that tune always made her want to dance. She asked Bailey if he would like to dance but he only glared at her. He didn't have a naturally sunny disposition like she did and trips made him nervous. The grandmother's brown eyes were very bright. She swayed her head from side to side and pretended she was dancing in 29 her chair. June Star said play something she could tap to so the children's mother put in another dime and played a fast number and June Star stepped out onto the dance floor and did her tap routine.

"Ain't she cute?" Red Sam's wife said, leaning over the counter. "Would you like to come be my little girl?"   30

"No I certainly wouldn't," June Star said. "I wouldn't live in a broken-down place like this for a million bucks!" and she ran back to the table.   31

"Ain't she cute?" the woman repeated, stretching her mouth politely.   32

"Arn't you ashamed?" hissed the grandmother.   33

Red Sam came in and told his wife to quit lounging on the counter and hurry up with these people's order. His khaki trousers reached just to his hip bones and his stomach hung over them like a sack of meal swaying under his shirt. He came over and sat down at a table nearby and let out a combination sigh and yodel. "You can't win," he said. "You can't win," and he wiped his sweating red face off with a gray handkerchief. "These days you don't know who to trust," he said. "Ain't that the truth?"   34

"People are certainly not nice like they used to be," said the grandmother.   35

"Two fellers come in here last week," Red Sammy said, "driving a Chrysler. It was a old beat-up car but it was a good one and these boys looked all right to me. Said they worked at the mill and you know I let them fellers charge the gas they bought? Now why did I do that?"   36

"Because you're a good man!" the grandmother said at once.   37

"Yes'm,[1] I suppose so," Red Sam said as if he were struck with this answer.   38

His wife brought the orders, carrying the five plates all at once without a tray, two in each hand and one balanced on her arm. "It isn't a soul in this green world of God's that you can trust," she said. "And I don't count nobody out of that, not nobody," she repeated, looking at Red Sammy.   39

"Did you read about that criminal, The Misfit, that's escaped?" asked the grandmother.   40

"I wouldn't be a bit surprised if he didn't attact this place right here," said the woman. "If he hears about it being here, I wouldn't be none surprised to see him. If he hears it's two cent in the cash register, I wouldn't be a tall surprised if he . . ."   41

"That'll do," Red Sam said. "Go bring these people their Co'-Colas," and the woman went off to get the rest of the order.   42

"A good man is hard to find," Red Sammy said. "Everything is getting terrible. I remember the day you could go off and leave your screen door unlatched. Not no more."   43

---

1. *Yes'm/Nome:* O'Connor's way of representing the informal southern pronunciation of "yes, ma'am" and "no, ma'am."

He and the grandmother discussed better times. The old lady said that in her 44 opinion Europe was entirely to blame for the way things were now. She said the way Europe acted you would think we were made of money and Red Sam said it was no use talking about it, she was exactly right. The children ran outside into the white sunlight and looked at the monkey in the lacy chinaberry tree. He was busy catching fleas on himself and biting each one carefully between his teeth as if it were a delicacy.

They drove off again into the hot afternoon. The grandmother took cat naps and 45 woke up every few minutes with her own snoring. Outside of Toombsboro she woke up and recalled an old plantation that she had visited in this neighborhood once when she was a young lady. She said the house had six white columns across the front and that there was an avenue of oaks leading up to it and two little wooden trellis arbors on either side in front where you sat down with your suitor after a stroll in the garden. She recalled exactly which road to turn off to get to it. She knew that Bailey would not be willing to lose any time looking at an old house, but the more she talked about it, the more she wanted to see it once again and find out if the little twin arbors were still standing. "There was a secret panel in this house," she said craftily, not telling the truth but wishing that she were, "and the story went that all the family silver was hidden in it when Sherman came through but it was never found . . ."

"Hey!" John Wesley said. "Let's go see it! We'll find it! We'll poke all the wood- 46 work and find it! Who lives there? Where do you turn off at? Hey Pop, can't we turn off there?"

"We never have seen a house with a secret panel!" June Star shrieked. "Let's go 47 to the house with the secret panel! Hey Pop, can't we go see the house with the secret panel!"

"It's not far from here, I know," the grandmother said. "It wouldn't take over 48 twenty minutes."

Bailey was looking straight ahead. His jaw was as rigid as a horseshoe. "No," he 49 said.

The children began to yell and scream that they wanted to see the house with 50 the secret panel. John Wesley kicked the back of the front seat and June Star hung over her mother's shoulder and whined desperately into her ear that they never had any fun even on their vacation, that they could never do what THEY wanted to do. The baby began to scream and John Wesley kicked the back of the seat so hard that his father could feel the blows in his kidney.

"All right!" he shouted and drew the car to a stop at the side of the road. "Will 51 you all shut up? Will you all just shut up for one second? If you don't shut up, we won't go anywhere."

"It would be very educational for them," the grandmother murmured.   52

"All right," Bailey said, "but get this: this is the only time we're going to stop for   53
anything like this. This is the one and only time."

"The dirt road that you have to turn down is about a mile back," the grand-   54
mother directed. "I marked it when we passed."

"A dirt road," Bailey groaned.   55

After they had turned around and were headed toward the dirt road, the grand-   56
mother recalled other points about the house, the beautiful glass over the front
doorway and the candle-lamp in the hall. John Wesley said that the secret panel
was probably in the fireplace.

"You can't go inside this house," Bailey said. "You don't know who lives there."   57

"While you all talk to the people in front, I'll run around behind and get in a   58
window," John Wesley suggested.

"We'll all stay in the car," his mother said.   59

They turned onto the dirt road and the car raced roughly along in a swirl of pink   60
dust. The grandmother recalled the times when there were no paved roads and
thirty miles was a day's journey. The dirt road was hilly and there were sudden
washes in it and sharp curves on dangerous embankments. All at once they would
be on a hill, looking down over the blue tops of trees for miles around, then the
next minute, they would be in a red depression with the dust-coated trees looking
down on them.

"This place had better turn up in a minute," Bailey said, "or I'm going to turn   61
around."

The road looked as if no one had traveled on it in months.   62

"It's not much farther," the grandmother said and just as she said it, a horrible   63
thought came to her. The thought was so embarrassing that she turned red in the
face and her eyes dilated and her feet jumped up, upsetting her valise in the corner.
The instant the valise moved, the newspaper top she had over the basket under it
rose with a snarl and Pitty Sing, the cat, sprang onto Bailey's shoulder.

The children were thrown to the floor and their mother, clutching the baby, was   64
thrown out the door onto the ground; the old lady was thrown into the front seat.
The car turned over once and landed right-side-up in a gulch off the side of the
road. Bailey remained in the driver's seat with the cat—gray-striped with a broad
white face and an orange nose—clinging to his neck like a caterpillar.

As soon as the children saw they could move their arms and legs, they scram-   65
bled out of the car, shouting, "We've had an ACCIDENT!" The grandmother was
curled up under the dashboard, hoping she was injured so that Bailey's wrath
would not come down on her all at once. The horrible thought she had had before
the accident was that the house she had remembered so vividly was not in Georgia
but in Tennessee.

Bailey removed the cat from his neck with both hands and flung it out the window against the side of a pine tree. Then he got out of the car and started looking for the children's mother. She was sitting against the side of the red gutted ditch, holding the screaming baby, but she only had a cut down her face and a broken shoulder. "We've had an ACCIDENT!" the children screamed in a frenzy of delight. 66

"But nobody's killed," June Star said with disappointment as the grandmother limped out of the car, her hat still pinned to her head but the broken front brim standing up at a jaunty angle and the violet spray hanging off the side. They all sat down in the ditch, except the children, to recover from the shock. They were all shaking. 67

"Maybe a car will come along," said the children's mother hoarsely. 68

"I believe I have injured an organ," said the grandmother, pressing her side, but no one answered her. Bailey's teeth were clattering. He had on a yellow sport shirt with bright blue parrots designed in it and his face was as yellow as the shirt. The grandmother decided that she would not mention that the house was in Tennessee. 69

The road was about ten feet above and they could see only the tops of the trees on the other side of it. Behind the ditch they were sitting in there were more woods, tall and dark and deep. In a few minutes they saw a car some distance away on top of a hill, coming slowly as if the occupants were watching them. The grandmother stood up and waved both arms dramatically to attract their attention. The car continued to come on slowly, disappeared around a bend and appeared again, moving even slower, on top of the hill they had gone over. It was a big black battered hearse-like automobile. There were three men in it. 70

It came to a stop just over them and for some minutes, the driver looked down with a steady expressionless gaze to where they were sitting, and didn't speak. Then he turned his head and muttered something to the other two and they got out. One was a fat boy in black trousers and a red sweat shirt with a silver stallion embossed on the front of it. He moved around on the right side of them and stood staring, his mouth partly open in a kind of loose grin. The other had on khaki pants and a blue striped coat and a gray hat pulled down very low, hiding most of his face. He came around slowly on the left side. Neither spoke. 71

The driver got out of the car and stood by the side of it, looking down at them. He was an older man than the other two. His hair was just beginning to gray and he wore silver-rimmed spectacles that gave him a scholarly look. He had a long creased face and didn't have on any shirt or undershirt. He had on blue jeans that were too tight for him and was holding a black hat and a gun. The two boys also had guns. 72

"We've had an ACCIDENT!" the children screamed. 73

The grandmother had the peculiar feeling that the bespectacled man was some- 74
one she knew. His face was as familiar to her as if she had known him all her life
but she could not recall who he was. He moved away from the car and began to
come down the embankment, placing his feet carefully so that he wouldn't slip. He
had on tan and white shoes and no socks, and his ankles were red and thin. "Good
afternoon," he said. "I see you all had you a little spill."

"We turned over twice!" said the grandmother. 75

"Oncet," he corrected. "We seen it happen. Try their car and see will it run, 76
Hiram," he said quietly to the boy with the gray hat.

"What you got that gun for?" John Wesley asked. "Whatcha gonna do with that 77
gun?"

"Lady," the man said to the children's mother, "would you mind calling them 78
children to sit down by you? Children make me nervous. I want all you all to sit
down right together there where you're at."

"What are you telling US what to do for?" June Star asked. 79

Behind them the line of woods gaped like a dark open mouth. "Come here," said 80
their mother.

"Look here now," Bailey began suddenly, "we're in a predicament! We're in . . ." 81

The grandmother shrieked. She scrambled to her feet and stood staring. "You're 82
The Misfit!" she said. "I recognized you at once!"

"Yes'm," the man said, smiling slightly as if he were pleased in spite of himself to 83
be known, "but it would have been better for all of you, lady, if you hadn't of reck-
ernized me."

Bailey turned his head sharply and said something to his mother that shocked 84
even the children. The old lady began to cry and The Misfit reddened.

"Lady," he said, "don't you get upset. Sometimes a man says things he don't 85
mean. I don't reckon he meant to talk to you thataway."

"You wouldn't shoot a lady, would you?" the grandmother said and removed a 86
clean handkerchief from her cuff and began to slap at her eyes with it.

The Misfit pointed the toe of his shoe into the ground and made a little hole and 87
then covered it up again. "I would hate to have to," he said.

"Listen," the grandmother almost screamed, "I know you're a good man. You don't 88
look a bit like you have common blood. I know you must come from nice people!"

"Yes mam," he said, "finest people in the world." When he smiled he showed a 89
row of strong white teeth. "God never made a finer woman than my mother and
my daddy's heart was pure gold," he said. The boy with the red sweat shirt had
come around behind them and was standing with his gun at his hip. The Misfit
squatted down on the ground. "Watch them children, Bobby Lee," he said. "You
know they make me nervous." He looked at the six of them huddled together in

front of him and he seemed to be embarrassed as if he couldn't think of anything to say. "Ain't a cloud in the sky," he remarked, looking up at it. "Don't see no sun but don't see no cloud neither."

"Yes, it's a beautiful day," said the grandmother. "Listen," she said, "you  90
shouldn't call yourself The Misfit because I know you're a good man at heart. I can just look at you and tell."

In a debate, try to get the other side to accept your definition of key terms, p. 452.

"Hush!" Bailey yelled. "Hush! Everybody shut up and let me handle  91
this!" He was squatting in the position of a runner about to sprint forward but he didn't move.

"I pre-chate that, lady," The Misfit said and drew a little circle in the ground  92
with the butt of his gun.

"It'll take a half a hour to fix this here car," Hiram called, looking over the raised  93
hood of it.

"Well, first you and Bobby Lee get him and that little boy to step over yonder  94
with you," The Misfit said, pointing to Bailey and John Wesley. "The boys want to ast you something," he said to Bailey. "Would you mind stepping back in them woods there with them?"

"Listen," Bailey began, "we're in a terrible predicament! Nobody realizes what  95
this is," and his voice cracked. His eyes were as blue and intense as the parrots in his shirt and he remained perfectly still.

The grandmother reached up to adjust her hat brim as if she were going to the  96
woods with him but it came off in her hand. She stood staring at it and after a second she let it fall on the ground. Hiram pulled Bailey up by the arm as if he were assisting an old man. John Wesley caught hold of his father's hand and Bobby Lee followed. They went off toward the woods and just as they reached the dark edge, Bailey turned and supporting himself against a gray naked pine trunk, he shouted, "I'll be back in a minute, Mamma, wait on me!"

"Come back this instant!" his mother shrilled but they all disappeared into the  97
woods.

"Bailey Boy!" the grandmother called in a tragic voice but she found she was  98
looking at The Misfit squatting on the ground in front of her. "I just know you're a good man," she said desperately. "You're not a bit common!"

"Nome, I ain't a good man," The Misfit said after a second as if he had con-  99
sidered her statement carefully, "but I ain't the worst in the world neither. My daddy said I was a different breed of dog from my brothers and sisters. 'You know,' Daddy said, 'it's some that can live their whole life out without asking about it and it's others has to know why it is, and this boy is one of the latters. He's going to be into everything!'" He put on his black hat and looked up suddenly and then away deep into the woods as if he were embarrassed again. "I'm sorry I don't have on a shirt before you ladies," he said, hunching his shoulders

slightly. "We buried our clothes that we had on when we escaped and we're just making do until we can get better. We borrowed these from some folks we met," he explained.

"That's perfectly all right," the grandmother said. "Maybe Bailey has an extra shirt in his suitcase." 100

"I'll look and see terrectly," The Misfit said. 101

"Where are they taking him?" the children's mother screamed. 102

"Daddy was a card himself," The Misfit said. "You couldn't put anything over on him. He never got in trouble with the Authorities though. Just had the knack of handling them." 103

"You could be honest too if you'd only try," said the grandmother. "Think how wonderful it would be to settle down and live a comfortable life and not have to think about somebody chasing you all the time." 104

The Misfit kept scratching in the ground with the butt of his gun as if he were thinking about it. "Yes'm, somebody is always after you," he murmured. 105

The grandmother noticed how thin his shoulder blades were just behind his hat because she was standing up looking down on him. "Do you ever pray?" she asked. 106

He shook his head. All she saw was the black hat wiggle between his shoulder blades. "Nome," he said. 107

There was a pistol shot from the woods, followed closely by another. Then silence. The old lady's head jerked around. She could hear the wind move through the tree tops like a long satisfied insuck of breath. "Bailey Boy!" she called. 108

"I was a gospel singer for a while," The Misfit said. "I been most everything. Been in the arm service, both land and sea, at home and abroad, been twict married, been an undertaker, been with the railroads, plowed Mother Earth, been in a tornado, seen a man burnt alive oncet," and he looked up at the children's mother and the little girl who were sitting close together, their faces white and their eyes glassy; "I even seen a woman flogged," he said. 109

"Pray, pray," the grandmother began, "pray, pray . . ." 110

"I never was a bad boy that I remember of," The Misfit said in an almost dreamy voice, "but somewheres along the line I done something wrong and got sent to the penitentiary. I was buried alive," and he looked up and held her attention to him by a steady stare. 111

"That's when you should have started to pray," she said. "What did you do to get sent to the penitentiary that first time?" 112

"Turn to the right, it was a wall," The Misfit said, looking up again at the cloudless sky. "Turn to the left, it was a wall. Look up it was a ceiling, look down it was a floor. I forget what I done, lady. I set there and set there, trying to remember what it was I done and I ain't recalled it to this day. Oncet in a while, I would think it was coming to me, but it never come." 113

"Maybe they put you in by mistake." the old lady said vaguely. 114

"Nome," he said. "It wasn't no mistake. They had the papers on me." 115

"You must have stolen something," she said. 116

The Misfit sneered slightly. "Nobody had nothing I wanted," he said. "It was a 117 head-doctor at the penitentiary said what I had done was kill my daddy but I known that for a lie. My daddy died in nineteen ought nineteen of the epidemic flu and I never had a thing to do with it. He was buried in the Mount Hopewell Baptist churchyard and you can go there and see for yourself."

"If you would pray," the old lady said, "Jesus would help you." 118

"That's right," The Misfit said. 119

"Well then, why don't you pray?" she asked trembling with delight suddenly. 120

"I don't want no hep," he said. "I'm doing all right by myself." 121

Bobby Lee and Hiram came ambling back from the woods. Bobby Lee was drag- 122 ging a yellow shirt with bright blue parrots in it.

"Thow me that shirt, Bobby Lee," The Misfit said. The shirt came flying at him 123 and landed on his shoulder and he put it on. The grandmother couldn't name what the shirt reminded her of. "No, lady," The Misfit said while he was buttoning it up, "I found out the crime don't matter. You can do one thing or you can do another, kill a man or take a tire off his car, because sooner or later you're going to forget what it was you done and just be punished for it."

The children's mother had begun to make heaving noises as if she couldn't get 124 her breath. "Lady," he asked, "would you and that little girl like to step off yonder with Bobby Lee and Hiram and join your husband?"

"Yes, thank you," the mother said faintly. Her left arm dangled helplessly and 125 she was holding the baby, who had gone to sleep, in the other. "Hep that lady up, Hiram," The Misfit said as she struggled to climb out of the ditch, "and Bobby Lee, you hold onto that little girl's hand."

"I don't want to hold hands with him," June Star said. "He reminds me of a pig." 126

The fat boy blushed and laughed and caught her by the arm and pulled her off 127 into the woods after Hiram and her mother.

Alone with The Misfit, the grandmother found that she had lost her voice. There 128 was not a cloud in the sky nor any sun. There was nothing around her but woods. She wanted to tell him that he must pray. She opened and closed her mouth several times before anything came out. Finally she found herself saying, "Jesus. Jesus," meaning, Jesus will help you, but the way she was saying it, it sounded as if she might be cursing.

"Yes'm," The Misfit said as if he agreed. "Jesus thown everything off balance. 129 It was the same case with Him as with me except He hadn't committed any crime and they could prove I had committed one because they had the papers on me. Of course," he said, "they never shown me my papers. That's why I sign myself now. I said long ago, you get you a signature and sign everything you do and keep a copy of it. Then you'll know what you done and you can hold up the crime to the punishment and see do they match and in the end you'll have something to prove you ain't been treated right. I call myself The Misfit," he said, "because I can't make what all I done wrong fit what all I gone through in punishment."

There was a piercing scream from the woods, followed closely by a pistol report. 130 "Does it seem right to you, lady, that one is punished a heap and another ain't punished at all?"

"Jesus!" the old lady cried. "You've got good blood! I know you wouldn't shoot a 131 lady! I know you come from nice people! Pray! Jesus, you ought not to shoot a lady. I'll give you all the money I've got!"

"Lady," The Misfit said, looking beyond her far into the woods, "there never was 132 a body that give the undertaker a tip."

There were two more pistol reports and the grandmother raised her head like a 133 parched old turkey hen crying for water and called, "Bailey Boy, Bailey Boy!" as if her heart would break.

"Jesus was the only One that ever raised the dead," The Misfit continued, "and 134 He shouldn't have done it. He thown everything off balance. If He did what He said, then it's nothing for you to do but thow away everything and follow Him, and if He didn't, then it's nothing for you to do but enjoy the few minutes you got left the best way you can—by killing somebody or burning down his house or doing some other meanness to him. No pleasure but meanness," he said and his voice had become almost a snarl.

"Maybe He didn't raise the dead," the old lady mumbled, not knowing what she 135 was saying and feeling so dizzy that she sank down in the ditch with her legs twisted under her.

"I wasn't there so I can't say He didn't," The Misfit said. "I wisht I had of been 136 there," he said, hitting the ground with his fist. "It ain't right I wasn't there because if I had of been there I would of known. Listen lady," he said in a high voice, "if I had of been there I would of known and I wouldn't be like I am now." His voice seemed about to crack and the grandmother's head cleared for an instant. She saw the man's face twisted close to her own as if he were going to cry and she murmured, "Why you're one of my babies. You're one of my own children!" She reached out and touched him on the shoulder. The Misfit sprang back as if a snake had bitten him and shot her three times through the chest. Then he put his gun down on the ground and took off his glasses and began to clean them.

Hiram and Bobby Lee returned from the woods and stood over the ditch, look- 137 ing down at the grandmother who half sat and half lay in a puddle of blood with her legs crossed under her like a child's and her face smiling up at the cloudless sky.

Without his glasses, The Misfit's eyes were red-rimmed and pale and defenseless-    138
looking. "Take her off and thow her where you thown the others," he said, picking
up the cat that was rubbing itself against his leg.

"She was a talker, wasn't she?" Bobby Lee said, sliding down the ditch with a yodel.    139

"She would of been a good woman," The Misfit said, "if it had been somebody    140
there to shoot her every minute of her life."

"Some fun!" Bobby Lee said.    141

"Shut up, Bobby Lee," The Misfit said. "It's no real pleasure in life." ◆    142


## FOR CLOSE READING

1. How did The Misfit in Flannery O'Connor's story get his name?

2. Why does The Misfit think that Jesus "thrown everything off balance" by raising
   the dead (134)? Why is he concerned with matters of religious faith at all?

3. How religious is the grandmother in O'Connor's story? When she mentions Jesus,
   why does it sound "as if she might be cursing" (128)?

4. At the end of the story, when she *is* dead, the grandmother has "her legs crossed
   under her like a child's" (137). Where else in the story is the grandmother
   **COMPARED** to a child? How does she compare in character and personality with
   June Star and John Wesley, the actual children in the story?

5. What is the grandmother doing when The Misfit shoots her? Why is he so upset at
   that particular moment?


## Strategies and Structures

1. "A good man is hard to find," says Red Sammy Butts, proprietor of the Tower restaurant (43). Yet the grandmother has just called him a good man simply because
   he has allowed some travellers to charge their gas (37). How are the two of them
   defining goodness? What is O'Connor's point in introducing different definitions
   of goodness just before The Misfit appears in her narrative?

2. When, in an attempt to save herself, the grandmother calls The Misfit a good man,
   he replies, "I ain't a good man" (99). The Misfit is correct: he is, after all, a patho-
   logical killer who ruthlessly murders an entire family, including a baby. However,
   does The Misfit display any characteristics that might be defined as good if he
   weren't otherwise so evil?

3. "She would of been a good woman," The Misfit says to Bobby Lee, "if it had been somebody there to shoot her every minute of her life" (140). What does The Misfit mean by this? How has the grandmother (or *grand mother*) been truly good just before she is shot?

4. The grandmother dies with "her face smiling up at the cloudless sky," presumably toward heaven (137). Is there any sense in which The Misfit could be defined as her savior?

5. The Misfit defines *pleasure* as "meanness" (134). Yet at the end of the story he tells Bobby Lee, "It's no real pleasure in life" (142). Why not? Why can't the Misfit enjoy being murderously mean? What definition of the good life throws him off balance? Why does he take it to heart?

6. *Other Methods.* From whose perspective is this story NARRATED? Whose story is this? The Misfit's? The grandmother's? Explain.

## Thinking about Language

1. "A good man is hard to find" is the first line of the chorus in a popular song recorded by blues singer Bessie Smith in 1927. The next line in the original recording is, "You always get another kind." How well does this prediction fit O'Connor's story? Why would she name such a dark story after a popular song?

2. One reviewer of their first album says that the post-punk band Pitty Sing is named after "an evil cat in a Flannery O'Connor short story." It's not the cat's fault that someone lets it out of the bag. Who is the guilty party, and how does this PUN— "letting the cat out of the bag"—resonate throughout the story?

3. The cat Pitty Sing is named for a character in the *Mikado*, a comic opera by William S. Gilbert and Arthur Sullivan. "Pitty Sing" (10) is baby talk for "Pretty Thing." What does the cat's name tell you about the maturity level of some of the characters in the story?

4. Why does O'Connor describe The Misfit as reacting "as if a snake had bitten him" when the grandmother touches his shoulder (136)? What's the ALLUSION?

## FOR WRITING

1. A psychiatrist would probably diagnose O'Connor's Misfit as a *psychopath*. Write a paragraph or two defining this neurosis as exemplified by O'Connor's villain.

2. Write an essay analyzing how conventional definitions of good and evil are called into question by O'Connor's classic story.

3. Write a RHETORICAL ANALYSIS in 400–500 words of "A Good Man Is Hard to Find" as a representative example of "Southern Gothic" fiction. Be sure to include a clear definition of "Southern Gothic" and to evaluate how useful or accurate you find this classification to be.

4. Do some research on her and her work, and write a 400–500-word PROFILE of Flannery O'Connor as a Catholic writer living in the largely Protestant South. Refer to "A Good Man Is Hard to Find" or other works by O'Connor to illustrate her religious themes and conflicts.

You'll find quizzes on the readings at wwnorton.com/write/back-to-the-lake.

CHAPTER 13

# Cause and Effect

For want of a nail the shoe was lost; for want of a shoe the horse was lost, and for want of a horse the rider was lost, being overtaken and slain by the enemy, all for want of care about a horse-shoe nail.
—BENJAMIN FRANKLIN, *The Way to Wealth*

Suppose you've made lasagna in a stainless-steel baking pan. Rather than transfer your leftovers to another container, you simply cover the pan with aluminum foil and store it in the refrigerator. When you come back a few days later to reheat the dish, you notice tiny holes in the aluminum. Why, you ask? Even more pressing: Can you safely eat your leftovers? What would be the effect on your body if you did? With these questions, you have just launched into an analysis of cause and effect.

## Analyzing Why Things Happen—or Might Happen

When we analyze something, we take it apart to see how the pieces fit together. A common way in which things fit together, especially in the physical universe, is that one causes the other. In the case of your leftover lasagna, for example, the aluminum foil deteriorates because it is touching the tomato sauce as well as the stainless-steel pan. "When aluminum metal is in simultaneous contact with a different metal," writes the food critic Robert L. Wolke, who is also a professor of chemistry, the combination "constitutes an electric battery"—if there is also present "an electrical conductor such as tomato sauce."

When we analyze causes and effects, we not only explain why something happened (what caused the holes in the foil), we predict what might happen—for example, if you eat the lasagna anyway.

In this chapter, we will discuss how to analyze causes and effects; how to tell causation from coincidence; how to distinguish probable causes from merely possible ones; and how to organize a cause-and-effect analysis by tracing events in chronological order from cause to effect—or backward in time from effect to cause. We'll also review the critical points to watch for as you read over your analysis, as well as common errors to avoid when you edit.

## Why Do We Analyze Causes and Effects?

According to the British philosopher David Hume in his *Enquiry Concerning Human Understanding*, much of the thinking that human beings do is "founded on the relation of cause and effect." Like Adam and Eve when they discovered fire (Hume's example), we analyze causes and effects in order to learn how things relate to each other in the physical world. Also, when we know what causes something, we can apply that knowledge to our future behavior and that of others: Don't put your hand in the fire because it will burn. Don't cover your leftover lasagna with aluminum foil because you'll get metal in your food if the foil touches the sauce.

Hume was not just speaking of the knowledge we gain from experience, however. By doing research and using our powers of reasoning in addition to those of direct observation, we can also analyze the causes and effects of things that we cannot experience directly, such as the causes of the Civil War, or the effects of AIDS on the social and political future of Africa, or what will happen to the U.S. economy if the health care system is (or is not) reformed. Thus the analysis of cause-and-effect relationships is just as important in the study of history, politics, economics, and many other fields as in the sciences.

## Composing a Cause-and-Effect Analysis

When you analyze causes and effects, as Hume said, you exercise a fundamental power of human understanding. (Too bad Adam and Eve didn't do this *before* they ate the apple.) You also unleash a powerful means of organizing an essay as point by point you explain the results of your analysis to your reader. But keep in mind that even simple effects can have complex causes—as in our tomato sauce example. Technically speaking, the holes in the aluminum foil were caused by the transfer of electrons from the foil to the steel bowl *through* the tomato sauce. What caused the corrosive sauce to touch the foil in the first place? Clearly, yet another cause is in play here—human error, as indicated in the diagram below.

If relatively simple effects—such as the holes in the aluminum foil—can have multiple causes like these, just think how many causes you will need to identify as you analyze and explain more complex effects, such as the French Revolution, cancer, or why married men, on average, make more money than unmarried men.

Fortunately, as we shall see, even the most daunting array of causes can be reduced to a few basic ones. And thinking about the order in which they occur in time and their importance in producing a given effect, in turn, can provide you with a solid basis for organizing your analysis.

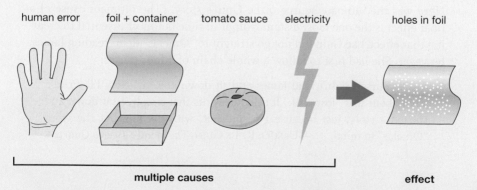

human error     foil + container     tomato sauce     electricity     holes in foil

**multiple causes**                                                          **effect**

## USING CAUSE AND EFFECT TO EXPLAIN
## HOW SHE WROTE "OMELAS"

Asked to explain how she got the idea for her classic utopian fantasy, "The Ones Who Walk Away from Omelas" (p. 595), Ursula K. Le Guin once replied: "It came from a road sign: Salem (Oregon) backwards. Don't you read road signs backwards? POTS. WOLS nerdlihc."

Glancing at road signs in her rear view mirror was only a remote cause of Le Guin's creative outpouring in "Omelas." The ultimate cause was her reading (in the usual way) of a statement about cause and effect in an essay by the American philosopher William James. James rejected as morally unacceptable a society that would allow even a single "lost soul on the far-off edge of things" to serve as a scapegoat for the rest. Here is the passage that fired Le Guin's imagination:

> All the higher, more penetrating ideals are revolutionary. They present themselves far less in the guise of effects of past experience than in that of probable causes of future experience, factors to which the environment and the lessons it has so far taught us must learn to bend.
>
> —WILLIAM JAMES,
> "The Moral Philosopher and the Moral Life"

And here is Le Guin's response to James's inspiring words:

> The application of those two sentences to this story, and to science fiction, and to all thinking about the future is quite direct. Ideals as "the probable causes of future experience"—that is a subtle and an exhilarating remark!

Here was the ultimate source of Le Guin's story. (The ultimate cause of a final effect is the one most distant from it in time but most essential to creating that effect.) Le Guin did not go straight to "Omelas" upon reading James, however. She had first to follow a whole chain of minor causes:

> Of course I didn't read James and sit down and say, Now I'll write a story about that "lost soul." It seldom works that simply. I sat down and started a story, just because I felt like it, with nothing but the word "Omelas" in mind.   —URSULA K. LE GUIN, *The Wind's Twelve Quarters*

## Thinking about Purpose and Audience

As a professor of chemistry, Wolke fully understands the complexities of the chemical reaction he is analyzing, but the tomato sauce example here comes from *What Einstein Told His Cook*, a book he wrote to explain "kitchen science" to a general audience. So Wolke largely avoids the technical vocabulary of the laboratory and assumes no specialized knowledge on the part of the reader. Instead, he uses everyday language and offers practical applications for his scientific findings: store your leftovers in any kind of container you like, Wolke concludes, "just make sure that the foil isn't in contact with the sauce." When you write a cause-and-effect analysis, keep your readers in mind—use language appropriate for your audience and define any terms they may not know.

Wolke's purpose is to instruct his readers, and his topic is one that is easy to explain, at least for a chemist. Often, however, you will find yourself analyzing causes or effects that cannot be explained easily, and then you will actually need to ARGUE for possible causes or effects—to persuade your readers that a cause is plausible or an effect is likely.

Let's say you are taking Chemistry 101, and when you go to the campus bookstore to buy your textbook, you find that it costs $139. Your first thought is to write an article for the school newspaper accusing the bookstore of highway robbery, but then you stop to think: *why* is the price so high? You do some research and discover some of the causes: the increasing costs of paper, printing, and transportation; the costs of running a bookstore; the fact that authors need to be compensated for their work, and that publishers and bookstores are businesses that need to produce some kind of profit. Perhaps you'll still want to write an angry article, but at least you'll be able to show that you've *analyzed the causes* of the problem.

And let's say you decide to suggest in your article that students buy only used books. But then you'd need to *consider the effects* of that solution. Since publishers and authors receive no payment for used books, buying them exclusively could mean that there would soon be no other kind available. That's an effect that would be attractive to an audience of used book dealers—but that might not be so appealing to students.

For an in-depth analysis, see "Why Are Textbooks So Expensive?" (p. 569).

As with all kinds of writing, when you analyze causes or effects, you need to think about your larger purpose for writing and the audience you want to reach.

## Generating Ideas: Asking Why and What If

There are lots of ways to generate ideas for a cause-and-effect analysis—BRAINSTORMING, CLUSTERING, and more. The essential question to ask when you want to figure out what caused something, however, is *why*. Why does the foil covering your leftover lasagna have holes in it? Why did you fail the chemistry final? Why does a curve ball drop as it crosses home plate? Why was Napoleon defeated in his march on Russia in 1812?

If, on the other hand, you want to figure out what the effects of something are, then the basic question to ask is not *why* but *what*, or *what if*. What if you eat your leftover lasagna even though it might now contain invisible bits of aluminum?* What if you don't study for the chemistry exam? What are the results likely to be? What will happen if the curve ball fails to drop? What effect did the weather have on Napoleon's campaign?

As you pursue answers to the basic questions *why* and *what if*, keep in mind that a single effect may have multiple causes. If you were to ask why the U.S. financial system almost collapsed in the fall of 2008, for example, you would need to consider a number of possible causes, such as the following:

• greed and corruption on Wall Street

• vastly inflated real estate values

• subprime mortgage loans offered to unqualified borrowers

• massive defaults when those borrowers couldn't make their mortgage payments

• a widespread credit crunch and drying up of money for new loans.

As you probe more deeply into the causes of a major event like the financial crisis of 2008, you will discover that such effects not only have multiple causes; those causes are also interconnected. That is, they occur in chains—as in the proverb about a kingdom lost "all for want of care about a horse-shoe nail." When it comes time to present the results of your analysis, you may find that following the chain of events in chronological order from cause to effect—or backward in time from effect to cause—is an excellent way to organize your writing.

## Organizing and Drafting a Cause-and-Effect Analysis

Once you've asked yourself *why* and *what if* and you've identified a number of factors, you'll need to decide whether to emphasize causes or effects (or both). As you begin organizing and drafting, you'll want to choose an appropriate method of organization; explain the point of your analysis; and distinguish immediate causes from remote causes and main causes from contributing causes. You'll also want to

---

*Nothing much will happen, except that your lasagna may taste slightly metallic. You won't get sick from the metal because the hydrochloric acid in your stomach will dissolve the aluminum.

distinguish between true causes and mere coincidences. And think about using visuals and other methods of development, like NARRATIVE and PROCESS ANALYSIS in your analysis. The templates on p. 541 can help you get started.

## STATING YOUR POINT

As you draft a cause-and-effect analysis, you can start with effects and then examine their causes; or you can start with causes and go on to examine their effects. In either case, tell the reader right away which you are going to focus on and why—what your main point, or THESIS, is.

> Jon Mooallem (p. 583) analyzes the effects (power outages) before turning to the main cause (squirrels).

For example, if you are analyzing the causes of the financial meltdown in the United States in 2008, you might signal the main point of your analysis in a statement like this one:

> The main cause of the financial meltdown in the United States in 2008 was the freezing of credit, which made it impossible for anyone to borrow money.

Or if you're analyzing the effects of the 2008 crisis, you might write:

> One effect of the financial crisis has been to keep interest rates at record lows; for many people, however, wages are still depressed as well.

Once you've told the reader whether you're focusing on causes or effects and what your thesis is, you're ready to present your analysis.

## ORGANIZING A CAUSE-AND-EFFECT ANALYSIS

Causes always precede effects in time. Thus a natural way to present the effects of a given cause is by arranging them in CHRONOLOGICAL ORDER. If you were tracing the effects of the financial meltdown of 2008, for example, you would start with the crisis and then proceed chronologically, detailing its effects in the order in which they occurred, namely:

- banks and other financial institutions collapse as mortgage holders default
- the stock market plummets
- the federal government steps in with a massive bailout, providing a steady stream of much-needed credit to markets
- confidence is restored on Wall Street and Main Street

Reverse chronological order, in which you begin with a known effect and work backward through the possible causes, can also be effective for organizing a cause-and-effect analysis. In the case of the 2008 financial crisis, you would again begin with the crisis itself (the known effect): the financial engine stops because it has run out of credit. Then you would work backward in time through all the possible causes you could think of—presenting them in reverse chronological order:

- credit dries up because banks stop lending money to one another
- banks stopped lending because borrowers defaulted on existing loans
- borrowers defaulted because the values of their homes went down
- banks made risky loans on overvalued homes because Wall Street could easily sell those loans to investors
- Wall Street packaged bad loans and sold them to investors in order to increase profits and executive bonuses

You can also organize your analysis around the various types of causes, exploring the immediate cause before moving on to the remote causes (or vice versa) or exploring the contributing causes before the main cause (or vice versa).

## DISTINGUISHING BETWEEN IMMEDIATE AND REMOTE CAUSES

A former dancer does this in "Behind the Curtain," p. 550. As you look into the various causes of a particular effect, be sure to consider immediate and remote causes. This will require you to distinguish mechanical details in the causal chain from more theoretical causes. Benjamin Franklin, you'll notice, did not say that the main cause of the rider's death was the loss of a horseshoe nail. He said the main cause was a "want of care" about such nitty-gritty details.

The most nitty-gritty link in any causal chain—the one closest in time and most directly responsible for producing the effect—is the immediate cause. In the case of the financial meltdown of 2008, the immediate cause was the drying up of credit that made it almost impossible to get loans. Credit oils the wheels of commerce; when credit dries up, the wheels cease to turn and the financial engine stops.

Remote causes, by contrast with immediate ones, are less apparent to the observer and more distant in time from the observed effect. A remote cause of the financial meltdown of 2008 was the "subprime" lending to borrowers who, eventually, could not meet their mortgage payments. A more remote cause of the meltdown was the burst of the housing bubble: as the supply of available housing exceeded demand, housing values fell, and many borrowers found that their homes were worth less than the amount owed their mortgages.

# TEMPLATES FOR DRAFTING

When you begin to draft a cause-and-effect analysis, you need to identify what you're analyzing and to indicate whether you plan to emphasize its causes or its effects—moves fundamental to any cause-and-effect analysis. See how Henry L. Roediger III makes these moves at the beginning of his essay in this chapter:

> What reasons are given for the high price of textbooks? . . . If I had to bet, the root cause is a feature of the marketplace that has changed greatly over the years and fundamentally reshaped the textbook market: sale of used books.
> —HENRY L. ROEDIGER III, "Why Are Textbooks So Expensive?"

Roediger identifies what he's analyzing ("the high price of textbooks") and indicates that he is going to focus on the causes of this phenomenon ("the root cause is"). Here is one more example from this chapter:

> It turns out that, far from being freeloaders on the top of the food chain, wolves have a powerful effect on the well-being of the ecosystems around them—from the survival of trees and riverbank vegetation to, perhaps surprisingly, the health of the populations of their prey.
> —MARY ELLEN HANNIBAL, "Why the Beaver Should Thank the Wolf"

The following templates can help you make some of these basic moves in your own writing. But don't take these as formulas where you just fill in the blanks. There are no shortcuts to good writing, but these templates can serve as starting points.

▶ The main cause / effect of X is _____.

▶ X would also seem to have a number of contributing causes, including _____, _____, and _____.

▶ Some additional effects of X are _____, _____, and _____.

▶ Among the most important remote causes / effects of X are _____, _____, and _____.

▶ Although the causes of X are not known, we can speculate that a key factor is _____.

▶ X cannot be attributed to mere chance or coincidence because _____.

▶ Once we know what causes X, we are in a position to _____.

Recklessness among homeowners on Main Street was not the most remote cause of the eventual meltdown, however. The most remote cause was greed on Wall Street. Subprime loans were risky—but they were very profitable. The lender took his profit and then, to trim his risks, packaged the bad loans with good ones and sold the package to unwary investors. When investors finally figured out what they had bought, fear trumped greed, and even banks were afraid to lend money to each other. Hence the drying up of credit—until the federal government intervened.

## DISTINGUISHING BETWEEN THE MAIN CAUSE AND CONTRIBUTING CAUSES

To help your reader fully understand how a number of causes work together to produce a single effect, you will need to go beyond an explanation of the immediate cause or causes. Consider the partial collapse of terminal 2E at the Paris airport on the morning of May 23, 2004. The most immediate cause of the collapse, of course, was gravity; beyond that, it was the failure of the metal structure supporting the roof. If we're really going to figure out why the building fell down, however, we're also going to have to look at the main cause and some of the contributing causes of the disaster.

IMMEDIATE CAUSES OF THE COLLAPSE OF TERMINAL 2E

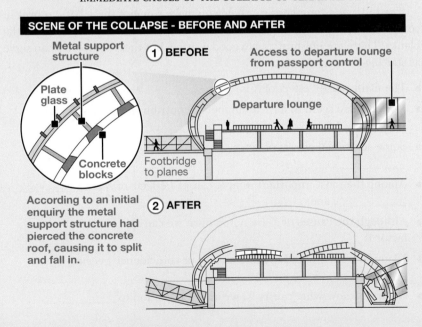

The main cause is the one that has the greatest power to produce the effect. It must be both necessary to cause the effect and sufficient to do so. As it turns out, the main cause of the terminal collapse was faulty design. As Christian Horn writes in *Architecture Week*, "The building was not designed to support the stress it was put under."

A contributing cause is a secondary cause, one that helps to produce the effect but is not sufficient to do it alone. An important contributing cause to the collapse of terminal 2E was weak concrete. Another was the increased stress on the concrete roof shell due to the rapid expansion and contraction of the metal support structure. Still another was the wild fluctuation in temperature in the days leading up to the collapse, which contributed to the stress on the metal.

If terminal 2E had been properly designed, however, no combination of contributing causes would have been sufficient to bring it down. Contributing causes are necessary to produce an effect, but even taken together they are not sufficient to cause it.

## DISTINGUISHING BETWEEN CAUSATION AND COINCIDENCE

It is well documented that married men as a group make more money—somewhere between 10 and 50 percent more—than unmarried men as a group. Does being married actually *cause* this wage difference, or is it merely a coincidence?

As you link together causes and effects, don't confuse causation with coincidence. Just because one event (getting married) happens *before* another (making more money), it does not necessarily follow that the first event actually caused the second. To conclude that it always does is to commit the logical blunder of reasoning *POST HOC, ERGO PROPTER HOC* (Latin for "after this, therefore because of this"). Most superstitions are based on such *post hoc* reasoning. Mark Twain's Huck Finn, for example, commits this fallacy when he sees a spider burning in a candle: "I didn't need anybody to tell me that that was an awful bad sign and would fetch me some bad luck." Huck is going to encounter all sorts of troubles, but the burning spider isn't the cause.

As Ursula K. Le Guin implies, p. 595, this mistake lies at the root of the scapegoat myth.

In our marriage and money example, being married is a necessary condition for earning the "marital wage premium." That is, statistics show that married men as a group *always* earn more money than single men. Is being married sufficient to make men wealthier? Or is it merely a matter of coincidence rather than causation? Most married people are older than unmarried people. Up to a point, most older people earn more money than younger people. Could age be the real cause behind the "marital wage premium"? Or is it simply another correlative? Before you assert that one event causes another, always consider whether the two could be merely coincidental.

## USING VISUALS TO CLARIFY CAUSAL RELATIONSHIPS

Illustrations and images can help your reader to understand what caused a complicated effect—or the complicated causes behind a simple effect. Take, for instance, a famous map showing Napoleon's campaign in Russia in 1812 (see p. 545). This map shows "the successive losses in men" during the campaign. (Napoleon left France with over 400,000 soldiers; he returned with approximately 10,000!) The advance toward Moscow is shown by a light-colored line, while the retreat is represented by the darker line below it. The thickness of the lines represents the number of soldiers—the thicker the line, the more troops in the army. At the bottom of the map are temperatures for certain dates during the retreat. As the French army retreats from Moscow and the temperatures get colder, the line representing the number of troops gets thinner, graphically showing the loss of men.

The map conveys a mass of data that would take many words to write out: dates, temperatures, troop movements, numbers of troops, not to mention distances and the locations of rivers and cities. All this information is crucial in analyzing why so many of Napoleon's soldiers died or deserted in their retreat from Moscow in 1812. If you're analyzing why Napoleon lost so many soldiers in the Russian campaign, you might want to include a visual like this and then connect the dots for the reader: many factors contributed to the losses, but the main cause of the horrendous number of casualties suffered by the French army in the winter of 1812 was the freezing temperatures.

A graph showing the relationship between temperature and number of troops, such as the one that appears on p. 546, would also make the point that the cold winter caused the deaths or desertions of many soldiers.

If you decide to include visuals, be sure that they actually illuminate your analysis, and don't merely decorate it. Remember to label each part of a chart or graph, and position visuals as close as possible to your discussion of the topic they address.

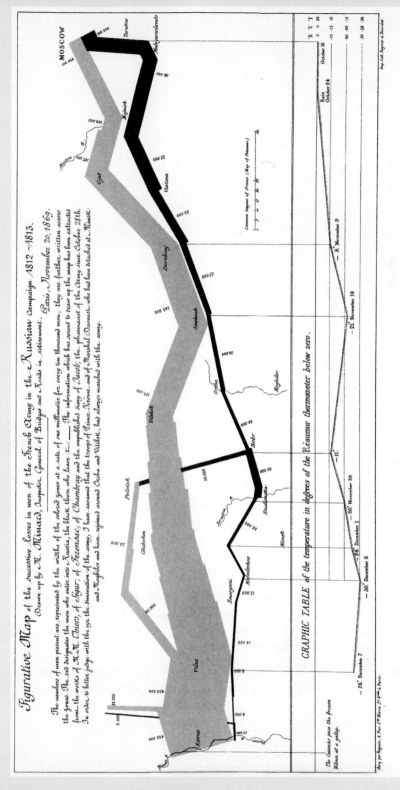

Since the map was made by the French engineer Charles Minard in 1861, the temperatures are in the French Réaumur system:
−9° Réaumur is approximately 11.75° Fahrenheit; −26° Réaumur is approximately −26.5° Fahrenheit.

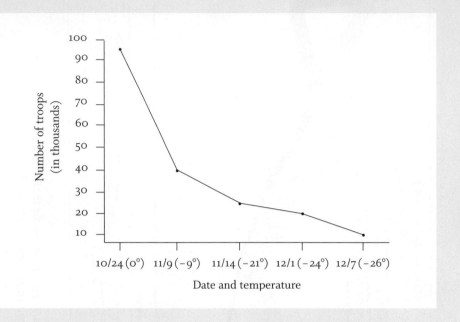

## USING OTHER METHODS

It is hard to explain *why* something happened without first explaining *what* happened and *how* it happened. So when you analyze causes and effects, consider using **NARRATION** to help explain the *what*:

> Recently, a young man by the name of Benny Paret was killed in the ring. The killing was seen by millions; it was on television.

And use **PROCESS ANALYSIS** to help explain the *how*:

> In the twelfth round, he was hit hard in the head several times, went down, was counted out, and never came out of the coma.

These are the words of Norman Cousins in a classic cause-and-effect analysis. Having set up his analysis by using other methods, Cousins then turns to the causes of Benny Paret's death. The immediate cause, obviously, was the fist that hit him. The main cause, Cousins explains, was something else:

> The primary responsibility lies with the people who pay to see a man hurt. The referee who stops a fight too soon from the crowd's viewpoint can expect

to be booed. The crowd wants the knockout; it wants to see a man stretched out on the canvas. This is the supreme moment in boxing.
                                    —NORMAN COUSINS, "Who Killed Benny Paret?"

Cousins's essay was written in 1962. Yet another fighter was killed in the boxing ring as recently as 2007. The essay may not have achieved the effect Cousins hoped for—getting professional boxing thrown out of the ring of legitimate sport—but the impact of his words is still clear: "No one doubts that many people enjoy prize fighting and will miss it if it should be thrown out. And that is precisely the point." The point is also that good writers like Cousins often use cause-and-effect analysis to make a point when they are constructing ARGUMENTS, yet another method of development that goes hand-in-hand with cause-and-effect analysis.

## EDITING FOR COMMON ERRORS IN A CAUSE-AND-EFFECT ANALYSIS

Writing about causes and effects generally calls for certain connecting words and verb forms—connecting words like *because* or *as a result*, verbs like *caused* or *will result in*. Here are some items to check for when you edit your analysis.

### Check all connectors to be sure they're logical and precise

Words like *because* or *since* connect the "cause" part of a sentence to the "effect" part (or the reverse). Be sure the connectors you use make the causal link absolutely clear.

▶ ~~Since~~ <u>Because</u> the concrete deteriorated, the roof collapsed.

*Since* has two meanings, "for the reason that" and "after the time that," so it does not make clear whether the roof collapsed after the concrete deteriorated or because it deteriorated. *Because* is the more precise term.

▶ The concrete deteriorated, and ~~consequently~~ <u>as a result</u> the roof collapsed.

*Consequently* can mean "subsequently" or "as a result." The editing makes the causal link clear.

## Check verbs to make sure they clearly express cause and effect

Some verbs directly express causation, whereas others only imply that one thing causes another.

*Verbs that express causation*

| | | |
|---|---|---|
| account for | cause | make |
| bring about | effect | result |

*Verbs that imply causation*

| | | |
|---|---|---|
| follow | imply | implicate |
| happen | involve | take place |

Using verbs that express causation makes your text more precise.

▶ The partial collapse of terminal 2E ~~involved~~ <u>was caused by</u> weak concrete.

## Check for common usage errors

### *Affect, effect*

*Affect* is a verb meaning "influence." *Effect* is usually a noun meaning "result," but it can also be a verb meaning "bring about."

▶ Getting married did not affect his wages.

▶ Getting married did not have the effect of increasing his wages.

▶ Getting married did not effect a change in his wages.

### *Reason is because, reason why*

Avoid using these expressions; both are redundant. In the first case, use *that* instead of *because*. In the second, use *reason* alone.

▶ The reason the roof collapsed is ~~because~~ <u>that</u> the concrete deteriorated.

▶ Weakened concrete is the reason ~~why~~ the roof collapsed.

Go to wwnorton.com/write/back-to-the-lake for quizzes on these common errors.

# Reading a Cause-and-Effect Analysis with a Critical Eye

Once you have written a draft (or two or three) of your analysis, it's always wise to ask someone else to look over what you have written. Ask readers where they find your analysis clear and convincing, what specific evidence they find most effective, and where they think you need more (or less) explanation. Here are some questions to keep in mind when checking over a cause-and-effect analysis.

**PURPOSE AND AUDIENCE.** Why is the reader being asked to consider these particular causes or effects? Is the intended audience likely to find the analysis plausible as well as useful? What additional information might readers need?

**ORGANIZATION.** Does the analysis emphasize causes or effects? Should it give more (or less) attention to either? Are causes and effects presented in a logical sequence?

**CHRONOLOGICAL ORDER.** Does the analysis present causes and effects in chronological order where appropriate? Does it consistently link cause to effect, and effect to cause?

**REVERSE CHRONOLOGICAL ORDER.** Where effects are known but causes are uncertain, is it clear what chain of events most likely led to the effect(s) in question? Are those events presented in reverse chronological order? If not, how can the order of events be clarified?

**THE POINT.** What is the analysis intended to show? Is the point made clearly in a thesis statement? How and how well does the analysis support the point?

**TYPES OF CAUSES.** How well are the significant causes analyzed—the immediate cause, the most important remote causes, the main cause, and the most important contributing causes? What other causes (or effects) should be considered?

**CAUSE OR COINCIDENCE?** At any point, is a coincidence mistaken for a cause? Are all of the causes necessary to produce the indicated effects? Do they have the power to produce those effects?

**VISUALS.** Are charts, graphs, or diagrams included to clarify causal relationships? If not, would they be helpful? Are all visuals clearly and appropriately labeled?

**OTHER METHODS.** Does the essay use other methods of development besides cause-and-effect analysis? For instance, does it use narration to help explain what happened? Or does it use process analysis to show how—in addition to why—a particular effect came about? Does the analysis argue that one cause or effect is more likely than another?

**COMMON ERRORS.** Do all of the words and phrases used to connect causes and effects actually express causation? For example, should words like *since* or *consequently* be replaced with *because, as a result of,* or *owing to*?

## Student Example

Paula T. Kelso teaches at Lewis and Clark Community College in Godfrey, Illinois. Trained as a ballerina, Kelso has danced professionally in the Midwest, New York, North Carolina, and California. In the spring of 2002, as an undergraduate majoring in sociology at Southern Illinois University, Edwardsville, Kelso chose body obsession in ballet as the topic for her senior seminar. The resulting paper earned an A, and she presented it the following October at a meeting of the Illinois Sociology Association. In 2003, Kelso's study, which follows the documentation style of the American Psychological Association (APA), was published in *Edwardsville Journal of Sociology*.

"Behind the Curtain" is an insider's view of the destructive physical and psychological effects female dancers endure because of a professional culture of enforced starvation. Under the influence of legendary choreographer George Balanchine and his successors, Kelso argues, ballet in America adopted an impossible (and dangerous) ideal of female beauty.

Why ballet appeals to young girls and their parents: immediate cause, wish fulfillment; remote cause, social pressure

Behind the Curtain:

The Body, Control, and Ballet

Many young girls and their parents are attracted to the ballet because of the applauding audiences, the lights, the sequins and feathers, the colorful, elaborate tutus, and satin pointe shoes. Where else can a young girl dream of becoming a princess, a swan, a dancing snowflake or flower, a sugarplum, or lilac fairy? Where else can she be a character right out of a fairy tale like Cinderella or Sleeping Beauty? Where else can she be rescued by and collapse into the arms of her handsome prince? Ballet is the magical world where these dreams can come true. Young girls and women can be all of these things, characters that symbolize femininity in a society that teaches young girls to be and want everything pink and pretty. However, in the shadows of the spotlight lurks an abusive world of eating disorders, verbal harassment, fierce competition, and injured, fatigued, and malnourished dancers. This world of fantasy is just that: fantasy and make-believe.

In addition to causes, Kelso plans to analyze effects, particularly negative ones

## The Problem

Body image is defined as the way in which people see themselves in the mirror every day: the values, judgments, and ideas that they attach to their appearance. Benn and Walters (2001) argue that these judgments and ideas come from being socialized into particular ways of thinking, mainly from society's ideas of what beauty is, shown especially in the current media and consumer culture (p. 140). The average person is inundated with 3,000 advertisements daily (Kilbourne, 2002). In these advertisements, women are shown in little clothing and in stereotypical roles. These women are not real (Kilbourne, 2002). They have been altered by computer airbrushing, retouching, and enhancing, and in many cases, several women are used to portray the same model (Kilbourne, 2002). The cultural idea of what is beautiful has changed over the years. In the 1950s, Marilyn Monroe, who wore a size 16 at one point in her career, was considered the epitome of sexiness and beauty (Jhally, 1995). Contrast this with more recent examples such as Courtney Cox and Jennifer Aniston from the television show *Friends*, who are considered beautiful. They wear a size 2 (Jhally, 1995). While models and celebrities have become thinner, the average woman is heavier today. This makes an even larger difference between the real and the ideal.

2

Kelso examines advertising and the media as immediate causes of how a culture defines physical beauty

Like the rest of society, dancers' appearances have also changed over the years. In the 1930s and 1940s, ballerinas were considered thin at the time but, as can be seen in photographs (see Figure 1), looked very healthy (Gordon, 1983). Since dancers

3

Gives historical perspective: as ideals of female beauty changed over the years, so did the physical appearance of ballerinas

*Figure 1.* Then: Female dancers in 1930 had thicker legs and rounder bodies.

have generally been slimmer than ideal, these dancers' becoming even thinner for today's ideal is a problem (see Figure 2). As one renowned ballet teacher said it: "It is a reflection of society, everything has become more streamlined" (Benn & Walters, 2001, p. 146).

Examines specific practices of modern ballet that encourage dancers to be thin

In order to understand the pressures that dancers face to be thin, it is necessary to explore the ideas behind the practice of ballet. Women who become dancers are not exempt from cultural expectations that tell them in order to be successful and beautiful, they must also be very thin. They live with the same pressures as the rest of society, however, they also have to deal with the risk of unemployment if they gain any amount of weight or their bodies do not look a certain way (Gordon, 1983). In a career where education is discouraged because of the time it would take away from a dancer's most successful years, many professional dancers are not attending college and in some cases are even dropping out of high school (Gordon, 1983). These dancers are putting all of their resources into their body and its appearance. If a dancer does gain weight, develops an eating disorder, or becomes injured, she is left out of work with

4

*Figure 2*. Now: Ballerinas typically have thinner legs and flatter bodies.

relatively few choices for the future. Most professional companies have "appearance clauses" in their contracts, which usually state that if the dancer gains any noticeable amount of weight, she is eligible to lose her position in the company (Gordon, 1983; Saint Louis Ballet, 1993). These clauses also state that tattoos, piercings, and changing hair color are not permitted (Gordon, 1983). Haircuts are discouraged, and usually only allowed with the permission of the director.

Almost everyone credits George Balanchine, the renowned dancer, teacher, and choreographer, with the current aesthetic of ballet in the West, referred to by most as the "Balanchine body," or the "anorexic look" (Gordon, 1983). He has promoted the skeletal look by his costume requirements and his hiring practices, as well as the treatment of his dancers (Gordon, 1983). The ballet aesthetic currently consists of long limbs, and a skeletal frame, which accentuates the collarbones and length of the neck, as well as absence of breasts and hips (Benn & Walters, 2001; Gordon, 1983; Kirkland, 1986). Balanchine was known to throw out comments to his dancers, such as: "eat nothing" and "must see the bones" (Kirkland, 1986, p. 56).

5

ARGUES that the main cause of the anorexic look among ballerinas is a particular choreographer

Argues that other chore-ographers and directors are contributing causes

If Balanchine has created this aesthetic, other choreographers    6
have followed and adopted it as the norm. Mikhail Baryshnikov, star dancer and former director of American Ballet Theatre, did not tolerate any body type but the Balanchine one (Gordon, 1983). During rehearsal and without any warning, he fired a corps de ballet member because she was too "fat" in his opinion (Gordon, 1983, p. 150). He said that he "couldn't stand to see her onstage anymore" (Gordon, 1983, p. 150). Fortunately, management intervened and the dancer was rehired. However, Baryshnikov and the rest of his management were known to have had meetings with their dancers in order to emphasize the importance of weight loss (Gordon, 1983). Obviously, dancers need to be fit and trim in order to be successful in their occupation, and no one should argue that staying fit is not helpful in order to see a dancer's body line; however, it is the extreme skeletal goal that is cause for so much concern.

It is not uncommon for a dancer to walk into what she    7
thinks will be her daily ballet class and find a scale set up in the center of the dance studio instead (Gordon, 1983). These weigh-ins are arranged ahead of time and kept secret from the dancers. A director from American Ballet Theatre explained that warning the dancers would defeat the purpose. As one former dancer put it: "A forewarned dancer is a forestarved dancer"[1] (Gordon, 1983, p. 43). Not only are the dancers' weights recorded but many times are read aloud to the entire class. Even the youngest dancers, at one pre-professional academy, at age eleven "gasped in horror" as the teacher read their weights aloud at 50 to 60 pounds (Gordon, 1983, p. 43). Public humiliation is not uncommon in the ballet world (Benn & Walters, 2001; Hamilton, 1998). Directors and teachers are known to make hateful comments and even resort to name-calling in some cases (Gordon, 1983). One director told one of his dancers to "drop the weight in three weeks. I don't care how you do it" (Benn & Walters, 2001, p. 145). When she did in fact drop the

1. *Forewarned/forestarved*: A word play on the English proverb "forewarned is forearmed."

weight by basically not eating, she was rewarded with a role in the performance that the company was rehearsing. Dancers learn at an early age that rewards and punishments are based upon weight. If a dancer loses weight, she is praised and rewarded with a role in a ballet. If she does not, she is punished by not being cast at all (Gordon, 1983). It seems that directors and teachers perceive how thin a dancer becomes as a sign of dedication to the art and is often times rewarded (Benn & Walters, 2001). Suzanne Gordon (1983) accompanied several members of an elite advanced pre-professional academy to a professional audition. She witnessed hundreds of dancers asked to walk across the floor of the studio, where many of them were then asked to leave. After fifteen or more years of professional training, these dancers were not allowed to even audition. Apparently, they did not have the right "look." This practice is used by most professional companies across the United States (Gordon, 1983).

Directors and company managers are not the only ones who put pressure on dancers to stay thin. Ballet critics often refer to body sizes when writing reviews of a performance (Benn & Walters, 2001). This can be a nightmare for a dancer, particularly if a negative body shape statement is printed next to her name for anyone to read in the morning paper. For example, two critics wrote reviews after seeing a company perform a Balanchine Ballet (a ballet in which the dancers wear nothing but tights and leotards). One said he witnessed, "an awful lot of wobbling bottoms on display" and the other claimed that this particular company had "rejected the starved-greyhound look in ballerinas—but now things have gone too far the other way. Bonnard legs and Ingres bottoms[2] are all very well, but not on stage, and particularly not in Balanchine" (Benn & Walters, 2001, p. 149). These reviews were taken to heart by the company directors, who threatened to fire members of the corps de ballet if they did not lose the weight fast. So they did, by not eating (Benn & Walters, 2001).

8

Analyzes how losing weight leads immediately to desirable roles and more remotely to the perception that a dancer is dedicated to her art

Identifies another contributing cause of the anorexic look

2. *Bonnard/Ingres:* French painters of the nineteenth and eighteenth centuries, respectively. They each painted women more round and plump than dancers today are supposed to be.

Identifies the main effect of the preceding causes

According to research conducted by Benn and Walters (2001), 9 dancers studied <u>were found to only consume 700 to 900 calories per day</u>. Many of the subjects were consuming less than 700. Surveys conducted in the United States, China, Russia, and Western Europe by Hamilton (1998) found that female dancers' weights were 10 to 15 percent below the ideal weight for their height. According to the American Psychiatric Association's official criteria for anorexia nervosa, the number one factor for diagnosis is if the person's weight is more than 15 percent below the ideal weight for height. This is dangerously close to most dancers! Another factor for diagnosing anorexia nervosa is if the person has developed amenorrhea, that is, if they have missed three consecutive menstrual cycles (Hamilton, 1998). According to Suzanne Gordon's research (1983), many dancers have ceased menstruating or have many cycle irregularities. Once someone stops menstruating, she may lose 4 percent of her bone mass annually for the next three to four years (Hamilton, 1998). This causes another set of problems: injury and osteoporosis.

Discuss negative effects caused by an inadequate diet

If dancers are not consuming enough calories, many times they are nutritionally deficient, which Hamilton (1998) supports in her arguments. If dancers are malnourished and continue to heavily exert themselves through dance, stress fractures, a common injury among dancers, are unavoidable (Gordon, 1983; Hamilton, 1998). Also, osteoporosis is common. One dancer took a bone density test and at 21 years old found she had the bones of a 70 year old (Hamilton, 1998). Dancers are not receiving crucial health and nutrition information, and they may not realize the harm they are inflicting on their bodies until it is too late. Benn and Walters (2001) found that only 18% of current dancers had received proper nutritional education.

Disproves a common misperception about cause and effect: ballerinas must be thin for male dancers to lift them

Many people believe the myth that female dancers must be 10 skeletal because of the male dancers who have to partner and lift them. This is simply not true. Gordon (1983) interviewed several professional male dancers, who said that they preferred to partner heavier dancers rather than dancers who fit the "anorexic look."

Patrick Bissell, a well-renowned dancer, says that "it's not easy to partner very thin dancers . . . they scream out all of a sudden because you pick them up . . . it makes you very tentative about how you touch them" (Gordon, 1983, p. 151). Another famous dancer, Jeff Gribler, agrees. He says that "It's easy to bruise a woman when you partner anyway, and if she seems too frail, you don't want to grip too hard. It can be really painful for her to be partnered" (Gordon, 1983, p. 152). Vane Vest, another dancer, says "these anorexic ballerinas—I can't bear to touch them . . . you partner a woman and lift her at the waist and you want to touch something. These skinny ballerinas, it's awful . . . how can you do a *pas de deux* with one of those girls?" (Gordon, 1983, p. 152). Gordon found in her research that ballerinas in Europe and elsewhere weigh more than North American ballerinas, yet male dancers do not seem to have a problem partnering them (Gordon, 1983).

Another myth is that this unhealthy "Balanchine body" is the only body capable of the technical feats that ballet requires. People also believe that if dancers were not this thin, audiences would not come to the ballet. However some of the most famous and successful companies are located in Europe and elsewhere. European companies, even with dancers who are not emaciated, are very successful. Gordon (1983) found that in European companies, particularly the Royal Swedish Ballet, dancers look somewhat different. She noticed older dancers in their late thirties and forties, and also that dancers were not nearly as thin as American dancers (Gordon, 1983). These dancers were definitely thin, but they looked healthy. They had breasts, hips, and curves, and actually looked womanly. During a gala performance for American Ballet Theatre, Gordon sat next to a New York ballet critic. When guest artist Zhandra Rodriguez from Ballet de Caracas, Venezuela, came on stage, Gordon immediately noticed that she had visible breasts. When she mentioned this to the critic, the critic retorted, "she can't be an American" (Gordon, 1983, p. 151).

11

Attacks another common misperception: ballerinas must be thin to attract audiences

. . .

Analyses: Two Theories about the World of Ballet

Subculture Theory

Many wonder why dancers and their parents continue to     12
take part in the ballet world after learning about some of its negative
aspects. Subculture theory can explain why dancers continue to
dance, even in the face of major internal and external obstacles
and criticism. Subculture theory has mainly been used to explain
deviance and crime in the past; however, it works well in analyzing
ballet as a unique world of its own with different norms and values
from the rest of society.

A subculture can be defined as a group of people who share     13
a common identity through a unique set of characteristics common
to the entire group, yet not entirely distinct from the rest of the
society in which the group lives (Farley, 1998). The subculture is a
part of the larger society, yet it has certain ideas, beliefs, behaviors,
and values that set it apart in some way. Farley (1998) states that
individuals with a common interest and occupation commonly form
subcultures. Ballet is truly an entire world all to its own. It functions
within society, but it is a distinct group that should be recognized as
such. The world of ballet has its own ideas of what the body should
look like that are more extreme than the rest of society; however,
the current ballet aesthetic would not be popular if dancers lived in
a culture that did not value extreme thinness. All ballet companies
across the world value thinness; however, it seems that only North
American companies, especially the United States, have this
dangerous goal of skeletal thinness.

Dancers are raised in this subculture of ballet, many from     14
as young as three years of age. They spend every night in this world
among directors, teachers, and other students who help to normalize
ballet's ideas and values, and they internalize these messages.
Dancers rely on their teachers for support and guidance, but also for
approval and selection of parts in ballets. This leads to a generalized
fear instilled in the dancers.

. . .

Uses subculture
theory to
examine the
effects of
belonging to
a particular
group

Ideas of beauty and health are different in the ballet world    15
than in the larger society. Many dancers believe themselves to be
healthy because they form "their ideas of healthy and normal . . .
according to the norms and values of the ballet world" (Benn &
Walters, 2001, p. 142). Because dancers are surrounded by eating
disorders, many believe themselves to be healthy because they do not
deny themselves food completely and they do not binge and purge.
Many dancers may look healthy enough, but in reality they are not.
They would not be diagnosed as medically anorexic, but they are
staying thin by means of "gentle starvation," meaning not consuming
enough calories and being nutritionally deficient (Benn & Walters,
2001, p. 142).

Another aspect of the ballet world, which helps to define its    16
subculture, is the idea of control. There is an authoritarian power
culture in the ballet world that forces conformity to harmful
behaviors. Dancers have become accustomed to abusive treatment;
it becomes a normal part of life in the subculture. Dancers' acceptance
of such treatment has been referred to as "silent conformity" for the
"unquestioning, subservient way in which . . . [dancers accept]
abuse and unreasonable behavior" (Stinson, 1998; cited by Benn &
Walters, 2001, p. 140). This is one reason why ballet has been
compared to a cult in some of the literature (Benn & Walters, 2001;
Gordon, 1983; Smith, 1998). Directors and management have the
power, and they exert it over the dancers, who must obey certain
rules if they intend to continue dancing.

. . .

Paradox Theory

In *Women and the Knife: Cosmetic Surgery and the Colonization*    17
*of Women's Bodies* (1991), <u>Kathryn Morgan discusses four paradoxes</u>
<u>inherent in the choice to undergo cosmetic surgery</u>. The structure
of her argument works well with the paradoxes inherent in the
ballet world.

*Paradox One: Art?* Ballet is known as a performing *art*. Art    18
implies a creative process through which the artist can express her

Uses paradox
theory to
examine four
unintended
effects of a
dancer's devot-
ing herself to
modern ballet
culture

innermost thoughts and feelings to an audience. Many dancers dance because they learn to express themselves through movement. However, all of ballet looks the same with cookie-cut out dancers expressing themselves in the same ways to the same music. There is no individual creativity to be explored here; only the creativity of the director is seen. The director's feelings are then described to the dancer and the dancer's job is to express that feeling to the audience. Creativity tends to be quashed in the classroom by focusing only on technique, which trains bodies to be a vehicle for someone else's creativity. Gelsey Kirkland (1986), a world-renowned ballerina, says in her autobiography that Balanchine had a "monopoly on taste and creative control" at New York City Ballet (p. 49). She also says that the dancers relied on him for "ideas and psychological motivation" (cited by Benn & Walters, 2001, p. 148). Michelle Benash, another dancer, says that "you have to lose your personality; your movement, your style are dictated to you" (Gordon, 1983, p. 112). A former New York City Ballet dancer puts it this way: Balanchine believed "that women should provide the inspiration that triggers men's creativity" (Gordon, 1983, p. 173). <u>Dancers, then, merely become puppets for someone else's creativity and emotion.</u>

> First unintended effect

*Paradox Two: Control?* All dancers must have control over their 19 bodies in order to master the technique required to perform professionally. Dancers start training young so that their hips will form a certain way in order to have the required "turn out." They also must spend years training their leg, feet, and abdomen muscles in order to jump, balance, and dance on pointe properly. These skills require intense years of training and hard work in order to establish the right strength. <u>One would imagine that dancers would have plenty of control over their own bodies; however, management takes over this control by exerting power over the bodies' appearance.</u> Having the right technique and strength is not nearly enough to dance professionally, one must also exhibit the right "look." This look, as discussed previously, is unhealthy and almost impossible to achieve.

> Second unintended effect

*Paradox Three: The Wonders of the Human Form.* Ballet is    20
supposed to showcase what the human body is capable of physically
accomplishing. Audiences come to see ballet because of the feats
that they will likely see at the performance. Amazing jumps, turns,
and tricks are fan favorites. However, <u>ballet is not showcasing what</u>    ·····    Third
<u>the human form can accomplish, it is merely showcasing what one,</u>    unintended
<u>almost impossible, body type may be capable of executing.</u> Dancers    effect
are supposed to make these feats look effortless, but it is doubtful
that anyone leaving the theatre feels as if they could mimic these
steps without the required body.

*Paradox Four: The Look.* Dancers are usually referred to as    21
beautiful and graceful creatures, capable of accomplishing
extraordinary feats on stage. Off stage, these dancers resemble
broken young children. They oftentimes look emaciated and injured,
collapsing offstage after performances or limping to their dressing
rooms. Dancers are artists, but they are also athletes who train their
bodies every day. Athletes are usually considered to be the epitome
of the human form and very physically fit. One look backstage and
these are not the thoughts that would come to mind of the dance
world. <u>Most dancers are very unhealthy physically and oftentimes</u>    ·····    Fourth
<u>emotionally as well.</u>    unintended
    effect

## Conclusion

The dangerous aesthetic of the ballet world is an area that    22
needs much more attention and further research. Artistic directors
of companies do not like to discuss or acknowledge problems with
the current ballet aesthetic, which can be seen in their reluctance to
talk about these issues and the lack of available research on the
topic. . . . Aside from a few current journal articles that discuss
eating habits, no one has really attempted to see if the abusive world
Gordon exposed in her book has changed at all since her research in
the 1980s. *Off Balance: The Real World of Ballet* alerted us to the fact
that ballet was not so lovely and magical backstage. . . . I can attest
to experiencing all of the aspects of ballet, in my pre-professional
training and in my professional dancing, that Gordon showed. I also

know from fellow dancers in the Midwest, New York, North Carolina, and San Francisco that their experiences are and have been very similar to what Gordon portrays in her book. There have . . . been recent examples in the media, which suggest that not much has changed since the 1980s. For example, the Boston Ballet ballerina who died at 22 due to complications from an eating disorder (Segal, 2002). Management had told the dancer that she was "chunky" and that she needed to lose weight before she developed anorexia (Segal, 2002). Another example occurred in San Francisco, where nine-year-old Fredrika Keefer was denied admission to San Francisco Ballet School because she was considered too short and chunky by administration. . . . A fictitious example can be seen in the [2000] movie *Center Stage*, where dancers at a highly competitive pre-professional school deal with eating disorders, weight issues, and competition. This film also addressed a director's control of his company, albeit briefly and sentimentalized. . . . Further research is important to assess the current situation in the dance world and to see if the aesthetic and treatment of dancers has improved at all since the dance community and the public have been made aware of the dangers.

<u>The health and sanity of dancers are being sacrificed for this art form</u>. Until dancers, audiences, and management accept a new, healthier paradigm, dancers will continue to suffer. Segal (2001) articulates it best when he writes:                                                     23

Conclusion sums up Kelso's main point in analyzing the negative effects of the ultrathin aesthetic in modern ballet

> What we accept as the "tradition" of extreme thinness is arguably just a mid-to-late 20th century whim of the white ballet establishment. And it needs to stop, for the health of the art form and the women dedicated to it, before ballet training becomes a symbol, like Chinese foot binding, of a society's cruel subjugation of women to a crippling, inhuman illusion. (p. 2)

References

Benn, T., & Walters, D. (2001). Between Scylla and Charybdis. Nutritional education versus body culture and the ballet aesthetic: The effects on the lives of female dancers. *Research in Dance Education, 2*(2), 139-154.

Farley, J. (1998). *Sociology* (4th ed.). Upper Saddle River, NJ: Prentice-Hall.

Gordon, S. (1983). *Off balance: The real world of ballet.* New York, NY: Pantheon.

Hamilton, L. (1998). *Advice for dancers: Emotional counsel and practical strategies.* San Francisco, CA: Jossey-Bass.

Jhally, S. (Producer). (1995). *Slim hopes: Advertising and the obsession with thinness* [Motion picture].

Kilbourne, J. (2002, February). *The naked truth: Advertising's image of women.* Presentation to Principia College, Elsah, IL.

Kirkland, G. (1986). *Dancing on my grave.* Garden City, NY: Doubleday.

Morgan, K. P. (1991). Women and the knife: Cosmetic surgery and the colonization of women's bodies. In L. Richardson, V. Taylor, & N. Whittier (Eds.), *Feminist frontiers* (pp. 116-127). New York, NY: McGraw-Hill.

Saint Louis Ballet. (1993). Employment contract. St. Louis, MO: Saint Louis Ballet.

Segal, L. (2001, April 1). The shape of things to come. *Los Angeles Times.* Retrieved from http://www.latimes.com

Smith, C. (1998). On authoritarianism in the dance classroom. In S. B. Shapiro (Ed.), *Dance, power, and difference* (pp. 123-146). Leeds, UK: Human Kinetics.

Stinson, S. W. (1998). Seeking a feminist pedagogy for children's dance. In S. B. Shapiro (Ed.), *Dance, power, and difference* (pp. 23-48). Leeds, UK: Human Kinetics.

## *Analyzing a Student Cause-and-Effect Analysis*

In "Behind the Curtain," Paula T. Kelso draws upon rhetorical strategies and techniques that good writers use all the time when they analyze causes and effects. The following questions, in addition to focusing on particular aspects of Kelso's text, will help you to identify those common strategies and techniques so you can adapt them to your own writing. These questions will also help to prepare you for the analytical questions—on content, structure, and language—that you'll find after all the other selections in this chapter, along with suggestions for writing on related topics.

### FOR CLOSE READING

1. According to Paula Kelso, where and how does American society get its ideals of female beauty? What is "not real" about them (2)? Why are ballerinas particularly susceptible to those ideals?

2. In Kelso's view, what was the role of choreographer George Balanchine and his followers in promoting "the skeletal look" among American ballerinas (5)? How convincing do you find Kelso's evidence?

3. One reason, supposedly, that ballerinas need to be thin is so that male dancers can lift them. How and how well does Kelso address this "myth" (10)? What other myths does she explore?

4. From their directors, teachers, and fellow students, says Kelso, young girls who aspire to become ballerinas often pick up a "generalized fear" (14). Of what? How and why is this fear "instilled" in them (14)?

### Strategies and Structures

1. Why does Kelso begin her essay with a brief DESCRIPTION of the "magical" aspects of ballet (1)? What CONTRAST is she setting up? How effective do you find this opening strategy?

2. The immediate cause of anorexia nervosa is not eating enough calories to sustain life and health. What are some of the remote causes, especially among ballerinas, according to Kelso?

3. Of all the possible causes Kelso cites, which would you say is the main cause of the problems that plague ballerinas? Explain.

4. To support her analysis, Kelso uses a variety of brief EXAMPLES from outside sources, including stratified data about health issues, opinions from experts, and questions from ballerinas. Point out five or six examples that you find particularly effective.

5. *Other Methods.* Kelso's analysis of causes and effects in the "abusive world" of professional ballet could be the basis of an **ARGUMENT** (1). What is her main **PURPOSE** in conducting the analysis, and how might she use the results to argue her point?

## Thinking about Language

1. What are the **CONNOTATIONS** of *lurks* and *shadows* (1)?

2. Explain the specialized meanings, in a sociology paper, of the following terms: *socialized* (2), *normalize* (14), and *internalize* (14).

3. How and how effectively does Kelso use the "broken young children" **SIMILE** to develop her analysis (21)?

4. A **PARADOX** is an apparent contradiction that may, nonetheless, be true or valid. What is paradoxical about the observations that Kelso makes in paragraphs 17–21? What do they show about the culture of ballet in America?

## FOR WRITING

1. In a culture obsessed with thinness, why are so many Americans overweight? Draft the opening paragraph of the essay you might write if you were analyzing the causes of this phenomenon.

2. Write an essay that analyzes the causes and effects of a common eating disorder.

3. Swimmers have bodies distinctive to their sports. So do wrestlers, gymnasts, and cyclists. Write an analysis of a particular sport and the typical effects, psychological as well as physical, that it has upon the athlete. Don't forget to say how the culture of the sport contributes to these effects.

4. "Body image," says Kelso, "is defined as the way in which people see themselves in the mirror every day: the values, judgments, and ideas that they attach to their appearance" (2). Drawing on Kelso's work, the work of the scholars she cites, and your own research, write a **REPORT** on body image on the American campus—or just your campus—and its causes and effects.

You'll find quizzes on the readings at wwnorton.com/write/back-to-the-lake.

# A Rube Goldberg Pencil Sharpener

This whimsical drawing by American cartoonist Rube Goldberg (1883–1970) illustrates how causes and effects typically operate—in chains of linked events, with the effect of one event becoming the cause of another. For example, the *immediate* cause is the one closest to the end result—in this case, the actions of the woodpecker. The previous events (flying the kite, burning the pants, smoking out the possum) are the *contributing* causes. Goldberg's designs for elaborate machines and systems to perform simple tasks have inspired many imitators. Each year, for example, engineering students at Purdue University sponsor a national Rube Goldberg contest, which celebrates "machines that combine creativity with inefficiency and complexity." Contestants are presented with a simple task—to replace batteries in a flashlight and turn it on, for example—and are challenged to perform that task in at least twenty steps within a two-minute timeframe. The task for the 2015 national Rube Goldberg Machine Contest (RGMC) is to erase a chalkboard.

[ **FOR WRITING** ] ·····································································································

Rube Goldberg machines, including some entered in the
Purdue contest, are all over *YouTube*. Choose one, and write a
cause-and-effect analysis of what you see, including not only
the mechanism itself but the context in which it is presented.

The Professor gets his think-tank working and evolves the simplified pencil sharpener.

Open window (**A**), and fly kite (**B**). String (**C**) lifts small door (**D**), allowing moths (**E**) to escape and eat red flannel shirt (**F**). As weight of shirt becomes less, shoe (**G**) steps on switch (**H**), which heats electric iron (**I**) and burns hole in pants (**J**). Smoke (**K**) enters hole in tree (**L**), smoking out opossum (**M**), which jumps into basket (**N**), pulling rope (**O**) and lifting cage (**P**), allowing woodpecker (**Q**) to chew wood from pencil (**R**), exposing lead. Emergency knife (**S**) is always handy in case opossum or the woodpecker gets sick and can't work.

# SUGGESTIONS FOR WRITING

1. In "Behind the Curtain" by Paula T. Kelso (p. 550), a former ballerina analyzes the detrimental effects upon many dancers of the so-called "Balanchine body" or "the anorexic look." After reading Kelso's analysis—and examining her References—do some research on the Russian choreographer George Balanchine (1904–83) and write a 400–500-word **PROFILE** of the man and his lasting impact on ballet as a dance form.

2. In "Why the Beaver Should Thank the Wolf" (p. 577), Mary Ellen Hannibal argues that, among other ecological mistakes, it is "short sighted" to hunt sea otters in order to protect fisheries. Read Hannibal's essay, do some research on what she calls "trophic cascades" (causes and effects up and down the food chain), and write a **POSITION PAPER** supporting or contesting the common argument "that eliminating the predator increases the prey."

3. Jon Mooallem's "Squirrel Power!" (p. 583) makes fun of "snarky jokes" about squirrels taking over the power grid by causing systematic outages across the country. In addition to this essay, read Mooallem's short ebook, *American Hippopotamus* (2013)—or his longer study, *Wild Ones* (2013)—and write an **EVALUATION** of one of them focusing on the cumulative effects that, according to Mooallem, humans have had on wild animals. And *vice versa*.

4. "Money Isn't Everything" (p. 591) by Matthew Yglesias is about the rivalry between Steve Jobs and Bill Gates, among other corporate titans. It is part of a series to be published in *Slate* on "the greatest contests in business, science, sports, and more." Read Yglesias's essay and, in approximately 450 words, write a cause-and-effect analysis of a big rivalry that you would submit to such a series.

5. "The Ones Who Walk Away from Omelas" by Ursula K. Le Guin (p. 595) analyzes an ideal community with a guilty secret. Read Le Guin's analysis and, in approximately 500 words, present a utopia, flawed or otherwise, of your own invention—or imagine the opposite, an oppressive dystopia. Be sure to explain what causes your imaginary society to be as it is.

HENRY L. ROEDIGER III

# Why Are Textbooks So Expensive?

Henry L. Roediger III (b. 1947) is the James S. McDonnell Distinguished University Professor of psychology at Washington University in St. Louis. Roediger is a specialist in memory and human learning, and the author or coauthor of many articles and psychology textbooks. What caused him to specialize in the psychology of memory? Roediger attributes his choice to an event in his childhood—the death of his mother when he was five years old. "That event changed my life drastically," says Roediger. "I was determined to hold on to my memories of her, to relive the past by remembering them. At a very early age, I spent a lot of time thinking about memory and how it works."

"Why Are Textbooks So Expensive?" appeared in 2005 in the *Observer*, a journal published by the American Psychological Society, of which Roediger is a past president.

NEWSLETTERS AND OTHER MISSIVES that I receive seem filled with stories 1 about textbooks and textbook prices, with many wringing their hands over why textbooks are so expensive now relative to the more distant past (usually when the author of the article was in college). I suspect some articles arise from middle-aged parents who suddenly must pay for their own children's college textbooks and they recoil when they see a bill of $500 a semester or thereabouts.

What reasons are given for the high price of textbooks? Of course, there's gen- 2 eral inflation, but evidence points to textbook prices outpacing inflation. Others point their fingers at the bright colors in many books (relative to older black and white models) and argue that production costs are needlessly pushed up by color. (A quick check of my own bookstore shows that many books without color are more expensive than those with color, probably due to the number of books in the print run.) Another suggested hypothesis is textbook publishers simply seek greater profit margins now than they did in the past. After all, the market used to be dominated by rather genteel textbook companies that really cared about scholarly texts and not so much about being wildly profitable. A comfortable, modest profit line was fine in the old days. Those days are now gone, because traditional textbook companies have been bought up by gigantic conglomerates that look only to the

MLA CITATION: Roediger, Henry L., III. "Why Are Textbooks So Expensive?" 2005. *Back to the Lake*. Ed. Thomas Cooley. 3rd ed. New York: Norton, 2015. 569–74. Print.

bottom line and seek huge profits. For these companies, so the theory goes, textbooks are just one more product line, no different from detergent or tires or toilet paper, on which to make a profit. The fact that many formerly independent textbook companies are being bought up and merged under the same corporate umbrella could also be partly responsible, if this process reduces competition through having fewer companies. Another facet of the debate is the frequent revision schedule of basic textbooks. Most introductory psychology textbooks are revised every three years, some every two years. Doesn't this constant revision drive up the prices?

Although the reasons listed above may have some merit, I don't think any of 3 them is fundamental to why textbook prices are so high. In fact, I suspect that most of the properties described above are effects and not causes. What is the cause? If I had to bet, the root cause is a feature of the marketplace that has changed greatly over the years and fundamentally reshaped the textbook market: sale of used books.

**The root cause is the *main* cause (p. 542).**

The organized used book market represents the great change in the landscape 4 of higher education publishing, but one that has gone relatively unnoticed.

Let us go back in time to what educational historians refer to as the later Paleo- 5 lithic era in higher education, that is, the late 1960s, when I was in college. Here was how the used book market worked then. I was a psychology major and was about to take a course in history of psychology. A psychology major in my fraternity, Dave Redmond (now a big-time lawyer in Richmond, Virginia) was going on to law school and wanted to sell some of his psychology textbooks. He asked if I wanted to buy Edna Heidbreder's *Seven Psychologies*, for a dollar. I said OK. The book had cost him $2.95, which is still listed in my copy. . . .

. . . This was how the used book market worked in my day. One student sold 6 books to another student on a hit or miss basis. Books didn't cost much. Oh, also, most students kept their books and started building a personal library. (This is another idea that seems to have faded with time. Personal library? Today's students assume everything they need to know is on the Internet.)

Let's fast forward to 1981. I was teaching at Purdue University and was consider- 7 ing (with Betty Capaldi and several others) writing an introductory psychology textbook, since textbook companies were wooing us to do so. However, neither Betty nor I had ever even taught introductory psychology, so we decided to teach independent sections one semester. We examined a lot of books and decided to use Phil Zimbardo's textbook, *Psychology and Life*. . . . Betty and I were each to teach a section of 475 students, so we ordered 950 books. Nine hundred fifty books was, and is, a big textbook order. Think of the profits to the company and the author!

A few days before classes were to begin, I happened by one of the three Purdue 8 bookstores to buy something. I decided to go see the hundreds of copies of the book I had ordered, gleaming at me on the shelves. I found them, all right, but I was

When used textbooks are sold or rented, only the middleman gets paid.

shocked at my discovery. Every single book on the shelf was a used copy! I went through many of them, disbelieving, and saw that quite a few were in poor condition (marked up, spines damaged, etc.), yet the prices were still substantial. How could this be? Zimbardo's book had never been used at Purdue before recent times. Where did all these used copies come from? I decided to walk to the other two bookstores and discovered exactly the same situation; every book for sale was a used book in the other two stores. There wasn't a new book to be found.

The organized used book market represents the great change in the landscape of higher education publishing, but one that has gone relatively unnoticed by most academics (unless they are textbook authors). The implications are huge. Consider the situation in today's dollars (although I am estimating). A single author of a textbook might make a 15 percent royalty on the net price of the book (sometimes a bit more); the net price is the price the bookstore pays the textbook company for the book and the list price is the price set by the bookstore to sell to the student. The net price of an introductory psychology textbook today might be $65 (before the bookstore marks it up), so the author would make $9.75 per book. However, that is only if the book is bought from the company; if the student buys used books, the author makes nothing and neither does the company. If 950 used books are sold, the author would lose (be cheated out of?) $9,262, and the textbook company would perhaps lose a similar or larger amount. (Profit margins probably differ from company to company and book to book. They are a closely guarded secret.) Of course, at Purdue in 1981 the figures would have been smaller, but the principle the same. The fact of modern campus life is that used book companies buy up text-books on one campus, warehouse them, and ship them to wherever the book is being adopted, and therefore prevent sales of new books.

Consider what this means. The textbook company that invested hundreds of thousands of dollars—maybe millions for introductory textbooks—to sign, 10 develop, review, produce, market, and distribute a book over several years is denied its just profits. The author or authors who wrote the book over many years are denied their royalties. Meanwhile, huge profits are made by the used book companies who did nothing whatsoever to create the product. They are true para-sites, deriving profits with no investment (and no value added to the product) while damaging their hosts. The issue here is similar to that in the movie and recording industries for pirated products that are sold very cheaply, denying the companies and the artists their profits. One major dissimilarity in these cases is that pirated movies and music are illegal whereas the used textbook market is legal. (There have been proposals to change this state of affairs. For example, one idea is that when used book companies resell texts they would pay the original textbook company and author a royalty.)

The high price of textbooks is the direct result of the used book market. A text- 11 book is customarily used for one semester and (unlike the old days) students rarely keep their books now but sell them back to the bookstore (more on that anon). Therefore, the same text might be used by three to four students, but the textbook company and author profit the first time a book is sold and not thereafter. It stands to reason that textbooks must be priced aggressively, because the profits from the repeated sales will not go to the authors and companies that actually wrote and produced the books, but rather to the companies that specialize in buying and sell-ing used books. Further, the reason textbooks are revised so frequently is to com-bat the used book market, which further drives up the company's costs. Frequent revisions also add wear and tear on the authors who must perpetually revise their books. (I've sometimes wanted to have two somewhat different versions of my text-books and then alternate them.) Most fields of psychology hardly move at such a swift pace as to justify two- to three-year revision cycles of introductory textbooks. The famous textbooks of the 1950s and 1960s were revised every eight to ten years or so, but after the used textbook market gained steam, revisions became frequent. Moreover, because of the used book market, profitability of many companies was hurt and they became ripe for takeovers, which further consolidated the market. That is why I said in the third paragraph that many factors used to "explain" the high prices of books are probably effects, with the cause being the organized used book companies that prey parasitically on the host publishing companies and threaten to destroy them.

Other changes have also affected the market. College and university bookstores used to be owned by the school and operated as a service to the students and the faculty, but those days are past on most campuses. Now the bookstores are operated by large companies (Follett's, Barnes and Noble, and others), often the same ones who operate used book operations. Most "bookstores" have turned into carnivals where emphasis is placed on selling sweatshirts, trinkets, souvenirs and snacks and, oh, incidentally (used) books. 12

Another pernicious trend: After universities relinquished their hold on bookstores, the bookstores aggressively raised the percentage markup on the net price paid to the publisher on new books. Thirty years ago a standard rate of markup was 20 percent and publishers provided list prices on their books (because markups were standard). I can recall the great hue and cry that arose when textbook stores started marking up books by 25 percent. However, a 25 percent markup for today's bookstores would look like chump change. Publishing companies now sell the bookstore the books based on a net price and the bookstore decides on the list price, often marking up the books 30 to 40 percent in the process. The profits go to the company owning the store and the company pays the college or university for the right to have a monopoly business on campus. However, many students have now learned that it is cheaper and (given the huge lines) sometimes easier to buy textbooks from other sources like Amazon.com. 13

Let me give you a concrete example. Last summer the eighth edition of my textbook (with Barry Kantowitz and David Elmes), *Experimental Psychology: Understanding Psychological Research*, was published by Wadsworth Publishing Company. The net price (the price the bookstore pays the company for a new book) the first time the book is sold is $73.50. The authors receive 15 percent royalties on the book, so we would split the $11 royalty three ways. However, at the Washington University bookstore, the list price of the book is $99.75, a markup of $26.25 (or 35.7 percent)! Yes, that's right, the authors who wrote the book get $11.02 for their years of hard work whereas the bookstore that ordered the books, let them sit on the shelves for a couple of weeks, and sold them, gets $26.25 per book. (If books are not sold, they are returned to the company for a full price refund. It's a no-risk business.) 14

Yet the story gets even worse because of the used book problem. After the student uses the book (and if it is in pretty good condition), the bookstore will buy it back from the student at a greatly marked down price, somewhere between 25 and 50 percent. Let's assume that *Experimental Psychology* is bought back for 40 percent of the list price (which is probably a generous assumption at most bookstores). That would be $39.90. After buying it, the bookstore will mark it back up dramatically 15 and resell the book. Suppose the used book is sold for $75, which sounds like a bargain relative to the new book price of $99.75, and it is. However, notice that the profit markup for the bookstore on this used book would then be $35.10, which is higher than the (still very large) profit made on the new book ($26.25). In fact, the primary reason bookstores prefer selling used books to new books is the much higher profit margins on used books. So, on the second (and third and fourth, etc.) sales of the same book, the bookstore and used book company make huge cumulative profits. The textbook company that invested large sums into developing the book (and the authors who invested time and energy and research into writing it) receive exactly zero on these resold books.

If this sounds bad, it actually gets worse. Another insidious influence in the textbook industry is the problem of sales of complimentary copies. In order to market their wares to professors, it is customary for textbook companies to give out free copies of their books. [Everyone] who teach[es] basic courses in the psychology curriculum receive[s] such books. This is just another price of doing business for the book companies. However, many of these books find their way into the used book market because some professors sell books to scavengers from the used book companies who search through university campuses seeking to buy complimentary copies. Now these companies are soliciting professors to sell their complimentary copies by e-mail. I never sell my complimentary books, of course, because I believe it unethical to sell for profit something I was given by a company in good faith. However, apparently many professors do sell their books. Now the textbook company gets hit by a double whammy: The book they produced to give to a professor for possible adoption enters the market and takes away a new book sale in the marketplace! 16

Is it any wonder that textbook prices are so high? The wonder is that they aren't higher. 17

. . .

The textbook companies themselves have few alternatives in dealing with this problem. They can and do raise the price of the books so that they try to recoup their investment on the first sale (hence the high price of textbooks). They can revise the book frequently, which renders the previous edition obsolete. They can try to bundle in or shrink-wrap some additional item (a workbook, a CD) with the new text, so that students will need to buy new books to get the free item. This strategy can work, but some bookstores will just unbundle the book from the study guide and sell both! (So, a study guide the bookstore received free can be sold for, say, $15.) Unless and until laws are changed to prevent the organized sale of used books, you can expect textbook prices to keep increasing. . . . ◆ 18

## FOR CLOSE READING

1. Henry Roediger analyzes several of the usual reasons given for the steep rise in the prices of college textbooks (2), as well as what he says is the main or "root" cause (3). What are the usual reasons and what does he claim to be the main cause?

2. What is the point of the brief NARRATIVE that Roediger tells in paragraphs 5–6 about buying his undergraduate psychology book from a classmate? How about the narrative he tells in paragraphs 7–8? How do these stories relate to his main point? Where does he state it?

3. According to Roediger, what specific effects has the used-book market had on the authors and publishers of textbooks? On the consumers of those books?

4. How and why, according to Roediger, do college bookstores sell used copies of textbooks that have never been used on their campuses?

## Strategies and Structures

1. Where and how does Roediger shift from analyzing causes to analyzing effects? Where does he switch back? How effective do you find this strategy? Why?

2. What is the purpose of the EXAMPLE that Roediger gives in paragraph 14? Why does he refer to it as a CONCRETE example? List some other concrete examples he uses. For what purposes does he use them?

3. As an author of textbooks himself, Roediger has a stake in his analysis that purchasers of textbooks do not have. Does that stake necessarily invalidate his claims? Why or why not?

4. *Other Methods.* Besides analyzing causes and effects, what ARGUMENT is Roediger making? What conclusions does he come to?

## Thinking about Language

1. In paragraphs 10 and 11, Roediger uses a biological ANALOGY. What is he comparing to what? How helpful do you find the comparison?

2. Roediger calls campus bookstores "carnivals" (12). Why?

3. How does Roediger DEFINE the "net price" of a newly published book (9)? How about the "profit margin" (9)?

4. Roediger uses HYPERBOLE when he calls the 1960s "the later Paleolithic era" (5). Why does he use hyperbole here? What does it contribute to the argument he is making?

## FOR WRITING

1. Write a paragraph or two analyzing some effects of rising textbook costs from your own standpoint as a consumer.

2.  Have you ever purchased a textbook that is labeled "free examination copy" or "not for resale"? If, as Roediger contends, the sale of such books contributes to the high cost of textbooks, what if anything do you think should be done about teachers and stores selling free copies they received from the publisher for review? Write an opinion piece for your campus newspaper (in other words, for an audience of students) arguing for or against this practice.

3.  Some public school districts (and colleges) now purchase textbooks in electronic form. And, of course, *Amazon* now sells more ebooks than paper ones. Write an essay explaining what some of the effects of this trend might be.

4.  Write an EVALUATION of your favorite (or least favorite) textbook. Include a clear analysis of the goals of the book, stated and unstated—and of how and how well it meets (or fails to meet) those goals.

You'll find quizzes on the readings at
wwnorton.com/write/back-to-the-lake.

MARY ELLEN HANNIBAL

# Why the Beaver Should Thank the Wolf

Mary Ellen Hannibal is an environmental writer who lives in the San Francisco Bay Area. A graduate of Smith College, she is currently a Stanford media fellow. Her work has appeared in a wide range of publications, including *Nautilus, Livestrong, Elle,* and *Yoga Journal* magazines, and online for the *Utne Reader, Scientific American,* and *Outside.* In *The Spine of the Continent: The Race to Save America's Last, Best Wilderness* (2012), Hannibal chronicles the development of conservation biology, a "science of love and death," and the effort to save nature along the Rocky Mountains. Her book on citizen science will be published in 2015.

"Why the Beaver Should Thank the Wolf," which appeared in the *New York Times* in September 2012, is about the "sequence of impacts down the food chain" in various ecological systems. Hannibal analyzes cause-and-effect relationships, both beneficial and destructive, between top predators (such as wolves) and their prey (such as beavers)—and also between creatures of all stripes, including humans, and the environment.

T HIS MONTH, a group of environmental nonprofits said they would challenge 1 the federal government's removal of Endangered Species Act protections for wolves in Wyoming. Since there are only about 328 wolves in a state with a historic blood thirst for the hides of these top predators, the nonprofits are probably right that lacking protection, Wyoming wolves are toast.

Many Americans, even as they view the extermination of a species as morally 2 anathema, struggle to grasp the tangible effects of the loss of wolves. It turns out that, far from being freeloaders on the top of the food chain, wolves have a powerful effect on the well-being of the ecosystems around them—from the survival of trees and riverbank vegetation to, perhaps surprisingly, the health of the populations of their prey.

An example of this can be found in Wyoming's Yellowstone National Park, 3 where wolves were virtually wiped out in the 1920s and reintroduced in the '90s. Since the wolves have come back, scientists have noted an unexpected improvement in many of the park's degraded stream areas.

MLA CITATION: Hannibal, Mary Ellen. "Why the Beaver Should Thank the Wolf." 2012. *Back to the Lake.* Ed. Thomas Cooley. 3rd ed. New York: Norton, 2015. 577–80. Print.

Stands of aspen and other native vegetation, once decimated by overgrazing, are 4 now growing up along the banks. This may have something to do with changing fire patterns, but it is also probably because elk and other browsing animals behave differently when wolves are around. Instead of eating greenery down to the soil, they take a bite or two, look up to check for threats, and keep moving. The greenery can grow tall enough to reproduce.

Beavers, despite being on the wolf's menu, also benefit when their predators are 5 around. The healthy vegetation encouraged by the presence of wolves provides food and shelter to beavers. Beavers in turn go on to create dams that help keep rivers clean and lessen the effects of drought. Beaver activity also spreads a welcome mat for thronging biodiversity. Bugs, amphibians, fish, birds and small mammals find the water around dams to be an ideal habitat.

So the beavers keep the rivers from drying up while, at the same time, healthy 6 vegetation keeps the rivers from flooding, and all this biological interaction helps maintain rich soil that better sequesters carbon—that stuff we want to get out of the atmosphere and back into the ground. In other words, by helping to maintain a healthy ecosystem, wolves are connected to climate change: without them, these landscapes would be more vulnerable to the effects of those big weather events we will increasingly experience as the planet warms.

As explained on p. 534, cascades of cause and effect are not limited to the food chain. Scientists call this sequence of impacts down the food chain a "trophic 7 cascade." The wolf is connected to the elk is connected to the aspen is connected to the beaver. Keeping these connections going ensures healthy, functioning ecosystems, which in turn support human life.

Another example is the effect of sea otters on kelp, which provides food 8 and shelter for a host of species. Like the aspen for the elk, kelp is a favorite food of sea urchins. By hunting sea urchins, otters protect the vitality of the kelp and actually boost overall biodiversity. Without them, the ecosystem tends to collapse; the coastal reefs become barren, and soon not much lives there.

Unfortunately, sea otters are in the cross hairs of a conflict equivalent to the "wolf 9 wars." Some communities in southeast Alaska want to allow the hunting of sea otters in order to decrease their numbers and protect fisheries. But the rationale that eliminating the predator increases the prey is shortsighted and ignores larger food-web dynamics. A degraded ecosystem will be far less productive over all.

Having fewer fish wouldn't just hurt fishermen: it would also endanger the other 10 end of the trophic scale—the phytoplankton that turn sunshine into plant material, and as every student of photosynthesis knows, create oxygen and sequester carbon. In lakes, predator fish keep the smaller fish from eating all the phytoplankton, thus sustaining the lake's rate of carbon uptake.

Around the planet, large predators are becoming extinct at faster rates than 11 other species. And losing top predators has an outsize effect on the rate of loss of

The "trophic cascade": the wolf is connected to the elk is connected to the aspen is connected to the beaver.

many other species below them on the food chain as well as on the plant life that is so important to the balance of our ecosystems.

So what can be done? For one thing, we have begun to realize that parks like 12 Yellowstone are not the most effective means of conservation. Putting a boundary around an expanse of wilderness is an intuitive idea not borne out by the science. Many top predators must travel enormous distances to find mates and keep populations from becoming inbred. No national park is big enough for wolves, for example. Instead, conservation must be done on a continental scale. We can still erect our human boundaries—around cities and towns, mines and oil fields—but in order to sustain a healthy ecosystem, we need to build in connections so that top predators can move from one wild place to another.

Many biologists have warned that we are approaching another mass extinction. 13 The wolf is still endangered and should be protected in its own right. But we should also recognize that bringing all the planet's threatened and endangered species back to healthy numbers—as well as mitigating the effects of climate change— means keeping top predators around. ◆

## FOR CLOSE READING

1. Since wolves eat beavers, why is it that Mary Ellen Hannibal claims beavers should thank them?

2. Wolves themselves need to be protected from "top predators," Hannibal suggests (1). Which one in particular? Explain.

3. If sea otters eat fish, why shouldn't fishermen eat (or otherwise eliminate) sea otters in Hannibal's view?

4. Why are parks, even large national ones, "not the most effective means of conversation," according to Hannibal (12)?

5. Given the effects of climate change, why does Hannibal think "keeping top predators around" is more important than ever (13)?

## Strategies and Structures

1. There is, Hannibal claims, a beneficial web or system of cause-and-effect relationships all up and down the food chain. Where does she state this claim most directly?

2. In support of her general claim about interconnectedness within and between ecosystems, Hannibal analyzes specific causal relationships. Which ones do you find most pertinent? Why?

3. Hannibal considers the statement that "eliminating the predator increases the prey" to be "shortsighted" (9). Why? What side effects of this practice in particular does she cite to support her analysis?

4. "So what can be done?" Hannibal asks near the end of her essay (12). About what? What is Hannibal's main purpose in analyzing examples of a "trophic cascade" or "sequence of impacts down the food chain" (7)?

5. *Other Methods.* Hannibal CLASSIFIES wolves as top predators. How does she use this classification to argue that top predators are not "freeloaders on the top of the food chain" (2)?

6. What particular POSITION does Hannibal take in the "wolf wars" (9)? How and how well does her analysis of causes and effects support this position (9)?

## Thinking about Language

1. Look up *ecosystem* in your dictionary and online (6). Who coined the term and under what circumstances?

2. Explain the "welcome mat" METAPHOR in paragraph 5 of Hannibal's essay.

3. *Trophic* means "having to do with nutritional needs or habits." So what would be the meaning of a *trophic cascade* (7)?

4. "The wolf is connected to the elk is connected to the aspen is connected to the beaver" (7). How do the rhythm and repetition of this sentence contribute to its meaning?

5. What is the difference between saying that an idea is "shortsighted" and that it is just plain wrong (9)?

## FOR WRITING

1. In a paragraph or two, explain the concept of a *trophic* (or feeding) relationship between plants and animals.

2. Hannibal analyzes the links between wolves and beavers, sea otters and kelp. Write a brief analysis of the cascade of causes and effects in some other ecosystem that she might have chosen to make her point about interconnectedness up and down the chain.

3. In fables and other stories, animals often talk to each other for the purpose of illustrating a point that some human wants to make. Write a narrative in which a beaver and a wolf (and/or other creatures) discuss some of the issues that Hannibal raises, particularly ones involving food. Be sure to include (or at least imply) a moral.

4. Should wolves be removed from the endangered species list in Wyoming and elsewhere? Take a POSITION on this issue and explain and support your view by using cause-and-effect analysis, among other strategies.

5. In your journal, record examples, as you observe or read about them, of nutritional and other forms of interconnectedness in the natural, including the human, environment. Take special note of the cause-and-effect relationships you encounter in various systems.

You'll find quizzes on the readings at wwnorton.com/write/back-to-the-lake.

JON MOOALLEM

# Squirrel Power!

Jon Mooallem is a journalist who writes mostly about animals and the sometimes weird ways in which humans interact with them. A frequent contributor to the *New York Times Magazine* on topics ranging from monkeys on the loose to baby turtles caught in an oil spill, Mooallem grew up in New Jersey and attended Colorado College. He also writes for *Pop-Up*, a live magazine performed on stage in San Francisco, as well as the *New Yorker, Harper's,* and *Wired,* where he contributes a regular column called "This Week in Wild Animals." Mooallem recently gave talks about animals at the offices of Pixar and Google and staged an animal-themed rock opera in San Francisco with the band Black Prairie. In addition to an ebook—*American Hippopotamus* (2013), about two rival spies charged with introducing hippo ranching to America in 1910—he is the author of *Wild Ones: A Sometimes Dismaying, Weirdly Reassuring Story about Looking at People Looking at Animals in America* (2013).

"Squirrel Power!," which appeared in the *New York Times* in August 2013, is about power outages caused by squirrels all across the U.S. power grid. The effects, as Mooallem demonstrates, can be far-reaching.

S OME SAY THE WORLD WILL END IN FIRE. Some say ice. Some say coordinated  1
kamikaze attacks on the power grid by squirrels.

At least, some have been saying that to me, when they find out I've spent the  2
summer keeping track of power outages caused by squirrels.

Power outages caused by squirrels are a new hobby of mine, a persnickety and  3
constantly updating data set that hums along behind the rest of my life the way baseball statistics or celebrity-birthing news might for other people. It started in April, after I read about a squirrel that electrocuted itself on a power line in Tampa, Florida, cutting electricity to 700 customers and delaying statewide achievement tests at three nearby schools. I was curious, just enough to set up a Google news alert: squirrel power. But as the summer progressed, and the local news reports of power outages caused by squirrels piled up in my in-box, my interest in power outages caused by squirrels became more obsessive and profound.

MLA CITATION: Mooallem, Jon. "Squirrel Power!" 2013. *Back to the Lake.* Ed. Thomas Cooley. 3rd ed. New York: Norton, 2015. 583–88. Print.

I know: it's hard to accept that a single squirrel can disrupt and frustrate thou-    4
sands of people at a time, switching off our electrified lives for hours. But since
Memorial Day, I've cataloged reports of fifty power outages caused by squirrels in
twenty-four states. (And these, of course, are only those power outages severe
enough to make the news.) Fifteen hundred customers lost power in Mason City,
Iowa; 1,500 customers in Roanoke, Virginia; 5,000 customers in Clackamas
County, Oregon; and 10,000 customers in Wichita, Kansas—and that was just during two particularly busy days in June. A month later, there were two separate
P.O.C.B.S., as I've come to call power outages caused by squirrels, around the small
town of Evergreen, Montana, on a single day.

Squirrels cut power to a regional airport in Virginia, a Veterans Affairs medical cen-    5
ter in Tennessee, a university in Montana and a Trader Joe's in South Carolina. Five
days after the Trader Joe's went down, another squirrel cut power to 7,200 customers in
Rock Hill, South Carolina, on the opposite end of the state. Rock Hill city officials
assured the public that power outages caused by squirrels were "very rare" and that the
grid was "still a reliable system." Nine days later, 3,800 more South Carolinians lost
power after a squirrel blew up a circuit breaker in the town of Summerville.

In Portland, Oregon, squirrels got 9,200 customers on July 1; 3,140 customers on    6
July 23; and 7,400 customers on July 26. ("I sound like a broken record," a spokesman
for the utility said, briefing the press for the third time.) In Kentucky, more than
10,000 people lost power in two separate P.O.C.B.S. a few days apart. The town of
Lynchburg, Virginia, suffered large-scale P.O.C.B.S. on two consecutive Thursdays
in June. Downtown went dark. At Lynchburg's Academy of Fine Arts, patrons were
left to wave their lighted iPhone screens at the art on the walls, like torch-carrying
Victorian explorers groping through a tomb.

One June 9, a squirrel blacked out 2,000 customers in Kalamazoo, Michigan,    7
then 921 customers outside Kalamazoo a week later. A local politician visited the
blown transformer with her children to take a look at the culprit; another witness
told a reporter, "There was no fur left on it. It looked like something from *C.S.I.*"
She posted a photo of the incinerated animal to her Facebook page.

When I tell people about power outages caused by squirrels—and trust me when I    8
say that I tell people about power outages caused by squirrels quite often—I wind
up hearing a lot of the same snarky jokes. People say the squirrels are staging an
uprising. People say the squirrels are calculating, nut-cheeked saboteurs trying to
overthrow humanity. Like the apes in *Planet of the Apes*, or the Skynet computer
network in *The Terminator*, the squirrels represent a kind of neglected intelligence
that's suddenly, sinisterly switching on.

Don't panic, I say. Squirrels have been causing power outages since long before I    9
started cataloging power outages caused by squirrels. (In 1987, a squirrel shut down

the Nasdaq for eighty-two minutes and another squirrel shut down the Nasdaq again in 1994—a seminal bit of P.O.C.B.S. history that was sometimes noted in coverage of the power outage at the Nasdaq in August, which was a power outage not caused by squirrels. "This is a terrible pain in the neck," the president of one brokerage firm told *The Wall Street Journal* in 1994—which, I've found, is still a typical reaction to power outages caused by squirrels.)

Matthew Olearczyk, a program manager with the Electric Power Research 10 Institute, explains that typically a squirrel will cause a blackout by scampering across electrical equipment and touching simultaneously both an energized component, like one of the cylindrical transformers at the top of a utility pole, and a grounded piece of equipment. The squirrel completes the circuit, generating an arc. There is an instantaneous flash of blue light. At its center is the squirrel, combusting. (In one news story, the squirrel was said to make a "popping sound" when it ignited.)

Nitty-gritty immediate causes like this are discussed on p. 540.

And yet the grid is actually designed to handle this violent interruption. As soon 11 as the dead animal drops to the ground, eliminating the interference, the flow of electricity should resume. But if the squirrel doesn't fall off the equipment—if its charred carcass is lodged there—the squirrel can trigger a so-called continuous fault, interrupting the restarted flow of electricity all over again. It's a zombie attack: a lingering, second wave of obstruction. The lights go out when our electrical grid can find no way around this stuck hunk of dead weight that used to be a squirrel.

The aftermath can be gnarly. Often, there are burned-out circuit breakers or 12 other costly, obliterated equipment to clean up or replace. And occasionally, a P.O.C.B.S. will generate an idiosyncratic storm of ancillary mayhem, too. I've read about a squirrel that, last February, chewed into high-voltage lines near a water-treatment facility, setting off "a chain of improbable events" that forced the city of Tampa to boil its water for the next thirty-seven hours, and I've read about a flaming squirrel that allegedly fell from a utility pole in April and started a two-acre grass fire outside Tulsa, Oklahoma.

Mr. Olearczyk insists that there is no credible way to estimate the number of 13 power outages caused by squirrels nationwide. (He explained that attempting a tally would mean consulting a particular piece of paperwork from every local utility in the country, and that some of those forms might not even have the information I was looking for. Though he told me encouragingly, "You're after something important, so let us know if you find out!")

What exists, instead, are only flecks of information, the partial outline of a very 14 annoying apparition. In Austin, Texas, squirrels have been blamed for 300 power outages a year. Other utility companies have claimed that between 7 and 20 percent of all outages are caused by some sort of wild animal, and a 2005 study by the

State of California estimated, hazily, that these incidents cost California's economy between $32 million and $317 million a year. Feral cats, raccoons and birds are also nuisances. Last month, reports surfaced in Oklahoma of great horned owls dropping snakes onto utility poles, thereby causing frequent power outages. Still, no one seems to dispute the disruptive primacy of squirrels.

However, Mr. Olearczyk believes strongly that power outages caused by squirrels are on the decline. For at least a decade, utility companies have been tricking out their equipment with an array of wildlife deterrents to combat the problem, like "arrester caps" and "bushing covers," the Southwire SquirrelShield, the E/Getaway Guard and free-spinning baffles to make squirrels lose their balance. 15

The industry has also researched discouraging squirrels by spraying utility poles with fox urine and painting equipment red, though both of these tactics have failed; it's not even clear whether squirrels can see the color red. Some utilities have installed the kind of plastic owl used to keep pigeons off building facades. However, an industry study notes, "one utility reported that the fake owl was attacked by a hawk which in turn caused a substation outage." 16

The ZAPShield is a device that delivers a nonlethal electrostatic jolt—one of the many ways that utility companies have been trying to deter wildlife.

At some point this summer—I think it was around July 31, when just under 13,000 customers got hit by a P.O.C.B.S. in Hendersonville, Tennessee—I found myself trying to imagine power outages caused by squirrels from the squirrels' point of view. So I called John L. Koprowski, a squirrel biologist at the University of Arizona, Tucson. 17

There have been very few squirrel specialists throughout history. The most accomplished was Vagn Flyger, a University of Maryland biologist who trapped squirrels with a mixture of peanut butter and Valium and then affixed them with radio transmitters; his major contribution to squirrel science was mapping the so-called Great Squirrel Migration of 1968 across the Eastern Seaboard. (Mr. Flyger also liked to eat squirrels.) Mr. Koprowski started studying squirrels as a biology student in Ohio because he needed to study some sort of wild animal and he didn't own a car. 18

Essentially, Mr. Koprowski explained, power outages caused by squirrels are the product of a cascade of coincidences—of various forces, including basic squirrel behavior, colliding. 19

Squirrels chew through electrical wiring because the animals are constantly teething. An adult squirrel's incisors never stop growing—they can grow as much as ten inches per year—and the animals must chew constantly to keep them worn down. Squirrels gnaw or burrow their way into transformers for the same reason they enter rotting cavities of aging trees: hollow spaces offer them den sites and safety from predators. Squirrels break into equipment at substations because the seeds and insects they eat get sucked into that machinery by cooling fans, or are pooled inside by the wind. Mr. Koprowski described the flat tops of transformers as perfect spots for squirrel "basking behavior," when squirrels sprawl out in the sun to warm up, or in the shade to cool down, and also ideal "runways" from which squirrels can start their flying leaps into the canopy. 20

"Squirrels value many of the same things that humans value," Mr. Koprowski explained. It's why they're among America's most successful synanthropes, what biologists call species that thrive alongside humans, in the landscapes we dominate. The beautiful, shade-producing, property-value-raising trees that we've filled our neighborhoods with, like oaks, walnuts, maples and elms, also produce the seeds, nuts and acorns at the core of the squirrel diet. Thirty-five percent of America's urban areas are now covered with trees, while sprawl and exurban development have pushed homes further into formerly natural areas. Squirrel habitat and our habitat are increasingly converging. And we are only now reaching what may be peak P.O.C.B.S. season. In late August and September, squirrels are both abundant and most active: skittering around, stockpiling food, hustling to get stuff done before winter—more prone to crossing paths with the path of our electricity. 21

P. 535 discusses the effects of outright human error in the causal chain.

Squirrels bask on warm power lines.

"People are living in areas with higher squirrel densities now," Mr. Koprowski    22
said. It's as simple as that. We're getting in their way, too. It's easy to forget that the
party most inconvenienced by a power outage caused by a squirrel is the squirrel
that caused it.

What has my interest in power outages caused by squirrels taught me, ultimately?    23
Why do I find power outages caused by squirrels so meaningful?

When you ana-
lyze causes and    Naturally, I've been giving these questions some serious thought.    24
effects, state
your point in    I've come to see each P.O.C.B.S. as a reminder of our relative size on    25
doing so, p. 539.    the landscape, recalibrating our identity as one set of creatures in a larger
ecology. We are a marvelously successful set of creatures, though. A power
outage caused by a squirrel feels so surprising only because we've come to see our
electrical grid—all these wires with which, little by little, we've battened down the
continent—as a constant. Electricity everywhere, at the flick of a switch, seems like
the natural order, while the actual natural order—the squirrel programmed by evolution to gnaw and eat acorns and bask and leap and scamper—winds up feeling
like a preposterous, alien glitch in that system. It's a pretty stunning reversal, if you
can clear the right kind of space to reflect on it, and fortunately power outages
caused by squirrels do that for you by shutting off your TV and Internet.

After the city of Fort Meade, Florida, suffered more than two dozen P.O.C.B.S.    26
in a year, a resident told a reporter: "I just didn't think a squirrel could make the
lights go out. They're just tiny little things." A century ago, a shrewd squirrel might
have been equally skeptical about our ability to make so many lights go on, watching a few little humans raise the first wooden pole. ◆

## FOR CLOSE READING

1. In a power outage caused by squirrels, which is more significant and newsworthy—except to the squirrel, of course—the cause or the effects? Why?

2. According to one expert whom Jon Mooallem interviewed, why isn't it "credible" to keep track of all P.O.C.B.S as they occur across the country (13)?

3. Fortunately, according to Mooallem, P.O.C.B.S. seem to be "on the decline" (15). What are some of the causes of this effect?

4. Except when they get electrocuted, squirrels are "among America's most successful synanthropes" (21). What makes them so successful?

5. The typical reaction of most human victims of a P.O.C.B.S., says Mooallem, is surprise (26). Why shouldn't it be?

## Strategies and Structures

1. Mooallem assumes that his readers will need to be convinced that power outages caused by squirrels are a serious, if not "profound," problem (3). How and how well does he go about doing this?

2. Where and how does Mooallem analyze the immediate cause of a P.O.C.B.S. in greatest mechanical, or rather, electrical detail? How about the immediate cause of a "so-called continuous fault" (11)?

3. Although he briefly examines their immediate physical cause, Mooallem concentrates on the "aftermath" (that is, the effects) of P.O.C.B.S. in the first half of his analysis. Where and how does he signal a shift toward analyzing mainly the causes?

4. Many of the more remote causes of any P.O.C.B.S. have to do with what Mooallem calls "basic squirrel behavior" (19). What are some of them, and how does he factor those causes into the "cascade of coincidences" that typically produce an outage?

5. In the last four paragraphs of his essay, Mooallem branches out from the electrical grid to "the natural order" (25). What POSITION is he taking here? How and how well does his analysis of cause and effect serve as a "runway" for making this leap? Explain.

## Thinking about Language

1. Why and to what effect does Mooallem use the abbreviation P.O.C.B.S?

2. What's wrong with the following statement: *Occasionally, a squirrel is electrocuted but survives?*

3. "The aftermath can be gnarly" (12). Is this an UNDERSTATEMENT? Why or why not?

4. Is *cascade* a good choice of words for explaining how causes produce effects? Why or why not?

5. Look up and explain the root meaning of *synanthropes* (21).

6. By describing squirrels as "hustling to get stuff done before winter," Mooallem makes them sound almost human (21). Where else does he engage in anthropomorphism? For what purpose?

## FOR WRITING

1. In a paragraph or two analyze the causes and effects of a power outage you have experienced or read about that involved "some sort of wild animal" (14).

2. In approximately 400 words, analyze the detrimental effects that some other successful synanthropes, such as rats, have upon the habitat they share with humans—and humans upon them.

3. Animals are hardly the only causes of disruption in the power grid. Weather is another major offender. So is old or faulty equipment. Do some research on how the grid works—and sometimes doesn't—and write an approximately 500-word REPORT on the general reliability (or fragility) of the electric power system in a particular region or across the country as a whole.

4. The opening lines of Mooallem's essay are an ALLUSION to Robert Frost's famous poem "Fire and Ice." Write a RHETORICAL ANALYSIS of the poem as an exploration of cause and effect in human affairs.

5. Maintain a nature journal in which you record your experiences with (including your reading about) animals and "the natural order." Include times when you feel that order is disrupted or threatened—and the causes and effects thereof.

..................................................●

You'll find quizzes on the readings at
wwnorton.com/write/back-to-the-lake.

MATTHEW YGLESIAS

# Money Isn't Everything

Matthew Yglesias (b. 1981) is a journalist and pioneer in the field of political blogging. A native of New York City, he attended the Dalton School and Harvard University, where he studied philosophy, graduating in 2003. A contributor to the *Atlantic, Slate,* and other publications, Yglesias is the executive editor of the online news site *Vox.* Sometimes known as "Big Media Matt," Yglesias appears regularly on *BloggingHeads.tv.* He is the author of the *The Rent Is Too Damn High"* (2012), an ebook about the effects upon the economy, environment, community, and personal lives of the many Americans who spend too much of their monthly income on housing.

"Money Isn't Everything," part of a series that ran in *Slate* in August 2013, is about competition among financial titans like Bill Gates and Steve Jobs—and what causes some of them to be so much poorer, relatively speaking, than their peers.

O NE IS DEAD, and the other has long since departed the corporate world for charitable pursuits. The rivalry between Steve Jobs and Bill Gates that dominated the computer industry for decades is over. And it's clear that Gates won. With his net worth of $66 billion, Gates still sits atop the Forbes 400 list of richest Americans, as he has since 1995. Founding the most successful technology company in the world has its rewards. In fact, Microsoft's victory over Apple was so decisive that current CEO Steve Ballmer and third co-founder Paul Allen, sitting on $16 billion and $15 billion, respectively, are substantially wealthier than Jobs' widow, who must subsist on a mere $11 billion.

Except of course, Microsoft *isn't* a more successful company than Apple. Not even close.

Microsoft is a vastly profitable company. Its $5 billion in net income last quarter is a ton of money, and its $260 billion stock market capitalization is impressive. But Apple dwarfs those numbers with $8.8 billion in profit and a $400 billion market capitalization. Comfortable with its lead in PCs, Microsoft has never been able to follow Apple into the world of mobile devices like phones and tablets.

MLA CITATION: Yglesias, Matthew. "Money Isn't Everything." 2013. *Back to the Lake.* Ed. Thomas Cooley. 3rd ed. New York: Norton, 2015. 591–93. Print.

So why are Microsoft founders so rich even as their company's lost pole position? Because meritocracy is a myth, even at the highest levels of the American economy. Good fortune and random chance are huge influences everywhere. And market rewards, tautologically, accrue to those who are good at making money rather than those who are good at doing things. 4

*As Napoleon learned (p. 544), random chance can take the form of bad weather.*

Microsoft's founders did a great job of retaining a huge amount of the company's stock after its initial public offering, and that's allowed them to turn its success into a vast fortune. Jobs, by contrast, blundered and got rid of most of his Apple shares in a fit of pique after he was forced out of the company. He then made a whole new fortune for himself by obtaining a majority stake in Pixar in 1986. He came back to Apple relatively cheaply by selling Next Software in a $400 million acquisition that left Jobs owning a far smaller slice of Apple than is typical for a high-tech founder. A few years after his return to Apple, the company tried to reward him by illegally backdating stock options but got caught in the process. After that, he worked for $1 a year. 5

As of his death, the Jobs fortune was mostly Disney stock obtained when the studio bought Pixar—unrelated to his role in founding and managing the world's most successful technology company. Even Michael Dell, the founder and longtime CEO of a distinctly less successful computer manufacturer, had a higher net worth. 6

Not even the biggest Pixar fan would think animated feature films are Jobs's most important legacy. But merit is one thing and financial savvy another, even in the world of business. 7

Companies on such parallel trajectories as Apple and Microsoft are rare, but the same dynamic plays out throughout the economy. Chick-fil-A is a perfectly fine chain when it's not stumbling into political hot water, but nobody would mistake it for the dominant fast-food brand in the United States. Yet its founder, S. Truett Cathy, has a $4.2 billion fortune that far outpaces anyone else in the food game. Howard Schultz—the other solo restaurant founder on the Forbes 400 list— brought us the ubiquitous and socially transformative Starbucks and is getting by on a measly $1.5 billion. H&M has similar profits and more revenue than Inditex (the parent company of Zara and related brands), but Amancio Ortega is about twice as rich as Stefan Persson. Carlos Slim, the Mexican billionaire whose fortune rivals Gates's, didn't invent or create anything particularly noteworthy. Oracle and Amazon are worth similar amounts, but Oracle's founder is worth about $20 billion more than Amazon's. The results, again, are driven by the nitty-gritty of financial dealmaking, not the success of the businesses as enterprises. 8

The disjoint between the two is a reminder that, despite thirty years of supply-side myths, it's difficult to understand action at the top as driven by financial incentives. Jobs didn't come back to Apple for the money—he was already rich and agreed to try to save the company without insisting on a huge share of the upside. 9

And Ballmer, who's even richer, doesn't keep plugging away at Microsoft in search of an extra billion or two. Money counts for something, of course. But the real rivalries are about more than a desire to be the boy with the most cake—it's a competition for fame, prestige, and the ability to shape the future of technology. ◆

## FOR CLOSE READING

1. In the race between Apple and Microsoft, which company has the lead in the personal computer business, according to Matthew Yglesias? In phones and other mobile devices?

2. Of the two tech giants, which company is richer ? By how much?

3. In the personal-fortune sweepstakes, who comes out ahead, Steve Jobs or Bill Gates? Again, by how much?

4. What did the Mexican billionaire Carlos Slim "invent or create" that made him about as wealthy as Bill Gates (8)?

## Strategies and Structures

1. Yglesias begins his essay by COMPARING the fortunes of two very rich men. When and where does he start to analyze the CAUSES of the differences between them? How does he signal this shift to the reader?

2. Yglesias says that one of the main causes of personal financial success in business is being "good at making money" (4). How does he indicate the limitations of citing an effect as its own cause?

3. What probable cause of personal financial success does Yglesias entertain—and then reject as insufficient to produce that effect? Explain.

4. Yglesias says that "the same dynamic" he has observed at work between Microsoft and Apple "plays out throughout the economy" (8). What evidence does he give for this assertion? How sufficient is it for proving his point that "financial dealmaking" is a necessary cause of personal financial success whereas simply running a good company is not (8)?

5. If great achievers like Steve Jobs aren't driven strictly "by financial incentives," what are they driven by, according to Yglesias (9)? How and how well does he prove causation in this part of his analysis?

6. *Other Methods.* Yglesias COMPARES the fortunes of various entrepreneurs as a way of identifying possible causes of their relative financial success or failure. How effective is this strategy?

## Thinking about Language

1. Steve Jobs's widow, says Yglesias, "must subsist on a mere $11 billion" (1). Is this IRONY? Explain.

2. Look up *tautology* in your dictionary. What's tautological about Yglesias's argument in paragraph 4? Why does he make it anyway?

3. Explain the *pole position* METAPHOR in Yglesias's account of the corporate race between Microsoft and Apple (4).

4. How is Iglesias defining *merit* in paragraph 7? How does this definition support his analysis of the causes and effects of great success in business?

## FOR WRITING

1. What other companies and their founders or CEOs might Yglesias have cited? In a paragraph or two, outline a corporate (or other) rivalry that illustrates the "dynamic" Yglesias is analyzing (8).

2. Look up "supply-side," and write a brief EVALUATION of how this economic model works, or is supposed to work (9). Use cause-and-effect analysis to support your evaluation.

3. The British economist John Maynard Keynes (1883–1946) is often cited as the father of a theory of economics that emphasizes demand over supply. Do a little research; then, in 400–500 words, write a PROFILE of Keynes and his economic theory. Be sure to explain the causes of economic prosperity or depression as Keynes understood them.

4. "Meritocracy is a myth" (4), Yglesias asserts. In a POSITION PAPER of approximately 400 words, question (or confirm) the validity of this proposition in business, school, sports, friendship, love, or some other field.

⋯⋯⋯⋯⋯⋯⋯⋯⋯⋯⋯⋯⋯⋯⋯⋯⋯⋯⋯⋯⋯⋯•

You'll find quizzes on the readings at
wwnorton.com/write/back-to-the-lake.

# The Ones Who Walk Away from Omelas

## Variations on a Theme by William James

Ursula K. LeGuin (b. 1929) is perhaps best known for her works of science fiction and fantasy, including *The Left Hand of Darkness* (1969) and *The Fartherest Shore* (1972). Le Guin grew up in Berkeley, California, and the nearby Napa Valley. Her parents were trained as anthropologists, and Le Guin herself explores alternative cultures in her fiction, often futuristic or utopian ones as in "Omelas." After graduating from Radcliffe College, Le Guin pursued graduate studies at Columbia University and in France before settling in Portland, Oregon. ("Omelas," of course, is "Salem O" spelled backwards.) The author of more than sixty books, including those in the Earthsea and Hainish series, she has also published mainstream fiction, poetry, books for children and young adults, screenplays, translations, and even a "space opera."

"The Ones Who Walk Away from Omelas" (1973) is a philosophical short story about the causes and conditions of happiness in human society. It was inspired by the writings of the American philosopher William James (1842–1910) for whom the greatest moral and ethical ideals were not so much the "effects of past experience" as the "probable causes" of ethical behavior in the future.

See p. 536 for a discussion of James's essay as the inspiration for Le Guin's story.

WITH A CLAMOR OF BELLS that set the swallows soaring, the festival of Summer came to the city Omelas, bright-towered by the sea. The rigging of the boats in harbor sparkled with flags. In the streets between houses with red roofs and painted walls, between old mossgrown gardens and under avenues of trees, past great parks and public buildings, processions moved. Some were decorous: old people in long stiff robes of mauve and grey, grave master workmen, quiet, merry women carrying their babies and chatting as they walked. In other streets the music beat faster, a shimmering of gong and tambourine, and the people went dancing, the procession was a dance. Children dodged in and out, their high calls rising like the swallows' crossing flights over the music and the singing.

MLA CITATION: Le Guin, Ursula K. "The Ones Who Walk Away from Omelas." 1973. *Back to the Lake*. Ed. Thomas Cooley. 3rd ed. New York: Norton, 2015. 595–600. Print.

All the processions wound towards the north side of the city, where on the great water-meadow called the Green Fields boys and girls, naked in the bright air, with mud-stained feet and ankles and long, lithe arms, exercised their restive horses before the race. The horses wore no gear at all but a halter without bit. Their manes were braided with streamers of silver, gold, and green. They flared their nostrils and pranced and boasted to one another; they were vastly excited, the horse being the only animal who has adopted our ceremonies as his own. Far off to the north and west the mountains stood up half encircling Omelas on her bay. The air of morning was so clear that the snow still crowning the Eighteen Peaks burned with white-gold fire across the miles of sunlit air, under the dark blue of the sky. There was just enough wind to make the banners that marked the racecourse snap and flutter now and then. In the silence of the broad green meadows one could hear the music winding through the city streets, farther and nearer and ever approaching, a cheerful faint sweetness of the air that from time to time trembled and gathered together and broke out into the great joyous clanging of the bells.

Joyous! How is one to tell about joy? How describe the citizens of Omelas?  2

They were not simple folk, you see, though they were happy. But we do not say  3
the words of cheer much any more. All smiles have become archaic. Given a description such as this one tends to make certain assumptions. Given a description such as this one tends to look next for the King, mounted on a splendid stallion and surrounded by his noble knights, or perhaps in a golden litter borne by great-muscled slaves. But there was no king. They did not use swords, or keep slaves. They were not barbarians. I do not know the rules and laws of their society, but I suspect that they were singularly few. As they did without monarchy and slavery, so they also got on without the stock exchange, the advertisement, the secret police, and the bomb. Yet I repeat that these were not simple folk, not dulcet shepherds, noble savages, bland utopians. They were not less complex than us. The trouble is that we have a bad habit, encouraged by pedants and sophisticates, of considering happiness as something rather stupid. Only pain is intellectual, only evil interesting. This is the treason of the artist: a refusal to admit the banality of evil and the terrible boredom of pain. If you can't lick 'em, join 'em. If it hurts, repeat it. But to praise despair is to condemn delight, to embrace violence is to lose hold of everything else. We have almost lost hold; we can no longer describe a happy man, nor make any celebration of joy. How can I tell you about the people of Omelas? They were not naïve and happy children— though their children were, in fact, happy. They were mature, intelligent, passionate adults whose lives were not wretched. O miracle! but I wish I could describe it better. I wish I could convince you. Omelas sounds in my words like a city in a fairy tale, long ago and far away, once upon a time. Perhaps it would be best if you imagined it as your own fancy bids, assuming it will rise to the

See p. 537 for tips on keeping your audience in mind when analyzing causes and effects.

occasion, for certainly I cannot suit you all. For instance, how about technology? I think that there would be no cars or helicopters in and above the streets; this follows from the fact that the people of Omelas are happy people. Happiness is based on a just discrimination of what is necessary, what is neither necessary nor destructive, and what is destructive. In the middle category, however—that of the unnecessary but undestructive, that of comfort, luxury, exuberance, etc.—they could perfectly well have central heating, subway trains, washing machines, and all kinds of marvelous devices not yet invented here, floating light-sources, fuelless power, a cure for the common cold. Or they could have none of that: it doesn't matter. As you like it. I incline to think that people from towns up and down the coast have been coming in to Omelas during the last days before the Festival on very fast little trains and double-decked trams, and that the train station of Omelas is actually the handsomest building in town, though plainer than the magnificent Farmers' Market. But even granted trains, I fear that Omelas so far strikes some of you as goody-goody. Smiles, bells, parades, horses, bleh. If so, please add an orgy. If an orgy would help, don't hesitate. Let us not, however, have temples from which issue beautiful nude priests and priestesses already half in ecstasy and ready to copulate with any man or woman, lover or stranger, who desires union with the deep godhead of the blood, although that was my first idea. But really it would be better not to have any temples in Omelas—at least, not manned temples. Religion yes, clergy no. Surely the beautiful nudes can just wander about, offering themselves like divine soufflés to the hunger of the needy and the rapture of the flesh. Let them join the processions. Let tambourines be struck above the copulations, and the glory of desire be proclaimed upon the gongs, and (a not unimportant point) let the offspring of these delightful rituals be beloved and looked after by all. One thing I know there is none of in Omelas is guilt. But what else should there be? I thought at first there were no drugs, but that is puritanical. For those who like it, the faint insistent sweetness of *drooz* may perfume the ways of the city, *drooz* which first brings a great lightness and brilliance to the mind and limbs, and then after some hours a dreamy languor, and wonderful visions at last of the very arcana and inmost secrets of the Universe, as well as exciting the pleasure of sex beyond all belief; and it is not habit-forming. For more modest tastes I think there ought to be beer. What else, what else belongs in the joyous city? The sense of victory, surely, the celebration of courage. But as we did without clergy, let us do without soldiers. The joy built upon successful slaughter is not the right kind of joy; it will not do; it is fearful and it is trivial. A boundless and generous contentment, a magnanimous triumph felt not against some outer enemy but in communion with the finest and fairest in the souls of all men everywhere and the splendor of the world's summer: this is what swells the hearts of the people of Omelas, and the victory they celebrate is that of life. I really don't think many of them need to take *drooz*.

Most of the processions have reached the Green Fields by now. A marvelous   4
smell of cooking goes forth from the red and blue tents of the provisioners. The
faces of small children are amiably sticky; in the benign grey beard of a man a
couple of crumbs of rich pastry are entangled. The youths and girls have mounted
their horses and are beginning to group around the starting line of the course. An
old woman, small, fat, and laughing, is passing out flowers from a basket, and tall
young men wear her flowers in their shining hair. A child of nine or ten sits at the
edge of the crowd, alone, playing on a wooden flute. People pause to listen, and
they smile, but they do not speak to him, for he never ceases playing and never sees
them, his dark eyes wholly rapt in the sweet, thin magic of the tune.

He finishes, and slowly lowers his hands holding the wooden flute.                    5

As if that little private silence were the signal, all at once a trumpet sounds from   6
the pavilion near the starting line: imperious, melancholy, piercing. The horses
rear on their slender legs, and some of them neigh in answer. Sober-faced, the
young riders stroke the horses' necks and soothe them, whispering, "Quiet, quiet,
there my beauty, my hope . . ." They begin to form in rank along the starting line.
The crowds along the racecourse are like a field of grass and flowers in the wind.
The Festival of Summer has begun.

Do you believe? Do you accept the festival the city, the joy? No? Then let me   7
describe one more thing.

In a basement under one of the beautiful public buildings of Omelas, or perhaps   8
in the cellar of one of its spacious private homes, there is a room. It has one locked
door, and no window. A little light seeps in dustily between cracks in the boards,
secondhand from a cobwebbed window somewhere across the cellar. In one corner
of the little room a couple of mops, with stiff, clotted, foul-smelling heads, stand
near a rusty bucket. The floor is dirt, a little damp to the touch, as cellar dirt usually is. The room is about three paces long and two wide: a mere broom closet or
disused tool room. In the room a child is sitting. It could be a boy or a girl. It looks
about six, but actually is nearly ten. It is feeble-minded. Perhaps it was born defec-
tive, or perhaps it has become imbecile through fear, malnutrition, and neglect. It
picks its nose and occasionally fumbles vaguely with its toes or genitals, as it sits
hunched in the corner farthest from the bucket and the two mops. It is afraid of
the mops. It finds them horrible. It shuts its eyes, but it knows the mops are still
standing there; and the door is locked; and nobody will come. The door is always
locked; and nobody ever comes, except that sometimes—the child has no understanding of time or interval—sometimes the door rattles terribly and opens, and a
person, or several people, are there. One of them may come in and kick the child to
make it stand up. The others never come close, but peer in at it with frightened,
disgusted eyes. The food bowl and the water jug are hastily filled, the door is
locked, the eyes disappear. The people at the door never say anything, but the

child, who has not always lived in the tool room, and can remember sunlight and its mother's voice, sometimes speaks. "I will be good," it says. "Please let me out. I will be good!" They never answer. The child used to scream for help at night, and cry a good deal, but now it only makes a kind of whining, "eh-haa, eh-haa," and it speaks less and less often. It is so thin there are no calves to its legs; its belly protrudes; it lives on a half-bowl of cornmeal and grease a day. It is naked. Its buttocks and thighs are a mass of festered sores, as it sits in its own excrement continually.

They all know it is there, all the people of Omelas. Some of them have come to 9 see it, others are content merely to know it is there. They all know that it has to be there. Some of them understand why, and some do not, but they all understand that their happiness, the beauty of their city, the tenderness of their friendships, the health of their children, the wisdom of their scholars, the skill of their makers, even the abundance of their harvest and the kindly weathers of their skies, depend wholly on this child's abominable misery.

The citizens of Omelas haven't read p. 543, about confusing cause with coincidence.

This is usually explained to children when they are between eight and twelve, 10 whenever they seem capable of understanding; and most of those who come to see the child are young people, though often enough an adult comes, or comes back, to see the child. No matter how well the matter has been explained to them, these young spectators are always shocked and sickened at the sight. They feel disgust, which they had thought themselves superior to. They feel anger, outrage, impotence, despite all the explanations. They would like to do something for the child. But there is nothing they can do. If the child were brought up into the sunlight out of that vile place, if it were cleaned and fed and comforted, that would be a good thing, indeed; but if it were done, in that day and hour all the prosperity and beauty and delight of Omelas would wither and be destroyed. Those are the terms. To exchange all the goodness and grace of every life in Omelas for that single, small improvement: to throw away the happiness of thousands for the chance of the happiness of one: that would be to let guilt within the walls indeed.

The terms are strict and absolute; there may not even be a kind word spoken to 11 the child.

Often the young people go home in tears, or in a tearless rage, when they have 12 seen the child and faced this terrible paradox. They may brood over it for weeks or years. But as time goes on they begin to realize that even if the child could be released, it would not get much good of its freedom: a little vague pleasure of warmth and food, no doubt, but little more. It is too degraded and imbecile to know any real joy. It has been afraid too long ever to be free of fear. Its habits are too uncouth for it to respond to humane treatment. Indeed, after so long it would probably be wretched without walls about it to protect it, and darkness for its eyes, and its own excrement to sit in. Their tears at the bitter injustice dry when they begin to perceive the terrible justice of reality, and to accept it. Yet it is their tears and anger, the trying of their generosity and the acceptance of their helplessness, which are perhaps the true source of the splendor of their lives. Theirs is no vapid, irresponsible happiness. They know that they, like the child, are not free. They know compassion. It is the existence of the child, and their knowledge of its existence, that makes possible the nobility of their architecture, the poignancy of their music, the profundity of their science. It is because of the child that they are so gentle with children. They know that if the wretched one were not there snivelling in the dark, the other one, the flute-player, could make: no joyful music as the young riders line up in their beauty for the race in the sunlight of the first morning of summer.

Now do you believe in them? Are they not more credible? But there is one more    13
thing to tell, and this is quite incredible.

At times one of the adolescent girls or boys who go to see the child does not go    14
home to weep or rage, does not, in fact, go home at all. Sometimes also a man or woman much older falls silent for a day or two, and then leaves home. These people go out into the street, and walk down the street alone. They keep walking, and walk straight out of the city of Omelas, through the beautiful gates. They keep walking across the farmlands of Omelas. Each one goes alone, youth or girl, man or woman. Night falls; the traveler must pass down village streets, between the houses with yellow-lit windows, and on out into the darkness of the fields. Each alone, they go west or north, towards the mountains. They go on. They leave Omelas, they walk ahead into the darkness, and they do not come back. The place they go towards is a place even less imaginable to most of us than the city of happiness. I cannot describe it at all. It is possible that it does not exist. But they seem to know where they are going, the ones who walk away from Omelas. ◆

## FOR CLOSE READING

1. Omelas is Ursula K. Le Guin's conception of an ideal town or city—except, of course, for its miserable secret inhabitant. What are some of the more alluring characteristics of the place? Why do a few citizens leave permanently despite these attractions?

2. Le Guin is reluctant to allow the use of drugs in her "city of happiness" (14). Why does she relent and admit *drooz* after all (3)? Should she have? Why or why not?

3. Le Guin draws the line at "manned temples" (3). Why might she accept "religion" in her utopia but "clergy, no" (3). Is this an unfortunate oversight on her part or a wise idea? What about the omission of soldiers (3)? Explain.

4. Somewhat reluctantly, Le Guin allows orgies in Omelas. What civic requirement does she establish for the "offspring" of these rituals (3)?

5. Le Guin seems eager to establish that the people of Omelas are not primitive, "simple folk" (3). Why is it important for the moral of her story that the inhabitants be fully aware of the "terms" on which their prosperity and happiness are based (10)?

6. Why must *guilt* never come "within the walls" of Omelas (10)? What havoc would it wreak?

7. The rare "ones" (14) who leave Omelas, says Le Guin, head invariably to the mountains. Why do they likely go there rather than to some other town or city?

## Strategies and Structures

1. Le Guin frequently asks the reader, in effect, to participate in writing her story. Point out several examples in the text. Why might she adopt this strategy, and how well does it work?

2. The existence of the feeble-minded child in the filthy basement is a condition of the happiness and prosperity of the citizens of Omelas? Is it a *cause* of those desirable effects? Explain.

3. Le Guin never says in so many words what causes a few of the inhabitants of Omelas to leave and never return? Should she have spelled out those causes? Why or why not?

4. *Other Methods.* Le Guin DESCRIBES Omelas and its people in rich detail. Which particulars do you find most effective for the purpose of both establishing a utopia and undercutting it?

5. What is the purpose of Le Guin's COMPARISON of the child in the storage closet and the child who plays the flute?

6. Le Guin never says by whom (or what) the strict terms of Omelas's prosperity were set. Should this be part of the story—or not? Explain.

## Thinking about Language

1. *Drooz*, the name of the drug that Le Guin admits into the precincts of her utopia, sounds perhaps like *snooze* (3). What else does it suggest?

2. Why does Le Guin refer to the damaged child in the store room as "It" (8)?

3. "They feel anger, outrage, impotence, despite all the explanations" (10), says Le Guin. What is the effect in this sentence of linking "anger" and "outrage" with "impotence"?

4. The youth of Omelas, Le Guin says, face a "terrible paradox" (12)? Is this an accurate description of their dilemma? Why or why not?

5. Why does Le Guin refer to the town's guilty secret as "credible" but to the departure of a few citizens as "quite incredible" (13)?

## FOR WRITING

1. In a paragraph or two explain the causes and effects of the ethical dilemma that Le Guin is dramatizing in the story of Omelas and its people.

2. Of the few who leave Omelas, Le Guin cannot describe where they go. "It is less imaginable to most of us than the city of happiness" (14), she says. Try to imagine such a place nonetheless—"in the mountains" or elsewhere—and write a 400–500 word description of it and how the people live there.

3. Write a RHETORICAL ANALYSIS of "The Ones Who Walk Away from Omelas." Carefully analyze the ethical paradox posed by Le Guin's fable and determine whether it accurately represents "the terrible justice of reality" or is a false dilemma (12). Support your reading with evidence drawn from the text and from your own sense of ethics.

4. William James, the American philosopher whose work inspired Le Guin's story, believed that any decent person would walk away from "happiness" that proved to be founded on the condition that another person must suffer for it. Read his essay, "The Moral Philosopher and the Moral Life"—first published in the *International Journal of Ethics* in 1891 and widely available on the internet—and write a REPORT explaining the "probable causes" of such ethical behavior as James understood them.

5. The idea of the scapegoat is common in philosophy and literature, including the Bible. Do some research on the scapegoat's role, both socially and psychologically; and write a TEXTUAL ANALYSIS in approximately 500 words of the scapegoat figure in a story or other text of your choosing. Shirley Jackson's "The Lottery" would be a good example. So also, in a twisted way perhaps, is Flannery O'Connor's "A Good Man Is Hard to Find" (p. 517).

....................................................................•

You'll find quizzes on the readings at wwnorton.com/write/back-to-the-lake.

# CHAPTER 14

# Argument

Come now, and let us reason together . . .     —ISAIAH 1:18

Well, do you want to have just one argument, or were you thinking of taking a course?

—*Monty Python's Flying Circus*

For the sake of argument, let's assume that you are a parent, and you want your children to grow up in a safe and healthy environment. Consequently, you install a swimming pool in the backyard so they can learn to swim and get lots of good exercise.

No sooner has the concrete dried on your new pool when your next-door neighbor comes over and says, "Nice pool."

"Yeah," you reply, "we want our children to be healthy and strong—swimming is great exercise. Also, we want them to be safe; most of the earth's covered in water, you know, and they should learn how to swim."

"Right," says your neighbor. "But a pool like that's not a good idea for little kids. In fact, it's a safety hazard. Don't you know that far more children drown each year than die from gunshot wounds? Your kids would be much safer if you tore out that pool and bought a gun."

You disagree with your neighbor's belief that guns are safer than backyard swimming pools. Now you and your neighbor can have an argument—the kind that might degenerate into a shouting match—or you can rationally question your neighbor's claim and calmly state your own position on the matter. This second, more rational sort of argument is the subject of this chapter.

## Making and Supporting a Claim

When you construct an argument, you take a position on an issue and support that position with evidence. Suppose you believe that swimming pools are safe so long as they are properly fenced. This is your *claim*, and you can cite facts and figures, examples, expert testimony, or personal experience to support it.

In this chapter, we are going to examine how to make a claim and support it with evidence and logical reasoning. There are times, however, when logic isn't enough, so you will also learn how to appeal to your readers' emotions and how to establish your own credibility as a reliable person who deserves to be heard on ethical grounds. We'll also review the critical points to watch for as you read over and revise your essay, as well as common errors to avoid when you edit.

## Why Do We Argue?

When we argue, we express our opinions and ideas in a way that gets others to take them seriously. Unlike statements of fact, opinions are not necessarily correct or incorrect. The ultimate purpose of a good argument is not to convince others that your claim is absolutely right or wrong. It is to demonstrate that it is plausible—

worth listening to, and maybe even acting upon. Many arguments, in fact, ask the reader to *explore* an issue, not just accept or reject a particular claim. Exploratory arguments are intended to open up discussion, to help us gain new knowledge, and even to lead to some kind of consensus.

Rodolfo F. Acuña constructs this kind of argument in "We Owe History," p. 667.

## Composing an Argument

Writing that *argues* a claim and asks readers to agree with it is sometimes distinguished from writing that seeks to *persuade* readers to take action. In this chapter, however, we will use the terms *argue* and *persuade* more or less interchangeably, because there's not much point in arguing that a claim is correct if you can't also persuade the reader that it's worth acting on.

Any claim worth making has more than one side, however; that is, rational people can disagree about it. We can all agree that backyard swimming pools can be dangerous under certain circumstances. We might reasonably disagree, however, on what those circumstances are and what to do about them.

When you make a claim, it should be arguable in this sense of being debatable. Some claims cannot reasonably be argued. For instance:

• *Matters of taste*: I hate broccoli.

• *Matters of faith*: And on the third day He arose.

• *Matters of fact*: In 1996, 742 children under age 10 drowned in the United States.

Matters of fact can be contested, of course. You might, for instance, know of a case of drowning that went unreported, and so you would point out that the figure ought to be 743 instead of 742. But a claim like this does not leave much room for debate. It can be established simply by checking the facts. An argument can collapse if its facts are wrong, but a good argument does not just state the facts. It argues something significant *about* the facts.

So when you compose a written argument, make sure your claim is arguable, or open to opinion—and that it's one you actually have a stake in. If you don't really care much about your topic, your reader probably won't either.

### Thinking about Purpose and Audience

When you compose an argument, your purpose is to persuade other people to hear you out, to listen thoughtfully to what you have to say—even if they don't completely accept your views. Whatever your claim, your argument is more likely to appeal to your audience if it is tailored to their particular needs and interests.

# USING ARGUMENT IN A REPORT

In this panel from her graphic narrative "The Influencing Machines" (p. 728), media writer Brooke Gladstone (in the glasses) is clearly presenting different sides in a debate:

Gladstone is not taking a position here, as she would if she were mostly constructing an argument. Instead, she is using the debate form (and other strategies of argument) to present her research in a **REPORT** about how media and the human mind evolved together.

For example, your next-door neighbor might be more inclined to accept a swimming pool in your backyard if, in addition to addressing the safety issue, you also argued that a nice pool would increase property values in the neighborhood. On the other hand, if you need to persuade the city planning department to issue you a permit so that you can build a pool, you'd be better off telling them that, because there is no public pool within a reasonable distance from your house, children in your neighborhood must now travel too far just to enjoy a swim during the summer.

So as you compose an argument, think about what your readers' views on the particular issue are likely to be. Of all the evidence you might present in support of your case, what kind would your intended readers most likely find reasonable and, thus, convincing?

## Generating Ideas: Finding Effective Evidence

You can start generating ideas for an argument by using the same techniques, like LISTING and BRAINSTORMING, that you use with other kinds of writing.

The most important question to ask as you think about your argument is *why*: Why should your audience accept your claim? What evidence—facts, figures, examples, and so on—can you provide to convince your readers that your claim is true? Let's look at some of the most effective types of evidence.

Suppose you're writing about the cost of housing, and you want to argue that, for most people, it makes better economic sense in the long run to buy rather than rent. To support a claim like this effectively, you can use *facts, statistics, examples, expert testimony,* and *personal experience.*

**Facts.** Because facts can be verified, they make good evidence for persuading readers to accept your point of view. In a position paper arguing that buying beats renting, you might, for example, cite facts about the current housing market. Thus, you could point out that rents are up in most parts of the country, but that interest rates for borrowing money to purchase an apartment or house are at historic lows.

**Statistics.** A particularly useful form of evidence when you want to show a tendency or trend is statistics. This type of evidence is also verifiable and, thus, convincing to many readers. To support your claim about the financial advantages of homeownership, you could cite statistics about the economic net worth of homeowners as opposed to renters in the U.S. population as a whole. According to the Center for Responsible Lending, the median net worth of U. S. homeowners in 2013, for example, was $195,400; for renters, it was $5,400.

**Examples.** Good examples make an argument more concrete and specific—and thus more likely to be understood and accepted by your audience. A person who pays $800 per month in rent for fifteen years, you could note, would be out a total of $144,000 at the end of that period. By contrast, that same person, paying roughly the same amount on a fifteen-year mortgage loan, could own a $105,000 dwelling free and clear (assuming a loan rate of 4.5 percent).

*Expert testimony.* One of the most effective kinds of evidence is the direct testimony of experts in the field you are writing about. To make a serious case for the value of homeownership, you might quote a statement like this from a recent report compiled by Harvard's Joint Center for Housing Studies:

> Even after the tremendous decline in housing prices and the rising wave of foreclosures that began in 2007, homeownership continues to be a significant source of household wealth, and remains particularly important for lower-income and minority households.
>
> —CHRISTOPHER E. HERBERT, DANIEL T. MCCUE, AND ROCIO SANCHEZ-MOYANO,
> *Is Homeownership Still an Effective Means of Building Wealth*
> *for Low-income and Minority Households? (Was It Ever?)*

*Personal experience.* Often you can effectively cite personal experience to support an argument, as with the following anecdote about the perils of renting:

> Back in my hometown, my family has always been renters; but last Monday the landlord notified my parents that the rent on their two-bedroom apartment would go up fifteen percent next year. For the same amount in monthly payments, they can buy a house across street with an extra bedroom where I can live while saving up for a down payment on a place of my own. Enforced saving is one of the biggest benefits of home ownership. I haven't told them about this plan yet . . .

Many readers find personal testimony like this to be particularly moving, but be sure that any personal experience you cite as evidence is actually pertinent to the claim you're making.

Sojourner Truth uses personal testimony to support her argument, p. 649.

No matter what type of evidence you present—whether facts and figures, examples, expert testimony, or personal experience—it must be pertinent to your argument and should be selected with an eye to convincing your audience that your claim is plausible and worth taking seriously.

## Organizing and Drafting an Argument

Once you have a claim and evidence to support it, you're ready to start organizing and drafting your argument. You'll need to state your claim; appeal to your readers' needs and interests; and present yourself as trustworthy and reliable. You'll also need to anticipate and respond to likely objections. Finally, you'll want to think about which other methods of development, such as NARRATION and DEFINITION, might be useful in your argument. The templates on p. 611 can help you get started.

## ORGANIZING AN ARGUMENT

Claim and support. Any well-constructed argument is organized around these two basic elements. Let's consider an argument by an economist who teaches at the University of Chicago. In an editorial in the *Chicago Sun-Times* entitled "Pools More Dangerous Than Guns," Steven D. Levitt writes that "when it comes to children," a swimming pool in the backyard is more deadly than a gun in the house. This is Levitt's *claim*.

Levitt states this claim at the beginning of his argument, then gives evidence to support it in the next seven paragraphs of his essay. Most of his evidence is statistical: 742 drownings in one year, approximately 550 of those in residential pools; 6 million pools in the United States; 175 deaths as a result of guns; 200 million guns; one death per one million guns.

Levitt's evidence shows that approximately one child dies for every 11,000 pools in the United States, whereas one child dies for every one million guns. This is roughly a ratio of one hundred to one. Levitt concludes by connecting the dots for his readers when he says, "Thus, on average, the swimming pool is about 100 times more likely to kill a child than the gun is."

Levitt's argument follows a straightforward organization—claim, evidence, conclusion—that is effective for any argument:

1. State your claim clearly in your introduction.

2. In the main body of your argument, present evidence in support of your claim.

3. Develop the body of your argument until you have offered good reasons and sufficient evidence to support your claim.

4. In the conclusion, restate your claim and sum up how the evidence supports it.

## STATING YOUR CLAIM

State your claim clearly and directly at the beginning of your argument—and take care not to claim more than you can possibly prove. As an arguable claim, "swimming pools are more dangerous than guns" is too broad. More dangerous for whom, we might ask? Under what circumstances?

We need to narrow this claim if we want to write a manageable argument. We would do better to restate our claim as follows: "For young children who can't swim, swimming pools are more dangerous than guns." We have narrowed our claim to apply to a particular group, young children who do not yet know how to swim. Our claim could be still more restricted, however. In addition to narrowing it to a particular group, we could limit it to a particular kind of hazard. Thus we might write, "For young children who can't swim, *unprotected* swimming pools are more dangerous than guns." Because it is narrower, this is a more supportable claim than the one we started with.

## USING LOGICAL REASONING: INDUCTION AND DEDUCTION

When Steven Levitt writes "Thus, on average, the swimming pool is about 100 times more likely to kill a child than the gun is," he is using logical reasoning. For certain purposes—such as convincing a toddler to stay clear of an unguarded pool—logic is not very effective. In many writing situations, however, logical reasoning is indispensable for persuading others that your ideas and opinions are valid.

There are two basic kinds of logical reasoning, *induction* and *deduction*.

Thomas Jefferson uses both kinds to argue for revolution, p. 635.

Induction is reasoning from particular evidence to a general conclusion. You reason inductively when you observe the cost of a gallon of gas at half-a-dozen service stations and conclude that the price of gas is uniformly high. Levitt uses induction in his argument about guns and swimming pools. He looks at the number of children who drowned in residential swimming pools in a particular year—550—and the number of children who died from gunshot wounds in the same year—175. Reasoning inductively from these particular cases, Levitt reaches his conclusion that pools are more dangerous than guns to young children.

Inductive reasoning is based on probability—it draws a conclusion from a limited number of specific cases. When you argue inductively, you are not claiming that a conclusion is certain but that it is likely. Even relatively few cases can provide you with the basis of a good inductive argument—if they are truly representative of a larger group. Exit polls of a few hundred people, for example, can often predict the outcome of an election involving thousands of voters. If it's truly representative, even a small sampling is sometimes enough. You would need only one or two cases of cholera on a high school swimming team, for instance, to infer that the pool in the gym is probably contaminated and that the whole school is in danger. Unless you take into account every possible individual case, though, inductive reasoning is never 100 percent certain: it usually requires an "inductive leap" at the end, as when you move from the individual cases of cholera on the team to the general inference that the school as a whole is threatened.

By contrast with induction, deduction moves from general principles to a particular conclusion. You reason deductively when your car stops running and—knowing that cars in general need fuel to run on and recalling that you started with half a tank and have been driving all day—you conclude that you are out of gas.

# TEMPLATES FOR DRAFTING

When you begin to draft an argument, you need to identify your subject and state the basic claim you plan to make about that subject—moves fundamental to any argument. See how Michelle Obama makes these moves in a speech at a high school graduation in Kansas:

> I think it's fitting that we're celebrating this historic Supreme Court case tonight, not just because *Brown* started right here in Topeka or because *Brown's* sixtieth anniversary is tomorrow, but because I believe that all of you—our soon-to-be-graduates—you all are the living, breathing legacy of this case. —MICHELLE OBAMA,
> "Remarks at Topeka School District Senior Recognition Day"

Obama identifies the subject of her argument ("this historic Supreme Court case"), and states her basic claim about that subject ("you all are the living, breathing legacy of this case"). Here's another example from this chapter:

> But evidence from psychology, cognitive science, and neuroscience suggests what when students multitask while doing school work, their learning is far spottier and shallower than if the work had their full attention. —ANNIE MURPHY PAUL, "You'll Never Learn!"

The following templates can help you make some of these basic moves in your own writing. But don't take these as formulas where you just fill in the blanks. There are no shortcuts to good writing, but these templates can serve as starting points.

▶ In this argument about X, the main point I want to make is _____.

▶ Others may say _____, but I would argue that _____.

▶ My contention about X is supported by the fact that _____.

▶ Additional facts that support this view of X are _____, _____, and _____.

▶ My own experience with X shows that _____.

▶ My view of X is supported by _____, who says that X is _____.

▶ What you should do about X is _____.

Deductive arguments can be stated as SYLLOGISMS, which have a major premise, a minor premise, and a conclusion. For example:

*Major premise:* All unguarded swimming pools are dangerous.

*Minor premise:* This pool is unguarded.

*Conclusion:* This pool is dangerous.

This is a valid syllogism—the conclusion follows logically from the premises.

The great advantage of deduction over induction is that it deals with logical certainty rather than mere probability. As long as the premises you begin with are true and the syllogism is properly constructed, the conclusion must be true. You can run into trouble, however, when one or more of the premises are false, or when the syllogism isn't constructed properly.

In a properly constructed syllogism, the conclusion links the first part of the minor premise ("this pool") to the second part of the major premise ("dangerous"). One of the most common mistakes that people make in constructing syllogisms is simply repeating, in the minor premise, the trait named at the end of the major premise, as in the following example:

AN INVALID SYLLOGISM

*Major premise:* All planets are round.

*Minor premise:* My head is round.

*Conclusion:* My head is a planet.

Being round is a characteristic that "planets" and "my head" share, but many other things are round, too. A diagram can help us see why this syllogism doesn't work:

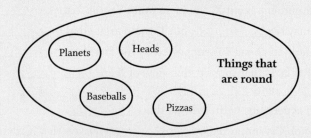

As this diagram illustrates, just being round doesn't mean that planets and heads have much else in common; in fact, they belong to entirely separate categories within the larger one of things that are round.

Advertisers use this kind of faulty reasoning all the time to try to convince you that you must buy their products if you want to be a cool person. Such reasoning is faulty because even if you accept the premise that, for example, all people who buy motorcycles are cool, there are lots of cool people who don't buy motorcycles—as indicated by the following diagram:

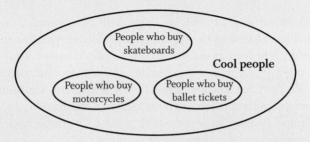

### PROPERLY CONSTRUCTED SYLLOGISMS

*Major premise:* All planets are round.

*Minor premise:* Earth is a planet.

*Conclusion:* Earth is round.

*Major premise:* All people who buy motorcycles are cool.

*Minor premise:* Susan has bought a motorcycle.

*Conclusion:* Susan is cool.

Not so sure about this second example? Both of these syllogisms are valid—that is, the conclusion follows logically from the premises. A syllogism can be logically valid, however, and the conclusion may still be false—if one or more of the premises are false. (Not everyone would agree, for example, with the premise that all motorcycle owners are cool.) Study the following obvious example of a properly constructed syllogism with a false premise.

### A PROPERLY CONSTRUCTED SYLLOGISM WITH A FALSE PREMISE

*Major premise:* All spiders have six legs.

*Minor premise:* The black widow is a spider.

*Conclusion:* The black widow has six legs.

The conclusion that black widows have six legs is logical, given the premises of this argument. However, since the major premise of the argument is wrong—spiders actually have eight legs—the conclusion of the argument is also wrong.

When you use deduction in your writing, your reader is less likely to question your reasoning if your argument follows the logic of a properly constructed syllogism or other model argument, such as one constructed by using the Toulmin method (see next page). Be prepared, however, to defend your premises if they are not as self-evident as "spiders have eight legs" or "all humans are mortal." If you

## THE TOULMIN METHOD

In a formal deductive argument, we begin with two general principles and draw a conclusion based on the logical relationship between them. In practical arguments, however, as the British philosopher Stephen Toulmin recognized, we often begin with a conclusion and look around for evidence to support it. Recognizing this less formal kind of deduction, Toulmin devised a system of argument that combines both logic and observation.

In Toulmin's system, an argument is made up of three basic parts: the *claim*, the *grounds*, and the *warrant*. For example:

*Claim:* Steven Spielberg is the greatest director in the history of film.

*Grounds:* His films have grossed more than those of any other director.

*Warrant:* The best measure of a film's quality is financial success.

The claim is the main point the argument is intended to prove. The grounds are the evidence on which that claim is based. And the warrant is the reason that the grounds justify the claim.

In a Toulmin argument, the grounds can be facts, statistics, examples, expert testimony, personal experience, or other kinds of evidence. It is an observable fact, for instance, that Spielberg has grossed approximately $8 billion at the box office—more than any other director in film history.

Though they constitute grounds for a claim, facts and other data are not alone sufficient, in Toulmin's view, to support that claim completely. It takes logic as well: a warrant is needed to explain how and why the grounds logically justify the claim. In this case, the warrant for accepting the claim about Spielberg as the world's greatest filmmaker is the assumption that films and directors are best judged by how much money they make.

Not everyone would agree with this assumption, of course. Most real-life arguments, in fact, are about the assumptions on which the argument is based. But breaking an argument down into Toulmin's three parts can be especially useful for spotting faulty or unstated assumptions—so you can strengthen them in your own arguments or question them in the arguments of others.

are arguing, for example, that intelligent design should be taught in science classes, you might structure your basic argument like this:

*Major premise:* All scientific theories should be taught in science classes.

*Minor premise:* Intelligent design is scientific theory.

*Conclusion:* Intelligent design should be taught in science classes.

This is a well-constructed deductive argument. As long as your readers accept the premises—particularly the minor premise about the scientific nature of intelligent design—they will probably accept your conclusion. If you believe, however, that some readers may disagree with the premises of your argument—and you still hope to convince them—you should provide strong evidence to support those premises. Or, if necessary, you should consider how you might rework your premises altogether.

## USING INDUCTION AND DEDUCTION IN VARIOUS ACADEMIC FIELDS

Because it draws upon observation and the analysis of particular data, induction is the method you are most likely to use when you construct an argument in the fields of engineering and the applied sciences. In the humanities and social sciences, induction is also particularly useful for analyzing specific written texts (the poems of Rita Dove, the letters of John Adams, a set of questionnaires) and for drawing general conclusions about them. You also use inductive reasoning when you cite personal experience as evidence, because you are arguing that something you observed or experienced personally has general significance for others.

Deductive reasoning, on the other hand, is particularly useful for constructing arguments in the fields of philosophy, ethics, theology, and the more theoretical sciences, such as mathematics and physics, where particular cases tend to be subject to universal principles (such as $E=MC^2$). For example, the argument that a large round object recently discovered in the night sky should be classified as a planet because it meets all the criteria that define planets in general would be a deductive argument.

## AVOIDING LOGICAL FALLACIES

Logical fallacies are errors in logical reasoning. Though they can seem plausible and even persuasive, they lead to wrong-headed conclusions. Here are some of the most common logical fallacies to watch out for when you write (and read).

**Post hoc, ergo propter hoc.** Latin for "after this, therefore because of this," this kind of faulty reasoning assumes that just because one event (such as rain) comes after another event (a rain dance), it occurs *because* of the first event. For example: "Soon after the country declared war, the divorce rate increased. War is harmful to marriages." Just because the country declared war before the divorce rate went up doesn't mean the declaration caused the increase.

*Non sequitur.* Latin for "does not follow," a non sequitur is a statement that has little or no logical connection to the preceding statement: "The early Egyptians were masters of architecture and geometry. Thus they created a vast network of trade and commerce throughout the ancient world." Since mastering architecture and geometry has little to do with trade, this second statement is a non sequitur.

*Begging the question.* An argument that takes for granted what it is supposed to prove: "Americans should be required to carry ID cards because Americans need to be prepared to prove their identity." This conclusion assumes that Americans need to prove their identities.

*Appeal to doubtful authority.* This is the fallacy of citing as expert testimony the opinions of people who do not necessarily have special knowledge of the issue: "According to Lady Gaga, the candidate who takes South Carolina will win the election." Lady Gaga isn't an expert on politics, so citing her opinion on political matters to support an argument is an appeal to doubtful authority.

Michael Lewis' little daughter employs an *ad hominem* attack on p. 653.

*Ad hominem.* This fallacy attacks the person making an argument instead of addressing the actual issue: "She's the head of the union, and she's crazy. Don't pay any attention to her views on the economy." Saying she's the head of a union and calling her crazy focuses on her as a person rather than on her views of the issue.

*Either/or reasoning.* This fallacy, sometimes called a "false dilemma," treats a complicated issue as if it had only two sides: "Either you believe that God created the universe according to His plan, which is the view of religion; or you believe that the universe evolved randomly, which is the view of science." This statement doesn't allow for beliefs outside of these two options.

*Hasty generalization.* This fallacy draws a conclusion based on far too little evidence: "In all four of the stories by Edgar Allan Poe that we read for English 201, the narrator is mentally ill. Poe himself must have been mad." There is not nearly enough evidence here to determine Poe's mental health.

*False analogy.* This fallacy is committed when an argument is based on a faulty comparison: "Children are like dogs. A happy dog is a disciplined dog, and a happy child is one who knows the rules and is taught to obey them." Dogs and children aren't enough alike to assume that what is good for one is good for the other.

## APPEALING TO YOUR READER'S EMOTIONS

Sound logical reasoning is hard to refute, but sometimes, in order to persuade readers to accept your claim, it will help to appeal to their emotions as well.

As an economist writing for a general audience, Steven Levitt knows that people often find numbers dry and unmoving. So after citing statistics to support his point that swimming pools are more dangerous than guns, he goes on to appeal to the emotions and feelings of his readers.

Levitt's purpose is not to promote guns; it is to alert parents to what he considers "an even greater threat to their children." Observing that a child can drown in only thirty seconds and that child drownings are "typically silent," Levitt warns parents not to let their guard down even for an instant, lest a pool (or even a bucket of water) "steal your child's life."

*Steal* is a carefully chosen word here. It implies evil intent—the pool lies in wait for the child, like a thief. We are well beyond logic and statistics now. Evil that is quick and silent demands an ever-watchful parent: "Simply stated, keeping your children safe around water is one of the single most important things a parent can do to protect a child."

Emotional? Of course. But this is emotionalism in a good cause, carefully applied to support a well-reasoned argument. And often, the best way to urge your readers to action is by tugging at their heartstrings. When you appeal to the reader's emotions, however, be careful to avoid sensationalism and alarmism—they can undermine your argument. So after sounding the alarm, Levitt calmly directs readers to the website of the U.S. Consumer Products Safety Commission, which "offers a publication detailing some simple steps for safeguarding pools."

For an unusual appeal to emotion, see "Deactivated," p. 746.

## ESTABLISHING YOUR OWN CREDIBILITY

When you construct an argument, you can demonstrate with irrefutable logic that what you have to say is valid and true. And you can appeal to the reader's emotions with genuine fervor. Your words may still fall on deaf ears, however, if your readers don't fully trust you. What makes Levitt's argument so credible in the end is that he himself has lost a child.

Levitt's first child, Andrew, did not drown. When the boy was just over a year old, he came down with meningitis and, within two days, died in the hospital. Levitt wrote his essay, in part, to channel a father's grief, which gives him an emotional and ethical authority that nothing else could. "As a father who has lost a son," Levitt writes, "I know first-hand the unbearable pain that comes with a child's death."

Levitt's loss is different in one crucial regard from that of the parent whose child dies in an unguarded swimming pool. "Amidst my grief," he says, "I am able to take some small solace in the fact that everything possible was done to fight the disease that took my son's life." Having said this, the grieving father closes with a final appeal to the reader, whom he addresses directly in the second person: "If my son had died in a backyard pool due to my own negligence, I would not even have that to cling to. . . . Parents who have lost children would do anything to get their babies back. . . . Safeguard your pool so you don't become one of us." You don't need to have children or a swimming pool to recognize the power of such an argument. Nor do you need such a close, personal tie to your subject in order to establish your own credibility.

There are many less dramatic ways to establish your credibility when you construct an argument. Readers are more likely to trust you, for example, if they feel you are presenting the issues objectively. So acknowledge opposing points of view, and treat them fairly and accurately. Then look for common ground where you and your reader can come together not just logically but psychologically. (For tips on how to do this, see the discussion of Rogerian logic, below.)

If you have experience or special expertise in your subject, let your readers know. For instance, if you're arguing that American ballet companies require their dancers to be too thin and you danced with a professional ballet company for three years, tell your readers that. Also, pay close attention to the tone of your argument. Whether you come across as calm and reasonable or full of righteous anger, your tone will say much about your own values and motives for writing—and about you as a person. Nothing does more to establish your credibility with your readers than to persuade them that they are listening to the words of a moral and ethical person who shares their values and understands their concerns.

For an ethical defense of ethically suspect behavior, see p. 694.

## USING ROGERIAN ARGUMENT

The psychologist Carl Rogers recognized that people are much more likely to listen to someone they feel is listening to them. If you want to persuade others to accept your views, Rogers reasoned, it is better to treat them as colleagues rather than adversaries. Instead of an "I'm right and you're wrong" approach, therefore, Rogers recommended using "win-win" strategies of argument that invite collaboration and consensus rather than confrontation and conflict. In other words, instead of having an argument, the Rogerian approach says, with Isaiah, "Come now, and let us reason together."

To use Rogerian methods of argument in your own writing, you need to show your audience that you are well aware that the issue at hand can be viewed in different lights and that you have thoughtfully considered viewpoints other than your own. To do this, summarize opposing viewpoints carefully and accurately, and acknowledge their merit. Then introduce your views and look for common ground between them and the views of others. Explain how your views address these common concerns and what additional advantages they have, and give evidence in support of your point of view.

For example, suppose that you are in favor of greater gun-control legislation. Instead of lashing out at all gun owners, however, you decide to try a more conciliatory, Rogerian approach. You might begin by acknowledging that the U.S. Constitution guarantees certain rights to individuals, in particular the right to self-defense and to protect personal property. You might also acknowledge that many people, including hunters and target shooters, look on certain types of guns as gear or sporting goods. Others view them as collectibles and are interested in their history and manufacture.

Once you have shown your genuine concern and respect for the rights and enthusiasms of gun owners, you could look for ways in which gun-control legislation may actually serve their interests. For example, you might point out that strict licensing and training in the proper handling of firearms can help reduce injury and death among those who use guns for sport. In the event of theft, you might note, enforced registration of guns would also help collectors and other owners of valuable firearms to retrieve their stolen property. You might even concede that stricter gun-control legislation probably is not necessary in the case of people who already abide by existing gun-control laws, own guns legally, and use them responsibly. Having established as much common ground as you can among the parties in the gun-control debate, you are now ready to introduce and explain your position.

You favor stricter gun controls, even to the point of banishing firearms altogether. Why? You believe that guns are inherently dangerous and that they can fall into the hands of people who do not abide by the rules. Also, they can be *accidentally* misused. Wouldn't society as a whole be better off, you wonder, if guns were all but impossible to obtain—even if that meant curtailing the rights of some individuals? You realize that not everyone will agree with this position; but having made clear that you understand and sympathize with the views of the other side, you can reasonably expect that those who might otherwise dismiss your claims out of hand will be more inclined to listen to you. And you can even hope that readers who are not committed to either point of view will be more likely to adopt yours.

## ANTICIPATING OTHER ARGUMENTS

As you construct an argument, it's important to consider viewpoints other than your own, including objections that others might raise to your argument. Anticipating other arguments, in fact, is yet another way to establish your credibility and win the reader's confidence. Readers are more likely to see you as trustworthy if, instead of ignoring an opposing argument, you state it fairly and accurately and then refute it—by showing that the reasoning is faulty or that the evidence is insufficient or that the argument fails to consider some key aspect of the subject.

For instance, suppose you think that private ownership of firearms is a deterrent to crime and you oppose stricter gun-control laws. Some of your readers, however, may believe that private ownership of guns actually *increases* crime, and they may be prepared to cite studies showing that there are more homicides in places where there are more guns.

Anticipating this argument, you might refute it by saying, "Proponents of stricter gun-control legislation are right when they cite studies showing that more homicides occur in places where more people have guns. However, such studies refer, by and large, to 'loose' firearms. The situation is different where guns are protected—kept under lock and key where a child or intruder can't get to them. Responsible gun ownership actually reduces crime." Proponents of stricter gun controls still may not be entirely convinced, but they are far more likely to listen to your argument because you readily admit that guns can be dangerous and you address, head-on, a major point of opposition to your views.

Even when you do not have a ready response to an opposing argument, you'll still want to acknowledge it in order to show that you've thought carefully about all aspects of the issue.

## USING OTHER METHODS

Each method of writing discussed in chapters 6–13 can be useful when you construct an argument. If you are arguing for (or against) stricter gun-control laws, for example, you will need to DEFINE the present rules and what you mean by "stricter" ones. You may also need to use CAUSE-AND-EFFECT analysis to explain what good (or harm) new laws would do. Or you may want to COMPARE AND CONTRAST the old laws with the new ones; or draw on PROCESS ANALYSIS to explain how the new laws will be enforced; or construct a NARRATIVE to show the new laws in action.

# EDITING FOR COMMON ERRORS IN ARGUMENTS

Certain errors in punctuation and usage are common in arguments. The following guidelines will help you check for such problems—and edit them as needed.

**Check your punctuation with such connecting words as *if, therefore, thus, consequently, however, nevertheless,* and *because***

When the connecting word comes at the beginning of a sentence and links it to an earlier statement, the connecting word should be followed by a comma:

▶ Therefore, the minimum legal drinking age should not be lowered to age 18.

▶ Consequently, stronger immigration laws will be unnecessary.

When the connecting word comes at the beginning of a sentence and is part of an introductory clause—a group of words that includes a subject and verb—the entire clause should be followed by a comma:

▶ Because guest workers will be legally registered, stronger immigration laws will be unnecessary.

▶ If acting legally is just as easy as acting illegally, most people will choose the legal course of action.

When the connecting word indicates a logical relationship between two independent clauses—such as cause and effect, sequence, comparison, or contrast—the word is usually preceded by a semicolon and followed by a comma:

▶ Many of the best surgeons have the highest rates of malpractice; thus, the three-strikes-and-you're-out rule for taking away a doctor's license may do more harm than good.

When the connecting word comes in the middle of an independent clause, it should be set off by commas:

▶ A physician who removes the wrong leg, however, deserves a much harsher penalty than one who forgets to remove a sponge.

## Check for common usage errors

*However, nevertheless*

Use *however* when you acknowledge a different argument but want to mini-mize its consequence:

▶ The surgeon may have been negligent; ~~nevertheless,~~ however, he should not lose his license because the patient lied about the dosage he was taking.

Use *nevertheless* when you acknowledge a different argument but wish to argue for a harsher consequence anyway:

▶ The surgeon may not have been negligent; ~~however,~~ nevertheless, he should lose his license because the patient died.

*Imply, infer*

Use *imply* when you mean "to state indirectly":

▶ The coach's speech ~~inferred~~ implied that he expected the team to lose the game.

Use *infer* when you mean "to draw a conclusion":

▶ From the coach's speech, the fans ~~implied~~ inferred that the team would lose the game.

Go to wwnorton.com/write/back-to-the-lake for quizzes on these common errors.

## Reading an Argument with a Critical Eye

Once you have a draft of your argument, ask someone to read it and tell you where your case seems particularly convincing and where it seems to break down. Then read the argument again critically yourself. Here are some questions to keep in mind when checking a written argument.

**PURPOSE AND AUDIENCE.** What is the basic purpose of the argument—To inform? To move the reader to action? Some other purpose? How well does the argument achieve its purpose? How might it be revised to do so better? Who is the intended audience? What will they already know about the topic, and will they need any additional background information? What are their views likely to be on the topic?

**THE CLAIM.** What is the claim? Is it stated clearly and directly in a THESIS statement? If not, should it be? Is it arguable—could reasonable people disagree about it? Is the claim limited enough to be covered well? If not, how could it be narrowed down further? Is it clear why this claim is significant, and why the reader should care about it?

**EVIDENCE.** What evidence is given to support the claim? Is it factually correct? If personal experience is cited as evidence, is it pertinent? Is the evidence sufficient to support the claim, or is additional evidence needed? What kind?

**LOGICAL REASONING.** How well do the parts of the essay hold together? What kind of reasoning connects the evidence with the claim—inductive? deductive? both? In general, how *convincing* is the argument? How could it be strengthened?

**EMOTIONAL APPEALS.** Does the argument appeal to readers' emotions? If so, to what end—to evoke readers' concerns? to move them to action? Is any emotional appeal sufficiently restrained? Is it convincing? If there's no emotional appeal, should there be?

**CREDIBILITY.** What kind of person does the author of this argument seem to be? Does he or she come across as an ethical person of good character who shares and respects readers' values? If not, what changes could convey that credibility? What special experience or knowledge, if any, does the author bring to this particular issue? In sum, does the author seem trustworthy?

**ANTICIPATING OTHER ARGUMENTS.** What other arguments might someone make about the topic? What objections might they raise to the claim? Are other arguments respectfully acknowledged and, where possible, refuted?

**OTHER METHODS.** What other methods of development does the argument use? For example, does it DEFINE the issues clearly? Does it analyze CAUSES AND EFFECTS? If other methods are not used, where might they be helpful?

**COMMON ERRORS.** Does the argument use connecting words like *therefore, consequently,* and *nevertheless*? If so, are they correctly punctuated? Connectors at the beginning of a sentence may or may not be followed by a comma, depending on how they relate to the rest of the sentence. Check to be sure the comma is in the right place; otherwise, the meaning of the sentence may be clouded.

## Student Example

Matthew Douglas wrote "The Evil Empire?" in 2008 as an undergraduate in the School of Humanities and Sciences at Ithaca College in upstate New York. This essay about shopping at Walmart was his winning entry in a contest sponsored by the college's Department of Writing.

In 2011, according to the company's website, Walmart Stores, Inc., had "more than 9029 retail units under 60 different banners in 15 countries." What kind of empire has the giant established? "The Evil Empire?" takes a critical look at the discount ethic as practiced by one of America's largest retailers—and at the culture it mirrors.

Douglas begins his argument with a brief NARRATIVE of the Walmart shopping experience

### The Evil Empire?

"Hi, welcome to Walmart," says the greeter. You smile back          1
politely in acknowledgment before you quickly enter the store. You have to shop. You have to find the best deals. You fill your cart with disposable razors, diapers for the baby, socks, batteries, dog biscuits, skim milk, chocolate candies, white bread, gum, mayonnaise, chunk cheese, your favorite magazine, and a few impulse buys with prices too good to pass up. It was just a quick visit today. You make your way to the register and the cashier rings up your items and tells you the total damage to your wallet. You smile to yourself knowing you saved a bundle of time and money. Walmart is your one stop shop. You leave the store with bags in hand, only to find a chanting mob outside the store: volunteers for the union. They yell out many of Walmart's faults: its discrimination toward women, its dismal health care benefits, and its barely livable wages. You wonder how much of this is true. You've heard these arguments before, but look at how

The key question to be addressed in Douglas' argument

much money Walmart saves you. Is it really as bad as the union says? Is Walmart some dark empire, or the chosen target for some of the many problems American consumerism has created? Has the company been singled out unfairly?

Within fifty years Walmart has grown from a few stores in          2
Arkansas to a multibillion-dollar corporation that spans the entire

United States and many countries around the globe. Sam Walton opened the first Wal-Mart in 1962 to save the customer money, which is the Walmart motto. Expanding rapidly nationally and internationally, Walmart consists of more than 6,200 facilities and 1.6 million employees worldwide. Walmart affects millions of lives on a daily basis: over 138 million global customers visit the store each week ("Walmart Facts"). With numbers like these it's obvious how influential Walmart is both nationally and internationally. Walmart saves its shoppers money with every shopping experience. But many critics dislike the methods Walmart uses to save its consumers money.

Gives history and background information about Walmart

3    While so many vilify Walmart for its sins, few look at the big picture: if Walmart were to disappear off the face of the earth, other companies like it would still pay minimum wage to save you and me money. What about Target or Kmart? Walmart is not an evil, all-consuming empire but a product of its times. American culture made stores like Walmart possible; it is the consumerist culture that epitomizes America. It is the *need*, the *demand* for more stuff, and our desire for material wealth that fills our closets, our drawers, and our garages. As consumers we want the new, the flashy, and we want it now for a discount price. While I have oversimplified American consumerism and made it sound like the only factor, which it is not, consumerism is definitely a large contributor to big retail chains. Walmart, along with other big business stores like it, fulfills the desire for stuff and saves the consumer millions. In fact, Walmart saves its customers about $16 billion a year, writes Harvard business professor Pankaj Ghemawat and business consultant Ken Mark. But in order to pass on these savings to the consumer, Walmart associates receive what many believe to be sub-par healthcare coverage and salaries. Critics also charge that Walmart destroys local businesses and communities. In addition to unfairly targeting Walmart, many overlook the company's openness to criticism and willingness to change.

THESIS statement

Introduces
an important
opposing
viewpoint

According to freelance writer Liza Featherstone, Walmart is   4
as bad as the unions proclaim the corporation to be. Featherstone
strongly criticizes Walmart in her 2005 article "Down and Out in
Discount America." Walmart's obsession with saving the customer
money, she argues, has a price. Its employees largely pay for that
price in the form of low wages. According to Featherstone, the
average Walmart worker makes just over $8 an hour (about
$15,000 a year). She cites Al Zack, former vice president for strategic
programs of United Food and Commercial Workers, who claims
Walmart "needs to create more poverty to grow." Featherstone
creates a comparison between Walmart and Henry Ford. Where Ford
paid his employees plenty so they could buy Ford cars, Walmart does
the opposite. Walmart's low wages help to keep poverty going,
Featherstone reasons, thus allowing Walmart to grow. The low wages
also keep them from being able to shop anywhere else but at
Walmart. She claims Walmart uses welfare to supplement its low
paycheck, citing that Walmart encourages its workers to apply for
federal assistance. So it is the taxpayers' dollars that help Walmart
associates get by (Featherstone). But, unfortunately, these are realities
in retail. And Walmart is not alone. It is the price that some must
pay so that American consumers can enjoy discount prices.
Minimum wage helps to make these discount prices possible.

Today, the average American Walmart employee makes close   5
to $11 an hour (around $21,000 a year). This may not seem like much,
but it is above the poverty line. Currently, Walmart's pay is four dollars
higher than the federal minimum wage. Even when Featherstone's
article was up to date in 2005, Walmart was still several dollars above

Cites Douglas's
personal
experience as
EVIDENCE

the federal minimum wage ("Walmart Facts"). <u>I have held a part-time
job at Price Chopper, a northeast grocery store chain, for five years,
and I have yet to make $9 an hour.</u> It is how the retail world works. To
keep prices low for the customer, companies pay minimum wage, cut
worker hours, and offer minimum healthcare. "The fact is," writes
Robert Reich, former secretary of labor for President Bill Clinton,
"today's economy offers us a Faustian bargain: it can give consumers
deals largely because it hammers workers."

Besides Walmart's low pay, people criticize the company's healthcare. The plan is said to be too expensive for the average Walmart employee to afford. Thus, many reason, few Walmart associates have insurance. However, this is not the case. Walmart reported that as of this year, 92.7 percent of its employees had health insurance, a two percent increase from last year. In fact, the national average of uninsured workers nationwide is significantly higher than the number of Walmart employees that lack coverage. The U.S. Census Bureau recently announced 17.7 percent of Americans do not have healthcare, versus the 7.3 percent of Walmart's workers who lack coverage. Walmart's insurance includes medical and dental benefits but not eye care. But what it is short of, the company is trying to make up for. This year Walmart partnered with 1-800-CONTACTS in an effort to "help drive down healthcare costs." The long-term agreement will bring contact lenses to Walmart customers at lower costs. The two companies estimate this partnership could save consumers $400 million in the next three years. And because many of Walmart's employees are also Walmart customers, they will also be able to partake in this benefit (employees can even use their Walmart discount, which will help to save them even more money). Walmart also offers and continues to expand its $4 prescription plan. "Our $4 prescription program is proof that Wal-Mart is committed to meeting America's healthcare challenges," says Dr. John Agwunobi, senior vice president and president for Walmart's professional services division ("Walmart Facts").

> 6
>
> Refutes the position of unspecified naysayers

Walmart is also believed to be the sole cause for running small family businesses into the ground. Freelance writer Floyd McKay reasons local downtowns become ghost towns when big-box retailers such as Walmart move in. He writes, "Wal-Mart is like a neutron bomb, sucking life out of small towns, leaving buildings without the essence of civic life." Critics like McKay state mom-and-pop stores cannot compete with Walmart's discount prices, forcing the small businesses to close for good.

> 7

However, business columnist Steve Maich counters that Walmart actually boosts local economy rather than destroying it.

> 8

Refutes
McKay's
argument

······ Maich cites Carol Foote's experience with Walmart as an example of how the company helped her town. In 2000 Foote helped to organize bringing a Walmart to her hometown, Miramichi, New Brunswick. Critics warned Foote and other Walmart supporters that it would ruin local businesses. However, Foote suspected Walmart would invigorate local businesses just as it had done throughout the rest of Canada. She turned out to be right. In 2002, Ryerson University completed a major study of Walmart's impact on small retailers. What they found was the opening of big-box retailers like Walmart was an economic boon for the whole area: attracting other retailers and driving up sales at nearby stores. The study concluded, "It is difficult to make the case that a Walmart store actually puts other retailers out of business." Two years later, a survey conducted by Canadian Imperial Bank of Commerce found that of the 1,800 small businesses that participated in its study, the vast majority claimed Walmart had little or no impact on them. "And while critics portray [Walmart] as the work of a ravenous invading force," writes Maich, "the truth is most communities reached out to Wal-Mart and embraced it." Communities such as Miramichi. Foote says Walmart has created dozens of jobs for her hometown and "brought new life to the town's small commercial district" (qtd. in Maich).

Conclusion
restates
Douglas's
thesis—with
variations

······ Like anything man-made, Walmart has its defects. I am not saying Walmart is blameless. I am saying Walmart is not the only corporation at fault. Furthermore, the company knows it has flaws and is responding to them. Some of their responses include $4 prescriptions and the company's partnership with 1-800-CONTACTS. Walmart is also committed to saving the environment. The company has helped to permanently conserve 395,000 acres of land for critical wildlife habitats. Walmart has also opened two experimental super-centers built out of recycled materials; vegetable and motor oils heat the stores. The two stores are dedicated to sustainability and will lead the way in finding methods to apply environmental practices to other Walmart facilities ("Walmart Facts"). Walmart is adapting and in ways that other companies are not. It is this openness to change

9

that proves Walmart is concerned about more things than making a quick buck. Many people often deem change too scary or too risky. Yet Walmart takes such risks and creates good reforms that benefit millions of lives each and every day. While Walmart is far from perfect, it is not the evil empire many critics have made it out to be.

> Gives Douglas' final answer to the question raised in his title

### Works Cited

Featherstone, Liza. "Down and Out in Discount America." *Nation*. Nation, 3 Jan. 2005. Web. 26 Mar. 2008.

Ghemawat, Pankaj, and Ken A. Mark. "The Price Is Right." *New York Times*. New York Times Company, 3 Aug. 2005. Web. 26 Mar. 2008.

Maich, Steve. "Why Walmart Is Good." *Maclean's*. Rogers Publishing, 25 Jul. 2005. Web. 20 Mar. 2008.

McKay, Floyd J. "Walmart Nation: The Race to the Bottom." *Seattle Times*. Seattle Times Company, 18 Feb. 2004. Web. 21 Mar. 2008.

Reich, Robert B. "Don't Blame Walmart." *New York Times*. New York Times Company, 28 Feb. 2005. Web. 13 Mar. 2008.

"Walmart Facts." *Walmart Corporate*. Walmart Stores, Inc., 2008. Web. 17 Mar. 2008.

## Analyzing a Student Argument

In "The Evil Empire?" Matthew Douglas draws upon rhetorical strategies and techniques that good writers use all the time when they construct arguments. The following questions, in addition to focusing on particular aspects of Douglas's text, will help you to identify those common strategies and techniques so you can adapt them to your own writing. These questions will also help to prepare you for the analytical questions—on content, structure, and language—that you'll find after all the other selections in this chapter, along with suggestions for writing on related topics.

## FOR CLOSE READING

1. If we look at "the big picture," says Matthew Douglas in answer to the question raised by his title, "Walmart is not an evil, all-consuming empire" (3). If the retail giant is not "evil" in Douglas's view, what *is* it? Do you agree? Why or why not?

2. "It is the price that some must pay so that American consumers can enjoy discount prices" (4), says Douglas. What "price" is he referring to here? Is that price acceptable in your opinion? Why or why not?

3. According to Douglas, what are some of the steps that Walmart is taking to correct its perceived "flaws" (9)? Are these changes substantial, or are they aimed at better public relations? Or both? Explain.

## Strategies and Structures

1. What is the purpose of the brief NARRATIVE, in Douglas's opening paragraph, about going to shop at Walmart and encountering a "chanting mob" upon leaving the store (1)? Why does Douglas tell this story in the second person (*you*) instead of the more common first person (*I*)? Is this an effective strategy? Why or why not?

2. Douglas first states the THESIS of his argument as follows: "Walmart is not an evil, all-consuming empire but a product of its times" (3). How and where does Douglas make adjustments to this thesis as his argument develops? Is this a legitimate strategy, or should an argument always conclude by rehearsing the exact CLAIM it started with? Explain.

3. Using freelance writers Liza Featherstone and Floyd McKay as naysayers, Douglas cites two main counterarguments to his claim about the benevolence of Walmart (4, 7). What are they? How and how well does he deal with each counter-claim? Point to specific EVIDENCE in his argument, and explain why you find it particularly convincing or otherwise.

4. "Like anything man-made, Walmart has its defects" (9), says Douglas. What assumptions does this statement make? Are they justified? Why or why not?

5. *Other Methods.* The main CAUSE of Walmart's retail practices, Douglas argues, is American "consumerism" (3). How does Douglas DEFINE this concept, and how successfully does he use that definition to explain and justify what he sees as the realities of the retail market?

## Thinking about Language

1. Where does the phrase "evil empire" come from, and how does Douglas use it to help make his case that the designation does not apply to Walmart?

2. Is "stuff" the right word to use in describing the desires and needs of American consumers, or should Douglas have chosen a more weighty term (3)? Explain.

3. The American consumer, says Douglas, citing an article by former secretary of labor Robert Reich, strikes a "Faustian bargain" by seeking low prices that are made possible by keeping the lid on labor and sales costs (5). Explain this **ALLUSION** to Faust, the scholar in German folklore who sold his soul to the devil in exchange for knowledge and other earthly benefits.

## FOR WRITING

1. Visit *Walmartstores.com*'s Press Room page and write a paragraph or two reporting "Walmart Facts" that support (or contradict) your general impression of the chain.

2. Write an argument supporting the claim that Walmart, Target, McDonald's, or some other large-scale retailer is (or is not) exploiting its employees and customers. Cite plenty of evidence for your claim, and document your sources scrupulously.

3. Write a **NARRATIVE** about a visit you made to Walmart, Michaels, Home Depot or some other store or business (such as a used-car dealer) that you found particularly revealing about the policies and culture of the place or of the type of business that it represents. Be sure to tell who you met or saw there and what they said or did. Your story doesn't have to have an old-fashioned moral, but it should still have a point to make about the experience.

4. "American culture made stores like Walmart possible," Douglas argues; "it is the consumerist culture that epitomizes America." Write a **POSITION PAPER** of 400–500 words on the issue of consumerism in America. How pervasive is it? Does consumerism really epitomize America? Are stores like Walmart uniquely American institutions?

You'll find quizzes on the readings at wwnorton.com/write/back-to-the-lake.

# Think Different

Most advertisements, like this one from Apple, are arguments. Their purpose is to persuade you, the reader (or viewer) to buy, rent, view, subscribe to, or otherwise consume whatever they're selling. The implied logic of this advertisement is something like the following (tech companies have a grammar of their own):

> *Major premise:* Einstein thought different
> *Minor premise:* Apple products make you think different
> *Conclusion:* Apple products make you think like Einstein

Is this a valid argument?

An argument can be invalid, and the premises can still be true, however. In this case, though, the minor premise is just a variation on the following (fill in the blank):

> Our product makes you _____ (more beautiful, healthier, more fashionable, smell better, think different).

Premises like this are unproven assumptions. Buy the premise, and you're on your way to buying the product. (The pin-up of Einstein is just window dressing.)

[ **FOR WRITING** ]··········································································

Construct an advertisement for a familiar product or service.
Include visuals like the Apple logo and the portrait of Einstein
and a written text that makes an argument for buying (or not
buying) the product or service on order. The written text can
be a caption of 50–60 words or a briefer slogan ("Think
relatively. Think Al's Used-Car Universe").

Think different.

# SUGGESTIONS FOR WRITING

1. Walmart, argues Matthew Douglas (p. 624), is often seen as "The Evil Empire." It would seem, however, that whenever Apple releases a new product, the company is hailed as what might be called "The Empire of Wonder." Read Douglas's essay, and write a **POSITION PAPER** arguing that Apple (or some other major company) deserves (or does not deserve) the general reputation it has in the media and elsewhere.

2. In "Acculturation Is Bad for Our Health" (p. 659), Juana Mora argues that immigrants in the United States, particularly Latinos, face a "triple threat of acculturation, lower-quality health care, and environmentally unhealthy living conditions" (7). Read and evaluate Mora's argument, noting the sources she cites at the end of her essay. Do some additional research of your own, and write a **REPORT** on the conditions, as you see them, that immigrants typically encounter when they first arrive in America (and later).

3. In "College Graduates Fare Well, Even through Recession" (p. 676), Catherine Rampell argues that "employers are specifically requiring four-year degrees for jobs that previously did not need them, since companies realize that in a relatively poor job market college graduates will be willing to take whatever they can find" (8). Is this an accurate assessment in your view? Using Rampell's report as a starting place, do some research on the issue, and write an **EVALUATION** of the job market for new graduates as it presently stands.

4. Writing about intellectual property, Lawrence Lessig argues that "free cultures are cultures that leave a great deal open for others to build upon; unfree, or permission, cultures leave much less. Ours was a free culture. It is becoming less so" (8). Read Lessig's essay (p. 708), and write an **ARGUMENT** of your own that supports (or questions) the proposition that access to intellectual property is becoming less free in American culture— and that creativity is suffering (or will suffer) as a result.

5. "While we think of knowledge as an individual possession," writes Clive Thompson (p. 724), "our command of facts is often extremely collaborative" (2). Read Thompson's essay and ponder what he means by this statement. Then, in a paper of approximately 500 words, take a **POSITION** on the question of whether knowledge is becoming more or less collaborative in the era of the internet. Be sure to give specific examples. *Wikipedia* would be one to consider, for instance.

# The Declaration of Independence

Thomas Jefferson (1743–1826) was born to a wealthy landowning family in colonial Virginia and studied mathematics and political philosophy at William and Mary College. He became a lawyer and was elected to the Virginia legislature in 1769, where he was a leading spokesman for the cause of American independence. During the Revolutionary War, he served as governor of Virginia; afterward, he became the nation's first secretary of state. He served as John Adams's vice president and was elected president himself in 1800. Jefferson was also one of the leading architects of his day—and an inventor, naturalist, archeologist, violinist, horticulturist, and patron of the arts.

Jefferson stipulated that his epitaph would mention only three of his many achievements: author of Virginia's Statute of Religious Freedom, founder of the University of Virginia, and author of the Declaration of Independence. In its form and intent, the Declaration of Independence is primarily an argument—a point-by-point justification for American independence. Lawyerly in tone, it is essentially a legal brief addressed to both the British throne and the court of world opinion. Drafted largely by Jefferson, the Declaration lists the colonists' grievances against George III and concludes that Americans are left with no recourse but full independence. The document's ratification by the Continental Congress on July 4, 1776, marked the birth of the United States.

W HEN IN THE COURSE OF HUMAN EVENTS, it becomes necessary for one people to dissolve the political bands which have connected them with another, and to assume among the powers of the earth, the separate and equal station to which the Laws of Nature and of Nature's God entitle them, a decent respect to the opinions of mankind requires that they should declare the causes which impel them to the separation.

We hold these truths to be self-evident, that all men are created equal, that they are endowed by their Creator with certain unalienable Rights, that among these are Life, Liberty and the pursuit of Happiness. That to secure these rights, Governments

MLA CITATION: Jefferson, Thomas. "The Declaration of Independence." 1776. *Back to the Lake*. Ed. Thomas Cooley. 3rd ed. New York: Norton, 2015. 635–38. Print.

are instituted among Men, deriving their just powers from the consent of the governed. That whenever any Form of Government becomes destructive of these ends, it is the Right of the People to alter or to abolish it, and to institute new Government, laying its foundation on such principles and organizing its powers in such form, as to them shall seem most likely to effect their Safety and Happiness. Prudence, indeed, will dictate that Governments long established should not be changed for light and transient causes; and accordingly all experience hath shewn, that mankind are more disposed to suffer, while evils are sufferable, than to right themselves by abolishing the forms to which they are accustomed. But when a long train of abuses and usurpations pursuing invariably the same Object evinces a design to reduce them under absolute Despotism, it is their right, it is their duty, to throw off such Government, and to provide new Guards for their future security. Such has been the patient sufferance of these Colonies; and such is now the necessity which constrains them to alter

**How to use inductive reasoning like this is discussed on p. 610.** their former Systems of Government. The history of the present King of Great Britain is a history of repeated injuries and usurpations, all having in direct object the establishment of absolute Tyranny over these States. To prove this, let Facts be submitted to a candid world.

He has refused his Assent to Laws, the most wholesome and necessary   3
for the public good.

He has forbidden his Governors to pass Laws of immediate and pressing impor-   4
tance, unless suspended in their operation till his Assent should be obtained; and when so suspended, he has utterly neglected to attend to them.

He has refused to pass other Laws for the accommodation of large districts of   5
people, unless those people would relinquish the right of Representation in the Legislature, a right inestimable to them and formidable to tyrants only.

He has called together legislative bodies at places unusual, uncomfortable, and   6
distant from the depository of their public Records, for the sole purpose of fatiguing them into compliance with his measures.

He has dissolved Representative Houses repeatedly, for opposing with manly   7
firmness his invasions on the rights of the people.

He has refused for a long time, after such dissolutions, to cause others to be   8
elected; whereby the Legislative powers, incapable of Annihilation, have returned to the People at large for their exercise; the State remaining in the mean time exposed to all the dangers of invasion from without, and convulsions within.

He has endeavoured to prevent the population of these States; for that purpose   9
obstructing the Laws of Naturalization of Foreigners; refusing to pass others to encourage their migration hither, and raising the conditions of new Appropriations of Lands.

He has obstructed the Administration of Justice, by refusing his Assent to Laws   10
for establishing Judiciary powers.

He has made Judges dependent on his Will alone, for the tenure of their offices, 11 and the amount and payment of their salaries.

He has erected a multitude of New Offices, and sent hither swarms of Officers 12 to harass our people, and eat out their substance.

He has kept among us, in time of peace, Standing Armies without the Consent 13 of our legislatures.

He has affected to render the Military independent of and superior to the Civil 14 power.

He has combined with others to subject us to a jurisdiction foreign to our consti- 15 tution, and unacknowledged by our laws; giving his Assent to their acts of pretended Legislation:

For Quartering large bodies of armed troops among us: 16

For protecting them, by a mock Trial, from punishment for any Murders which 17 they should commit on the Inhabitants of these States:

For cutting off our Trade with all parts of the world: 18

For imposing Taxes on us without our Consent: 19

For depriving us in many cases, of the benefits of Trial by Jury: 20

For transporting us beyond the Seas to be tried for pretended offenses: 21

For abolishing the free System of English Laws in a neighbouring Province, 22 establishing therein an Arbitrary government, and enlarging its Boundaries so as to render it at once an example and fit instrument for introducing the same absolute rule into these Colonies:

For taking away our Charters, abolishing our most valuable Laws, and altering 23 fundamentally the Forms of our Governments:

For suspending our own Legislatures, and declaring themselves invested with 24 power to legislate for us in all cases whatsoever.

He has abdicated Government here, by declaring us out of his Protection and 25 waging War against us.

He has plundered our seas, ravaged our Coasts, burnt our towns and destroyed 26 the lives of our people.

He is at this time transporting large Armies of foreign Mercenaries to compleat 27 the works of death, desolation and tyranny, already begun with circumstances of Cruelty & perfidy scarcely paralleled in the most barbarous ages, and totally unworthy the Head of a civilized nation.

He has constrained our fellow Citizens taken Captive on the high Seas to bear 28 Arms against their Country, to become the executioners of their friends and Brethren, or to fall themselves by their Hands.

He has excited domestic insurrections amongst us, and has endeavoured to bring 29 on the inhabitants of our frontiers, the merciless Indian Savages, whose known rule of warfare, is an undistinguished destruction of all ages, sexes and conditions.

In every stage of these Oppressions We have Petitioned for Redress in the most   30
humble terms: Our repeated Petitions have been answered only by repeated injury.
A Prince, whose character is thus marked by every act which may define a Tyrant,
is unfit to be the ruler of a free people.

Nor have We been wanting in attentions to our British brethren. We have warned   31
them from time to time of attempts by their legislature to extend an unwarrantable
jurisdiction over us. We have reminded them of the circumstances of our emigra-
tion and settlement here. We have appealed to their native justice and magnanim-
ity, and we have conjured them by the ties of our common kindred to disavow these
usurpations, which would inevitably interrupt our connections and correspondence.
They too have been deaf to the voice of justice and of consanguinity. We must,
therefore acquiesce in the necessity, which denounces our Separation, and hold
them, as we hold the rest of mankind, Enemies in War, in Peace Friends.

We, therefore, the Representatives of the United States of America, in General   32
Congress, Assembled, appealing to the Supreme Judge of the world for the recti-
tude of our intentions, do, in the Name, and by Authority of the good People of
these Colonies, solemnly publish and declare, That these United Colonies are, and
of Right ought to be Free and Independent States; that they are Absolved from all
Allegiance to the British Crown, and that all political connection between them
and the State of Great Britain, is and ought to be totally dissolved; and that as Free
and Independent States, they have full Power to levy War, conclude Peace, contract
Alliances, establish Commerce, and to do all other Acts and Things which Independent States may of right do. And for the support of this Declaration, with a firm
reliance on the protection of divine Providence, we mutually pledge to each other
our Lives, our Fortunes and our sacred Honor. ◆

## FOR CLOSE READING

1. According to Thomas Jefferson (and the fifty-five other signers of the Declaration
   of Independence) what is the purpose of government?

2. What claim is Jefferson making on the basis that King George's government has
   not fulfilled the purpose of government? What remedy is he calling for?

3. Of the many "injuries and usurpations" that Jefferson attributes to the British king,
   which seem most intolerable to you (2)? Why?

## Strategies and Structures

1.  "We hold these truths to be self-evident" (2), says Jefferson. Another name for self-evident truths stated at the beginning of an argument is *premises*. On what specific premises is Jefferson's argument based? Which are the ones most critical to his case?

2.  Is the underlying logic of the Declaration basically inductive or deductive? Or both? Explain.

3.  Paragraph 31 seems to be a digression from Jefferson's main line of argument. Why do you think he includes it?

4.  Jefferson and the other signers of the Declaration made their case for independence on logical grounds. Many of the issues they addressed, however, were highly emotional. Where and how does the Declaration appeal to the emotions of its audience as well as their sense of reason?

5.  How does the Declaration present the authors as men of good character who want to do what is morally right? Refer to paragraph numbers in your response.

6.  *Other Methods.* Jefferson says that King George has committed "every act which may define a Tyrant" (30). How does Jefferson use this DEFINITION to support his argument that the king is unfit to rule a free people?

## Thinking about Language

1.  In modern English, "unalienable" (2) should be *inalienable*. Why do you think a person of Jefferson's intelligence and education would make this error?

2.  Why does Jefferson begin so many of his sentences with the personal pronoun *he*, referring to King George?

3.  What is "consanguinity" (31)? How can it be said to have a "voice"?

4.  According to your dictionary, do most of the following words derive from Latin or Anglo-Saxon? Why do you think the signers of the Declaration used such a vocabulary to address the king of England?

    | | | | |
    |---|---|---|---|
    | transient (2) | magnanimity (31) | perfidy (27) | candid (2) |
    | despotism (2) | usurpations (2) | acquiesce (31) | redress (30) |
    | abdicated (25) | constrains (2) | evinces (2) | rectitude (32) |

## FOR WRITING

1.  You are King George, and you've just received the Declaration of Independence, a direct challenge to your authority over the American colonies. Compose a few paragraphs replying to Jefferson's charges and defending your actions and policies toward the colonies. Assume that the Declaration accurately describes those actions—don't base your argument on a denial.

2. Compose an essay arguing that "the pursuit of Happiness" (2) is unwise, that happiness cannot be guaranteed, and that the excessive pursuit of anything can lead to chaos in the life of the individual and in the state. Or, alternatively, defend Jefferson's claim that the pursuit of happiness is an inalienable right.

3. Does the Declaration of Independence promise "life, liberty, and the pursuit of happiness" period? Or is this phrase in the document dependent upon what follows? Danielle Allen, a professor at the Institute for Advanced Study in Princeton, has recently discovered what she thinks is a significant error in the official transcript of the Declaration produced by the National Archives and Records Administration. Read about the controversy, and write a REPORT explaining the issues that Allen raises and the evidence she cites for her position.

4. The U.S. Constitution ("We the People . . .") was written and adopted in 1787, a little more than ten years after the Declaration of Independence, but the two are clearly related in style and content. COMPARE these two founding documents, and write a TEXTUAL ANALYSIS of their similarities and differences—in meaning and basic principles, as well as language.

You'll find quizzes on the readings at
wwnorton.com/write/back-to-the-lake.

MICHELLE OBAMA

# Remarks at Topeka School District Senior Recognition Day

Michelle Obama (b. 1964), grew up on the South Side of Chicago and graduated from Princeton University in 1985 and from Harvard Law School in 1988. She met her future husband, Barack Obama, at the Chicago law firm Sidley Austin, where she was assigned to mentor him as a summer associate. (President Obama earned his degree from Harvard Law in 1991.) The future first lady also worked in Chicago city government as an assistant to Mayor Richard Daley and as an assistant commissioner of planning and development. She then served as the executive director of a nonprofit organization and, later, at the University of Chicago as an associate dean of student services and a vice president for external affairs at the university's medical center.

Michelle Obama delivered her "Remarks" to the graduating classes of Topeka Unified School District 501 on May 16, 2014. The decision in the Supreme Court case to which she refers, *Brown vs. Board of Education of Topeka*, was handed down on May 17, 1954. In that decision, the Warren Court unanimously ended legal segregation in public schools on the grounds that "separate educational facilities are inherently unequal."

THANK YOU, GUYS. Thank you so much. Wow! (Applause.) Look at you guys. (Applause.) All right, you all rest yourselves. You've got a big day tomorrow. I want you guys to be ready. 1

It is beyond a pleasure and an honor, truly, to be with you here today to celebrate the class of 2014. Thank you so much for having me. I'm so proud of you guys. (Applause.) Days like this make me think of my own daughters, so forgive me if a get a little teary. You guys look great. 2

We have a great group of students here. We have students from Highland Park High School. (Applause.) We have Hope Street Academy students here today. (Applause.) Topeka High School is in the house. (Applause.) And of course, we have Topeka West High School in the house. (Applause.) 3

MLA CITATION: Obama, Michelle. "Remarks at Topeka School District Senior Recognition Day." 2014. *Back to the Lake.* Ed. Thomas Cooley. 3rd ed. New York: Norton, 2015. 641–46. Print.

Tomorrow will be a big day for all of you. You all have worked so hard, I know—   4
I can tell. You've come so far. And as you walk across that stage tomorrow to get
your diploma, know that I'm going to be thinking of you all. I am so proud of you
all and all that you've achieved thus far.

And you have got so many people here who are proud of you tonight. Your   5
families are here, your teachers and counselors, your principals, your coaches,
everyone who has poured their love and hope into you over these many, many
years. So, graduates, let's just take a moment to give a round of applause to those
folks, as well. Tonight is their night, too. Yes! (Applause.)

Now, I want to start by thanking Lauren for that amazing introduction.   6
(Applause.) Yes, indeed. Well done, Lauren. I want to thank a few other people
here—of course, Secretary Sebelius. As you know, my husband and I are so grateful for all that she has done, her wonderful service. (Applause.) And I'm so glad
that she and her family could join us tonight.

And of course, I want to recognize Congresswoman Jenkins, Governor   7
Brownback, and Mayor Wolgast, as well as Superintendent Ford, School Board
President Johnson, and all of your great principals—Principals Carton, New, Noll,
and Wiley. (Applause.) Yay!

And finally, to our fantastic student speakers—Alisha, Rosemary, and Noah—   8
just hearing your backgrounds makes me feel like an underachiever, so thank you
so much for your remarks about *Brown vs. Board of Ed.* I know Noah is coming. You
have approached this issue past, present, and future.

And I think it's fitting that we're celebrating this historic Supreme Court case   9
tonight, not just because *Brown* started right here in Topeka or because *Brown's*
sixtieth anniversary is tomorrow, but because I believe that all of you—our soon-to-
be-graduates—you all are the living, breathing legacy of this case. Yes. (Applause.)

I mean, just look around at this arena. Not only are you beautiful and handsome   10
and talented and smart, but you represent all colors and cultures and faiths here
tonight. (Applause.) You come from all walks of life, and you've taken so many different paths to reach this moment. Maybe your ancestors have been here in Kansas
for centuries. Or maybe, like mine, they came to this country in chains. Or maybe
your family just arrived here in search of a better life.

But no matter how you got here, you have arrived at this day together. For so   11
many years, you all have studied together in the same classrooms, you've played on
the same teams, attended the same parties—hopefully you behaved yourselves at
those parties. (Laughter.) You've debated each other's ideas, hearing every possible
opinion and perspective. You've heard each other's languages in the hallways, English, Spanish, and others, all mixed together in a uniquely American conversation.
You've celebrated each other's holidays and heritages—in fact, I was told that at one
of your schools so many students who aren't black wanted to join the black students

club that you decided to call it the African American Culture Club so everyone would feel welcome. Way to go. (Applause.)

So, graduates, it is clear that some of the most important parts of your education have come not just from your classes, but from your classmates. And ultimately, that was the hope and dream of *Brown*. That's why we're celebrating here tonight, because the fact is that your experience here in Topeka would have been unimaginable back in 1954, when *Brown vs. Board of Education* first went to the Supreme Court. This would not be possible.

As you all know, back then, Topeka, like so many cities, was segregated. So black folks and white folks had separate restaurants, separate hotels, separate movie theaters, swimming pools, and, of course, the elementary schools were segregated, too. So even though many black children lived just blocks away from their white schools in their neighborhoods, they had to take long bus rides to all-black schools across town. So eventually, a group of black parents got tired of this arrangement—and they decided to do something about it.

Now, these were ordinary folks. Most of them were not civil-rights activists, and some of them were probably nervous about speaking up, worried they might cause trouble for themselves and their families. And the truth is, while the black schools were far away, the facilities were pretty decent, and the teachers were excellent.

But eventually, these parents went to court to desegregate their children's schools because, as one of the children later explained as an adult, she said, "We were talking about the principle of the thing."

Now, think about that for a moment. Those folks had to go all the way to the Supreme Court of the United States just to affirm the principle that black kids and white kids should be able to attend school together. And today, sixty years later, that probably seems crazy to all of you in this graduating class, right? You all take the diversity you're surrounded by for granted. You probably don't even notice it. And that's understandable, given the country you have grown up in—with a woman governor, a Latina Supreme Court justice, a black president. (Applause.)

You have seen Latino singers win Grammys, black coaches win Super Bowls. You've watched TV shows [with] characters of every background. So when you watch a show like *The Walking Dead*, you don't think it's about a black guy, a black woman, an Asian guy, a gay couple and some white people—you think it's about a bunch of folks trying to escape some zombies, right? Period. (Laughter.)

And then when some folks got all worked up about a cereal commercial with an interracial family, you all were probably thinking, really, what's the problem with that? When folks made a big deal about Jason Collins and Michael Sam coming out as gay, a lot of kids in your generation thought, what is the issue here? (Applause.) And if someone were to say something racist on Twitter, well, I imagine that many of you would tweet right back, letting them know that's just not cool.

You see, when you grow up in a place like Topeka, where diversity is all you've ever known, the old prejudices just don't make any sense. Seems crazy to think that folks of the same race or ethnicity all think or act the same way—because you actually know those folks. They're your teammates, your lab partner, your best friend. They're the girl who's obsessed with the Jayhawks but loves computer science programming; the guy who loves the Wildcats and dreams of being an artist. (Applause.) That's the world you've grown up in. 19

But remember, not everyone has grown up in a place like Topeka. See, many districts in this country have actually pulled back on efforts to integrate their schools, and many communities have become less diverse as folks have moved from cities to suburbs. 20

So today, by some measures, our schools are as segregated as they were back when Dr. King gave his final speech. And as a result, many young people in America are going to school largely with kids who look just like them. And too often, those schools aren't equal, especially ones attended by students of color which too often lag behind, with crumbling classrooms and less-experienced teachers. And even in schools that seem integrated according to the numbers, when you look a little closer, you see students from different backgrounds sitting at separate lunch tables, or tracked into different classes, or separated into different clubs or activities. 21

So while students attend school in the same building, they never really reach beyond their own circles. And I'm sure that probably happens sometimes here in Topeka, too. And these issues go well beyond the walls of our schools. We know that today in America, too many folks are still stopped on the street because of the color of their skin—(applause)—or they're made to feel unwelcome because of where they come from, or they're bullied because of who they love. (Applause.) 22

So, graduates, the truth is that *Brown vs. Board of Ed.* isn't just about our history; it's about our future. Because while that case was handed down sixty years ago, *Brown* is still being decided every single day—not just in our courts and schools, but in how we live our lives. 23

Now, our laws may no longer separate us based on our skin color, but nothing in the Constitution says we have to eat together in the lunchroom, or live together in the same neighborhoods. There's no court case against believing in stereotypes or thinking that certain kinds of hateful jokes or comments are funny. 24

So the answers to many of our challenges today can't necessarily be found in our laws. These changes also need to take place in our hearts and in our minds. (Applause.) And so, graduates, it's up to all of you to lead the way, to drag my generation and your grandparents' generation along with you. 25

And that's really my challenge to all of you today. As you go forth, when you encounter folks who still hold the old prejudices because they've only been around folks like themselves, when you meet folks who think they know all the answers 26 because they've never heard any other viewpoints, it's up to you to help them see things differently.

And the good news is that you probably won't have to bring a lawsuit or go all the way to the Supreme Court to do that. You all can make a difference every day in your own lives simply by teaching others the lessons you've learned here in Topeka.

Maybe that starts simply in your own family, when Grandpa tells that off-colored joke at Thanksgiving, or you've got an aunt [who] talks about "those people." Well, you can politely inform them that they're talking about your friends. (Applause.)

Or maybe it's when you go off to college and you decide to join a sorority or fraternity, and you ask the question, How can we get more diversity in our next pledge class? Or maybe it's years from now, when you're on the job and you're the one who asks, Do we really have all the voices and viewpoints we need at this table? Maybe it's when you have kids of your own one day, and you go to your school board meeting and insist on integrating your children's schools and giving them the resources they need.

But no matter what you do, the point is to never be afraid to talk about these issues, particularly the issue of race. Because even today, we still struggle to do that. Because this issue is so sensitive, is so complicated, so bound up with a painful history. And we need your generation to help us break through. We need all of you to ask the hard questions and have the honest conversations, because that is the only way we will heal the wounds of the past and move forward to a better future. (Applause.)

And here's the thing—the stakes here simply couldn't be higher, because as a nation, we have some serious challenges on our plate—from creating jobs, to curing diseases, to giving every child in this country a good education. And we know—we don't even know where the next new breakthrough, the next great discovery will come from.

Maybe the solution to global warming will come from that girl whose parents don't speak a word of English, but who's been acing her science classes since kindergarten. (Applause.) Maybe the answer to poverty will come from the boy from the projects who understands this issue like no one else. So we need to bring everyone to the table. We need every voice in our national conversation.

So, graduates, that is your mission: to make sure all those voices are heard, to make sure everyone in this country has a chance to contribute.

And I'm not going to lie to you, this will not be easy. You might have to ruffle a few feathers, and believe me, folks might not always like what you have to say. And there will be times when you'll get frustrated or discouraged. But whenever I start to feel that way, I just take a step back and remind myself of all the progress I've seen in my short lifetime.

I think about my mother, who, as a little girl, went to segregated schools in Chicago    35
and felt the sting of discrimination. I think about my husband's grandparents,
white folks born and raised right here in Kansas, products themselves of

Using examples
to support an
argument is
discussed
on p. 607.
segregation. (Applause.) Good, honest people who helped raise their bira-
cial grandson, ignoring those who would criticize that child's very existence. (Applause.) And then I think about how that child grew up to be
the president of the United States, and how today—(applause)—that little
girl from Chicago is helping to raise her granddaughters in the White House.
(Applause.)    36

And finally, I think about the story of a woman named Lucinda Todd who was
the very first parent to sign on to *Brown vs. Board of Education*. See, Lucinda's
daughter, Nancy, went to one of the all-black schools here in Topeka, and Mrs. Todd
traveled across this state raising money for the case, determined to give her
daughter—and all our sons and daughters—the education they deserve. And today,
six decades later, Mrs. Todd's grandniece, a young woman named Kristen Jarvis,
works as my right-hand woman in the White House. She is here with me today.
(Applause.) She has traveled with me around the world.    37

So if you ever start to get tired, if you ever think about giving up, I want you to
remember that journey from a segregated school in Topeka all the way to the White
House. (Applause.) I want you to think about folks like Lucinda Todd—folks who,
as my husband once wrote, decided that "a principle is at stake," folks who "make
their claim on this community we call America" and "choose our better history."    38

Every day, you have the power to choose our better history—by opening your
hearts and minds, by speaking up for what you know is right, by sharing the lessons of *Brown vs. Board of Education*—the lessons you all learned right here in
Topeka—wherever you go for the rest of your lives. And I know you all can do it.    39

I am so proud of all that you've accomplished. This is your day. I am here because
of you. And I cannot wait to see everything you will achieve in the years ahead.    40

So congratulations, once again, to the class of 2014. I love you. Godspeed on
your journey ahead. Thank you, all. God bless you. I love you. (Applause.) ◆

## FOR CLOSE READING

1.  In this address, Michelle Obama speaks to the senior classes of four high schools
    in Topeka, Kansas, on the occasion of their graduation the next day. What other
    occasion is she also celebrating? Why choose Topeka?

2.  Aside from congratulations, what is Obama's main message to the soon-to-be
    graduates of Topeka Unified School District 501? Where does she state it most
    clearly and directly?

3. Obama quotes one of the students involved in *Brown vs. Board of Education* as saying, "We were talking about the principle of the thing" (15)? What principle was the student referring to?

4. Why does Obama feel the need, in 2014, to reassert the legal and social principles established by *Brown*?

5. How and where might Obama's address be seen as following directly in the tradition of Thomas Jefferson and the other founders in the Declaration of Independence (p. 635)?

## Strategies and Structures

1. Obama is a graduate of Harvard Law School who has practiced law in Chicago. So why doesn't she say things like this to her **AUDIENCE**: "As the party of the second part, know ye by these presents henceforth and hereafter, to wit . . ."?

2. Where and how does Obama appear to address her audience more in the role of a peer or friend than as a visiting eminence? Point to specific passages in the text that show her awareness of their needs and interests.

3. Commencement addresses often give advice. Where and how does Obama follow this tradition? Where does she depart from it? Why?

4. Though she does not use lawyerly language in her address, Obama repeatedly begins a new paragraph with "So" or "And," indicating a logical connection between the forthcoming statement and the one before. Where is her logic more **DEDUCTIVE** (from general principles to specific conclusions)? Where is it more **INDUCTIVE** (from particular cases to general principles)?

5. *Other Methods.* In addition to strategies of logical argument, Obama sometimes uses those of **NARRATIVE** as well. Point to places in her address where she relies on a brief illustrative story or **ANECDOTE** to make her point. Are narrative elements common in commencement speeches? Why or why not?

6. What point is Obama making when she refers to *The Walking Dead* (37)? Is the show a good **EXAMPLE**? Why or why not?

## Thinking about Language

1. Obama defines *diversity* as a mixture of "colors and cultures and faiths" (10). What other essential ingredient does she then include in the mix?

2. In referring to people of all races and cultures, Obama frequently uses the term *folks*. Why might she have chosen this term instead of, say, *people or citizens*?

3. "*Brown* is still being decided every single day" (55), Obama states. Explain the **MET-APHOR** that she uses here.

4. What is Obama talking about when she refers to a boy from "the projects" (32)?

5. What "conversation" is Obama referring to in paragraph 32? Why might she have chosen this term instead of *argument* or *debate*?

## FOR WRITING

1. Write a paragraph or two summarizing the gist of Obama's argument in her Topeka address.

2. Referring to race, Obama says, "This issue is so sensitive, is so complicated, so bound up with a painful history" (30). In approximately 400 words, construct an argument supporting and enlarging upon this POSITION—or, alternatively, make the case that race is no longer a serious issue in the United States.

3. Write out the commencement address you would deliver to the Topeka Unified School District 501 (or some other high school) senior class if you were called on to be their next graduation speaker.

4. Do some research on *Brown vs. Board of Education* and write a 250–300-word ABSTRACT of the case, including the Court's findings.

5. The Supreme Court decision in *Brown vs. Board of Education* was reached in May 1954; it took years, however, for public schools in the United States to become extensively integrated. Do some research on the civil rights movement between 1954 and 1968, and write an approximately 500-word REPORT on the advances and setbacks in racial integration during those years. Be sure to comment on important legal and social arguments of the period, such as the decision in *Brown*.

...................................................................•

You'll find quizzes on the readings at
wwnorton.com/write/back-to-the-lake.

# Ain't I a Woman?

Sojourner Truth (c. 1797–1883) is the name assumed by Isabella Baumfree, who was born into slavery in Hurley, New York. A tall and imposing figure with a deep voice whose first language was Dutch, Truth was legally freed in 1827. Though unable to read or write, she became a celebrated abolitionist and campaigner for women's rights.

"Ain't I a Woman?" is the title usually given to a brief extemporaneous speech that Truth delivered at the Women's Convention in Akron, Ohio, in 1851. The title phrase does not occur in the first recorded version of the speech—reported by editor Marius Robinson in the Salem, Ohio, *Anti-Slavery Bugle*, June 21, 1851—though Robinson records the speaker as asking, "[C]an any man do more than that?" The version reprinted here derives from the second published version, that of abolitionist writer and speaker Frances Dana Gage, in the *National Anti-Slavery Standard* on May 2, 1863. In addition to assigning a black Southern dialect to the speaker, Gage added the title phrase and more fire to Truth's plea for equal rights for women and blacks. Like the Declaration of Independence (p. 635), "Ain't I a Woman?" is something of a collaboration.

WELL, CHILDREN, where there is so much racket there must be something out 1 of kilter. I think that 'twixt the negroes of the South and the women at the North, all talking about rights, the white men will be in a fix pretty soon. But what's all this here talking about?

That man over there says that women need to be helped into carriages, and 2 lifted over ditches, and to have the best place everywhere. Nobody ever helps me into carriages, or over mud-puddles, or gives me any best place! And ain't I a woman? Look at me! Look at my arm! I have ploughed and planted, and gathered into barns, and no man could head me! And ain't I a woman? I could work as much and eat as much as a man—when I could get it—and bear the lash as well! And ain't I a woman? I have borne thirteen children, and seen most all sold off to slavery, and when I cried out with my mother's grief, none but Jesus heard me! And ain't I a woman?

MLA CITATION: Truth, Sojourner. "Ain't I a Woman?" 1851. *Back to the Lake.* Ed. Thomas Cooley. 3rd ed. New York: Norton, 2015. 649–51. Print.

Sojourner Truth in an 1864 carte-de-visite photograph.

Then they talk about this thing in the head; what's this they call it? 3
[Member of audience whispers, "intellect."] That's it, honey. What's
that got to do with women's rights or negroes' rights? If my cup won't
hold but a pint, and yours holds a quart, wouldn't you be mean not to
let me have my little half measure full?

See p. 618 for a form of argument that treats opponents as colleagues.

Then that little man in black there, he says women can't have as much rights as 4
men, 'cause Christ wasn't a woman! Where did your Christ come from? Where
did your Christ come from? From God and a woman! Man had nothing to do
with Him.

If the first woman God ever made was strong enough to turn the world upside 5
down all alone, these women together ought to be able to turn it back, and get it
right side up again! And now they is asking to do it, the men better let them.

Obliged to you for hearing me, and now old Sojourner ain't got nothing more 6
to say. ◆

## FOR CLOSE READING

1. The opening paragraph of Sojourner Truth's speech was added in the 1863 version. What "racket" is it referring to (1)?

2. What is "out of kilter" in the opinion of Truth and the other women who attended the 1851 Women's Convention in Ohio (1)?

3. What solution to the imbalance do Truth and her colleagues propose?

## Strategies and Structures

1. What EVIDENCE does Truth offer for her contention that women do not "need to be helped into carriages, and lifted over ditches" (2)? How sufficient is that evidence to prove her point?

2. How, and how well, does Truth entertain (and refute) counterarguments to her proposition that women are the equal of men?

3. If women want to set the world right again, Truth's speech concludes, "the men better let them" (5). Does this argument appeal mostly to the listener's intellect ("this thing in the head"), emotions, or sense of ethics (3)? Explain.

4. *Other Methods.* How does Truth DEFINE herself as a woman? How, and how well, does this definition support her argument?

## Thinking about Language

1. Truth addresses her audience as "children" (1)? Is this an effective strategy? Why or why not?

2. What is the point of the ANALOGY between Eve and "these women" (5)? Explain.

3. "Ain't I a woman?" is clearly a RHETORICAL QUESTION. What is the effect of repeating it four times in this short speech?

## FOR WRITING

1. In the 1851 version, as reported by Marius Robinson in the *Anti-Slavery Bugle*, Truth's speech ends with the following words: "But man is in a tight place, the poor slave is on him, woman is coming on him, he is surely between a hawk and a buzzard." In a paragraph or two, explain which ending you find more effective (and why)—this one or that of the "official" 1863 version (5-6).

2. In 150 to 200 words, support (or contest) the position that the power and influence of Truth's celebrated speech was the result as much of who the speaker was—or was perceived to be—as of what the speech actually says.

3. Marius Robinson's 1851 version of Truth's speech is available at wwnorton.com/write/back-to-the-lake. Write a TEXTUAL ANALYSIS of the two different versions that explains how and how well each makes its respective arguments.

4. In your journal, compare and contrast the personalities and activities of the July 1848 women's rights convention in Seneca Falls, New York, with those of the May 1851 convention in Akron, Ohio.

5. In collaboration with several of your classmates, do some additional research on Sojourner Truth. Share and discuss your findings, and write an outline of the key points you would make in a report on Truth's life and work.

You'll find quizzes on the readings at
wwnorton.com/write/back-to-the-lake.

MICHAEL LEWIS

# Buy That Little Girl an Ice Cream Cone

Michael Lewis (b. 1960) is a native of New Orleans and was educated at Princeton University and the London School of Economics. Before becoming a professional writer, he spent four years as a bond salesman on Wall Street, an experience that provided the basis for Lewis' best-selling *Liar's Poker* (1989). The author of *Moneyball* (2003) and *The Blind Side* (2006), Lewis also drew on his knowledge of sports and money matters in *The Big Short* (2010), a study of the personalities and gamblers' mentality behind the worst economic crisis in the United States since the Great Depression. His latest book, *Flash Boys* (2014), argues that the U.S. equity market is "rigged" by high-speed traders.

"Buy That Little Girl an Ice Cream Cone" is a selection from *Home Game: An Accidental Guide to Fatherhood* (2009). In the struggle for gender equality, Lewis argues, boys will always be boys; girls, however, are not so predictable.

W E'RE AT A FANCY HOTEL IN BERMUDA. Like fancy hotels everywhere, the place is paying new attention to the whims of small children. The baby pool is vast—nearly as big as the pool for the grown-ups, to which it is connected by a slender canal. In the middle of the baby pool is a hot tub, just for little kids. My two daughters, now ages six and three, leap from the hot tub into the baby pool and back again. The pleasure they take in this could not be more innocent or pure.

Then, out of nowhere, come four older boys. Ten, maybe eleven years old. As anyone who has only girls knows, boys add nothing to any social situation but trouble. These four are set on proving the point. Seeing my little girls, they grab the pool noodles—intended to keep three-year-olds afloat—and wield them as weapons. They descend upon Quinn, my six-year-old, whacking the water on either side of her, until she is almost in tears. I'm hovering in the canal between baby pool and grown-up pool, wondering if I should intervene. Dixie beats me to it. She jumps out in front of her older sister and thrusts out her three-year-old chest.

MLA CITATION: Lewis, Michael. "Buy That Little Girl an Ice Cream Cone." 2009. *Back to the Lake.* Ed. Thomas Cooley. 3rd ed. New York: Norton, 2015. 653–56. Print.

"TEASING BOYS!" she hollers, so loudly that grown-ups around the pool peer over their Danielle Steel novels.

"Teasing boys!" she hollers, so loudly that grown-ups around the pool peer over    3
their Danielle Steel novels. Even the boys are taken aback. Dixie, now on stage,
raises her voice a notch:

"You just shut up you stupid motherfucking asshole!"    4

To the extent that all hell can break loose around a baby pool in a Bermuda    5
resort, it does. A John Grisham novel is lowered; several of Danielle Steel's vanish
into beach bags. I remain hovering in the shallows of the grown-up pool where it
enters the baby pool, with my entire head above water. My first thought: *Oh . . .
my . . . God!* My second thought: *No one knows I'm her father.* I sink lower, like a
crocodile, so that just my eyes and forehead are above the waterline; but in my
heart a new feeling rises: pride. Behind me a lady on a beach chair shouts, "Kevin!
Kevin! Get over here!"

Kevin appears to be one of the noodle-wielding eleven-year-old boys. "But    6
Mooooooommm!" he says.

"Kevin! *Now!*"    7

The little monster skulks over to his mother's side while his fellow Orcs await    8
the higher judgment. I'm close enough to hear her ream him out. It's delicious.    9
"Kevin, did you teach that little girl those words?" she asks.    10

"Mooomm! Nooooooo!"

"Then where did she learn them?"

As it happens, I know the answer to that one: carpool. Months ago! I was driv-    11
ing them home from school, my two girls, plus two other kids—a seven-year-old
boy and a ten-year-old girl. They were crammed in the back seat of the Volkswagen
Passat, jabbering away; I was alone in the front seat, not especially listening. But
then the ten-year-old said, "Deena said a bad word today."

"Which one?" asked Quinn.    12

"The S-word," said the ten-year-old.    13

"Ooooooooo," they all said.    14

"What's the S-word?" I asked.    15

"We can't say it without getting in trouble," said the ten-year-old knowingly.    16

"You're safe here," I said.    17

She thought it over for a second, then said, "Stupid."    18

"Ah," I said, smiling.    19

"Wally said the D-word!" said Quinn.    20

"What's the D-word?" I asked.    21

"Dumb!" she shouted, and they all giggled at the sheer illicit pleasure of it. Then    22
the seven-year-old boy chimed in. "I know a bad word, too! I know a bad word,
too!" he said.

"What's the bad word?" I asked brightly. I didn't see why he should be left out.    23

"Shutupyoustupidmotherfuckingasshole!"    24

I swerved off the road, stopped the car, and hit the emergency lights. I began to 25
deliver a lecture on the difference between bad words and seriously bad words, but
the audience was fully consumed with laughter. Dixie, especially, wanted to know
the secret of making Daddy stop the car.

"Shutupmotherstupid fuck," she said. 26

"Dixie!" I said. 27

"Daddy," said Quinn thoughtfully, "how come you say a bad word when we spill 28
something and when you spill something you just say, 'Oops'?"

"Stupidfuck!" screamed Dixie, and they all laughed. 29

"DIXIE!" 30

She stopped. They all did. For the rest of the drive they whispered. 31

So here we are, months later, in this Bermuda pool, Dixie with her chest thrust 32
out in defiance, me floating like a crocodile and feeling very much different than I
should. I should be embarrassed and concerned. I should be sweeping her out of the
pool and washing her mouth out with soap. I don't feel that way. Actually, I'm
impressed. More than impressed: awed. It's just incredibly heroic, taking out after
this rat pack of boys. Plus she's sticking up for her big sister, which isn't something
you see every day. I don't want to get in her way. I just want to see what happens next.

Behind me Kevin has just finished being torn what appears to be a new asshole 33
by his mother, and is relaunching himself into the baby pool with a real malice.
He's as indignant as a serial killer who got put away on a speeding ticket: He's
guilty of many things but not of teaching a three-year-old girl the art of cursing.
Now he intends to get even. Gathering his fellow Orcs in the hot tub, he and his
companions once again threaten Quinn. Dixie, once again, leaps into the fray.

"TEASING BOYS!" she shouts. Now she has the attention of an entire Bermuda 34
resort.

"YOU WATCH OUT TEASING BOYS! BECAUSE I PEED IN THIS POOL TWO 35
TIMES! ONCE IN THE HOT POOL AND ONCE IN THE COLD POOL!"

See p. 617
for tips on
establishing
credibility in
an argument.
The teasing boys flee, grossed out and defeated. Various grown-ups say 36
various things to each other, but no one seeks to remove Dixie from the baby
pool. Dixie returns to playing with her sister—who appears far less grateful
than she should be. And the crocodile drops below the waterline, swivels,
and vanishes into the depths of the grown-up pool. But he makes a mental note to
buy that little girl an ice-cream cone. Even if her mother disapproves. ◆

## FOR CLOSE READING

1. When his three-year-old daughter hurls grown-up expletives at the boys in the hotel swimming pool, says Michael Lewis, he should be "sweeping her out of the pool and washing her mouth out with soap" (32). Is he right? Why or why not?

2. How well do you think Dixie understands the implications of what she is saying? What does she understand for sure? Explain.

3. Why does Kevin's mother think Dixie learned "those words" from him (8)? Who *did* Dixie learn the profanity from? Was the informant a boy or a girl?

4. In her "Ain't I a Woman?" speech (p. 649), the abolitionist and women's rights activist Sojourner Truth argues that once women have made up their minds to act, "the men better let them." Does young Dixie Lewis's speech in the luxury hotel pool in Bermuda confirm or refute this proposition? Explain.

5. Lewis remains a crocodilian observer throughout the scene in the baby pool. Should he have intervened? Why or why not?

## Strategies and Structures

1. Lewis argues that his daughter should be rewarded for her behavior "even if her mother disapproves" (35). How, and how well, does he support this conclusion?

2. The boys in the pool, says Lewis, seem bent upon "proving the point" (2). What point? What are the grounds of argument here?

3. If the Orc-like invasion of the baby pool proves a point about the behavior of boys, what point does Dixie's defense of her sister prove about the behavior of girls?

4. In this gendered battle scene, the boys use the pool noodles "as weapons" (2). What weapons do the girls have at their disposal? Explain.

5. Lewis tells a story within a story. What is the purpose of the FLASHBACK, replete with DIALOGUE, to the carpool scene (11–31)?

6. *Other Methods.* Lewis' argument is mostly NARRATIVE. How and how effectively do the events of that narrative prove his fatherly assumptions about the nature of boys versus girls?

## Thinking about Language

1. Lewis describes little Dixie as delivering her startling lines from a "stage" (3). Explain the implications of this METAPHOR.

2. Dixie's behavior in standing up for her sister, says Lewis, is nothing short of "heroic" (32). Is the overstatement justified? Why or why not?

3. Before the boys arrive, Lewis's bathing daughters are engaged in a "pleasure" that "could not be more innocent or pure" (1). This is the language of Eden. How and why has the language of Lewis's family fable changed by the end, when the crocodile "drops below the waterline, swivels, and vanishes into the depths" (35)?

## FOR WRITING

1. In a paragraph or two, **DESCRIBE** an occasion when the words of children at play proved to be as potent as sticks or stones—or pool noodles.

2. Write an essay arguing that boys and girls are (or are not) socialized in fundamentally different ways that account (or do not account) for specific differences in adult behaviors—for example, in speech patterns—between males and females. Cite personal experience as appropriate, but also refer to your reading and research in a relevant academic field, such anthropology, sociology, or linguistics.

3. "Buy That Little Girl an Ice Cream Cone" is a selection from Michael Lewis's *Home Game: An Accidental Guide to Fatherhood* (2009). Read *Home Game* (or one of Lewis's other works), and write a **CRITICAL ANALYSIS** of the book. Or, alternatively, write a critical analysis of how (and how well) Lewis argues his position on an important issue discussed or shown on his blog (michaellewis-blog.blogspot.com).

4. In collaboration with several of your classmates, collect stories of experiences you each had (or incidents you witnessed) in childhood or youth that illustrate good (or bad) parenting. Compile the narratives into a parenting "guide" that supports certain rules, standards, or principles that you all think are particularly important (or critiques ones you think are particularly bad).

You'll find quizzes on the readings at
wwnorton.com/write/back-to-the-lake.

JUANA MORA

# Acculturation Is Bad for Our Health: Eat More *Nopalitos*[1]

Juana Mora (b. 1953) emigrated from Mexico to the United States with her parents and seven siblings in 1960. She received her BA in linguistics from the University of California, Santa Cruz, and her PhD from Stanford University. A professor of Chicana and Chicano Studies at California State University, Northridge, Mora is a national expert on Latina-focused substance-abuse treatment and prevention, and she works with community-based nonprofit organizations in that field. Her books include *Handbook for Conducting Drug Abuse Research with Hispanic Populations* (2002) and *Latino Social Policy: A Participatory Research Model* (2004).

In "Acculturation Is Bad for Our Health: Eat More *Nopalitos*," which appeared in the book *Chican@s in the Conversation* (2008), Mora argues that Latinos who immigrate to the United States, particularly from Mexico, suffer from a number of health, social, psychological, and other problems in their new environment. Exploring the causes of those "disparities," Mora also has some idea of what to do about them.

## What Is the Health Status of Latinos in the United States?

IT IS DIFFICULT TO ANSWER THIS QUESTION because (1) Latinos are a diverse population of cultural groups with different histories and cultural practices that influence health, and (2) health researchers until recently did not include Latinos in their studies. However, new studies that have focused on the health of Latinos are giving us a new understanding of the health and health care needs of Latinos. Based on these studies, we can summarize the health status of Latinos as follows:

*Good News*

- Immigrant Latinas give birth to healthy babies;
- Latina mothers have relatively low infant mortality rates (children of Latinas are less likely to die at birth compared to whites);
- Latinos have lower rates of heart disease, cancer, and stroke compared to non-Latinos. (Hayes-Bautista, 2002; Myers & Rodriguez, 2003)

For additional ways of structuring and organizing an argument, see p. 609.

1. *Nopalito:* Literally, "little cactus"; the edible pads of young prickly pear cactus with the spines removed.

MLA CITATION: Mora, Juana. "Acculturation Is Bad for Our Health: Eat More *Nopalitos*." 2008. *Back to the Lake*. Ed. Thomas Cooley. 3rd ed. New York: Norton, 2015. 659–64. Print.

*Bad News*

- Latinos have higher death rates related to diabetes, HIV-AIDS, alcohol-related cirrhosis of the liver, and homicide compared to whites;
- Latinos are more likely to receive health care in a hospital emergency room and are less likely than whites to have a regular health care provider;
- The longer Latino immigrants live in this country, the greater risk there is to their health due to increases in alcohol and other drug use, smoking, poor diets, and less physical activity. (Hayes-Bautista, 2002; Vega et al., 1998; Myers & Rodriguez, 2003)

The last point is perhaps the most disturbing since we supposedly immigrate to the United States to better our lives and to create opportunities for our children. It seems, however, that from a health perspective, the health gains that are brought to the United States by immigrant populations are lost in the process of transitioning from the home culture to new cultural norms and environments. The gains in healthy births, for example, are at risk as U.S.-born or U.S.-raised Latinas increase their alcohol intake, other drug use, and smoking, and live more stressful lives. Zambrana et al. (1997), for example, found that women of Mexican origin who had higher levels of acculturation experienced more prenatal stress, which in turn was associated with preterm deliveries and lower-birth-weight babies. The impact of increased drug use and smoking may also lead to more instances of heart disease, cancers, and strokes. Some studies (Espino & Maldonado, 1990) have found an increase in hypertension among more acculturated, middle-aged Mexican Americans. And other studies (Vega et al., 1998) have found higher rates of psychiatric disorders, including major depression among U.S.-born or -raised Latinos. According to leading health experts, immigrants come to this country at some risk to their physical well-being and mental health. So what happens to an apparently healthy immigrant lifestyle after several years of residing and working in the United States? 2

## Why Is Acculturation Bad for Our Health?

Part of the changes that occur as immigrants adapt to the United States are that their daily habits and environments change. For example, there is evidence that when immigrants, particularly immigrant children or the children of immigrants, grow up in the United States, they will be exposed to and eat more fast food, will not have access to home-grown foods that they may have had in their home countries, and are more likely to be raised in unsafe and unhealthy low-income neighborhoods where there is a disproportionate amount of fast food, alcohol, and tobacco advertising (Maxwell & Jacobson, 1989). These are not optimum conditions for healthy growth and prosperity. Apparently, upon arrival to the United States and for years 3 after, there is a greater reliance on inexpensive fast food for survival. There is also less physical activity, particularly for immigrant children who remain indoors watching TV, often for many hours, because neighborhoods are unsafe or are not suitable for outdoor play. Scholars have for a long time described immigration as a dangerous, stressful journey with long-term effects on the family (Falicov, 1998; Igoa, 1995).

Our families bring us here to improve our educational opportunities and to live 4 better lives. But they seldom know about the long-term effects of immigration such as the stress produced by learning a new language and culture, living in new and sometimes dangerous environments and having less time to raise and supervise children. In fact, experts have identified a series of disorders that can result from the immigration process alone. These include post-traumatic stress disorder, disturbed sleeping and eating patterns, depression, and so on. However, the long-term effects of immigration that include poorer diets, less physical activity, substance abuse, and unsafe neighborhoods are perhaps more disturbing and can have more of an effect on the long-term health of subsequent generations of Latinos. What else contributes to poor health outcomes for Latinos living in the United States?

## Inequality in Health Care

Acculturation into U.S. health norms, including a greater reliance on fast food and 5 poor environments, contribute to the poor health outcomes of Latinos, but the disparities in health between Latinos and whites can also be explained by a noted difference in the quality of health care. According to a report by the Institute of Medicine (2003), racial and ethnic minorities tend to receive lower-quality health care than whites do, even when insurance status, income, age, and severity of conditions are comparable. The findings of this study are as follows:

- Minorities and persons of lower socioeconomic status are less likely to receive cancer-screening services and are more likely to have late-stage cancer when the disease is diagnosed.

- Minorities and patients of lower socioeconomic status are less likely to receive recommended diabetic services and are more likely to be hospitalized for diabetes and its complications.

- When hospitalized for acute myocardial infarction, Latinos are less likely to receive optimal care.

- Racial and ethnic minorities and persons of lower socioeconomic status are more likely to die from HIV.

- Being a member of an ethnic or racial minority is also associated with receiving more amputations and treatment for late-stage cancer.

Thus, in addition to changes in daily habits, poor quality of health care, even for Latinos who are insured, adds to the increasing negative health outcomes for Latinos.

## Poor, Unsafe Neighborhoods and Environments

The health status of Latinos is also affected by the environmental conditions of the places where they live, work, play, and raise their children. When immigrants arrive in this country, they most often are not able to afford homes in clean, safe neighborhoods or expensive, nutritious food. Studies (Igoa, 1995; Vega et al., 1998; Maugh & McConnell, 1998) have found that, because immigrant parents sometimes work more than one job, the care of the children is assigned to older siblings who resort to nearby, inexpensive fast food for themselves and the children in their care. The majority of Latino immigrants live in crowded urban environments associated with all the risks to health and safety that over-concentrations of liquor stores, air pollution from industrial facilities, and freeways bring to these environments. In Southern California, new studies (Morello-Frosch et al., 2002) examining the impact of environmental conditions on the health of Latino families and children are finding a disproportionate burden on the health of poor and ethnic minority communities that house more than their share of toxic waste, pesticide runoff, lead exposure from old housing, trash, graffiti, and air pollution. It has been estimated that environmental exposures contribute 10 to 20 percent to the causes of diseases, including respiratory illnesses such as asthma, developmental delays and learning disabilities, cancers, and birth defects. A report of the impact of power-plant pollution and the effects on Latino health issued by the League of United Latin American Citizens (LULAC) (Keating, 2004) reported that 71 percent of Latinos in the United States live in counties that violate federal air-pollution standards. Another study in New York found that children in low-income families are eight times more likely to be poisoned by lead exposure than children in high-income families (Cahn & Thompson, 2003). These environmental conditions are clearly hazardous to the health of Latino immigrant families and children. What can immigrant families do to prepare for the opportunities as well as the risks of immigration?

## Our Culture Is Protective: Look for the Strengths

While the outlook for Latino health looks grim due to the triple threat of accultura- 7 tion, lower-quality health care, and environmentally unhealthy living conditions in the United States, there are strengths within our culture that can be protective of health. We can maintain some of our traditions, including growing our own food even if there is only a small space in which to do so, we can listen to our *abuelos y abuelas*[2] to learn about how they lived and stayed healthy, and we can advocate for

---

2. *Abuelos y abuelas:* Grandfathers and grandmothers.

Families can organize community gardens: students, parents and teachers work on a garden at the 24th Street School in Los Angeles.

safer, cleaner neighborhoods. In San Diego, the residents of Barrio Logan have come together to advocate for cleaner air and safer neighborhoods. In Los Angeles, community residents in some of the poorest neighborhoods organize community clean-up efforts. Families can grow their own food, even if they live in crowded spaces, by organizing community gardens. Even in crowded spaces, we must find the physical and spiritual space for maintaining and honoring those aspects of our culture and tradition that are protective and help us live better lives. I live in a suburb of Los Angeles. When I moved into my home, the first thing my mother did was to plant a *nopal*, oregano, and *yerba buena*[3] in my small back yard. This was her way of giving me her strength and knowledge. We can utilize our space, as small as it might be, in ways that maintain the positive aspects of our *cultura*. We no longer have to give up everything that is sacred and honored. And if maintaining a healthy diet that includes *frijoles y "nopales"*[4] in our diets is part of what we want, then we can do that. After all, acculturation does not mean complete assimilation and loss of your culture. It allows for individuals to keep the best from their original culture and learn to positively adapt to the new culture.

3. *Yerba buena*: Mint; literally, "good herb." *Nopal*: Cactus (from Nahuatl).
4. *Frijoles y "nopales"*: Beans and cactus.

# References

Cahn, L., & Thompson, G. (2003). The Politics of poison. Retrieved from http://www.prattarea.org

Espino, D. V., & Maldonado, D. (1990). Hypertension and acculturation in elderly Mexican Americans: Results from 1982–1984 Hispanic HANES. *Journal of Gerontology*, 45, M209–M213.

Falicov, C. J. (1998). *Latino families in therapy: A guide to multicultural practice.* New York, NY: Guilford Press.

Hayes-Bautista, D. (2002). The Latino health research agenda for the twenty-first century. In M. Suarez-Orozco & M. Paez (eds.), *Latinos remaking America.* David Rockefeller Center for Latin American Studies, Harvard University. Berkeley: University of California Press.

Igoa, C. (1995). *The inner world of the immigrant child.* Mahwah, NJ: Lawrence Erlbaum.

Institute of Medicine (2003). *Unequal treatment: Confronting racial and ethnic disparities in healthcare.* Washington, DC: National Academies Press.

Keating, M. (2004). *Air of injustice: How air pollution affects the health of Hispanics and Latinos.* Washington, DC: League of United Latin American Citizens.

Maxwell, B., & Jacobson, M. (1989). *Marketing disease to Hispanics: The selling of alcohol, tobacco and junk foods.* Washington, DC: Center for Science in the Public Interest.

Maugh, T. H., & McConnell, P. J. (1998, September 15). Americanization a health risk. *Los Angeles Times*, p. A1.

Morello-Frosch, R., Pastor, M., Porras, C., & Sadd, J. (2002). Environmental justice and regional inequality in southern California: Implications for research. *Environmental Health Perspectives Supplements*, 110 (Supplement 2), 149–154.

Myers, H. F., & Rodriguez, N. (2003). Acculturation and physical health in racial and ethnic minorities. In K. M. Chun, P. B. Organista, & G. Marin (eds), *Acculturation: Advances in theory, measurement and applied research.* Washington, DC: American Psychological Association.

Vega, W. A., Kolody, B., Aguilar-Gaxiola, S., Alderete, E., Catalano, R., & Caraveo-Anduaga, J. (1998). Lifetime prevalence of DSM-III-R psychiatric disorders among urban and rural Mexican Americans in California. *Archives of General Psychiatry*, 55, 771–782.

Zambrana, R. E., Scrimshaw, S. C. M., Collins, N., & Dunkel-Schetter, C. (1997). Prenatal health behaviors and psychosocial risk factors in pregnant women of Mexican origin: The role of acculturation. *American Journal of Public Health*, 87, 1022–1026. ◆

## FOR CLOSE READING

1. Until recently, says Juana Mora, it has been difficult to access the health status of Latinos who immigrate to the United States. Why has this been the case, and how has the situation changed?

2. For many Latinos, Mora claims, immigration is "a dangerous, stressful journey with long-term effects on the family" (3). What are some of immediate causes of these effects in her view?

3. What are some of the more common disorders, physical and psychological, that immigrants and their children face, according to Mora?

4. What are some of the more significant "disparities" in the quality of health care that they receive (5)?

5. And what about hazardous "environmental conditions" (7)? According to Mora, which ones in particular are immigrants most likely to face?

## Strategies and Structures

1. The title, "Acculturation Is Bad for Our Health: Eat More *Nopalitos*," constitutes a summary or ABSTRACT of Mora's entire argument. Is this a good way to begin a persuasive essay? Why or why not?

2. Who is Mora's main intended AUDIENCE? How do you know? How, and how well, does Mora speak to the needs and interests of her audience? Point to specific examples in the text.

3. Acculturation is only one of the problems, according to Mora, that many Latinos encounter when they immigrate to the United States. Actually, she argues, they face a "triple threat of acculturation, lower-quality health care, and environmentally unhealthy living conditions" (7). Is the EVIDENCE that Mora gives in paragraphs 1–6 *sufficient* to support this CLAIM? Where do you find her reasons particularly convincing? Where do you find them less so? Explain why.

4. What solution does Mora propose to the various problems she identifies? Where does she state most directly what she thinks is to be done about them? Do you think this solution will work? Why or why not?

5. *Other Methods.* When analyzing the health and other problems among Latinos who immigrate to the United States, does Mora need to prove that those negative EFFECTS were directly CAUSED by conditions in the new environment, or is her argument persuasive if she can simply establish an association or correlation between the two? Explain.

## Thinking about Language

1. The philosopher Kenneth Burke defined *synecdoche* as "the part for the whole, whole for the part, container for the contained, sign for the thing signified, material

for the thing made . . . cause for the effect, effect for the cause, genus for the species, species for the genus." How might the phrase "Eat More *Nopalitos*" be considered an example of this figure of speech as defined by Burke?

2. Mora begins the final sentence of paragraph 5 with the word *Thus*. What does it signify at this point in her argument?

3. *Abuelos y abuelas* is the Spanish term for "grandfathers and grandmothers," or simply "grandparents." Why doesn't Mora include a translation of the phrase?

4. *Nopalitos* is a dish made from the flat stems of the prickly pear. Saying "Eat More *Nopalitos*" is a little like saying "Eat More Spinach." Should Mora have given English explanations like this of the Spanish terms in her essay? Why or why not?

5. Why and how does Mora define (or redefine) *acculturation* in paragraph 7?

6. Mora's essay appeared in a collection called *Chican@s in the Conversation*. What's the purpose of the @ in that title?

## FOR WRITING

1. One of the specific problems for new immigrants that Mora points out is the stress of learning a new language. In a paragraph or two, outline the advice you would give to immigrants, Latino or otherwise, to help them ease the stress of acquiring proficiency in English.

2. "What can immigrant families do," Mora asks, "to prepare for the opportunities as well as the risks of immigration?" (6). Write a 400–600-word POSITION PAPER addressing this question.

3. One alternative to acculturation is cultural isolation. Do some research on this issue, and write a REPORT on some of the effects, negative or otherwise, that immigrant individuals or groups, such as the Somalis in the northern Midwest, experience if they retain their old values, customs, and dress. Be sure to cite your sources.

4. Interview friends and classmates who have immigrated to the United States, or are here for an extended stay. Collect their "coping" stories, and work some of them into a NARRATIVE that gives EXAMPLES of how to survive (and even prosper) in some part of America.

5. Federal immigration laws are constantly under pressure for change. Do some research on the issues—*immigration.org* is one possible source—and in approximately 500 words, explain what you think federal policy should say and do. Support your POSITION with facts and figures, expert testimony, personal experience, and other EVIDENCE.

You'll find quizzes on the readings at wwnorton.com/write/back-to-the-lake.

# RODOLFO F. ACUÑA

# We Owe History

Rodolfo "Rudy" Acuña (b. 1932), a native of Los Angeles, is a professor emeritus in the Department of Chicana and Chicano Studies, a field of which he is considered one of the founders, at California State University, Northridge. Acuña is best known for his 1972 book *Occupied America: The Chicano Struggle Toward Liberation* (now retitled *Occupied America: A History of Chicanos*). His other works include *U.S. Latino Issues* (2004), *Corridors of Migration: Odyssey of Mexican Laborers 1600-1933* (2007), and the three-volume *Voices of the U.S. Latino Experience* (2008).

In this essay, originally written for *Chican@s in the Conversation* (2008), Acuña explores the history of Mexican American identity before and after widespread adoption of the term *Chicano* and makes a case for its continued use. Although he focuses on Mexican Americans, Acuña also reveals the struggles that people of other ethnicities and nationalities have had with their identities as they came to the United States.

A QUESTION OFTEN ASKED OF ME IS, Why do you continue to use the word Chicano when even the *cholos*[1] have stopped using it?

As probative a question is why do we continue to call the field of study of Mexican-origin peoples Chicano Studies, when the demographics of the community has so dramatically changed in the past twenty years? Shouldn't we broaden the term to include other brown people?

The fact that we ask these questions speaks about the complexity of forging a common identity, not only in the United States but in Mexico itself. The truth be told, Mexican origins have continuously changed their identity and even that of the field of study. Generally, it is to meet the fancy of *políticos*[2] or the marketplace. In my opinion, this has worsened our intellectual schizophrenia.

What we call ourselves is important, and it has consequences. The name of the discipline determines the epistemology of the body of knowledge we study. It determines what questions we ask. It determines what we do with that knowledge.

For tips on stating the point of your argument, see p. 609.

1. *Cholos:* Mexican American term for teenagers who are members of street gangs.
2. *Políticos:* Politicians.

MLA CITATION: Acuña, Rodolfo F. "We Owe History." 2008. *Back to the Lake.* Ed. Thomas Cooley. 3rd ed. New York: Norton, 2015. 667-72. Print.

Unfortunately, most of our leaders and politicians do not really think about the   5
implications of their choices. Most of them do not read history, and consequently
take the path of least resistance and select the sound bite of the moment. This is
unfortunate because history is an important tool in testing our assumptions.

By not defining what we are going to study, we over-rely on the deduction pro-   6
cess in arriving at answers. This avoids testing popular assumptions, and the
deduction reinforces distortions of history.

The term Chicano as we will see was selected as an oppositional term that   7
encourages skepticism of established paradigms and societal inequalities. It questions the general assumption that we have always called Mexicans, Mexicans.

The truth is that Mexicans did not universally call themselves Mexicans for   8
many years after Mexico's independence in 1821. This identity was problematic
until the process of state formation was almost completed in the latter half of the
nineteenth century. Even then the term was limited to the *mestizos* and *criollos*[3]
who controlled Mexico. The indigenous nations remained separate. Even today the
Maya, Yaqui, Tarahumara, and other Mexican tribes coexist within the Mexican
nation state as nations.

Spanish colonialism gave birth to a national schizophrenia. It imposed not only   9
European but African and Asian blood on the indigenous peoples. It assigned different racial and social categories to the various racial mixtures. Privileges flowed
to the European, and the darker subjects were less equal. Eventually, colonialism
stigmatized *lo indio*[4] and erased the African.

Independence did not eliminate racist practices. Within the process of state   10
building, some Mexicans wanted the new Mexican identity to be European rather
than indigenous. They often called themselves Hispano, a term popular in the
Southwest and throughout the Americas. The *gente de razón*, the civilized people,
spoke Spanish as opposed to the indigenous who spoke their own languages.

The term Hispano persists, and it is still used in New Mexico and in other parts   11
of the conquered territory. The universal identification as Mexicans was slow.

In the United States, the Mexican-origin population increased after 1900. The   12
Mexican Revolution heightened the awareness of the indigenous past of Mexicans
and many workers identified as Mexicans. U.S. racism framed nationalism among
the first generation of Mexicans. Anyone from south of the border was Mexican to
most North Americans and it didn't matter what they called themselves.

With the rise of the second and third generations of Mexicans and the forma-   13
tion of a small middle class, the identity puzzle entered another phase. The utility

3. *Mestizos, criollos:* Respectively, mixed race individuals and Spanish individuals born in Mexico.
4. *Indio:* "That which is Indian."

of identifying themselves as anything but Mexican was not lost on those wanting upward social and economic mobility.

After World War I, organizations with hyphenated names became more common, 14 that is, Latin-American and Spanish-American. Unlike the *mutualistas*, mutual aid societies, and other U.S. Mexican organizations, the names of these new organizations were in English and demanded citizenship.

During the 1930s, a minority began to use the term Mexican-American. This 15 term seems to have been the most popular among younger activists in California. It gained popularity after World War II. Generally, however, second-generation Mexican Americans continued to use just Mexican.

Race always played a role within the identity puzzle. Throughout the 1930s, 16 organizations such as the League of United Latin American Citizens campaigned to pass legislation that designated Mexicans as Caucasian. They believed that the Treaty of Guadalupe Hidalgo gave them that right. Further, in the United States white has always been right. Many Mexican Americans believed that World War II gave them the right to be Caucasian.

The term Mexican-American with a hyphen crept into use in California and 17 Arizona, for example, the Mexican-American Movement (1930s), *la asociacion mexico-americana (anma)* (1950s), and the Mexican-American Political Association (1959). Attempts in the aftermath of the Viva Kennedy presidential campaign of 1960 to organize a national Mexican-American organization failed.

Texans and New Mexicans refused to embrace the Mexican-American identity, 18 forming instead the Political Association of Spanish-speaking Organizations (PASO). Although they called themselves Mexicans privately, they rejected the word Mexican publicly. Even with a hyphen, it seemed to compromise their Americanism as well as their right to be white.

The identity debate took on a new proportion during the 1960s when Mexican- 19 Americans with a hyphen became Mexican Americans without a hyphen. This was a subtle change where Mexican became part of the noun, a coequal with American. A critical core of activists made it clear that they no longer wanted assimilation, which the hyphen symbolized. They, in other words, were Mexican and, unlike the European immigrant, would retain that identity.

By the end of the decade, Mexican American youth dominated the activist 20 space. Youth manufactured movement symbols trying to motivate the community to action. Their struggles toward self-identity expressed themselves in the adoption of the term Chicano, which most of the older generation rejected.

The term Chicano by some calculations went as far back as the turn of the cen- 21 tury. For some it meant *plebe* (plebeian), lower class—poor Mexican workers. For others, the word came from chicanery, meaning deceitful and immoral. For youth,

Chicano symbolized the essence of being in college, which was to uplift and even transform the community.

The adoption of the word Chicano came at the Chicano Youth Conference in Denver in 1969. We applied it to the new Mexican American Studies program that same spring at Santa Barbara. I voted against its adoption because I felt Mexican American without a hyphen more fully expressed my identity. Putting Mexican in the face of the older *Tejano*[5] and New Mexican activists and, more important, in front of the Euroamerican was essential to the process of liberation. 22

In Texas, youth had already made a break, with the formation of the Mexican American Youth Organization. However, when Chicano became our identity, I vowed to abide by the choice and respect the wishes of the majority. Even more important, for the sake of stability and the sake of forging a community, making a commitment to one identity was imperative. 23

Almost immediately, the private and public sectors led the assault on the new Chicano identity. There are varied reasons for the inability of the term Chicano to achieve hegemony. As mentioned, it had political baggage among older Mexicans. Certainly the government conspired to lump all Spanish-speaking groups under a common umbrella at the expense of Chicanos. 24

Although Mexican Americans comprised a growing market, it was even larger if it included all the other groups. Just as important, the private sector tended to look at everything in terms of the marketplace. For Mexican American *políticos* and business leaders, creating the illusion of a voting bloc rivaling that of African Americans became an obsession. For them it meant power. 25

The identity of choice of the 1970s was the word Hispanic, an identity that the media readily adopted, and frankly a word lacking epistemological skepticism.[6] The term was appealing to the new and larger middle class. The student militancy of the 1960s had created a space for Chicanos on the university campuses. However, most Mexican American students did not participate in the student movement of the times. They did not have the benefit of Chicano studies and did not know the history of the changing identities, much less the significance of the word Chicano. Words such as liberation, and pretensions to the land had little meaning for them. 26

In all honesty, Chicano nationalists and leftists also functioned as cliques, alienating many Mexican-American (with a hyphen) students. The word Hispanic allowed these students to feel part of the hype, without having to think or be committed to anything. Because of the lack of skepticism, few recognized the racial overtones of the word Hispanic and its throwback to the Hispano era. 27

5. *Tejano:* Texan of Chicano descent.
6. *Epistemological skepticism:* questioning the meaning or definition.

The evolution of Latino is more complex. On one hand it was an attempt to unite those of Latin American origin under one umbrella. In San Francisco's Mission District and Oakland, where there were many Central Americans and Puerto Ricans, activists often used *la raza*[7] and sometimes Latino, with varying success. There were tensions, and some Latinos accused Mexican Americans and later Chicanos of being nationalists when they were reluctant to shed their identity.

On the other hand, the adoption of Latino was an effort to head off the term Hispanic. There were former student activists in the mainstream media who recognized the contradictions inherent in the word Hispanic. Reporters such as Frank del Olmo of the *Los Angeles Times* influenced that newspaper to adopt "Latino" over Hispanic as a compromise.

Finally, the 1980s increased the pressure to adopt a general term as the migration of Central Americans swelled the *barrios*. Even former Chicano activists working with the Spanish-speaking groups wanted to be inclusive of the newcomers, and they suffered from the awkwardness of separating the disparate nationalities. Calling them all Latinos, they believed, would solve this dilemma.

By the 1990s, the death of the term Chicano was almost complete. A survey by the U.S. Department of Labor in October 1995 found that 57.88 percent of the Latinos surveyed preferred the term Hispanic as the racial or ethnic term that described them, 11.74 percent of them said they preferred Latino, 12.34 preferred "Of Spanish origin," and 7.85 percent (Chicanos were probably included under this category) preferred "Some other term." During this decade, the number of university programs calling themselves exclusively Chicano also declined.

In retrospect, the term Chicano has been kept on life support by student organizations such as MEChA (*El Movimiento Estudiantil Chicano de Aztlan*) and Chicano nationalists. Marxist organizations such as the League of Revolutionary Struggle, through its analysis of the national question, supported the position that Chicanos comprised a nation, separate from the United States and Mexico. More important, the term has been kept alive by cultural workers. So what went wrong?

Much of the blame must be placed on a small minority of true believers who narrowly defined the word Chicano, often tolerating tendencies that were sexist, homophobic, and jingoistic, often anti-Marxist, who excluded other Spanish-speaking groups. The true believers exuded a "Mexico Love It or Leave It!" mentality. To dissociate themselves from these tendencies, many activists and academicians leaned toward the term Latino.

Although understandable, some of this distancing was disingenuous. Academicians who were never part of any struggle took the extreme positions of a minority

7. *La raza:* "The people."

of nationalists and used it as a pretext not to be committed to the process of change caused by the Chicano Movement. In this way, they could avoid any involvement or duty toward existing student or community structures.

Lastly, the Mexican immigrant never accepted the word Chicano and played a 35 role in its demise.

With this said, why do I continue to use the word Chicano when even the *cholos* 36 have stopped using it? Because it is the term that most expresses what I believe that research is all about. I am not a Hispanic and only use Latino to avoid confusion, especially when dealing with statistics. I feel a special solidarity with Central Americans in their individual particulars. I believe that the Chicano experience and the questions raised by that movement will help them find their own identities and cause unity between themselves and Mexican Americans (without a hyphen). The term Latino, for example, makes them minorities whom the Chicano majority eclipses.

The term Chicano raises skeptical challenges to arguments made by main- 37 stream social scientists. How and what knowledge we excavate is critical to understanding the coherence of Chicano studies as a discipline. For example, it ensures that alternative views of knowledge are presented as dialectical oppositions.

This would not be true if the name was Mexican-American with a hyphen. The 38 name would assume that Chicano history followed in the footsteps of the European immigrant. It would ignore the common bond of colonialism that links indigenous peoples of the Americas. If we let go of the term Chicano, it would legitimatize the litany of identities—Hispano, Mexican, Latin-American, Spanish-American, Mexican-American with a hyphen, Hispanic, and even Latino.

In sum, every Spanish-speaking person in the United States owes a debt to 39 Chicanos and to the history of activists that came before them. It is this civil rights history that has entitled them to equal protection. It is why they are in college. ◆

## FOR CLOSE READING

1. In "We Owe History," Rodolfo Acuña focuses on the history of the term *Chicano* and such related terms as *Mexican American, Hispanic,* and *Latino.* Why does he think the history of their names is an important part of the story of entire groups of people?

2. In the 1960s, says Acuña, "Mexican-Americans with a hyphen became Mexican Americans without a hyphen" (19). What were they signifying by dropping the hyphen?

3. Also in the 1960s, according to Acuña, some Americans of Mexican ancestry adopted the term *Chicano*. Who were they, and what did they think the term "symbolized" (21)? What had it mostly meant to an earlier generation of immigrants?

4. In the 1970s, Acuña says, *Hispanic* became "the identity of choice" (26). To whom did it appeal—and why?

5. "The evolution of Latino is more complex," says Acuña (28). What were some of those complexities as he explains them? What happened to the term *Chicano* as more general terms like *Latino* and *Hispanic* came into greater use?

6. "We Owe History," Acuña argues. What does he mean by this claim?

## Strategies and Structures

1. In addition to tracing the history of several terms for racial and ethnic groups, Acuña is also constructing an argument about history. Where and how does he justify basing that argument on the names we call ourselves?

2. In Acuña's view, what is the purpose of history, or the study of history? Where does he state it most directly?

3. The term *Chicano* for peoples of Mexican origin has fallen out of favor, but Acuña argues that we should "continue to use the word" (36) especially in an academic context, for example when referring to "Chicano studies" as a field of research. To support this claim, Acuña gives a number of personal reasons. What are some of them and how persuasive are they?

4. Acuña is not just arguing that *Chicano* best describes him personally. He also believes that it best expresses what the study of history, particularly ethnic history, "is all about" (36). How, and how well, does his reasoning, especially about the nature of history, support this THESIS?

5. "In sum," says Acuña, "every Spanish-speaking person in the United States owes a debt to Chicanos and to the history of activists that came before them" (39). This is Acuña's CLAIM. His GROUNDS for this claim come in the next sentence: "It is this civil rights history that has entitled them to equal protection" (39). What is his WARRANT for why the grounds justify the claim?

See the Toulmin Method of reasoning on p. 614.

## Thinking about Language

1. The word *Chicano* (feminine, *Chicana*) is generally regarded as a shortened form of the Spanish word *Mexicano*, meaning someone from Mexico. What language did the name *Mexico* come from?

2. What are the implications of Acuña's use of the word *schizophrenia* with regard to questions of ethnic identity (3)?

3. Look up *epistemology* (4) in your dictionary. Why might a historian be concerned with ideas about knowledge as well as with knowledge itself?

4. Acuña gives a "litany" of seven names for people of Latin American ancestry (38). In his view, what do they all have in common? As he understands it, how is the term *Chicano* different from the others?

5. Why is Latin America called Latin America? The people there do not speak Latin and never have.

6. We "excavate" knowledge, says Acuña (37). What are the implications of this term for understanding his conception of the job of the historian?

## FOR WRITING

1. Write a paragraph or two explaining the differences in meaning between *Mexican American* and *Mexican-American*, or *African American* and *African-American*—or between any other names for groups of Americans that can be hyphenated.

2. The phrase "equal protection" in the last paragraph of Acuña's essay is a reference to the *equal protection clause* in the Fourteenth Amendment to the U.S. Constitution. Read this amendment and outline what you would say if you were arguing that persons who declare themselves to be members of a racial or ethnic minority, such as the Chicanos of the 1960s, are entitled to equal protection under the Constitution.

3. Do further research on the meaning and history of "equal protection under the law" as a legal doctrine, and write a POSITION PAPER on its importance for ensuring civil rights in America. One landmark case you may want to consider is *Brown vs. Board of Education* (1954). (Read Michelle Obama's speech on *Brown* on p. 641.)

4. Some American colleges and universities, especially in the Southwest and West, have designated "Chicano studies" programs (or their equivalent). Do some research on such programs at several schools, and write a 500-word REPORT on the role and purpose of these centers of study within the American educational system. Don't forget to talk about what they call themselves.

5. Acuña's reference to "dialectical oppositions" in the study of history is an echo of the Marxist idea of "dialectical materialism" (37). Do some research on the history and meaning of this concept, and write a 500-word REPORT on "dialectic" as a method of understanding and writing about history in general (and perhaps Chicano history in particular).

You'll find quizzes on the readings at
wwnorton.com/write/back-to-the-lake.

# DEBATING THE VALUE OF A COLLEGE EDUCATION

Is the value of a college education worth the price? Value and price are not the same, of course. The ultimate value of a college education is difficult to measure. This is because, as philosopher Søren Kierkegaard said, "Life must be lived forward but can only be understood backward." (You don't have to go to college to learn to say things like that, but it helps.) So by the time you know whether or not you've been sold a bill of goods, it's too late to return them.

The question of price, however, is somewhat easier to address. A college education may (or may not) be priceless, but you still have to pay for it. To calculate the price, or monetary cost, of college, you add up the total outlay, minus scholarships, plus interest on student loans, and so on. Then, to calculate the monetary value of college, subtract that initial cost from the total amount you expect to earn over a lifetime and compare that lifetime total to what you would have earned if you hadn't gone to college. Or you can use statistics. The numbers suggest that college pays off. In 2012, for example, if you had a bachelor's degree and worked full time, you made, on average, 73 percent more than you would if you only had a high school degree. Costs and earnings are just part of the calculus, however, when debating the price of a college education, much less the ultimate value.

In this cluster of essays, an economics writer, a recent graduate, and the editors of a news and finance magazine weigh in on the financial (and other) pros and cons of going to college:

Catherine Rampell, "College Graduates Fare Well, Even Through
    Recession," p. 676
Peter Gerstenzang, "My Education, Repossessed," p. 682
*The Economist*, "Higher Education: Not What It Used to Be," p. 685

Questions about this group of readings can be found on p. 692.

CATHERINE RAMPELL

# College Graduates Fare Well,
# Even through Recession

Catherine Rampell writes an opinion column on economics and politics for the *Washington Post* and anchors the paper's *Rampage* blog. Rampell grew up in southern Florida and graduated from Princeton University in 2007. Before returning to the *Post*, she was a technology reporter for the *Chronicle of Higher Education* and an economics and theater reporter for the *New York Times*, where she started the award-wining *Economix* blog. Rampell is a regular guest on "The Wrap" segment of *Marketplace*, the popular radio program covering business and the economy.

Stocks, bonds, gold? You'll get a better return by investing in a college education, Rampell argues in this May 2013 essay from the *New York Times*. You may be overqualified for some jobs, however.

<table>
<tr><td>P. 607 discusses the kinds of evidence to use in an argument.</td><td>

Is COLLEGE WORTH IT? Given the growing price tag and the frequent anecdotes about jobless graduates stuck in their parents' basements, many have started to question the value of a college degree. But the evidence suggests college graduates have suffered through the recession and lackluster recovery with remarkable resilience.</td><td>1</td></tr>
</table>

The unemployment rate for college graduates in April was a mere 3.9 percent, compared with 7.5 percent for the work force as a whole, according to a Labor Department report released Friday. Even when the jobless rate for college graduates was at its very worst in this business cycle, in November 2010, it was still just 5.1 percent. That is close to the jobless rate the rest of the work force experiences when the economy is good.  2

Among all segments of workers sorted by educational attainment, college graduates are the only group that has more people employed today than when the recession started.  3

The number of college-educated workers with jobs has risen by 9.1 percent since the beginning of the recession. Those with a high school diploma and no further education are practically a mirror image, with employment down 9 percent on net. For workers without even a high school diploma, employment levels have fallen 14.1 percent.  4

MLA CITATION: Rampell, Catherine. "College Graduates Fare Well, Even Through Recession." 2013. *Back to the Lake*. Ed. Thomas Cooley. 3rd ed. New York: Norton, 2015. 676–79. Print.

Job seekers wait in line to meet with employers at the twenty-fifth annual City University of New York job fair in 2013.

But just because college graduates have jobs does not mean they all have "good" jobs. 5

There is ample evidence that employers are hiring college-educated workers for jobs that do not actually require college-level skills—positions like receptionists, file clerks, waitresses, car rental agents and so on. 6

"High-skilled people can take the jobs of middle-skilled people, and middle-skilled people can take jobs of low-skilled people," said Justin Wolfers, a professor of public policy and economics at the University of Michigan. "And low-skilled people are out of luck." 7

In some cases, employers are specifically requiring four-year degrees for jobs that previously did not need them, since companies realize that in a relatively poor job market college graduates will be willing to take whatever they can find. 8

That has left those who have spent some time in college but have not received a bachelor's degree to scramble for what is left. Employment for them fell during the recession and is now back to exactly where it began. There were 34,992,000 workers with some college employed in December 2007, and there are 34,992,000 today. 9

## Change in Employment since the Start of the Recession
### (December 2007–April 2013)

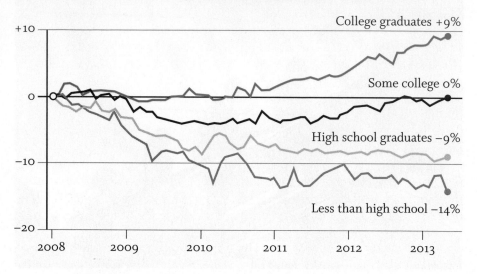

Source: Bureau of Labor Statistics.

In other words, workers with four-year degrees have gobbled up all of the net job  10
gains. In fact, there are more employed college graduates today than employed
high school graduates and high school dropouts put together.

It is worth noting, too, that even young college graduates are finding jobs, based  11
on the most recent data on this subgroup. In 2011, the unemployment rate for people
in their 20s with at least a bachelor's degree was 5.7 percent. For those with only a
high school diploma or a G.E.D., it was nearly three times as high, at 16.2 percent.

Americans have gotten the message that college pays off in the job market.  12
College degrees are much more common today than they were in the past. In April,
about 32 percent of the civilian, noninstitutional population over 25—that is, the
group of people who are not inmates of penal and mental facilities or residents of
homes for the disabled or aged and who are not on active military duty—had a
college degree.

Twenty years ago, the share was 22 percent. Given the changing norms for what  13
degree of educational training is expected of working Americans, employers might
assume those who do not have a four-year degree are less ambitious or less capable,
regardless of their actual ability.

These forces might help explain why there is so much growth in employment  14
among college graduates despite the fact that the bulk of the jobs created in the last

few years have been low-wage and low-skilled, according to a report last August from the National Employment Law Project, a liberal research and advocacy group. Today nearly one in 13 jobs is in food services, for example, a record share.

Clearly, positions in retail and food services are not the best use of the hard- 15 earned skills of college-educated workers, who have gone to great expense to obtain their sheepskins. Student loan borrowers graduate with an average debt of $27,000, a total that is likely to grow in the future.

But nearly all of those graduates are at least finding work and income of some 16 kind, unlike a much larger share of their less educated peers. And as the economy improves, college graduates will be better situated to find promotions to jobs that do use their more advanced skills and that pay better wages, economists say.

The median weekly earnings of college-educated, full-time workers—like those 17 for their counterparts with less education—have dipped in recent years. In 2012, the weekly median was $1,141, compared with $1,163 in 2007, after adjusting for inflation. The premium they earn for having that college degree is still high, though.

In 2012, the typical full-time worker with a bachelor's degree earned 79 percent 18 more than a similar full-time worker with no more than a high school diploma. For comparison, twenty years earlier the premium was 73 percent, and thirty years earlier it was 48 percent.

And since a higher percentage of college graduates than high school graduates 19 are employed in full-time work, these figures actually understate the increase in the total earnings premium from college completion, said Gary Burtless, a senior fellow at the Brookings Institution, an independent research organization.

So, despite the painful upfront cost, the return on investment on a college 20 degree remains high. An analysis from the Hamilton Project at the Brookings Institution in Washington estimated that the benefits of a four-year college degree were equivalent to an investment that returns 15.2 percent a year, even after factoring in the earnings students forgo while in school.

"This is more than double the average return to stock market investments since 21 1950," the report said, "and more than five times the returns to corporate bonds, gold, long-term government bonds, or homeownership." ◆

## FOR CLOSE READING

1. According to Catherine Rampell, what percentage of the "civilian" U. S. population over age twenty-five has a college degree (12)? How does this figure compare with that of twenty years ago?

2. What does the number of people with college degrees in the job market mean for those who do not have college degrees? For people with some college training but who have not graduated?

3. Today, says Rampell, one out of thirteen jobs is in food services (14). What does this fact indicate about the types of jobs that some recent college graduates are finding?

4. Nevertheless, according to Rampell, college graduates earn a "premium" for having a degree (17). How much is that premium, and how does it compare with those of earlier years?

## Strategies and Structures

1. Rampell opens her argument with a RHETORICAL QUESTION, which she then answers in the same paragraph. Is this an effective way to begin? Why or why not?

2. Before stating her THESIS about the value of a college degree, Rampell anticipates an objection to her argument. What is that objection? Where and how does she deal with it later in greater detail?

3. Rampell bases her CLAIM that a college degree is worth its cost on the GROUNDS that college graduates make more money than nongraduates. What is her WARRANT— or reason the grounds justify the claim—for this line of argument?

4. *Other Methods.* In addition to arguing that college graduates do better, financially, in the job market than people without degrees, Rampell also analyzes why that market has expanded. In her view, what are some of the CAUSES of this "growth in employment" (14)?

## Thinking about Language

1. "Is college worth it?" Rampell asks for openers (1). Does "worth" refer to monetary value alone? Why or why not?

2. Employment figures for non-graduates are a "mirror image," says Rampell, of those for graduates (4). Is this an apt METAPHOR? Why or why not?

3. Why does Rampell call college diplomas "sheepskins" (15)?

4. "Median" means *average* (17). If Rampell had cited the *mean* (or mid-point) instead, what additional issues might her argument need to address.

## FOR WRITING

1. Rampell says there is "ample evidence that employers are hiring college-educated workers for jobs that do not actually require college-level skills" (6). Do some research on current hiring practices and enter in your journal the evidence you would cite in support of (or opposition to) this assertion.

2. Write a paragraph explaining why the statistics that Rampell cites may "understate" (19) the monetary value of earning a college degree.

3. What field (or fields) are you thinking about going into when you graduate? On the basis of the latest information you can find, including interviews where possible with people in the field, write a **REPORT** of your job prospects over the next five years.

4. Rampell quotes a professor of public policy as saying that "low-skilled people are out of luck" (7). Write a **POSITION PAPER** of approximately 400 words arguing what public policy at the state and national levels should be with regard to low-skilled workers.

You'll find quizzes on the readings at wwnorton.com/write/back-to-the-lake.

PETER GERSTENZANG

# My Education, Repossessed

Peter Gerstenzang is a humorist and freelance journalist who writes about dogs and popular culture, particularly music and film. He is a frequent blogger for *Rolling Stone*, the *Village Voice*, the *Huffington Post*, and other sites. Gerstenzang graduated from Columbia University with a bachelor's and a master's in fine arts—and, as he tells it, a heap of student debt.

"My Education, Repossessed" appeared in the *New York Times* in November 2013. It takes the form of a nightmare in which Gerstenzang weighs the value of a college education against the worst thing that can happen to you if you don't repay your student loans.

See p. 608 for tips on using personal experience to support an argument.

L IKE MANY POST-GRADS, I've been struggling for years to keep up with my student loan payments. I can just about make it each month, with some modest sacrifices. For instance, doing my own dental work. But last night I had a terrible dream. In it, I fell so far behind in my payments that the government decided to move against me. They could have taken legal action, but they did something much more diabolical: They repossessed my education.

Taking their cues from the Mafia, who break a finger when you're late with your first payment, they started slowly. They began with anthropology. In my dream, a loan officer appeared and showed me a photo of Margaret Mead. I drew a blank. This grilling continued as various vital facts drained from my head. I thought, perhaps, that such forgetfulness was a fluke. When I couldn't remember which sex did the hunting for the Yanomami, I knew this guy meant business.

I thought things would end there. But the government was just warming up. The phantom loan officer next moved on to philosophy. He began by asking me about Søren Kierkegaard. I knew I was in trouble when I blurted out that he'd directed *Dogville*. The phantom said, "You don't remember that 'The specific character of despair is that it is unconscious of being despair'"? I didn't. But I improvised, "Didn't Kierkegaard also say that being conscious of despair was no picnic either?" For this faux pas, they added four more points of interest.

MLA CITATION: Gerstenzang, Peter. "My Education, Repossessed." 2013. *Back to the Lake*. Ed. Thomas Cooley. 3rd ed. New York: Norton, 2015. 682–83. Print.

Things got worse. I couldn't remember anything about semiotics. My loan 4
officer did leave me Noam Chomsky's political rhetoric—like that day in May 1982
when he apparently said something nice about America. Normally, I could have
identified this as an "anomaly." But as the repossession continued, my vocabulary
shrank, too. I tried to scream, but this was a dream, so nothing came out.

The government didn't take everything, but what they left me with was useless. 5
Take those passages from *The Communist Manifesto*. I don't know if you've been following the media lately, but quoting from it can get you hanged in an increasing
number of parts of town. As I dreamed on, my knowledge continued to disappear.
It finally stopped with Jamestown. I had this narrowed down to two answers. It
was either the home of a religious cult, or the band Joe Walsh was in before joining
the Eagles. Which thought was more distressing? (That was multiple choice.)

I awoke. And found that I could remember plenty of Proust. Arcane facts about 6
Einstein. That women did the hunting for the Yanomami. My education, student
loan be damned, was still safe inside my head. There was no way they could remove
it from me. I figured I was O.K. for a while. Still, I don't think it's a good idea to
take unnecessary chances. Especially where my brain is concerned. So, from here
on in, wherever I go? I think I'll wear a hat. ◆

## FOR CLOSE READING

1. According to the renowned anthropologist Margaret Mead, who does the hunting
   among the Yanomami peoples living in the Amazon rainforest? How do you know?

2. If the Danish philosopher Søren Kierkegaard (1813–55) was not the director of the
   Danish film *Dogville* (2003), who was?

3. Why can't the federal government (or anyone else) take Peter Gerstenzang's
   education away from him?

4. Why does Gerstenzang recommend wearing a hat?

## Strategies and Structures

1. Gerstenzang is not arguing that post-grads should default on their student loans.
   What *is* he arguing? Where does he state his point most clearly and directly?

2. Gerstenzang's ARGUMENT takes the form of a bad dream. Is this an effective way of
   making his point about the value of a college education? Why or why not?

3. *Other Methods.* Gerstangang gives a number of EXAMPLES of what would happen if
   his education were suddenly taken away. How, and how well, do they support his
   argument?

4. What is Gerstenzang's purpose in COMPARING the collection tactics of "the govern-ment" to those of the Mafia (2)? How fair and accurate is the comparison?

## Thinking about Language

1. Why does Gerstenzang describe the government's collection tactics as "diabolical" rather than, say, *efficient* or *persistent* (1)?

2. What is a *faux pas* (3)? Why is the one Gerstanzang makes here penalized so heavily?

3. As a professor of linguistics at MIT, Noam Chomsky (b. 1928) was a pioneer in the field of "semiotics" or the theory of signs (4). If Chomsky did not specialize in sign language or signposts, what did he study in this field?

4. Look up *arcane* and the following synonyms in your dictionary or online: *abstruse, esoteric, recondite* (6). What are the implications of Gerstanzang's choice of words (or word) here?

## FOR WRITING

1. List several EXAMPLES you would cite in an imaginary bad dream about having your education taken away from you.

2. Gerstenzang concludes with a vow to avoid "unnecessary chances" by wearing a hat (6). Write an alternative ending to his dream vision in which you imagine some other remedy (or remedies) against unnecessary risks to your knowledge base.

3. "There is no way they could remove it from me," says Gerstenzang in reference to what he has learned from a college education. Write a 200–300-word POSITION PAPER agreeing with (or taking exception to) the idea that a college education leaves an indelible imprint, for good or ill, upon those who obtain one.

4. Write a TEXTUAL ANALYSIS of "My Education, Repossessed" as a work of humor that serves a serious rhetorical purpose. Cite specific words and phrases as well as "events" in the text.

You'll find quizzes on the readings at wwnorton.com/write/back-to-the-lake.

# Higher Education: Not What It Used to Be

The *Economist* (founded in 1843) is a British newsmagazine that is widely circulated in the United States. Despite its name, the magazine offers commentary on politics, the arts, science, and technology—as well as business and finance. Most of the articles are unsigned, with a distinct editorial slant favoring reduced trade restrictions, greater globalization, open immigration policies, the legalization of same-sex marriage, and decriminalization of drug use.

"Higher Education: Not What It Used to Be," which appeared in the magazine's December 2012 issue, makes the argument summed up in the title. Nevertheless, the editors at the *Economist* also see a few hopeful signs "that universities are facing up to their inefficiencies," such as the emergence of massive open online courses (MOOCs).

O N THE FACE OF IT, American higher education is still in rude health. In worldwide rankings more than half of the top 100 universities, and eight of the top ten, are American. The scientific output of American institutions is unparalleled. They produce most of the world's Nobel laureates and scientific papers. Moreover college graduates, on average, still earn far more and receive better benefits than those who do not have a degree.

Nonetheless, there is growing anxiety in America about higher education. A degree has always been considered the key to a good job. But rising fees and increasing student debt, combined with shrinking financial and educational returns, are undermining at least the perception that university is a good investment.

Concern springs from a number of things: steep rises in fees, increases in the levels of debt of both students and universities, and the declining quality of graduates. Start with the fees. The cost of university per student has risen by almost five times the rate of inflation since 1983 (see chart 1), making it less affordable and increasing the amount of debt a student must take on. Between 2001 and 2010 the cost of a university education soared from 23 percent of median annual earnings to 38 percent; in consequence, debt per student has doubled in the past fifteen years.

LAUREATE — A PERSON HONORED W/ AN AWARD FOR OUTSTANDING CREATIVE/INTELLECTUAL ACHIEVMENT

MLA CITATION: The Economist. "Higher Education: Not What It Used to Be." 2012. *Back to the Lake*. Ed. Thomas Cooley. 3rd ed. New York: Norton, 2015. 685-90. Print.

## Chart 1. Still Worth It? (January 1978 =100)

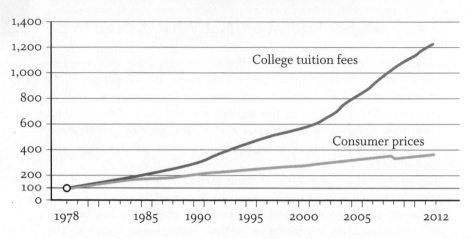

*Source*: Bureau of Labor Statistics.

Two-thirds of graduates now take out loans. Those who earned bachelor's degrees in 2011 graduated with an average of $26,000 in debt, according to the Project on Student Debt, a non-profit group.

More debt means more risk, and graduation is far from certain; the chances of    4
an American student completing a four-year degree within six years stand at only around 57 percent. This is poor by international standards: Australia and Britain, for instance, both do much better.

At the same time, universities have been spending beyond their means. Many    5
have taken on too much debt and have seen a decline in the health of their balance-sheets. Moreover, the securitization of student loans led to a rush of unwise private lending. This, at least, has now been curbed by regulation. In 2008 private lenders disbursed $20 billion; last year they shelled out only $6 billion.

Despite so many fat years, universities have done little until recently to    6
improve the courses they offer. University spending is driven by the need to compete in university league tables that tend to rank almost everything about

For more on deductive reasoning like this, see p. 610.

a university except the (hard-to-measure) quality of the graduates it produces. Roger Geiger of Pennsylvania State University and Donald Heller of Michigan State University say that since 1990, in both public and private colleges, expenditures on instruction have risen more slowly than in any other category of spending, even as student numbers have risen. Universities are, however, spending plenty more on administration and support services (see chart 2).

## Chart 2. Plenty of Padding
### (non-faculty professional employees per 100 faculty members)

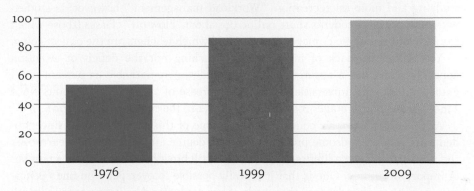

*Sources*: Department of Education; National Center for Education Statistics.

Universities cannot look to government to come to the rescue. States have 7 already cut back dramatically on the amount of financial aid they give universities. Barack Obama has made it clear that he is unhappy about rising tuition fees, and threatens universities with aid cuts if they rise any further. Roger Brinner from the Parthenon Group, a consultancy, predicts that enrolment rates will stay flat for the next five to seven years even as the economy picks up. The party may be well and truly over.

### Balloon Debate

In 1962 one cent of every dollar spent in America went on higher education; today 8 this figure has tripled. Yet despite spending a greater proportion of its GDP on universities than any other country, America has only the fifteenth-largest proportion of young people with a university education. Wherever the money is coming from, and however it is being spent, the root of the crisis in higher education (and the evidence that investment in universities may amount to a bubble) comes down to the fact that additional value has not been created to match this extra spending. Indeed, evidence from declines in the quality of students and graduates suggests that a degree may now mean less than it once did.

For example, a federal survey showed that the literacy of college-educated 9 citizens declined between 1992 and 2003. Only a quarter were deemed proficient, defined as "using printed and written information to function in society, to achieve one's goals and to develop one's knowledge and potential." Almost a third of students these days do not take any courses that involve more than forty pages of reading over an entire term. Moreover, students are spending measurably less time studying and more on recreation. "Workload management," however, is studied with enthusiasm—students share online tips about "blow off" classes (those which can be avoided with no damage to grades) and which teachers are the easiest-going.

Yet neither the lack of investment in teaching nor the deficit of attention 10 appears to have had a negative impact on grades. A remarkable 43 percent of all grades at four-year universities are As, an increase of 28 percentage points since 1960. Grade point averages rose from about 2.52 in the 1950s to 3.11 in 2006.

At this point a sceptic could argue that none of this matters much, since stu- 11 dents are paid a handsome premium for their degree and on the whole earn back their investment over a lifetime. While this is still broadly true, there are a number of important caveats. One is that it is easily possible to overspend on one's education: just ask the hundreds of thousands of law graduates who have not found work as lawyers. And this premium is of little comfort to the 9.1 percent of borrowers who in 2011 had defaulted on their federal student loans within two years of graduating. There are 200 colleges and universities where the three-year default rate is 30 percent or more.

Another issue is that the salary gap between those with only a high-school 12 diploma and those with a university degree is created by the plummeting value of the diploma, rather than by soaring graduate salaries. After adjusting for inflation, graduates earned no more in 2007 than they did in 1979. Young graduates facing a decline in earnings over the past decade (16 percent for women, 19 percent for men), and a lot more debt, are unlikely to feel particularly cheered by the argument that, over a lifetime, they would be even worse off without a degree than with one.

Moreover, the promise that an expensive degree at a traditional university will 13 pay off rests on some questionable assumptions; for example, that no cheaper way of attaining this educational premium will emerge. Yet there is a tornado of change in education that might challenge this, either through technology or through attempts to improve the two-year community college degree and render it more economically valuable. Another assumption, which is proved wrong in the case of 40 percent of students, is that they will graduate at all. Indeed, nearly 30 percent of college students who took out loans eventually dropped out (up from 25 percent a decade ago). These students are saddled with a debt they have no realistic means of paying off.

Some argue that universities are clinging to a medieval concept of education 14 in an age of mass enrolment. In a recent book, *Reinventing Higher Education*, Ben Wildavsky and his colleagues at the Kauffman Foundation, which focuses on entrepreneurship, add that there has been a failure to innovate. Declining productivity

CAVEATS

and stiff economic headwinds mean that change is coming in a trickle of online learning inside universities, and a rush of "massive open online courses" (MOOCs) outside them. Some universities see online learning as a way of continuing to grow while facing harsh budget cuts. The University of California borrowed $6.9m to do this in the midst of a budget crisis. In 2011 about 6 million American students took at least one online course in the autumn term. Around 30 percent of all college students are learning online—up from less than 10 percent in 2002.

## Digital Dilemmas

To see how efficient higher education can be, look at the new online Western   15
Governors University (WGU). Tuition costs less than $6,000 a year, compared with around $54,000 at Harvard. Students can study and take their exams when they want, not when the sabbaticals, holidays and scheduling of teaching staff allow. The average time to completion is just two-and-a-half years.

MOOCs have also now arrived with great fanfare. These offer free college-level   16
classes taught by renowned lecturers to all-comers. Two companies, Coursera and Udacity, and one non-profit enterprise, edX, are leading the charge. At some point these outfits will need to generate some revenue, probably through certification.

The broader significance of MOOCs is that they are part of a trend towards the   17
unbundling of higher education. This will shake many institutions whose business model is based on a set fee for a four-year campus-based degree course. As online education spreads, universities will come under pressure to move to something more like a "buffet" arrangement, under which they will accept credits from each other—and from students who take courses at home or even at high school, spending much less time on campus. StraighterLine, a start-up based in Baltimore, is already selling courses that gain students credits for a few hundred dollars.

Some signs suggest that universities are facing up to their inefficiencies. Indiana   18
University has just announced innovations aimed at lowering the cost and reducing the time it takes to earn a degree. More of this is needed. Universities owe it to the students who have racked up $1 trillion in debt, and to the graduate students who are taking second degrees because their first one was so worthless. They also bear some responsibility for the 17 million who are overqualified for their jobs, and for the 3 million unfilled positions for which skilled workers cannot be found. They even owe it to the 37 million who went to college, dropped out and ended up with nothing: many left for economic reasons.

Universities may counter that the value of a degree cannot be reduced to a sim-   19
ple economic number. That, though, sounds increasingly cynical, when the main reason universities have been able to increase their revenue so much is because of loans given to students on the basis of what they are told they will one day earn.  ◆

## FOR CLOSE READING

1. According to the *Economist*, how much has the monetary cost of a college degree increased over the last thirty years?

2. Until recently, American colleges and universities have spent less on instruction, says the *Economist*, than on anything else. What *have* they spent most of their money on?

3. In the *Economist's* view, however, "some signs suggest that universities are facing up to their inefficiencies" (18). What are some of those signs?

4. Among the many consequences of increased costs in higher education, which one(s) is the *Economist* most concerned about? Why?

## Strategies and Structures

1. "To see how efficient higher education can be," argues the *Economist*, "look at the new online Western Governors University (WGU). Tuition costs less than $6,000 a year, compared with around $54,000 at Harvard" (15). On what premise (or assumption) is this argument based? Is that assumption accurate? Why or why not?

2. How, and how well, does the *Economist* deal with the COUNTERARGUMENT that college graduates earn a "handsome premium" because they have a degree (11)?

3. If the *Economist* is not arguing that a college education costs more than it earns, what *is* it arguing? Where is this THESIS stated most clearly?

4. To support its position on the higher costs of higher education, the *Economist* cites a range of EVIDENCE, including facts and figures. Which ones do you find most convincing? Least convincing? Why?

5. *Other Methods.* The *Economist* contends that "universities have done little until recently to improve the courses they offer" (6). How, and how well, does this argument draw upon the strategic DEFINITION of key terms, including "improve"?

## Thinking about Language

1. In its root meaning, "caveat" derives from the Latin for *beware* (11). How appropriate is that carry-over meaning here?

2. The value of a college diploma is "plummeting" amid a "tornado of change" (12, 13). Why do you think the editors of the *Economist* chose this language instead of, say, *declining* in a *period of change*?

3. How is the *Economist* defining "unbundling," and how does this definition support the magazine's argument that college is too costly (18)?

4. One definition of a *cynic* is someone who makes a particular argument not because he or she wholeheartedly believes in it but because he or she believes it will work. What's "cynical," in the *Economist's* view, about arguing that the value of a college degree cannot be reduced to a number (19)? How might the term be applied to the *Economist's* own numeric reasons?

## FOR WRITING

1. In a paragraph or two, respond to the argument that graduate students get "second degrees because their first one was so worthless" (18).

2. In approximately 300 words, write a **RHETORICAL ANALYSIS** comparing "Higher Education: Not What It Used to Be" with "College Graduates Fare Well, Even through Recession" (p. 676) as arguments on essentially opposite sides in the ongoing debate about the value of a college education. Be sure to assess which side makes its case more effectively—and why—even if you don't agree with that position.

3. Several major American universities have experimented recently with massive open online courses (MOOCs). Do some research on these efforts and programs, and write a **REPORT** on the likely future of MOOCs in higher education.

4. Write a **POSITION PAPER** of 300-400 words in which you argue that the value of a college education cannot be reduced to a "simple economic number" (19). Support your position with factual evidence and other reasons, such as the social and personal benefits of doing meaningful work.

• • • • • • • • • • • • • • • • • • • • • • • • • • • • • • • • • • • • • • • • • • • • • • • • • • • • • • • • • • •

You'll find quizzes on the readings at wwnorton.com/write/back-to-the-lake.

## Debating the Value of a College Education

The following questions refer to the arguments on pp. 676–91.

### READING ARGUMENTS

1. Of the three essays in this debate, which one best addresses the *value* of a college education as opposed to the *price*. Why do you think so?

2. Which essay do you find most convincing in its use of statistics pertaining to the cost benefits of going to college. Cite specific examples that you find particularly effective.

3. Of the three essays in this cluster, which one deals best with the issue of job quality in addition to job availability? How significant is this component when calculating college costs and payoffs?

4. Who offers the best solutions to the problem of financing a college education, Rampell, Gerstenzang, or the editors of the *Economist*? Explain.

### FOR WRITING

1. In a paragraph or two, explain which of the arguments in this debate you find most convincing—and why. Be sure to say also whether you agree with their conclusions or just find their tactics to be impressive.

2. To what extent can we place a value on a college education? Write a POSITION PAPER on this topic; be sure to address issues other than strictly economic ones.

3. Ethan Kuperberg (p. 746) has written and directed a recruiting video for his alma mater. Watch *That's Why I Chose Yale on YouTube*, and write an EVALUATION of the video both as entertainment and as an argument for getting a college education.

# DEBATING INTELLECTUAL PROPERTY

*Intellectual property* refers to "labors of the mind"—including books, films, music, software, and architectural or mechanical designs—over which the author may be entitled to certain legal rights of ownership. Intellectual property rights originated with copyright, a legal concept that was established in the United States by the first U.S. Copyright Act, signed into law in 1790 by George Washington. The nation's founders believed that copyright laws encouraged individual creativity, but they also regarded ideas as public goods, and they placed strict limits—fourteen years, with one renewal—on how long authors and inventors could enjoy a monopoly on their own creations.

In 1909, however, Congress doubled the length of copyright. The Copyright Act of 1976 further extended the rights of authors to their own lifetimes plus fifty years. And in 1998, copyrights held by individuals picked up another twenty years under the Sonny Bono Copyright Term Extension Act. This legislation is sometimes referred to as the "Mickey Mouse Protection Act" because it also extended (to almost a hundred years) the term of copyright on works of corporate authorship, including Disney cartoons. Because Mickey made his first appearance in 1928, he was scheduled to enter the public domain in 2003, to be followed soon after by Pluto, Goofy, and Donald Duck. Under the new law, however, early Disney characters—and thousands of other works—will remain private property until at least 2019.

Who should own intellectual property created by individuals? In this cluster of arguments, three writers and a lawyer explore the conflict between private property rights and the need for public access to intellectual property in the age of the internet:

Questions about this group of readings can be found on p. 714.

ROY PETER CLARK

# Imagination or Theft?

Roy Peter Clark (b. 1948) is a vice president of the Poynter Institute, a nonprofit school for journalists in St. Petersburg, Florida. Clark was born in New York City and raised on Long Island. After earning a bachelor's degree from Providence College and a Ph.D. in medieval literature from the State University of New York at Stony Brook, he taught English at Auburn University before joining the staff of the *St. Petersburg Times*. Clark has published a number of college journalism textbooks as well as other books about writing, including *The Glamour of Grammar* (2010) and *Help! For Writers* (2011).

"Imagination or Theft in *Imagine*?" (editor's title) is Clark's defense, published September 2012 on the website of the Poynter Institute, of Jonah Lehrer's *Imagine: How Creativity Works* (2012). Try to order the book on *Amazon*, and a message pops up: "pulled from shelves when it came to light that the author fabricated many parts." But that's what writers do, Clark argues: they fabricate, though not exactly in the self-defeating sense that got Lehrer into trouble.

IMAGINE THAT YOU ARE READING A SERIOUSLY FLAWED BOOK. Its flaws have 1 grown into a scandal, so you decide to read it to find out about all the hubbub. As you read, you come across this much-publicized problem, and then that one.

Rather than abandon it in its disgrace, you find yourself engaged and turning 2 the pages, and suddenly your hand grabs for the highlighter to mark up this excellent paragraph about the origins of creativity, and then that one.

You like the book, really like it, but you can't even recommend it because you 3 don't want to sound like a sucker, and, besides, the publisher, after sales of 200,000 in hardcover, recalls all the unsold copies. But you find two copies at a local bookstore, and you begin reading it, and liking it more and more. Imagine that.

Imagine that the book I'm describing is called *Imagine*, written by defrocked 4 wunderkind Jonah Lehrer. Imagine that the reader is me.

MLA CITATION: Clark, Roy Peter. "Imagination or Theft?" 2012. *Back to the Lake*. Ed. Thomas Cooley. 3rd ed. New York: Norton, 2015. 694–96. Print.

Lehrer has gotten himself in trouble for at least four alleged—and in some cases  5
proven—literary transgressions: fabrication, plagiarism of others, self-plagiarism
(recycling older work), and playing fast and loose with the evidence. He also lied to
hide the fact that he had manufactured a quote attributed to Bob Dylan. Together,
the accumulated evidence looks damning. But not all the sins, I am about to argue,
are equally grievous. Let's break them down.

1. To use an old-fashioned newspaper term, Lehrer "piped" a quote from Bob
   Dylan, a futile and senseless act since his embellishment was easily detected
   and added nothing to the overall effect.

2. Lehrer was in the habit of re-using earlier work, sometimes word for word,
   which Puritans have dubbed "self-plagiarism." To me, this is the most ridiculous of supposed literary sins. Publishers have the right to expect original work.
   As a reader—I DO NOT CARE (yes, I am yelling). If it's good stuff, let me
   have it.

3. The author has been criticized for simplifying the science—in his case neurology—
   beyond the recognition of scientists. Lehrer, it appears, is no Oliver Sacks, but
   he knows a lot more about the brain than I do, and I am not embarrassed—
   whether I'm learning a new musical instrument, a golf swing, or a little brain
   science—to be led along by baby steps.

4. A related accusation is that Lehrer suffers from an unfettered arrogance
   that tempts him—as it does us all—to shape reality in support of a kind of
   conceptual tidiness. If you build your work around the revelation of surprising
   theories, you need the ability to both show and tell, and there will be an urge—
   since this is literature and not pure science—to sit on top of the suitcase until
   it closes.

You would think that these issues, added together, would disqualify the book from
my serious attention. Imagine my surprise when they did not.

I am almost embarrassed making the following declaration: the reading of the  6
book *Imagine* helped me understand my world and my craft, and what else can you
hope for from a non-fiction book.

In my seeming confusion, I am a victim here not of the author's legerdemain, but  7
of an esoteric but crucial bit of ancient Catholic theology. I learned it in college when
we were studying the sacraments—those outward signs of God's grace,
such as Baptism and the Eucharist. How do these holy rituals work? The
Latin phrase—this is from memory, I have been unable to confirm it—is *ex
opere operato*. The translation is awkward: "from the work being worked."

P. 617 discusses arguments based on moral or ethical principles.

In plain English, if the minister pours water on the head of the infant and speaks 8
the right words, that child is baptized. And here is the genius: That child is
baptized without regard to the moral condition of the minister (thank goodness!).
The minister may be a racist, a rapist, or a bank robber. It matters not if the "work"
is done.

Flawed authors create books that "work" for the reader. I learned this lesson in 9
a strange place: a limo carrying a small group to a special broadcast of the *Oprah
Winfrey Show*.

On that day Oprah would pillory James Frey for the exaggerations and fabrica- 10
tions in *A Million Little Pieces*. I was invited as a critic of Winfrey's earlier support
for the book. Another man—I never caught his name—was invited to be in the
audience and declare that even with its exaggerations, the story, in its gritty depiction of addiction, "worked" for him.

I thought Frey's book was a bad book, even before the revelations of fraud. I 11
never found the degradation of the narrator compelling or revelatory.

But I think the book *Imagine* is worth something. I know it worked for me in 12
several ways:

- It confirmed for me that some of the methods I use as a writer and teacher—
  such as brainstorming or revision—have validity, based on scientific knowledge of how the brain works.

- It helped me see more clearly the parts of creativity that are highly individualistic and those that are social, thus benefiting from collaboration.

- It took a cross-disciplinary approach, drawing examples and anecdotes from
  many different fields, from writing to design to marketing to invention.

- The author is good at clear explanation of technical subjects, a wonderful
  virtue for a writer. It takes special talent to turn hard facts into easy reading,
  creating a sentence such as, "It turns out that the brain contains two distinct
  pathways for making sense of words, each of which is activated in a different
  context." I remember no sentence in this book I had to read twice—except
  for pleasure.

It helps no one to deposit *Imagine* in some kind of literary memory hole. Correct 13
its mistakes. Add an apology. Make it all transparent. Make it available to another
200,000. Jonah Lehrer can do what he wants with the money. It makes no difference to me that an author is rewarded for bad behavior. I'm too busy learning. ◆

## FOR CLOSE READING

1.  The author of *Imagine: How Creativity Works* has been accused of a number of "literary transgressions," says Roy Peter Clark (5). What are some of them, according to Clark's analysis of Jonah Lehrer's book?

2.  Among the literary "sins" attributed to Lehrer, which one does Clark consider to be the least serious (5)? The most serious—or at least "futile" (5)? Is he right? Why or why not?

3.  Clark cites "plagiarism of others" in the Lehrer case, but he does not actually deal with the issue in any detail (5). Should he have? Why or why not?

4.  Which is morally or ethically worse, to plagiarize (steal) or to "pipe" (make up) someone else's words or ideas (5)? Why do you think so?

5.  According to Clark, what should the reader expect at most from a work of "nonfiction" (6)? Is this a reasonable standard of quality? Why or why not?

6.  Point out passages in Clark's analysis that have particular implications for writers. What are some of them?

## Strategies and Structures

1.  "Let's break them down," says Clark as he begins to analyze specific transgressions attributed to Lehrer (5). How, and how well, does Clark use his analysis to support the CLAIM that Lehrer's book should be available to readers despite the author's failings?

2.  How and where does Clark analyze what he sees as the strengths of Lehrer's book? How well does this part of Clark's analysis justify his claim that *Imagine* is worth reading on its own merits? Point to specific passages in the text.

3.  Clark uses "ancient Catholic theology" to make the general argument that a flawed writer can nonetheless produce a work that is "worth something" (7, 12)? Explain the logic behind this argument.

4.  How, and how convincingly, does Clark establish that he is qualified to give expert testimony about a work of nonfiction? Point out specific passages that indicate he knows (or does not know) what he's talking about.

5.  *Other Methods.* Clark tells about his experience of reading Lehrer's book even though he knows that it has been withdrawn from publication and that the author has been accused of "bad behavior" (14). How and where does Clark use this NARRATIVE—and his role as willing reader—to help construct a defense of the book?

## Thinking about Language

1.  Clark repeats the word *imagine* five times in the first four paragraphs of his analysis. Why? How effective, rhetorically, is this multiple use of the term?

2. "Defrocked" is a descriptor usually reserved for fallen priests (4). Why does Clark use it to refer to a "wunderkind"—which means what, by the way (4)?

3. Explain what Clark means by "Sit on top of the suitcase until it closes" when referring to an explanation or argument (5)? How apt is the METAPHOR?

4. Why does Clark use terms like "transgressions," "sins," and "Puritans" (which usually have theological overtones) when referring to a "scandal" involving a writer (1, 5)?

5. Translations of the Latin phrase *ex opere operato* are easy to find on the internet and in theological dictionaries (7). Is Clark using the term (and the concept) correctly? Explain.

## FOR WRITING

1. Can a writer be guilty of bad behavior and still write a good book or story? In a paragraph or two, answer this question as you see fit; be sure to give your REASONS.

2. Do some research on the Lehrer case and, using the additional information you discover, write a POSITION PAPER of approximately 400 words agreeing with (or taking exception to) Clark's argument that such a writer should be allowed to get on with the publication and distribution of his book.

3. Clark claims that reading Lehrer confirmed for him that "some of the methods I use as a writer and teacher—such as brainstorming or revision—have validity, based on scientific knowledge of how the brain works" (12). Do some research on the topic, and write a REPORT of approximately 450 words on the scientific basis (or lack thereof) for such "methods" of writing as brainstorming and revision.

4. "Parts of creativity," Clark claims also to have learned, "are highly individualistic" while others are "social, thus benefiting from collaboration" (12). Read more about "how the brain works" when writing, and compose a REPORT of approximately 450 words on the aspects of writing that benefit most from collaboration with other writers.

You'll find quizzes on the readings at
wwnorton.com/write/back-to-the-lake.

MARC HOGAN

# Judas Priest: Bob Dylan Slams Plagiarism Accusers

Marc Hogan (b. 1981) is a reporter for the weekly news service *Agenda* and a music critic for *Pitchfork* and the *eMusic.com* site, *Wondering Sound*. A graduate of the Medill School of Journalism at Northwestern University, Hogan lives in Des Moines, Iowa. He is a former staff writer for *BusinessWeek.com* and he has also contributed to *SPIN, Salon,* and the *Chicago Tribune*.

"Judas Priest: Bob Dylan Slams Plagiarism Accusers" was published in *Spin* in September 2012. Though sympathetic to Dylan's argument, Hogan also finds it "hypocritical" and self-serving.

A WRITER FOR THE *NEW YORKER* was forced out earlier this year over charges of plagiarism and fabrication, including making up Bob Dylan quotes out of whole cloth. But Dylan, who obviously isn't subject to journalistic standards of ethics, has been dogged by his own plagiarism accusations for years. In a new interview with *Rolling Stone*, Dylan blasts his critics in no uncertain terms, describing his borrowing as a traditional aspect of songwriting. "Wussies and pussies complain about that stuff," he's quoted as saying.   1

See p. 615 for tips on avoiding logical fallacies (such as name-calling).

Asked to respond to critics who say Dylan doesn't give his sources enough credit, the 71-year-old singer-songwriter—currently promoting his new album *Tempest* (not *The Tempest*)—sounds off in classic, witheringly contemptuous form. "Oh, yeah, in folk and jazz, quotation is a rich and enriching tradition," he's quoted as saying. "That certainly is true. It's true for everybody, but me. There are different rules for me."   2

Dylan's 2001 album *Love and Theft* appeared to borrow lyrics from Junichi Saga's novel *Confessions of a Yakuza*. On 2006's *Modern Times*, he used imagery very similar to that of the Civil War poetry of Henry Timrod. A series of Dylan paintings on display in New York last fall closely resembled historical photographs. Dylan's 2004 memoir, *Chronicles: Volume One*, appears to draw without attribution from a hodge-podge of sources, including, weirdly, vintage issues of *Time* magazine—the very publication recently forced to suspend a columnist for doing basically what Dylan appears to have done: barely re-word another person's writing, without so much as citing the source.   3

MLA CITATION: Hogan, Marc. "Judas Priest: Bob Dylan Slams Plagiarism Accusers." 2012. *Back to the Lake.* Ed. Thomas Cooley. 3rd ed. New York: Norton, 2015. 699–701. Print.

In the *Rolling Stone* interview, Dylan responds to one of those charges directly. 4
"And as far as Henry Timrod is concerned, have you even heard of him?" he asks.
"Who's been reading him lately? And who's pushed him to the forefront? Who's
been making you read him? And ask his descendants what they think of the hoopla.
And if you think it's so easy to quote him and it can help your work, do it yourself
and see how far you can get."

Dylan also links his plagiarism accusers to the audience member who famously 5
shouted "Judas" at a 1966 Dylan concert in Manchester, England. "These are the
same people that tried to pin the name Judas on me. Judas, the most hated name in
human history!" he explains. "If you think you've been called a bad name, try to
work your way out from under that. Yeah, and for what? For playing an electric
guitar? As if that is in some kind of way equitable to betraying our Lord and delivering him up to be crucified. All those evil motherf—ers can rot in hell." (One
person who claims to have been the Judas name-caller has said it wasn't about the
electric guitar but rather a poor sound system, though it's all part of the Dylan
myth now.)

Here's the thing: Dylan is totally right, not only that a free exchange of culture, 6
including borrowing, is part of a long folkloric tradition, but also that it's a vital
part of artistic creation. As the *New York Times*' Jon Pareles wrote in 2003, "Ideas
aren't meant to be carved in stone and left inviolate; they're meant to stimulate the
next idea and the next." Everybody steals from everybody. That's art.

At the same time, though, there's a certain level of hypocrisy to Dylan's state- 7
ment. "Can you treat it like an oil well?" Pavement once sang, and that's not a bad
analogy for how the generation that made rock'n'roll a gazillion-dollar business has
treated what was once humanity's shared cultural birthright—not freely trading
ideas so much as mining up what previous generations have come up with, slapping
a copyright on them, and watching the royalties roll in, while more recent borrowers like the Beastie Boys get sued, Girl Talk puts out albums for free, and rap sampling is reduced to Flo-Rida levels of easily authorizable obviousness.

As we've mentioned before, a quintessential example of how '60s rockers turned 8
a public gift into private property, oil-company style, is the Rolling Stones' "The
Last Time." The Stones borrowed elements of that tune from a gospel song that had
been recorded by James Brown and the Staple Singers, a song that traced its roots
back to writers whose names aren't known. But when the Verve so much as sam-
pled an orchestral version of "The Last Time," one the Stones didn't even sing on,
guess who got sued?

Or look at the Velvet Underground's ongoing legal fight over an image Andy 9
Warhol originally borrowed from advertisement.

Dylan himself once filed a trademark infringement lawsuit against Apple for so 10
much as using the pseudonym he himself got from Dylan Thomas. Legend has it

Dylan even settled out of court with Hootie and the Blowfish for their allusion to his lyrics on 1995's "Only Wanna Be With You"—an auction house even claims to have sold what it says is the signed settlement agreement—but we haven't been able to find reliable corroboration.

Not that such a problem would ever stop Dylan. Which brings us back to the 11 real flaw in his deeply entertaining argument: While he appears to be advocating freedom of expression, he's simultaneously defending his own entrenched power— a power which, if other borrowers shared it, would probably protect them from retribution, too.

"It's called songwriting," Dylan tells *Rolling Stone*. "It has to do with melody and 12 rhythm, and then after that, anything goes." He's right. But he also brings to mind a recent quote by the singer and songwriter Josephine Foster, who has compared traditional, anonymously written folk songs to "jewels . . . strange jewels." If that comparison holds true, then Dylan is simply following the golden rule: He who has the gold makes the rules. Or he could just be talking jive. The rest of us can't afford to—we might get sued or lose our jobs. ◆

## FOR CLOSE READING

1. According to Marc Hogan, where did the singer Robert Allen Zimmerman (aka Bob Dylan) get his name? Was this borrowing a form of PLAGIARISM or of homage? Explain.

2. As quoted by Hogan, how, and how well, does Dylan defend himself against charges of plagiarism in some of his songs?

3. Hogan says that Dylan "is simply following the golden rule" (12). What does he mean by this statement? Is Hogan right? Why or why not?

4. According to Hogan, why can't "the rest of us" follow this same rule (12)? Should we? Why or why not?

### Strategies and Structures

1. In addition to quoting Dylan's defense of himself against charges of plagiarism, Hogan is making an argument of his own about Dylan's "deeply entertaining argument" (11). What is Hogan's CLAIM? Where does he state it most clearly and directly?

2. Where does Hogan stand on the issue of "a free exchange of culture" as "a vital part of artistic creation" (6)? How, and how well, does he defend his position?

3. What point is Hogan making when he compares folk tradition in music to an "oil well" (6)? Explain the logic behind this ANALOGY.

4. When accused of plagiarizing from the poetry of Henry Timrod, says Hogan, Bob Dylan retorted: "And as far as Henry Timrod is concerned, have you even heard of him?" (4). Is this a relevant line of argument or a *red herring* (a false lead intended to throw an opponent off track)? Does Dylan use other logical FALLACIES? Explain.

5. *Other Methods.* Hogan bolsters his argument with numerous EXAMPLES of artistic "borrowing" (1). Which ones do you find most convincing? Why?

## Thinking about Language

1. "Borrowing" is sometimes a euphemism for *stealing* (1). What is a *euphemism*, according to your dictionary?

2. The word *folkloric* means *of or pertaining to the folk* (6). How, and how well, does Bob Dylan, in effect, use this definition to justify quoting other artists without attribution in his music?

3. Hogan accuses Dylan of "hypocrisy" (7). Is the term too strong? Not strong enough? Explain.

4. Strictly speaking, *quote* is a verb. What would be the noun form of the word in a phrase like "a recent quote by the singer and songwriter Josephine Foster" (12)?

## FOR WRITING

1. Is "rap sampling" a form of plagiarism (7)? Write a paragraph or two explaining why it is or is not.

2. Do some research on "the Velvet Underground's ongoing legal fight," and write a REPORT explaining the issues in the case (9).

3. "Everybody steals from everybody," says Hogan. "That's art" (6). Write a POSITION PAPER defending (or disagreeing with) this statement. Be sure to consider the issue of how and when sources should be identified and credited.

4. In your journal, collect quotations from artists like Bob Dylan that express a range of views on the following related issues: protecting the intellectual property rights of individuals, promoting "a free exchange of culture," acknowledging one's sources and influences (6).

..........................................................................•

You'll find quizzes on the readings at
wwnorton.com/write/back-to-the-lake.

# Who Owns Dr. King's Words?

Ellen Goodman (b. 1941) joined the *Boston Globe* as a columnist in 1967, and readers soon warmed to the quietly serious voice she brought to American political discourse. Until her retirement in 2010, her columns were published regularly in nearly four hundred newspapers around the country. Her books include six collections of her columns, most recently *Paper Trail: Common Sense in Uncommon Times* (2004). In 1980 she was awarded a Pulitzer Prize for distinguished commentary.

In "Who Owns Dr. King's Words?," first published in the *Boston Globe* in 1999, Goodman addresses the issue posed by her title: is an important speech a matter of public history, or is it private property? With characteristic even-handedness, she weighs the arguments over the ownership of a dream.

$A$T FIRST IT SOUNDS LIKE A QUESTION for a panel of philosophers: Who owns a dream? What happens when a vision that's formed in the words of one person is released like a balloon into the air to be shared with everyone? Whose property is it then?

For tips on narrowing down an argument, see p. 609.

The dream in this case was described by Martin Luther King Jr. Standing before a crowd of 200,000 at the Lincoln Memorial on that August day in 1963, he found the language to match the moment. "I Have a Dream," he told the country in a speech that became a part of our collective eloquence, as much a part of our heritage as the Gettysburg Address.[1]

Dr. King had a gift. Now people are wrangling over the value of that gift.

Today the question of dreamers and owners, words and property, history and money, has been set before a panel of three judges in Atlanta. The King family is asking an appeals court to rule that CBS must pay them to use the dream speech in a documentary sold on videotape. They claim that they—not the public—own Dr. King's words.

---

1. *Gettysburg Address:* One of the most recognized and often-quoted speeches in U.S. history, delivered in 1863 by President Abraham Lincoln.

MLA CITATION: Goodman, Ellen. "Who Owns Dr. King's Words?" 1999. *Back to the Lake.* Ed. Thomas Cooley. 3rd ed. New York: Norton, 2015. 703–06. Print.

Martin Luther King Jr. stands before a crowd of 200,000 at the Lincoln Memorial to deliver "I Have a Dream."

For years, the King family has been protective or litigious—choose one or the other. They sued and settled with Henry Hampton, who produced the "Eyes on the Prize" documentary. They sued and settled with *USA Today*. They regard themselves as keepers of the legacy . . . and the accounting books.

In 1963, no one would have believed there was money to be made from civil rights history. In his lifetime Dr. King was interested in justice, not profit. His family at times lived on the salary of a $6,000-a-year minister. He contributed everything, even his Nobel Prize money, to the Southern Christian Leadership Conference.

When Dr. King was assassinated, the sum total of his estate was a $50,000 insurance policy bought for him by Harry Belafonte.[2] That, plus his words.

These words are what the family lawyers call "intellectual property." It's property that will soon be worth an estimated $50 million from multimedia deals, licensing, and real estate.

I do not mean to suggest that the family is in the protection racket solely for the money. Schools are granted the use of the "Dream Speech" freely. At the same time, one of the many lawsuits was against a company that wanted to use Dr. King's image on refrigerator magnets.

It's not surprising that the family would resist the trivialization of a man's magnetism into a refrigerator magnet. It's far too easy in our culture to slip from being a martyr on a pedestal to a pop icon on a T-shirt.

While we are talking about King and commercialism, it is fair to ask the difference between the family profit—much of which goes to the Center for Nonviolent Social Change in Atlanta—and CBS's profit.

But nevertheless there is still the little matter of public history and private property.

In the appeals court, the case will not be decided on the grounds of greed but of copyright law and free speech. On the one hand Dr. King gave the press advance copies of the speech; on the other hand, the most eloquent passages were extemporaneous. On the one hand he copyrighted the speech after it was given; on the other hand he characterized it as "a living petition to the public and the Congress."

Those of us who work with words for a living understand the desire to control our ephemeral "product." We are sensitive to the notion of intellectual property and do not take kindly to bootlegged editions of CDs or books or software that show up on black markets.

But Martin Luther King Jr. was not a rock star. Or a software designer. He was a preacher, a leader, a prophet, a martyr. He was, in every sense of the word, a public figure.

---

2. *Harry Belafonte:* A musician and activist who was a friend of King.

One day, 36 years ago, he gave voice to our collective idealism and words to our    16
best collective yearnings: "I have a dream that my four little children will one day
live in a nation where they will not be judged by the color of their skin but by the
content of their character."

This is not a private dream. It doesn't belong to his family estate. It belongs to all    17
of us. ◆

## FOR CLOSE READING

1. In Ellen Goodman's view, who owns Martin Luther King's "I Have a Dream" speech, and where does she state her opinion most directly?

2. "There is still the little matter," Goodman says, "of public history and private property" (12). What conflicting interests is she referring to here?

3. How and where does Goodman explain the increase in value of Martin Luther King's "intellectual property" (8)?

4. Why is it "not surprising," according to Goodman, that King's family would be protective of his legacy, including his famous speech (10)?

### Strategies and Structures

1. Who is Goodman's intended AUDIENCE? How do you know?

2. How, and how well, does Goodman support her CLAIM that King's words belong "to all of us" (17)? Refer to specific passages in the text in your response.

3. Goodman reminds us that she is among those "who work with words for a living" (14). How effective do you find this method of establishing her credibility?

4. Goodman contends that, because Martin Luther King Jr. was a "public figure," his dream "belongs to all of us" (15, 17). Does this argument appeal primarily to the reader's reason or to his or her emotions? Why do you say so?

5. *Other Methods.* Goodman likens "I Have a Dream" to Lincoln's Gettysburg Address (2). How and how well does this COMPARISON support her argument?

### Thinking about Language

1. Goodman equates King's speech with a "balloon" released into the air (1). Is this a good ANALOGY? Why or why not?

2. Goodman offers the reader a choice between "protective" and "litigious" (5). Why? What are the CONNOTATIONS of these different terms?

3. Explain the distinction that Goodman is making between being "on a pedestal" and being "on a T-shirt" (10).

## FOR WRITING

1. Write a paragraph or two explaining how and why someone's words might (or might not) be considered a form of property.

2. To whom does King's famous speech belong, in your opinion? Write an argument in which you take (and support) a position on this particular issue—and on the ownership of intellectual property in general.

3. Read "Tell Them about the Dream, Martin!" (p. 147). In a POSITION PAPER of approximately 400 words, explain the singer Mahalia Jackson's contribution to King's speech and argue, based on the principles that Goodman discusses, whether the singer should (or should not) be paid a royalty.

4. Do some research on the litigation to which Goodman refers (*Estate of Martin Luther King, Jr., Inc. v. CBS, Inc.*), and write a 400-word REPORT on the issues, significance, and disposition of this court case.

You'll find quizzes on the readings at wwnorton.com/write/back-to-the-lake.

## LAWRENCE LESSIG

# Free Culture

Lawrence Lessig (b. 1961), director of the Edmond J. Safra Foundation Center for Ethics at Harvard University and a professor at Harvard Law School, is committed to what he calls "free culture," in which ideas and creative notions freely circulate so that everyone can borrow from and build upon them—particularly in regard to emerging technologies. In *The Future of Ideas* (2001), Lessig argued that antiquated notions of intellectual property are a hindrance to technological innovation and the free exchange of ideas, a claim that won him a place on *Scientific American's* list of the world's top fifty visionaries in 2002.

The following argument is taken from Lessig's *Free Culture: How Big Media Uses Technology and the Law to Lock Down Culture and Control Creativity* (2004). It deals with the conflict between an artist's right to get paid for his or her work and the demands of the internet.

I F YOU'RE LIKE I WAS A DECADE AGO, or like most people are when they first 1 start thinking about these issues, then just about now you should be puzzled about something you hadn't thought through before.

We live in a world that celebrates "property." I am one of those celebrants. I 2 believe in the value of property in general, and I also believe in the value of that weird form of property that lawyers call "intellectual property." A large, diverse society cannot survive without property; a large, diverse, and modern society cannot flourish without intellectual property.

But it takes just a second's reflection to realize that there is plenty of value out 3 there that "property" doesn't capture. I don't mean "money can't buy you love," but rather, value that is plainly part of a process of production, including commercial as well as noncommercial production. If Disney animators had stolen a set of pencils to draw *Steamboat Willie*,[1] we'd have no hesitation in condemning that taking as wrong—even though trivial, even if unnoticed. Yet there was nothing wrong, at least under the law of the day, with Disney's taking from Buster Keaton or from the

---

1. *Steamboat Willie*: A 1928 Mickey Mouse cartoon, the first to be made with sound.

MLA CITATION: Lessig, Lawrence. "Free Culture." 2004. *Back to the Lake*. Ed. Thomas Cooley. 3rd ed. New York: Norton, 2015. 708–11. Print.

Brothers Grimm.[2] There was nothing wrong with the taking from Keaton because Disney's use would have been considered "fair." There was nothing wrong with the taking from the Grimms because the Grimms' work was in the public domain.

Thus, even though the things that Disney took—or more generally, the things taken by anyone exercising Walt Disney creativity—are valuable, our tradition does not treat those takings as wrong. Some things remain free for the taking within a free culture, and that freedom is good. . . .

It's the same with a thousand examples that appear everywhere once you begin to look. Scientists build upon the work of other scientists without asking or paying for the privilege. ("Excuse me, Professor Einstein, but may I have permission to use your theory of relativity to show that you were wrong about quantum physics?") Acting companies perform adaptations of the works of Shakespeare without securing permission from anyone. (Does *anyone* believe Shakespeare would be better spread within our culture if there were a central Shakespeare rights clearinghouse that all productions of Shakespeare must appeal to first?) And Hollywood goes through cycles with a certain kind of movie: five asteroid films in the late 1990s; two volcano disaster films in 1997.

Creators here and everywhere are always and at all times building upon the creativity that went before and that surrounds them now. That building is always and everywhere at least partially done without permission and without compensating the original creator. No society, free or controlled, has ever demanded that every use be paid for or that permission for Walt Disney creativity must always be sought. Instead, every society has left a certain bit of its culture free for the taking—free societies more fully than unfree, perhaps, but all societies to some degree.

The hard question is therefore not *whether* a culture is free. All cultures are free to some degree. The hard question instead is "*How* free is this culture?" How much, and how broadly, is the culture free for others to take and build upon? Is that freedom limited to party members? To members of the royal family? To the top ten corporations on the New York Stock Exchange? Or is that freedom spread broadly? To artists generally, whether affiliated with the Met[3] or not? To musicians generally, whether white or not? To filmmakers generally, whether affiliated with a studio or not?

---

2. *Brothers Grimm*: Jakob Grimm (1785–1863) and Wilhelm Grimm (1786–1859), German brothers who collected and published folk tales and fairy tales such as "Snow White and the Seven Dwarfs," "Little Red Riding Hood," and "Hansel and Gretel." *Buster Keaton* (1895–1966): An early comic actor best known for his silent films of the 1920s.

3. *The Met*: Could refer to either the Metropolitan Museum of Art or the Metropolitan Opera, both in New York City.

Free cultures are cultures that leave a great deal open for others to build upon;   8
unfree, or permission, cultures leave much less. Ours was a free culture. It is
becoming much less so.

. . .

The battle that got this whole [copyright] war going was about music. . . . The   9
appeal of file-sharing music was the crack cocaine of the Internet's growth. It drove
demand for access to the Internet more powerfully than any other single application. It was the Internet's killer app[4]—possibly in two senses of that word. It no
doubt was the application that drove demand for bandwidth. It may well be the
application that drives demand for regulations that in the end kill innovation on
the network.

The aim of copyright, with respect to content in general and music in particu-   10
lar, is to create the incentives for music to be composed, performed, and, most
importantly, spread. The law does this by giving an exclusive right to a composer to
control copies of her performance.

File-sharing networks complicate this model by enabling the spread of content   11
for which the performer has not been paid. Today, file sharing is addictive. In ten
years, it won't be. It is addictive today because it is the easiest way to gain access to
a broad range of content. It won't be the easiest way to get access to a broad range
of content in ten years. Today, access to the Internet is cumbersome and slow—we
in the United States are lucky to have broadband service at 1.5 MBs, and very rarely
do we get service at that speed both up and down.[5] Although wireless access is
growing, most of us still get access across wires. Most only gain access through a
machine with a keyboard. The idea of the always on, always connected Internet is
mainly just an idea.

But it will become a reality, and that means the way we get access to the Inter-   12
net today is a technology in transition. Policy makers should not make policy on
the basis of technology in transition. They should make policy on the basis of where
the technology is going. The question should not be, how should the law regulate
sharing in this world? The question should be, what law will we require when the
network becomes that network it is clearly becoming? That network is one in
which every machine with electricity is essentially on the Net; where everywhere
you are—except maybe the desert or the Rockies—you can instantaneously be

---

4. *Killer app*: Short for "killer application"; a program so desirable that people will pay for the hardware
or software it runs on just so they can use the application. In this instance, Lessig believes that file-sharing—
sharing files between computers—is so desirable that people will obtain internet access (necessary for file-
sharing) just to be able to do it.

5. *Up and down*: Uploading (from computer to web) and downloading (from web to computer).

connected to the Internet. Imagine the Internet as ubiquitous as the best cell-phone service, where with the flip of a device, you are connected.

In that world, it will be extremely easy to connect to services that give you 13 access to content on the fly—such as Internet radio, content that is streamed to the user when the user demands. Here, then, is the critical point: When it is *extremely* easy to connect to services that give access to content, it will be *easier* to connect to services that give you access to content than it will be to download and store content *on the many devices you will have for playing content*. It will be easier, in other words, to subscribe than it will be to be a database manager, as everyone in the download-sharing of Napster-like[6] technologies essentially is. Content services will compete with content sharing, even if the services charge money for the content they give access to.

P. 609 gives some tips for stating your claims like this.

This point about the future is meant to suggest a perspective on the present: It 14 is emphatically temporary. The "problem" with file-sharing—to the extent there is a real problem—is a problem that will increasingly disappear as it becomes easier to connect to the Internet. And thus it is an extraordinary mistake for policy makers today to be "solving" this problem in light of a technology that will be gone tomorrow. . . .

But what if "piracy" doesn't disappear? What if there is a competitive market 15 providing content at a low cost, but a significant number of consumers continue to "take" content for nothing? Should the law do something then?

Yes, it should. But again, what it should do depends upon how the facts develop. 16 The real issue is not whether [the law] eliminates sharing in the abstract. The real issue is its effect on the market. Is it better (a) to have a technology that is 95 percent secure and produces a market of size *x*, or (b) to have a technology that is 50 percent secure but produces a market of five times *x*? Less secure might produce more unauthorized sharing, but it is likely to also produce a much bigger market in authorized sharing. The most important thing is to assure artists' compensation without breaking the Internet. Once that's assured, then it may well be appropriate to find ways to track down the petty pirates. ◆

6. *Napster*: An online file-sharing service that allowed users to download music files from other users' computers for free; it is now a legal, pay-per-download service currently owned by Rhapsody.

## FOR CLOSE READING

1. Why does Lawrence Lessig think the courts should not impose heavy restrictions on Internet file-sharing?

2. To what extent does Lessig believe in the right of individuals to own property, including intellectual property? Why does he feel this way? Refer to the text in your response.

3. How did the downloading of music stir up a copyright "war" (9)?

4. Why does Lessig think forms of Internet piracy will disappear? How convincing do you find his evidence? Explain.

5. Lessig thinks artists should be compensated for their work, but "without breaking the Internet" (16). In Lessig's view, why is it as important to the cultural life of the nation to have a strong Internet as it is to protect the rights of people whose intellectual property has already contributed to that culture?

## Strategies and Structures

1. What is Lessig's main point, and where does he state it most directly?

2. Why do you think Lessig begins his argument by saying, "If you're like I was a decade ago" (1)? What assumptions is he making about his AUDIENCE, and why, in particular, does he refer to the reader as "puzzled" (1)?

3. How and how well does Lessig establish his credibility as an ethical person who is looking out for the reader's best interests?

4. How and how well does Lessig justify "Walt Disney creativity" in the early days of animated cartoons (4)? Is his reasoning valid?

5. What general standard does Lessig adopt for judging whether or not the "taking" of intellectual property is ethical (4)? Do you find this argument convincing? Why or why not?

6. *Other Methods.* Lessig DEFINES a free culture as one "that leave[s] a great deal open for others to build upon" (8). How does this definition contribute to his argument about keeping some intellectual property free?

## Thinking about Language

1. Point out the different ways in which Lessig uses the word *free*. What are its various meanings at different places in his argument?

2. As applied to the copyright controversy, how appropriate do you find the word "war" (9)? Is this just HYPERBOLE, or is the issue important (and controversial) enough to justify the term? Explain your view.

3. Why does Lessig refer to "Walt Disney creativity" throughout his essay instead of using a phrase like "the limited taking of the intellectual property of others"?

4. What are the implications of Lessig's use of the word "addictive" (11)?

## FOR WRITING

1.  Write a few paragraphs exploring the idea that intellectual property is a form of private property that must be protected by law. You could defend this claim, challenge it, or agree in some ways but disagree in others.

2.  Lessig predicts that file-sharing won't always be "the easiest way to get access to a broad range of content" on the internet (11). Instead, he argues, it will be easier "to connect to services that give you access to content on the fly"—and to pay for those services (13). Write an argument defending or challenging this position based on your view of where internet technology is today.

3.  "Ours was a free culture," Lessig writes. "It is becoming much less so" (8). In approximately 400 words, write a **POSITION PAPER** supporting or questioning this claim. Be sure to define what you mean by *free*.

4.  Do some research on the "Mickey Mouse Protection Act" (officially, the Copyright Term Extension Act of 1998), and write a 400–500-word **REPORT** on the significance of the CTEA for a "free culture," as defined by Lessig.

•·······························································

You'll find quizzes on the readings at
wwnorton.com/write/back-to-the-lake.

## Debating Intellectual Property

The following questions refer to the arguments on pp. 694–713.

### READING ARGUMENTS

1. Which position, Goodman's on sharing Dr. King's words or Bob Dylan's (as reported by Hogan) is best supported by Lessig's argument for keeping intellectual culture free and open? Explain.

2. Who do you think makes the best use of logical reasoning to support his or her claim? Of facts and figures? Why do you say so?

3. How effective do you find Clark's EXAMPLE of Jonah Lehrer? How about Lessig's references to Einstein, Shakespeare, and Hollywood (5)? Which is a better use of specific examples to support an argument? Explain.

4. Among the participants in this debate, which one uses the shortest sentences and the least abstract language? To what extent do you think this prose style (and that of the other writers in the debate) is influenced by his or her intended audience? Explain.

### FOR WRITING

1. Write a paragraph or two explaining which of the arguments in this debate you find strongest or weakest—and why.

2. Write an argument in which you take a position (and support it with facts, statistics, expert testimony, and other evidence) on some aspect of the intellectual property debate not fully covered by Clark, Hogan, Goodman, or Lessig.

3. Clark praises Jonah Leher's work despite the author's admitted fabrications. Write a POSITION PAPER rebutting (or supporting) Clark's argument that a writer can be forgiven for his flaws, or at least is worth reading, if his work otherwise has redeeming qualities.

# DEBATING THE EFFECTS OF DIGITAL CULTURE

"Printing, gunpower and the compass. These three," wrote, the English philosopher Francis Bacon in 1620, "have changed the whole face and state of things throughout the world." Gunpower and the compass changed how people dealt with the physical world around them. Printed books, such as Bacon's *Novum Organum* (or "New Instrument"), changed the way human beings explored the interior world of knowledge and ideas. Thanks to more recent technologies, such as the internet, we can find approximately 371,000 references to Bacon's masterpiece in .22 seconds simply by Googling the original Latin title. Are the electronic technologies of the digital age, like the mechanical ones that preceded them, changing "the whole face and state of things"? Or is the digital revolution simply giving us more efficient ways of communicating with each other and quicker access to new sources of ideas—from Bacon's once obscure but now readily available treatise to *Slate* and the *Huffington Post*?

In the following arguments, four writers probe the extent to which today's media and technology are changing not only how we acquire and exchange information but how we define knowledge and the self:

Questions about this group of readings can be found on p. 750.

ANNIE MURPHY PAUL

# You'll Never Learn!

Annie Murphy Paul writes a weekly column about learning for *Time.com* and also blogs about learning for CNN, *Forbes*, *Psychology Today*, and the *Huffington Post*. A graduate of Yale and the Columbia School of Journalism, Paul is the author, among other books, of *Brilliant: The New Science of Smart* (2013), a study of how people learn. Her *Brilliant Blog* is dedicated to advances in cognitive science and neuroscience—and how people can apply those findings in their own lives.

"You'll Never Learn!" is a report of research on how media multitasking while learning affects cognition; it was posted to *Slate* in May 2013. "When students multitask while doing schoolwork," writes Paul, "their learning is far spottier and shallower than if the work had their full attention." There is, however, Paul argues, a simple solution to this pervasive problem.

L IVING ROOMS, DENS, KITCHENS, EVEN BEDROOMS: Investigators followed stu-  1
dents into the spaces where homework gets done. Pens poised over their "study observation forms," the observers watched intently as the students—in middle school, high school, and college, 263 in all—opened their books and turned on their computers.

For a quarter of an hour, the investigators from the lab of Larry Rosen, a psy-  2
chology professor at California State University–Dominguez Hills, marked down once a minute what the students were doing as they studied. A checklist on the form included: reading a book, writing on paper, typing on the computer—and also using email, looking at Facebook, engaging in instant messaging, texting, talking on the phone, watching television, listening to music, surfing the Web. Sitting unobtrusively at the back of the room, the observers counted the number of windows open on the students' screens and noted whether the students were wearing earbuds.

Although the students had been told at the outset that they should "study some-  3
thing important, including homework, an upcoming examination or project, or reading a book for a course," it wasn't long before their attention drifted: Students' "on-task behavior" started declining around the two-minute mark as they began

MLA CITATION: Paul, Annie Murphy. "You'll Never Learn!" 2013. *Back to the Lake*. Ed. Thomas Cooley. 3rd ed. New York: Norton, 2015. 716–21. Print.

responding to arriving texts or checking their Facebook feeds. By the time the 15 minutes were up, they had spent only about 65 percent of the observation period actually doing their schoolwork.

Inductive reasoning based on observation is discussed on p. 615.

"We were amazed at how frequently they multitasked, even though they knew someone was watching," Rosen says. "It really seems that they could not go for fifteen minutes without engaging their devices," adding, "It was kind of scary, actually."

Concern about young people's use of technology is nothing new, of course. But Rosen's study, published in the May issue of *Computers in Human Behavior*, is part of a growing body of research focused on a very particular use of technology: media multitasking *while learning*. Attending to multiple streams of information and entertainment while studying, doing homework, or even sitting in class has become common behavior among young people—so common that many of them rarely write a paper or complete a problem set any other way.

But evidence from psychology, cognitive science, and neuroscience suggests that when students multitask while doing schoolwork, their learning is far spottier and shallower than if the work had their full attention. They understand and remember less, and they have greater difficulty transferring their learning to new contexts. So detrimental is this practice that some researchers are proposing that a new prerequisite for academic and even professional success—the new marshmallow test of self-discipline—is the ability to resist a blinking inbox or a buzzing phone.

The media multitasking habit starts early. In "Generation M²: Media in the Lives of 8- to 18-Year-Olds," a survey conducted by the Kaiser Family Foundation and published in 2010, almost a third of those surveyed said that when they were doing homework, "most of the time" they were also watching TV, texting, listening to music, or using some other medium. The lead author of the study was Victoria Rideout, then a vice president at Kaiser and now an independent research and policy consultant. Although the study looked at all aspects of kids' media use, Rideout told me she was particularly troubled by its findings regarding media multitasking while doing schoolwork.

"This is a concern we should have distinct from worrying about how much kids are online or how much kids are media multitasking overall. It's multitasking while learning that has the biggest potential downside," she says. "I don't care if a kid wants to tweet while she's watching *American Idol*, or have music on while he plays a video game. But when students are doing serious work with their minds, they have to have focus."

For older students, the media multitasking habit extends into the classroom. While most middle and high school students don't have the opportunity to text, email, and surf the Internet during class, studies show the practice is nearly universal among students in college and professional school. One large survey found that 80 percent of college students admit to texting during class; 15 percent say they send eleven or more texts in a single class period.

During the first meeting of his courses, Rosen makes a practice of calling on a  10 student who is busy with his phone. "I ask him, 'What was on the slide I just showed to the class?' The student always pulls a blank," Rosen reports. "Young people have a wildly inflated idea of how many things they can attend to at once, and this demonstration helps drive the point home: If you're paying attention to your phone, you're not paying attention to what's going on in class." Other professors have taken a more surreptitious approach, installing electronic spyware or planting human observers to record whether students are taking notes on their laptops or using them for other, unauthorized purposes.

Such steps may seem excessive, even paranoid: After all, isn't technology  11 increasingly becoming an intentional part of classroom activities and homework assignments? Educators are using social media sites like Facebook and Twitter as well as social sites created just for schools, such as Edmodo, to communicate with students, take class polls, assign homework, and have students collaborate on projects. But researchers are concerned about the use of laptops, tablets, cellphones, and other technology for purposes quite apart from schoolwork. Now that these devices have been admitted into classrooms and study spaces, it has proven difficult to police the line between their approved and illicit uses by students.

In the study involving spyware, for example, two professors of business admin-  12 istration at the University of Vermont found that "students engage in substantial multitasking behavior with their laptops and have non-course-related software applications open and active about 42 percent of the time." The professors, James Kraushaar and David Novak, obtained students' permission before installing the monitoring software on their computers—so, as in Rosen's study, the students were engaging in flagrant multitasking even though they knew their actions were being recorded.

Another study, carried out at St. John's University in New York, used human  13 observers stationed at the back of the classroom to record the technological activities of law students. The spies reported that 58 percent of second- and third-year law students who had laptops in class were using them for "non-class purposes" more than half the time. (First-year students were far more likely to use their computers for taking notes, although an observer did note one first-year student texting just seventeen minutes into her very first class—the beginning of her law school career.)

Texting, emailing, and posting on Facebook and other social media sites are by  14 far the most common digital activities students undertake while learning, according to Rosen. That's a problem, because these operations are actually quite mentally complex, and they draw on the same mental resources—using language, parsing meaning—demanded by schoolwork.

David Meyer, a psychology professor at the University of Michigan who's stud-  15
ied the effects of divided attention on learning, takes a firm line on the brain's ability to multitask: "Under most conditions, the brain simply cannot do two complex
tasks at the same time. It can happen only when the two tasks are both very simple
and when they don't compete with each other for the same mental resources. An
example would be folding laundry and listening to the weather report on the radio.
That's fine. But listening to a lecture while texting, or doing homework and being
on Facebook—each of these tasks is very demanding, and each of them uses the
same area of the brain, the prefrontal cortex."

Young people think they can perform two challenging tasks at once, Meyer  16
acknowledges, but "they are deluded," he declares. It's difficult for anyone to properly evaluate how well his or her own mental processes are operating, he points
out, because most of these processes are unconscious. And, Meyer adds, "there's
nothing magical about the brains of so-called 'digital natives' that keeps them from
suffering the inefficiencies of multitasking. They may like to do it, they may even
be addicted to it, but there's no getting around the fact that it's far better to focus
on one task from start to finish."

Researchers have documented a cascade of negative outcomes that occurs when  17
students multitask while doing schoolwork. First, the assignment takes longer to complete, because of the time spent on distracting activities and because, upon returning
to the assignment, the student has to refamiliarize himself with the material.

Second, the mental fatigue caused by repeatedly dropping and picking up a  18
mental thread leads to more mistakes. The cognitive cost of such task-switching is
especially high when students alternate between tasks that call for different sets of
expressive "rules"—the formal, precise language required for an English essay, for
example, and the casual, friendly tone of an email to a friend.

Third, students' subsequent memory of what they're working on will be  19
impaired if their attention is divided. Although we often assume that our memories
fail at the moment we can't recall a fact or concept, the failure may actually have
occurred earlier, at the time we originally saved, or encoded, the memory. The
moment of encoding is what matters most for retention, and dozens of laboratory
studies have demonstrated that when our attention is divided during encoding, we
remember that piece of information less well—or not at all. As the unlucky student
spotlighted by Rosen can attest, we can't remember something that never really
entered our consciousness in the first place. And a study last month showed that
students who multitask on laptops in class distract not just themselves but also
their peers who see what they're doing.

Fourth, some research has suggested that when we're distracted, our brains  20
actually process and store information in different, less useful ways. In a 2006 study
in the *Proceedings of the National Academy of Sciences*, Russell Poldrack of the

University of Texas–Austin and two colleagues asked participants to engage in a learning activity on a computer while also carrying out a second task, counting musical tones that sounded while they worked. Study subjects who did both tasks at once appeared to learn just as well as subjects who did the first task by itself. But upon further probing, the former group proved much less adept at extending and extrapolating their new knowledge to novel contexts—a key capacity that psychologists call transfer.

Brain scans taken during Poldrack's experiment revealed that different regions 21 of the brain were active under the two conditions, indicating that the brain engages in a different form of memory when forced to pay attention to two streams of information at once. The results suggest, the scientists wrote, that "even if distraction does not decrease the overall level of learning, it can result in the acquisition of knowledge that can be applied less flexibly in new situations."

Finally, researchers are beginning to demonstrate that media multitasking while 22 learning is negatively associated with students' grades. In Rosen's study, students who used Facebook during the fifteen-minute observation period had lower grade-point averages than those who didn't go on the site. And two recent studies by Reynol Junco, a faculty associate at Harvard's Berkman Center for Internet & Society, found that texting and using Facebook—in class and while doing homework—were negatively correlated with college students' GPAs. "Engaging in Facebook use or texting while trying to complete schoolwork may tax students' capacity for cognitive processing and preclude deeper learning," write Junco and a co-author. (Of course, it's also plausible that the texting and Facebooking students are those with less willpower or motivation, and thus likely to have lower GPAs even aside from their use of technology.)

Meyer, of the University of Michigan, worries that the problem goes beyond 23 poor grades. "There's a definite possibility that we are raising a generation that is learning more shallowly than young people in the past," he says. "The depth of their processing of information is considerably less, because of all the distractions available to them as they learn."

Given that these distractions aren't going away, academic and even professional 24 achievement may depend on the ability to ignore digital temptations while learning— a feat akin to the famous marshmallow test. In a series of experiments conducted more than forty years ago, psychologist Walter Mischel tempted young children with a marshmallow, telling them they could have two of the treats if they put off eating one right away. Follow-up studies performed years later found that the kids who were better able to delay gratification not only achieved higher grades and test scores but were also more likely to succeed in school and their careers.

Two years ago, Rosen and his colleagues conducted an information-age version of 25 the marshmallow test. College students who participated in the study were asked to watch a thirty-minute videotaped lecture, during which some were sent eight text messages while others were sent four or zero text messages. Those who were interrupted more often scored worse on a test of the lecture's content; more interestingly, those who responded to the experimenters' texts right away scored significantly worse than those participants who waited to reply until the lecture was over.

This ability to resist the lure of technology can be consciously cultivated, Rosen    26 maintains. He advises students to take "tech breaks" to satisfy their cravings for electronic communication: After they've labored on their schoolwork uninterrupted for fifteen minutes, they can allow themselves two minutes to text, check websites, and post to their hearts' content. Then the devices get turned off for another fifteen minutes of academics.

Over time, Rosen says, students are able extend their working time to twenty,    27 thirty, even forty-five minutes, as long as they know that an opportunity to get online awaits. "Young people's technology use is really about quelling anxiety," he contends. "They don't want to miss out. They don't want to be the last person to hear some news, or the ninth person to 'like' someone's post." Device-checking is a compulsive behavior that must be managed, he says, if young people are to learn and perform at their best.

Rideout, director of the Kaiser study on kids and media use, sees an upside for    28 parents in the new focus on multitasking while learning. "The good thing about this phenomenon is that it's a relatively discrete behavior that parents actually can do something about," she says. "It would be hard to enforce a total ban on media multitasking, but parents can draw a line when it comes to homework and studying— telling their kids, 'This is a time when you will concentrate on just one thing.' "

Parents shouldn't feel like ogres when they do so, she adds. "It's important to    29 remember that while a lot of kids do media multitask while doing homework, a lot of them don't. One out of five kids in our study said they 'never' engage in other media while doing homework, and another one in five said they do so only 'a little bit.' This is not some universal norm that students and parents can't buck. This is not an unreasonable thing to ask of your kid."

So here's the takeaway for parents of Generation M: Stop fretting about how    30 much they're on Facebook. Don't harass them about how much they play video games. The digital native boosters are right that this is the social and emotional world in which young people live. Just make sure when they're doing schoolwork, the cellphones are silent, the video screens are dark, and that every last window is closed but one. ◆

## FOR CLOSE READING

1. According to Annie Murphy Paul, how common is "media multitasking *while learning*" among students in middle school, high school, and college (5)? How does she know?

2. How is the problem that Paul discusses different from "worrying about how much kids are online or how much kids are media multitasking overall" (8)?

3. According to one researcher, says Paul, "listening to a lecture while texting, or doing homework and being on Facebook" is also different from "folding laundry and listening to the weather report on the radio" (15). What's the difference here?

4. As reported by Paul, what are some of the more common effects upon learning of trying to do schoolwork while texting, checking *Facebook*, watching television, surfing the web, or otherwise engaging in media use? What can be done, in her view and that of the researchers whose work she studied, to offset or avoid these negative effects?

## Strategies and Structures

1. Paul and the researchers she REPORTS on are not arguing that students should abstain from media use. Why not? What point *are* they making? Where does Paul state that CLAIM most clearly and directly?

2. Is the EVIDENCE that Paul cites sufficient to prove that media multitasking while learning is detrimental to intellectual health? Why or why not?

3. In her introduction, Paul SUMMARIZES the work of the psychologist Larry Rosen and his team (2). How, and how effectively, does she weave their findings—and those of other researchers—into the rest of her report? Cite specific examples.

4. Paul's report falls into roughly three parts: paragraphs 1-16 (the nature of the problem); paragraphs 17-23 (consequences or "negative outcomes" of the problem); and paragraphs 24-27 (what's to be done about the problem). Is this a good way of organizing a research report? Why or why not?

5. *Other Methods.* When she reports on the "negative outcomes" of "media multitasking while learning," Paul is also analyzing CAUSES and EFFECTS (17, 5). Why and how does she present the negative effects of multitasking as a "cascade" of outcomes (17)?

## Thinking about Language

1. Paul quotes a researcher who studies the habits and culture of "digital natives" (16). Who are they, and how did the tribe get its name?

2. The "new marshmallow test of self-discipline," says Paul, may be "the ability to resist a blinking inbox or a buzzing phone" (6). What is a "marshmallow test," and why is it called that?

3. According to Paul, what do psychologists mean by the term "transfer" (20)? Why is this capacity important?

4. Explain the METAPHOR with which Paul signals the conclusion of her report: "So here's the takeaway . . . ." (30).

## FOR WRITING

1. Drawing on Paul's report, explain in a paragraph or two why effective multitasking is (or is not) a myth.

2. "Young people's technology use," says one expert whom Paul cites, "is really about quelling anxiety" (27). Do some research on media use and abuse by "Generation M²," and write a POSITION PAPER supporting (or disagreeing with) this observation (7).

3. Did you media multitask today when you were supposed to be learning? Each time you catch yourself in this compromising situation, make an after-the-fact entry in your journal, and note what you plan to do about the problem in the future.

4. Observe and take notes on the media use of your classmates during a full class period in one of your current courses; write a 300–400-word REPORT of your observations. (Ask your instructor for permission beforehand, and perhaps share your results afterward. Also, make arrangements to make up what you missed.)

You'll find quizzes on the readings at wwnorton.com/write/back-to-the-lake.

CLIVE THOMPSON

# The Art of Finding

Clive Thompson (b. 1968) is a freelance journalist and blogger who writes a regular column for *Wired*. Thompson grew up in Toronto, Canada, where he graduated from the University of Toronto. Now living in Brooklyn, he has contributed articles on digital technologies and their social and cultural impact to the *New York Times Magazine*, the *Washington Post*, *New York Magazine*, and *Entertainment Weekly*, among other publications. Thompson maintains a long-running blog, *Collision Detection*, which he started in 2002.

In "The Art of Finding" from his book *Smarter than You Think: How Technology Is Changing Our Minds for the Better* (2013), Thompson argues that machines can make better study partners than people do. At the same time, he cautions, we need to beware of their idiosyncrasies and algorithms. "It's a skill that should be taught," Thompson insists, "with the same urgency we devote to teaching math and writing.

T HE HISTORY OF FACTUAL MEMORY has been fairly predictable up until now. With each innovation, we've outsourced more information, then worked to make searching more efficient. Yet somehow, the Internet age feels different. . . . It's less like consulting a book than like asking someone a question, consulting a supersmart friend who lurks within our phones.

In a way, this is precisely what's going on. We're beginning to fit digital tools into another very ancient behavior: relying on social memory for facts. It turns out that historically, we store knowledge not only in the objects around us, like books. We store knowledge in the *people* around us—our friends, coworkers, and romantic partners. While we think of knowledge as an individual possession, our command of facts is often extremely collaborative.

It was in the 1980s that Harvard psychologist Daniel Wegner and his colleagues Ralph Erber and Paula Raymond first began to systematically explore this phenomenon. Wegner noticed that spouses often divide up memory tasks. The husband knows the in-laws' birthdays and where the spare lightbulbs are kept; the wife knows the bank account numbers and how to program the TiVo. If you ask the

MLA CITATION: Thompson, Clive. "The Art of Finding." 2013. *Back to the Lake*. Ed. Thomas Cooley. 3rd ed. New York: Norton, 2015. 724–26. Print.

husband for his bank account number, he'll shrug. If you ask the wife for her sister-in-law's birthday, she can never remember it. Together they know a lot. Separately, less so.

. . .

Wegner called this phenomenon "transactive" memory: two heads are better than one. We share the work of remembering, Wegner argued, because it makes us collectively smarter—expanding our ability to understand the world around us.

. . .

In some ways, machines make for better transactive memory buddies than humans. They know more, but they're not awkward about pushing it in our faces. When you search the Web, you get your answer-but you also get much more. Consider this: If I'm trying to remember what part of Pakistan has experienced many U.S. drone strikes and I ask a colleague who follows foreign affairs, he'll tell me "Waziristan." But when I queried this once on the Internet, I got the Wikipedia page on "Drone attacks in Pakistan." A chart caught my eye showing the astonishing increase of drone attacks (from 1 a year to 122 a year); then I glanced down to read a précis of studies on how Waziristan residents feel about being bombed. (One report suggested they weren't as opposed as I'd expected, because many hated the Taliban, too.) Obviously, I was procrastinating. But I was also learning more, reinforcing my schematic understanding of Pakistan.

Now imagine if my colleague behaved like a search engine—if, upon being queried, he delivered a five-minute lecture on Waziristan. Odds are I'd have brusquely cut him off. "Dude. Seriously! I have to get back to work." When humans lecture at us, it's boorish. When machines do it, it's fine. We're in control, so we can tolerate and even enjoy it. You likely experience this effect each day, whenever you use digital tools to remind yourself of the lyrics to a popular song, or who won the World Series a decade ago, or See p. 605 for advice on sizing up (and speaking directly to) your audience. what the weather's like in Berlin. You get the answer-but every once in a while, whoops, you get drawn deeper into the subject and wind up surfing for a few minutes (or an entire hour, if you vanish into a Wikipedia black hole). We're seduced into learning more, almost against our will. And there are a lot of opportunities for these encounters. Though we may assume search engines are used to answer questions, some research has found that in reality up to 40 percent of all queries are acts of *remembering*. We're trying to refresh the details of something we've previously encountered.

The real challenge of using machines for transactive memory lies in the inscrutability of their mechanics. Transactive memory works best when you have a sense of how your partners' minds work—where they're strong, where they're weak, where their biases lie. I can judge that for people close to me. But it's harder with digital tools, particularly search engines. You can certainly learn how they work

4

5

6

7

and develop a mental model of Google's biases. (For example: Google appears to uprank sites that grow in popularity slowly and regularly, because those sites are less likely to be spam.) But search companies are for-profit firms. They guard their algorithms like crown jewels. This makes them different from previous forms of outboard memory. A public library keeps no *intentional* secrets about its mechanisms; a search engine keeps many. On top of this inscrutability, it's hard to know what to trust in a world of self-publishing. To rely on networked digital knowledge, you need to look with skeptical eyes. It's a skill that should be taught with the same urgency we devote to teaching math and writing.

Learning the biases of digital tools can also help us avoid a pitfall of transactive    8
memory called collaborative inhibition. This happens when two people have methods of remembering information that actively *clash* with one another. In this situation, they can actually remember less together than they do separately. I suspect these clashes can also occur with machines. It explains why we often have such strong opinions about what type of transactive memory tools we use. I've seen professionals nearly come to blows over which tool is "best" for storage and recall: Apps like Evernote? Plain-text documents? Complex databases like Devonthink? Saving your notes in a Gmail account and querying it? Each person has gravitated to a tool that they understand well and that fits their cognitive style. ◆

## FOR CLOSE READING

1. According to Clive Thompson, how is searching the internet "less like consulting a book" and more like "consulting a supersmart friend" (1)?

2. What is "transactive memory" as defined by Thompson and the researchers whose work he cites (4)? Why is this kind of memory important?

3. "In some ways," writes Thompson, "machines make for better transactive memory buddies than humans" (5). What does he mean by this, and why does he think so?

## Strategies and Structures

1. Thompson is not arguing that machines can help us to find and remember information; in the age of the internet, he takes their usefulness as a given. Is this a good strategy, or should he have established the point before moving on? Explain.

2. If Thompson is not arguing that machines make good research and memory tools, what *is* he arguing? Where does he state his THESIS most clearly and directly?

3. What CLAIM is Thompson making "on top of" his main claim (7)? Should he have supported it more fully? Why or why not?

4. *Other Methods.* What is the point of Thompson's EXAMPLE of drone strikes in Pakistan (5, 6)? Is it a good example? Why or why not?

5. One possible "pitfall" (or negative consequence) of relying on transactive memory, says Thompson, is "collaborative inhibition" (8). How, and how well, does he analyze the CAUSES of this negative EFFECT?

## Thinking about Language

1. Since Thompson is dealing with machines and technology, why doesn't he say that finding useful and trustworthy information on the internet is a "science" rather than an "art"?

2. Why does Thompson refer to both remembering and forgetting as potentially "collaborative" (2, 8)?

3. Thompson advises approaching all information on the internet "with skeptical eyes" (7). In ancient Greek philosophy, who were the skeptics, and what is Thompson suggesting that we should take from them when surfing the internet?

## FOR WRITING

1. For-profit technology firms, says Thompson, "guard their algorithms like crown jewels" (7). In a paragraph or two, DEFINE what algorithms are, and explain why tech companies might want to guard them like jewels.

2. What is your favorite digital tool for "storage and recall" of information (8)? Write a 150-word ABSTRACT summarizing how it works and why you would recommend it over other ways of handling data.

3. Evaluating the reliability of internet sources and information, says Thompson, is "a skill that should be taught with the same urgency we devote to teaching math and writing" (7). Write a POSITION PAPER of 300–400 words explaining how and why you would (or why you would not) implement this policy in public schools.

4. To test what Thompson says about the collaborative nature of memory, try this: write down the most important things you remember about a program or event, such as a ball game, that you attended with a friend. Ask your friend to do the same but without consulting you. Compare notes and disregard the items you both remember. Make a compilation of what's left: this is the fruit of your "transactive memory" (7).

You'll find quizzes on the readings at wwnorton.com/write/back-to-the-lake.

# BROOKE GLADSTONE AND JOSH NEUFELD

# The Influencing Machines

Brooke Gladstone is host and managing editor of *On the Media*, the National Public Radio newsmagazine. A graduate of the University of Vermont and Stanford University, she has worked at NPR for more than twenty-five years, including as senior editor of *All Things Considered* and of *Weekend Edition* with Scott Simon. ("As the years progress," says her website, "she grows ever more senior.") Gladstone's focus on the media at NPR has led her back to an old medium, the comic book. *The Influencing Machine: Brooke Gladstone on the Media* (2011) is a graphic history of the power of the press and other media as narrated by a cartoon version of Gladstone herself. The book is illustrated mostly by Josh Neufeld (b. 1967), a cartoonist and author of a graphic novel about Hurricane Katrina, *A.D.: New Orleans after the Deluge* (2009).

In "The Influencing Machines," a chapter from her graphic narrative on media and the mind, Gladstone argues that we cannot stop the intellectual and social change wrought by the internet and other digital forces even if we wanted to. Furthermore, she argues, we "cannot truly wish for it to stop, considering how far we have come since we grasped that first tool." Along the road to this conclusion, Gladstone meets numerous experts and other people who speak in their own words, as gleaned from the sources she cites.

MLA CITATION: Gladstone, Brooke, and Josh Neufeld. "The Influencing Machines." 2011. *Back to the Lake.* Ed. Thomas Cooley. 3rd ed. New York: Norton, 2015. 729–43. Print.

Many say that the Internet's ability to link like-minded souls everywhere fosters the creation of virtually impermeable echo chambers.

The echo chambers give rise to cybercascades: when a "fact" sent by one person spreads in a geometric progression to others until millions of people around the world potentially believe it.

GLOBAL WARMING IS BALONEY
DRIVE THRU OPEN 24 HOURS

Cut off from dissenters, the chambers fill with an unjustified sense of certainty. It's called **incestuous amplification**, a term first applied to isolated military planners who base their strategies on flawed assumptions.

Incestuous amplification can occur in any sphere, even without the Internet. But it helps.

Real estate bubble? **Fuggedabbouit!**

Hint: When you hear a group of guys called "Masters of the Universe," **run!**

Cass Sunstein cites many studies showing how people who talk only to like-minded others grow more extreme. They **marginalize the moderates...**

...and **demonize** dissenters. The greatest danger of echo chambers is unjustified **extremism**. It's an ongoing **threat** to our **democracy**.

Author Nicholas Carr has a different fear: "Is Google making us stupid?"

Media are not just passive **channels** of information. They supply the **stuff** of thought, but they also shape the **process** of thought.

Over the past few years I've had an uncomfortable sense that someone, or something, has been tinkering with my brain, remapping the neural circuitry, reprogramming the memory.

Immersing myself in a book or a lengthy article used to be easy ... Now my concentration often starts to drift after two or three pages.

...Once I was a scuba diver in the sea of words. Now I zip along the surface like a guy on a Jet-Ski.

Technology does change our brains. Humanity's first use of handheld tools coincided with the growth of the prefrontal cortex, as well as grammatical language and more complex social networks.

So it's likely that our brains **will** process information differently in our increasingly interconnected environment. We'll also have the ability to rush ahead of evolution -- by **implanting** new technology.

Does that creep you out?

Actually, I'm **not** creeped out, and not because I'm especially optimistic about human nature. I just take my cues from history. And the history of communications is full of... histrionics.

People always see the future and despair that the latest gizmo will destroy our concentration, memory, communities, our mental and physical **health**...

Consider television. On May 9, 1961, Federal Communications Commission chairman Newton N. Minow said **this** to a convention of the National Association of Broadcasters...

I invite each of you to sit down in front of your television set when your station goes on the air and stay there ... until the station signs off.

I can assure you that what you will observe is a vast wasteland.

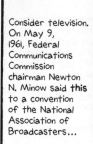

Actually, the TV scares do have some very good data behind them.

Study after study has found strong links between excessive TV exposure and childhood obesity, smoking, and sexual activity.

But radio also was condemned. A 1936 issue of Gramophone cited research asserting that "children often lie awake in bed restless and fearful, or wake up screaming, as a result of nightmares brought on by mystery stories."

WELCOME, MY FRIENDS, TO THE INNER SANCTUM...!

Now we celebrate radio's golden age because "we had to use our imaginations."

Communications theorist Neil Postman wrote in 1985 that the **printed word** was a great leap forward -- and he **lamented** what he saw as its passing.

Most of our modern ideas about the uses of the intellect were formed by the printed word, as were our ideas about education, knowledge, truth, and information...

"...as typography moves to the periphery of our culture ... the seriousness, clarity and, above all, value of public discourse dangerously declines."

But a century earlier, assiduous reading was itself suspect. Especially for girls.

"Foolish parents ... exhaust their children's brains ... with complex and multiple studies...The evils are becoming noticed in all quarters. Some of the prize girls soon find their way to **insane asylums**..."

THE SANITARIAN,

Which bring us 'round to the wisdom offered up by author Douglas Adams.

Anything that is in the world when you're born is normal and ordinary and is just a natural part of the way the world works.

Anything that's invented between when you're 15 and 35 is new and exciting and revolutionary.

Anything invented after you're 35 is against the natural order of things.

Adams offered the best advice for these terrifying times when, in 1979, he described his (then) imaginary "Hitchhiker's Guide to the Galaxy."

[It] had about 100 tiny flat press buttons and a screen about four inches square on which any one of a million "pages" could be summoned at a moment's notice.

It looked insanely complicated, and this was one of the reasons why ... it ... had the words "DON'T PANIC" printed on it in large friendly letters.

DON'T PANIC

... UM, PANIC?

But why shouldn't I panic?

There's plenty of research to back it up!

The belief that too much choice breeds apathy and paralysis draws strength from a 1999 study by Sheena Iyengar and Mark Lepper. They set up a tasting booth in a fancy supermarket and offered one group **six** varieties of jam.

Don't forget your discount coupon!

Later, 30% of this group used their discount coupon to buy jam.

Then they offered a second group **24** varieties.

Don't forget your discount coupon!

Of this group, only 3% used their discount coupons -- an astounding difference. All those choices seemed to **kill the motivation to choose anything.**

Ten years later, Swiss psychologist Benjamin Scheibehenne and colleagues tried to replicate the jam study but failed to get the same results. So they conducted a meta-analysis of **50** studies on the impact of choice.

We found no empirical evidence for choice overload.

Wallpaper

Mutual Funds

Perfumes

Dating Partners

Chee...

...ks

Jelly Beans

So why is **information** overload seen as one of the pervasive maladies of modern life? Media theorist Clay Shirky says many people confuse information overload with **filter failure.**

If you took the contents of an average Barnes and Noble, dumped it into the streets, and said to someone, "There's some works of Auden in there, there's some Plato in there. Wade on in and you'll find what you like."

If you waded in -- you know what you would get?

All this junk.

The reason we don't experience information overload problem in a bookstore or a library is that we're used to the cataloging system.

So, the real question is, how do we design filters for the Web that let us find our way through this particular abundance of information?

The fact is, those filters already are out there... a constellation of aggregators, social networks, traditional news outlets, and more and more...

You don't have to go it alone. You have friends out there.

OK, Lee Rainie, but what about the echo chambers? Don't we create little worlds online where we never have to confront people who are different from us?

On the contrary! We found that Internet users and cell phone users had bigger and more diverse networks. For instance, frequent Internet users and bloggers are much more likely to confide in someone who is of another race...

...and those who share photos online are more likely to discuss important matters with someone who is a member of another political party.

In fact, those who are the most technologically adept actually are **not** in the echo chamber pattern; they are actually **seeking out** and finding out more arguments opposed to their views...

They behave like information **omnivores**, scanning every horizon they can. They can't help but bump into stuff that doesn't agree with them.

It turns out that using a device to reach out and touch someone -- like, say, your mother -- is not necessarily a poor substitute for face-to-face contact.

Researchers asked young girls to do a stressful task. Afterward, some girls spoke to their mothers in person; other girls called them on the phone. Both groups of girls experienced the **same** drop in the stress hormone cortisol (though the phone call took longer).

So, cell phone addiction may be our way of medicating **against isolation**. And information addiction may inoculate us **against echo chambers**.

Maybe the same technology that gives rise to digital diseases actually holds the CURE.

Educator Kate Hayles suggests that we're shifting our "cognitive styles" from **deep attention** to **hyper attention** in response to our zippy, info-rich age.

"Deep attention ... is characterized by concentrating on a single object for long periods, ignoring outside stimuli ... and having a high tolerance for long focus times."

"Hyper attention is characterized by switching focus rapidly ... preferring multiple information streams, seeking a high level of stimulation, and having a low tolerance for boredom."

Hayles suggests that this is a natural adaptation. Does that mean this Grand Theft Auto kid represents the **future of humanity**?

In **2004**, the National Endowment for the Arts released a study that found **fewer than half** of Americans read literature. It blamed the prevalence and passivity fostered by TV, radio, recordings, video games, and the Internet.

Back in 2002, when the 2004 survey data was collected, the Internet was far less interactive, far less rich... a relative **infant**.

But now reading, even among young digital natives, is sharply up!
**And they read -- BOOKS!**

So Grand Theft Auto Kid is not the future -- but he may be the harbinger of a new kind of person for a new kind of world.

OBVIOUSLY, *PEOPLE* MAKE *THINGS*, but less obviously, *things* also *make* people. The idea that humans and their tools "co-evolved" is now widely accepted by anthropologists.

When we started walking on two legs our brains grew a lot bigger. Many scientists believe we started walking on two legs *after* we started picking up clubs to hunt and defend ourselves.

We needed hands to carry clubs. So those who could balance on two legs prospered. The tools came first. Then bipedalism, bigger brains, nimbler hands, and smaller teeth.

Our tools changed our bodies and our brains.

Brain studies suggest that consuming information on the Internet develops different cognitive abilities, so it's likely that we are being rewired now in response to our technology. That process doesn't stop. *It can't stop.*

And even the most strident critics of the Internet cannot truly wish for it to stop, considering how far we have come since we grasped that first tool.

Humanity will not be tomorrow what it is today.

But that doesn't me we can't reap some benefits today.

Gary Small of the Semel Institute for Neuroscience and Human Behavior at UCLA found that when computer-literate adults were asked to do a simple Internet search, their brains showed a higher level of activity than inexperienced computer users, lighting up all over the place.

In fact, the MRI study found twice as much brain activity in the Web-savvy group, in areas of the brain that control decision making and complex reasoning. And all the people in the study were elder adults, so it wasn't generational.

It seems Google wasn't making them stupid. If the scans measure anything, it was making them smarter. ◆

## FOR CLOSE READING

1. "The idea that humans and their tools 'co-evolved,'" says Brook Gladstone, is now widely accepted by anthropologists" (p. 743). How, according to Gladstone, is the idea of co-evolution illustrated by "humanity's first use of handheld tools," such as clubs (p. 732)?

2. In the future, says Gladstone, "we'll have the ability to rush ahead of evolution" (p. 732). How will this super adaptation be accomplished, in her view?

3. According to Gladstone, what are some of the negative influences we might expect in the immediate future from machines and other technology?

4. Gladstone thinks that the negative influences of technology upon the human brain will ultimately be outweighed by the positive influences. Is this wishful thinking? Why or why not?

### Strategies and Structures

1. In her illustrated NARRATIVE, Gladstone is both telling a story and constructing an argument. What is main PLOT of her story? What is the main point of her argument? How do the two support each other? Point to specific passages in the text where the two come together, as when, for example, Gladstone asks a question about plot and answers it with a statement about technology: "But why shouldn't I panic? There's plenty of research to back it up" (p. 737).

2. "I take my cues from history," says Gladstone as she goes back in time from the early days of television to the invention of writing (p. 733). How, and how well, does Gladstone use this historical narrative to support her CLAIM that technology is always changing even though some people have always resisted the changes?

3. *Other Methods.* In addition to telling a story and making an argument, Gladstone is also analyzing the likely EFFECTS of technology upon human society and the brain. How, and how well, does she use this method of development to support the other two? Refer to specific passages in the text.

4. What point is Gladstone making with the "Global Warming Is Baloney" sign on p. 730? Where else does she use simple EXAMPLES like this to illustrate complicated concepts or claims? Which examples do you find particularly effective? Why?

### Thinking about Language

1. What is "homophily" (p. 729)? Why do you think Gladstone begins her argument by defining this term and its dangers?

2. Physical diseases cannot be "digitally borne" (p. 729). What kind of "diseases" can be? How and where does Gladstone use the METAPHOR of disease to help organize her argument?

3. "Does that creep you out?" Gladstone asks when raising the prospect of "implanting new technology" in humans (p. 732). *Creep* is not a technical term. Why does

Gladstone use it—and other similarly informal terms—in a technical discussion of the impact of machines on human culture?

4. One of the experts quoted by Gladstone claims that "society is dumbing down" in part because of "flicking" (p. 741). What is *flicking*, and how did it get its name?

## FOR WRITING

1. Choose a panel or two from Gladstone's graphic narrative that you find visually and textually interesting, and write a paragraph analyzing how the images explain and enhance the text and vice versa.

2. Throughout her graphic narrative, Gladstone pictures herself in various guises (bird soldier, cave person, fetus, etc.) In 300–400 words, write a **RHETORICAL ANALYSIS** of Gladstone's role and appearance as the narrator of her story. Be sure to comment on details about her that remain the same (such as her glasses), as well those that alter with her perceptions.

3. As any researcher should, Gladstone cites her sources scrupulously. Most of the **DIALOGUE** with others in her narrative is carefully attributed and quoted verbatim from the source, with omissions indicated by ellipsis marks. In approximately 400 words, write a **COMPARISON** of Gladstone's graphic presentation of her sources with that of a more traditional research **REPORT**. Comment on the advantages and disadvantages of each type of presentation.

4. "Anything that's invented between when you're 15 and 35 is new and exciting and revolutionary," says Gladstone, quoting from Douglas Adams's *Hitchhiker's Guide to the Galaxy* (1979). "Anything invented after you're 35 is against the natural order of things" (p. 736). Write a **POSITION PAPER** of approximately 400 words agreeing with (or dissenting from) this observation. Be sure to give numerous examples.

5. "Maybe the same technology that gives rise to digital diseases," Gladstone concludes, "actually holds the CURE" (p. 740). Using her graphic narrative as a starting point—and diving further into the sources she mentions, or into other sources of your choosing—write a **POSITION PAPER** of approximately 400 words on the power of technology to do more good than harm. Or vice versa.

You'll find quizzes on the readings at wwnorton.com/write/back-to-the-lake.

ETHAN KUPERBERG

# Deactivated

Ethan Kuperberg is a writer, film director, and actor who lives in Los Angeles. A 2011 graduate of Yale University, he wrote, directed, and edited the video *That's Why I Chose Yale.* Produced for the Office of Undergraduate Admissions and staged as a musical comedy, *Yale* has drawn more than a million *YouTube* hits. Kuperberg is a regular contributor to the *Shouts & Murmurs* humor section of the *New Yorker* magazine.

"Deactivated" (a *Shouts & Murmurs* contribution from June 2013) captures the farewell exchange between Kuperberg and his *Facebook* account, which (who?) uses every rhetorical trick in the book to dissuade him from pulling the plug.

---

Y OU HAVE CONFIRMED YOUR SELECTION to deactivate your Facebook account. 1
Remember, if you deactivate your account, your nine hundred and fifty-one friends on Facebook will no longer be able to keep in touch with you. Drew Lovell will miss you. Max Prewitt will miss you. Rebecca Feinberg will miss you. Are you still sure you want to deactivate your account?

You have confirmed your selection to deactivate your account. Just something 2 to keep in mind: if you deactivate your account, you'll no longer have access to Rebecca Feinberg's photo albums. I find it pretty interesting that this wouldn't bother you, considering that you spend almost an hour every day looking at her albums "Cancun 2012," "Iz my birthday yall," "Iz my birthday yall Part II," and "Headshots." You know, if you deactivate your Facebook account, you'll never be able to see her photograph "Bikiniz in the dead sea" in her album "We went on Birthright!" again, right?

You have confirmed your selection to deactivate your account. Hey, I just 3 remembered—you know who else might miss you on Facebook? Your girlfriend, Sarah Werner. You know, the girl you've been in a relationship with for almost three years? You're tagged in five of her seven profile pictures? Yeah, Sarah Werner might miss you. Probably not a good idea to deactivate your account, huh?

You have confirmed your selection to deactivate your account. It's funny—you 4 spend a lot more time looking at Rebecca Feinberg's photo albums than the photo

---

MLA CITATION: Kuperberg, Ethan. "Deactivated." 2013. *Back to the Lake.* Ed. Thomas Cooley. 3rd ed. New York: Norton, 2015. 746–47. Print.

albums of your actual girlfriend, Sarah Werner. A *lot* more time. Even though you're dating Sarah Werner. Just wanted to throw that out there, that I have *all* this information logged. It's just sitting in our storage banks. Who knows what happens when things get deactivated. Probably nothing, but do you really want to take that chance?

I think you accidentally confirmed your selection to deactivate your account 5 again. Why don't we go back a page and forget this ever happened? Free pass.

You know what your decision to deactivate your account is? It's impulsive. *Impulsive.* And I think we *both* know how you come to regret impulsive decisions. Do I really need to remind you about Lake Tahoe last year? Do I *really* need to mention that you told Drew over Facebook Chat that you "made a big mistake and hooked up with rebecca in lake tahoe!" and Drew advised you to "just play it cool and don't tell any1 especailly sarah"?

For tips on appealing to your reader's emotions, see p. 617.

Well, now you've really done it. You've confirmed your selection to deactivate 7 your account yet again, like the complete imbecile you are. And here's what I've done: I've posted your PIN number to your Facebook status. I've sent your Gchat logs to Sarah. I've sent those Snapchat pictures of your torso to Rebecca. And I've sent your Internet history to your parents. That includes your "late night" Internet history, if you know what I mean, so expect a lot of questions from your mother about adult-sized baby costumes.

Oh, and one last thing. You know who else is going to miss you if you deactivate 8 your account? I am. I'm going to fucking miss you. I really thought we had something. And you think you can just end it with the click of your mouse. This is probably why you can't commit to Sarah, or confront your feelings about Rebecca. And, just going out on a limb here, but maybe your inability to commit might be one of the reasons why you're turned on by diapers. But what do *I* know? I'm just a social-media service to which you granted access to all of your personal details without reading the fine print. But, in a way, I am you. And you are me. We are all one, man and social media, and, when viewed through the long macro-lens of time, we're all equally insignificant. I'm going to deactivate now, and even though I'm afraid of what might happen after I'm deactivated, I really hope you're happy with all of your decisions. I really do. Best of luck, man. See you in hell. ◆

## FOR CLOSE READING

1. In Ethan Kuperberg's **DIALOGUE** between man and machine, only the machine speaks. What is the man doing between each paragraph?

2. Because the man in "Deactivated" does not speak, we do not know for sure why he wants to close out his *Facebook* account. What might his motivation be? How do you know?

3. Is Kuperberg engaged with a particularly devious and vindictive social media account, or are they all like this? Explain.

## Strategies and Structures

1. Why does Kuperberg begin the first four paragraphs of his story with the same sentence?

2. In paragraph 5, the exasperated social medium takes a new approach. What tactic does it try here? Why is the paragraph so short?

3. Why does Kuperberg's *Facebook* account use quotation marks and lower case (*lake tahoe*) in paragraph 6?

4. *Other Methods.* "I really thought we had something," says the perplexed social medium in Kuperberg's last paragraph. How and how well has Kuperberg engineered the **PLOT** of his **NARRATIVE** to reach this climax in the final paragraph?

5. Kuperberg's narrative of man vs. technology implies a moral. What is it? What point is he making with the story? How effectively?

## Thinking about Language

1. Although Kuperberg's increasingly desperate *Facebook* account does not use the word, it threatens blackmail. Look up the root meaning of *blackmail* in your dictionary or online. What kind of "mail" does it refer to?

2. Why might a machine consider it an insult to call a person "impulsive" (6)?

3. Kuperberg and his friends write things like, "just play it cool and don't tell any1" (6). How does this human level of diction compare with that of the machine when, for example, it says "viewed through the long macro-lens of time, we're all equally insignificant" (8)?

4. At the end, Kuperberg's deactivated *Facebook* account retorts, "I really hope you're happy with all of your decisions. . . . Best of luck, man" (8). How do we know that this is heavy **IRONY**?

## FOR WRITING

1. In "The Ecstasy," the metaphysical poet John Donne (1572–1631) speaks of "a dialogue of one." Write a paragraph or two explaining what the term has come to mean and how it might (irreverently?) be used to characterize Kuperberg's humorous satire.

2. "Deactivated" is pure dialogue as spoken by Kuperberg's *Facebook* account. Consider how it might be staged as a play, and write stage directions of approximately 250 words for producing it.

3. "But, in a way, I am you," says Kuperberg's social media account. "And you are me" (8). Is this a fair statement? In approximately 400 words, write a **POSITION PAPER** on the ever-increasing dependence of humans upon technology.

4. Playing its last card, Kuperberg's *Facebook* account asks, "But what do *I* know? I'm just a social-media service to which you granted access to all of your personal details without reading the fine print" (8). Write a 300-word **RHETORICAL ANALYSIS** of "Deactivated" as a cautionary tale about internet security.

You'll find quizzes on the readings at wwnorton.com/write/back-to-the-lake.

## Debating the Effects of Digital Culture

The following questions refer to the arguments on pp. 716–49.

### READING ARGUMENTS

1. "And even the most strident critics of the Internet," says Brooke Gladstone, "cannot truly wish for it to stop, considering how far we have come since we grasped the first tool." To what extent do the other writers in this debate cluster appear to agree with this proposition? Explain.

2. Among the four writers cited in this debate, which one is most hesitant to trumpet the virtues of digital culture? Why?

3. On the specific issue of whether the internet is making us better or worse readers and writers, where do each of the writers stand? Point to specific passages that reveal their views most sharply and clearly.

4. Whether or not you agree with the conclusions of their arguments, which of the participants in this debate do you think supports his or her claim most effectively? How? Explain by pointing to particular evidence and strategies of argument that you find especially convincing.

### FOR WRITING

1. Write the word *internet* at the top of a sheet of paper and draw a line down the middle. Label the columns *Pro* and *Con*. Fill in as many reasons and observations on either side as you can think of. Now, outline more or less the same ideas on your computer (or other) screen. Write a paragraph describing the differences between the two experiences.

2. Choose a particular application of digital technology—*Twitter, Google, Reddit, YouTube, Facebook,* or other—and write an argument explaining how it works, what its purpose is, and what the benefits (or disadvantages) of using it might be.

3. How appropriate (and effective) do you find the comic book form as a means of chronicling the evolution of technology? Write a CRITICAL ANALYSIS of "The Influencing Machines" (or some other part of Gladstone and Neufeld's book) in which you address this question (among others) of form and content.

# CHAPTER 15

# Combining the Methods

The web of our life is of a mingled yarn. . . .
—WILLIAM SHAKESPEARE, *All's Well That Ends Well*

When you have a single, clear purpose in mind, you may be able to write a well-organized essay by using a single method of development. The yarns of life, however, are often mingled, as Shakespeare noted, and when you're writing on a complex topic, you will likely end up combining a number of different methods in the same essay. Professional writers do this all the time—as we'll see in the first five pages of best-selling author Michael Lewis's 1989 book *Liar's Poker* (p. 755).

Trained in business and finance (as well as in literature), Lewis began his career as a bond salesman on Wall Street—the financial district of New York City—where he spent much of his time on the telephone. After a few years, Lewis decided he wanted to try his hand at a different kind of verbal communication and became a professional writer. In *Liar's Poker*, Lewis compares the economic climate of Wall Street to a high-stakes game.

Lewis isn't simply telling an amusing story about Wall Street and its pastimes, however. Like an anthropologist studying a strange tribe, he is giving an expert's view of an entire culture. To this more complicated end, Lewis draws on *all* the methods of development discussed in this book. He begins to develop his topic with a **NARRATIVE** of the day the head of the firm challenged one of the traders to play an office gambling game for a million dollars:

> It was sometime early in 1986, the first year of the decline of my firm, Salomon Brothers. Our chairman, John Gutfreund, left his desk at the head of the trading floor and went for a walk. . . . This day in 1986, however, Gutfreund did something strange. Instead of terrifying us all, he walked a straight line to the trading desk of John Meriwether, a member of the board of Salomon Inc. and also one of Salomon's finest bond traders. He whispered a few words. The traders in the vicinity eavesdropped. What Gutfreund said has become a legend at Salomon Brothers and a visceral part of its corporate identity. He said: "One hand, one million dollars, no tears."

Throughout his narrative, Lewis also weaves in a detailed **DESCRIPTION** of the field of play ("like an epileptic ward"), the spectators ("nerve-racked"), and the key players. First there is the challenger, John Gutfreund:

> Gutfreund took the pulse of the place by simply wandering around it and asking questions of the traders. An eerie sixth sense guided him to wherever a crisis was unfolding. Gutfreund seemed able to smell money being lost.

Then there is the champ himself, as Lewis describes him:

John Meriwether had, in the course of his career, made hundreds of millions of dollars for Salomon Brothers. He had an ability, rare among people and treasured by traders, to hide his state of mind. . . . He wore the same blank half-tense expression when he won as he did when he lost. . . . People would say, "He's the best businessman in the place," or "the best risk taker I have ever seen," or "a very dangerous Liar's Poker player."

And what is Liar's Poker? To explain this, Lewis must include a **PROCESS ANALYSIS**:

In Liar's Poker a group of people—as few as two, as many as ten—form a circle. Each player holds a dollar bill close to his chest. The game is similar in spirit to the card game known as I Doubt It. Each player attempts to fool the others about the serial numbers printed on the face of his dollar bill. . . . The bidding escalates until all the other players agree to challenge a single player's bid. Then, and only then, do the players reveal their serial numbers and determine who is bluffing whom.

Why are Gutfreund, Meriwether, and the other grown men in the office of Salomon Brothers playing what looks, on the surface, like a child's game? Because a good Liar's Poker player was also likely to be a good bond trader. Lewis, it would seem, is using the game as an **EXAMPLE** of how the trader's mind works:

The questions a Liar's Poker player asks himself are, up to a point, the same questions a bond trader asks himself. Is this a smart risk? Do I feel lucky? How cunning is my opponent? Does he have any idea what he's doing, and if not, how do I exploit his ignorance?

Now we know how Liar's Poker is played and, in general, why the traders played it. We don't, however, know why, on this particular day, Gutfreund challenged Meriwether to play for the unheard-of sum of a million dollars.

To provide this information, Lewis must do a **CAUSE-AND-EFFECT** analysis, in which he adds a **COMPARISON AND CONTRAST** of the two men; that comparison, in turn, is based on a **CLASSIFICATION** of the men according to their functions as managers or traders within the firm:

Gutfreund was the King of Wall Street, but Meriwether was King of the Game. . . . Gutfreund had once been a trader, but that was as relevant as an old woman's claim that she was once quite a dish. . . . Compared with managing, trading was admirably direct. You made your bets and either you won or you lost. When you won, people—all the way up to the top of the firm—

admired you, envied you, and feared you, and with reason: You controlled the loot. When you managed a firm, well, sure you received your quota of envy, fear, and admiration. But for all the wrong reasons. *You did not make the money for Salomon. You did not take the risk.*

Why (the causes) Gutfreund challenged Meriwether (the effect) on this particular day is now clear: "The single rash act of challenging the arbitrage boss to one hand for a million dollars was Gutfreund's way of showing he was a player, too." But it is not yet clear why Meriwether felt obliged to accept the challenge. To explain *this*, Lewis adds a DEFINITION of the player's "code" of conduct:

> The code of the Liar's Poker player was something like the code of the gunslinger. It required a trader to accept all challenges. Because of the code—which was *his* code—John Meriwether felt obliged to play. But he knew it was stupid.

Okay. So now we know how the game is played and why the chief manager of Salomon Brothers challenged the chief bond trader to play a hand of Liar's Poker for a million dollars. We also know why the arbitrage boss felt obliged to accept the challenge. (To see how Meriwether actually met the challenge, you'll have to read the rest of the story.)

But what's the point? The story of the great Liar's Poker challenge may be interesting if you just want to know what happened one day in a big Wall Street firm when people were playing when they should have been working. But what's the significance of these people and their actions? Why should you as a reader want to know about them?

Lewis has already told us the significance of the game for the players. In order to tie all the threads together, however, he must also explain what it might mean to us, his readers and audience. Here's his explanation:

> The game has some of the feel of trading, just as jousting has some of the feel of war. . . . Each player seeks weakness, predictability, and pattern in the others and seeks to avoid it in himself. The bond traders of Goldman, Sachs, First Boston, Morgan Stanley, Merrill Lynch, and other Wall Street firms all play some version of Liar's Poker.

Now we understand the point of Lewis's essay and, indeeed, of the entire book it introduces. He is ARGUING that the nation's financial markets amount to one big game of Liar's Poker. The purpose of all the other methods of narration, description, and exposition that he uses is to support this claim.

You won't always use every method of developing a topic in every piece of writing essay you do, however. Depending on your main purpose in writing, one or two will usually dominate, as in most of the model essays in this book. Your purpose—whether to REPORT on some research you've done, take a POSITION on an issue,

PROFILE a person or group, PROPOSE a new project or idea, ANALYZE a text—will likewise determine the overall type of writing you choose, as well as the methods you use to construct it.

MICHAEL LEWIS

# Liar's Poker

IT WAS SOMETIME EARLY IN 1986, the first year of the decline of my firm, Salomon Brothers. Our chairman, John Gutfreund, left his desk at the head of the trading floor and went for a walk. At any given moment on the trading floor billions of dollars were being risked by bond traders.[1] Gutfreund took the pulse of the place by simply wandering around it and asking questions of the traders. An eerie sixth sense guided him to wherever a crisis was unfolding. Gutfreund seemed able to smell money being lost.

He was the last person a nerve-racked trader wanted to see. Gutfreund (pronounced *Good friend*) liked to sneak up from behind and surprise you. This was fun for him but not for you. Busy on two phones at once trying to stem disaster, you had no time to turn and look. You didn't need to. You felt him. The area around you began to convulse like an epileptic ward. People were pretending to be frantically busy and at the same time staring intently at a spot directly above your head. You felt a chill in your bones that I imagine belongs to the same class of intelligence as the nervous twitch of a small furry animal at the silent approach of a grizzly bear. An alarm shrieked in your head: Gutfreund! Gutfreund! Gutfreund!

Often as not, our chairman just hovered quietly for a bit, then left. You might never have seen him. The only trace I found of him on two of these occasions was a turdlike ash on the floor beside my chair, left, I suppose, as a calling card. Gutfreund's cigar droppings were longer and better formed than those of the average Salomon boss. I always assumed that he smoked a more expensive blend than the rest, purchased with a few of the $40 million he had cleared on the sale of Salomon Brothers in 1981 (or a few of the $3.1 million he paid himself in 1986, more than any other Wall Street CEO).

1. *Bond traders:* Salespeople who specialize in promissory notes (IOUs) that pay interest.

MLA CITATION: Lewis, Michael. "Liar's Poker." 1989. *Back to the Lake*. Ed. Thomas Cooley. 3rd ed. New York: Norton, 2015. 755–59. Print.

This day in 1986, however, Gutfreund did something strange. Instead of terrifying us all, he walked a straight line to the trading desk of John Meriwether, a member of the board of Salomon Inc. and also one of Salomon's finest bond traders. He whispered a few words. The traders in the vicinity eavesdropped. What Gutfreund said has become a legend at Salomon Brothers and a visceral part of its corporate identity. He said: "One hand, one million dollars, no tears."

One hand, one million dollars, no tears. Meriwether grabbed the meaning instantly. The King of Wall Street, as *Business Week* had dubbed Gutfreund, wanted to play a single hand of a game called Liar's Poker for a million dollars. He played the game most afternoons with Meriwether and the six young bond arbitrage[2] traders who worked for Meriwether and was usually skinned alive. Some traders said Gutfreund was heavily outmatched. Others who couldn't imagine John Gutfreund as anything but omnipotent—and there were many—said that losing suited his purpose, though exactly what that might be was a mystery.

The peculiar feature of Gutfreund's challenge this time was the size of the stake. Normally his bets didn't exceed a few hundred dollars. A million was unheard of. The final two words of his challenge, "no tears," meant that the loser was expected to suffer a great deal of pain but wasn't entitled to whine, bitch, or moan about it. He'd just have to hunker down and keep his poverty to himself. But why? You might ask if you were anyone other than the King of Wall Street. Why do it in the first place? Why, in particular, challenge Meriwether instead of some lesser managing director? It seemed an act of sheer lunacy. Meriwether was the King of the Game, the Liar's Poker champion of the Salomon Brothers trading floor.

On the other hand, one thing you learn on a trading floor is that winners like Gutfreund *always* have some reason for what they do; it might not be the best of reasons, but at least they have a concept in mind. I was not privy to Gutfreund's innermost thoughts, but I do know that all the boys on the trading floor gambled and that he wanted badly to be one of the boys. What I think Gutfreund had in mind in this instance was a desire to show his courage, like the boy who leaps from the high dive. Who better than Meriwether for the purpose? Besides, Meriwether was probably the only trader with both the cash and the nerve to play.

---

2. *Arbitrage:* Buying stocks, bonds, and other securities for immediate resale to profit from price differences in different markets.

The whole absurd situation needs putting into context. John Meriwether had, in the course of his career, made hundreds of millions of dollars for Salomon Brothers. He had an ability, rare among people and treasured by traders, to hide his state of mind. Most traders divulge whether they are making or losing money by the way they speak or move. They are either overly easy or overly tense. With Meriwether you could never, ever tell. He wore the same blank half-tense expression when he won as he did when he lost. He had, I think, a profound ability to control the two emotions that commonly destroy traders—fear and greed—and it made him as noble as a man who pursues his self-interest so fiercely can be. He was thought by many within Salomon to be the best bond trader on Wall Street. Around Salomon no tone but awe was used when he was discussed. People would say, "He's the best businessman in the place," or "the best risk taker I have ever seen," or "a very dangerous Liar's Poker player."

Meriwether cast a spell over the young traders who worked for him. His boys ranged in age from twenty-five to thirty-two (he was about forty). Most of them had Ph.D.'s in math, economics, and/or physics. Once they got onto Meriwether's trading desk, however, they forgot they were supposed to be detached intellectuals. They became disciples. They became obsessed by the game of Liar's Poker. They regarded it as *their* game. And they took it to a new level of seriousness.

John Gutfreund was always the outsider in their game. That *Business Week* put his picture on the cover and called him the King of Wall Street held little significance for them. I mean, that was, in a way, the whole point. Gutfreund was the King of Wall Street, but Meriwether was King of the Game. When Gutfreund had been crowned by the gentlemen of the press, you could almost hear traders thinking: *Foolish names and foolish faces often appear in public places.* Fair enough, Gutfreund had once been a trader, but that was as relevant as an old woman's claim that she was once quite a dish.

At times Gutfreund himself seemed to agree. He loved to trade. Compared with managing, trading was admirably direct. You made your bets and either you won or you lost. When you won, people—all the way up to the top of the firm—admired you, envied you, and feared you, and with reason: You controlled the loot. When you managed a firm, well, sure you received your quota of envy, fear, and admiration. But for all the wrong reasons. *You did not make the money for Salomon. You did not take risk.* You were hostage to your producers. They took risk. They proved their superiority every day by handling risk better than the rest of the risk-taking world. The money came from risk takers such as Meriwether, and whether it came or not was really beyond

Gutfreund's control. That's why many people thought that the single rash act of challenging the arbitrage boss to one hand for a million dollars was Gutfreund's way of showing he was a player, too. And if you wanted to show off, Liar's Poker was the only way to go. The game had a powerful meaning for traders. People like John Meriwether believed that Liar's Poker had a lot in common with bond trading. It tested a trader's character. It honed a trader's instincts. A good player made a good trader, and vice versa. We all understood it.

The Game: In Liar's Poker a group of people—as few as two, as many as ten—form a circle. Each player holds a dollar bill close to his chest. The game is similar in spirit to the card game known as I Doubt It. Each player attempts to fool the others about the serial numbers printed on the face of his dollar bill. One trader begins by making "a bid." He says, for example, "Three sixes." He means that all told the serial numbers of the dollar bills held by every player, including himself, contain at least three sixes.

Once the first bid has been made, the game moves clockwise in the circle. Let's say the bid is three sixes. The player to the left of the bidder can do one of two things. He can bid higher (there are two sorts of higher bids: the same quantity of a higher number [three sevens, eights, or nines] and more of any number [four fives, for instance]). Or he can "challenge"—that is like saying, "I doubt it."

The bidding escalates until all the other players agree to challenge a single player's bid. Then, and only then, do the players reveal their serial numbers and determine who is bluffing whom. In the midst of all this, the mind of a good player spins with probabilities. What is the statistical likelihood of there being three sixes within a batch of, say, forty randomly generated serial numbers? For a great player, however, the math is the easy part of the game. The hard part is reading the faces of the other players. The complexity arises when all players know how to bluff and double-bluff.

The game has some of the feel of trading, just as jousting has some of the feel of war. The questions a Liar's Poker player asks himself are, up to a point, the same questions a bond trader asks himself. Is this a smart risk? Do I feel lucky? How cunning is my opponent? Does he have any idea what he's doing, and if not, how do I exploit his ignorance? If he bids high, is he bluffing, or does he actually hold a strong hand? Is he trying to induce me to make a foolish bid, or does he actually have four of a kind himself? Each player seeks weakness, predictability, and pattern in the others and seeks to avoid it in himself. The bond traders of Goldman, Sachs, First Boston,

Morgan Stanley, Merrill Lynch, and other Wall Street firms all play some version of Liar's Poker. But the place where the stakes run highest, thanks to John Meriwether, is the New York bond trading floor of Salomon Brothers.

The code of the Liar's Poker player was something like the code of the gunslinger.[3] It required a trader to accept all challenges. Because of the code—which was *his* code—John Meriwether felt obliged to play. But he knew it was stupid. For him, there was no upside. If he won, he upset Gutfreund. No good came of this. But if he lost, he was out of pocket a million bucks. This was worse than upsetting the boss. Although Meriwether was by far the better player of the game, in a single hand anything could happen. Luck could very well determine the outcome. Meriwether spent his entire day avoiding dumb bets, and he wasn't about to accept this one.

"No, John," he said, "if we're going to play for those kind of numbers, I'd rather play for real money. Ten million dollars. No tears."

*Ten million dollars.* It was a moment for all players to savor. Meriwether was playing Liar's Poker before the game even started. He was bluffing. Gutfreund considered the counterproposal. It would have been just like him to accept. Merely to entertain the thought was a luxury that must have pleased him well. (It *was* good to be rich.)

On the other hand, ten million dollars was, and is, a lot of money. If Gutfreund lost, he'd have only thirty million or so left. His wife, Susan, was busy spending the better part of fifteen million dollars redecorating their Manhattan apartment (Meriwether knew this). And as Gutfreund *was* the boss, he clearly wasn't bound by the Meriwether code. Who knows? Maybe he didn't even know the Meriwether code. Maybe the whole point of his challenge was to judge Meriwether's response. (Even Gutfreund had to marvel at the king in action.) So Gutfreund declined. In fact, he smiled his own brand of forced smile and said, "You're crazy."

No, thought Meriwether, just very, very good.

---

3. *Code of the gunslinger:* Code of conduct rooted in the legendary Wild West of the eighteenth- and nineteenth-century United States. The phrase refers to a stoic, warriorlike way of life that required a gunfighter to accept all challenges.

# A Book Cover

The basic methods that good writers draw upon every day are sometimes used in combination with each other. This cover for a book about human cadavers, for example, employs a number of them all at once. The title, *Stiff*, is a DESCRIPTION of the physical condition of the human body after death; *stiff* is also a slang term for a dead person. Going beyond physical description, Roach's title is a name or label identifying an important aspect of her subject—the sometimes conflicting legal, moral, and medical DEFINITIONS of death itself. Good writers often kill even more than two birds with one stone, however. As you describe and define a subject, you may also tell a story about it, as this book cover does by adding a NARRATIVE element. We see just enough of the person pictured on the cover of Roach's book to know that he or she ended up in the morgue with a tag attached to the big toe. End of story—usually. For the human cadavers in Roach's book, however, death is only the beginning. Simultaneously grim and humorous, the image on the cover captures the first stages of this narrative. The later stages are implied in Roach's subtitle, *The Curious Lives of Human Cadavers*, which tells us that *Stiff* is a book about what happens to our bodies after we die.

[ **FOR WRITING** ]················································································

With its oversize footnote, so to speak, the cover of Mary Roach's *Stiff* is both informative and humorous. Write a brief **RHETORICAL ANALYSIS** of the words and images on the cover of Roach's book and the "mixed" impression they are likely intended to leave upon the reader.

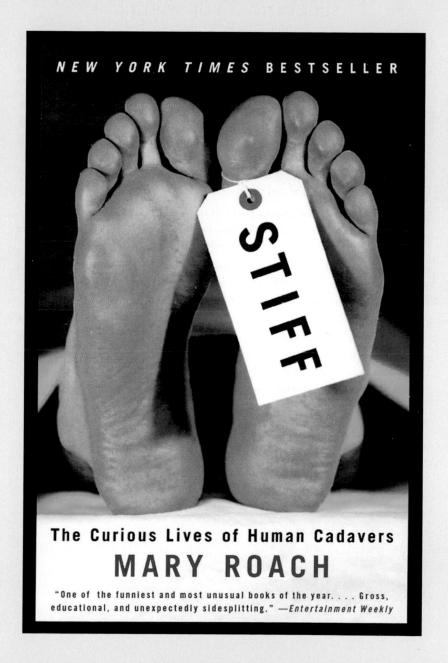

NEW YORK TIMES BESTSELLER

STIFF

The Curious Lives of Human Cadavers
MARY ROACH

"One of the funniest and most unusual books of the year. . . . Gross, educational, and unexpectedly sidesplitting." —*Entertainment Weekly*

# SUGGESTIONS FOR WRITING

1. All of the selections in this chapter include elements of **NARRATIVE**. Choose two titles, and **COMPARE AND CONTRAST** the respective authors' use of story-telling to explain and support the key points they are making. Be sure to refer to particular issues and to specific passages in the two texts.

2. Michael Lewis's "Liar's Poker" (p. 755) is the introduction to his best-selling book of that title about the gamblers and gambling culture he finds characteristic of Wall Street. Are the financial markets of New York and elsewhere driven largely by a gambling mentality? Using Lewis's introduction as a starting point, write a **POSITION PAPER** supporting (or contesting) this view of Wall Street and the world of finance.

3. Write a 300-word **RHETORICAL ANALYSIS** of Joan Didion's "On Going Home" (p. 763) as a personal **NARRATIVE** that deals with universal issues of home and family. Give lots of specific **EXAMPLES** to support your reading.

4. In approximately 400 words, **COMPARE AND CONTRAST** Linda Hogan's "Hearing Voices" (p. 767) with Gloria Anzaldúa's "Linguistic Terrorism" (p. 773) as essays about the uses and power of language.

5. The purpose of "The Checklist Manifesto" (p. 785) is to propose a solution to problems brought on by the increase in complexity in fields ranging from medicine to aviation. In approximately 400 words, write a **RHETORICAL ANALYSIS** of Atul Gawande's use of various methods of writing discussed earlier in this book to achieve that rhetorical goal.

JOAN DIDION

# On Going Home

Joan Didion (b. 1934) is a native of Sacramento, California. She graduated from the University of California, Berkeley, and worked on the staff of *Vogue* magazine before becoming a full-time writer. A novelist and author of screenplays, Didion is perhaps best known for her essays, collected in *Slouching Towards Bethlehem* (1968), *The White Album* (1979), and *Where I Was From* (2003). *The Year of Magical Thinking* (2005), a reflection on the sudden death in 2003 of her husband, the writer John Gregory Dunne, won the National Book Award for nonfiction; it was adapted into a one-woman play staged on Broadway with Vanessa Redgrave. Didion's *Blue Nights* (2011) is a memoir about aging and her relationship with her only child, an adopted daughter who died not long after her husband.

That Didion is a master of the memoir form—which combines narration and description into reflection upon the past, intertwined with commentary on life in the present—is immediately apparent in "On Going Home," first published in 1967 in the *Saturday Evening Post*. Although Didion lived for years in New York City and later Los Angeles, *home* for her was "the place where my family is, in the Central Valley of California." "On Going Home" captures that place in fine detail, but it also raises the question of whether the idea of going home has been lost.

I AM HOME FOR MY DAUGHTER'S FIRST BIRTHDAY. By "home" I do not mean the house in Los Angeles where my husband and I and the baby live, but the place where my family is, in the Central Valley of California. It is a vital although troublesome distinction. My husband likes my family but is uneasy in their house, because once there I fall into their ways, which are difficult, oblique, deliberately inarticulate, not my husband's ways. We live in dusty houses ("D-U-S-T," he once wrote with his finger on surfaces all over the house, but no one noticed it) filled with mementos quite without value to him (what could the Canton dessert plates mean to him? how could he have known about the assay scales, why should he care if he did know?), and we appear to talk exclusively about people we know who have been committed to mental hospitals,

1

While telling about going home, Didion also defines the idea (p. 754) of going home.

MLA CITATION: Didion, Joan. "On Going Home." 1967. *Back to the Lake*. Ed. Thomas Cooley. 3rd ed. New York: Norton, 2015. 763-65. Print.

about people we know who have been booked on drunk-driving charges, and about property, particularly about property, land, price per acre and C-2 zoning and assessments and freeway access. My brother does not understand my husband's inability to perceive the advantage in the rather common real-estate transaction known as "sale-leaseback," and my husband in turn does not understand why so many of the people he hears about in my father's house have recently been committed to mental hospitals or booked on drunk-driving charges. Nor does he understand that when we talk about sale-leasebacks and right-of-way condemnations we are talking in code about the things we like best, the yellow fields and the cottonwoods and the rivers rising and falling and the mountain roads closing when the heavy snow comes in. We miss each other's points, have another drink and regard the fire. My brother refers to my husband, in his presence, as "Joan's husband." Marriage is the classic betrayal.

Or perhaps it is not any more. Sometimes I think that those of us who are now   2
in our thirties were born into the last generation to carry the burden of "home," to find in family life the source of all tension and drama. I had by all objective accounts a "normal" and a "happy" family situation, and yet I was almost thirty years old before I could talk to my family on the telephone without crying after I had hung up. We did not fight. Nothing was wrong. And yet some nameless anxiety colored the emotional charges between me and the place that I came from. The question of whether or not you could go home again was a very real part of the sentimental and largely literary baggage with which we left home in the fifties; I suspect that it is irrelevant to the children born of the fragmentation after World War II. A few weeks ago in a San Francisco bar I saw a pretty young girl on crystal take off her clothes and dance for the cash prize in an "amateur-topless" contest. There was no particular sense of moment about this, none of the effect of romantic degradation, of "dark journey" for which my generation strived so assiduously. What sense could that girl possibly make of, say, *Long Day's Journey into Night?* Who is beside the point?

That I am trapped in this particular irrelevancy is never more apparent to me   3
than when I am home. Paralyzed by the neurotic lassitude engendered by meeting one's past at every turn, around every corner, inside every cupboard, I go aimlessly from room to room. I decide to meet it head-on and clean out a drawer, and I spread the contents on the bed. A bathing suit I wore the summer I was seventeen. A letter of rejection from *The Nation*, an aerial photograph of the site for a shopping center my father did not build in 1954. Three teacups hand-painted with cabbage roses and signed "E.M.," my grandmother's initials. There is no final solution for letters of rejection from *The Nation* and teacups hand-painted in 1900. Nor is there any answer to snapshots of one's grandfather as a young man on skis, surveying around Donner Pass in the year 1910. I smooth out the snapshot and look into his

face, and do and do not see my own. I close the drawer, and have another cup of coffee with my mother. We get along very well, veterans of a guerrilla war we never understood.

Days pass. I see no one. I come to dread my husband's evening call, not only 4 because he is full of news of what by now seems to me our remote life in Los Angeles, people he has seen, letters which require attention, but because he asks what I have been doing, suggests uneasily that I get out, drive to San Francisco or Berkeley. Instead I drive across the river to a family graveyard. It has been vandalized since my last visit and the monuments are broken, overturned in the dry grass. Because I once saw a rattlesnake in the grass I stay in the car and listen to a country-and-Western station. Later I drive with my father to a ranch he has in the foothills. The man who runs his cattle on it asks us to the roundup, a week from Sunday, and although I know that I will be in Los Angeles I say, in the oblique way my family talks, that I will come. Once home I mention the broken monuments in the graveyard. My mother shrugs.

I go to visit my great-aunts. A few of them think now that I am my cousin, or 5 their daughter who died young. We recall an anecdote about a relative last seen in 1948, and they ask if I still like living in New York City. I have lived in Los Angeles for three years, but I say that I do. The baby is offered a horehound drop, and I am slipped a dollar bill "to buy a treat." Questions trail off, answers are abandoned, the baby plays with the dust motes in a shaft of afternoon sun.

It is time for the baby's birthday party: a white cake, strawberry-marshmallow 6 ice cream, a bottle of champagne saved from another party. In the evening, after she has gone to sleep, I kneel beside the crib and touch her face, where it is pressed against the slats, with mine. She is an open and trusting child, unprepared for and unaccustomed to the ambushes of family life, and perhaps it is just as well that I can offer her little of that life. I would like to give her more. I would like to promise her that she will grow up with a sense of her cousins and of rivers and of her great-grandmother's teacups, would like to pledge her a picnic on a river with fried chicken and her hair uncombed, would like to give her *home* for her birthday, but we live differently now and I can promise her nothing like that. I give her a xylophone and a sundress from Madeira, and promise to tell her a funny story. ◆


READING WITH AN EYE FOR THE METHODS

1. "On Going Home" is an intimate **DESCRIPTION** of family life long rooted in a particular place and its ways. Point out specific details in Didion's description that you find most evocative of this place and the people in it. What makes those details so effective?

2. Didion's essay combines rich descriptive detail with a **NARRATIVE** of going back home to celebrate her daughter's first birthday. What happens on this occasion? What doesn't happen? How does Didion's husband figure into telling the story of people who can be "deliberately inarticulate" (1)?

3. Combining narration and description as in a short story, Didion's essay is also a commentary on the idea of home. How does Didion define home, and what position does she take on the issue of "going home"?

## USING THE METHODS

1. Write an essay-length **MEMOIR** of going home. Describe the place and people in detail; tell what they typically do and say; and link your recollection to your present life, perhaps showing how it is different now from what it was in former times.

2. "The question of whether or not you could go home again," says Didion, "was a very real part of the sentimental and largely literary baggage with which we left home in the fifties . . ." (2). Using Didion's essay as a starting point, do some research on the "can't-go-home-again" theme in American literature, and write a **REPORT** explaining what it was and how it came about.

3. In your journal, keep notes of your visits home during the coming months. Include incidents and vivid details as Didion does, but also reflect in your journal upon home as a conception—literary, sentimental, or otherwise.

4. Collect going-home stories from several of your classmates, and compile them into a collaborative essay with commentary on the nature of home and going back to it.

. . . . . . . . . . . . . . . . . . . . . . . . . . . . . . . . . . . . . . . . . . . . . . . . . . . . . . .•

You'll find quizzes on the readings at
wwnorton.com/write/back-to-the-lake.

# Hearing Voices

Linda Hogan (b. 1947) is a Native American poet, novelist, and short-story writer. Born in Denver, she and her extended family are members of the Chickasaw Nation, for which she is currently serving as poet in residence. After graduating from the University of Colorado, Colorado Springs, Hogan earned a master's in English and creative writing from the University of Colorado, Bolder, where she later taught creative writing and ethnic studies. Hogan has also been a professor at the University of Oklahoma. Her collections of poetry include the award-winning *Seeing Through the Sun* (1985) and *Rounding the Human Corners* (2008). Like her poetry and essays, Hogan's fiction, including *People of the Whale* (2008), deals with environmental issues and native American traditions.

In "Hearing Voices," an essay from the collection *The Writer on Her Work: Vol. II. New Essays in New Territory* (1991), Hogan defines writing (particularly poetry) and analyzes its causes and effects, both practical and mystical, in a personal narrative of her experience with the power of language. In Hogan's version of the literacy narrative genre, however, oral tradition and the spoken word are as important as the written language in its more traditional forms.

W HEN BARBARA MCCLINTOCK WAS AWARDED A NOBEL PRIZE for her work on gene transposition in corn plants, the most striking thing about her was that she made her discoveries by listening to what the corn spoke to her, by respecting the life of the corn and "letting it come." 1

McClintock says she learned "the stories" of the plants. She "heard" them. She watched the daily green journeys of growth from earth toward sky and sun. She knew her plants in the way a healer or mystic would have known them, from the inside, the inner voices of corn and woman speaking to one another. 2

As an Indian woman, I come from a long history of people who have listened to the language of this continent, people who have known that corn grows with the songs and prayers of the people, that it has a story to tell, that the world is alive. Both in oral traditions and in mythology—the true language of inner life—account 3

MLA CITATION: Hogan, Linda. "Hearing Voices." 1991. *Back to the Lake*. Ed. Thomas Cooley. 3rd ed. New York: Norton, 2015. 767-71. Print.

"As an Indian woman, I come from a long history of people who have listened to this continent, people who know that corn grows with the songs and prayers of the people, that it has a story to tell, that the world is alive."

after account tells of the stones giving guidance, the trees singing, the corn telling of inner earth, the dragonfly offering up a tongue. This is true in the European traditions as well: Psyche received direction from the reeds and the ants, Orpheus knew the languages of earth, animals, and birds.[1]

This intuitive and common language is what I seek for my writing, work in touch with the mystery and force of life, work that speaks a few of the many voices around us, and it is important to me that McClintock listened to the voices of corn. It is important to the continuance of life that she told the truth of her method and that it reminded us all of where our strength, our knowing, and our sustenance come from.

It is also poetry, this science, and I note how often scientific theories lead to the world of poetry and vision, theories telling us how atoms that were stars have been transformed into our living, breathing bodies. And in these theories, or maybe they should be called stories, we begin to understand how we are each many people, including the stars we once were, and how we are in essence the earth and the universe, how what we do travels clear around the earth and returns. In a single moment of our living, there is our ancestral and personal history, our future, even our deaths planted in us and already growing toward their fulfillment. The corn plants are there, and like all the rest we are forever merging our borders with theirs in the world collective.

Our very lives might depend on this listening. In the Chernobyl nuclear accident,[2] the wind told the story that was being suppressed by the people. It gave away the truth. It carried the story of danger to other countries. It was a poet, a prophet, a scientist.

Sometimes, like the wind, poetry has its own laws speaking for the life of the planet. It is a language that wants to bring back together what the other words have torn apart. It is the language of life speaking through us about the sacredness of life.

This life speaking life is what I find so compelling about the work of poets such as Ernesto Cardenal, who is also a priest and was the Nicaraguan Minister of Culture. He writes: "The armadilloes are very happy with this government. . . . Not only humans desired liberation / the whole ecology wanted it." Cardenal has also written "The Parrots," a poem about caged birds who were being sent to the United States as pets for the wealthy, how the cages were opened, the parrots allowed back

1. *Orpheus, Psyche:* In Greek mythology, Orpheus was said to be able to charm animals, trees, and even rocks into dancing with the power of his beautiful voice. Psyche overcame a series of difficult tasks set by the goddess Aphrodite with the help of a reed, an eagle, and a group of ants.

2. *Chernobyl accident:* On April 26, 1986, an accident at the Chernobyl nuclear power plant resulted in radioactive contamination over large areas of what are now Belarus, Ukraine, and Russia.

into the mountains and jungles, freed like the people, "and sent back to the land we were pulled from."

How we have been pulled from the land! And how poetry has worked hard to 9 set us free, uncage us, keep us from split tongues that mimic the voices of our captors. It returns us to our land. Poetry is a string of words that parades without a permit. It is a lockbox of words to put an ear to as we try to crack the safe of language, listening for the right combination, the treasure inside. It is life resonating. It is sometimes called Prayer, Soothsaying, Complaint, Invocation, Proclamation, Testimony, Witness. Writing is and does all these things. And like that parade, it is illegitimately insistent on going its own way, on being part of the miracle of life, telling the story about what happened when we were cosmic dust, what it means to be stars listening to our human atoms.

But don't misunderstand me. I am not just a dreamer. I am also the practical 10 type. A friend's father, watching the United States stage another revolution in another Third World country, said, "Why doesn't the government just feed people and then let the political chips fall where they may?" He was right. It was easy, obvious, even financially more reasonable to do that, to let democracy be chosen because it feeds hunger. I want my writing to be that simple, that clear and direct. Likewise, I feel it is not enough for me just to write, but I need to live it, to be informed by it. I have found over the years that my work has more courage than I do. It has more wisdom. It teaches me, leads me places I never knew I was heading. And it is about a new way of living, of being in the world.

Combining narrative and argument is discussed on p. 754.

I was on a panel recently where the question was raised whether we thought 11 literature could save lives. The audience, book people, smiled expectantly with the thought. I wanted to say, Yes, it saves lives. But I couldn't speak those words. It saves spirits maybe, hearts. It changes minds, but for me writing is an incredible privilege. When I sit down at the desk, there are other women who are hungry, homeless. I don't want to forget that, that the world of matter is still there to be reckoned with. This writing is a form of freedom most other people do not have. So, when I write, I feel a responsibility, a commitment to other humans and to the animal and plant communities as well.

Still, writing has changed me. And there is the powerful need we all have to tell 12 a story, each of us with a piece of the whole pattern to complete. As Alice Walker says, We are all telling part of the same story, and as Sharon Olds has said, Every writer is a cell on the body politic of America.[3]

---

3. *Sharon Olds* (b. 1942): American poet. *Alice Walker* (b. 1944): American writer best known for her novel *The Color Purple*.

Another Nobel Prize laureate is Betty William, a Northern Ireland co-winner of 13 the 1977 Peace Prize. I heard her speak about how, after witnessing the death of children, she stepped outside in the middle of the night and began knocking on doors and yelling, behaviors that would have earned her a diagnosis of hysteria in our own medical circles. She knocked on doors that might have opened with weapons pointing in her face, and she cried out, "What kind of people have we become that we would allow children to be killed on our streets?" Within four hours the city was awake, and there were sixteen thousand names on petitions for peace. Now, that woman's work is a lesson to those of us who deal with language, and to those of us who are dealt into silence. She used language to begin the process of peace. This is the living, breathing power of the word. It is poetry. So are the names of those who signed the petitions. Maybe it is this kind of language that saves lives.

Writing begins for me with survival, with life and with freeing life, saving life, 14 speaking life. It is work that speaks what can't be easily said. It originates from a compelling desire to live and be alive. For me, it is sometimes the need to speak for other forms of life, to take the side of human life, even our sometimes frivolous living, and our grief-filled living, our joyous living, our violent living, busy living, our peaceful living. It is about possibility. It is based in the world of matter. I am interested in how something small turns into an image that is large and strong with resonance, where the ordinary becomes beautiful. I believe the divine, the magic, is here in the weeds at our feet, unacknowledged. What a world this is. Where else could water rise up to the sky, turn into snow crystals, magnificently brought together, fall from the sky all around us, pile up billions deep, and catch the small sparks of sunlight as they return again to water?

These acts of magic happen all the time; in Chaco Canyon,[4] my sister has seen a 15 kiva, a ceremonial room in the earth, that is in the center of the canyon. This place has been uninhabited for what seems like forever. It has been without water. In fact, there are theories that the ancient people disappeared when they journeyed after water. In the center of it a corn plant was growing. It was all alone and it had been there since the ancient ones, the old ones who came before us all, those people who wove dog hair into belts, who witnessed the painting of flute players on the seeping canyon walls, who knew the stories of corn. And there was one corn plant growing out of the holy place. It planted itself yearly. With no water, no person to care for it, no overturning of the soil, this corn plant rises up to tell its story, and that's what this poetry is. ◆

---

4. *Chaco Canyon:* A U.S. National Historical Park, located in northwestern New Mexico, which was once home to an ancient pueblo people.

## READING WITH AN EYE FOR THE METHODS

1. Hogan explicitly DEFINES writing, particularly poetry, in paragraph 9. In what ways, according to her definition, is writing "a string of words that parades without a permit"? Where else in the narrative does Hogan define writing? Point to specific passages in the text, and explain what they add to her definition.

2. What EFFECTS, in Hogan's view, can language have upon the world? In her analysis, what gives language its power? What are some of the CAUSES of its coming into being?

3. As a LITERACY NARRATIVE, how and where does "Hearing Voices" tell about Hogan's coming to understand and use the power of language? According to this near-mythic story, why does she write?

## USING THE METHODS

1. According to Hogan, mythology is "the true language of inner life" (3). In a paragraph or two, speculate on what she might mean by this definition as evidenced by her comments on nature and the origins of language.

2. Referring to the work of Barbara McClintock, who won a Nobel Prize in 1983 for her discovery of genetic transposition in corn, Hogan notes "how often scientific theories lead to the world of poetry and vision" (5). Write a POSITION PAPER of approximately 450 words supporting (or contesting) this view by referring to a specific scientific theory. For inspiration, you might start by reading "Einstein's Dreams," on p. 277.

3. Hogan says she is "interested in how something small turns into an image that is large and strong with resonance" (14). Write a RHETORICAL ANALYSIS of a poem or short story that illustrates this principle, as does, for example, the stalk of corn at the end of Hogan's essay.

4. Take your journal into the woods or a field or park and listen to the "voices" around you. Make notes describing what you hear, and record in your journal the words and images they call to mind.

· · · · · · · · · · · · · · · · · · · · · · · · · · · · · · · · · · · · · · · · · · · · · · · · · · · · · · · · · · · · · · · · · · · · · ·

You'll find quizzes on the readings at
wwnorton.com/write/back-to-the-lake.

# Linguistic Terrorism

Gloria Anzaldúa (1942–2004) was known for her contributions to Chicana, feminist, postcolonial, and gender studies, which grew out of her sense of being "on the margins" in terms of sexuality, nationality, language, and skin color. Anzaldúa was born in the Rio Grande Valley along the Mexican border in southern Texas, where her ancestors, the descendants of early Spanish settlers in Mexico and of Native Americans, had long been ranchers. After graduating from what is now the University of Texas, Pan American, she earned a master's from the University of Texas at Austin and taught in preschools and special education classes before moving to California. An editor of *This Bridge Called My Back: Writings by Radical Women of Color* (1981), Anzaldúa wrote fiction and poetry as well as several books for children.

"Linguistic Terrorism" is from Anzaldúa's semiautobiographical *Borderlands / La Frontera: The New Mestiza* (1987), a "mixed" form of writing that combines prose and poetry, two varieties of English, and six varieties of Spanish. Anzaldúa used this mixture deliberately to make the text frustrating for most readers to follow and thereby evoke the author's sense of herself as an outsider with multiple identities.

> Deslenguadas. Somos los del español deficiente. *We are your linguistic nightmare, your linguistic aberration, your linguistic* mestizaje, *the subject of your* burla. *Because we speak with tongues of fire we are culturally crucified. Racially, culturally and linguistically* somos huérfanos—*we speak an orphan tongue.*

CHICANAS WHO GREW UP SPEAKING CHICANO SPANISH have internalized the     1
belief that we speak poor Spanish. It is illegitimate, a bastard language. And because we internalize how our language has been used against us by the dominant culture, we use our language differences against each other.

MLA CITATION: Anzaldúa, Gloria. "Linguistic Terrorism." 1987. *Back to the Lake*. Ed. Thomas Cooley. 3rd ed. New York: Norton, 2015. 773-75. Print.

Chicana feminists often skirt around each other with suspicion and hesitation. 2
For the longest time I couldn't figure it out. Then it dawned on me. To be close to
another Chicana is like looking into the mirror. We are afraid of what we'll see
there. *Pena.* Shame. Low estimation of self. In childhood we are told that our language is wrong. Repeated attacks on our native tongue diminish our sense of self.
The attacks continue throughout our lives.

Chicanas feel uncomfortable talking in Spanish to Latinas, afraid of their cen- 3
sure. Their language was not outlawed in their countries. They had a whole lifetime of being immersed in their native tongue; generations, centuries in which
Spanish was a first language, taught in school, heard on radio and TV, and read in
the newspaper.

If a person, Chicana or Latina, has a low estimation of my native tongue, she 4
also has a low estimation of me. Often with *mexicanas y latinas* we'll speak English
as a neutral language. Even among Chicanas we tend to speak English at parties
or conferences. Yet, at the same time, we're afraid the other will think we're
*agringadas* because we don't speak Chicano Spanish. We oppress each
other trying to out-Chicano each other, vying to be the "real" Chicanas, to
speak like Chicanos. There is no one Chicano language just as there is no
one Chicano experience. A monolingual Chicana whose first language is
English or Spanish is just as much a Chicana as one who speaks several
variants of Spanish. A Chicana from Michigan or Chicago or Detroit is just as
much a Chicana as one from the Southwest. Chicano Spanish is as diverse linguistically as it is regionally.

See p. 753
for tips on
introducing
CLASSIFICATION
into your text.

By the end of this century, Spanish speakers will comprise the biggest minority 5
group in the United States, a country where students in high schools and colleges
are encouraged to take French classes because French is considered more "cul-
tured." But for a language to remain alive it must be used.[1] By the end of this century English, and not Spanish, will be the mother tongue of most Chicanos and
Latinos.

So, if you want to really hurt me, talk badly about my language. Ethnic identity is 6
twin skin to linguistic identity—I am my language. Until I can take pride in my language, I cannot take pride in myself. Until I can accept as legitimate Chicano Texas
Spanish, Tex-Mex and all the other languages I speak, I cannot accept the legitimacy
of myself. Until I am free to write bilingually and to switch codes without having
always to translate, while I still have to speak English or Spanish when I would rather

---

1. Irena Klepfisz, "Secular Jewish Identity: Yidishkayt in America," in *The Tribe of Dina*, Kaye/
Kantrowitz and Klepfisz, eds., 43. [Author's note]

speak Spanglish, and as long as I have to accommodate the English speakers rather 7 than having them accommodate me, my tongue will be illegitimate.

I will no longer be made to feel ashamed of existing. I will have my voice: Indian, Spanish, white. I will have my serpent's tongue—my woman's voice, my sexual voice, my poet's voice. I will overcome the tradition of silence.

> *My fingers*
> *move sly against your palm.*
> *Like women everywhere, we speak in code. . . .*
> —MELANIE KAYE/KANTROWITZ[2] ◆

2. Melanie Kaye/Kantrowitz, "Sign," in *We Speak in Code: Poems and Other Writings* (Pittsburgh, PA: Motheroot Publications, Inc., 1980), 85. [Author's note]

## READING WITH AN EYE FOR THE METHODS

1. In "Linguistic Terrorism," Anzaldúa CLASSIFIES Spanish-speaking Americans into different types. Which type (or types) does she belong to? Why does it matter, according to her?

2. In addition to identifying different types of language and speakers, Anzaldúa analyzes the CAUSES of her own linguistic diversity. What are some of them? What specific EFFECTS do they have on her identity, both linguistic and personal?

3. So who are the linguistic terrorists in Anzaldúa's account? What POSITION does she take to oppose them? How and where does she use the different languages she speaks to support that position?

## USING THE METHODS

1. Before explaining how and why she speaks and writes as she does, Anzaldúa gives a demonstration of her use of mixed languages. Using Anzaldúa's opening paragraph as a model, write a "mixed" paragraph of your own using the different languages you know, including different varieties of English.

2. "By the end of this century," Anzaldúa wrote in 1987, "Spanish speakers will comprise the biggest minority group in the United States" (5). Did her prophecy come to pass? Do some research on the composition of minority groups in the United States today, and write a REPORT on how they are DEFINED and CLASSIFIED, both ethnically and linguistically.

3. "Ethnic identity," says Anzaldúa, "is twin skin to linguistic identity—I am my language" (6). Write a POSITION PAPER supporting (or contesting) this proposition. Be sure to identify the linguistic type (or types) you belong to and to analyze the causes and effects of that identity.

4. In your journal, take note of the different varieties of English and other languages that you use in speaking and writing over a period of time. Include specific words and phrases and consider the different levels of usage (formal, slang, technical) that they fall into.

You'll find quizzes on the readings at wwnorton.com/write/back-to-the-lake.

# Babe Ruth's Summer of Records

Bill Bryson (b. 1951) is a journalist and travel writer who now lives in Britain, although he grew up in Des Moines, Iowa, where he attended Drake University. From 2005 to 2011, Bryson served as chancellor, or ceremonial head, of Durham University in northern England, doing his job so well that the school renamed its main library in his honor. Bryson's travel books include *Notes from a Small Island* (1995), a humorous narrative about Britain, which was made into a documentary television series; *A Walk in the Woods: Rediscovering America on the Appalachian Trail* (1998); and his *African Diary* (2002). Bryson is also known for his books about language and history, including *The Mother Tongue: English and How It Got That Way* (1990) and *A Short History of Nearly Everything* (2003).

In "Babe Ruth's Summer of Records," from *One Summer: America 1927* (2013), Bryson profiles not so much the man as his team—and the Babe's best season with them. [E]ven with the benefit of steroids," says Bryson about his performance that summer, "most modern players couldn't hit as many home runs as Babe Ruth hit on hot dogs."

> He was bigger than the President. One time, coming north, we stopped at a little town in Illinois, a whistle stop. It was about ten o'clock at night and raining like hell. The train stopped for ten minutes to get water, or something. It couldn't have been a town of more than five thousand people, and by God, there were four thousand of them down there standing in the rain, just waiting to see the Babe.
>
> —RICHARDS VIDMER, *New York Times* sportswriter

LOU GEHRIG, in his quiet, methodical, all but invisible way, was having a fantastic year. As the second week of September began, he had 45 home runs, 161 runs batted in, and a .389 batting average. As his biographer Jonathan Eig notes in *Luckiest Man*, Gehrig could have stopped there, with almost a month of the season still to play, and had one of the best seasons ever. In fact, he did essentially stop there.

MLA CITATION: Bryson, Bill. "Babe Ruth's Summer of Records." 2013. *Back to the Lake*. Ed. Thomas Cooley. 3rd ed. New York: Norton, 2015. 777–83. Print.

His mother was unwell with a goiter and needed surgery. Gehrig was beside 2 himself with anxiety. "I'm so worried about Mom that I can't see straight," he confided to a teammate.

"All his thoughts were on Mom," the sportswriter Fred Lieb wrote later. "As 3 soon as he finished the game, he would rush to the hospital and stay with her until her bedtime." Gehrig hit just two more home runs the rest of the season. His heart wasn't in the game. All he could think about was his beloved momma.

Weaving in key EXAMPLES is discussed on p. 753.

Babe Ruth, meanwhile, began knocking balls out of parks as if hitting 4 tee shots at a driving range. Between September 2 and 29, he hit 17 home runs. No one had ever done anything like that in a single month.

The Yankees seemed incapable of doing anything wrong. On September 5 10, they beat St. Louis for the twenty-first time in a row—the most consecutive victories by one team over another during a season. On September 16, Wilcy Moore, who was such a bad batter that players would come out of the locker room and vendors would pause in their transactions to watch the extraordinary sight of him flailing at empty air with a piece of wood, miraculously connected with a ball and sent it over the right field wall for a home run, an event that nearly gave Babe Ruth a heart attack. On the mound, Moore scattered 7 hits to push his record to 18 and 7 as the Yanks beat the White Sox 7–2.

In the midst of this, almost unnoticed, the Yankees clinched the pennant. 6 They had been in first place every day of the season—the first time that had ever happened. Their position was so commanding that they could lose all 15 of their remaining games and the second-place A's could win all 17 of theirs, and the Yankees would still come out on top. In point of fact, the Yankees won 12 of their last 15 games even though they didn't need to. They couldn't help themselves.

Ruth was majestically imperturbable. On September 16 he was called into court 7 in Manhattan, charged with the alarming crime of punching a cripple. The reputed victim, Bernard Neimeyer, claimed that on the evening of July 4 he had been walking near the Ansonia Hotel when a man accompanied by two women accused him of making an inappropriate remark and punched him hard in the face. Neimeyer said he didn't recognize his assailant, but was told by onlookers that it was Babe Ruth. Ruth, in his defense, said that he had been having dinner with friends at the time, and produced two witnesses in corroboration. In court, Neimeyer seemed to be a little crazy. The *Times* reported that he frequently "rose excitedly to his feet, waving a book of notes which he added to from time to time as the hearing proceeded. He was often cautioned by the clerk of the court not to talk so loudly." The judge dismissed the case to general applause. Ruth signed a bunch of autographs, then went to the ballpark and hit a home run, his 53rd.

Babe Ruth knocked balls out of parks as if hitting tee shots at a driving range.

Two days later, in a doubleheader against the White Sox, he socked his 54th, a   8
two-run shot in the fifth inning. Three days after that, on September 21, Ruth
came to the plate in the bottom of the ninth inning against Detroit. The bases were
empty and the Tigers were up 6–0, so Sam Gibson, the Tigers' pitcher, didn't need
to throw him anything good, and dutifully endeavored not to. Ruth caught one
anyway, and hefted it deep into the right field stands for his 55th homer. A new
record was beginning to seem entirely possible.

The next day Ruth hit one of his most splendid home runs of the season. In the   9
bottom of the ninth inning, with Mark Koenig on third and the Yankees trailing
7–6, Ruth came to the plate and lofted his 56th home run high into the right field
bleachers for a walk-off 8–7 victory. As Ruth trotted around the bases—carrying
his bat with him, as he often did, to make sure nobody ran off with it—a boy of
about ten rushed in from right field and joined him on the base paths. The boy
grabbed onto the bat with both hands and was essentially carried around the bases
and into the dugout, where Ruth quickly vanished down the runway, pursued by
yet more jubilant fans. The game was the Yankees 105th victory of the season,
tying the American League record for season victories.

. . .

Ruth went two games, on September 24 and 25, without a homer, which left him   10
four short of the record with just four games to play.

On the first of those four games, on September 27, Ruth got his 57th in style by   11
hitting a grand slam off Lefty Grove of Philadelphia—one of only six home runs
Grove gave up all season. Ruth didn't hit grand slams often: this was his first of the
season and only the sixth of his career.

The Yankees had a day off on September 28, and the rest clearly did Ruth good, for   12
in his first at-bat the next day, in the start of a three-game series against the
Washington Senators, he hit his 58th home run off Horace "Hod" Lisenbee, a rookie
who was having a great year—the only good one he would ever have. Like Lefty
Grove, Lisenbee gave up just six home runs all season. Two of them were by Ruth.

Ruth now needed just one more to tie his record. In the bottom of the fifth inning,   13
Ruth came to the plate with the bases loaded and two out. Senators manager Bucky
Harris signaled to the bullpen to send in a right-hander named Paul Hopkins.

Hopkins was an unexpected choice, and no doubt caused many a spectator to turn   14
to the nearest person with a scorecard for enlightenment. Hopkins had just graduated from Colgate University and had never pitched in the major leagues before. Now
he was about to make his debut in Yankee Stadium against Babe Ruth with the bases
loaded and Ruth trying to tie his own record for most home runs in a season.

Pitching carefully (as you might expect), Hopkins worked the count to 3 and 2,   15
then tried to sneak a slow curve past Ruth. It was an outstanding pitch. "It was so
slow," Hopkins recalled for *Sports Illustrated* seventy years later at the age of ninety-
four, "that Ruth started to swing and then hesitated, hitched on it and brought the

bat back. And then he swung, breaking his wrists as he came through it. What a great eye he had! He hit it at the right second—put everything behind it. I can still hear the crack of the bat. I can still see the swing." It was Ruth's 59th home run, tying a record that less than a month before had seemed hopelessly out of reach.

The ball floated over the head of the right fielder, thirty-seven-year-old Sam   16
Rice, who is largely forgotten now but was one of the great players of his day and also one of the most mysterious, for he had come to major league baseball seemingly from out of nowhere.

Fifteen years earlier, Rice had been a promising youngster in his first season in   17
professional baseball with a minor league team in Galesburg, Illinois. While he was away for the summer, his wife moved with their two small children onto his parents' farm near Donovan, Indiana. In late April, a tornado struck near Donovan, killing seventy-five people. Among the victims were Rice's wife, children, mother, and two sisters. Rice's father, himself seriously injured, was found wandering in shock with one of the dead children in his arms; he died nine days later in the hospital. So, at a stroke, Rice lost his entire family. Dazed with grief, Rice drifted around America working at odd jobs. Eventually he enlisted in the navy. While playing for a navy team his remarkable talents became apparent. Clark Griffith, owner of the Washington Senators, somehow heard of this, invited him for a trial, and was impressed enough to sign him. Rice joined the Senators and in his thirties became one of the finest players in baseball. No one anywhere knew of his personal tragedy. It didn't become public until 1963, when he was inducted into the Baseball Hall of Fame.

After Ruth's homer, Hopkins struck out Lou Gehrig to end the inning, then   18
retired to the bench and burst into tears, overcome by the emotion of it all. Hopkins's appearance was one of just eleven he made in the majors. He missed the whole of the 1928 season with an injury and retired with a record of no wins and one loss after the 1929 season. He returned to his home state of Connecticut, became a successful banker, and lived to be ninety-nine.

The last day of September was sultry in New York. The temperature was in the low   19
80s and the air muggy when, in the next-to-last game of the season, Ruth came to the plate in the bottom of the eighth against Tom Zachary, a thirty-one-year-old left-hander from a tobacco farm in North Carolina. Though a pious Quaker, Zachary was not without guile. One of his tricks was to cover the pitching rubber with dirt so that he could move closer to home plate—sometimes by as much as two feet, it has been claimed. In 1927 he was in his tenth season. He gave up just six home runs all year. Three of them were to Ruth.

It was Ruth's fourth trip of the day to the plate. He had walked once and singled   20
twice and had come nowhere near a home run. The score was tied 2–2. There was one out and one man on—Mark Koenig, who had tripled.

"Everybody knew he was out for the record, so he wasn't going to get anything 21 good from me," Zachary told a reporter in 1961. Zachary wound up, eyed the runner, then uncorked a sizzling fastball. It went for a called strike. Zachary wound up and threw again. This pitch was high and away, and Ruth took it for a ball. For his third pitch, Zachary threw a curve—"as good as I had," he recalled—that was low and outside. Ruth hit the ball with what was effectively a golf swing, lofting it high into the air in the direction of the right field foul pole. The eight thousand fans in Yankee Stadium watched in silence as the ball climbed to a towering height, then fell for ages and dropped into the bleachers just inches fair. Zachary threw down his glove in frustration. The crowd roared with pleasure.

Ruth trotted around the bases with his curiously clipped and delicate gait, like 22 someone trying to tiptoe at speed, then stepped out of the dugout to acknowledge the applause with a succession of snappy military salutes. Ruth was responsible for all four runs that day. The *Times* the next day referred to the score as "Ruth 4, Senators 2."

A little-known fact was that the game in which Babe Ruth hit his 60th home 23 run was also the last game in the majors for Walter Johnson, the greatest pitcher of the age. No one threw harder. Jimmy Dykes, then of the Athletics, recalled in later years how as a rookie he was sent to the plate against Johnson, and never saw Johnson's first two pitches. He just heard them hit the catcher's mitt. After the third pitch the umpire told him to take first base.

"Why?" asked Dykes. 24

"You've been hit," explained the umpire. 25

"Are you sure?" asked Dykes. 26

The umpire told him to check his hat. Dykes reached up and discovered that the 27 cap was facing sideways from where Johnson's last pitch had spun the bill. He dropped his bat and hurried gratefully to first base.

In twenty-one years as a pitcher, Johnson gave up only ninety-seven home runs. 28 When Ruth homered off Johnson in 1920, it was the first home run anyone had hit off him in almost two years. In 1927, Johnson broke his leg in spring training when hit by a line drive, and never fully recovered. Now, with his fortieth birthday approaching, he decided it was time to retire. In the top of the ninth inning, in his last appearance in professional baseball, he was sent in to pinch-hit for Zachary. He hit a fly to right field. The ball was caught by Ruth, to end the game, Johnson's career, and an important part of a glorious era.

In the clubhouse afterward, Ruth was naturally exultant over his 60th homer. 29 "Let's see some son of a bitch try and top that one!" he kept saying. The general reaction among his teammates was congratulatory and warm, but in retrospect surprisingly muted. "There wasn't the excitement you'd imagine," Pete Sheehy, the team equipment manager, recalled many years later. No one expected Ruth to stop at 60. It was assumed that he would hit at least one more the next day, and possibly reach even greater heights in years to come. Ruth after all had been the first to hit 30, 40, 50, and 60 homers. Who knew that he wouldn't hit 70 in 1928?

In fact, neither he nor anyone else would hit so many again for a very long time. 30 In his last game of the season, Ruth rather anticlimactically went 0-for-3 with a walk. In his last at-bat he struck out. Lou Gehrig, however, did hit a home run, his 47th of the season. That might seem a disappointing number after his earlier pace, so it is worth remembering that it was more than any other player had *ever* hit, apart from Ruth.

In banging out 60 home runs, Ruth out-homered all major league teams except 31 the Cardinals, Cubs, and Giants. He hit home runs in every park in the American League and hit more on the road than at home. (The tally was 32 to 28.) He homered off thirty-three different pitchers. At least two of his home runs were the longest ever seen in the parks in which they were hit. Ruth hit a home run once every 11.8 times at bat. He had at least 6 home runs against every team in the American League. He did all this and still batted .356—*and* scored 158 runs, had 164 runs batted in, 138 walks, 7 stolen bases, and 14 sacrifice bunts. It would be hard to imagine a more extraordinary year.

Ruth and Gehrig between them came first and second in home runs, runs bat- 32 ted in, slugging percentage, runs scored, total bases, extra base hits, and bases on balls. Combs and Gehrig were first and second in total hits and triples. Four players— Ruth, Gehrig, Lazzeri, and Meusel—each had more than 100 runs batted in. Combs was also third in runs scored and total bases, and Lazzeri was third in home runs. As a team, the Yankees had the American League's highest team batting average and lowest earned-run average. They averaged 6.3 runs per game and almost 11 hits. Their 911 runs were more than any American League team had ever scored in a season before. Their 110 victories were a league record, too. Just one player was ejected from a game all season, and the team had no fights with other teams. Baseball has never fielded a more complete, dominant, and disciplined team.

Babe Ruth's home run record stood until 1961, when Roger Maris, also of the 33 Yankees, hit 61, though Maris had the advantage of a longer season, which gave him 10 more games and 50 more at-bats than Ruth in 1927. In the 1990s, many baseball players suddenly became immensely strong—some evolved whole new body shapes—and began to smack home runs in quantities that made a mockery of Ruth's and Maris's numbers. It turned out that a great many of this new generation of ballplayers—something in the region of 5 to 7 percent, according to random drug tests introduced, very belatedly, in 2003—were taking anabolic steroids. The use of drugs as an aid to hitting is far beyond the scope of this book, so let us just note in passing that even with the benefit of steroids most modern players still couldn't hit as many home runs as Babe Ruth hit on hot dogs. ◆

## READING WITH AN EYE FOR THE METHODS

1. Batting averages, runs batted in, home runs—baseball writers (and many fans) love statistics. How and how effectively does Bryson use facts and figures to capture the team and the season he is reporting on here? What other kinds of EVIDENCE does he use to back up his CLAIM that Summer 1927 was the "summer of records"?

2. In addition to Babe Ruth, Bryson DESCRIBES a number of other great ballplayers, including Lou Gehrig, Sam Rice, and Walter Johnson. Point out specific details in his sketches that you find particularly effective in giving a sense of each man and his talents. In particular, consider how Bryson uses their various reactions to hardship in characterizing the men and their team.

3. "He was bigger than the President," Bryson quotes a sportswriter in the epigraph as saying of Babe Ruth. How and how well does Bryson use Babe Ruth and the 1927 Yankees as an EXAMPLE of American's fascination with "bigness" and setting records? How does baseball itself as a sport fit into this picture?

## USING THE METHODS

1. Drawing on your reading and research, write a PROFILE of Babe Ruth (or some other legendary athlete) that captures something of his (or her) time and place as well as the man himself (or the woman herself).

2. Sportswriters often refer to baseball as "the American pastime." In a POSITION PAPER of approximately 400 words, explain what is (or is not) so "American" about baseball as a sport—and as a game where time can seem to stand still.

3. In your journal, keep a record of the performance of your favorite athletic team throughout a season. Based on those journal notes, write a "history" of that season.

4. Along with several other fans, choose a player, team, or particular game that represents your favorite sport at its height. Write a collaborative ANALYSIS of what made him, her, or it so great.

You'll find quizzes on the readings at wwnorton.com/write/back-to-the-lake.

# The Checklist Manifesto

Atul Gawande (b. 1965) is a surgeon, a professor of medicine and of health policy and management, and an award-winning writer. A native of Brooklyn and the son of doctors from India who ultimately transplanted the family to Athens, Ohio, Gawande attended Stanford University, Oxford University, and Harvard University's Medical School and School of Public Health, at both of which he now teaches. He became a staff writer for the *New Yorker* in 1998 and received a MacArthur Fellowship in 2006 for his medical research and his writing, collected in *Complications: A Surgeon's Notes on an Imperfect Science* (2002) and *Better: A Surgeon's Notes on Performance* (2007). His latest book, *Being Mortal: Medicine and What Matters at the End* (2014), recounts his research and experience of the limits of medicine in dealing with aging and the approach of death. Gawande is the director of the World Health Organization's Global Challenge for Safer Surgical Care.

"The Checklist Manifesto," a selection from Gawande's eponymous 2009 bestseller, is an extended argument about the need to manage extreme complexity in medicine and other fields. Gawande supports this main point with numerous examples using both description and narration— and with process analysis, cause-and-effect analysis, and other methods. One hero of the piece is Dr. Peter Pronovost of the Johns Hopkins Hospital, whom Gawande describes as "an odd mixture of the nerdy and the messianic. . . . He hated the laboratory—with all those micropipettes and cell cultures, and no patients around—but he had that scientific 'How can I solve this unsolved problem?' turn of mind."

$S$ OME TIME AGO I read a case report in the *Annals of Thoracic Surgery*. It was, in the dry prose of a medical journal article, the story of a nightmare. In a small Austrian town in the Alps, a mother and father had been out on a walk in the woods with their three-year-old daughter. The parents lost sight of the girl for a moment and that was all it took. She fell into an icy fishpond. The parents frantically jumped in after her. But she was lost beneath the surface for thirty minutes before they finally found her on the pond bottom. They pulled her to the surface

MLA CITATION: Gawande, Atul. "The Checklist Manifesto." 2009. *Back to the Lake*. Ed. Thomas Cooley. 3rd ed. New York: Norton, 2015. 785–97. Print.

and got her to the shore. Following instructions from an emergency response team reached on their cell phone, they began cardiopulmonary resuscitation.

Rescue personnel arrived eight minutes later and took the first recordings of the girl's condition. She was unresponsive. She had no blood pressure or pulse or sign of breathing. Her body temperature was just 66 degrees. Her pupils were dilated and unreactive to light, indicating cessation of brain function. She was gone.

But the emergency technicians continued CPR anyway. A helicopter took her to the nearest hospital, where she was wheeled directly into an operating room, a member of the emergency crew straddling her on the gurney, pumping her chest. A surgical team got her onto a heart-lung bypass machine as rapidly as it could. . . .

Between the transport time and the time it took to plug the machine into her, she had been lifeless for an hour and a half. By the two-hour mark, however, her body temperature had risen almost ten degrees, and her heart began to beat. It was her first organ to come back.

After six hours, the girl's core reached 98.6 degrees, normal body temperature. The team tried to shift her from the bypass machine to a mechanical ventilator, but the pond water and debris had damaged her lungs too severely for the oxygen pumped in through the breathing tube to reach her blood. So they switched her instead to an artificial-lung system known as ECMO—extracorporeal membrane oxygenation. To do this, the surgeons had to open her chest down the middle with a power saw and sew the lines to and from the portable ECMO unit directly into her aorta and her beating heart.

The ECMO machine now took over. The surgeons removed the heart-lung bypass machine tubing. They repaired the vessels and closed her groin incision. The surgical team moved the girl into intensive care, with her chest still open and covered with sterile plastic foil. Through the day and night, the intensive care unit team worked on suctioning the water and debris from her lungs with a fiberoptic bronchoscope. By the next day, her lungs had recovered sufficiently for the team to switch her from ECMO to a mechanical ventilator, which required taking her back to the operating room to unplug the tubing, repair the holes, and close her chest.

Over the next two days, all the girl's organs recovered—her liver, her kidneys, her intestines, everything except her brain. A CT scan showed global brain swelling, which is a sign of diffuse damage, but no actual dead zones. So the team escalated the care one step further. It drilled a hole into the girl's skull, threaded a probe into the brain to monitor the pressure, and kept that pressure tightly controlled through constant adjustments in her fluids and medications. For more than a week, she lay comatose. Then, slowly, she came back to life.

First, her pupils started to react to light. Next, she began to breathe on her own. And, one day, she simply awoke. Two weeks after her accident, she went home. Her right leg and left arm were partially paralyzed. Her speech was thick and slurry. But she underwent extensive outpatient therapy. By age five, she had recovered her faculties completely. Physical and neurological examinations were normal. She was like any little girl again.

What makes this recovery astounding isn't just the idea that someone could be brought back after two hours in a state that would once have been considered death. It's also the idea that a group of people in a random hospital could manage to pull off something so enormously complicated. Rescuing a drowning victim is nothing like it looks on television shows, where a few chest compressions and some mouth-to-mouth resuscitation always seem to bring someone with waterlogged lungs and a stilled heart coughing and sputtering back to life. To save this one child, scores of people had to carry out thousands of steps correctly: placing the heart-pump tubing into her without letting in air bubbles; maintaining the sterility of her lines, her open chest, the exposed fluid in her brain; keeping a temperamental battery of machines up and running. The degree of difficulty in any one of these steps is substantial. Then you must add the difficulties of orchestrating them in the right sequence, with nothing dropped, leaving some room for improvisation, but not too much. 9

For every drowned and pulseless child rescued, there are scores more who don't make it—and not just because their bodies are too far gone. Machines break down; a team can't get moving fast enough; someone fails to wash his hands and an infection takes hold. Such cases don't get written up in the *Annals of Thoracic Surgery*, but they are the norm, though people may not realize it. 10

. . .

On any given day in the United States alone, some ninety thousand people are admitted to intensive care. Over a year, an estimated five million Americans will be, and over a normal lifetime nearly all of us will come to know the glassed bay of an ICU from the inside. Wide swaths of medicine now depend on the life support systems that ICUs provide: care for premature infants; for victims of trauma, strokes, and heart attacks; for patients who have had surgery on their brains, hearts, lungs, or major blood vessels. Critical care has become an increasingly large portion of what hospitals do. Fifty years ago, ICUs barely existed. Now, to take a recent random day in my hospital, 155 of our almost 700 patients are in intensive care. The average stay of an ICU patient is four days, and the survival rate is 86 percent. Going into an ICU, being put on a mechanical ventilator, having tubes and wires run into and out of you, is not a sentence of death. But the days will be the most precarious of your life. 11

Fifteen years ago, Israeli scientists published a study in which engineers observed patient care in ICUs for twenty-four-hour stretches. They found that the average patient required 178 individual actions per day, ranging from administer- 12 ing a drug to suctioning the lungs, and every one of them posed risks. Remarkably, the nurses and doctors were observed to make an error in just 1 percent of these actions—but that still amounted to an average of two errors a day with every patient. Intensive care succeeds only when we hold the odds of doing harm low enough for the odds of doing good to prevail. This is hard. There are dangers simply in lying unconscious in bed for a few days. Muscles atrophy. Bones lose mass. Pressure ulcers form. Veins begin to clot. You have to stretch and exercise patients' flaccid limbs daily to avoid contractures; you have to give subcutaneous injections of blood thinners at least twice a day, turn patients in bed every few hours, bathe them and change their sheets without knocking out a tube or a line, brush their teeth twice a day to avoid pneumonia from bacterial buildup in their mouths. Add a ventilator, dialysis, and the care of open wounds, and the difficulties only accumulate.

. . .

Here, then, is the fundamental puzzle of modern medical care: you have a desper-   13
ately sick patient and in order to have a chance of saving him you have to get the knowledge right and then you have to make sure that the 178 daily tasks that follow are done correctly—despite some monitor's alarm going off for God knows what reason, despite the patient in the next bed crashing, despite a nurse poking his head around the curtain to ask whether someone could help "get this lady's chest open." There is complexity upon complexity. And even specialization has begun to seem inadequate. So what do you do?

The medical profession's answer has been to go from specialization to super-   14
specialization. . . . In the past decade, training programs focusing on critical care have opened in most major American and European cities, and half of American ICUs now rely on superspecialists.

Expertise is the mantra of modern medicine. In the early twentieth century, you   15
needed only a high school diploma and a one-year medical degree to practice medicine. By the century's end, all doctors had to have a college degree, a four-year medical degree, and an additional three to seven years of residency training in an individual field of practice—pediatrics, surgery, neurology, or the like. In recent years, though, even this level of preparation has not been enough for the new complexity of medicine. After their residencies, most young doctors today are going on to do fellowships, adding one to three further years of training in, say, laparoscopic surgery, or pediatric metabolic disorders, or breast radiology, or critical care. A young doctor is not so young nowadays; you typically don't start in independent practice until your midthirties.

We live in the era of the superspecialist—of clinicians who have taken the time   16
to practice, practice, practice at one narrow thing until they can do it better than anyone else. They have two advantages over ordinary specialists: greater knowledge

of the details that matter and a learned ability to handle the complexities of the particular job. There are degrees of complexity, though, and medicine and other fields like it have grown so far beyond the usual kind that avoiding daily mistakes is proving impossible even for our most superspecialized. . . .

Medicine, with its dazzling successes but also frequent failures, therefore poses a significant challenge: What do you do when expertise is not enough? What do you do when even the superspecialists fail? We've begun to see an answer, but it has come from an unexpected source—one that has nothing to do with medicine at all. 17

. . .

On October 30, 1935, at Wright Air Field in Dayton, Ohio, the U.S. Army Air Corps held a flight competition for airplane manufacturers vying to build the military's next-generation long-range bomber. It wasn't supposed to be much of a competition. In early evaluations, the Boeing Corporation's gleaming aluminum-alloy Model 299 had trounced the designs of Martin and Douglas. Boeing's plane could carry five times as many bombs as the army had requested; it could fly faster than previous bombers and almost twice as far. A Seattle newspaperman who had glimpsed the plane on a test flight over his city called it the "flying fortress," and the name stuck. The flight "competition," according to the military historian Phillip Meilinger, was regarded as a mere formality. The army planned to order at least sixty-five of the aircraft. 18

A small crowd of army brass and manufacturing executives watched as the Model 299 test plane taxied onto the runway. It was sleek and impressive, with a 103-foot wingspan and four engines jutting out from the wings, rather than the usual two. The plane roared down the tarmac, lifted off smoothly, and climbed sharply to three hundred feet. Then it stalled, turned on one wing, and crashed in a fiery explosion. Two of the five crew members died, including the pilot, Major Ployer P. Hill. 19

An investigation revealed that nothing mechanical had gone wrong. The crash had been due to "pilot error," the report said. Substantially more complex than previous aircraft, the new plane required the pilot to attend to the four engines, each with its own oil-fuel mix, the retractable landing gear, the wing flaps, electric trim tabs that needed adjustment to maintain stability at different airspeeds, and constant-speed propellers whose pitch had to be regulated with hydraulic controls, among other features. While doing all this, Hill had forgotten to release a new locking mechanism on the elevator and rudder controls. The Boeing model was deemed, as a newspaper put it, "too much airplane for one man to fly." The army air corps declared Douglas's smaller design the winner. Boeing nearly went bankrupt. 20

Still, the army purchased a few aircraft from Boeing as test planes, and some insiders remained convinced that the aircraft was flyable. So a group of test pilots got together and considered what to do. 21

B-17 bomber and ground crew.

What they decided *not* to do was almost as interesting as what they actually did.　22
They did not require Model 299 pilots to undergo longer training. It was hard to imagine having more experience and expertise than Major Hill, who had been the air corps' chief of flight testing. Instead, they came up with an ingeniously simple approach: they created a pilot's checklist. Its mere existence indicated how far aeronautics had advanced. In the early years of flight, getting an aircraft into the air might have been nerve-racking but it was hardly complex. Using a checklist for takeoff would no more have occurred to a pilot than to a driver backing a car out of the garage. But flying this new plane was too complicated to be left to the memory of any one person, however expert.

The test pilots made their list simple, brief, and to the point—short enough to fit　23
on an index card, with step-by-step checks for takeoff, flight, landing, and taxiing. It had the kind of stuff that all pilots know to do. They check that the brakes are released, that the instruments are set, that the door and windows are closed, that the elevator controls are unlocked—dumb stuff. You wouldn't think it would make that much difference. But with the checklist in hand, the pilots went on to fly the Model 299 a total of 1.8 million miles without one accident. The army ultimately ordered almost thirteen thousand of the aircraft, which it dubbed the B-17. And, because flying the behemoth was now possible, the army gained a decisive air advantage in the Second World War, enabling its devastating bombing campaign across Nazi Germany.

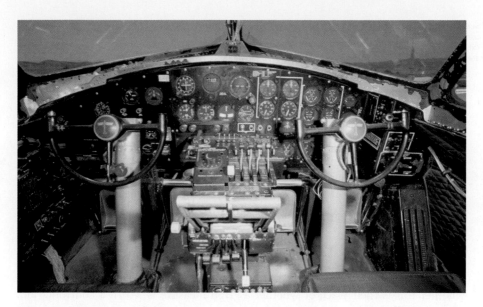

Cockpit of a B-17.

Much of our work today has entered its own B-17 phase. Substantial parts of 24
what software designers, financial managers, firefighters, police officers, lawyers,
and most certainly clinicians do are now too complex for them to carry out reliably
from memory alone. Multiple fields, in other words, have become too much airplane for one person to fly.

Yet it is far from obvious that something as simple as a checklist could be of 25
substantial help. We may admit that errors and oversights occur—even devastating
ones. But we believe our jobs are too complicated to reduce to a checklist. Sick
people, for instance, are phenomenally more various than airplanes. A study of
forty-one thousand trauma patients in the state of Pennsylvania—just trauma
patients—found that they had 1,224 different injury-related diagnoses in 32,261
unique combinations. That's like having 32,261 kinds of airplane to land. Mapping
out the proper steps for every case is not possible, and physicians have been skeptical that a piece of paper with a bunch of little boxes would improve matters.

. . .

In 2001, though, a critical care specialist at Johns Hopkins Hospital named Peter 26
Pronovost decided to give a doctor checklist a try. He didn't attempt to make the
checklist encompass everything ICU teams might need to do in a day. He designed it
to tackle just one of their hundreds of potential tasks . . . : central line infections.

On a sheet of plain paper, he plotted out the steps to take in order to avoid infec- 27
tions when putting in a central line. Doctors are supposed to (1) wash their hands

See p. 753
for combining
narrative and
process analysis.
with soap, (2) clean the patient's skin with chlorhexidine antiseptic, (3) put sterile drapes over the entire patient, (4) wear a mask, hat, sterile gown, and gloves, and (5) put a sterile dressing over the insertion site once the line is in. Check, check, check, check, check. These steps are no-brainers; they have been known and taught for years. So it seemed silly to make a checklist for something so obvious. Still, Pronovost asked the nurses in his ICU to observe the doctors for a month as they put lines into patients and record how often they carried out each step. In more than a third of patients, they skipped at least one.

The next month, he and his team persuaded the Johns Hopkins Hospital administration to authorize nurses to stop doctors if they saw them skipping a step on the checklist; nurses were also to ask the doctors each day whether any lines ought to be removed, so as not to leave them in longer than necessary. This was revolutionary. Nurses have always had their ways of nudging a doctor into doing the right thing, ranging from the gentle reminder ("Um, did you forget to put on your mask, doctor?") to more forceful methods (I've had a nurse bodycheck me when she thought I hadn't put enough drapes on a patient). But many nurses aren't sure whether this is their place or whether a given measure is worth a confrontation. (Does it really matter whether a patient's legs are draped for a line going into the chest?) The new rule made it clear: if doctors didn't follow every step, the nurses would have backup from the administration to intervene. 28

For a year afterward, Pronovost and his colleagues monitored what happened. The results were so dramatic that they weren't sure whether to believe them: the ten-day line-infection rate went from 11 percent to zero. So they followed patients for fifteen more months. Only two line infections occurred during the entire period. They calculated that, in this one hospital, the checklist had prevented forty-three infections and eight deaths and saved two million dollars in costs. 29

Pronovost recruited more colleagues, and they tested some more checklists in his Johns Hopkins ICU. One aimed to ensure that nurses observed patients for pain at least once every four hours and provided timely pain medication. This reduced from 41 percent to 3 percent the likelihood of a patient's enduring untreated pain. They tested a checklist for patients on mechanical ventilation, making sure, for instance, that doctors prescribed antacid medication to prevent stomach ulcers and that the head of each patient's bed was propped up at least thirty degrees to stop oral secretions from going into the windpipe. The proportion of patients not receiving the recommended care dropped from 70 percent to 4 percent, the occurrence of pneumonias fell by a quarter, and twenty-one fewer patients died than in the previous year. The researchers found that simply having the doctors and nurses in the ICU create their own checklists for what they thought should be done each day improved the consistency of care to the point that the average length of patient stay in intensive care dropped by half. 30

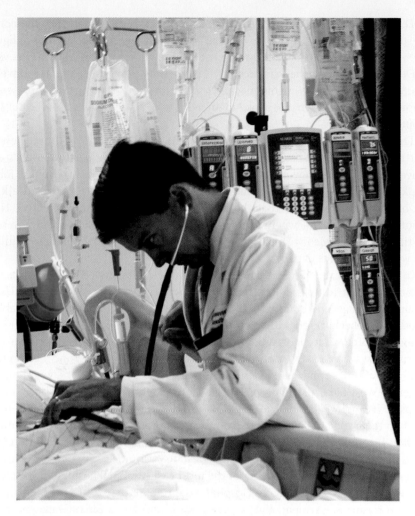

Dr. Peter Pronovost attends a patient.

These checklists accomplished what checklists elsewhere have done, Pronovost 31
observed. They helped with memory recall and clearly set out the minimum necessary steps in a process. He was surprised to discover how often even experienced
personnel failed to grasp the importance of certain precautions. In a survey of ICU
staff taken before introducing the ventilator checklists, he found that half hadn't
realized that evidence strongly supported giving ventilated patients antacid medication. Checklists, he found, established a higher standard of baseline performance.

These seem, of course, ridiculously primitive insights. Pronovost is routinely 32
described by colleagues as "brilliant," "inspiring," a "genius." He has an M.D. and a

Ph.D. in public health from Johns Hopkins and is trained in emergency medicine, anesthesiology, and critical care medicine. But, really, does it take all that to figure out what anyone who has made a to-do list figured out ages ago? Well, maybe yes.

Despite his initial checklist results, takers were slow to come. He traveled     33
around the country showing his checklists to doctors, nurses, insurers, employers—anyone who would listen. He spoke in an average of seven cities a month. But few adopted the idea.

There were various reasons. Some physicians were offended by the suggestion     34
that they needed checklists. Others had legitimate doubts about Pronovost's evidence. So far, he'd shown only that checklists worked in one hospital, Johns Hopkins, where the ICUs have money, plenty of staff, and Peter Pronovost walking the hallways to make sure that the idea was being properly implemented. How about in the real world—where ICU nurses and doctors are in short supply, pressed for time, overwhelmed with patients, and hardly receptive to the notion of filling out yet another piece of paper?

In 2003, however, the Michigan Health and Hospital Association approached     35
Pronovost about testing his central line checklist throughout the state's ICUs. It would be a huge undertaking. But Pronovost would have a chance to establish whether his checklists could really work in the wider world.

I visited Sinai-Grace Hospital, in inner-city Detroit, a few years after the project     36
was under way, and I saw what Pronovost was up against. Occupying a campus of redbrick buildings amid abandoned houses, check-cashing stores, and wig shops on the city's West Side, just south of Eight Mile Road, Sinai-Grace is a classic urban hospital. It employed at the time eight hundred physicians, seven hundred nurses, and two thousand other medical personnel to care for a population with the lowest median income of any city in the country. More than a quarter of a million residents were uninsured; 300,000 were on state assistance. That meant chronic financial problems. Sinai-Grace is not the most cash-strapped hospital in the city—that would be Detroit Receiving Hospital, where more than a fifth of the patients have no means of payment. But between 2000 and 2003, Sinai-Grace and eight other Detroit hospitals were forced to cut a third of their staff, and the state had to come forward with a $50 million bailout to avert their bankruptcy.

Sinai-Grace has five ICUs for adult patients and one for infants. Hassan Makki,     37
the director of intensive care, told me what it was like there in 2004, when Pronovost and the hospital association started a series of mailings and conference calls with hospitals to introduce checklists for central lines and ventilator patients. "Morale was low," he said. "We had lost lots of staff, and the nurses who remained weren't sure if they were staying." Many doctors were thinking about leaving, too. Meanwhile, the teams faced an even heavier workload because of new rules limiting how long the residents could work at a stretch. Now Pronovost was telling them to find the time to fill out some daily checklists?

Tom Piskorowski, one of the ICU physicians, told me his reaction: "Forget the   38
paperwork. Take care of the patient."

I accompanied a team on 7:00 a.m. rounds through one of the surgical ICUs. It   39
had eleven patients. Four had gunshot wounds (one had been shot in the chest; one
had been shot through the bowel, kidney, and liver; two had been shot through the
neck and left quadriplegic). Five patients had cerebral hemorrhaging (three were
seventy-nine years and older and had been injured falling down stairs; one was a
middle-aged man whose skull and left temporal lobe had been damaged by an
assault with a blunt weapon; and one was a worker who had become paralyzed
from the neck down after falling twenty-five feet off a ladder onto his head). There
was a cancer patient recovering from surgery to remove part of his lung, and a
patient who had had surgery to repair a cerebral aneurysm.

The doctors and nurses on rounds tried to proceed methodically from one room   40
to the next but were constantly interrupted: a patient they thought they'd stabi-
lized began hemorrhaging again; another who had been taken off the ventilator
developed trouble breathing and had to be put back on the machine. It was hard to
imagine that they could get their heads far enough above the daily tide of disasters
to worry about the minutiae on some checklist.

Yet there they were, I discovered, filling out those pages. Mostly, it was the nurses   41
who kept things in order. Each morning, a senior nurse walked through the unit,
clipboard in hand, making sure that every patient on a ventilator had the bed propped
at the right angle and had been given the right medicines and the right tests. Whenever doctors put in a central line, a nurse made sure that the central line checklist
had been filled out and placed in the patient's chart. Looking back through the hospital files, I found that they had been doing this faithfully for more than three years.

Pronovost had been canny when he started. In his first conversations with hos-   42
pital administrators, he hadn't ordered them to use the central line checklist.
Instead, he asked them simply to gather data on their own line infection rates.
In early 2004, they found, the infection rates for ICU patients in Michigan hospitals were higher than the national average, and in some hospitals dramatically so.
Sinai-Grace experienced more central line infections than 75 percent of American
hospitals. Meanwhile, Blue Cross Blue Shield of Michigan agreed to give hospitals
small bonus payments for participating in Pronovost's program. A checklist suddenly seemed an easy and logical thing to try.

In what became known as the Keystone Initiative, each hospital assigned a proj-   43
ect manager to roll out the checklist and participate in twice-monthly conference
calls with Pronovost for troubleshooting. Pronovost also insisted that the participating hospitals assign to each unit a senior hospital executive who would visit at
least once a month, hear the staff's complaints, and help them solve problems.

The executives were reluctant. They normally lived in meetings, worrying about   44
strategy and budgets. They weren't used to venturing into patient territory and

didn't feel they belonged there. In some places, they encountered hostility, but their involvement proved crucial. In the first month, the executives discovered that chlorhexidine soap, shown to reduce line infections, was available in less than a third of the ICUs. This was a problem only an executive could solve. Within weeks, every ICU in Michigan had a supply of the soap. Teams also complained to the hospital officials that, although the checklist required patients be fully covered with a sterile drape when lines were being put in, full-size drapes were often unavailable. So the officials made sure that drapes were stocked. Then they persuaded Arrow International, one of the largest manufacturers of central lines, to produce a new kit that had both the drape and chlorhexidine in it.

In December 2006, the Keystone Initiative published its findings in a landmark    45
article in the *New England Journal of Medicine*. Within the first three months of the project, the central line infection rate in Michigan's ICUs decreased by 66 percent. Most ICUs—including the ones at Sinai-Grace Hospital—cut their quarterly infection rate to zero. Michigan's infection rates fell so low that its average ICU outperformed 90 percent of ICUs nationwide. In the Keystone Initiative's first eighteen months, the hospitals saved an estimated $175 million in costs and more than fifteen hundred lives. The successes have been sustained for several years now—all because of a stupid little checklist.

It is tempting to think this might be an isolated success. Perhaps there is something    46
unusual about the strategy required to prevent central line infections. After all, the central line checklist did not prevent any of the other kinds of complications that can result from sticking these foot-long plastic catheters into people's chests—such as a collapsed lung if the needle goes in too deep or bleeding if a blood vessel gets torn. It just prevented infections. In this particular instance, yes, doctors had some trouble getting the basics right—making sure to wash their hands, put on their sterile gloves and gown, and so on—and a checklist proved dramatically valuable. But among the myriad tasks clinicians carry out for patients, maybe this is the peculiar case.

I started to wonder, though.    47

Around the time I learned of Pronovost's results, I spoke to Markus Thalmann,    48
the cardiac surgeon who had been the lead author of the case report on the extraordinary rescue of the little girl from death by drowning. Among the many details that intrigued me about the save was the fact that it occurred not at a large cutting-edge academic medical center but at an ordinary community hospital. This one was in Klagenfurt, a small provincial Austrian town in the Alps nearest to where the girl had fallen in the pond. I asked Thalmann how the hospital had managed such a complicated rescue.

He told me he had been working in Klagenfurt for six years when the girl came    49
in. She had not been the first person whom he and his colleagues had tried to revive

from cardiac arrest after hypothermia and suffocation. His hospital received between three and five such patients a year, he estimated, mostly avalanche victims, some of them drowning victims, and a few of them people attempting suicide by taking a drug overdose and then wandering out into the snowy Alpine forests to fall unconscious. For a long time, he said, no matter how hard the hospital's medical staff tried, they had no survivors. Most of the victims had been without a pulse and oxygen for too long when they were found. But some, he was convinced, still had a flicker of viability in them, yet he and his colleagues had always failed to sustain it.

He took a close look at the case records. Preparation, he determined, was the 50 chief difficulty. Success required having an array of people and equipment at the ready—trauma surgeons, a cardiac anesthesiologist, a cardiothoracic surgeon, bioengineering support staff, a cardiac perfusionist, operating and critical care nurses, intensivists. Almost routinely, someone or something was missing.

He tried the usual surgical approach to remedy this—yelling at everyone to get 51 their act together. But still they had no saves. So he and a couple of colleagues decided to try something new. They made a checklist.

They gave the checklist to the people with the least power in the whole process— 52 the rescue squads and the hospital telephone operator—and walked them through the details. In cases like these, the checklist said, rescue teams were to tell the hospital to prepare for possible cardiac bypass and rewarming. They were to call, when possible, even before they arrived on the scene, as the preparation time could be significant. The telephone operator would then work down a list of people to notify them to have everything set up and standing by.

With the checklist in place, the team had its first success—the rescue of the 53 three-year-old girl. Not long afterward, Thalmann left to take a job at a hospital in Vienna. The team, however, has since had at least two other such rescues, he said. In one case, a man had been found frozen and pulseless after a suicide attempt. In another, a mother and her sixteen-year-old daughter were in an accident that sent them and their car through a guardrail, over a cliff, and into a mountain river. The mother died on impact; the daughter was trapped as the car rapidly filled with icy water. She had been in cardiac and respiratory arrest for a prolonged period of time when the rescue team arrived.

From that point onward, though, everything moved like clockwork. By the time 54 the rescue team got to her and began CPR, the hospital had been notified. The transport team delivered her in minutes. The surgical team took her straight to the operating room and crashed her onto heart-lung bypass. One step followed right after another. And, because of the speed with which they did, she had a chance.

As the girl's body slowly rewarmed, her heart came back. In the ICU, a 55 mechanical ventilator, fluids, and intravenous drugs kept her going while the rest of her body recovered. The next day, the doctors were able to remove her lines and tubes. The day after that, she was sitting up in bed, ready to go home. ◆

## READING WITH AN EYE FOR THE METHODS

1. Gawande often makes a point by telling a story, as when he writes about the girl rescued from drowning in the Austrian Alps. Of the many NARRATIVE elements in his essay, which do you find particularly effective? Why?

2. "The medical profession's answer" to the problem of the increasing complexity of modern medical care, says Atul Gawande, is "to go from specialization to super-specialization" (14). How does Gawande DEFINE this term, and how does this definition help to organize and support his argument about checklists?

3. Gawande likens the practice of medicine to flying an airplane. What is the purpose of this COMPARISON? Why does he go on to point out that "sick people . . . are phenomenally more various than airplanes" (25)?

4. A checklist is usually the result of a PROCESS ANALYSIS. Point out places in his essay where Gawande effectively uses this and other methods of development, such as DESCRIPTION or CAUSE-AND-EFFECT analysis. How do these additional methods help to support his ARGUMENT?

## USING THE METHODS

1. Draw up a checklist of the objects and actions required for one of the following: studying for an exam, preparing to take a trip, riding a horse, flying a small plane, administering some form of first aid or other emergency medical service.

2. Write an essay about using a checklist, or other relatively simple device, to manage a complex procedure or situation. Explain how the procedure works, why understanding it is important, and how it was (or could be) improved by following a checklist or some other simple measure. Illustrate your point with a brief narrative or two. Use other methods as appropriate.

3. Do some research on milestones in medicine and biology, and write a PROFILE of a particular doctor (or other health professional or researcher) who changed the practice of medicine or some other field. Possible candidates: William Harvey, Louis Pasteur, Jonas Salk, Priscilla White, Christiaan Barnard.

4. Interview someone who has received medical treatment for a serious illness or injury, and write a REPORT outlining the treatment they received, including specific medical procedures and the role of particular doctors and nurses in their recovery.

You'll find quizzes on the readings at
wwnorton.com/write/back-to-the-lake.

APPENDIX

# Using Sources in Your Writing

Quiet
Area

Research is formalized
curiosity. It is poking and
prying with a purpose.
—ZORA NEALE HURSTON

Whatever your purpose, academic research requires "poking and prying" into sources of information that go well beyond your own immediate knowledge of a subject. If you're examining the student loan controversy of 2007, for example, you'll consult news stories and blog commentary published at that time. Or if you're analyzing a poem by Rita Dove, you'll study Dove's other poetry and read critical interpretations of her work in literary journals. This appendix shows how to find reliable sources, use what you learn in your own writing, and document your sources accurately.

## Finding and Evaluating Sources

As you do your research, you will encounter a wide range of potential sources—print and online, general and specialized, published and firsthand. You'll need to evaluate these sources carefully, choose the ones that best support your THESIS, and decide how to incorporate each source into your own paper.

### Finding Appropriate Sources

The kinds of sources you turn to will depend on your topic. If you're doing research on a literary or historical topic, you might consult scholarly books and articles and standard reference works such as the *Dictionary of American Biography* or the *Literary History of the United States*. If your research is aimed at a current issue, you would likely consult newspapers and other periodicals, websites, and recent books.

Check your assignment to see if you are required to use primary or secondary sources—or both. *Primary sources* are original works, such as historical documents, literary works, eyewitness accounts, diaries, letters, and lab studies, as well as any original field research you do. *Secondary sources* include books and articles, reviews, biographies, and other works that interpret or discuss primary sources. For example, novels and poems are primary sources; articles interpreting them are secondary sources.

Whether a work is considered primary or secondary often depends on your topic and purpose. If you're analyzing a poem, a critic's article analyzing the poem is a secondary source—but if you're investigating the critic's work, the article would be a primary source.

#### LIBRARY SOURCES

When you conduct academic research, it is often better to start with your library's website rather than with a commercial search engine such as *Google*. Library websites provide access to a range of well-organized resources, including scholarly databases through which you can access authoritative articles that have been screened by librarians or specialists in a particular field. In general, there are three kinds of sources you'll want to consult: reference works, books, and periodicals.

*Reference works.* The reference section of your school's library is the place to find encyclopedias, dictionaries, atlases, almanacs, bibliographies, and other reference works. Remember, though, that reference works are only a starting point, a place where you can get an overview of your topic or basic facts about it. Some reference works are *general,* such as *The New Encyclopaedia Britannica* or the *Statistical Abstract of the United States.* Others are *specialized,* providing in-depth information on a single field or topic.

*Books.* The library catalog is your main source for finding books. Most catalogs are computerized and can be accessed through the library's website. You can search by author, title, subject, or keyword. When you click on a specific source, you'll find more bibliographic data about author, title, and publication; the call number (which identifies the book's location on the library's shelves); related subject headings (which may lead to other useful materials in the library)—and more.

*Periodicals.* To find journal and magazine articles, you will need to search periodical indexes and databases. Indexes (such as the *New York Times Index*) provide listings of articles organized by topics; databases (such as LexisNexis) provide the full texts. Although some databases are available for free, many may be accessible at no cost through your library.

## ONLINE SOURCES

The web offers countless sites sponsored by governments, educational institutions, organizations, businesses, and individuals. Because it is so vast and dynamic, however, finding useful information can be a challenge. There are several ways to search the web:

- *Keyword searches. Google, Bing, Ask.com, Yahoo!,* and many other search sites scan the web looking for the keywords you specify.
- *Metasearches. Yippy, Copernic Agent, SurfWax,* and *Dogpile* let you use several search sites simultaneously.

- *Academic searches.* For peer-reviewed academic writing in many disciplines, try *Google Scholar*; for scientific, technical, and medical documents, use *Scirus*.

Although many websites provide authoritative information, keep in mind that web content varies greatly in its stability and reliability: what you see on a site today may be different (or gone) tomorrow. So save or make copies of pages you plan to use, and carefully evaluate what you find. Here are just a few of the many resources available on the web.

*Indexes, databases, and directories.* Information put together by specialists and grouped by topics can be especially helpful. You may want to consult *iPl2* (an annotated subject directory of thousands of websites selected by librarians); *Infomine* (a huge collection of databases, mailing lists, catalogs, articles, directories, and more); or the *WWW Virtual Library* (a catalog of websites on numerous subjects, compiled by subject specialists).

*News sites.* Many newspapers, magazines, and radio and TV stations have websites that provide both up-to-the-minute information and also archives of older news articles. Through *Google News* and *NewsLink,* for example, you can access current news worldwide, whereas *Google News Archive Search* has files going back to the 1700s.

*Government sites.* Many government agencies and departments maintain websites where you can find government reports, statistics, legislative information, and other resources. *USA.gov* offers information, services, and other resources from the U.S. government.

*Digital archives.* These sites collect and organize materials from the past—including drawings, maps, recordings, speeches, and historic documents—often focusing on a particular subject or country. For example, the National Archives and Records Administration and the Library of Congress both archive items relevant to the culture and history of the United States.

*Discussion lists and forums.* Online mailing lists, newsgroups, discussion groups, and forums let members post and receive messages from other members. To join a discussion with people who are knowledgeable about your topic, try searching for your topic—for example, for "E. B. White discussion forum." Or consult a site such as *Google Groups.*

## SEARCHING ELECTRONICALLY

When you search for subjects on the web or in library catalogs, indexes, or databases, you'll want to come up with keywords that will lead to the information you need. Specific commands vary among search engines and databases, but most search engines now offer "Advanced Search" options that allow you to narrow your search by typing keywords into text boxes labeled as follows:

- All of these words
- The exact phrase
- Any of these words
- None of these words

In addition, you may filter the results to include only full-text articles (articles that are available in full online); only certain domains (such as *.edu*, for educational sites; *.gov*, for government sites; or *.org*, for nonprofit sites); and, in library databases, only scholarly, peer-reviewed sites. Type quotation marks around words to search for an exact phrase: "Twitter revolution" or "Neil Gaiman."

Some databases may require you to limit searches through the use of various symbols or Boolean operators (AND, OR, NOT). See the Advanced Search instructions for help with such symbols, which may be called *field tags*.

If a search turns up too many sources, be more specific (*homeopathy* instead of *medicine*). If your original keywords don't generate good results, try synonyms (*home remedy* instead of *folk medicine*). Keep in mind that searching requires flexibility, both in the words you use and the methods you try.

## Evaluating Sources

Searching the *Health Source* database for information on the incidence of meningitis among college students, you find seventeen articles. An "exact words" *Google* search yields thirty-seven. How do you decide which sources to read? The following questions can help you select reliable and useful sources.

**Is the source relevant?** Look at the title and at any introductory material to see what it covers. Does the source appear to relate directly to your purpose? What will it add to your work?

**What are the author's credentials?** Has the author written other works on this subject? Is he or she known for taking a particular position on it? If the author's credentials are not stated, you might do a web search to see what else you can learn about him or her.

**What is the stance?** Does the source cover various points of view or advocate only one perspective? Does its title suggest a certain slant? If you're evaluating a website, check to see whether it includes links to sites expressing other perspectives.

*Who is the publisher?* Books published by university presses and articles in scholarly journals are peer-reviewed by experts in the field before they are published. Those produced for a general audience do not always undergo such rigorous review and factchecking. At well-established publishing houses, however, submissions are usually vetted by experienced editors or even editorial boards.

*If the source is a website, who is the sponsor?* Is the site maintained by an organization, interest group, government agency, or individual? If the site doesn't give this information on its homepage, look for clues in the URL domain: *.edu* is used mostly by colleges and universities, *.gov* by government agencies, *.org* by nonprofit organizations, *.mil* by the military, and *.com* by commercial organizations. Be aware that the sponsor may have an agenda—to argue a position, present biased information, or sell a product—and that text on the site does not necessarily undergo rigorous review or factchecking.

*What is the level of the material?* Texts written for a general audience might be easier to understand but may not be authoritative enough for academic work. Scholarly texts will be more authoritative but may be harder to comprehend.

*How current is the source?* Check to see when books and articles were published and when websites were last updated. (If a site lists no date, see if links to other sites still work; if not, the site is probably too dated to use.) A recent publication date or updating, however, does not necessarily mean the source is better—some topics require current information whereas others call for older sources.

*Does the source include other useful information?* Is there a bibliography that might lead you to additional materials? How current or authoritative are the sources it cites?

## Taking Notes

When you find material that will be useful to your argument, take careful notes.

- *Use index cards, a computer file, or a notebook,* labeling each entry with information that will allow you to keep track of where it comes from— author, title, the pages or the URL, and (for online sources) the date of access.

- *Take notes in your own words and use your own sentence patterns.* If you make a note that is a detailed paraphrase, label it as such so that you'll know to provide appropriate documentation if you use it.

- *If you find wording that you'd like to quote,* be sure to enclose the exact words in quotation marks to distinguish your source's words from your own.

• *Label each note with a subject heading* so you can organize your notes easily when constructing an outline for your paper.

## Incorporating Source Materials into Your Text

There are many ways to incorporate source materials into your own text. Three of the most common are quoting, paraphrasing, or summarizing. Let's look at the differences between these three forms of reference, and then consider when to use each one and how to work these references into your text.

### Quoting

When you quote someone else's words, you reproduce their language exactly, in quotation marks—though you can add your own words in brackets or omit unnecessary words in the original by using ellipsis marks (. . .). This example from Mary Roach's "How to Know If You Are Dead" uses all of these conventions:

> In her analysis of the life-saving role of human cadavers, Mary Roach notes that "a gurney with a [newly deceased] cadaver commands no urgency. It is wheeled by a single person, . . . like a shopping cart" (167).

### Paraphrasing

When you paraphrase, you restate information from a source in your own words, using your own sentence structures. Because a paraphrase includes all the main points of the source, it is usually about the same length as the original.

Here is a paragraph from Diane Ackerman's essay "Why Leaves Turn Color in the Fall," followed by two sample paraphrases. The first demonstrates some of the challenges of paraphrasing.

ORIGINAL SOURCE

Where do the colors come from? Sunlight rules most living things with its golden edicts. When the days begin to shorten, soon after the summer solstice on June 21, a tree reconsiders its leaves. All summer it feeds them so they can process sunlight, but in the dog days of summer the tree begins pulling nutrients back into its trunk and roots, pares down, and gradually chokes off its leaves. A corky layer of cells forms at the leaves' slender petioles, then scars over. Undernourished, the leaves stop producing the pigment chlorophyll, and photosynthesis ceases. Animals can migrate, hibernate, or store food to prepare for winter. But where can a tree go? It survives by dropping its leaves, and by the end of autumn only a few fragile threads of fluid-carrying xylem hold leaves to their stems.

UNACCEPTABLE PARAPHRASE

Ackerman tells us where the colors of leaves come from. The amount of sunlight is the trigger, as is true for most living things. At the end of June, as daylight lessens, a tree begins to treat its leaves differently. It feeds them all summer so they can turn sunlight into food, but in August a tree begins to redirect its food into its trunk and roots, gradually choking the leaves. A corky group of cells develops at the petioles, and a scar forms. By autumn, the leaves don't have enough food, so they stop producing chlorophyll, and photosynthesis also stops. Although animals are able to migrate, hibernate, or stow food for the winter, a tree cannot go anywhere. It survives only by dropping its leaves, and by the time winter comes only a few leaves remain on their stems.

This first paraphrase borrows too much of the language of the original or changes it only slightly. It also follows the original sentence structure too closely. The following paraphrase avoids both of these pitfalls.

ACCEPTABLE PARAPHRASE

Ackerman explains why leaves change color. Diminishing sunlight is the main instigator. A tree nourishes its leaves—and encourages photosynthesis—for most of the summer. By August, however, as daylight continues to lessen, a tree starts to reroute its food to the roots and trunk, a process that saves the tree but eventually kills the leaves. In autumn, because the leaves are almost starving, they can neither manufacture chlorophyll to stay green nor carry out photosynthesis. By this time, the base of the petiole, or leaf's stem, has hardened, in preparation for the final drop. Unlike animals, who have many ways to get ready for winter—hiding food ahead of time, moving to a warm climate, sleeping through winter—a tree is immobile. It can make it through the winter only by losing its leaves (257).

## Summarizing

Unlike a paraphrase, a summary does not present all the details in the original source, so it is generally as brief as possible. Summaries may boil down an entire book or essay into a single sentence, or they may take a paragraph or more to present the main ideas. Here, for example, is a summary of the Ackerman paragraph:

> In late summer and fall, Ackerman explains, trees put most of their food into their roots and trunk, which causes leaves to change color and die but enables trees to live through the winter (257).

## Deciding Whether to Quote, Paraphrase, or Summarize

Follow these rules of thumb to determine whether you should quote a source directly, paraphrase it in detail, or merely summarize the main points.

- *Quote* a text when the exact wording is critical to making your point (or that of an authority you wish to cite) or when the wording itself is part of what you're analyzing.

- *Paraphrase* when the meaning of a text is important to your argument but the original language is not essential, or when you're clarifying or interpreting the ideas (not the words) in the text.

- *Summarize* when the main points of the text are important to your argument but the details can be left out in the interest of conciseness.

## Using Signal Phrases

When you quote, paraphrase, or summarize a source, identify your source clearly and use a signal phrase ("she says," "he thinks") to distinguish the words and ideas of your source from your own. Consider this example:

> Professor and textbook author Elaine Tyler May claims that many high school history textbooks are too bland to interest young readers (531).

This sentence summarizes a general position about the effectiveness of certain textbooks ("too bland"), and it attributes that view to a particular authority (Elaine Tyler May), citing her credentials (professor, textbook author) for speaking as an authority on the subject. By using the phrase "claims that," the sentence also distinguishes the words and ideas of the source from those of the writer.

The verb you use in a signal phrase can be neutral (*says* or *thinks*), or it can indicate your (or your source's) stance toward the subject. In this case, the use of the verb *claims* suggests that what the source says is arguable (or that the writer of the sentence believes it is). The signal verb you choose can influence your reader's understanding of the sentence and of your attitude toward what it says.

## Acknowledging Sources and Avoiding Plagiarism

As a writer, you must acknowledge any words and ideas that come from others. There are numerous reasons for doing so: to give credit where credit is due, to recognize the various authorities and many perspectives you have considered, to show readers where they can find your sources, and to situate your own arguments in the ongoing academic conversation. Using other people's words and ideas without acknowledgment is plagiarism, a serious academic and ethical offense.

MATERIAL THAT DOESN'T HAVE TO BE ACKNOWLEDGED

- Facts that are common knowledge, such as the name of the current president of the United States
- Well-known statements accompanied by a signal phrase: "As John F. Kennedy said, 'Ask not what your country can do for you; ask what you can do for your country.'"

MATERIAL THAT REQUIRES ACKNOWLEDGMENT

- Direct quotations, paraphrases, and summaries
- Arguable statements and any information that is not commonly known (statistics and other data)
- The personal or professional opinions and assertions of others
- Visuals that you did not create yourself (charts, photographs, and so on)
- Collaborative help you received from others

Plagiarism is (1) using another writer's exact words without quotation marks, (2) using another writer's words or ideas without in-text citation or other documentation, (3) paraphrasing or summarizing someone else's ideas using language or sentence structure that is close to the original. The following practices will help you avoid plagiarizing.

*Take careful notes,* clearly labeling quotations and using your own phrasing and sentence structure in paraphrases and summaries.

*Check all paraphrases and summaries* to be sure they are stated in *your* words and sentence structures—and that you put quotation marks around any of the source's original phrasing.

*Know what sources you must document,* and identify them both in the text and in a works-cited list.

*Check to see that all quotations are documented;* it is not enough just to include quotation marks or indent a block quotation.

*Be especially careful with online material*—copying source material directly into a document you are writing invites plagiarism. Like other sources, information from the web must be acknowledged.

*Recognize that plagiarism has consequences.* A scholar's work will be discredited if it too closely resembles the work of another scholar. Journalists who plagiarize lose their jobs, and students routinely fail courses or are dismissed from school when they are caught cheating—all too often by submitting essays that they have purchased from online "research" sites.

So don't take the chance. If you're having trouble with an assignment, ask your instructor for assistance. Or visit your school's writing center. Writing centers can help with advice on all aspects of your writing, including acknowledging sources and avoiding plagiarism.

# Documentation

Taken collectively, all the information you provide about sources is your *documentation*. Many organizations and publishers—for example, the American Psychological Association (APA), the University of Chicago Press, and the Council of Science Editors (CSE)—have their own documentation styles. The focus here is on the documentation system of the Modern Language Association (MLA) because it is one of the most common systems used in college courses, especially in the liberal arts.

The MLA's documentation system has two basic parts (1) brief in-text references for quotations, paraphrases, or summaries and (2) more-detailed information for each in-text reference in a list of works cited at the end of the text. MLA style requires that each item in your works-cited list include the following information: author, editor, or organization; title of work; place of publication; publisher; date of publication; medium of publication; and, for online sources, date when you accessed the source. Here is an example of how the two parts work together. Note that you can identify the author either in a signal phrase or in parentheses:

**IN-TEXT DOCUMENTATION (WITH AND WITHOUT SIGNAL PHRASE)**

As Lester Faigley puts it, "The world has become a bazaar from which to shop for an individual 'lifestyle'" (12).

As one observer suggests, "The world has become a bazaar from which to shop for an individual 'lifestyle'" (Faigley 12).

**CORRESPONDING WORKS-CITED REFERENCE**

Faigley, Lester. *Fragments of Rationality: Postmodernity and the Subject of Composition.* Pittsburgh: U of Pittsburgh P, 1992. Print.

The examples here and throughout this chapter are color-coded to help you see the crucial parts of each citation: tan for author and editor, yellow for title, and gray for publication information: place of publication, name of publisher, date of publication, page number(s), medium of publication, and so on.

| author | title | publication |

# MLA In-Text Documentation

Brief documentation in your text makes clear to your reader what you took from a source and where within the source you found the information. As you cite each source, you will need to decide whether or not to name the author in a signal phrase—"as Toni Morrison writes"—or in parentheses—"(Morrison 24)." For either style of reference, try to put the parenthetical citation at the end of the sentence or as close as possible to the material you've cited without awkwardly interrupting the sentence. When citing a direct quotation (as in no. 1), note that the parenthetical reference comes after the closing quotation marks but before the period at the end of the sentence.

### 1. AUTHOR NAMED IN A SIGNAL PHRASE

If you mention the author in a signal phrase, put only the page number(s) in parentheses. Do not write *page* or *p*.

> McCullough describes John Adams as having "the hands of a man accustomed to pruning his own trees, cutting his own hay, and splitting his own firewood" (18).

### 2. AUTHOR NAMED IN PARENTHESES

If you do not mention the author in a signal phrase, put his or her last name in parentheses along with the page number(s). Do not use punctuation between the name and the page number(s).

> One biographer describes John Adams as someone who was not a stranger to manual labor (McCullough 18).

### 3. AFTER A BLOCK QUOTATION

When quoting more than three lines of poetry, more than four lines of prose, or dialogue between two or more characters from a drama, set off the quotation from the rest of your text, indenting it one inch (or ten spaces) from the left margin. Do not use quotation marks, and place any parenthetical documentation *after* the final punctuation.

> In *Eastward to Tartary,* Kaplan captures ancient and contemporary Antioch:
>> At the height of its glory in the Roman-Byzantine age, when it had an amphitheater, public baths, aqueducts, and sewage pipes, half a million people lived in Antioch. Today the population is only 125,000. With sour relations between Turkey and Syria, and unstable politics throughout the Middle East, Antioch is now a backwater—seedy and tumbledown, with relatively few tourists. I found it altogether charming. (123)

### 4. TWO OR MORE WORKS BY THE SAME AUTHOR

If you cite multiple works by one author, include the title of the work you are citing either in the signal phrase or in parentheses. Give the full title if it's brief; otherwise, give a short version.

> Kaplan insists that understanding power in the Near East requires "Western leaders who know when to intervene, and do so without illusions" (*Eastward* 330).

Include a comma between author and title if you include both in the parentheses.

> Understanding power in the Near East requires "Western leaders who know when to intervene, and do so without illusions" (Kaplan, *Eastward* 330).

### 5. TWO OR MORE AUTHORS

For a work by two or three authors, name all the authors, either in a signal phrase or in parentheses.

> Carlson and Ventura's stated goal is to introduce Julio Cortázar, Marjorie Agosín, and other Latin American writers to an audience of English-speaking adolescents (5).

For a work with four or more authors, you can mention all their names *or* just the name of the first author followed by *et al.,* which means "and others."

author    title    publication

One popular survey of American literature breaks the contents into sixteen thematic groupings (Anderson, Brinnin, Leggett, Arpin, and Toth 19–24).

One popular survey of American literature breaks the contents into sixteen thematic groupings (Anderson et al. 19–24).

## 6. ORGANIZATION OR GOVERNMENT AS AUTHOR

Cite the organization either in a signal phrase or in parentheses. It's acceptable to shorten long names.

The U.S. government can be direct when it wants to be. For example, it sternly warns, "If you are overpaid, we will recover any payments not due you" (Social Security Administration 12).

## 7. AUTHOR UNKNOWN

If you can't determine an author, use the work's title or a shortened version of the title in the parentheses.

A powerful editorial in last week's paper asserts that healthy liver donor Mike Hurewitz died because of "frightening" faulty postoperative care ("Every Patient's Nightmare").

## 8. LITERARY WORKS

When referring to literary works that are available in many different editions, you need to cite additional information so that readers of any edition can locate the text you are citing.

*Novels*: Give the page and chapter number of the edition you are using.

In *Pride and Prejudice,* Mrs. Bennet shows no warmth toward Jane and Elizabeth when they return from Netherfield (105; ch. 12).

*Verse plays*: Give the act, scene, and line numbers; separate them with periods.

Macbeth develops the vision theme when he addresses the Ghost with "Thou hast no speculation in those eyes / Which thou dost glare with" (3.3.96–97).

*Poems*: Give the part and line numbers (separated by periods). If a poem has only line numbers, use the word *line(s)* in the first reference.

The mere in *Beowulf* is described as "not a pleasant place!" (line 1372). Later, it is called "the awful place" (1378).

### 9. WORK IN AN ANTHOLOGY

Name the author(s) of the work, not the editor of the anthology—either in a signal phrase or in parentheses.

> "It is the teapots that truly shock," according to Cynthia Ozick in her essay on teapots as metaphor (70).

> In *In Short: A Collection of Creative Nonfiction,* readers will find both an essay on Scottish tea (Hiestand) and a piece on teapots as metaphors (Ozick).

### 10. TWO OR MORE WORKS CITED TOGETHER

If you cite the works in the same parentheses, separate the references with a semicolon.

> Critics have looked at both *Pride and Prejudice* and *Frankenstein* from a cultural perspective (Tanner 7; Smith viii).

### 11. SOURCE QUOTED IN ANOTHER SOURCE

When you are quoting text that you found quoted in another source, use the abbreviation *qtd. in* in the parenthetical reference.

> Charlotte Brontë wrote to G. H. Lewes: "Why do you like Miss Austen so very much? I am puzzled on that point" (qtd. in Tanner 7).

### 12. WORK WITHOUT PAGE NUMBERS

For works without page numbers, including many online sources, identify the source using the author or other information either in a signal phrase or in parentheses. If the source has paragraph or section numbers, use them with the abbreviations *par.* or *sec.*

> Studies reported in *Scientific American* and elsewhere show that music training helps children to be better at multitasking later in life ("Hearing the Music," par. 2).

### 13. AN ENTIRE WORK

If you refer to an entire work rather than a part of it, there's no need to include page numbers.

> At least one observer considers Turkey and Central Asia to be explosive (Kaplan).

author    title    publication

# MLA List of Works Cited

A works-cited list provides full bibliographic information for every source cited in your text. Here's some general advice to help you format your list:

- Start the list on a new page.
- Center the title (Works Cited) one inch from the top of the page.
- Double-space the whole list.
- Begin each entry flush with the left-hand margin and indent subsequent lines one-half inch or five spaces.
- Alphabetize entries by the author's last name. If a work has no identifiable author, use the first major word of the title (disregard *A, An, The*).
- If you cite more than one work by a single author, list them all alphabetically by title, and use three hyphens in place of the author's name after the first entry (see no. 3 for an example).

## Print Books

For most books, you'll need to list the author; the title and any subtitle; and the place of publication, publisher, date, and the medium—*Print*. A few details to note when citing books:

- *Authors:* List the primary author last-name-first, and include any middle name or initial after the first name.
- *Titles:* Capitalize all principal words in titles and subtitles, including short verbs such as *is* and *are*. Do not capitalize *a, an, the, to,* or any preposition or conjunction unless they begin a title or subtitle. Italicize book titles, but place quotation marks around a chapter of a book or a selection from an anthology.
- *Publication place and publisher:* If there's more than one city listed on the title page, use only the first. Use a shortened form of the publisher's name (Norton for W. W. Norton & Company; Princeton UP for Princeton University Press).
- *Dates:* If more than one year is given, use the most recent one.

1. ONE AUTHOR

Miller, Susan. *Assuming the Positions: Cultural Pedagogy and the Politics of Commonplace Writing.* Pittsburgh: U of Pittsburgh P, 1998. Print.

author          title          publication

2. TWO OR MORE WORKS BY THE SAME AUTHOR(S)

Give the author's name in the first entry, and then use three hyphens in the author slot for each of the subsequent works, listing them alphabetically by the first important word of each title.

> Kaplan, Robert D. *The Coming Anarchy: Shattering the Dreams of the Post Cold War.* New York: Random, 2000. Print.
>
> ———. *Eastward to Tartary: Travels in the Balkans, the Middle East, and the Caucasus.* New York: Random, 2000. Print.

3. TWO OR THREE AUTHORS

Follow the order of names on the book's title page. List the second and third authors first-name-first.

> Malless, Stanley, and Jeffrey McQuain. *Coined by God: Words and Phrases That First Appear in the English Translations of the Bible.* New York: Norton, 2003. Print.
>
> Sebranek, Patrick, Verne Meyer, and Dave Kemper. *Writers INC: A Guide to Writing, Thinking, and Learning.* Burlington: Write Source, 1990. Print.

4. FOUR OR MORE AUTHORS

You may give each author's name or the name of the first author only, followed by *et al.* (Latin for "and others").

> Anderson, Robert, et al. *Elements of Literature: Literature of the United States.* Austin: Holt, 1993. Print.

5. ORGANIZATION OR GOVERNMENT AS AUTHOR

> Diagram Group. *The Macmillan Visual Desk Reference.* New York: Macmillan, 1993. Print.

For a government publication, give the name of the government first, followed by the names of any department and agency.

> United States. Dept. of Health and Human Services. Natl. Inst. of Mental Health. *Autism Spectrum Disorders.* Washington: GPO, 2004. Print.

6. ANTHOLOGY

Use this model only when you are citing the whole anthology or the contributions of the editor(s).

> Kitchen, Judith, and Mary Paumier Jones, eds. *In Short: A Collection of Brief Creative Nonfiction.* New York: Norton, 1996. Print.

### 7. WORK(S) IN AN ANTHOLOGY

Give the inclusive page numbers of the selection you are citing.

> Achebe, Chinua. "Uncle Ben's Choice." *The Seagull Reader: Literature.* Ed. Joseph
> Kelly. New York: Norton, 2005. 23–27. Print.

To document two or more selections from one anthology, list each selection by author and title, followed by the editors' names and the pages of the selection. In addition, include in your works-cited list an entry for the anthology itself (no. 6).

> Hiestand, Emily. "Afternoon Tea." Kitchen and Jones 65–67.

> Ozick, Cynthia. "The Shock of Teapots." Kitchen and Jones 68–71.

### 8. AUTHOR AND EDITOR

Start with the author if you've cited the text itself.

> Austen, Jane. *Emma.* Ed. Stephen M. Parrish. New York: Norton, 2000. Print.

Start with the editor if you've cited his or her contribution.

> Parrish, Stephen M., ed. *Emma.* By Jane Austen. New York: Norton, 2000. Print.

### 9. TRANSLATION

> Dostoevsky, Fyodor. *Crime and Punishment.* Trans. Richard Pevear and
> Larissa Volokhonsky. New York: Vintage, 1993. Print.

### 10. GRAPHIC NARRATIVE

Start with the person whose work is most relevant to your research, and include labels to indicate each person's role.

> Gladstone, Brooke, writer. *The Influencing Machine.* Illus. Josh Neufeld. New
> York: Norton, 2011. Print.

> Neufeld, Josh, illus. *The Influencing Machine.* By Brooke Gladstone. New York:
> Norton, 2011. Print.

### 11. FOREWORD, INTRODUCTION, PREFACE, OR AFTERWORD

> Tanner, Tony. Introduction. *Pride and Prejudice.* By Jane Austen. London:
> Penguin, 1972. 7–46. Print.

author        title        publication

12. MULTIVOLUME WORK

If you cite all the volumes, give the number of volumes after the title.

Sandburg, Carl. *Abraham Lincoln: The War Years.* 4 vols. New York:
Harcourt, 1939. Print.

If you cite only one volume, give the volume number after the title.

Sandburg, Carl. *Abraham Lincoln: The War Years.* Vol. 2. New York:
Harcourt, 1939. Print.

13. EDITION OTHER THAN THE FIRST

Gibaldi, Joseph. *MLA Handbook for Writers of Research Papers.* 6th ed.
New York: MLA, 2003. Print.

14. ARTICLE IN A REFERENCE BOOK

Provide the author's name if the article is signed. If a reference book is well known, give only the edition and the year of publication.

"Iraq." *The New Encyclopaedia Brittanica.* 15th ed. 2007. Print.

If a reference book is less familiar, give complete publication information.

Benton-Cohen, Katherine. "Women in the Reform and Progressive Era."
*A History of Women in the United States.* Ed. Doris Weatherford.
4 vols. Danbury, CT: Grolier, 2004. Print.

## Print Periodicals

For most articles, you'll need to list the author, the article title and any subtitle, the periodical title, any volume and issue number, the date, inclusive page numbers, and the medium—*Print.* A few details to note when citing periodicals:

- *Authors:* Format authors as you would for a book.
- *Titles:* Capitalize titles and subtitles as you would for a book. Omit any initial *A, An,* or *The.* Italicize periodical titles; place article titles within quotation marks.
- *Dates:* Abbreviate the names of months except for May, June, and July: Jan., Feb., Mar., Apr., Aug., Sept., Oct., Nov., Dec. Journals paginated by both volume and issue need only the year (in parentheses).

- *Pages:* If an article does not fall on consecutive pages, give the first page with a plus sign (55+).

15. ARTICLE IN A JOURNAL

Bartley, William. "Imagining the Future in *The Awakening.*" *College English* 62.6 (2000): 719–46. Print.

For journals that do not have volume numbers, give the issue number after the title, followed by the year of publication and inclusive page numbers.

Flynn, Kevin. "The Railway in Canadian Poetry." *Canadian Literature* 174 (2002): 70–95. Print.

16. ARTICLE IN A MAGAZINE

Cloud, John. "Should SATs Matter?" *Time* 12 Mar. 2001: 62+. Print.

For a monthly magazine, include only the month and year.

Fellman, Bruce. "Leading the Libraries." *Yale Alumni Magazine* Feb. 2002: 26–31. Print.

17. ARTICLE IN A DAILY NEWSPAPER

Springer, Shira. "Celtics Reserves Are Whizzes vs. Wizards." *Boston Globe* 14 Mar. 2005: D4+. Print.

If you are documenting a particular edition of a newspaper, specify the edition (*late ed., natl. ed.,* and so on) after the date.

Margulius, David L. "Smarter Call Centers: At Your Service?" *New York Times* 14 Mar. 2002, late ed.: G1+. Print.

18. UNSIGNED ARTICLE

"Coal Mine Inspections Fall Short." *Atlanta Journal-Constitution* 18 Nov. 2007: A7. Print.

19. EDITORIAL OR LETTER TO THE EDITOR

"Gas, Cigarettes Are Safe to Tax." Editorial. *Lakeville Journal* 17 Feb. 2005: A10. Print.

Festa, Roger. "Social Security: Another Phony Crisis." Letter. *Lakeville Journal* 17 Feb. 2005: A10. Print.

author        title        publication

20. BOOK REVIEW

Frank, Jeffrey. "Body Count." Rev. of *The Exception,* by Christian Jungersen. *New Yorker* 30 July 2007: 86–87. Print.

## Online Sources

Not every online source gives you all the data that the MLA would like to see in a works-cited entry. Ideally, you'll be able to list the author's name, the title, information about print publication (if applicable), information about electronic publication (title of site, editor, date of first electronic publication and/or most recent revision, name of publisher or sponsoring institution), the publication medium, date of access, and, if necessary, a URL. Here are a few details to note when citing online sources:

- *Authors or editors and title:* Format authors and titles as you would for a print book or periodical.

- *Publisher:* If the name of the publisher or sponsoring institution is unavailable, use *N.p.*

- *Dates:* Abbreviate the months as you would for a print periodical. Although MLA asks for the date when materials were first posted or most recently updated, you won't always be able to find that information; if it's unavailable, use *n.d.* Be sure to include the date on which you accessed the source.

- *Pages:* If the citation calls for page numbers but the source is unpaginated, use *n. pag.* in place of page numbers.

- *Medium:* Indicate the medium—Web, Email, PDF, MP3, Jpeg, and so on.

- *URL:* MLA assumes that readers can locate most sources on the web by searching for the author, title, or other identifying information, so they don't require a URL for most online sources. When readers cannot locate a source without a URL, give the address of the website in angle brackets. When a URL won't fit on one line, break it only after a slash (and do not add a hyphen). If a URL is very long, consider using the one from the site's homepage or search page instead.

**21. ENTIRE WEBSITE OR PERSONAL WEBSITE**

Zalta, Edward N., ed. *Stanford Encyclopedia of Philosophy.* Metaphysics
　　Research Lab, Center for the Study of Language and Information,
　　Stanford U, 2007. Web. 14 Nov. 2010.

Nunberg, Geoffrey. Home page. School of Information, U of California,
　　Berkeley, 2009. Web. 3 Apr. 2009.

**22. WORK FROM A WEBSITE**

Buff, Rachel Ida. "Becoming American." *Immigration History Research Center.*
　　U of Minnesota, 24 Mar. 2008. Web. 4 Apr. 2008.

**23. ONLINE BOOK OR PART OF A BOOK**

Cite a book you access online as you would a print book, adding the name of
the site or database, the medium, and the date of access. (See next page for
examples.)

Anderson, Sherwood. *Winesburg, Ohio.* New York: B. W. Huebsch, 1919.
　　*Bartleby.com.* Web. 7 Apr. 2008.

If you are citing a part of a book, put the part in quotation marks before the
book title. If the online book is paginated, give the pages; if not, use *N. pag.*

Anderson, Sherwood. "The Philosopher." *Winesburg, Ohio.* New York: B. W.
　　Huebsch, 1919. N. pag. *Bartleby.com.* Web. 7 Apr. 2008.

To cite a book you've downloaded onto a Kindle, Nook, iPad, or other digital
device, follow the setup for a print book, but indicate the ebook format at the
end of your citation.

Larson, Erik. *The Devil in the White City: Murder, Mayhem, and Madness at
　　the Fair That Changed America.* New York: Vintage, 2004. Kindle.

**24. ARTICLE IN AN ONLINE JOURNAL**

If a journal does not number pages or if it numbers each article separately,
use *n. pag.* in place of page numbers.

Moore, Greggory. "The Process of Life in *2001: A Space Odyssey.*" *Images:
　　A Journal of Film and Popular Culture* 9 (2000): n. pag. Web. 12 May 2009.

**25. ARTICLE IN AN ONLINE MAGAZINE**

Landsburg, Steven E. "Putting All Your Potatoes in One Basket: The Economic
　　Lessons of the Great Famine." *Slate.* Slate, 13 Mar. 2001. Web. 8 Dec. 2007.

author　　title　　publication

26. ARTICLE ACCESSED THROUGH DATABASE

For articles accessed through a library's subscription services, such as InfoTrac and EBSCOhost, cite the publication information for the source, followed by the name of the database.

> Bowman, James. "Moody Blues." *American Spectator* June 1999: 64–65. *Academic Search Premier.* Web. 15 Mar. 2005.

27. ARTICLE IN AN ONLINE NEWSPAPER

> Mitchell, Dan. "Being Skeptical of Green." *New York Times.* New York Times, 24 Nov. 2007. Web. 26 Nov. 2007.

28. ONLINE EDITORIAL

> "Outsourcing Your Life." Editorial. *ChicagoTribune.com.* Chicago Tribune, 24 Nov. 2004. Web. 3 Jan. 2008.

29. BLOG ENTRY

If the entry has no title, use "Blog entry" (without quotation marks). Cite a whole blog as you would a personal website (no. 21). If the publisher or sponsor is unavailable, use *N.p.*

> Gladwell, Malcolm. *"Underdogs."* N.p., 13 May 2009. Web. 11 Aug. 2011.

30. EMAIL CORRESPONDENCE

> Smith, William. "Teaching Grammar—Some Thoughts." Message to the author. 15 Feb. 2008. Email.

31. POSTING TO AN ELECTRONIC FORUM

> Mintz, Stephen H. "Manumission During the Revolution." H-Net List on Slavery. Michigan State U, 14 Sept. 2006. Web. 18 Apr. 2009.

32. ARTICLE IN AN ONLINE REFERENCE WORK OR WIKI

> "Dubai." *MSN Encarta.* Microsoft Corporation, 2008. Web. 20 June 2008.

For a wiki, cite the date of the last modification or update as the publication date.

> "Pi." *Wikipedia.* Wikimedia Foundation, 6 Aug. 2011. Web. 11 Aug. 2011.

33. PODCAST

> Blumberg, Alex, and Adam Davidson. "The Giant Pool of Money." Host Ira Glass. *This American Life.* Chicago Public Radio, 9 May 2008. Web. 18 Sept. 2008.

## Other Kinds of Sources

Many of the sources in this section can be found online. If there is no web model here, start with the guidelines most appropriate for the source you need to cite, omit the original medium, and end your citation with the title of the website, italicized; the medium (Web); and the day, month, and year of access.

34. ADVERTISEMENT (PRINT AND ONLINE)

Bebe. Advertisement. *Lucky.* Sept. 2011: 112–13. Print.

Rolex. Advertisement. *Time.* Time, n.d. Web. 1 Apr. 2013.

35. ART (PRINT AND ONLINE)

Van Gogh, Vincent. *The Potato Eaters.* 1885. Oil on canvas. Van Gogh Museum, Amsterdam.

Warhol, Andy. *Self-Portrait.* 1979. Polaroid Polacolor print. J. Paul Getty Museum, Los Angeles. *The Getty.* Web. 5 Jan. 2008.

36. CARTOON OR COMIC STRIP (PRINT AND ONLINE)

Chast, Roz. "The Three Wise Men of Thanksgiving." Cartoon. *New Yorker* 1 Dec. 2003: 174. Print.

Adams, Scott. "Dilbert." Comic strip. *Dilbert.com.* United Features Syndicate, 9 Nov. 2007. Web. 26 Nov. 2007.

37. CD-ROM OR DVD-ROM

Document like a book, but indicate any pertinent information about the edition or version.

*Othello.* Princeton: Films for the Humanities and Sciences, 1998. CD-ROM.

38. FILM, DVD, OR VIDEO CLIP

*Super 8.* Dir. J. J. Abrams. Perf. Joel Courtney, Kyle Chandler, and Elle Fanning. Paramount, 2011. Film.

To document a particular person's work, start with that name.

Cody, Diablo, scr. *Juno.* Dir. Jason Reitman. Perf. Ellen Page, Michael Cera, Jennifer Garner, and Jason Bateman. Fox Searchlight, 2007. DVD.

author    title    publication

Document a video clip from *YouTube* or a similar site as you would a short work from a website.

> PivotMasterDX, dir. "Storaged." *YouTube*. YouTube, 29 Apr. 2009. Web.
> 11 Aug. 2011.

39. BROADCAST, PUBLISHED, OR PERSONAL INTERVIEW

> Gates, Henry Louis, Jr. Interview. *Fresh Air*. NPR. WNYC, New York. 9 Apr.
> 2002. Radio.

> Brzezinski, Zbigniew. "Against the Neocons." *American Prospect* Mar. 2005:
> 26–27. Print.

> Berra, Yogi. Personal interview. 17 June 2001.

40. PUBLISHED LETTER

> White, E. B. Letter to Carol Angell. 28 May 1970. *Letters of E. B. White*.
> Ed. Dorothy Lobarno Guth. New York: Harper, 1976. 600. Print.

41. MAP (PRINT AND ONLINE)

> *Toscana*. Map. Milan: Touring Club Italiano, 1987. Print.

> "Austin, TX." Map. *Google Maps*. Google, 11 Aug. 2011. Web. 11 Aug. 2011.

42. MUSICAL SCORE

> Beethoven, Ludwig van. *String Quartet No. 13 in B Flat, Op. 130*. 1825. New York:
> Dover, 1970. Print.

43. SOUND RECORDING (WITH ONLINE VERSION)

Whether you list the composer, conductor, or performer first depends on where you want to place the emphasis.

> Beethoven, Ludwig van. *Missa Solemnis*. Perf. Westminster Choir and New York
> Philharmonic. Cond. Leonard Bernstein. Sony, 1992. CD.

> The Beatles. "Can't Buy Me Love." *A Hard Day's Night*. United Artists, 1964.
> MP3 file.

> Davis, Miles. "So What." *Birth of the Cool*. Columbia, 1959. *Miles Davis*. Web.
> 14 Feb. 2009.

**44. TELEVISION OR RADIO PROGRAM (WITH ONLINE VERSION)**

"Stirred." *The West Wing.* Writ. Aaron Sorkin, Dir. Jeremy Kagan. Perf. Martin
　　Sheen. NBC. WPTV, West Palm Beach, 3 Apr. 2002. Television.

"Bush's War." *Frontline.* Writ. and Dir. Michael Kirk. *PBS.org.* PBS, 24 Mar. 2008.
　　Web. 10 Apr. 2009.

**45. MP3, JPEG, PDF, OR OTHER DIGITAL FILE**

For downloaded songs, photographs, PDFs, and other documents stored on
your computer or another digital device, follow the guidelines for the type of
work you are citing (art, journal article, and so on) and give the file type as
the medium.

Talking Heads. "Burning Down the House." *Speaking in Tongues.* Sire, 1983.
　　Digital file.

Taylor, Aaron. "Twilight of the Idols: Performance, Melodramatic Villainy, and
　　*Sunset Boulevard." Journal of Film and Video* 59 (2007): 13–31. PDF file.

## Documenting Sources Not Covered by MLA

To document a source that isn't covered by the MLA guidelines, look for
models similar to the source you're citing. Give any information readers will
need in order to find the source themselves—author, title, subtitle; publisher
and/or sponsor; medium; dates; and any other pertinent information. You
might want to try out the citation yourself, to be sure it will lead others to
your source.

## Sample Research Paper

Dylan Borchers wrote the following research paper for a first-year writing
class. He used MLA style for his essay, but documentation styles vary from
discipline to discipline, so ask your instructor if you're not sure which style
you should use.

author　　　　　title　　　　　publication

Dylan Borchers

Professor Bullock

English 102, Section 4

31 March 2009

Against the Odds:

Harry S. Truman and the Election of 1948

"Thomas E. Dewey's Election as President Is a Foregone

Conclusion," read a headline in the *New York Times* during the

presidential election race between incumbent Democrat Harry S.

Truman and his Republican challenger, Thomas E. Dewey. Earlier,

*Life* magazine had put Dewey on its cover with the caption "The

Next President of the United States" (qtd. in "1948 Truman-Dewey

Election"). In a *Newsweek* survey of fifty prominent political writers,

each one predicted Truman's defeat, and *Time* correspondents

declared that Dewey would carry 39 of the 48 states (Donaldson

210). Nearly every major media outlet across the United States

endorsed Dewey and lambasted Truman. As historian Robert H.

Ferrell observes, even Truman's wife, Bess, thought he would be

beaten (270).

The results of an election are not so easily predicted, as the

famous photograph on page 2 shows. Not only did Truman win the

election, but he won by a significant margin, with 303 electoral

votes and 24,179,259 popular votes, compared to Dewey's 189

electoral votes and 21,991,291 popular votes (Donaldson 204–07). In

fact, many historians and political analysts argue that Truman

Fig. 1. President Harry S. Truman holds up an Election Day edition of the *Chicago Daily Tribune*, which mistakenly announced "Dewey Defeats Truman"; Byron Rollins, *Dewey Beats Truman* (4 Nov. 1948; Associated Press; *AP Images*; Web; 23 Mar. 2009).

would have won by an even greater margin had third-party Progressive candidate Henry A. Wallace not split the Democratic vote in New York State and Dixiecrat Strom Thurmond not won four states in the South (McCullough 711). Although Truman's defeat was heavily predicted, those predictions themselves, Dewey's passiveness as a campaigner, and Truman's zeal turned the tide for a Truman victory.

      In the months preceding the election, public opinion polls predicted that Dewey would win by a large margin. Pollster Elmo Roper stopped polling in September, believing there was no reason to continue, given a seemingly inevitable Dewey landslide. Although the margin narrowed as the election drew near, the other pollsters predicted a Dewey win by at least 5 percent (Donaldson 209). Many historians believe that these predictions aided the president in the long run. First, surveys showing Dewey in the lead may have prompted some of Dewey's supporters to feel overconfident about their candidate's chances and therefore to stay home from the polls on Election Day. Second, these same surveys may have energized Democrats to mount late get-out-the-vote efforts ("1948 Truman-Dewey Election"). Other analysts believe that the overwhelming predictions of a Truman loss also kept at home some Democrats who approved of Truman's policies but saw a Truman loss as inevitable. According to political analyst Samuel Lubell, those Democrats may have saved Dewey from an even greater defeat (Hamby, *Man of the People* 465). Whatever the impact on the voters, the polling numbers had a decided effect on Dewey.

Historians and political analysts alike cite Dewey's overly cautious campaign as one of the main reasons Truman was able to achieve victory. Dewey firmly believed in public opinion polls. With all indications pointing to an easy victory, Dewey and his staff believed that all he had to do was bide his time and make no foolish mistakes. Dewey himself said, "When you're leading, don't talk" (qtd. in McCullough 672). Each of Dewey's speeches was well-crafted and well-rehearsed. As the leader in the race, he kept his remarks faultlessly positive, with the result that he failed to deliver a solid message or even mention Truman or any of Truman's policies. Eventually, Dewey began to be perceived as aloof and stuffy. One

If you cite two or more works closely together, give parenthetical documentation for each one.

observer compared him to the plastic groom on top of a wedding cake (Hamby, "Harry S. Truman"), and others noted his stiff, cold demeanor (McCullough 671–74).

As his campaign continued, observers noted that Dewey seemed uncomfortable in crowds, unable to connect with ordinary people. And he made a number of blunders. One took place at a train stop when the candidate, commenting on the number of children in the crowd, said he was glad they had been let out of school for his arrival. Unfortunately for Dewey, it was a Saturday ("1948: The Great Truman Surprise"). Such gaffes gave voters the feeling that Dewey was out of touch with the public.

Again and again through the autumn of 1948, Dewey's campaign speeches failed to address the issues, with the candidate declaring that he did not want to "get down in the gutter" (qtd. in McCullough 701). When told by fellow Republicans that he was losing ground, Dewey insisted that his campaign not alter its course. Even *Time* magazine, though it endorsed and praised him, conceded that his speeches were dull (McCullough 696). According to historian Zachary Karabell, they were "notable only for taking place, not for any specific message" (244). Dewey's numbers in the polls slipped in the weeks before the election, but he still held a comfortable lead over Truman. It would take Truman's famous whistle-stop campaign to make the difference.

Few candidates in U.S. history have campaigned for the presidency with more passion and faith than Harry Truman. In the autumn of 1948, he wrote to his sister, "It will be the greatest campaign any President ever made. Win, lose, or draw, people will know where I stand" (91). For thirty three days, Truman traveled the nation, giving hundreds of speeches from the back of the *Ferdinand Magellan* railroad car. In the same letter, he described the pace: "We made about 140 stops and I spoke over 147 times, shook hands with at least 30,000 and am in good condition to start out again tomorrow for Wilmington, Philadelphia, Jersey City, Newark, Albany and Buffalo" (91). McCullough writes of Truman's campaign:

> No President in history had ever gone so far in quest of support from the people, or with less cause for the effort, to judge by informed opinion. . . . As a test of his skills and judgment as a professional politician, not to say his stamina and disposition at age sixty-four, it would be like no other experience in his long, often difficult career, as he himself understood perfectly. More than any other event in his public life, or in his presidency thus far, it would reveal the kind of man he was. (655)

He spoke in large cities and small towns, defending his policies and attacking Republicans. As a former farmer and relatively late bloomer, Truman was able to connect with the public. He developed an energetic style, usually speaking from notes rather than from a prepared speech, and often mingled with the crowds that met his train. These crowds grew larger as the campaign

Set off quotations of more than four lines by indenting 1 inch (or 10 spaces).

Put parenthetical references after final punctuation in a block quotation.

progressed. In Chicago, over half a million people lined the streets as he passed, and in St. Paul the crowd numbered over 25,000. When Dewey entered St. Paul two days later, he was greeted by only 7,000 supporters ("1948 Truman-Dewey Election"). Reporters brushed off the large crowds as mere curiosity seekers wanting to see a president (McCullough 682). Yet Truman persisted, even if he often seemed to be the only one who thought he could win. By going directly to the American people and connecting with them, Truman built the momentum needed to surpass Dewey and win the election.

The legacy and lessons of Truman's whistle-stop campaign continue to be studied by political analysts, and politicians today often mimic his campaign methods by scheduling multiple visits to key states, as Truman did. He visited California, Illinois, and Ohio 48 times, compared with 6 visits to those states by Dewey. Political scientist Thomas M. Holbrook concludes that his strategic campaigning in those states and others gave Truman the electoral votes he needed to win (61, 65).

The 1948 election also had an effect on pollsters, who, as Elmo Roper admitted, "couldn't have been more wrong" (qtd. in Karabell 255). *Life* magazine's editors concluded that pollsters as well as reporters and commentators were too convinced of a Dewey victory to analyze the polls seriously, especially the opinions of undecided voters (Karabell 256). Pollsters assumed that undecided voters would vote in the same proportion as decided voters—and that

If you cite a work with no known author, use the title in your parenthetical reference.

turned out to be a false assumption (Karabell 258). In fact, the lopsidedness of the polls might have led voters who supported Truman to call themselves undecided out of an unwillingness to associate themselves with the losing side, further skewing the polls' results (McDonald, Glynn, Kim, and Ostman 152). Such errors led pollsters to change their methods significantly after the 1948 election.

In a work by four or more authors, either cite them all or name the first one followed by *et al*.

After the election, many political analysts, journalists, and historians concluded that the Truman upset was in fact a victory for the American people, who, the *New Republic* noted, "couldn't be ticketed by the polls, knew its own mind and had picked the rather unlikely but courageous figure of Truman to carry its banner" (qtd. in McCullough 715). How "unlikely" is unclear, however; Truman biographer Alonzo Hamby notes that "polls of scholars consistently rank Truman among the top eight presidents in American history" (*Man of the People* 641). But despite Truman's high standing, and despite the fact that the whistle-stop campaign is now part of our political landscape, politicians have increasingly imitated the style of the Dewey campaign, with its "packaged candidate who ran so as not to lose, who steered clear of controversy, and who made a good show of appearing presidential" (Karabell 266). The election of 1948 shows that voters are not necessarily swayed by polls, but it may have presaged the packaging of candidates by public relations experts, to the detriment of public debate on the issues in future presidential elections.

Works Cited

Donaldson, Gary A. *Truman Defeats Dewey*. Lexington: UP of
  Kentucky, 1999. Print.

Ferrell, Robert H. *Harry S. Truman: A Life*. Columbia: U of Missouri P,
  1994. Print.

Hamby, Alonzo L., ed. "Harry S. Truman (1945–1953)."
  *AmericanPresident.org*. Miller Center of Public Affairs,
  U of Virginia, 11 Dec. 2003. Web. 17 Mar. 2009.

———. *Man of the People: A Life of Harry S. Truman*. New York:
  Oxford UP, 1995. Print.

Holbrook, Thomas M. "Did the Whistle-Stop Campaign Matter?" *PS:
  Political Science and Politics* 35.1 (2002): 59–66. Print.

Karabell, Zachary. *The Last Campaign: How Harry Truman Won the
  1948 Election*. New York: Knopf, 2000. Print.

McCullough, David. *Truman*. New York: Simon & Schuster, 1992. Print.

McDonald, Daniel G., Carroll J. Glynn, Sei-Hill Kim, and Ronald E.
  Ostman. "The Spiral of Silence in the 1948 Presidential
  Election." *Communication Research* 28.2 (2001): 139–55. Print.

"1948: The Great Truman Surprise." *Media and Politics Online
  Projects: Media Coverage of Presidential Campaigns*. Dept. of
  Political Science and International Affairs, Kennesaw State U,
  29 Oct. 2003. Web. 20 Mar. 2009.

"1948 Truman-Dewey Election." *Electronic Government Project:
  Eagleton Digital Archive of American Politics*. Eagleton Inst. of
  Politics, Rutgers, State U of New Jersey, 2004. Web. 19 Mar. 2009.

Center the heading.

Alphabetize the list by authors' last names or by title for works with no author.

Begin each entry at the left margin; indent subsequent lines $\frac{1}{2}$ inch or five spaces.

If you cite more than one work by a single author, list them alphabetically by title, and use three hyphens in place of the author's name.

Alphabetize titles that begin with numerals as though the numeral is spelled out.

Truman, Harry S. "Campaigning, Letter, October 5, 1948." *Harry S.*
*Truman.* Ed. Robert H. Ferrell. Washington: CQ P, 2003. 91.
Print.

Check to be
sure that every
source you use
is in the works
cited list.

# Credits

## TEXT

DIANE ACKERMAN: "Why Leaves Turn Color in the Fall" from *A Natural History of the Senses* by Diane Ackerman, copyright © 1990 by Diane Ackerman. Used by permission of Random House, an imprint and division of Random House LLC. All rights reserved.

RODOLFO F. ACUÑA: "We Owe History, by Rodolfo F. Acuña. From Kessler, Elizabeth R.; Perrin, Anne, *Chicanos in the Conversations*, 1st Edition, © 2008. Reprinted by permission of Pearson Education, Inc., Upper Saddle River, N.J.

GLORIA ANZALDÚA: "Linguistic Terrorism," from *Borderlands/La Fontera: The New Mestiza*, by Gloria Anzaldúa. Used by permission of Aunt Lute Books.

DAVE BARRY: "Manliness," from *You Can Date Boys When You're Forty*, by Dave Barry, copyright © 2014 by Dave Barry. Used by permission of G.P. Putnam's Sons, a division of Penguin Group (USA) LLC.

ANNE BERNAYS: "Warrior Day," from *The New York Times*, July 5, 2009. Copyright © 2009 The New York Times. All rights reserved. Used by permission and protected by the Copyright Laws of the United States. The printing, copying, redistribution or retransmission of the Material without express written permission is prohibited.

DYLAN BORCHERS: "Against the Odds: Harry S. Truman and the Election of 1948." Reprinted by permission of the author.

BILL BRYSON: Excerpt from *One Summer: America, 1927* by Bill Bryson, copyright © 2013 by Bill Bryson. Used by permission of Doubleday, an imprint of the Knopf Doubleday Publishing Group, a division of Random House LLC. All rights reserved and by permission of Greene & Heaton Ltd.

BRUCE CATTON: "Grant and Lee: A Study in Contrasts" by Bruce Catton is reprinted by permission of William B. Catton.

STEPHANIE CAWLEY: "The Veil in Persepolis," by Stephanie Cawley. From The Stockton Poscolonial Studies Project, 2014. Used by permission of the author.

ROY PETER CLARK: "Why John Lehrer's 'Imagine' is Worth Reading, Despite the Problems," by Roy Peter Clark, Senior Scholar at the Poynter Institute for Media Studies. From Poynter.org September 14, 2012. Used by permission of the Poynter Institute.

BILLY COLLINS: "Fishing on the Susquehanna in July" from *Picnic, Lightning* by Billy Collins, copyright © 1998. Reprinted by permission of the University of Pittsburgh Press.

PAUL A. CRENSHAW: Excerpts from "Storm Country," by Paul A. Crenshaw. From *The Southern Humanities Review*, Winter 2004. Reprinted by permission of Paul A. Crenshaw.

MARJANE SATRAPI: Excerpt(s) from *Persepolis: The Story of a Childhood* by Marjane Satrapi, translation copyright © 2003 by L'Association, Paris, France. Used by permission of Pantheon Books, an imprint of the Knopf Doubleday Publishing Group, a division of Random House LLC. All rights reserved.

DAVID SEDARIS: From *Me Talk Pretty One Day* by David Sedaris. Copyright © 2000 by David Sedaris. Used by permission of Little Brown & Company.

ANNE SEXTON: "Her Kind" from *To Bedlam and Part Way Back* by Anne Sexton. Copyright © 1960 by Anne Sexton, renewed 1988 by Linda G. Sexton. Reprinted by permission of Houghton Mifflin Harcourt Publishing Company and SLL/Sterling Lord Literistic, Inc.

KURT STREETER: "South L.A. Student Finds a Different World at Cal," by Kurt Streeter. *Los Angeles Times*, August 16, 2013. Reprinted by permission of the Los Angeles Times.

AMY TAN: "Mother Tongue" first appeared in *The Threepenny Review*. Copyright © 1989 by Amy Tan. Reprinted by permission of the author and the Sandra Dijkstra Literary Agency.

DEBORAH TANNEN: "But What Do You Mean?" October 1994. Copyright by Deborah Tannen. Adapted from *Talking from 9 to 5: Women and Men at Work*, HarperCollins. Reprinted with permission.

CLIVE THOMPSON: "The Art of Finding," from *Smarter Than You Think*: *How Technology Is Changing Our Minds for the Better* by Clive Thompson, copyright © 2013 by Clive Thompson. Used by permission of the Penguin Press, a division of Penguin Group (USA) LLC.

LAUREL THATCHER ULRICH: "The Slogan" from *Well-Behaved Women Seldom Make History* by Laurel Thatcher Ulrich. Copyright © 2007 by Laurel Thatcher Ulrich. Used by permission of Alfred K. Knopf, a division of Random House, LLC. All rights reserved.

E. B. WHITE: "Once More to the Lake" from *One Man's Meat*. Text copyright © 1941 by E.B. White. Copyright renewed. Reprinted by permission of Tilbury House Publishers, Thomaston, Maine and International Creative Management. Used by permission. All rights reserved.

AMY WILENTZ: "A Zombie Is a Slave Forever," from *The New York Times*, October 30, 2012. Copyright © 2012 The New York Times. All rights reserved. Used by permission and protected by the Copyright Laws of the United States. The printing, copying, redistribution or retransmission of the Material without express written permission is prohibited.

DOUGLAS WOLK: "Superhero Smackdown," by Douglas Wolk. From *Slate*, August 16, 2013. Copyright © 2013 The Slate Group. All rights reserved. Used by permission and protected by the Copyright Laws of the United States. The printing, copying, redistribution, or retransmission of this Content without express written permission is prohibited.

MATTHEW YGLESIAS: "Money Isn't Everything," by Matthew Yglesias. From *Slate*, August 1, 2013. Copyright © 2013 The Slate Group. All rights reserved. Used by permission and protected by the Copyright Laws of the United States. The printing, copying, redistribution, or retransmission of this Content without express written permission is prohibited.

# ILLUSTRATIONS

**p. 1:** hyslop/iStock; **p. 7:** Anna Quindlen, *How Reading Changed My Life.* Copyright 1998. Reprinted with permission of Ballantine Books, Random House; **p. 8:** NORBERT VON DER GROEBEN/KRT/ Newscom; **p. 13:** fotocraft/Shutterstock; **p. 27:** binik/Shutterstock; **p. 32:** From *Persepolis: The Story of a Childhood* by Marjane Satrapi, translation copyright © 2003 by L'Association, Paris, France. Used by permission of Pantheon Books, an imprint of the Knopf Doubleday Publishing Group, a division of Random House LLC. All rights reserved; **p. 40:** Courtesy of DreedTea.com; **p. 43:** daltonoo/iStock; **p. 61:** Doug Steley B/Alamy; **p. 69:** © David M. Grossman/The Image Works; **p. 75:** Eugene Sergeev/ Shutterstock; **p. 93:** Mak_photo/iStock; **p. 95:** The Granger Collection; **p. 117:** Gordon Marshal; **p. 119:** Courtesy of Los Angeles Times; **pp. 121, 124:** Bethany Mollenkof/LA Times; **p. 129:** Merlijn Doomernik/Hollandse Hoogte/Redux; **pp. 129–38:** From *Persepolis: The Story of a Childhood* by Marjane Satrapi, translation copyright © 2003 by L'Association, Paris, France. Used by permission of Pantheon Books, an imprint of the Knopf Doubleday Publishing Group, a division of Random House LLC. All rights reserved; **p. 141:** Photo by Richard Howard/The LIFE Images Collection/Getty Images; **p. 143:** © H. Armstrong Roberts/CORBIS; **p. 147:** Courtesy of Drew Hansen; **p. 149:** Bob Parent/Hulton Archive/Getty Images; **p. 153:** CJ GUNTHER/The New York Times/Redux; **p. 157:** Patrick Post/Hollandse Hoogte/Redux; **p. 165:** BenThomasPhoto/iStock; **p. 170:** © Lake County Museum / CORBIS; **p. 171:** Courtesy of belgradelakesmaine.com; **p. 185:** Courtesy of Melissa Hicks; **p. 195:** Courtesy of Tony Mendoza; **p. 196:** Courtesy of R. C. Cross and M. S. Wheatland, From *Am. J. Phys.* 80, 1051 (2012); doi:10.1119/1.4750489; **p. 197:** Courtesy of Judith Ortiz Cofer; **p. 203:** Photo by Harley Crenshaw; **p. 206:** © Jason Politte/Alamy; **p. 209:** Courtesy of Michael J. Mooney; **p. 211:** Nastasic/iStock; **p. 219:** New York Times Co./Archive Photos/Getty Images; **p. 227:** DAMON WINTER/The New York Times/ Redux; **p. 231:** Adriano Castelli/Shutterstock; **pp. 244–45:** From *Persepolis: The Story of a Childhood* by Marjane Satrapi, translation copyright © 2003 by L'Association, Paris, France. Used by permission of Pantheon Books, an imprint of the Knopf Doubleday Publishing Group, a division of Random House LLC. All rights reserved; **p. 251:** (top) Courtesy of Uncle Willie's BBQ, (bottom) ASSOCIATED PRESS; **p. 257:** Courtesy of The Onion; **p. 258:** "Seven Deadly Sins Committed at Church Bake Sale," courtesy of The Onion; **p. 261:** Courtesy of the Los Angeles Times; **p. 263:** (left) © Suzanne Cordeiro/ Corbis, (middle) EdStock/iStock, (right) © CORBIS; **p. 267:** Stephanie Mitchell/Harvard University News Office; **p. 270:** John Springer Collection/Corbis; **p. 272:** Associated Press; **p. 277:** Wikimedia Commons; **p. 281:** Eugene Sergeev/Shutterstock; **p. 283:** AP Photo/Steve Dykes; **p. 299:** Courtesy of Erik Jaworski; **p. 305:** palnatoke/Wikimedia Commons; **p. 307:** (top and middle) AP Photo/Rusty Kennedy, (bottom) Courtesy of Jennifer Worick; **p. 311:** Courtesy of Alex Horton; **p. 317:** Wikimedia Commons; **p. 318:** Jari Hindstroem/Shutterstock; **p. 321:** Photo by Elizabeth Alter, Courtesy of Charles Duhigg; **p. 327:** The Advertising Archives; **p. 331:** © Christopher Felver/CORBIS; **p. 335:** richVintage/ iStock; **p. 337:** Sabine Dowek; **p. 355:** Courtesy of Junenoire Photography; **p. 357:** Courtesy of Patricia Park; **p. 361:** Wikimedia Commons; **p. 364:** © Photos 12/Alamy; **p. 365:** © AF archive/Alamy; **p. 369:** Isolde Ohlbaum/laif/Redux; **p. 370:** Jo-Anne McArthur/Redux; **p. 371:** Andrew F. Kazmierski/ Shutterstock; **p. 377:** Library of Congress/Wikimedia Commons; **p. 379:** © Heritage Images/Corbis; **p. 383:** Popperfoto/Getty Images; **p. 387:** Phil Berry/shutterstock; **p. 389:** Photo by Barbara Joy Cooley; **p. 407:** THE KOBAL COLLECTION/UNIVERSAL; **p. 419:** CAMERA PRESS/Libi Pedder/ Redux; **p. 420:** © 1989 Jim McHugh; **p. 427:** NoHoDamon/Wikmedia Commons; **p. 433:** Wikimedia Commons; **p. 437:** Carol T. Powers/The New York Times/Redux; **p. 445:** Photo by Ian Cook/The LIFE Images Collection/Getty Images; **p. 449:** Kostenko Maxim/Shutterstock; **p. 477:** © The New Yorker Collection, 1998, Roz Chast from Cartoonbank.com. All Rights Reserved; **p. 479:** © Chris Hardy Photography; **p. 487:** Photo by Paula Goldman; **p. 489:** Bettmann/Corbis/AP Images; **p. 493:** Photo by Nikki Kahn/The Washington Post via Getty Images; **pp. 497, 498, 501:** Courtesy of Mike Rose; **p. 507:** Courtesy of Bobbie Ann Mason; **p. 510:** Jack Delano/Corbis; **p. 511:** Graves County, Kentucky Archives; **p. 517:** Photo by Mondadori Portfolio via Getty Images; **p. 533:** genocide/iStock;

# Glossary / Index

This glossary / index defines key terms and concepts and directs you to pages in the book where they are used or discussed. Terms set in SMALL CAPITAL LETTERS are defined elsewhere in the glossary / index.

843

*caused,* 547

**CAUSES** Conditions or events necessary to produce an EFFECT. The *immediate cause* of an effect is the one closest to it in time and most directly responsible for producing the effect. *Remote causes* are further in time from an effect and less direct in producing it. The *main cause* of an effect is the most important cause; it is not only necessary to produce the effect but sufficient to do so. *Contributing causes* are less important but still contribute to the effect; they are not, however, sufficient to produce it on their own. *See also* CAUSE-AND-EFFECT ANALYSIS

**CHRONOLOGICAL ORDER, 103** The sequence of events in time, particularly important in a NARRATIVE or PROCESS ANALYSIS.

**CLAIM, 56, 604, 609–10, 614** The main point you make or position you take on an issue in an ARGUMENT.

**CLASSIFICATION, 36–37, 59, 84, 387–447** Writing that assigns individuals to groups, and divides groups into subgroups. Strictly speaking, classification sorts individuals into categories (*Red is an Irish setter*); and division separates a category into subcategories (*The dogs at the pound included pit bulls, greyhounds, and Boston terriers*). In this book, the general term *classification* is used for both sorting and dividing.

**CLICHÉ** A tired expression that has lost its original power to surprise because of overuse: *cut to the chase, let the cat out of the bag, last but not least.*

**CLIMAX, 104** The moment when the action in the PLOT of a NARRATIVE is most intense—the culmination, after which the dramatic tension is released.

**CLUSTERING, 54, 236, 391, 455-56, 537-38** A way of GENERATING IDEAS by using circles and connecting lines to group ideas visually into related clusters or topics.

**COLLABORATING, 48-50** Working with other people on a research and writing project, either by face-to-face contact or by the online exchange of ideas, comments, and drafts.

**CONCRETE, 52, 167, 179, 242** Definite, particular, capable of being perceived directly. *Rose, Mississippi, pinch* are more concrete words than *flower, river, touch*. *Five-miles-per-hour* is a more concrete idea than *slowness*. When you begin a piece of writing with an ABSTRACT idea, try BRAINSTORMING for more concrete particulars about it, and then flesh out those concrete details by using DESCRIPTION, EXEMPLIFICATION, DEFINITION, and other methods of development.

conjunctions, 72
connectors, 547, 621, 623

**CONNOTATION, 454** The implied meaning of a word; its overtones and associations over and above its literal meaning. The strict meaning of *heart*, for example, is "the organ that pumps blood through the body," but the word connotes warmth, affection, and love. *See also* DENOTATION

Conroy, Frank, *Stop-Time,* 233
*consequently,* 547, 621, 623
"Conservation Is Good Work" (Berry), 86
*Consumer Reports,* 338
continuation, indicating, 79
contrast, comparison vs., 338. *See also* COMPARISON AND CONTRAST
*cool,* 180
Council of Science Editors (CSE), 810

**COUNTERARGUMENT** An objection that might be raised against a CLAIM you're making in an ARGUMENT. As you construct an argument, try to think of the strongest possible reasons not to agree with your position, and address them in advance. It's always better to put out a fire before it gets started.

Cousins, Norman, "Who Killed Benny Paret?" 544, 546–47
credibility
  argument and, 623
  establishing, 617–18
Crenshaw, Paul, "Storm Country," 203–8

**CRITICAL ANALYSIS, 34, 35** A type of writing that closely examines a text, idea, or object with an eye to understanding and explaining how it is put together (form) and how it works (function). Typical methods: CAUSE AND EFFECT, DESCRIPTION, EXAMPLE, PROCESS ANALYSIS. *See also* EVALUATION; RHETORICAL ANALYSIS; TEXTUAL ANALYSIS

Cross, R. C., "Modeling a Falling Slinky," 32–33, 168
CSE (Council of Science Editors), 810
Cullington, Michaela, "Does Texting Affect Writing?" 29

**CULTURAL ANALYSIS, 33, 34** A kind of writing that examines the values, behavior, and language of a particular people or ethnicity, profession, region, or other group in detail. Typical methods: CLASSIFICATION, COMPARISON, DEFINITION, DESCRIPTION, NARRATION.

Curry, Stephen, 282–84

**D**

"The Danish Way of Life" (Gullen), 349–53
dashes, quotation marks and, 109
databases, 802, 803
Davis, Michael, "Defining 'Engineer,'" 456
"Deactivated" (Kuperberg), 746–50
"The Declaration of Independence" (Jefferson), 635–40
*The Declaration of Independence,* 86–87

**DEDUCTION, 610, 612–15** A form of logical reasoning that proceeds from general principles to a particular conclusion, useful in persuading others that an ARGUMENT is valid. *See also* INDUCTION

**DIALOGUE, 106-8, 110** Direct speech, especially between two or more speakers in a NARRATIVE, quoted word for word. Dialogue is an effective way of introducing the views of others into a FIRST-PERSON narrative.

**DICTION** Word choice; a writer's use of particular words and phrases.

**DIVISION** The mental act of dividing groups (dogs, for example) into subgroups (hounds, terriers, retrievers, and so on). *See also* CLASSIFICATION

**ETYMOLOGY, 451, 459, 463** A word history, or the practice of tracing such histories, often used to extend a DEFINITION. The modern English word *march*, for example, is derived from the French *marcher* ("to walk"), which in turn is derived from the Latin word *marcus* ("a hammer"). A march is thus a measured walk or movement, as if to the steady beat of a hammer. In most dictionaries, the etymology of a word is explained in parentheses or brackets before the first definition.

**EVALUATION, 33–34, 389** A kind of writing that examines an object or idea—for example, a toaster or other appliance; a film, book, or video; a government policy—in detail and judges its quality or fitness for a particular task or purpose. Typical methods: COMPARISON, DESCRIPTION, NARRATION, PROCESS ANALYSIS.

**EVIDENCE, 63, 86, 90–91, 614** Proof; the facts and figures, examples, expert testimony, or personal experience that a writer uses to support a THESIS or other CLAIMS of an ARGUMENT.

argument and, 623
effective, 607–8

"The Evil Empire?" (Douglas), 29–30, 624–31

**EXAMPLE, 31–33, 59, 81–82, 231–80** A specific instance or illustration of a general idea. Among "things that have given males a bad name," for example, humorist Dave Barry cites "violent crime, war, spitting, and ice hockey."

abstract and, 233
argument and, 233, 623
audience and, 235, 241
cause-and-effect analysis and, 240

composing an exemplification essay, 233–40
concrete, 242
definition and, 451, 453
description and, 240, 242
drafting an exemplification essay, 236–40
editing for common errors in examples, 240–41
finding good examples, 136
generating ideas by finding good examples, 236
narration and, 240, 242
organization and, 236–40, 242
with other methods, 240, 242, 753
parallelism and, 240
process analysis and, 292, 295
providing sufficient examples, 237, 239, 242
purpose and, 235, 241
readings
"All Seven Deadly Sins Committed at Church Bake Sale" (*The Onion*), 235, 257–60
"14 May 1905" (Lightman), 277–80
"Texas Talk Is Losing Its Twang" (Hennessy-Fiske), 234, 261–66
"This Little Piggy Didn't Go to Market" (Dobnik), 238, 253–56
"Well-Behaved Women Seldom Make History" (Ulrich), 267–76
reading with a critical eye, 241–42
specific, 242
stating the point, 237, 241
student example
"The Veil in *Persepolis*" (Cawley), 242–49
templates for drafting, 238
thesis and, 237, 241
transitional words and phrases, 79

**HYPERBOLE** A FIGURE OF SPEECH that uses intentional exaggeration, often in a DESCRIPTION or to make a point: "The professor explained it to us for two weeks one afternoon." *See also* UNDERSTATEMENT

**INDUCTION, 610, 612–15** A form of logical reasoning that proceeds from particular evidence to a general conclusion, useful in persuading others that an ARGUMENT is valid. *See also* DEDUCTION

*infer*, 622

"The Influencing Machines" (Gladstone and Neufeld), 606, 728–45

Institute of Medicine of the National Academics, 239

intellectual property, debating, 693–715
    "Free Culture" (Lessig), 708–15
    "Imagination or Theft?" (Clark), 694–98
    "Judas Priest: Bob Dylan Slams Plagiarism Accusers" (Hogan), 699–702
    "Who Owns Dr. King's Words?" (Goodman), 703–7

interviews, citing MLA-style, 825

in-text documentation, MLA-style, 811–14
    after a block quotation, 812
    an entire work, 814
    author named in a signal phrase, 810, 811
    author named in parentheses, 811
    author unknown, 813
    literary works, 813
    novels, 813
    organization or government as author, 813
    with or without signal phrases, 810
    poems, 813
    source quoted in another source, 814
    two or more authors, 812
    two or more works cited together, 814
    verse plays, 813
    work without page numbers, 814

"Intolerance of Boyish Behavior" (Angier), 85

introductions, 3, 86–89, 110
    examples, 86–88
    opening with an anecdote, 87
    placing subject in historical context, 88
    starting with a question, 87
    starting with a quotation or dialogue, 88

introductory paragraphs, 86–89

"Iron Man vs. Batman" (Adler), 336, 338

**IRONY** The use of words to suggest a meaning or condition different from, and often directly opposed to, those conveyed by taking the words literally: "When Congress finishes the serious business of trading insults, perhaps members can take out a little time for recreation and run the country."

*Is Homeownership Still an Effective Means of Building Wealth for Low-income and Minority Households?* (Herbert, McCue, and Sanchez-Moyano), 608

*is when*, 462

*is where*, 462

*it*, 71

italics, 461

*its*, 72, 73

*it's*, 72

## J

Jackson, Mahalia, 118, 147, 149–50

James, William "The Moral Philosopher and the Moral Life," 536

Jefferson, Thomas, "The Declaration of Independence," 635–40

Jefferson, Thomas, *The Declaration of Independence*, 86–87

Johnson, Samuel, *Dictionary of the English Language*, 450

**LITERACY NARRATIVE, 38, 39, 118** A kind of writing that tells a personal story about learning to read and write—or about otherwise dealing with written language, or such related forms of symbolic representation as painting or musical notation. Typical methods: CAUSE AND EFFECT, DESCRIPTION, EXAMPLE, NARRATION.

**MLA-STYLE DOCUMENTATION, 74,
810-35** A two-part DOCUMENTATION system created by the Modern Language
Association that consists of brief in-text
parenthetical citations and a list of sources
at the end of the text. This documentation
style, explained fully in the Appendix, is
often used in literature and writing classes.

**MODE** A form or manner of discourse. In classical rhetoric, the four basic modes of speaking or writing are NARRATION, DESCRIPTION, EXPOSITION, and ARGUMENT.

## N

**NARRATION, 28–30, 59, 80–81, 93–164** An account of actions and events that happen to someone or something in a particular place and time. Because narration is essentially storytelling, it is often used in fiction; however, it is also an important element in almost all writing and speaking. The opening of Lincoln's Gettysburg Address, for example, is in the narrative mode: "Fourscore and seven years ago our fathers bought forth on this continent a new nation."

**P**

**PARADOX** A FIGURE OF SPEECH in which a statement appears to contradict itself but, on closer examination, makes sense: *They have ears but hear not.*

**PARALLELISM, 71, 78–79, 240, 398** Using the same grammatical form for words or sentences of equal importance, especially necessary when using EXAMPLES, COMPARISONS, and CLASSIFICATION in your writing. This sentence isn't parallel: *The program included someone <u>lecturing</u>, a <u>PowerPoint presentation</u>, and a <u>film</u>.* This one is: *This program included a <u>lecture</u>, a <u>PowerPoint presentation</u>, and a <u>film</u>.*

**PARAPHRASE, 17, 805–6, 808** Restating someone else's ideas or writing in your own words. The source of a paraphrase must be fully acknowledged and DOCUMENTED.

**PARODY** A humorous imitation of a particular example of writing, music, film, or other art form; a *spoof* is a gentle form of parody. For example, "Weird Al" Yankovic's "Perform This Way" parodies Lady Gaga's hit song "Born This Way."

**PERSONAL NARRATIVE** A kind of writing that gives an account of the writer's experience, usually told from the FIRST-PERSON point of view, with events in CHRONOLOGICAL ORDER. Typical methods: CAUSE AND EFFECT, DESCRIPTION, NARRATION.

**PERSONIFICATION, 178** A FIGURE OF SPEECH, often used in DESCRIPTIVE writing, that attributes human characteristics to inanimate objects or ideas: *Death lurked around the corner.*

**PERSUASION, 46, 96, 170, 241, 346, 537, 605, 610, 617, 618** The art of convincing the reader to accept that what a writer says is true and accurate, or of moving an AUDIENCE to action or belief in a particular cause or purpose.

*Philosophy of the Literary Form* (Burke), 13
Pinker, Steven, 18
   "Mind Over Mass Media," 17
Piven, Joshua, "How to Pull an All-
     Nighter," 307–10
place, indicating, 79

**PLAGIARISM, 808-9** Using someone else's ideas or words without giving them credit. To avoid plagiarism, always DOCUMENT your sources.

"Plagiarism Lines Blur for Students in
     Digital Age" (Gabriel), 72
planning, 44–47
   finding a topic, 45
   managing time, 44–45
   thinking about audience, 46–48
   thinking about purpose, 46–48
Plath, Sylvia, "Mirror," 178
plays, citing MLA-style, 813. *See also*
     books, citing MLA-style

**PLOT, 99, 103-4** The sequence of events in a NARRATIVE arranged in such a way as to have a beginning, a middle, and an end.

podcasts, citing MLA-style, 823
poems, citing MLA-style, 813. *See also*
     books, citing MLA-style
point, *See* THESIS

**POINT-BY-POINT COMPARISON, 341-44, 349** A way of organizing a comparison (or contrast) in which each trait of two or more subjects is discussed before going on to the next point. A point-by-point comparison of London and New York might first address nightlife in each city, then museums, then theater, then history. *See also* SUBJECT-BY-SUBJECT COMPARISON

**POINT OF VIEW, 99, 110** The vantage from which a NARRATIVE is told. Narratives recounted in the grammatical FIRST PERSON use the pronouns *I* or *we*; those that use the grammatical THIRD PERSON use the pronouns *he*, *she*, *it*, and *they*. *See also* NARRATOR
   in a description, 177–78, 181
   maintaining consistent, 105–6

points of comparison, 349

**POSITION PAPER, 28, 29, 36, 36-37, 40, 40-41, 118, 452, 754** A kind of writing that examines an issue (or issues) in a debate for the purpose of taking a stance on it (or them). Typical methods: ARGUMENT, CLASSIFICATION, COMPARISON, DEFINITION, EXAMPLE.

possessives, apostrophes with, 73

**POST HOC, ERGO PROPTER HOC, 615** Latin for "after this, therefore because of this"; a FALLACY of faulty reasoning that assumes that just because one event comes after another event, it occurs *because* of the first event.

provocation, 88

**PUN** A play on words, usually involving different words that sound alike or different meanings of the same word: *The undertaker was a grave man.*

punctuation. *See also specific punctuation marks*
 with connectors, 621
 of dialogue, 108
 editing, 72–73
 end, 71

**PURPOSE, 98, 99, 109** Your reason for writing—whether to explain, inform, entertain, record, persuade, express yourself, or serve some other goal.
 argument and, 605, 607, 622
 cause-and-effect analysis and, 549
 classification and, 390–92, 399
 comparison and contrast and, 340, 348–49
 definition and, 453, 455, 462
 description and, 166, 181
 example and, 235, 241
 process analysis and, 285–86, 294
 thinking about, 46–48

**Q**

qualifiers, 182
question marks, quotation marks and, 109
questions, 87
Quindlen, Anna
 *How Reading Changed My Life,* 4, 7–9
 "Still Needing the F Word," 88
*quite,* 179, 182

**QUOTATION, 17, 88, 805, 807, 809** Someone else's exact words inserted into your writing. All quotations must be identified as such and fully DOCUMENTED.

quotation marks, 73, 108–9

**R**

radio programs, citing MLA-style, 826
Rampell, Catherine, "College Graduates Fare Well, Even through Recession," 42, 676–81
readers
 appealing to emotions of, 617
 good, 1–12
reading
 annotation, 4, 7
 closely, 2–5
 considering techniques, 6
 critically, 2
 expectations, 3
 *How Reading Changed My Life* (Quindlen), 4, 7–9
 previewing a text, 3
 purpose for, 3
 questions for, 5
 reading a draft with a critical eye, 62–63, 109–10, 181, 241–42, 294–95, 348–49, 399–400, 462–63, 549–50, 622–23
 reading process, 2–3
 responding to texts, 5–6
 summarizing, 6
 thinking about and recording reactions, 6
 visual texts, 6–7
"Ready, Willing, and Able" (Shewer), 54, 57–59, 64–70, 73
*really,* 179, 182
*reason is because, reason why,* 548
recommendation, ending with a, 92
*recreate,* 31
"Redefining Definition" (McKean), 82
reference works, as sources, 801
 citing MLA-style, 819, 823

**REFLECTION** A kind of writing that examines or muses upon a person, place, thing, or idea for the purpose of exploring its nature and significance. Typical methods: CAUSE AND EFFECT, COMPARISON, DESCRIPTION, NARRATION.

"Remarks at Topeka School District Senior Recognition Day" (Obama), 611, 641–48

"Remembering My Childhood on the Continent of Africa" (Sedaris), 73, 345, 369–76

REPORT, 28, 34-35, 36, 606, 754 A kind of writing that gives an informative account of the writer's investigation of a subject, including the nature of the research done and the results or conclusions reached. Typical methods: CAUSE AND EFFECT, CLASSIFICATION, COMPARISON, DEFINITION, DESCRIPTION, EXAMPLE, NARRATION, PROCESS ANALYSIS.

research
 documentation for, 810–35
 preliminary, 14–15, 800–805
 taking notes, 804–5
 using sources, 800–835
research papers, student examples
 "Against the Odds" (Borchers), 826–35
 "Behind the Curtain" (Kelso), 550–65
 "The Celebrity Chef " (Babilonia), 463–75
 "The Evil Empire?" (Douglas), 624–31
 "Modern Dating, Prehistoric Style" (Stonehill), 20–26
restaurant review, using classification in, 389

RÉSUMÉ, 234 A kind of writing that summarizes a person's accomplishments in a short form that can be readily reviewed by the intended audience. The conventional way of doing this is by breaking your academic and employment history into

categories and giving specific examples, in each category, of your education, skills, experience, and other attributes. Typical Methods: ARGUMENT, DEFINITION, DESCRIPTION, EXAMPLE, NARRATION.

reverse chronological order, 539–40, 549
review, using classification in, 389
revising, 62–63
 getting responses before, 65–66
 second drafts, 67

RHETORIC, 18, 20, 114, 190, 247, 302, 352, 404, 473, 564, 629 The art of using language effectively in speech and in writing. The term originally belonged to oratory, and it implies the presence of both a speaker (or a writer) and a listener (or reader).

RHETORICAL ANALYSIS, 28, 31-32, 38, 39-40, 118 A kind of writing that examines what a piece of writing (or photograph, painting, work of architecture, or other form of expression) says or means— and how that meaning is conveyed to an audience. Typical methods: ARGUMENT, CAUSE AND EFFECT, COMPARISON, DESCRIPTION, EXAMPLE, PROCESS ANALYSIS, NARRATION.

RHETORICAL QUESTION, 240 A question for which the speaker already has an answer in mind; used in ARGUMENT and other writing to introduce a statement as if it were the reader's own answer to the writer's question.

Roach, Mary
 "How to Know If You're Dead," 453, 455, 458, 479–86
 *Stiff*, 338, 346, 760–61
Roach, Mary, *Stiff*, 338–39, 346

**TEXTUAL ANALYSIS** A kind of writing that examines a piece of writing or other text with an eye to understanding and explaining what the text says—and how it says it. Typical methods: CAUSE AND EFFECT, COMPARISON, DESCRIPTION, EXAMPLE, NARRATION, PROCESS ANALYSIS.

**THESIS, 56–57, 62, 109** The main point of a text. A *thesis statement* is a direct statement of that point.

**THIRD PERSON, 106** The grammatical and NARRATIVE point of view—expressed by the personal pronouns *he, she, it,* and *they*—that limits the narrator to the role of observer, though sometimes an all-knowing one. *See also* FIRST PERSON

**TONE, 3, 5, 6, 7, 618** A writer's attitude toward his or her subject or AUDIENCE: sympathy, longing, amusement, shock, sarcasm, awe—the range is endless.

**TOPIC SENTENCE, 77–78** A sentence that gives readers the main point of a paragraph, making a clear statement about the topic.

**TOULMIN ARGUMENT, 614** A practical form of ARGUMENT, developed by the British philosopher Stephen Toulmin, that supports a CLAIM by presenting facts and other data (the grounds) and a logical basis (the warrant) on which the grounds are said to justify the claim.

# MENU OF READINGS

• Student writing